The SIMS 2 UNIVERSITY

EXPANSION PACK

PRIMA Official Game Guide

Greg Kramer

Prima Games
A Division of Random House, Inc.

3000 Lava Ridge Court
Roseville, CA 95661
1-800-733-3000
www.primagames.com

PRIMA OFFICIAL GAME GUIDE

Product Manager: Jill Hinckley
Editorial Supervisor: Christy Seifert

ISBN: 0-7615-4636-7
Library of Congress Catalog Card Number: 2004116621
Printed in the United States of America
05 06 07 08 AA 10 9 8 7 6 5 4 3 2 1

Acknowledgements

Prima would like to thank JP Dolan, Charles Gast, Kevin Gibson, Jack Greaves, Kevin Hogan, Hunter Howe, Julie Kanarowski, Beverly Lam, Charles London, Lyndsay McGaw, Seth Olshfski, Frank Simon, and Thomas Vu for their help with this guide.

Contents

The SIMS™ 2
UNIVERSITY

EXPANSION PACK

Part 1

Chapter 1

What's New in *The Sims™ 2 University*?

Are your Sims ready for a whole new phase of life? If so, the exciting world of college awaits: that heady time between the teenage years and adulthood when Sims learn to spread their wings and fly...or plummet with a sickening (but oddly amusing) thud.

Until now, Sims went straight from high school to the adult world with the snuffing of a birthday candle. Now it's possible to spend some time in young adulthood gaining skills, meeting dozens of new friends, earning money, and opening new career vistas. It's a time to carve out your Sim's future while enjoying a casual environment in which a good time is always at hand and no one's a stranger—just a friend you haven't met.

The rewards of a successful college experience are many: career advantages, large friendship networks, time to develop skills, otherwise unavailable social advantages, and increased ability to control the actions of other Sims.

The following list introduces all the new features in this expansion and the following chapters provide everything you need to know to get the most out of your Sim's college experience.

CHANGES TO THE CORE GAME

Most of the features described in this guide apply only to Sims who are in or who have been to college, but there are several new or changed features that impact all Sims. Some, like the newly introduced Influence, benefit college graduates, but all Sims, old and new, can take advantage of that power.

◆ Influence: Sims can accumulate a new power called "Influence" through the acquisition (and retention) of friends and the fulfillment of certain Wants. In turn, you can use this to make otherwise uncontrollable Sims do what your Sim commands.

◆ New Socials: Though there are a few Socials only available to young adult Sims, this game introduces 17 new Socials that most Sims can use.

◆ Career outfits: Whenever your Sims reach a new level in their career, the outfit they acquire is added to every wardrobe object on the property. Mom's astronaut uniform can be worn anytime she wants!

◆ Lifetime Want: When a Sim chooses an Aspiration, they are randomly assigned a Lifetime Want—an extremely hard-to-achieve Want that, though optional, can guide the choices they make throughout life. When this Want is achieved, the Sim gains a gigantic infusion of Aspiration Reward points and Influence points and attains *permanent* Platinum Aspiration—and with it, a lifetime of unshakeable good mood.

◆ Household merging: Previously, the only way to move Sims from one household (or family) to another was through social interactions. Now, any family in the Family Bin (in regular neighborhoods) or the Student Bin (in college neighborhoods) can be moved into an existing household and, space permitting, become part of it. Merged Sims retain their own surnames.

New foods: Sims have two new food options. Sims with a microwave can now cook a Cup O' Ramen for lunch or dinner or may order Chinese food delivery any time of day (be careful, it's fattening!).

Computers: Computers now feature a new way to replenish Fun and Social and build Daily Relationship with another Sim on the same lot. With two or more computers, you can hold a LAN party to enjoy multiplayer gaming right in your Sims' own homes. Computers in houses with teens sport new functions for getting teens college scholarships and moving them to college.

Telephones: If a household has teens in it, the telephone has new functions for earning scholarships and gaining admission to college.

Bartenders and Baristas: Community lots can feature commercial juice and coffee bars manned by Bartender and Barista NPCs.

New objects: You can use many of the expansion's new objects in neighborhoods. These objects include novel versions of existing objects as well as completely new and powerful items. New items include new Body skill objects, Fun objects, group showers, collaborative musical instruments, and decorative objects.

Sports party: This new kind of party celebrates the glory of watching sports while eating and drinking with other Sims.

New TV channel: The new SimStation Sports channel features round-the-clock sports coverage.

Personal electronic devices: Sims can purchase a cell phone, a handheld game, or an MP3 player.

COLLEGE FEATURES

With the advent of the Sims' university life comes dozens of new features and changes that enliven, enrich, and entertain your educated Sims. This list, though not comprehensive, gives you an idea of how much there is in store.

Young adult Sims: A totally new age group created just for college life. College towns feature a young adult—only Create A Sim tool, and an updated *The Sims™ 2 Body Shop* application permits cloning and creation of parts for young adults.

Grading and academics: College Sims have the freedom to earn their grades in several ways with a new grading system. Choose your Sim's major, achieve the skills required for each semester, and earn grades by doing research or assignments, going to class, writing term papers, cheating, or getting friendly with professors. Be in a good mood, however—happy Sims earn high grades more easily.

New Want and Fear slots and locks: College students can earn up to two additional Want slots and a second Want/Fear lock. Dropouts gain an additional Fear slot.

New careers and career advantages: College graduates have access to four new career tracks. These tracks generally pay more and have more days off than the original eight *The Sims™ 2* careers but demand more skills and friends. Additionally, graduating with honors can provide a potential automatic boost in any career track, new or old.

New career objects: Each of the four new careers come with a new career object. These objects enable Sims to change their faces, take posed photographs, resurrect dead Sims, or (shudder) use other Sims to increase their own lifespan.

- New parties: In addition to the sports party (also available in neighborhoods), there are two other parties available only in college. All graduated Sims can throw a final blowout in honor of their achievement, and Greek houses can throw the extra special toga party.

- New self-interactions: Sims can now streak or Perform Freestyle.

- New lot types: College towns have three new lot types. Dorms are large, special-purpose residential lots. Greek houses are also residential but Sims can live on them only by getting a charter for their non-Greek residence or by undergoing a rush procedure. College community lots are different from regular community lots, allowing some unique services. There's also the mysterious secret society lot found in every university...but no one talks about *those* (except, of course, in Chapter 29).

- College-only socials: A few of the new social interactions can only be performed by Sims in college or Sims who have graduated. Sims back in the neighborhood or who've left college early simply can't do, for example, School Cheer.

- Student jobs: College students don't go to work like other Sims. Money can be earned hourly by doing jobs on a residential or community lot. Students can work for the cafeteria, serve coffee, serve drinks, tutor other students, or serve as Personal Trainers. They can also play in a band, hustle pool, or freestyle for tips.

- New Aspiration Reward object: With this new Aspiration Reward object, your Sims can print their own simoleans.

- New nonplayer Sims: Several new nonplayer Sims populate this expanded world, including the Lunch Server, Barista, Professor, Coach, Cheerleader, Mascot (and Evil Mascot), and Streaker.

- New Build mode tools: Builders can now utilize the power of multistory columns and doors, columns that connect with a lovely archway, "smart fences" that realistically space posts in long runs of fence, or build walls directly atop other walls. This guide even contains a cheat to allow editing of dorms.

NEIGHBORHOODS AND COLLEGE TOWNS

The Sims™ 2 University introduces a new kind of neighborhood—the college town—that's distinct from but crucially linked to the core game's residential neighborhoods. The differences between these two

locales are extremely important, but the terminology used in the game can be confusing.

For the purposes of this guide, we use a standard terminology for the sake of clarity:

♦ "Neighborhood" refers to the base residential neighborhoods that were the exclusive locations used in the original *The Sims™ 2*.

♦ "College town" refers to the new dependent neighborhoods in which Sims attend college.

♦ "Household" refers to the collection of playable Sims on a single lot. In *The Sims™ 2*, this grouping was formally called a "family," although Sims not related by blood or marriage could be part of it. In college towns, however, all such groupings are called households.

College towns are separate from, but linked to, your base neighborhoods. Each neighborhood can have several colleges linked to it; its teens can go there for higher education, and they can be summoned there to visit. When a Sim graduates from a college, he or she returns to the base neighborhood associated with his or her college by way of the neighborhood's Family Bin.

Remember that the same college template can be associated with several or all of your core neighborhoods, but various incarnations of an individual college have no relation to the same college town linked to another neighborhood. For example, Jim Simmons (a teen from Pleasantview) may attend Sim State and Tim Simpson (a teen from Strangetown)

may also attend Sim State, but they don't both exist in each other's version of Sim State. Sims who graduate from a college can only return to the neighborhood to which the college is linked, even if another version of that college is linked to another neighborhood.

WHY GO TO COLLEGE?

The vast majority of this guide is dedicated to this question, but it helps to see reasons laid out in one place.

♦ Sims who go to college have lengthy opportunities to build skills and make friends before becoming adults.

♦ Sims leave college with several otherwise unavailable social interactions.

♦ Graduates gain four new challenging and more rewarding career tracks, and each has a new (and extremely desirable) career object.

♦ Graduates with high grades get a boost in their chosen careers in career tracks old and new.

♦ Sims who get through at least sophomore year gain up to two new Want slots and a new Want lock. Getting past junior year offers the once-in-a-lifetime chance to change Aspiration.

♦ More time to make friends means more time to build Influence.

♦ More time to amass Aspiration Reward points means you can buy powerful reward objects later in life.

Chapter 2
Anatomy of a Young Adult Sim

In the original *The Sims™ 2* game, there were six ages of Sims: babies, toddlers, children, teens, adults, and elders. Traditionally, when teens reached the end of their high school years, they went directly to the working world of adult responsibilities, opportunities, and privileges. Now there's something between the freewheeling teen years and the rich but demanding adult world: college.

note

You can always tell an adult or elder who has been to college from one who hasn't. Look at the icons around the Sim's current age. If there are six icons (toddler, child, teen, young adult, adult, elder), they've at least been to—if not graduated from—college. If there are only five icons, they've never attended college.

If the Sim has dropped out or has been booted from college, they have the extra young adult icon but there is a yellow line through it.

If, on the other hand, the Sim has graduated—and with honors—a star appears near the young adult icon.

Sims who've been to college have an extra age icon under their portrait.

With this new challenge comes a new age of Sim life: the young adult. In reality, young adult Sims are similar to adults, but the few differences are important.

A DEFINITION

A young adult Sim is any Sim who is currently attending college. Sims who don't attend college by the end of their teen years transition straight into adults just as they always have.

Traditionally, teens went straight from high school to adulthood with the celebration of a birthday.

Essentially, young adult Sims don't exist in the game outside of college towns except when summoned as nonplayable visitors or party guests to households in traditional neighborhoods. They cannot be part of any normal neighborhood household until they graduate and (automatically) become adults. The young adult age, then, is an optional detour rather than an actual age group.

Now, Sims arrive at college as teens but immediately transition into sturdier, but still youthful, young adults.

The implications of this are important, especially if a young adult has been imported as a teen from the linked neighborhood. When a Sim leaves a neighborhood for college, they are removed from their neighborhood household exactly as if they were an adult who opted to find their own place. While playing your departed Sim at college, the family back home does not age at all!

ADULTS AND YET NOT

Young adult Sims are, in most ways, identical to adult Sims. There are only a few things adults can do that young adults cannot:

♦ Get Married/Joined

♦ Try for Baby

♦ Adopt

♦ Hold adult careers

Beyond these limitations, most things about young adults is covered in Chapter 6. They, for example, deplete their Needs at the same rate as adults (accelerated Hunger and Hygiene depletion), and all their Needs (except Energy) tend to weigh equally on their overall Mood.

YOUNG ADULT LIFESPAN

The young adult lifespan isn't measured in days as are other age groups, but rather in semesters.

The young adult age is measured by progress in school, not by passage of time.

A young adult stays a young adult:

1. As long it takes to finish four years of college plus two free days after graduation, or

2. Until they drop out or are expelled.

Barring academic probation (which forces the Sim to repeat a semester), a Sim can be a young adult for about twenty-six days (three days per semester plus two days of postgraduate celebrating).

This period can be elongated if the Sim goes on academic probation (fails to make at least a D+ in a semester). Sims on academic probation must repeat the semester and are expelled if they don't earn at least a C- on their second try. Thus, the maximum time a Sim can possibly be a young adult—repeating every semester without getting booted—is fifty days.

The young adult age is cut short if the Sim voluntarily or involuntarily departs college before graduation or if a graduating Sim departs college before the end of the two-day post-school break.

YOUNG ADULT SOCIALS

Generally, young adults have access to the same social interactions as adults (with the notable marital and procreative exceptions listed above). However, here are some socials that young adults can do that adults (who haven't been to college) cannot:

♦ Hang Out: A group talk interaction for up to six Sims. Sims lounge in various seated and reclining positions and chat. Teens may do this too.

♦ School Cheer: Entertain interaction that only a young adult Sim or adult/elder who has been to college can do (even if dropped out or expelled).

♦ Secret Handshake: For members of the Secret Society or by adults/elders who've both been to college and been Secret Society members.

- Streak: A self-interaction only for college towns (they won't Streak autonomously when visiting home neighborhoods).
- Talk about Major: Talk interaction between young adults only or between young adults and college town NPCs.

After Sims leave college, they won't have time to really Hang Out anymore. Pity, really.

Even after they leave campus, college alumni can still do the School Cheer. It works best, though, with other graduates.

YOUNG ADULT NEEDS

Though young adults and adults share the same approach to their Needs and overall Mood, there is a difference in how the Need/Mood game is played with young adults. This difference has more to do with class-time demands, which is different from career-shift demands.

Sims in college must spend tremendous amounts of time keeping their Fun Need satisfied because the rigorous classes are so draining.

The difference is, when a young adult returns from class, their Fun Need is *greatly* depleted. No adult career has so dramatic an effect. This regular depletion of Fun makes young adults behave differently when acting autonomously: they spend more time autonomously having Fun and interacting with other Sims than would an adult. If you're directing a young adult Sim, much more of your time will be spent replenishing Fun.

note

Note that this is a difference in AUTONOMOUS action. If you dictate every move your Sim makes, the effect of this difference will not manifest.

YOUNG ADULT "CREATE A SIM"

You may import your playable and teen Sims to populate your college town or you may design your own young adults from scratch. You cannot, however, create young adults in the regular neighborhood Create A Sim tool.

The Create New Students button is the doorway to young adult Create a Sim.

Instead, there's a specialized young adult Create A Sim tool available only in college towns. It is in the same location as the standard Create A Sim tool, under the Students menu (called "families" in regular neighborhoods) via the Create New Students button. Here you find several differences from the standard Create a Family environment.

Groupings of Sims in college towns are called "households" instead of "families."

The first difference is the décor, but that's just window dressing (in this case, literally). More important, however, is the change from "Family Name" to "Household Name."

> **note**
>
> Whether you begin a household in an unoccupied dorm or in private housing, the household retains (and the dorm assumes) its name. If, however, you move the household into an already inhabited property or dorm, you must merge them with the existing household. The new household switches to the old household's name. Each Sim's individual surnames remain unchanged.
>
> You can name your household anything you want.

Young adults get two name-entry fields because they require a first and last name.

Click on the Create A Sim button to begin a Sim. The only real difference between this and regular Create A Sim is the addition of an extra name slot that permits creation of both a first and last name for your new Sim.

Young adults have their own style.

> **note**
>
> The only other change in young adult Create A Sim results from the tool's specialization. Randomizing, Choosing an Existing Sim, and Heads (Step 2) all draw exclusively from young adult content.

Young adult Sims' relationships can only be set to Roomie or Sibling.

When you're done forging your Sim, it's time to add more Sims or set relationships among those you already have. The Household Relationships button can only establish two kinds of relationships: Roomie and Sibling. Anything beyond that (engaged, love, etc.), you must earn in the game.

> **note**
>
> Sims in a student household are presumed to be Roomies, so you don't have to specify this. The only relationship you must specify is "Sibling."

THE SIMS™ 2 BODY SHOP

The Sims™ 2 Body Shop application has changed as well. New Sims can be made as young adults. Build a new Sim or Clone an existing one and click the new Young Adult button on the Change Age wheel. All genetics, clothing, and other content for young adults is available for your tinkering pleasure.

THE SIMS™ 2 BODY SHOP now contains a control to create young adult Sims.

Likewise, forge young adult parts in the Create Parts tool. When making skin tones, note that there is no specific young adult version of the Sim's skin and face in the project folder. Structurally, a young adult has a gender-appropriate adult body structure and adult skin with their teen face. Therefore, when you create a new skin tone project for young adults, you are actually making changes to the Sim's teen facial file and to the adult body and hair files.

Chapter 3

Influence and Lifetime Wants

Every Sim, whether in college or not, has more to do than they have time for, and each craves a way to make others do their bidding. Moreover, they all have one thing they desperately desire (above all else) so much that achieving it would make them happy forever.

These lofty wishes are now a reality in the form of Influence and Lifetime Wants.

INFLUENCE

> ### note
>
> Let's clear up one possible bit of confusion. Chapter 19 of this guide refers to "influence" as one of the three goals of THE SIMS™ 2's generational game. In that context, "influence" (with a lowercase "i") refers to an older Sim's general ability to foster skill (by Teaching) and personality changes (by Encouraging) in younger Sims.
>
> The new concept of Influence (with an uppercase "I") refers to the ability to direct uncontrollable Sims to do a specific action.

Sims can now direct another Sim to do something by using the "Influence to ..." interaction and choosing an action for the other Sim to perform. If necessary, they can specify which Sim they should perform it upon.

> ### note
>
> Every Sim—except babies—has Influence.

Now, this kind of power has to be earned. Gaining Influence requires two things:

1. Influence capacity 2. Influence points

Influence Capacity

Influence capacity determines the maximum number of Influence points a Sim can accumulate.

The Influence meter is located on your control panel to the Aspiration meter's left.

> ### note
>
> The Influence meter is divided into five levels, each of which can hold 2,000 Influence points.
>
> At full capacity, the Influence meter can contain 10,000 Influence points; to gain this capacity, however, your Sim must win and retain at least twelve friends.

Initially, every controllable Sim has an Influence meter capacity of 2,000 (Level 1). At this initial level, they may accumulate up to 2,000 points, enough for several low-cost actions. To go further, however, they must increase their Influence capacity.

> ### tip
>
> Winning Influence points when your Sim's Influence meter is full is a waste since your Sim lacks more room to retain them. Like excess Aspiration points, any points above your Sim's maximum capacity are lost forever.
>
> Therefore, if your Sim is at full capacity and is close to gaining the next level in Influence capacity, consider locking any Influence-scoring Wants in his or her Wants panel and saving them until you have room to hold their benefit.

Influence capacity is built by the accumulation of personal (not household) friends (Daily Relationship >50 for both Sims). Gaining the requisite number of friends earns another level of Influence capacity. Thus, a Sim with zero friends has an Influence

capacity level of 1 (2,000 points). A Sim with one to three friends is Level 2 (4,000 points). Ultimately, a Sim with 12 or more friends has full Influence capacity of Level 5 (10,000) and can exert the most expensive Influence actions.

The number of a specific Sim's friends (not household friends) determines that Sim's Influence capacity.

note

The friends requirement for Influence is different from the requirement for career advancement. For careers, any friend of anyone in the household counts as a friend for any individual Sim. For Influence, only a friend belonging to a specific Sim counts toward their Influence level.

Since Influence level is connected to your Sim's *current* number of friends, losing a friend could result in a loss of Influence capacity. If the Sim's friend count drops below the requirement of the current Influence level, capacity will fall until the friend is recovered or another made.

Point at the Influence meter to see your Sim's current Influence moniker, Influence capacity, and how many friends they need in order to gain the next Influence level.

Every level of Influence capacity displays a moniker indicating a Sim's level of potential Influence.

Influence Level	Friends Required	Influence Capacity	Influence Moniker
1	0	0–2,000	Puny Pleader
2	1	2,001–4,000	Common Cajoler
3	3	4,001–6,000	Suave Stringpuller
4	6	6,001–8,000	Powerful Persuader
5	12	8,001–10,000	Master Manipulator

Finally, gaining Influence capacity, by itself, doesn't give your Sim any power over other Sims. To actually Influence anyone, they must gain Influence points.

Influence Points

Influence points are the currency that buys Influenced actions. They are gained by fulfilling certain Wants and are lost by realizing certain Fears.

Wants and Fears that earn Influence are surrounded by a blue box.

The Wants and Fears system in the game designates certain Wants and Fears as Influence Wants and Fears. These Wants and Fears tend to revolve around things that would give a Sim bragging rights. Thus, gaining a skill for a Knowledge Sim or going steady for a Romance Sim would likely earn each Sim a measure of Influence points.

Wants and Fears that will, if achieved, affect your Sim's total Influence points are indicated in the Wants and Fears panel by a blue frame around the Want/Fear's icon. Watch for these Wants and lock them whenever you have the opportunity; big Influence Wants are precious, so cling to them as they arise.

note

Sims who complete their sophomore year in college are rewarded with a second Want/Fear lock. This comes in very handy in the Influence game.

Influenced Actions

There are a variety of actions that are compelled by Influence. Every Influenced action costs a certain amount of Influence points. The more risky and powerful an action, the more Influence is required to compel another Sim to do it. For example, it takes very little Influence to convince a Sim to tell a joke but quite a bit to persuade them to do someone else's schoolwork.

All possible Influenced actions are shown in the "Influence to ..." menu. Actions that your Sim lacks the accumulated Influence to use are grayed out.

All possible Influenced actions are listed here with their Influence point cost.

- ◆ Appreciate (500)
- ◆ Entertain (500)
- ◆ Talk (500)
- ◆ Flirt (1,000)
- ◆ Play (1,000)
- ◆ Prank (1,000)
- ◆ Fight (1,500)
- ◆ Hug (1,500)
- ◆ Kiss (1,500)
- ◆ Do My Assignment (2,000)
- ◆ Garden (2,000)
- ◆ Repair (2,000)
- ◆ Clean (2,500)
- ◆ Cook (2,500)
- ◆ Do My Term Paper (2,500)

This amount is deducted from your Sim's Influence point total the moment the Influenced Sim accepts the challenge.

While these are all the possible Influenced actions, they are not always available or even visible.

Only actions that are possible will appear in the "Influence to..." menu. Repair, for example, only appears when there's something broken on the lot.

If nothing's broken, the Influenced action is deemed impossible and won't be shown on the menu.

Actions that are possible but cost more than the Sim's current total of Influence points appear in the menu but are grayed out.

Types of Influenced Actions

There are two kinds of Influenced Actions: social actions and object-based actions.

Social Actions

When Influencing a social action, you must choose the action and then the Sim to whom it will be done.

Social actions involve Influencing a Sim to perform a social interaction on a third Sim.

> ### note
>
> One Sim can't Influence another Sim to perform a social interaction on the first Sim. They can only be directed toward a third party.

To begin such actions:

1. Successfully do the "Influence to..." interaction on a Sim.
2. Indicate which category of action (i.e. Talk, Prank, Hug) you want them to perform.
3. Specify on which third Sim you'd like them to do it.

After you achieve all three steps, your actions (if accepted) take effect.

You cannot dictate the precise interaction you want a Sim to perform, only its category. The influenced Sim randomly chooses which of the interactions of that kind they'll do. This is important because, as we'll see later, the interaction the Influenced Sim picks may be doomed to backfire.

Object-Based Actions

Object-based actions entail instructing a Sim to perform some action on an unspecified object on the lot.

House a mess? Use Influence to get someone else to clean it.

Thus, you can Influence a Sim to cook a group meal, pull any weeds they find and water dry plants, clean any messes they see, or repair any broken objects. You can't control which objects they choose or produce. For example, a Sim Influenced to cook chooses randomly from the meals available from their skill and the cooking objects on the lot.

Coaxing someone into doing your Sim's term paper is a real timesaver but it costs big Influence points.

College Sims can Influence others to do their schoolwork for them (freeing them up to pursue friendships or build skills):

♦ Do Assignment: Influenced Sims randomly choose an assignment book from any lying about the lot. If no book is on the lot (on a desk, table, or on the floor), the action won't appear in the Influence menu. If your Sim has a partially completed assignment on the lot (when clicked on, books display a completion percentage), make sure it's the only one the Influenced Sim can choose by deleting any other stray books owned by your Sim.

♦ Do My Term Paper: Influenced Sim goes to the nearest free computer and writes a term paper on your Sim's behalf until the project is done or until they are forced to stop by their own Mood

or Needs. This action is available even if all computers on the lot are being used. However, if the Influenced Sim can't get use of any computer, they eventually abandon the Influenced action— you won't, however, get your 2,500 Influence points back for the aborted effort.

> **tip**
>
> When Influencing Sims to do your Sims' schoolwork, make sure your Sims have the grade capacity to benefit from the completion of the work. For example, a Sim with only one of the three skill requirements for his major for the current semester can't reap the full benefit of a finished term paper, wasting an otherwise massive boost in his semester grade. See Chapter 5 for details.

Influence Acceptance and Rejection

There is no guarantee that a Sim will accept your Sim's exercise of Influence. Whether they agree to perform the action you request depends on their Daily Relationship with your Sim. The requirement is, however, quite light: Daily Relationship must be greater than -50.

Sure you can get her to deliver a kiss, but there's no guarantee the other Sim will appreciate it.

After the Influenced action is accepted, its cost is deducted from your Sim's Influence total. Whether the ensuing action is completed *successfully*, however, depends on a number of factors.

For social actions, the Influenced Sim is always able to initiate the social interaction (unless barred by the recipient's age or a family connection) even if they'd be unable to attempt it independently.

If, for example, the Influenced Sim and the target of the action had never met, the first Sim would normally be unable to do any action that required a positive Lifetime Relationship; it would simply be unavailable. Under Influence, however, any relationship score-based availability rules are suspended and pose no obstacle.

Availability, however, does not guarantee acceptance; the target of a social interaction decides whether to accept or reject the interaction just as they normally would. Thus, sending someone to kiss a stranger results in an inevitable rejection, but your Sim is charged for the exertion of Influence regardless of the outcome, predictable or not.

tip

A rejected kiss, for example, may seem like a waste of Influence. If, however, damaging the relationship between two Sims is your goal, then an inevitable rejection could be Influence well spent.

For nonsocial actions (i.e., Gardening, Repairing, Doing Assignments, and so on), there's a different limitation: the Influenced Sim's Mood and Needs. When your Sim undertakes any of these actions, he is eventually kicked out of the action if his Mood drops below zero (red) or if Hunger, Energy, Comfort (if not seated), or Bladder Needs descend too low. Likewise, an Influenced Sim only continues his task until his Mood or Needs require him to stop. Therefore, be careful which Sims you choose to Influence; a Sim in Need distress will agree to serve your Sim, but can't for very long.

tip

Before Influencing a Sim, see if they are displaying any Need thought or scream balloons and whether they've recently tended to their Needs. A Sim who's just been to the bathroom may be a better servant than one who's just arisen from a few hours in front of the TV.

Big Sim on Campus

Many Sims have a Want to be "Big Sim on Campus." What they actually want is to achieve *Level 5 Influence* capacity while still *in college*. Only this combination of conditions satisfies the Want.

LIFETIME WANT

The Lifetime Want is displayed when you point at your Sim's Aspiration meter.

Sims' lives can be largely driven by their chosen Aspiration. Now they have a more specific long-term goal with the addition of the Lifetime Want.

note

Aspiration is chosen in several ways:

1. When Sim age transitions to teen
2. When Sim is created in Create A Sim
3. When Sim becomes a junior in college (this is the only way Aspiration can be changed after initially chosen)

When an Aspiration is chosen—or, in one specific instance, changed—one of the Lifetime Wants associated with the Aspiration is randomly chosen for the Sim.

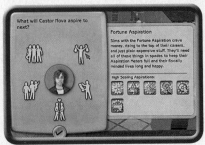

At the start of a Sim's junior year, they have the chance to change Aspiration.

The assigned Lifetime Want can be changed only if the Sim changes Aspiration (upon starting his junior college year).

Lifetime Wants are extremely long-term and are very difficult to achieve. They usually involve reaching the top of a profession, reaching certain familial, popularity, financial, or romantic goals, or by maxing out several skills.

Rewards for Lifetime Want

When a Sim achieves his Lifetime Aspiration, he receives 25,000 Aspiration Reward points, 10,000 Influence points, and is blessed with *permanent Platinum Aspiration level*! In other words, he gets a permanent perfect Mood for the rest of his life. The benefits of a constant top-drawer Mood are many.

When a Lifetime Want is realized, the Sim gets permanent Platinum Aspiration and Mood and a huge influx of Influence points. They also get a new Lifetime Want to earn more Reward and Influence points.

After realizing a Lifetime Want, the Sim is randomly assigned another. If he achieves another Lifetime Want, he gets another 25,000 Aspiration Reward points. This kind of Reward-point wealth makes Aspiration Reward objects easy to afford. This, in turn, has further benefits that make other things (including the achievement of additional Lifetime Wants) easier.

note

After a Lifetime Want is achieved, it is marked with a green check mark.

Lifetime Want Catalog

Lifetime Wants include:

Knowledge
◆ Max 5 skills
◆ Become Hospital Chief of Staff (Medicine career)
◆ Become Cult Leader (Paranormal career)
◆ Become Ecological Guru (Natural Scientist career)
◆ Have 10 children abducted by aliens
◆ Become Mad Scientist (Science career)
◆ Become Criminal Mastermind (Criminal career)

Fortune
◆ Earn §100,000
◆ Become Hospital Chief of Staff (Medicine career)
◆ Become Hall of Famer (Sports career)
◆ Become Tycoon (Business career)
◆ Become Criminal Mastermind (Criminal career)

Family
◆ Graduate 10 children from college
◆ Have 10 grandchildren
◆ Marry off 10 children
◆ Reach golden anniversary
◆ Become Captain Hero (Law Enforcement career)

Romance
◆ Become Professional Party Guest (Slacker career)
◆ Become Visionary (Artist career)
◆ Become Hall of Famer (Sports career)
◆ WooHoo with 10 different Sims
◆ Have 10 simultaneous lovers
◆ Become Celebrity Chef (Culinary career)

Popularity
◆ Become Cult Leader (Paranormal career)
◆ Become Icon (Show Business career)
◆ Become General (Military career)
◆ Become Hall of Famer (Sports career)
◆ Become Mayor (Politics career)
◆ Become Celebrity Chef (Culinary career)
◆ Have 10 simultaneous best friends
◆ Become Captain Hero (Law Enforcement career)

Chapter 4
Getting Into College

In the world of *The Sims™ 2*, getting into college is the easy part. Thanks to the wonders of universal higher education, all Sims with a high school average of D- or better are guaranteed admission into any college they choose. Not all may *want* to go to college, and it may not be the right move for everyone, but they are certainly free to choose.

There are various ways to get a student into college, each with its own mechanics and strategies. Moreover, there are several things a teen Sim can do to make the transition to college easier, both academically and financially. This chapter covers all pre-college quandaries and procedures.

note

Teens with an F average in school can't apply for college by phone or computer (the College menu on these objects won't appear), and their names won't appear in the available Teens list in the Send Sims to College tool.

STUDENT SOURCES

There are four sources of students for your colleges:

- Young adults created in the college town's Create A Sim tool.
- The Send Sims to College tool found in neighborhoods and in college towns (in the Families or Students control panel, respectively).
- Via phone or computer from a neighborhood household.
- Preassembled households from the Student Bin or already on a lot (in either private or Greek housing).

College Create A Sim

Young adults generated in a college town's Create A Sim tool can be grouped into households and assembled, ready to matriculate, in the town's Student Bin (*Sims™ 2 University*'s answer to the Family Bin).

Assemble the ideal Freshman class in young adult Create A Sim.

These students are just like any others, save three crucial details: skills, Influence capacity, and Aspiration Reward points. Since they have not grown up organically in the game, they enter college with *no* skills, no accumulated Aspiration Reward points, and no friends (which dictate Influence point capacity). As such, playing them is more difficult than playing a continuing teen Sim who's already built skills, amassed Aspiration points, and established friendships.

Create A Sim products arrive in college fresh off the proverbial turnip truck, with no skill development and only starting friendships with their household mates.

When playing with a young adult built in the college town's Create A Sim, you have the luxury of choosing an Aspiration with college in mind. Knowledge Sims tend to have the easiest time in college since learning skills simultaneously satisfy their most common Wants (raising their Aspiration bar into Platinum level, making them able to study longer and meet skill requirements more easily).

Moreover, a seasoned Sim will likely have accumulated some store of Reward Points that can be spent on objects that aid in college life (the Thinking Cap for fast skill building or the Cool Shades for amplified relationship development).

With Romance, Popularity, Wealth, and Family Sims, education is more difficult since their Wants tend to pull them AWAY from their studies. If you dedicate them to school, their Aspiration level will be difficult to maintain, and they won't be able to study as long as they would with a Platinum good Mood.

The trick is this: you get to choose a new Aspiration for any Sim who finishes Junior year. If you want your young adults to graduate with an Aspiration other than Knowledge, start them as Knowledge Sims and change them later to whatever you feel is their destiny.

Send Sims to College

The Send Sims to College button is available in both the neighborhood and college town via the Families and Students console, respectively. Through it, you can quickly assemble a household of teens from the college town's linked neighborhood.

Located in the Students console in college towns or in the Family console in neighborhoods, the Send Sims to College tool is an easy way to assemble households of preexisting teens.

This three-panel tool lets you handpick which teens in a neighborhood will make the big move from family life to college. All selected teens are simultaneously removed from their individual households (if they have one) and assembled as a household in the Student Bin of every college.

Since the move to college involves an age transition, existing teens moved to college retain all of their skills, Aspiration Reward points, Personality profiles, family connections, and relationships. Two things, however, do change:

◆ Crush/Go Steady status: Since teens can only develop romantic relationships with other teens, age transitioning erases any existing romantic relationships, even if the teens become young adults together. To remedy this, verify that the teens retain the requisite Daily and/or Lifetime relationship minimums between them and do a romantic interaction to reestablish the bond.

◆ Aspiration Level: As discussed in Chapter 21, when Sims age transition, the scale of their Aspiration meter expands and the Sim's previous Aspiration Level drops. This isn't a penalty, just a necessity of the greater challenge of maintaining high Aspiration in a new age.

Every qualifying teen from the home neighborhood is listed in the Send Sims to College tool.

Every teen (with a D- average or better) in the neighborhood is listed in the left-hand pane, including playable, NPC, and Townie teen Sims. Teens that were actively playable in the home neighborhood are highlighted with a green Plumbob jewel to the left of their name.

There are several ways to get originally playable teens into college, but Townie and NPC Sims from the home neighborhood can only be enrolled via the Send Sims to College tool. This, too, is one of the easiest ways to convert an otherwise unplayable Townie Sim into a full-fledged playable Sim.

Townie and NPC Sims, unlike newly created young adults, usually arrive with some skills developed and possibly several relationships. They'll have an Aspiration but it will begin at neutral level with no accumulation of Reward points. They may even have some memories.

When a teen's name is clicked, his or her picture appears in the middle pane along with the amount of starting money for college. This figure includes $500 (grant given to all teens to start college) and the sum of any scholarships awarded the teen (see the "Scholarships" section later in this chapter).

tip

Though this tool is the easiest way to move teens to college, it pays to first see if any of your playable teens are eligible for scholarship funds. Go into each playable house containing a teen and have him or her use the phone or computer to apply for scholarships. Then, save the households and return to the Send Sims to College tool. The new funds (if any) will have been added for the big move.

Students with scholarship money will display a higher total of funds.

The right-hand pane lists all students you've selected to be in the household. To add the selected Sim to the college household, click on the right-facing arrow (with the "+" in it).

To remove a Sim, highlight the Sim's name and click the left-facing arrow (with the "-" in it). Here you may also input the college household's name and preview how much money they'll have together. With that, the teen's moved out, and the household is created and added to every linked college's Student Bin.

From Neighborhood Lots

Teen Sims may enroll in college individually from their own home lots if they have a D- or better average in high school.

Enrolling can be done from either any house or cell phone, or from any computer.

The application process is a breeze: pick up the phone and ask.

With either object, select the College menu and select "Move to College." The remaining residents of the household bid farewell to the departing teen, and a taxi ships the teen off to school.

After the departing Sim's cab leaves, the Sim is removed from the household. The rest of the family, however, continues without the departing student, going on with the business of life.

tip

When a student is moved out to college, you can undo the decision by exiting the household and choosing NOT to save it. When you reenter the house, the student will be restored and everything will be back the way it was at the last save.

To rejoin your incoming Freshman at college, choose a school and locate the teen in the Student Bin.

note

If a teen qualifies, he or she may be eligible for one or more scholarships to add to starting school funds. To find out, make the first phone call or computer connection to the "Apply for Scholarship" selection in the College menu. After taking care of that business, the teen can enroll in college with the maximum possible resources.

Prefabricated Households

Each college's Student Bin comes with several premade college households that you can move in or merge into college housing. These Sims are fully realized with some (but not much) skill development and a few preexisting relationships.

The college town Student Bins are brimming with student households eager to get to school.

Additionally, each college has several households already moved in and ready to play. Mostly, these households are in the more expensive private housing rather than dorms. Almost every college also has two Greek houses that you're free to play (but can't merge any other household into).

Established households are even more developed than premade Student Bin households. Don't be shy about dropping in on them.

> **note**
>
> Sim Greek houses, even if called "fraternity" or "sorority," are not gender discriminatory. Any Sim, regardless of gender, may be invited to move into any Greek house.

If you don't want to build your own Sims in Create A Sim and don't wish to uproot your neighborhood teen Sims, these households are a good way to get a feel for college life in the Sims' world.

MOVING SIMS IN

Regardless of how a student household is assembled, all are deposited in the Student Bin. From there, they can be moved or merged as playable Sims into any occupied dorm or private residence. They cannot, however, be moved directly into a Greek house, as those lots require an in-game invitation before a Sim may move in. For more on this procedure, see Chapter 6.

Select a Sim from the Student Bin and place him or her in an empty residential lot, or merge the Sim into an occupied one.

> **note**
>
> The Student Bin is shared between all college towns connected with a neighborhood.

All playable Sims in a household (even when merged with an already established household) will share their collective funds. Nonplayable Sims may not expend these funds, but any one member of the household may draw from them freely.

The difference between a dorm and private housing is largely a matter of money. Monthly bills in dorms are lower (regardless of dorm size) than in private housing.

No matter how much money a household has, it can't ever move directly from the Student Bin into a Greek house.

19

On the upside, dorms offer far more amenities than private housing, and full residential food service is included in the cost of residence. Students in private homes must cook for themselves.

GRANTS AND SCHOLARSHIPS

All teen Sims (above an F grade) who desire it are guaranteed admission to college, and all students get automatic grants to get them started financially while away at school.

Upon admission, all Sims receive grants of §500. This money is added to the collective funds of their new college household.

Scholarships

Sims can get off to an even better financial start at college if they can win one or more scholarships. Each scholarship awarded adds §1,000 to the Sim's starting college funds.

Scholarships are awarded either by phone or computer to qualifying teens.

Getting scholarship money requires two things:

◆ Meeting the scholarship's qualifications
◆ Applying for scholarships by computer or phone

Available Scholarships

SCHOLARSHIP	QUALIFICATION	AWARD
Hogan Award for Athletics	Level 8 or higher Body skill	§750
Bain-Gordon Communications Fellowship	Level 8 or higher Charisma skill	§750
Kim Metro Prize for Hygienics	Level 8 or higher Cleaning skill	§750
London Culinary Arts Scholarship	Level 8 or higher Cooking skill	§750
Will Wright Genius Grant	Level 8 or higher Logic skill	§750
Bui Engineering Award	Level 8 or higher Mechanical skill	§750
Quigley Visual Arts Grant	Level 8 or higher Creative skill	§750
SimCity Scholar's Grant	A- or better in high school	§1,000
Extraterrestrial Reparations Grant	Abducted by aliens	§1,500
Young Entrepreneurs Award	Level 3 in any teen career	§750
Undead Educational Scholarship	Teen is a Zombie	§1,500
Phelps-Wilsonoff Billiards Prize	Level 8 Pool skill	§1,000
Tsang Footwork Award	Level 8 Dancing skill	§1,000
Orphaned Sims Assistance Fund	Sim has no living parents	§1,500

note

Pool and Dancing skills are invisible skills developed by using the pool table and partner dancing with other Sims, respectively. These skills are built by spending time and accomplishing special moves in each of these activities and provide access to greater performance and more advanced tricks. There is, however, no way to view your Sim's status in either skill, so qualifying for these scholarships is a matter of trial and error; if you don't qualify, dance or shoot pool more and try the scholarship again. For details on Dancing and Pool skills, see the "Hidden Skills" section in Chapter 22 and the "Corner Pocket Pool Table" section in Chapter 8, respectively.

The Zombie scholarship is available automatically if a teen has been returned from the dead as a Zombie. For more info on Zombies, see Chapter 8.

PRE-COLLEGE WANTS AND FEARS

Every teen *can* go to college, but not every teen *wants* to go to college. Some don't really care, some want it, and some want it so badly, they fear *not* going to college.

Likewise, the parents and grandparents of teens can get wrapped up in their offspring's college prospects, also wanting them to advance to higher education and, in some cases, fearing they'll miss out.

College can, thus, be a major Aspiration-scoring opportunity for some Sims.

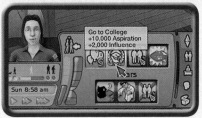

All teen Sims want to go to college, though only those who REALLY want it will show it in their Wants panel. Satisfy this desire and they arrive at college with a huge boost to Aspiration score and Influence points.

Generally, all Sims have a Want to go to college, but some want it more than others based on personality and Aspiration.

Pre-College Wants and Fears

Who?	Want or Fear?	What?	If	Want or Fear Power Amplified By
Teens	Want	To go to college	—	Outgoing/Shy, Wealth, or Knowledge Aspiration. If Knowledge, increased further if teen gets a scholarship
Knowledge or Wealth teen	Fear	Not going to college		Grade drops to F or adult transition nearing Outgoing/Shy
Parents/Grandparents of teens	Want	Teen to go to college	High Lifetime relationship with teen	If Parents/Grandparents are Knowledge or Family Sims
Parents/Grandparents of teens	Fear	Teen not going to college	High Lifetime Relationship, teen grades drop to F, or teen's adult transition approaching.	If Parents/Grandparents are Knowledge or Family Sims
Teens/Parents/Grandparents	Want	Apply for any scholarship	Teen is nearly qualified or has qualified but not applied for any scholarship	For Parent/Grandparents, if they're Wealth Sims
Teen Wealth Sim	Want	Collect multiple scholarships	Has already gotten one	—

---

note

Keep in mind that when discussing the "power" or "strength" of a Want or Fear, we're talking not about how many Reward points it's worth or how much it will raise the Aspiration score, but how loudly it advertises itself to be shown in the Want/Fears panel. The top four strongest Wants and the top three strongest Fears are the ones displayed in the panel, so a Want or Fear must be pretty potent relative to all others to appear and be scorable.

note

Wants and Fears about going to college will also build Influence. Make sure your Knowledge and Wealth Sims have enough Influence capacity to absorb the Influence benefit of these Wants.

Chapter 5
Majors, Grades, and All Things Academic

Not every Sim needs to make the dean's list to consider their college experience a success, but they must have a measure of academic achievement to remain on campus and to, in career terms, make the experience worth the effort. Whether you want your Sims to score straight As or just squeak by and party to the max, you gotta know how to work the system.

This chapter describes the standards by which Sims are evaluated and rewarded for their academic toils and describes the choices and advantages implicit in choosing a major.

YEAR STRUCTURE AND SEMESTER SYSTEM

note

In college towns, there's no way to know precisely what day of the week it is (the console shows only the year, semester, and time of day), but it doesn't matter. Classes are held seven days a week, and when your Sim chooses to unwind is up to them.

Unlike the basic game of *The Sims™ 2*, the college experience isn't measured in days but rather in academic years and semesters. The college experience is divided into the four traditional academic years: Freshman (Fr), Sophomore (So), Junior (Jr), and Senior (Sr). Academic years are divided into two grading periods ("semesters") during which your Sim must earn passing grades. Each semester lasts approximately three days.

note

More precisely, your Sim's first exam is exactly 72 hours after they arrive at college, and each subsequent exam is 72 hours after that.

During each three-day semester, Sims must build their "academic potential" (by meeting skill requirements) and accumulate "Class Performance" (by doing things that earn grade points).

Each semester concludes with a final exam that is your Sim's last chance to contribute to the semester's Class Performance. At this exam's end (whether your Sim attends or not), the Sim's semester grade and grant are announced and awarded, and their GPA is raised or lowered as the new grade is factored. They then move to the next semester; however, if they scored below a C-, they must repeat the previous semester.

When Sims are promoted to a new academic year, they are also awarded an additional bonus that affects their Aspiration and Wants.

Upon successful completion of Senior year's second semester, the Sim graduates and receives his final grant, the Senior year Aspiration award, and final GPA. If the GPA is high enough, the Sim graduates with honors and may receive a level boost in any postcollege career.

After graduation, the Sim can remain on campus for two days to do whatever they wish: have fun, socialize, build skills, etc. They depart college for their base neighborhood by letting this time expire, summoning a taxi, or throwing a Graduation Party.

COLLEGE CONSOLE AND THE PERSONAL ACADEMIC CLOCK

As previously mentioned, the console for young adults is a bit different than for Sims in the neighborhoods. There's also an difference in the way the clock works for timing the Sim's final exams.

Academic Year Indicator

When you select a Sim, his portrait appears in the console. Below this is his Academic Year indicator (in lieu of his Age indicator). The Sim's current year is (just as with Sims' current age group back in the neighborhoods) expanded and then split into two halves representing the two semesters of the current year. Other years (past and future) are abbreviated and the Semester indicator is combined into a single small circle; if the circle is blue, the year was completed.

The Academic Year indicator is below the active Sim's portrait. The current year is split into two (semesters), and past and future years are minimized to small dots.

Point at the Academic Year indicator to see the number of hours until the Sim's final exam for the current semester. This is how much time you have left to build this Sim's Class Performance.

Point to the Academic Year indicator and a pop-up tells you when the active Sim's next exam is.

The Personal Exam Clock

Every Sim has an invisible clock that indicates when their exams take place. This is linked to your Sim's home clock, which is based on how often and for how long your Sim leaves their lot to visit others. As a result, Sims who arrived on campus together may start to have exams at wildly different times, even in the middle of the night.

To further explain, when a Sim leaves a lot and goes to another, the clock on the previous lot freezes

the moment the Sim departs. When the Sim arrives at the new lot, the clock there runs as long as that lot is loaded. Then, when the Sim returns home, the clock picks up where it left off, as if the Sim never left.

This "time warp" means a Sim can leave their home lot at the semester's beginning, go to a community lot, do all their skill and class work on the community lots, return home, and be ready for their exam with little or no time coming off the home lot clock. For this reason, exams are scheduled by the Sim's "personal clock," which continues to run whenever the Sim is playable.

Don't, therefore, rely on the day clock time or when the exams of other playable Sims are supposed to occur. When the exam is less than five hours away, announcements are made and the Sim's Skills and Major panel changes to show when the next exam will be. Let these be your guide.

MAJORS

All Sim universities offer eleven majors of specialized study (plus four semesters of an Undeclared curriculum). Each major offers different classes (with differing times and durations), requires development of a different combination of skills, and connects to a distinct selection of three adult careers.

Class Schedules

Each major (including Undeclared) offers one class per semester, meeting every day at the same time for the same duration. Most classes are two hours but some require three.

A Sim's current class title and time are shown in the Skills and Major panel.

Class attendance isn't mandatory, but it goes a long way toward your Sims' semester grades.

Punctuality and a good Mood (+55 or higher) earn your Sims the most points for their class time. From the time a Sim leaves for classes until they return, their Needs shift:

◆ Bladder: -5 per hour
◆ Comfort: -5 per hour
◆ Energy: -2 per hour
◆ Fun: -5 per hour

◆ Hunger: -5 per hour
◆ Hygiene: -5 per hour
◆ Social: +2 per hour

Skills

Every new semester, a student must meet certain skill requirements in up to three skills. As skill levels rise and take longer to acquire, Junior- and Senior-year semesters only require two targets.

Skill levels needed for the current semester are outlined in the Skills and Majors panel. As you meet these requirements, the Class Performance meter expands to accommodate more grade points.

Each major features one skill most prominently, and each major tends to coincide with careers that emphasize the same skill. Smart planning of a Sim's future takes into account:

◆ Which majors spotlight which skills
◆ Which careers a major favors
◆ Which careers and majors share the most common skills

Ideal Careers

Each major prepares graduates for three careers. Graduating with the skills needed to succeed in your chosen career is an obvious benefit.

When choosing a major, its ideal postcollege careers are displayed.

Less obvious is the extra bonus of moving into a career with the proper major. If a Sim graduates with honors *and* goes into one of the three ideal careers for their major, they begin one level higher than they would in nonaligned careers.

The Majors

Here are the 12 possible majors for a young adult Sim. Each major includes an icon, the skills it requires, its ideal careers, and its class title and schedule.

Undeclared

◆ Primary skill: None
◆ Other required skills: All
◆ Linked careers: None

Classes

Semester	Class Title	Cooking	Mechanical	Charisma	Body	Logic	Creativity	Cleaning	Hours
Freshman 1	The World: A Survey of Everything That Ever Happened	1	—	—	—	1	1	—	3 p.m.–5 p.m.
Freshman 2	Academic Argument: Beyond "Did Not, Did Too"	—	1	—	1	—	—	1	8 a.m.–11 a.m.
Sophomore 1	Workshop: Writing More Goodly	—	2	1	—	2	—	—	8 p.m.–10 p.m.
Sophomore 2	Intro to Philosophy: Your Insignificant Place in the Universe	2	—	—	—	—	2	2	6 p.m.–8 p.m.

> **note**
>
> Sims must declare a major before they begin Junior year. If they remain Undeclared at this point, the major switches automatically to Philosophy (see the "Philosophy" section).

Art

- Primary skill: Creativity
- Other required skills: Cooking, Mechanical, Charisma
- Linked careers: Artist, Slacker, Culinary

Classes

Semester	Class Title	Cooking	Mechanical	Charisma	Body	Logic	Creativity	Cleaning	Hours
Freshman 1	Stick Figures: Lowering the Bar	—	1	—	—	—	1	1	2 p.m.–4 p.m.
Freshman 2	Life Drawing: An Excuse to See Naked People	—	—	1	1	1	—	—	5 p.m.–7 p.m.
Sophomore 1	Underwater Basket Weaving: Art Meets Fitness	1	—	2	—	—	2	—	10 a.m.–1 p.m.
Sophomore 2	Oil Painting and Other Ways to Poison Oneself	2	2	—	—	—	3	—	7 p.m.–9 p.m.
Junior 1	Art History 1: Artists You'll Never Be as Good As	—	3	3	—	—	—	—	4 p.m.–6 p.m.
Junior 2	Art History 2: Artists You're Already Way Better Than	3	—	—	—	—	4	—	9 a.m.–11 a.m.
Senior 1	Impressionism and Other Blurry Movements	4	4	—	—	—	—	—	7 p.m.–10 p.m.
Senior 2	Conceptual Art: No, Really. It's Art	—	—	4	—	—	5	—	8 a.m.–10 a.m.

Biology

- Primary skill: Logic
- Other required skills: Mechanical, Body, Cleaning
- Linked careers: Natural Scientist, Law Enforcement, Medicine

Classes

Semester	Class Title	Cooking	Mechanical	Charisma	Body	Logic	Creativity	Cleaning	Hours
Freshman 1	Lab Techniques 1: Poking at Things with Tweezers	1	1	—	—	1	—	—	5 p.m.–7 p.m.
Freshman 2	Beginning Dissection: Why the Frog Hates You	—	—	1	1	—	1	—	4 p.m.–7 p.m.
Sophomore 1	Enzymes: Ase Up Your Life	—	—	—	2	2	—	1	9 a.m.–11 a.m.
Sophomore 2	The Lysozome: Everybody's Favorite Trash-Eater	—	2	—	3	—	—	2	10 a.m.–12 p.m.
Junior 1	Inhibitor Molecules: Nature's Bureaucrats	—	3	—	—	—	—	3	3 p.m.–6 p.m.
Junior 2	Borborygmic Digestion	—	—	—	4	3	—	—	6 p.m.–8 p.m.
Senior 1	Xenobiology: Who's Probing Who NOW?	—	4	—	—	4	—	—	8 p.m.–10 p.m.
Senior 2	Senior Thesis: The Laganaphyllis Simnovorii	—	—	—	—	5	—	4	3 p.m.–5 p.m.

Drama

- ◆ Primary skill: Charisma
- ◆ Other required skills: Body, Logic, Creativity
- ◆ Linked careers: Show Business, Politics, Athletic

Classes

Semester	Class Title	Cooking	Mechanical	Charisma	Body	Logic	Creativity	Cleaning	Hours
Freshman 1	The History of Ancient Drama: When Every Play Ended with Death	1	1	1	—	—	—	—	10 a.m.–12 p.m.
Freshman 2	Improvisation: Because Scripts Are for Wusses	—	—	—	1	—	1	1	7 p.m.–9 p.m.
Sophomore 1	Pratfalls and Other Ways to Give Up Your Dignity	—	—	2	2	1	—	—	11 a.m.–1 p.m.
Sophomore 2	Costume Design: Because Naked Actors Are Distracting	—	—	3	—	2	2	—	2 p.m.–4 p.m.
Junior 1	Moving Pretentiously: A Modern Dance Workshop	—	—	—	3	—	3	—	6 p.m.–9 p.m.
Junior 2	Stage Combat without Killing Your Peers	—	—	—	4	3	—	—	5 p.m.–7 p.m.
Senior 1	The One-Sim Show: Drama for Those Who Don't Play Well with Others	—	—	4	—	—	4	—	11 a.m.–2 p.m.
Senior 2	Characterization: Becoming Someone More Interesting Than You	—	—	5	—	4	—	—	3 p.m.–5 p.m.

Economics

- ◆ Primary skill: Charisma
- ◆ Other required skills: Mechanical, Logic, Creativity
- ◆ Linked careers: Business, Politics, Show Business

Classes

Semester	Class Title	Cooking	Mechanical	Charisma	Body	Logic	Creativity	Cleaning	Hours
Freshman 1	Why Money Does Grow on Some Trees	1	—	1	—	—	1	—	5 p.m.–7 p.m.
Freshman 2	Work Is for Losers: A Counterfeiting Workshop	—	1	—	1	—	1	—	6 p.m.–9 p.m.
Sophomore 1	Economic Forecasting: Guessing Never Hurt Anybody	—	—	2	—	1	2	—	4 p.m.–6 p.m.
Sophomore 2	Laissez-Faire and Other Lazy Policies	—	2	3	—	2	—	—	12 p.m.–3 p.m.
Junior 1	Econometrics: Graphs a' Plenty	—	3	—	—	—	3	—	2 p.m.–4 p.m.
Junior 2	Converting Video Game Money Into Real Simoleans	—	4	4	—	—	—	—	8 p.m.–10 p.m.
Senior 1	Exploiting the Environment for Fun and Profit	—	—	—	—	3	4	—	12 p.m.–2 p.m.
Senior 2	Senior Project Internship: Coffeemaking at Landgraab Enterprises	—	—	5	—	4	—	—	2 p.m.–4 p.m.

History

- ◆ Primary skill: Logic
- ◆ Other required skills: Mechanical, Charisma, Creativity
- ◆ Linked careers: Military, Artist, Politics

Classes

Semester	Class Title	Cooking	Mechanical	Charisma	Body	Logic	Creativity	Cleaning	Hours
Freshman 1	Intro to History: People More Important Than You	1	—	—	1	1	—	—	8 p.m.–10 p.m.
Freshman 2	Civilization: Why It's Rarely Very Civil	—	1	—	—	1	1	1	3 p.m.–5 p.m.
Sophomore 1	Revisionism: It's Not Libel If They're Dead	—	—	1	—	2	2	—	4 p.m.–6 p.m.
Sophomore 2	Memorizing Names and Dates: An Alternative to Learning	—	2	2	—	3	—	—	12 p.m.–2 p.m.
Junior 1	Ethnography: Why Those People Seem Strange	—	—	3	—	—	3	—	1 p.m.–3 p.m.
Junior 2	Political Science Majors: Why You Should Hate Them	—	3	—	—	4	—	—	3 p.m.–6 p.m.
Senior 1	Anthropology: Not as Cool as in the Movies	—	4	—	—	—	4	—	5 p.m.–7 p.m.
Senior 2	Historic Pessimism: Why We'll Never Learn	—	—	4	—	5	—	—	1 p.m.–3 p.m.

Literature

- ◆ Primary skill: Creativity
- ◆ Other required skills: Mechanical, Charisma, Body
- ◆ Linked careers: Criminal, Slacker, Show Business

Classes

Semester	Class Title	Cooking	Mechanical	Charisma	Body	Logic	Creativity	Cleaning	Hours
Freshman 1	How to Judge a Book By Its Cover	—	1	—	—	1	1	—	1 p.m.–3 p.m.
Freshman 2	Haiku: Form Over Function	1	—	—	1	—	—	1	12 p.m.–3 p.m.
Sophomore 1	Words Ending with -eth: A Shakespearean Study	—	—	1	2	—	2	—	2 p.m.–4 p.m.
Sophomore 2	The Girl from Nantucket and Other Famous Limericks	—	2	2	—	—	3	—	11 a.m.–1 p.m.
Junior 1	Iambic Pentameter: DaDUM DaDUM DaDUM DaDUM DaDUM	—	3	—	—	—	4	—	2 p.m.–4 p.m.
Junior 2	Understanding C. London's Complete Works: Good Luck, Kid	—	—	3	3	—	—	—	9 a.m.–11 a.m.
Senior 1	Using Bizarre Metaphors: Life Is Feeding Baked Alaska to Zombies	—	4	—	4	—	—	—	2 p.m.–5 p.m.
Senior 2	Senior Project: Translations from the Simlish	—	—	4	—	—	5	—	3 p.m.–5 p.m.

Mathematics

$$\frac{1 + \sqrt{5}}{2}$$

◆ Primary skill: Logic

◆ Other required skills: Mechanical, Creativity, Cleaning

◆ Linked careers: Natural Science, Science, Criminal

Classes

Semester	Class Title	Cooking	Mechanical	Charisma	Body	Logic	Creativity	Cleaning	Hours
Freshman 1	Remedial Addition: The Fingers and Toes Technique	—	1	—	1	1	—	—	1 p.m.–3 p.m.
Freshman 2	P = NP and other Straightforward Proofs	1	—	—	—	—	1	1	3 p.m.–6 p.m.
Sophomore 1	PEMDAS and You	—	2	1	—	2	—	—	11 a.m.–1 p.m.
Sophomore 2	Stopping Robot Hordes: Dividing by Zero	—	—	—	—	3	2	2	6 p.m.–8 p.m.
Junior 1	3D Geometry: Re-imagining the Plumb Bob	—	3	—	—	—	3	—	3 p.m.–6 p.m.
Junior 2	Reasoning with Irrational Numbers	—	—	—	—	4	—	3	7 p.m.–9 p.m.
Senior 1	Mathematics in Nature: Pinecones and the Golden Ratio	—	4	—	—	—	—	4	11 a.m.–1 p.m.
Senior 2	1337 Ways to Write a Lemma	—	—	—	—	5	4	—	1 p.m.–3 p.m.

Philosophy

◆ Primary skill: Logic

◆ Other required skills: Cooking, Charisma, Creativity

◆ Linked careers: Slacker, Culinary, Paranormal

Classes

Semester	Class Title	Cooking	Mechanical	Charisma	Body	Logic	Creativity	Cleaning	Hours
Freshman 1	What Is the Meaning of This?!	—	1	—	—	1	—	1	10 a.m.–12 p.m.
Freshman 2	The Refrigerator Light: Proof vs. Faith	1	—	1	—	—	1	—	6 p.m.–8 p.m.
Sophomore 1	Old Dead Guys Who Thought Stuff	—	—	—	1	2	2	—	12 a.m.–2 a.m.
Sophomore 2	Optimists and Other Idiots	2	—	2	—	3	—	—	4 p.m.–6 p.m.
Junior 1	Philosophy's Place in the Neighborhood: Anywhere?	—	—	—	—	4	3	—	9 a.m.–12 p.m.
Junior 2	Existentialism: Depressing Yourself on Purpose	3	—	—	—	—	4	—	11 a.m.–2 p.m.
Senior 1	Who Controls the Pie Menu and Why?	—	—	3	—	5	—	—	4 p.m.–6 p.m.
Senior 2	Senior Project: Preparing for the Fast Food Industry	4	—	4	—	—	—	—	10 a.m.–12 p.m.

Physics

- ◆ Primary skill: Mechanical
- ◆ Other required skills: Logic, Creativity, Cleaning
- ◆ Linked careers: Science, Medicine, Paranormal

Classes

Semester	Class Title	Cooking	Mechanical	Charisma	Body	Logic	Creativity	Cleaning	Hours
Freshman 1	Newtonian Physics 1: Measuring Falling Stuff	1	1	1	—	—	—	—	9 a.m.–11 a.m.
Freshman 2	Newtonian Physics 2: Measuring Rolling Stuff	—	—	—	1	1	1	—	1 p.m.–3 p.m.
Sophomore 1	Lasers: Ruining Your Eyesight	—	2	—	—	—	2	1	5 p.m.–8 p.m.
Sophomore 2	General Relativity: Pretending to Understand	—	3	—	—	2	—	2	7 p.m.–10 p.m.
Junior 1	Quantum Mechanics: Why You're Wrong	—	—	—	—	3	—	3	8 a.m.–10 a.m.
Junior 2	Lab: Plasma Is Fun	—	4	—	—	—	—	4	7 p.m.–9 p.m.
Senior 1	Stellar Astrophysics: Too Far Away to Matter	—	—	—	—	4	3	—	11 a.m.–1 p.m.
Senior 2	The Strange Charm of Quarks	—	5	—	—	—	4	—	10 a.m.–12 p.m.

Political Science

- ◆ Primary skill: Charisma
- ◆ Other required skills: Body, Creativity, Cleaning
- ◆ Linked careers: Politics, Show Business, Military

Classes

Semester	Class Title	Cooking	Mechanical	Charisma	Body	Logic	Creativity	Cleaning	Hours
Freshman 1	The Soapbox and You	—	—	1	—	1	1	—	8 a.m.–10 a.m.
Freshman 2	Feudalism: Serf's Up!	1	1	—	1	—	—	—	6 p.m.–8 p.m.
Sophomore 1	Patriotism: Why Every Country Is Worse Than Yours	—	—	2	—	—	2	1	9 a.m.–11 a.m.
Sophomore 2	Lab: Making Your Own Monarchy	—	—	3	2	—	—	2	7 p.m.–10 p.m.
Junior 1	Plutocracy: Buying the Vote	—	—	—	—	—	3	3	5 p.m.–8 p.m.
Junior 2	Protesters: When to Repress	—	—	4	3	—	—	—	12 p.m.–2 p.m.
Senior 1	History Majors: Why You Should Hate Them	—	—	—	4	—	—	4	5 p.m.–7 p.m.
Senior 2	Senior Project: Questionable Fundraising Internship	—	—	5	—	—	4	—	10 a.m.–12 p.m.

Psychology

- ◆ Primary skill: Logic
- ◆ Other required skills: Charisma, Creativity, Cleaning
- ◆ Linked careers: Paranormal, Law Enforcement, Business

Classes

Semester	Class Title	Cooking	Mechanical	Charisma	Body	Logic	Creativity	Cleaning	Hours
Freshman 1	Introduction to Psychology: We Are Too a Science!	—	—	—	1	1	1	—	4 p.m.–6 p.m.
Freshman 2	Animal Behavior: Of Mazes and Cheeses	1	1	—	—	—	—	1	9 a.m.–11 a.m.
Sophomore 1	Abnormal Psychology: A Guide to Misdiagnosing Your Friends	—	—	1	—	2	2	—	12 p.m.–2 p.m.
Sophomore 2	The Prefrontal Lobe and Other Optional Brain Parts	—	—	2	—	3	—	2	7 p.m.–10 p.m.
Junior 1	Cognitive Dissonance: Recognizing How Broken Your Brain Is	—	—	—	—	3	—	3	2 p.m.–4 p.m.
Junior 2	Emotions: Don't Fear the Amygdala	—	—	3	—	4	—	—	4 p.m.–7 p.m.
Senior 1	Negative Interactions: What Happened to Deviance?	—	—	4	—	—	4	—	11 a.m.–1 p.m.
Senior 2	Advanced Autonomy: Finding the Best Action	—	—	—	—	5	—	4	6 p.m.–8 p.m.

Choosing a Major

There are many ways to select a major for your Sim. Here are a few:

- ◆ Existing skills: Choosing a major that emphasizes skills your Sim already has lightens his or her workload considerably, leaving more time for socializing, working on grades, and making money.
- ◆ Lifetime Want: If a Sim's Lifetime Want points toward reaching the top of a particular career and you want them to pursue that Want, put them in a major that favors the desired career.
- ◆ Desired career/career object: To enter a particular career or to obtain a particular career object, choose an aligned major to make attaining those goals easier.
- ◆ Aspiration: If your Sim's Aspiration favors a certain career (see Chapter 21), major in an aligned area to make satisfying the Sim's career-related Wants much easier.

- ◆ Personality: If your Sim has a personality that learns certain skills at an increased rate, choose a major that includes one or more of your Sim's personality-accelerated skills. For example, a Sim with Playful 10 learns the Creative skill quickly, so choose Art or Literature to meet class requirements faster.

Declaring Major

Sims may declare a major any time, but must declare one before the beginning of their Junior year.

Declaring your Sim's major is just a phone call or mouse click away.

Declare your major by contacting the Registrar (under the College menu) via telephone, cell phone, or computer. The option to call the Registrar disappears after the start of Senior year. If you opt not to immediately declare a major, your Sim may be Undeclared for the first two years of college. This "major" has specific class times and skill requirements like any other. If you do not select a major by the start of Junior year, the Sim automatically becomes a Philosophy major.

> ### tip
>
> The Undeclared major doesn't focus on any skills in particular, ultimately requiring a Level 2 skill in all except Body (1) and Charisma (1). Though the experience is broad, all other majors require a Level 3 in one skill by the start of Junior year. If, therefore, you stick to the Undeclared major and accomplish only its required skill levels, your Sim will be behind at the start of Junior year in whatever major he or she chooses.

Changing Majors

You can change your major any time until the start of a Sim's Senior year. Just contact the Registrar by phone, cell phone, or computer.

> ### note
>
> When a Sim becomes a Senior, the Registrar options disappear from the phones and computer.

Keep in mind that changing your major can have a negative effect on your Sims' academic progress; if they lack enough skill for the current semester of the new major, they have to acquire any old skill requirements plus all for the current semester to have any hope of a high grade. Failure to make up this lost ground results in academic probation.

GRADING

To be promoted to the next semester, Sims must achieve at least a C-. Better grades are rewarded with progressively larger academic grants, and finishing college with a cumulative GPA of 3.7 or better yields substantial career benefits. To snare these top grades while leaving your Sims free to socialize, have fun, and make money, you must understand how the grading system functions and how it can be used most efficiently.

> ### GRADES AND TIME MANAGEMENT
>
> Sims must spend, on average, a certain number of hours per day on schoolwork of some kind. To give you an idea of the commitment required to excel and the minimum effort your Sims must exert to avoid probation:
>
> ◆ A: Seven hours per day
>
> ◆ C-: Two hours per day
>
> Early years require less than the average time, while later years may require more.

GPA vs. Grades

There are two measures of how well your Sim is doing in college: GPA and grades.

GPA is shown in the Skills and Major panel.

GPA is always viewable in the Sim's Skills and Major panel and is the cumulative measure of all completed semesters (not including the current one). This figure is used, at the conclusion of college, to determine if a Sim graduates with honors—a distinction that can earn big Aspiration Rewards and a boost in postcollege employment.

Grade is the final letter grade for a semester. Grade is determined by the level of the Class Performance meter in the Skills and Major panel after the conclusion of the current semester's final exam. Grades correspond to the number of grade points the Sim accumulated over the course of the semester.

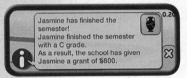

Jasmine has finished the semester!
Jasmine finished the semester with a C grade.
As a result, the school has given Jasmine a grant of §600.

At a semester's end, a Sim's grade and monetary grant are announced.

Grades also correspond to a sliding scale of financial rewards ("grants") for student performance. When a Sim's final semester grades are calculated (they return home from their final exam), they're immediately awarded the corresponding grant. Thus, an A+ student could earn §9,600 over four school years just for doing well in college.

Grading Scale

Letter Grade	Numerical Grade	Minimum Score Required	Grant
A+	4.0	1,000	§1,200
A	3.9	975	§1,100
A-	3.7	925	§1,000
B+	3.3	825	§800
B	3.0	750	§700
B-	2.7	675	§600
C+	2.2	575	§500
C	2.0	500	§400
C-	1.7	425	§300
D+	1.3	325	§0
D	1.0	250	§0
D-	0.7	175	§0
F	0.0	less than 175	§0

Academic Potential & Class Performance

To succeed (or in later years, just survive) in college, students must tend to two things: their academic potential and Class Performance.

This Class Performance bar is not at full potential; the open portion is about a third full (below the pass/fail line). This Sim must expand the capacity by learning required skills or no amount of Class Performance will earn him a passing grade.

This bar, on the other hand, is fully open, enabling the Sim to earn top grades.

Both academic potential and performance are displayed in the Class Performance meter in the Skills and Major panel. The unlocked portion of this vertical bar grows upward as potential is built and fills in as performance is accumulated. It resets at each semester's start as higher new requirements are set.

At a semester's start, the Class Performance meter is empty. Filling the meter involves earning Class Performance Points by doing assignments, attending classes, writing term papers, etc. Adding points, however, when the meter is less than full is a waste if the points exceed the meter's capacity. In other words, partial academic potential puts a lid on how high your Sim's grade can possibly go, no matter how much schoolwork they do.

note

The white horizontal line (the "pass/fail" line) on the Class Performance meter shows the grade needed to pass the semester. When Class Performance Points are BELOW this line, the student is in danger of failing and having to repeat the semester. When points rise above this line, the bar turns blue-gray and the student can be (mostly) assured of a passing mark.

Building Academic Potential

Before many points can be earned, however, you must increase the *capacity* of the bar (aka, academic potential). Do this by achieving the semester's skill levels for the Sim's major. The required skill levels are highlighted with a blue outline.

tip

Spend the first day of a semester working on building academic potential. Anything that speeds skill acquisition reduces the required work for each semester and lets you get on with earning a grade.

Choosing a major that matches your Sim's existing skills or having a personality extreme that speeds needed skills eases this process. Likewise, using Aspiration Reward points to purchase the skill-speeding Thinking Cap reward object is a good expenditure of resources. However, only use it when your Sim has Gold or Platinum Aspiration or you'll risk LOSING random skill points.

Each required skill point proportionally increases the Class Performance's size or capacity. In the Freshman and Sophomore years, *three* skill levels are required for full academic potential, so each one earned increases the meter by one quarter. In Junior and Senior years, only *two* skill levels are mandated (since higher skills take longer to earn), so each opens one third of the meter.

Thus, a Junior with only one of two skills required for their major can only manage a C+, no matter how much work they do.

Class Performance

Class Performance is built by doing coursework or related activities. *How* your Sim earns these points is up to you; there's no right way. You can earn high grades without ever attending class, though that may not be the most time-efficient route. To understand how to efficiently earn high grades, you must know the things that build Class Performance and how they do it. Earn Class Performance (or "grade points") by doing any of the following (in order of grade-points-per-hour efficiency):

Activity	Grade Points
Hacking grades via computer	180 per hour
Attending final exam	168 per hour
Group research	120 per hour with 5 Sims
Writing term paper	108 per hour
Group research	105 per hour with 4 Sims
Completing assignments with a tutor	90 points and 50 minutes per assignment or 108 per hour
Attending scheduled classes	100 per hour
WooHoo with Prof.	100 per hour or 50 per WooHoo
Completing assignments	90 per hour
Group research	90 per hour with 3 Sims
Group research	75 per hour with 2 Sims
Building relationship with Professor(s) in major	Points per Daily and Lifetime point
Solo research	60 per hour
Ask for tutoring	4 per conversation exchange
Talk about major	2 per conversation exchange

Each activity earns a number of grade points that are added to the current semester's Class Performance meter. The number of points accrued during the semester represent the Sim's final semester grade. Any points earned in excess of the Sim's current academic potential—which is less than 100 percent if the Sim hasn't achieved all the current semester's skill requirements—are not counted.

Class Attendance

Attending class earns up to 100 grade points per hour. Thus, a two-hour class can be worth 200 and a three-hour class can be worth 300.

note

Simply attending all three classes for the semester in a good Mood is worth at least 600 of the 1,000 points a Sim needs for an A+. If the class for the semester is a three-hour class, perfect attendance could net 900 of the 1,000 needed points.

How much of the potential total your Sim earns, however, depends on two things:

◆ Mood   ◆ Punctuality

Mood

Your Sim's Mood when they leave for class affects how many grade points they'll get.

A Sim's Mood when they leave for class determines the maximum number of points they can receive for attending, potentially reducing it by up to half.

◆ Good Mood (+55 or above): 100 per hour
◆ Medium Mood (-20 to +55): 75 per hour
◆ Bad Mood (-20 or below): 50 per hour

Punctuality

Just as with careers, classes are scheduled for specific times and Sims (Mood permitting) will leave the lot automatically (unless you prevent them) to arrive on time.

Unlike careers, however, a Sim can be late to a class, leaving the lot any time until the class has concluded.

note

If a Sim's Mood is extremely bad (less than -30), they won't automatically go to class. You MUST direct them to do so.

Late students don't, however, get the full benefit of the class. Points for class attendance are calculated by the amount of time the Sim spends in class. An on-time student gets a full point total, while a Sim who arrives half an hour late for a two-hour class gets only 75 percent of the points. The later they arrive, the fewer grade points they earn.

tip

Sims will attempt to leave for class at the first opportunity, starting one hour before the class start time. They don't, however, get any extra credit for being early, so manage your Sim in the hour before a class. Use the time to feed Needs, do assignments or research, work on a term paper, socialize, build skills, or earn money. Twenty minutes before class, disengage the Sim from activity, click on the Sim, select the College menu, and choose "Go to Class."

note

A Sim in a bad Mood going to a two-hour class on time will snag 100 grade points out of a possible 200. If he's a half hour late, however, he gets only 75 points.

Completing Assignments

Assignments are activities that require one hour's work and earn the Sim 90 grade points each.

Sims will look for a desk or table to do assignments.

Assignments can be done any time (Mood and Needs permitting) via a self-interaction. Click on your Sim and select "College" and "Do Assignment." The Sim pulls out an assignment book and looks for the nearest table or desk. If the Sim is unable to find a useable surface, he or she tries to find a spot on the floor. While doing assignments, a light blue progress bar appears above the Sim's head.

Click on an assignment book to see who owns it and how much of it is complete. If the book belongs to the active Sim, it won't have a name attached.

Assignments can also be initiated if a Sim has left an assignment book somewhere on the lot; just click on the book. The interaction menu shows what percentage of the assignment has been completed.

tip

Assignment books can be moved like any other object in Buy mode and can be deleted. If a book is left in an inaccessible place (i.e., in a locked room belonging to another Sim), entering Buy mode and moving it may be the only way to retrieve it.

Up to three assignment books per Sim are allowed on a lot. When all three are situated some-where, the self-interaction Do Assignment disappears until one of the three books is completed (by clicking on the books themselves) or until they're deleted.

note

Click on books to see who they belong to. If the menu reads "Do Assignment," it belongs to the selected Sim. If it reads, "Do Sim X's Assignment," it belongs to Sim X. Sims are free to do other Sims' assignments, but the grade points go to the Sim to whom the assignment belongs. This is a generous act and a good way to help a roommate improve his grades while he's doing other things.

Just as with skill-building activities, Sims stop doing assignments if their Mood falls below -20 or if their Fun, Hunger, Comfort, Bladder, or Energy drop too low.

Influence lets Sims do assignments with a hands-off approach.

If your Sim has enough Influence points (2,000), they can Influence another Sim to do their assignment for them, leaving your Sim free to pursue other

activities while earning valuable grade points. For the Influenced Sim to be successful, however, there must be an assignment book belonging to your Sim located somewhere accessible to the Influenced Sim (i.e., not in a locked room).

tip

Influenced Sims randomly choose among all accessible assignment books. If you want them to work on a specific one among several, move the others (in Buy mode) into an inaccessible place or delete them.

Assignments take an hour to complete, but this time can be shortened (by half) if the Sim asks another playable Sim for help or tutoring. These interactions, available via assignment books, cause your Sim to approach a specified Sim to ask for help. If the other Sim accepts, he or she coaches the requesting Sim until the assignment is done or until the tutor's own Mood or critical Needs force an exit.

note

Your playable Sims can make money by offering to tutor a Sim working on an assignment. See "Earning Money at College," in Chapter 6. The tutor may also help another Sim for free by clicking on the Sim's book and choosing "Help with Assignment."

Doing Research

Do Research is an interaction available on any book-shelf or unreturned book (i.e., the Study interaction for Mechanical, Cooking, and Cleaning skills) via the College menu.

Research is doubly productive when done with four other Sims. The learning never stops!

Periodically during research, your Sim displays his major icon and plus signs to indicate he's earned some grade points.

Research is a joinable interaction for up to five Sims. You can direct your Sims to join another Sim engaged in research or invite other Sims (playable or not) to join your Sim. With each Sim added to the study group, the rate of grade point acquisition increases by 15 (up to a max of 120). Sims doing research alone earn only 60 grade points per hour.

◆ 1 Sim: 60 per hour
◆ 2 Sims: 75 per hour
◆ 3 Sims: 90 per hour
◆ 4 Sims: 105 per hour
◆ 5 Sims: 120 per hour

As a bonus, all Sims in the study group will group talk, feeding their Social Need simultaneously.

Write Term Paper

Write Term Paper is an interaction available on any computer under the College menu and can be done only *once per semester.*

Toil away on one masterwork a semester and you'll be on your way toward that A.

Term papers take three hours to complete, and a Sim stops writing if Mood or critical Needs drop too low. A light blue progress bar appears above your Sim's head while writing term papers. If the Sim stops before the paper is completed, the progress is saved. Any term papers unfinished at a semester's end, however, are thrown out. Finishing a term paper is worth 325 grade points (about 108 points per hour).

note

Term papers are an efficient way to earn grade points, but make sure you have enough academic capacity to absorb all those points before the job is done. To be safe, save term paper work until after you've met all the semester's skill requirements.

Unlike assignments, Sims can't select to do another Sim's term paper nor can anyone help speed the process. Your Sims can, however, use their Influence points (2,500) to Influence other Sims to write papers for them. If the Influenced Sim accepts the request and completes the project, your Sim gets the full grade point benefit with no actual effort. There's no better reason to amass large batches of Influence in college!

tip

Since term paper writing is such a lengthy process, make sure the Sim you're Influencing is in a good Mood and is showing no signs of Need distress. If they're displaying Hunger thought balloons, your Influence will only produce a partially completed term paper. The cost in Influence is the same regardless, so invest only in Sims who are up to the task.

Relationships with Professors

Sims earn grade points from having relationships with their Professors. Every Daily and Lifetime Relationship point with any Professor in your Sim's major earned during the current term adds grade points (five per Daily point up to 340 and six per Lifetime point up to 475) to your Sim's Class Performance.

Sims don't NEED to be romantic with Professors to improve their grades, but it does work well.

On the first day of class or the first day in a new major, the names of a Sim's current Professors are announced; write them down! These Professors are added to your Sim's Relationship panel but aren't distinguished from any other Professors your Sim has met. Since only Relationship points with Professors within your Sim's major affect Class Performance, know which Profs are the right ones.

Relationships with major Professors, however, can also cause your Sim to *lose* grade points. Daily or Lifetime Relationship points lost during a semester due to negative or rejected social interactions drop your grade by five or six points, respectively. Therefore, maintain relationships (a daily phone call is a good relationship investment) once established and beware employing high-risk interactions.

Ask For Tutoring/Talk about Major

One social interaction, in addition to building relationship and fulfilling Social Need, also builds class performance. When it's available and how fast it boosts grades depends on whom it's being used.

Asking a Professor for tutoring earns grade points from the tutoring and for any relationship increases during the chat.

The Ask for Tutoring interaction can only be done with Professors in the Sim's current major, and it increases class performance at a rate of four points per conversation exchange. Your Sim is also increasing the Daily Relationship with the Professor simultaneously, so the Sim gains grade points that way too.

When Sims in the same major talk about that major, they earn grade points.

Talk about Major is available only with other young adult Sims in the *same major*; it boosts class performance by two points per conversation exchange.

WooHoo with Professor

Good relationships are fine, but the most efficient way to wring academic benefit from a Professor is with a good, old-fashioned WooHoo.

Sims earn grade points by relating with Professors and even more grade points by RELATING with Professors.

Every WooHoo with a Professor in your Sim's current major earns 50 grade points per encounter.

tip

Perhaps the Love Tub Aspiration reward object could help woo a Professor! On the other hand, if your Sim gets rejected for WooHoo, you can probably kiss the dean's list good-bye.

Hacking Grades

After a Sim is a member of the Secret Society (see the "Secret Society" section in Chapter 6), they gain the ability to Hack Grades on any computer.

Hacking is dangerous business. Keep your eyes on that Risk Level and quit out of the interaction if it gets too high.

Hacking grades is a fast way to earn grade points but it's risky. Start by interacting with a computer and select "College" and "Hack Grades."

> ### tip
>
> If you're hacking and fear getting caught, place objects to obstruct the police from reaching the computer. You still lose the grade points and get tagged with the fine, but the cops won't be able to confiscate the computer.

Every minute your Sim hacks, his or her grade climbs. The longer the Sim hacks, the better his grade. Hacking, however, must be done with care. Your Sim trips a random number of security alerts every minute he or she hacks. This number changes periodically, but each alert is added together and reflected in the displayed Risk Level. The higher your Sim's Logic skill, the fewer alerts he or she is likely to raise each interval and, thus, the longer the Sim can go before the Risk Level becomes dangerous.

> ### note
>
> Hacking becomes more difficult as a grade increases. Getting from a D to a C is much faster than getting from a B to an A. Also, the Risk Level rises with the level of the grade so that hacking B to A is inherently riskier than hacking a D to a C.

Even high Logic skill Sims can get nabbed in the early stages of hacking. Because the number of alerts is random, any Sim *could* trip enough to raise the Risk Level on the first try. The probability of this happening drops as Logic skill rises, but it never disappears.

Busted. Hope you weren't too attached to that computer.

Getting caught hacking undoes any grade increase your Sim achieved, imposes a §450 fine, and results in the confiscation of the computer (if the police can physically reach the object). If, however, you stop hacking (by clicking on the interaction's icon in the queue or closing the hacking dialog box) before the Risk Level rises too high, your Sim gets away with the crime. Your Sim may then reengage and start the process over to improve the grade further with the Risk Level back to normal for their current grade level (the higher the grade, the greater the risk).

Attending Final Exam

The final exam is one of the biggest contributors to your Sim's semester grade. Missing it denies your Sim the grade increase of attending, and it costs a large number of earned grade points.

> ### note
>
> If an exam conflicts with a regular class time, the class is cancelled.

The Skills and Major panel changes in the last five hours before an exam to call attention to the pending final.

Just like regular classes, the grade score increases from attending the final exam is based on your Sim's Mood when he or she leaves for the exam and the time the Sim spends at the exam. Compared to regular classes, however, the two-hour exam can earn up to (with Good Mood and on-time attendance):

◆ Good Mood (+55 or above): 336
◆ Medium Mood (-20 to +55): 264
◆ Bad Mood (-20 or below): 168

Late arrivals receive a proportional percentage of this score. Missing the exam entirely gives your Sim no points for the exam but also inflicts a penalty of -350. The lesson: even if your Sims attend no other classes, make sure they go to the final.

PROMOTION AND ACADEMIC PROBATION

To be promoted at a semester's end, your Sim must have a grade of C- or higher. Sims who fail to meet this requirement go on academic probation or, if they make a habit of it, get kicked out.

Promotion

Getting a passing grade promotes the Sim automatically to the next semester. When the Sim returns from the final exam, the semester grade is tabulated, the monetary grant for it is added to the household funds, and their cumulative GPA is updated.

Whenever a Sim successfully finishes a year of college, he or she gets a special bonus to keep for life:

◆ Freshman: One additional Want slot
◆ Sophomore: One additional Want/Fear lock
◆ Junior: Opportunity to change Aspiration
◆ Senior: Another additional Want slot

To start a new semester, the Class Performance meter is reset to zero points and its capacity is reduced based on how many of the semester's skill requirements are already met. Time to earn that A+ all over again.

Probation and Expulsion

If Sims fail to make passing grades, they go on academic probation and must repeat the semester. If they get a passing grade on the second try, they move out of probation and onto the next semester.

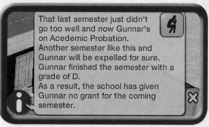

Sims who can't muster a passing grade get no money and must repeat the semester. They also get that embarrassing red "Academic Probation" label until they prove themselves.

Sims who can't muster a C- or higher while on academic probation are immediately kicked out of college. They are returned to the Family Bin of their original neighborhood and, as a badge of failure, given an third Fear slot.

note

Sims can fail (below C-) every semester and still complete four years as long as they get a passing grade while on academic probation. Such a Sim would, in effect, do every semester twice and spend about 48 days as a young adult. If you enjoy campus life, this is a good way to prolong it. Just don't imagine your Sim graduating with honors.

GRADUATION

Sims graduate from college when they successfully complete all eight semesters. From there they get to hang out on campus for a bit and prepare for the real world with the advantages college has given them.

Graduating with Honors

Sims with very high cumulative GPA graduate with honors. There are three levels of academic honors:

◆ 3.7 GPA: cum laude

◆ 3.9 GPA: magna cum laude

◆ 4.0 GPA: summa cum laude

Graduating with honors allows Sims a boost in their postcollege career tracks. How much of a boost, however, depends on what level of honors they achieved and which career they select.

Career Benefits

College graduates have several legs up in the working world.

New Careers

Sims who graduate college have access to jobs in four new career tracks:

◆ Artist   ◆ Paranormal

◆ Natural Scientist   ◆ Show Business

Sims who haven't graduated can't take jobs in these tracks. These expansion careers generally pay higher and offer more days off, but getting promoted in them requires relatively higher levels of skill and more friends. See Chapter 7 for full details.

Initial Job Level

All Sims who finish college get some advantage over nongraduates even in one of the original career tracks. How much of a boost, however, depends on how well they did in college and whether they're entering a career aligned with their major.

Nonhonors Graduates

Sims who graduate with a cumulative grade point average of less than 3.7 gain a privilege not available to nongraduate Sims.

> **note**
>
> Upper-level job offerings are available only by computer. Job listings in the newspaper are always Level 1.

Traditionally, adult Sims entering a new career track follow the rules laid out in Chapter 23. If they qualify for a Level 6 or lower job in a career, they'll be offered a job *two levels below* their qualifications. If they qualify for a Level 7 or higher job, they'll always be offered the Level 6 job.

All college graduates (even those with honors) are subject to the -2 rule but are not limited by the Level 6 cap. Thus, if a college graduate qualifies for a Level 9 job, he is offered a Level 9 job. By contrast, a nongraduate with the same skills and friends would only be offered a Level 6 job.

Cum Laude Graduates

Cum laude graduates (3.7 GPA) have the same benefits as nonhonors graduates in that they can, if they qualify, get jobs above Level 6 in a new career track. Also, like non-honors graduates, honors graduates qualifying for jobs below Level 6 will be offered two levels below the level for which they're qualified.

Where they differ from normal graduates is when they choose a career track that's aligned with their major. If they seek a job in any of the three tracks tied to their final major, they get +1 job level. For example, a Biology major who graduated cum laude and has all qualifications for a Level 7 Natural Scientist job would be offered a Level 8 job. By contrast, the same Sim seeking a job in Business would be offered a Level 7 job. Likewise, a cum laude Biology

graduate who qualifies for a Level 4 job would be offered a Level 3 job (-2 levels + 1 level) and a non-honors Biology graduate with Level 4 qualifications would be offered a Level 2 job.

Magna Cum Laude

Sims graduating magna cum laude (3.9 GPA) get similar benefits as cum laude graduates, but they get +1 level for careers outside their major and +2 for careers aligned with their major.

Summa Cum Laude

Summa cum laude (4.0 GPA) graduates receive similar benefits as magna cum laude but they get +2 level for careers outside their major and +3 for careers aligned with their major.

GRADUATION

When all the classes, exams, term papers, Professor schmoozing, and homework are done, it's time for Sims (at least those who got a C- or better) to enjoy their graduation.

To give the happy graduates some time to unwind, colleges permit their students to remain on campus for 48 hours after their last final exams. During this period, they can work on skills, socialize, satisfy Wants (they now have six glorious Want slots and two locks to work with, after all), or do anything else they care to try.

There are three ways that this carefree period—and, with it, the Sim's tenure as a young adult—can come to a close:

◆ Expiration of the postgraduate break: When the clock runs out, a taxi automatically arrives to take Sims back to their neighborhoods. There isn't much fanfare, just an age transition to adult and a cab ride.

◆ Summoning a taxi: Sims anxious to get on with life can call a taxi to take them back to their neighborhoods any time. Other than the timing, this is identical to waiting for the clock to expire.

◆ Graduation Party: Graduating Sims can throw a Graduation Party via the Throw Party menu on the phone. At the party's end, you'll see the otherwise unavailable graduation cinematic and your Sim rides off amidst much fanfare.

Graduation Party

The Graduation Party is a variation on the standard House Party that can give the inviting Sim a good (or, if things don't go well, bad) party memory, possibly satisfy a Want, and a cinematic send-off no other college departure can trigger.

The Graduation Party allows a Sim to depart campus in style.

The host of the party immediately switches into a cap and gown, as do any invited guests with a high Lifetime Relationship with the host.

At its conclusion, the party is scored and the appropriate Memory (good or bad) is entered, any Wants or Fears associated with the party are registered, and the graduation cinematic unspools. Your Sim gloriously age transitions to adulthood and gets a royal send-off for a triumphant return to the neighborhood.

note

A Graduation Party always ends a Sim's college career even if the 48-hour break is not over. If you want to spend maximum time at college, wait until near that time's end to throw the party.

Returning Home

Graduating, dropped-out, or kicked-out Sims are each placed individually in the Family Bin of their home neighborhood.

To get started in their adult life, they return with either:

◆ §20,000, or

◆ Their share of their college household funds when they graduated (if more than §20,000).

You may merge these graduates into any inhabited household or buy them their own place. If you wish your graduates to move in together, have one buy a house and merge the others individually.

tip

If you want to buy a property worth more than §20,000, create an empty lot, move one graduate onto it, save and exit the lot, merge any other graduates (or any Family Bin Sim) into the household, collectively move them out of the lot, and then buy the property you really want them to own.

College Buddies

The friendships and loves Sims built in their carefree college days are not lost when they graduate. To continue the relationships, Sims must make the first move. How to do this depends on whether the other Sim is a playable or nonplayable Sim.

If the Sim was playable, he or she may only be brought into a Sim's household by merging from the Family bin. Thus, if the other Sim hasn't yet finished college (by whatever route),

that Sim must be played out at college (to graduation, drop out, or be kicked out) and returned to the neighborhood before he or she can become playable in the neighborhood.

If the other Sim was nonplayable, the Sim can be brought from college no matter where he or she was in a college career when your Sim left. How the Sim returns to the neighborhood depends on how the Sim who summons them left college:

1. Invite the nonplayable Sim over a phone or wait for the Sim to visit.

2. Use the Propose—Move In interaction. The other Sim will accept based generally on Lifetime and Daily Relationship, Mood, and (if those are low) how high the Nice/Grouchy trait is (see Chapter 24 for specifics).

3. If the Sim accepts, the Sim age transitions to adulthood and becomes part of the household.

Since the other Sim didn't leave college naturally, that Sim assumes a status determined by the status of the inviting Sim:

◆ If the proposing Sim was a graduate, the new household member is also deemed a graduate.

◆ If the proposing Sim dropped out, the new household member is also deemed a drop out.

◆ If the proposing Sim was kicked out, the new household member is deemed a drop out.

Chapter 6
Living at College

The vista of college presents you and your Sims with many choices. Navigating these choices effectively requires a little inside info. This chapter deals with all the non-academic considerations of life at college.

RESIDENTIAL OPTIONS

In college towns, there are three different living styles available to college Sims, but not all college Sims are eligible (due to either money or membership).

Dorm life is the classic entry point for young scholars.

Sims of any academic year may reside in:

◆ Dorms

◆ Private housing

◆ Greek housing

WHERE SHOULD A FRESHMAN LIVE?

Upon arrival on campus, dorm dwelling isn't mandatory, but economics make it the only reasonable choice for all but a few.

Sims who lack scholarship money cannot (alone) move into private housing and must earn their way into a Greek house. With most houses requiring upwards of §2,500 to move in, it takes many roommates or an astonishing collection of scholarships to even get in the door.

Therefore, do what students everywhere do: have them spend some time in the dorms. Have them get good enough grades and/or work hard enough at jobs to bank up some money, and move out at the first opportunity.

Each kind of residence has advantages and disadvantages. The most obvious of these is financial. Dorm and Greek housing have no move-in fees, and private housing has a reduced (compared to normal neighborhood housing) but still significant up-front cost.

Bills differ among the housing types. From lowest to highest, they typically are:

1. Dorm

2. Private housing

3. Greek housing

Other features revolve around amenities, social opportunities, and nonbill expenses. Decide what you want your Sim to achieve. Studious Sims, for example, who want to live where they can work on skills without having to buy new objects, should live in a dorm, while a more gregarious Sim, who craves several social options and wants to meet many new Sims, should live in a Greek house.

> ### tip
> A Sim's Aspiration can be a guide to the best housing for them.

Dorms

Features:

◆ Low bills

◆ No move-in cost

◆ Free food service

◆ Not convertible into Greek house

◆ Most in-house Fun/skill objects

◆ Can't change architecture

> ### note
> The number of PLAYABLE Sims in the house has no effect on the per-Sim-share of the bills, though it raises the gross amount of the bills.

The price is right and the food is free, but dorms don't offer much privacy.

Dorm dwellers can add objects to their home, but the objects' purchase prices come out of the household funds and increase bills. However, since your Sims are "sharing" the total bills with all the nonplayable Sims living on the lot (aka, "Dormies"), the increase isn't as much as on a neighborhood lot.

tip

The more Sims living in a dorm, the more demanding it is on your computer's hardware. Players with slower computers may want to stick to smaller dorms.

Build mode tools are limited in dorms.

While you can't make any major changes to a dorm (i.e., build and demolish walls), there are a limited set of Build tools, such as the Design Mode tool and wall covering, flooring, terrain, and garden center.

note

There are cheats that allow you to alter or create dorms from scratch. You must follow several rules for your creations to function. These are covered in Chapter 13.

Every built-in campus has three or more dorms of varying sizes. Though they differ in their design and overall contents, all dorms contain at least one of the following objects:

- Bookshelf
- Cafeteria stove
- Computer
- Counter island (any kind)
- Desk
- Garbage can (inside)
- Garbage can (outside)
- Lights
- Mailbox
- Minifridge
- Refrigerator
- Sprinkler
- Stereo (any kind)
- Telephone
- Dresser

Claiming Rooms

A Sim's first order of business is claiming the dorm room of their choice.

When moving into a dorm, each playable Sim must quickly claim a room. Your Sims are alone on the lot for one hour before the rest of the students arrive and begin claiming rooms. To get your desired rooms, immediately click on the room's door and select "Claim Door." Your Sim's picture appears on the door and gives them the exclusive right to lock the door.

note

Claiming a room doesn't mean other Sims can't use objects in the room or even enter as they please. They will treat your Sims' rooms like any other space unless you lock the door.

Each claimed room is private, so, in Live mode, you can't see inside any nonplayable Sim's room. The contents of the room become visible only if your Sim is permitted inside.

If you merge Sims into an inhabited dorm, space is made by randomly kicking out the needed number of nonplayable Dormies. If, for example, a dorm has ten rooms with four playable Sims and you want to merge in three more, three of the dorm's six nonplayable Sims will vacate, leaving the new arrivals three rooms to claim.

When a nonplayable Sim is in their room or the room is locked, the room displays a thought bubble informing you what the room's owner is doing.

A Dormie can be sleeping (Bed icon) ...

having Fun in the dorm (TV-Fun icon) ...

or be away at class (Green chalkboard icon).

note

Nonplayable Sims ALWAYS lock their doors when they're sleeping or at class and always leave them unlocked when they're doing things on the lot.

Peek into locked rooms by switching the game into Buy or Build mode. From here you can move objects out of other Sims' rooms or sell them for cash. Selling your dormmates' beds is most uncool, unless you like your dorm floor cluttered with snoozing scholars.

tip

If house bills are placed in a room that's subsequently locked (as will happen if the room contains the closest uncluttered surface to the mailbox), retrieve them by switching into Buy mode and moving them somewhere your Sim can go.

Locking Rooms

To prevent other Sims from using your Sims' rooms when your Sim is away or asleep, click on the door and select "Look Door."

To shut out disturbances and interlopers, Sims can lock their dorm doors.

When a door is locked, only the room's owner may pass through it without knocking.

note

Rooms needn't be locked every time your Sim goes in or out; they remain locked until your Sim unlocks them.

Even sleeping Sims answer if they have a well-established relationship with the person knocking. If not, they express their displeasure.

If a nonplayable Sim is in their room with the door locked, your Sim can try to gain access by knocking (click on the door and select "Knock on Door"). Even if the Sim is asleep, they answer the door if their Lifetime Relationship toward the knocking Sim is above 20. If Lifetime Relationship is too low, they refuse to answer (displayed by a thought bubble with your Sim's face crossed by an X).

Entering a Dormie's unlocked room while they're inside may get a Sim shooed out, depending on how high Daily Relationship is between the Sims.

Eating in Dorms

Every dorm is equipped with two primary sources for food: the cafeteria and a self-serve kitchenette.

Dorms have twenty-hour-a-day food service. The food is free, paid for in advance by your Sims' bill payments. No other college living spaces have this service, though it is available on some college community lots.

There's always at least some space in dorms for Sims to prepare simple meals, even when the Cafeteria Worker has command of the kitchen.

Dorm denizens also have access to a minifridge (which can double as a prep surface) and, in many dorms, a microwave or toaster oven. Some even come with self-serve coffee machines. Find full details on college food service in the "Eating at College" section.

> ### note
> Sims can vacate the dorm by moving to a Greek house after they've gained membership (see following) or by using the phone or computer to "Find Own Place."

Private Housing

Features:

◆ Medium bills

◆ Steep move-in cost

◆ No food service

◆ Convertible into Greek house

◆ Few in-house Fun/skill objects

It's more expensive to live in a private house than a dorm. First, there's the move-in cost. At least four or five non-scholarship Sims in their first semester would have to pool their money to afford even the least expensive private home. Then they must have enough money left to pay the bills.

Those bills are typically higher than dorm bills. They're less than bills on Greek houses (which include Greek dues), but the financial burden is still heavier.

Unlike dorms, there is no free food service; Sims must cook for themselves, live off expensive delivery food, or travel to community lots for free food-service meals. There are also no dorm doors with their elaborate access rules.

Turning Greek

The most interesting and useful feature of private homes is that they can be converted into Greek houses.

Getting a Greek charter is easy: just call and pay.

Check your Greek house's status by clicking on any Greek letter adorning the walls.

Direct a Sim to pick up any house (or cell) phone, use the Greek House menu, and select "Apply for Charter." If the house can part with the §20 national organization fee, Greek life can be theirs.

With this change, the household bills rise, but the myriad of benefits of Greekdom begin to flow. To unlock these treats, however, you must know how Greek houses work.

Greek Housing

Features:

◆ Highest bills

◆ Toga Parties

◆ Increased walk-bys and higher chance Sims are greeted automatically

◆ Influence new pledges without spending Influence points

◆ Hunger, Energy, Comfort, Bladder, and Hygiene Needs decay more slowly as Greek house level increases, while Social and Fun decay more quickly

◆ Residents can elect to "Sleep on Floor"

◆ Members may occasionally wander off lot and bring back free pizza and "borrowed" objects

Whether you convert a house into Greek housing or use a prebuilt Greek house, it pays to know how the houses work and how to make one great.

Although all the Greek lots in the three built-in colleges follow the traditional single-sex model, you can change this. Your pre-built Greek houses can also be either.

View Greek house status by clicking on any Greek letter decoration (if there is one) and select "Check Greek House Status." This tells you:

◆ Greek house level

◆ # of members

◆ # of pledges

◆ # of family friends

◆ # of family friends needed to gain the next house level

◆ Maximum # of members at current level

Greek houses grow and prosper based on how many friends the household members collectively make. The more "family friends" the residents have, the higher their Greek house's level and the more members (including nonresident members) they can have.

Greek House Levels

Every Greek house has a rating based on the resident members' collective number of family friends.

> **note**
>
> Household Sims don't count as family friends.

To get beyond Level 1, the house must have at least one Greek letter decoration (found under the Wall Hangings submenu). Purchase this or wait for a member to wander off the lot and bring one back for free (happens within the house's first few days). Without this item, no number of friends will raise the house's level. With each increase in level, the house's maximum number of members rises.

Greek House Levels

LEVEL	# OF FAMILY FRIENDS	MEMBER MAX
1	0	8
2	3	10
3	5	15
4	7	20
5	10	30
6	15	32,000

> **note**
>
> Friends of nonresident members do not contribute to the family friend count.

More members means more Sims who can move in and make friends, adding to the house's collective count of family friends. If, for example, the house has four residents and each of these Sims has two unique friends, the Greek house gets credit for eight friends, enough to raise the house to Level 4.

> **note**
>
> When a resident member graduates, his or her unique (not shared by any other members) friendships are lost from the family friend count, possibly causing the house's demotion. Alternatively, if a friend graduates or drops out, he or she is still counted as a friend even though they've moved off campus. Friends in the base neighborhood do count for Greek house level.

Beyond raising the member limit, Greek house levels offer additional benefits. Each level retains the benefits of lower levels:

◆ Level 1: Members may randomly wander off the lot and return with a Greek letter object (if there isn't one on the lot already).

◆ Level 2: Members may randomly wander off the lot and return with pizza.

◆ Level 3: No bonuses, raises member maximum

◆ Level 4: Elevated chance of Cheerleader and Mascot NPCs visiting lot.

◆ Level 5: Elevated chance of Evil Mascot NPC visiting the lot.

◆ Level 6: Members may randomly wander off the lot and return with inexpensive objects to add to the lot.

Greek Houses and Needs

As the house rises in prestige, all Needs other than Fun and Social decay more slowly. This means Sims can spend less time tending to their essential Needs and more time having Fun, socializing, building skill, or doing schoolwork.

Social and Fun Needs for any Sim on the lot decay more quickly as the Greek house level increases. This drives all Sims to autonomously do Fun activities and socialize more often.

Pledging and Getting New Members

There are two ways for a Greek house to gain new members:

1. Members can recruit members on the Greek house lot with the "Ask to Pledge" interaction.

2. Nonmember Sims can submit themselves for consideration on their own or community lots by doing the "Ask to Join Greek House" interaction with visiting house members or over the phone (home lot only). This triggers the Pledge scenario.

Pledging on Greek House Lot

You can use the "Ask to Pledge" interaction to direct Greek lot residents to invite visitors to become a house member.

Every visitor to a Greek house is a potential Pledge.

The visitor accepts the invitation if:

1. The house has, by virtue of its level, any space for new members, and

2. There's sufficient relationship between the prospective Pledge and the member who invited them (see following).

Specifically, the visitor accepts the invitation if the visitor's:

1. Outgoing/Shy >5, Daily with the member >50, and Lifetime with the member >10, or,

2. Outgoing/Shy <5, Daily with the member >40, and Lifetime with the member >5.

> ## note
>
> Becoming a member of a Greek house has no mandatory effect on a Sim's housing situation. Members can, but don't have to, move into the Greek house lot.

When a Sim becomes a member in this fashion, they immediately become a "Pledge." Pledges are still autonomous, nonplayable Sims but, as prospective members, they get extra visitor privileges (they can use beds to restore Energy and can get more than snack food from the refrigerator).

Because they're Pledges, however, they are indirectly controllable via Influence. In fact, one of the requirements of a Pledge is that they spend their pledgehood (14 hours after accepting the offer to join) doing resident members' bidding—resident members can issue Influence To commands to Pledges without expending their Influence points. After spending 14 hours on the Greek house lot, Pledges become full-fledged members and can no longer be Influenced for free.

> ## tip
>
> If they keep a constant stream of new Pledges around, resident members shouldn't ever have to write a term paper or do an assignment. Thus, being in a Greek house can be leveraged to get high grades.

After the expiration of this "servile" period, a Pledge becomes a full member and any house members gather round to cheer.

Ask to Join Greek House

In this alternative route into Greek membership, the potential member (not the house member) is the playable Sim. If ever a house member is encountered as a visitor (on a residential or community lot), playable Sims can use the "Ask to Join Greek House" interaction to begin the process.

When a Sim really wants to join a Greek house, the most direct way is to just invite the members over and show them your stuff. Befriend the members beforehand and the job gets even easier.

Alternatively, playable Sims can start the process by using their house or cell phone (on their home lot only). Select the Greek House menu, then select "Join..." and the house you want them to join.

Be ready to charm them because the members come ready for Fun.

Immediately, several members arrive at the Sim's lot (dressed in togas) and the Pledging scenario begins. The playable Sim has six Sim hours to reach specified Daily Relationship targets with each of the house members on the lot.

> ## note
>
> If the playable Sim has a preexisting relationship with any or all of the members, these scores are considered. Thus, the Sim may be able to satisfy the scenario immediately based on socializing they've already done.

Kicky Bag is a great way to build relationships with several members at once.

It is not your Sim's relationship to the member that matters. It's the member's Daily Relationship to your Sim. Normally this score is invisible (as when Sims socialize with nonplayable Sims), but here it's shown in the scenario's tracking box. Looking at your own Sim's Relationship panel is, therefore, not an entirely accurate measure of progress.

tip

Draw several Greek house members into Hang Out to simultaneously build relationship with all of them. When relationship is a bit higher, involve several of them in a game of Kicky Bag. The more efficiently you build relationships, the faster you complete the scenario.

If your Sim builds all relationships to or beyond the target scores, he immediately becomes a member of the Greek house, and the members gather around to cheer and then depart.

Charm everyone from the Greek house in time and membership is as good as yours.

Sims who join in this way never become Pledges who can be freely Influenced.

Benefits for Nonresident Members

After a nonresident Sim is a member (by either method), several things change:

◆ When you're playing the Greek house, nonresident members frequently walk by and usually are greeted autonomously.

◆ Nonresident members visiting the Greek house can use objects normally off-limits to visitors. They can use beds for sleep or make meals from the refrigerators.

◆ Nonresident-member visitors can move to the Greek house from their home lot by using the phone (cell or house), selecting the Greek House menu, and then "Move into Greek House."

◆ When a nonresident member visits the Greek house, resident members can invite them to move in with the "Ask to Move In" interaction.

Greek House Life

If at least one member resides in a Greek house, that lot can remain a Greek house eternally. Since, however, college forces Sims to eventually move on, it's essential to keep a steady flow of younger members to take over the house as older ones graduate.

If all playable Sims move out of a Greek house, it loses its Greek charter and reverts to a private residence. To restore its status, move in Sims and reapply for a charter via phone.

EATING AT COLLEGE

There are several food sources in college towns, but some are only available in certain locations.

Food Service

Dorms and some college town community lots are equipped with an industrial cooktop and a Cafeteria Worker who constantly prepares group meals between 4 a.m. and midnight.

If the ShinyTyme Cooktop is placed on a residential or Greek lot in college towns or on any lot in base neighborhoods, it isn't manned by a Cafeteria Worker and serves as a standard cooker. It, however, can only make stovetop-cooked meals.

In dorms and some community lots, nourishing food is free from the Cafeteria Worker.

Sims can eat food-service meals at no cost, but the meals tend to be low-skill meals that don't provide much Hunger satisfaction. The Cafeteria Worker prepares three different meals each day. Occasionally, the Cafeteria Worker makes a "special"—a higher-skill meal that offers more Hunger satisfaction:

Meal	Standard	Special
Breakfast	Pancakes	Omelets
Lunch	Macaroni and Cheese	Chili Con Carne
Dinner	Macaroni and Cheese	Spaghetti

tip

When a playable Sim takes over the Cafeteria Worker's job (see the "Earning Money at College" section), they make the same dishes the Cafeteria Worker would. If the menu calls for a special, however, they only make that dish if they have Cooking skill of 5 or higher.

Home Cooking

On private residences and Greek lots with fully equipped kitchens, residents can prepare meals within their Cooking skill. Visitors to these lots can eat for free from any served meal residents prepare.

note

With a bit of cash, you can upgrade the dorm's self-serve kitchen facilities to allow residents to prepare any kind of meal.

Dorms are usually equipped with limited kitchens from which residents can cook meals any time of day (usually with a provided microwave or toaster oven). While the Cafeteria Worker is on duty, residents may make cold meals or take snacks from the dorm's full-sized refrigerator. Between midnight and 4 a.m. they can prepare stovetop-only meals in accordance with their individual Cooking skill.

note

Self-serve meals and snacks from dorm refrigerators deplete refrigerator stocks and must be replenished with groceries from community lot stores or the grocery delivery service (summoned by computer, house phone, or cell phone). Meals prepared by the Cafeteria Worker DO NOT deplete refrigerators stocks.

Cup O' Ramen

If a residential lot has a refrigerator and a microwave, Sims can create a new meal: the Cup O' Ramen.

◆ Food Points: 55
◆ Cost: §2

Cup O' Ramen is perfect college food: quick and cheap.

The meal requires no skill and can be prepared in college town and neighborhood residential lots by children and older.

Delivery

Sims can order (by house or cell phone) delivered food from any kind of college town lot. Cost is §30–§40 for eight servings.

Chinese Food (§30)

In addition to pizza, all Sims (in college towns or neighborhoods) can order Chinese food delivery.

Order up some Chinese food for some really good cram fuel!

Functionally, Chinese food is identical to pizza in terms of Hunger satisfaction and efficiency but slightly cheaper than pizza.

It does, however, have a hidden cost that Sims, especially those fearful of the "freshman 15," should know. Chinese food is very fattening. Normally, a Sim only loses Fitness when they eat with Hunger fully satisfied. With Chinese food, however, they lose Fitness just for eating it.

BILLS

Sims living at college get bills just like regular Sims, but several factors beyond the value of objects on the lot affect their amount.

In general:

◆ Bills in dorms cost the least.

◆ Bills in private residences are the next highest.

◆ Greek house bills are the highest.

Bills arrive in the same way and with the same frequency as in neighborhoods.

tip

As in neighborhoods, it pays to drop an end table near the mailbox to provide a convenient place to deposit bills as they arrive and await payment. Keep this place clear and bills will never get lost (locked inside a Dormie's room).

BILL CALCULATION

Bills are computed by the following formula: standard bills × (playable Sims ÷ total resident Sims) × housing-type factor.

The division of playable Sims by total residents is only a factor in dorms where there are many objects on the lot that don't benefit your playable Sims. Thus, their bills are reduced according to their "share" of the object value. In any other college residence, the number of playable Sims and total Sims is identical and, therefore, has no effect on the calculation.

The housing-type factor scales the amount of the bills to the lot's housing type. Bills (adjusted by the number of playable Sims among the residents) are modified as follows:

◆ Dorms: multiplied by 6

◆ Private residence: multiplied by 1.6

◆ Greek housing: multiplied by 1.8

Though the housing-type factor for dorms seems high, the result (along with dividing the bills by the number of residents) usually works out less than the per Sim bills in other housing.

EARNING MONEY AT COLLEGE

Although they can't hold conventional jobs, college students must earn regular income so they can pay the bills, buy objects, order groceries and food delivery, and play arcade games.

There are several ways of earning cash at college, and no one way is right for everybody.

Starting Money: Grants and Scholarships

Every entering Freshman gets a §500 grant upon enrollment in a college. If they're a teen from the base neighborhood, they can apply for various scholarships that add significantly to this starting reserve.

> **note**
>
> Scholarships are detailed in Chapter 4.

College Jobs

College Sims don't have careers like teens, adults, and elders in the neighborhoods, but they can earn money doing odd jobs at various college facilities.

Cafeteria, Barista, Bartender

Anywhere there's a working Cafeteria Worker, Barista, or Bartender NPC, you can take over for them by interacting with either them or their object (stove, espresso machine, or juice bar, respectively) and selecting "Work as...."

It's not the best-paying job, but for dorm dwellers, working in the cafeteria is a way to make money right at home.

Your Sim assumes the job's uniform and takes the NPC's position behind the object, behaving precisely as the NPC does at work. You can't direct your Sim to do anything else while they're working one of these jobs.

> **note**
>
> While your Sim works hard for the money, the relieved NPC stays on the lot, behaving like a regular visitor.

Slinging coffee can't be done at home, but it pays somewhat better.

The longer your Sim works, the more money they make:

◆ Barista: §80 per hour

◆ Bartender: §80 per hour

◆ Cafeteria Worker: §50 per hour

Meanwhile, however, their Needs and overall Mood slowly deplete.

When you've stayed long enough, cancel the job interaction and the NPC retakes their post. If critical Needs or Mood fall too low, your Sim exits the job autonomously.

Every few Sim minutes, the Sim receives an infusion of cash for their labors.

Tutoring

Helping another Sim do their assignments lets that Sim complete their schoolwork faster. Tutoring has the same effect and makes money for your Sim. The longer the tutoring session, the more money you earn.

Helping less successful students is a good way for smart Sims to earn a few extra simoleans.

Take a high Body skill Sim to the campus gym and they can make money and work out at the same time.

If you click on another Sim's assignment book and your Sim has a high enough GPA, your Sim can "Tutor Sim for Simoleans." Sims can't tutor during their first semester since they don't yet have a GPA. After that, however, tutoring an NPC is available if your Sim has a C or better GPA. To tutor a playable Sim, the tutoring Sim's GPA need only be *higher* than the Sim being tutored.

When the assignment is done, the tutoring Sim gets their cash (§60 per hour).

tip

The most fruitful place to make money tutoring is the library.

Personal Training

Similar to tutoring, a Sim can make money training other Sims on exercise machines.

note

Part of being a Personal Trainer is demonstrating how to do the exercise. Thus, the training Sim is also building their Body skill while making money.

To train a Sim with lower Body skill, interact with them or their machine while they use an exercise machine. The trainee Sim earns Body skill faster while being trained.

tip

The best place to make money as a Personal Trainer is at the campus gym.

The longer the Sim acts as Trainer, the more money they earn (§70 per hour). When you choose to stop training, when the trained Sim exits, or when your Sim's critical Needs or Mood forces them to stop, the session ends and your Sim collects their pay.

tip

Being a Personal Trainer to another playable Sim is doubly efficient since it gives the trainee more Body skill in less time and earns the trainer money. If both trainer and trainee share the same funds, no money comes out of the household funds to pay the training Sim. Tutoring or being a Personal Trainer, in the end, is a financial gain for the household.

Money for Grades

Your Sim's current semester grade entitles them to a grant awarded at each semester's end.

Semester Grants

Grade	Earning	Grade	Earning
A+	§1,200	B-	§600
A	§1,100	C+	§500
A-	§1,000	C	§400
B+	§800	C-	§300
B	§700	D+ (or below)	§0

Other Ways to Earn Money

There are several other ways to earn spending money:

- **Counterfeit Machine:** If your Sim is a member of the Secret Society (see the "Secret Society" section later in this chapter), they can use the Society's Counterfeit Machine to print simoleans. There's a risk of getting busted by the police, but working diligently at this device earns the equivalent of a mid-level career job. Sims not in the Secret Society can also get a Counterfeit Machine as an Aspiration Reward for their homes, but it costs §27,750 Aspiration Reward points.

- **Money Tree:** With enough Reward points, your Sim can own a Money Tree. The tree requires frequent tending or it dies, but the money's not bad (about the equivalent of a low-level job).

- **Hustle Pool:** If your Sim has played a lot of pool, they can profitably Hustle Pool at any pool table object. The larger the difference between your Sim and their competitor's Pool skill, the greater the odds of your Sim winning. If your Sim has high skill and plays for the biggest possible stakes, they'll make some of the best money on campus.

- **Freestyle for Tips:** The self-interaction Freestyle (under the Entertain menu) can be done for tips. Your Sim puts down a tip jar and does their thing. The higher their Charisma, the better their tips. Try to perform on community lots where there are plenty of other Sims.

- **Perform in a Band:** Performing (rather than practicing) any of the musical instruments is done with a tip jar nearby. Any Sims who like the music put cash in the jar. The higher your Sim's Creativity (and the higher the Nice/Grouchy of passersby), the more simoleans they're likely to make. Playing with other Sims in a band attracts more observers; check out clubs on campus that have a full complement of instruments and an open mike policy.

COLLEGE PARTIES

There are two new kinds of college parties: the Sports Party and the Toga Party. They are both initiated and scored like other parties (the more social interaction, the better the party) but are distinct in their own way.

Sports Party

You can throw Sports Parties on residential lots in college towns or neighborhoods, if there's a television somewhere on the lot.

While the party is going on, Sims turn the TV to the new SimStation Sports channel, boo or cheer at the TV, talk about sports, and do the School Cheer. If there's a juice barrel on the lot, they'll guzzle juice from cups and directly from the tap.

If the party is going particularly well, the Mascot or Cheerleader NPC shows up.

Toga Party

This classic party is only available on Greek lots.

The Toga Party is a special party with a special dress code.

The main feature of the Toga Party is guest attire. This depends on personality:

- **Sexy Clothes:** If Outgoing/Shy is more than 8, they'll wear a "sexy" outfit (lingerie for women and shirtless for men).

◆ Toga: If Outgoing/Shy is 2–8, they'll wear togas.

◆ Everyday: If Outgoing/Shy is less than 2, they'll wear their Everyday outfit.

The Sim throwing the party changes into a toga as soon as they invite others and hang up the phone (they're *really* excited) and other household residents change when the party begins.

CAMPUS DIRECTORY

The campus directory is available via the phone (under the College menu) and lists all Sims on campus whether or not the caller has met them. This allows Sims to *initiate* relationships via phone.

SECRET SOCIETY

Every campus has a shadowy organization lurking below the surface. Its members seem to have advantages other students lack, like snazzy black blazers with embroidered llama crests. Who wouldn't want to be a member?

Gaining Membership

To be inducted into the Secret Society, your Sim must become friends with *three* Secret Society members (Daily >50 for both Sims in each relationship). That may not be as easy as it sounds. How do you find Secret Society members? Your Sim may know them already. When they're hanging around your residence or visiting the homes of others, they wear their normal clothes. It's entirely possible to gain admission into the Secret Society without ever seeing a Sim in their member outfit. It could be a total surprise if your Sim just happens to befriend the right Sims.

To take a more aggressive approach, you can often find Secret Society members in their telltale outfits on community lots. When you arrive, keep your eyes peeled for Sims wearing black blazers with the Society's crest on the pocket. There's almost always at least one about.

Engage them in conversation and build a relationship with them as quickly as possible. When your Sim returns home, have them call, talk to, or invite the member to build the relationship further.

You can never be sure when "they" will come for your Sim.

After your Sim has three friends in the Society, the Society comes to your Sim. When a limo pulls up to the door and your Sim is handcuffed and led away, you know it's time.

After their abduction, the Sim is brought to the hidden Secret Society house and welcomed by the members. You are henceforth a Society member.

This place is a well-kept secret for good reason: it contains some of the most powerful and hard-to-get objects around.

Benefits of Membership

There are several benefits to being in the Secret Society:

◆ Your Sim can use any computer to Hack Grades. This dishonest endeavor boost grades quickly but it's risky. The higher the Sim's Logic, the less

likely they are to get caught and the more likely they'll have time to significantly affect their grades.

♦ Your Sim may go to the Secret Society lot at any time by using a house or cell phone, selecting the Transportation menu, and choosing "Go to Secret Society." The limo picks up the Sim shortly.

♦ The Secret Society lot has the powerful Counterfeiting Machine. Use this object to print your own simoleans, but beware the twin dangers of police intervention and fire (the machine gets really hot).

♦ There are always several Sims on the lot with which to socialize.

♦ Depending on which Secret Society lot is on campus, the houses come with a selection of otherwise unavailable career objects, including ones that build skill faster.

♦ Your Sim gets the snazzy Secret Society outfit added to their Everyday wardrobe.

♦ Your Sim can do the Secret Handshake interaction (under Play) with any other Society members. This interaction is only accepted by other members who have a good relationship with your Sim or who are very Playful or Active. See Chapter 9 for all the details. Nonmembers look upon this arcane display with shock and bewilderment, so know who you're dealing with before offering this interaction. Sims keep this interaction after graduation.

note

The Secret Society clubhouse does not appear in the college town view because it's, you know, secret. The only way to get there is by summoning the limo.

BURGLARS

The high level of security in college towns tends to deter burglars, so thefts are rare (but not nonexistent).

SCHOOL/WORK/ SOCIALIZING BALANCE

The greatest challenge in the college game is to balance all the demands on your college Sim and choose which opportunities they can pursue. Having it all (success in school, work, and socializing) is just not possible. Still, with skill, practice, and determination, it is possible to come close.

Consider this as a goal: by playing well and using all you learn in this book, you can succeed at two of the three pursuits. You can, for example, be very good at school and earn lots of cash, but not have time for making friends. On the other hand, you can gain lots of green to buy cool objects and make lots of friends, but your grades will suffer.

Chapter 7
New Careers

The Sims™ 2 University boasts four brand-new career tracks, but they're a little different from the old careers. Not every Sim is equipped to undertake the increased challenge they entail, and only Sims who've graduated from college may even apply. The rewards, however, are tremendous, with greater pay, more free time, and four of the most powerful objects ever.

NEW CAREERS, NEW CHALLENGES

In most ways, the four new careers in The Sims™ 2 University are identical to any other Sims career. They feature 10 increasingly lucrative jobs to which your Sims must go several times a week, they reward achievement with an exclusive career reward object, and they require your Sims to improve themselves by gaining greater skill levels and amassing large circles of family friends.

The differences, however, arise in the details:

- Availability: New career tracks are only available to Sims who have *graduated* college.
- Number of skills: The Sims™ 2 University careers require development in *four* rather than the traditional three skill areas.
- More friends: The new careers require larger numbers of family friends at nearly every level and begin to require friends at lower levels.
- Days per week: Beginning at about Level 7, the new careers require fewer days per week than the 10 core jobs. At Level 10, one career pays more per week than any of the 10 originals while requiring only one day of work!

- Less demanding: The expansion careers deplete your Sim's Needs less while they're at work, requiring less replenishing time after hours. Many of the highest-level jobs substantially fill some Needs while the Sim is at work.
- New reward objects: Four new reward objects can create posed photographs suitable for framing, alter your Sims' facial features, resurrect dead Sims, and provide a particularly morbid way to add days to your Sims' life (see "Cow Plant" later in this chapter).
- Chance cards: New careers have chance cards but not at every level.

NEW CAREER OVERVIEW

Every career requires development in four skill areas, which are listed in the following table. The personality traits that allow Sims to learn those skills more quickly are also presented here. Sims with accelerated skill building are best suited for careers that demand those skills.

The following tables also include the college majors that feed into each career, new and old. Sims who graduate with honors receive a substantial level boost if they enter a career affiliated with their major.

New Career Tracks, Featured Skills, Majors, and Helper Personalities

CAREER TRACK	SKILL 1 (PERS.)	SKILL 2 (PERS.)	SKILL 3 (PERS.)	SKILL 4 (PERS.)	MAJOR(S)
Artist	Creativity (Playful)	Mechanical (None)	Charisma (Outgoing)	Cooking (None)	Art, History
Natural Scientist	Logic (Serious)	Body (Active)	Mechanical (None)	Cleaning (Neat)	Biology, Mathematics
Paranormal	Creativity (Playful)	Charisma (Outgoing)	Cooking (None)	Cleaning (Neat)	Psychology, Philosophy, Physics
Show Business	Logic (Serious)	Body (Active)	Creativity (Playful)	Cleaning (Neat)	Drama, Economics, Literature, Political Science

Core Careers and Majors

CAREER TRACK	MAJOR(S)
Athletic	Drama
Business	Psychology, Economics
Criminal	Mathematics, Literature
Culinary	Philosophy, Art
Law Enforcement	Psychology, Biology

Core Careers and Majors

CAREER TRACK	MAJOR(S)
Medicine	Biology, Physics
Military	History, Political Science
Politics	Political Science, History, Drama
Science	Physics, Mathematics
Slacker	Art, Philosophy, Literature

JOBS BY CAREER LEVEL

Artist

Level	Job Name	Logic	Body	Creativity	Mechanical	Charisma	Cooking	Cleaning	Friends	Hours
1	Canvas Stretcher	0	0	0	0	0	0	0	0	7 a.m.–2 p.m.
2	Street Caricaturist	0	0	1	0	0	0	0	0	11 a.m.–6 p.m.
3	Souvenir Whittler	0	0	3	2	0	0	0	1	9 a.m.–4 p.m.
4	Comic Book Penciller	0	0	4	3	0	1	0	2	10 a.m.–5 p.m.
5	Wedding Photographer	0	0	5	4	3	2	0	4	8 a.m.–3 p.m.
6	Art Forger	0	0	5	5	4	3	0	5	2 p.m.–9 p.m.
7	Fashion Photographer	0	0	6	6	6	3	0	8	10 a.m.–5 p.m.
8	Acclaimed Muralist	0	0	7	7	7	4	0	9	12 a.m.–7 p.m.
9	Conceptual Artist	0	0	9	8	7	5	0	10	10 a.m.–5 p.m.
10	Visionary	0	0	10	0	7	6	0	13	1 p.m.–6 p.m.

Natural Scientist

Level	Job Name	Logic	Body	Creativity	Mechanical	Charisma	Cooking	Cleaning	Friends	Hours
1	Ratkeeper	0	0	0	0	0	0	0	0	9 a.m.–4 p.m.
2	Algae Hunter	0	1	0	1	0	0	1	0	8 a.m.–3 p.m.
3	Clam Wrangler	0	3	0	2	0	0	2	0	9 a.m.–4 p.m.
4	Scatmaster	0	4	0	3	0	0	3	1	11 a.m.–6 p.m.
5	Soil Identifier	1	5	0	4	0	0	5	2	9 a.m.–4 p.m.
6	Rogue Botanist	3	5	0	6	0	0	6	4	10 a.m.–5 p.m.
7	Animal Linguist	6	5	0	6	0	0	6	6	10 a.m.–5 p.m.
8	Unnatural Crossbreeder	8	5	0	7	0	0	7	8	9 a.m.–4 p.m.
9	Dinosaur Cloner	10	6	0	9	0	0	8	10	11 a.m.–6 p.m.
10	Ecological Guru	10	8	0	10	0	0	8	12	12 p.m.–9 a.m.

Days Off	# Work Days	Daily Salary	Weekly Average	Energy	Bladder	Hygiene	Social	Hunger	Fun	Comfort
Mon. & Wed.	5	§231	§1,155	-8	-8	-10	-3	-4	-10	-3
Mon. & Sat.	5	§357	§1,785	-8	-8	-10	-3	4	-7	3
Tue. & Thur.	5	§483	§2,415	-8	-8	-8	-4	-4	-6	-5
Sun. & Fri.	5	§630	§3,150	-8	-8	-3	-3	-5	-4	-5
Sun. & Tue.	5	§808	§4,040	-6	-8	-8	-2	5	-4	6
Sun., Fri., & Sat.	4	§1,339	§5,356	-4	-8	-5	-2	-5	-5	-3
Sun., Tue., & Thu.	4	§1,785	§7,140	-5	-8	-4	-2	6	-4	4
Sun., Wed., Fri.,& Sat.	3	§2,232	§6,696	-5	-8	-7	-2	-6	-7	-1
Sun., Thur., Fri., & Sat.	3	§2,625	§7,875	-4	-8	-2	-2	-6	-4	-3
Sun., Mon., Wed., & Fri.	3	§4,549	§13,647	-4	-8	-2	-2	8	-4	2

Days Off	# Work Days	Daily Salary	Weekly Average	Energy	Bladder	Hygiene	Social	Hunger	Fun	Comfort
Sun. & Fri.	5	§325	§1,625	-8	-8	-10	-3	-4	-10	-3
Mon. & Fri.	5	§483	§2,415	-8	-8	-10	-3	-4	-7	-3
Sun. & Wed.	5	§672	§3,360	-8	-8	-8	-3	-4	-6	5
Sun. & Sat.	5	§787	§3,935	-8	-8	-10	-3	-5	-4	-5
Mon. & Thu.	5	§945	§4,725	-6	-8	-10	-2	-5	-4	-6
Tue. & Thu.	5	§1,134	§5,670	-4	-8	-5	-2	-5	-5	3
Sun. & Sat.	4	§1,344	§5,376	-5	-8	-4	-2	6	-4	4
Tue. & Thu.	4	§1,554	§6,216	-5	-8	-7	-2	6	-7	1
Sun., Mon., & Sat.	4	§2,283	§9,132	-4	-8	-2	-2	-6	-4	3
Mon., Tues., Thurs., Fri., Sat., & Sun.	1	§10,497	§10,497	10	10	-10	10	10	10	10

Paranormal

Level	Job Name	Logic	Body	Creativity	Mechanical	Charisma	Cooking	Cleaning	Friends	Hours
1	Psychic Phone Pal	0	0	0	0	0	0	0	0	8 p.m.–3 a.m.
2	Conspiracy Theorist	0	0	2	0	1	0	0	0	5 p.m.–12 a.m.
3	Tarot Card Reader	0	0	4	0	2	0	0	1	6 p.m.–1 a.m.
4	Hypnotist	0	0	5	0	3	0	0	2	11 a.m.–6 p.m.
5	Medium	0	0	5	0	3	1	1	4	5 p.m.–12 a.m.
6	Douser	0	0	6	0	3	3	3	6	5 p.m.–12 a.m.
7	Police Psychic	0	0	7	0	4	4	6	8	1 p.m.–7 p.m.
8	UFO Investigator	0	0	7	0	5	4	7	9	10 a.m.–5 p.m.
9	Exorcist	0	0	8	0	6	5	8	10	9 p.m.–3 a.m.
10	Cult Leader	0	0	10	0	10	7	9	13	6 p.m.–3 a.m.

Show Business

Level	Job Name	Logic	Body	Creativity	Mechanical	Charisma	Cooking	Cleaning	Friends	Hours
1	Screen Test Stand-In	0	0	0	0	0	0	0	0	10 a.m.–5 p.m.
2	Body Double	0	1	0	0	1	0	0	0	1 p.m.–8 p.m.
3	Bit Player	0	2	0	0	2	0	0	0	9 a.m.–4 p.m.
4	Commercial Actor/Actress	0	3	0	0	3	0	0	1	8 a.m.–5 p.m.
5	Cartoon Voice	1	3	2	0	4	0	0	3	1 p.m.–8 p.m.
6	Supporting Player	2	5	3	0	5	0	0	5	6 p.m.–1 a.m.
7	Broadway Star	3	7	4	0	6	0	0	7	6 p.m.–1 a.m.
8	Leading Man/Lady	4	10	5	0	7	0	0	9	1 p.m.–7 p.m.
9	Blockbuster Director	5	10	7	0	9	0	0	11	10 a.m.–5 p.m.
10	Icon	6	10	9	0	10	0	0	14	4 p.m.–9 p.m.

Days Off	# Work Days	Daily Salary	Weekly Average	Energy	Bladder	Hygiene	Social	Hunger	Fun	Comfort
Sun. & Wed.	5	§252	§1,260	-8	-8	-10	-3	4	-10	-3
Mon. & Thurs.	5	§375	§1,875	-8	-8	-10	-3	-4	-7	-3
Sun. & Tue.	.5	§525	§2,625	-8	-8	-8	-3	-4	-6	-5
Sun. & Wed.	5	§672	§3,360	-8	-8	-3	-3	-5	-4	5
Sun. & Fri.	5	§840	§4,200	-6	-8	-8	-2	-5	-4	-6
Sun. & Tue.	5	§1,092	§5,460	-4	-8	-5	-2	-5	-5	-3
Sun. & Sat.	5	§1,386	§6,930	-5	-8	-4	-2	-6	-4	-4
Sun., Tue., & Sat.	4	§2,100	§8,400	-5	-8	-7	-2	6	-7	1
Mon., Tues., Thurs., & Sat.	3	§2,494	§7,482	-4	-8	-2	-2	6	-4	-3
Sun., Mon., Wed., Thurs., & Fri.	2	§4,725	§9,450	5	-8	3	4	10	5	10

Days Off	# Work Days	Daily Salary	Weekly Average	Energy	Bladder	Hygiene	Social	Hunger	Fun	Comfort
Mon. & Sat.	5	§420	§2,100	-8	-8	-10	-3	4	-10	3
Mon. & Fri.	5	§577	§2,885	-8	-8	-10	-3	4	-7	3
Sun. & Wed.	5	§714	§3,570	-8	-8	-8	-3	4	-6	5
Sun. & Mon.	5	§861	§4,305	-8	-8	-3	-3	5	-4	5
Sun. & Sat.	5	§1,008	§5,040	-6	-8	-8	-2	5	-4	6
Sun. & Fri.	5	§1,155	§5,775	-4	-8	-5	-2	5	-5	3
Mon., Wed., & Fri.	4	§1,312	§5,248	-5	-8	-4	-2	6	-4	4
Sun., Wed., Fri., & Sat.	3	§2,205	§6,615	-5	-8	-7	-2	6	-7	5
Sun., Wed., Fri., & Sat.	3	§3,051	§9,153	-4	-8	-2	-2	6	-4	3
Sun., Mon., Fri., & Sat.	3	§5,022	§15,066	-4	-8	-2	-2	10	-4	10

CAREER OUTFITS

A new feature in *The Sims™ 2 University* allows Sims to keep their super-cool (and not-so-cool) career outfits as wardrobe options. After a Sim reaches any job level, the costume associated with that job level becomes a selectable Everyday outfit, if your Sim owns a wardrobe object.

Some work clothes are too cool not to wear around the house. Now your Sims can slap on the duds of any job they've ever held.

Go to the wardrobe and Plan Outfit for Everyday. Select the work clothing of your choice and it becomes your Sim's default duds.

CAREER REWARD OBJECTS

note

Career objects appear in the Rewards panel when Sims reach their career's reward level. Place the object on the lot or save it until later.

With the new careers comes a slate of new career reward objects. Like career objects in *The Sims™ 2*, these objects are awarded at job Level 5 or 6, depending on the career. Unlike the 10 original job objects, however, they are not skill builders. They instead offer extremely powerful new abilities for college-educated, successful Sims.

Dr. Vu's Automated Cosmetic Surgeon

Dr. Vu's Automated Cosmetic Surgeon

◆ Career: Show Business (Level 6)

This Sim is pleased with the results.

Interactions:

◆ Modify Facial Structure: Can be used by young adults and older. Sims can now change their facial features using the facial controls found in Create A Sim. These changes have no effect on genetics if the Sim later reproduces; the resulting offspring will receive genes from the altered Sim's original facial features. Each time Sims alter their facial structure, there is a 20 percent chance that they will emerge absurdly disfigured; however, using the machine again can undo the damage.

Vanity has its price.

Laganaphyllis Simnovorii (aka "Cow Plant")

Laganaphyllis Simnovorii

◆ Career: Natural Scientist (Level 6)

Interactions:

◆ Feed: Costs §35. Child or older only. The Lagana-phyllis Simnovorii is an extraordinary example of botanical engineering. Feed it regularly (at §35 per feeding) and it's a nice, harmless (if freakishly huge and bovine in appearance) bit of home vegetation. Let it go hungry for 12 hours, however, and it becomes extremely dangerous or extremely useful (or both, depending on your view). Feeding the plant while it's in "cake mode" (see next bullet) causes it to retract its lure and go dormant for 12 hours.

◆ Grab Cake: Kills visitor Sims. Can only be done by teen or older. Unfed, the Cow Plant takes matters into its own hands...er...leaves, extending a birthday-cake-shaped "tongue" (complete with lit candle) from its maw. The cake calls to hungry visitors (household Sims will not autonomously grab the cake), drawing them into devouring range. Within seconds, the ravenous plant gulps down the unwary visitor and unceremoniously regurgitates a tombstone.

◆ Milk: Adds five days to current age. Can only be used by child or older. To use your new ferocious flora for your Sims' benefit, leave it unfed somewhere visitors are likely to go. After feeding on Sim flesh, the Cow Plant's udders become engorged; milking them provides an elixir that adds five days to the current age of the Sim who drinks it.

tip

If you don't want your Sims' visitors (including friends) periodically digested, keep the Cow Plant well fed and somewhere inaccessible. Also, the Cow Plant will not eat a Sim with very low hygiene, which is a way to avoid ingestion.

Feeding the Cow Plant.

note

If a family friend is eaten, it may affect your Sims' career promotion qualifications by reducing the friend count.

After eating a Sim, the Cow Plant remains dormant for 12 hours before extending its cake lure again.

The cow's got a sucker on the line, comes in for a sniff, and... supper time!

Turn one Sim's misfortune into another's longevity.

Luminous Pro Antique Camera

Luminous Pro Antique Camera

◆ Career: Artist (Level 5)

Posed Sims turn their heads to look at the camera as you change the view's angle.

Position Sims anywhere (the location of the camera doesn't matter) in whatever goofy pose you choose. Frame the scene and press C to snap.

To get into camera mode, press [Tab].
Interactions:

◆ Shoot Picture: Select either portrait or landscape and any picture effects (Normal, Lighting Bloom, Film Grain, Letterbox, or Vignette). This brings up the picture-framing box. Follow the onscreen instructions for shooting. The camera object's position is irrelevant to the picture you create; you can shoot anywhere on the lot from any angle. With the framing box up, position your view anywhere you like (even utilizing Cameraman mode) and press C to take the shot. First,

however, have your Sims strike a pose. Note that the Sim taking the picture cannot be posed, though the photographer will appear in the photo (standing at the camera) if they're within the framing box.

◆ Pose: Any selectable Sim on the lot can do the Pose interaction. Position the Sim within the framing box (direct the Sim to "Walk Here") and click on the Camera to select "Pose." Choose any of the zany poses for your Sim.

Posed Sims' Needs decay while posing, so they eventually bail out if Mood or critical Needs drop enough. Left-click on the Pose icon in the queue to unpose a Sim.

◆ Stand Next To: With another Sim selected, click on a posed Sim and position the selected Sim somewhere in relation to the posed Sim. Now you can pose this Sim, too.

◆ Sell Picture: After you take the picture, any Sim can click on the camera and select "Sell Picture." The picture disappears and §40 is added to the household funds.

Continuous picture-taking results in the same time commitment and income as a low-level job. Alternatively, you may hang the picture in your Sims' home. Switch the game to Buy mode, use the Hand tool to grab the picture from the camera's side, and place it somewhere on the lot. If you hold the picture near a wall, it switches to a hanging frame. Hold it over a surface and it becomes a tabletop frame. You can sell the picture any time, but it does not depreciate or gain value from the photographer's Creative skill (as would easel paintings).

The memories from photos are worth more than §40; hang this family portrait on the wall or place it on a table.

tip

For information on Camera mode and effects (see the "Cinematic Cheats" section in Chapter 9).

note

The picture-taking system on the camera object is very similar to the Paint Portraits/Still Life interactions on the easel. See Chapter 5 for details.

Resurrect-O-Nomitron

Resurrect-O-Nomitron

◆ Career: Paranormal (Level 5)

Choose your resurrection budget carefully; the price of frugality may be quite high.

Interactions:

◆ Call Grim Reaper: Child or older Sim places a call to the hereafter to revive any Sim whose tombstone/urn exists in the neighborhood or college town. The amount of money you pay for a resurrection dictates how the deceased comes back (see the Note) as a household member. This interaction is unavailable if there are already eight Sims in the household, since the resurrection adds more than the lot can hold.

Zombies spend a lot of time thinking of brains.

note

The amount of money you spend on a resurrection affects the quality of the resurrection:

◆ §1–§987: Resurrection fails and money paid is forfeit.

◆ §988–§4,127: Sims return in their previous age group but as zombies. Zombies' Needs are badly depleted and they're extremely angry at the Sim doing their poor resurrection, causing a -20 Daily/ -15 Lifetime point reduction in relationship with the caller. They lose most of their skills and get the "zombie personality."

◆ §4128–§8,512: Sims return but with all skills reduced by three levels and all personality factors reversed (low becomes high and vice versa). Imperfect Sims are nevertheless happy to be back and experience a +10 Daily/+5 Lifetime point increase in relationship with the caller.

◆ §8,513–§10,000: Sims return exactly as they were at the time of death. Perfectly resurrected Sims are ecstatic to be risen and get a +35 Daily/ +25 Lifetime point increase in Daily Relationship with the caller.

If the resurrected Sims are children, they can only come back perfectly or not at all. Offering less than §987 gets you nothing but §1,000 poorer. Above §1,000 yields the same perfect children, just as you knew them.

tip

Don't spend more than §8,513 on a resurrection, since spending more won't have any additional benefit.

ZOMBIE LIFE

Zombie Sims, not surprisingly, have several limitations but also a few advantages:

◆ Skin tone and change of face: All zombies come back with distorted facial features and a special zombie skin tone. They also have a special portrait when their interaction menu appears; don't make them look in one direction for too long. When idle, they occasionally have trouble keeping their head up.

◆ Shamble: Zombies can't run, walk, or skip, no matter how far you direct them to travel, the level of their personality, or how you direct them to go. They always move with the zombie shamble.

◆ WooHoo and Procreation: Zombie Sims can WooHoo but cannot Try for Baby. If, however, a Sim expired while pregnant, she (or he, via alien abduction) will return pregnant and give birth to a normal (or normal alien) baby.

◆ Age Transition: Zombies don't age and are, effectively, immortal. Thus, they have unlimited time to work on skills and pursue other self-improvements. This makes them fantastic resources as skill teachers or personality encouragers. There is one exception to

zombies' inability to age and it pertains to college (see College bullet below). Zombies can, however, die accidentally (electrocution, starvation, etc.)

◆ Skills: Some skills are lost.

◆ Personality: All zombies return with the same personality. Generally, they're Mean, a bit Outgoing, very Sloppy, and a bit Playful and Active.

◆ Thoughts: Zombies have frequent thoughts of brains.

◆ College: Teen Zombie Sims can go to college. In fact, there's a special scholarship just for Zombies. In this one case, zombies WILL age; they become young adults in college and adults upon graduation. They don't, however, advance in age any further.

Zombies can WooHoo but don't expect to start a family.

Chapter 8
New Objects

A new world like college requires new objects to make it come alive. How does over 100 new objects sound? This chapter provides stats for each one. We also detail the new trio of personal inventory objects (think pocket-sized electronics).

OBJECT DIRECTORY

Object	Price and Depreciation				Needs					
	Price	Initial Depreciation	Daily Depreciation	Depreciation Limit	Hunger	Comfort	Hygiene	Energy	Fun	Environment
A-maz-ing Matey!	§1,050	§157	§105	§420	0	0	0	0	6	0
ADD Disco Dining Chair	§320	§48	§32	§128	0	4	0	0	0	0
ADD Disco Dining Table	§755	§113	§75	§302	0	0	0	0	0	2
Blinding Soldier Wall Lamp	§230	§34	§23	§92	0	0	0	0	0	1
Blooms & Boomers End Table	§120	§18	§12	§48	0	0	0	0	0	0
Blossoming Heart	§485	§0	§0	§0	0	0	0	0	0	4
Cafeteria-Style Steelate Counter Island	§810	§121	§81	§324	0	0	0	0	0	2
Circle of Light Friendship Lamp	§215	§32	§21	§86	0	0	0	0	0	1
Club Room Countertop	§600	§90	§60	§240	0	0	0	0	0	0
College Public Phone	§550	§82	§55	§220	0	0	0	0	0	0
Corner Pocket Pool Table	§1,800	§270	§180	§720	0	0	0	0	10	0
Cornerstone Veritable Vanity	§1,200	§180	§120	§480	0	0	0	0	0	0
Cozmo MP3 Player	§195	§0	§0	§0	0	0	0	0	7	0
Dahlen Library Bookcases	§700	§105	§70	§280	0	0	0	0	1	0
Deceptico Plano Glass	§580	§87	§58	§232	0	0	0	0	0	3
Don Meswitthis Bunny Pennant	§65	§0	§0	§0	0	0	0	0	0	1
Downbeat Kit	§3,100	§585	§390	§1,560	0	0	0	0	10	3
Dr. Vu's Automated Cosmetic Surgeon	§0	§0	§0	§0	0	0	0	0	0	0
Exerto Butterfly Exercise Machine	§900	§135	§90	§360	0	0	0	0	1	2
Exerto Free Press Exercise Machine	§900	§135	§90	§360	0	0	0	0	1	2
Exerto Leg Extension Exercise Machine	§900	§135	§90	§360	0	0	0	0	1	2
Fallorayne Fountain	§625	§0	§0	§0	0	0	0	0	0	10
Fearless Flyin' 4000 Treadmill	§2,250	§337	§225	§900	0	0	0	0	5	2
Fighting Llamas Pennant	§65	§0	§0	§0	0	0	0	0	0	1
Fighting Llamas Tri-Pennant Combo	§65	§0	§0	§0	0	0	0	0	0	1
Fighting Piranhas Tri-Pennant Combo	§65	§0	§0	§0	0	0	0	0	0	1
Fists of Bunny Poster	§45	§0	§0	§0	0	0	0	0	0	1

Skills				Room Sort								Community Sort			
Charisma	Creativity	Body	Function	Kids	Study	Dining Room	Outside	Living Room	Bathroom	Bedroom	Kitchen	Miscellaneous	Outdoor	Shopping	Food
			Electronics					X		X		X			
			Comfort	X	X						X			X	X
			Surfaces		X						X				X
			Lighting		X			X	X	X		X		X	
			Surfaces					X		X				X	
			Decorative	X			X					X	X		
			Surfaces								X	X			
			Lighting	X	X			X		X		X		X	
			Surfaces						X		X	X			
			Electronics												
			Hobbies					X				X			
			Surfaces							X					
			Personal												
			Hobbies		X			X		X		X			
X			Decorative					X	X	X				X	
	X		Decorative		X					X				X	
			Hobbies					X				X			
			Career Rewards												
		X	Hobbies		X		X					X			
		X	Hobbies		X		X					X			
		X	Hobbies		X		X					X			
			Decorative				X					X	X		
		X	Hobbies		X		X					X			
			Decorative		X					X				X	
			Decorative		X					X				X	
			Decorative		X					X				X	
			Decorative		X		X			X				X	

Object Directory continued

	Price and Depreciation				Needs					
	Price	Initial Depreciation	Daily Depreciation	Depreciation Limit	Hunger	Comfort	Hygiene	Energy	Fun	Environment
Flickering Mercenary Table Lamp	§195	§29	§19	§78	0	0	0	0	0	1
Flowin' Protozoan Double Bed	§620	§93	§62	§248	0	3	0	3	0	1
Flowin' Protozoan Single Bed	§520	§78	§52	§208	0	3	0	3	0	0
Fusty Hors D'oeuvres Gym Lockers	§700	§105	§70	§280	0	0	0	0	0	4
Genuine Buck's Famous Counterfeiting Machine	§0	§0	§0	§0	0	0	0	0	0	0
Groovy Dresser by Keen Co.	§425	§63	§42	§170	0	0	0	0	0	4
Impresso Espress-o-Matic	§1,495	§224	§149	§598	0	0	0	0	0	0
Industrial Steelate Counter	§560	§84	§56	§224	0	0	0	0	0	0
It's Reggae, Mon Poster	§45	§0	§0	§0	0	0	0	0	0	1
Laganaphyllis Simnovorii	§0	§0	§0	§0	0	0	0	0	0	0
LeTournament Decahedron XS	§245	§0	§0	§0	0	0	0	0	0	0
Locker Room CounterFeet	§90	§13	§9	§36	0	0	0	0	0	0
Luminous Pro Antique Camera	§0	§0	§0	§0	0	0	0	0	0	0
Magnificently Medieval Armchair	§1,000	§150	§100	§400	0	9	0	0	0	2
Majestically Medieval Double Bed	§3,400	§510	§340	§1,360	0	8	0	8	0	6
Masterfully Medieval Sofa	§840	§126	§84	§336	0	8	0	2	0	0
Maturely Medieval Single Bed	§1,100	§165	§110	§440	0	5	0	6	0	2
Mediocre Medieval Loveseat	§1,350	§202	§135	§540	0	8	0	2	0	0
Merry-making Dining Table	§1,025	§153	§102	§410	0	0	0	0	0	2
Mini-Disco Dinette Table	§255	§38	§25	§102	0	0	0	0	0	0
MMM Mini Fridge	§350	§52	§35	§140	10	0	0	0	0	0
Modest Medieval End Table	§355	§53	§35	§142	0	0	0	0	0	0
Myne Cafeteria Table	§380	§57	§38	§152	0	0	0	0	0	0
Mysteriously Medieval Dining Chair	§950	§142	§95	§380	0	7	0	0	0	2
NOYIN 2680 Cellular Phone	§149	§0	§0	§0	0	0	0	0	0	0
Orbs of Connectedness Ceiling Lamp	§180	§27	§18	§72	0	0	0	0	0	1
Party Juice Barrel	§145	§21	§14	§58	1	0	0	0	6	0
Pimp Viking 3D Arcade Game	§1,050	§157	§105	§420	0	0	0	0	6	0
Psychedelic SimAtri Coffee Table	§145	§0	§0	§0	0	0	0	0	0	0
Really Distressed Loveseat by Club Distress	§165	§24	§16	§66	0	5	0	2	0	0
Resurrect-O-Nomitron	§0	§0	§0	§0	0	0	0	0	0	0
Retro Bodacious Loveseat	§615	§92	§61	§246	0	7	0	2	0	0
Retro Overeasy Eggseater	§620	§93	§62	§248	0	7	0	0	0	0
Retro Overeasy Eggseater Recliner	§640	§96	§64	§256	0	7	0	2	0	0
Revolutionary Rebellion Poster	§45	§0	§0	§0	0	0	0	0	0	1
Rugged Llamas of the North Souvenir Rugby Jersey	§115	§0	§0	§0	0	0	0	0	0	1

Skills				Room Sort								Community Sort			
Charisma	Creativity	Body	Function	Kids	Study	Dining Room	Outside	Living Room	Bathroom	Bedroom	Kitchen	Miscellaneous	Outdoor	Shopping	Food
			Lighting	X	X	X		X		X		X			
			Comfort							X					
			Comfort							X					
			Miscellaneous							X		X			
			Aspiration Rewards												
			Miscellaneous							X					
			Appliances									X	X		X
			Surfaces								X			X	
			Decorative		X					X				X	
			Career Rewards												
			Personal												
			Surfaces								X			X	
			Career Rewards												
			Comfort					X				X		X	
			Comfort							X					
			Comfort					X						X	
			Comfort							X					
			Comfort					X				X			
			Surfaces			X					X				X
			Surfaces			X							X		X
			Appliances								X				
			Surfaces					X		X					
			Surfaces		X										X
			Comfort		X	X					X			X	X
			Personal												
			Lighting		X			X	X	X	X	X		X	X
			Miscellaneous		X		X					X	X		
			Electronics					X		X		X			
			Surfaces					X		X				X	
			Comfort					X						X	
			Career Rewards												
			Comfort					X				X			
			Comfort					X				X		X	
			Comfort					X				X			
			Decorative		X					X				X	
			Decorative		X					X				X	

Object Directory continued

	Price and Depreciation				Needs					
	Price	Initial Depreciation	Daily Depreciation	Depreciation Limit	Hunger	Comfort	Hygiene	Energy	Fun	Environment
Save the Sheep Faux Sheepskin Diploma	§0	§0	§0	§0	0	0	0	0	0	0
Sellafone Gadget Kiosk	§2,500	§375	§250	§1,000	0	0	0	0	4	7
Shining Knight Standing Lamp	§315	§47	§31	§126	0	0	0	0	0	2
ShinyTyme Cooktop	§900	§135	§90	§360	10	0	0	0	0	0
Simbic Bisectaur Bass	§1,800	§525	§350	§1,400	0	0	0	0	10	2
SimCity Championship Roster 1984-85 Season Poster	§55	§0	§0	§0	0	0	0	0	0	1
Simgreek Letter Sign—Cham	§100	§14	§9	§39	0	0	0	0	0	0
Simgreek Letter Sign—Hoh	§100	§14	§9	§39	0	0	0	0	0	0
Simgreek Letter Sign—Urele	§100	§14	§9	§39	0	0	0	0	0	0
Simgreek Letter Sign—Annya	§100	§14	§9	§39	0	0	0	0	0	0
Simgreek Letter Sign—Fruhm	§100	§14	§9	§39	0	0	0	0	0	0
Simgreek Letter Sign—Nagard	§100	§14	§9	§39	0	0	0	0	0	0
Simgreek Letter Sign—Oresha	§100	§14	§9	§39	0	0	0	0	0	0
Simgreek Letter Sign—Var	§100	§14	§9	§39	0	0	0	0	0	0
Skimmer Securities Ceiling Sprinkler	§245	§36	§24	§98	0	0	0	0	0	0
Space Oddity	§50	§0	§0	§0	0	0	0	0	0	1
Spaceship Spacious Fountain	§6,250	§0	§0	§0	0	0	0	0	0	10
Stack-O-Flames Bonfire	§245	§0	§0	§0	0	0	0	0	0	10
Stick 'Em Up Bulletin Board	§75	§0	§0	§0	0	0	0	0	0	1
Strut Your Stuff Communal Shower	§425	§63	§42	§170	0	0	7	0	0	0
Superflux Über UV Guitar	§2,500	§375	§250	§1,000	0	0	0	0	10	3
Surfing the Universe Poster	§59	§0	§0	§0	0	0	0	0	0	1
The Truth is Somewhere	§55	§0	§0	§0	0	0	0	0	0	1
Tushugger Cushy Chair	§380	§57	§38	§152	0	7	0	0	0	0
Way Coolinary Countertop	§410	§61	§41	§164	0	0	0	0	0	0
Way Coolinary Fluid Island Bar	§1,850	§277	§185	§740	0	0	0	0	3	0
Way Coolinary Island	§810	§121	§81	§324	0	0	0	0	0	2
We Call It Football Limited Edition Prints	§75	§0	§0	§0	0	0	0	0	0	1
White Rabbit Nirvana Blower	§1,720	§258	§172	§688	0	6	0	0	8	0
Wornable Easy Chair	§180	§27	§18	§72	0	7	0	0	0	0
Wornable Fridge	§375	§56	§37	§150	10	0	0	0	0	0
Wornable Sofa	§195	§27	§18	§72	0	5	0	2	0	0
Wrath of Sack Man Pinball	§1,750	§262	§175	§700	0	0	0	0	10	2

Charisma	Creativity	Body	Function	Kids	Study	Dining Room	Outside	Living Room	Bathroom	Bedroom	Kitchen	Miscellaneous	Outdoor	Shopping	Food
Skills				**Room Sort**								**Community Sort**			
			Career Rewards												
			Electronics									X		X	
			Lighting		X	X		X		X		X		X	
			Appliances								X				X
	X		Hobbies					X				X			
			Decorative		X					X				X	
			Decorative				X	X							
			Decorative				X	X							
			Decorative				X	X							
			Decorative				X	X							
			Decorative				X	X							
			Decorative				X	X							
			Decorative				X	X							
			Decorative				X	X							
			Miscellaneous								X	X			X
			Decorative		X					X				X	
			Decorative				X					X	X		
			Miscellaneous				X					X	X		
			Decorative		X					X				X	
			Plumbing						X			X			
	X		Hobbies					X				X			
			Decorative		X					X				X	
			Decorative		X					X				X	
			Comfort					X				X		X	
			Surfaces					X			X	X			
			Miscellaneous									X			X
			Surfaces								X	X			
			Decorative		X					X				X	
			Miscellaneous		X		X							X	
			Comfort					X				X		X	
			Appliances								X				
			Comfort					X						X	
			Electronics					X				X			

OBJECT CATALOG
Comfort
Dining Chairs

AOD Disco Dining Chair
◆ Price: §320
◆ Need Effects: Comfort 4

Mysteriously Medieval Dining Chair
◆ Price: §950
◆ Need Effects: Comfort 7, Environment 2

Living Chairs

Wornable Easy Chair
◆ Price: §180
◆ Need Effects: Comfort 7

Tushugger Cushy Chair
◆ Price: §380
◆ Need Effects: Comfort 7

Retro Overeasy Eggseater
◆ Price: §620
◆ Need Effects: Comfort 7

Magnificently Medieval Armchair
◆ Price: §1,000
◆ Need Effects: Comfort 9, Environment 2

Recliners

Retro Overeasy Eggseater Recliner
◆ Price: §640
◆ Need Effects: Comfort 7, Energy 2 (Nap)
◆ Need Max: Energy up to 80 (Nap)

Sofas & Loveseats

Really Distressed Loveseat by Club Distress
◆ Price: §165
◆ Need Effects: Comfort 4 (Sit), Comfort 5 (Lounge), Energy 2 (Nap), Fun 4 (Play)
◆ Need Max: Energy up to 20 (Nap)

Wornable Sofa
◆ Price: §195
◆ Need Effects: Comfort 4 (Sit), Comfort 5 (Lounge), Energy 2, Fun 4 (Play)
◆ Need Max: Energy up to 20 (Nap)

Retro Bodacious Loveseat
◆ Price: §615
◆ Need Effects: Comfort 6 (Sit), Comfort 7 (Lounge), Energy 2 (Nap), Fun 4 (Play)
◆ Need Max: Energy up to 60 (Nap)

Masterfully Medieval Sofa
◆ Price: §840
◆ Need Effects: Comfort 7 (Sit), Comfort 8 (Lounge), Energy 2 (Nap), Fun 4 (Play)
◆ Need Max: Energy up to 55 (Nap)

Mediocre Medieval Loveseat
- ◆ Price: $1,350
- ◆ Need Effects: Comfort 7 (Sit), Comfort 8 (Lounge), Energy 2 (Nap), Fun 4 (Play)
- ◆ Need Max: Energy up to 85 (Nap)

Beds

Flowin' Protozoan Single Bed
- ◆ Price: $520
- ◆ Need Effects: Comfort 3, Energy 3, Environment 1, Fun 2 (Jump)
- ◆ Need Max: Fun up to 70 (Jump)

Flowin' Protozoan Double Bed
- ◆ Price: $620
- ◆ Need Effects: Comfort 2, Energy 3, Environment 1, Fun 2 (Jump)
- ◆ Need Max: Fun up to 70 (Jump)

Maturely Medieval Single Bed
- ◆ Price: $1,100
- ◆ Need Effects: Comfort 5, Energy 6, Environment 2, Fun 2 (Jump)
- ◆ Need Max: Fun up to 80 (Jump)

Majestically Medieval Double Bed
- ◆ Price: $3,400
- ◆ Need Effects: Comfort 8, Energy 8, Environment 6
- ◆ Need Max: Fun up to 80 (Jump)

Surfaces
Counters

Locker Room CounterFeet
- ◆ Price: $90

Way Coolinary Countertop
- ◆ Price: $410

Industrial Steelate Counter
- ◆ Price: $560

Club Room Countertop
- ◆ Price: $600

note

In the original THE SIMS™ 2, this countertop had only one variation. This expansion pack adds the singe-drawer/cabinet model.

Cafeteria-Style Steelate Counter Island
- ◆ Price: $810
- ◆ Need Effects: Environment 2

Way Coolinary Island
- ◆ Price: $810
- ◆ Need Effects: Environment 2

Tables

Mini-Disco Dinette Table
◆ Price: §255

Myne Cafeteria Table
◆ Price: §380

AOD Disco Dining Table
◆ Price: §755
◆ Need Effects: Environment 2

Merry-Making Dining Table
◆ Price: §1,025
◆ Need Effects: Environment 2

End Tables

Blooms & Boomers End Table
◆ Price: §120

Modest Medieval End Table
◆ Price: §355

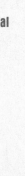

Coffee Tables

Psychedelic SimAtri Coffee Table
◆ Price: §145

Miscellaneous

Cornerstone Veritable Vanity
◆ Price: §1,200
◆ Need Effects: Fun 2 (Look at Self)
Interactions:
◆ Change Appearance: Works just like standard mirror.
◆ Makeover: Allows you to Change Appearance of other Sims, including NPCs and Townies.

Decorative
Wall Hangings

Fists of Bunny Poster
◆ Price: §45
◆ Need Effects: Fun 3 (View), Environment 1
◆ Need Max: Fun up to 95 (View)

It's Reggae, Mon Poster
◆ Price: §45
◆ Need Effects: Fun 3 (View), Environment 1
◆ Need Max: Fun up to 95 (View)

Revolutionary Rebellion Poster
◆ Price: §45
◆ Need Effects: Fun 3 (View), Environment 1
◆ Need Max: Fun up to 95 (View)

Space Oddity
- Price: §50
- Need Effects: Fun 3 (View), Environment 1
- Need Max: Fun up to 95 (View)

SimCity Championship Roster 1984–85 Season Poster
- Price: §55
- Need Effects: Fun 3 (View), Environment 1
- Need Max: Fun up to 95 (View)

The Truth Is Somewhere
- Price: §55
- Need Effects: Fun 3 (View), Environment
- Need Max: Fun up to 95 (View)

Surfing the Universe Poster
- Price: §59
- Need Effects: Fun 3 (View), Environment 1
- Need Max: Fun up to 95 (View)

Don Meswitthis Bunny Pennant
- Price: §65
- Need Effects: Fun 3 (View), Environment 1
- Need Max: Fun up to 95 (View)

Fighting Llamas Pennant
- Price: §65
- Need Effects: Fun 3 (View), Environment 1
- Need Max: Fun up to 95 (View)

Fighting Llamas Tri-Pennant Combo
- Price: §65
- Need Effects: Fun 3 (View), Environment 1
- Need Max: Fun up to 95 (View)

Fighting Piranhas Tri-Pennant Combo
- Price: §65
- Need Effects: Fun 3 (View), Environment 1
- Need Max: Fun up to 95 (View)

Stick 'Em Up Bulletin Board
- Price: §75
- Need Effects: Fun 3 (View), Environment 1
- Need Max: Fun up to 95 (View)

We Call It Football Limited Edition Prints
- Price: §75
- Need Effects: Fun 3 (View), Environment 1
- Need Max: Fun up to 95 (View)

Simgreek Letter Signs
- Price: §100
- Need Effects: Fun 3 (View), Environment 0
- Need Max: Fun up to 95 (View)

Rugged Llamas of the North Souvenir Rugby Jersey
- Price: §115
- Need Effects: Fun 3 (View), Environment 1
- Need Max: Fun up to 95 (View)

PRIMA OFFICIAL GAME GUIDE

Sculpture

Blossoming Heart
◆ Price: §485
◆ Need Effects: Fun 3 (View), Environment 4
◆ Need Max: Fun up to 95 (View)

Fallorayne Fountain
◆ Price: §625
◆ Need Effects: Fun 3 (View), Environment 10
◆ Need Max: Fun up to 95 (View)

Interactions:
◆ View: Look at fountain for Fun.
◆ Add Soap: Sims adds detergent to fountain to make it sudsy.
Outdoor only.

Spaceship Spacious Fountain
◆ Price: §6,250
◆ Need Effects: Fun 3 (View), Environment 10
◆ Need Max: Fun up to 95 (View)

Interactions:
◆ View: Look at fountain for Fun.
◆ Add Soap: Sims adds detergent to fountain to make it sudsy.
Outdoor only.

Mirrors

Deceptico Piano Glass
◆ Price: §580
◆ Skill: Charisma (Practice Romance or Practice Speech)
◆ Need Effects: Environment 3

Plumbing
Showers and Tubs

Strut Your Stuff Communal Shower
◆ Price: §425
◆ Skill: Mechanical (Repair)
◆ Need Effects: Hygiene 7 (Take a Shower), Bladder 2 (Take a Shower, Sloppy only)

If the communal shower is on a noncollege lot, young adults and older will shoo away younger Sims who enter the room containing the shower.

Appliances
Cooking

ShinyTyme Cooktop
◆ Price: §900
◆ Need Effects: Hunger 10

This stove can only be used to cook stovetop foods; anything that goes in the oven will be unavailable.

Though it can be placed on dorm, residential, or community lots in either home neighborhoods or college towns, the lot type dictates how the stove can be used:

◆ Residential lots in neighborhoods: stovetop-only foods but otherwise normal.
◆ Community lots in neighborhoods: self-serve stovetop-only foods but otherwise normal.
◆ Dorm or college community lots: From 6 a.m. to 11 p.m., the NPC Cafeteria Worker comes to the lot and takes over the stove. He or she serves group meals constantly throughout the day. Playable Sims can only use the stove when the Cafeteria Worker is off duty and then only for stovetop foods. They can use it during serving hours if they Work in Cafeteria. See the "Eating at College" and "College Jobs" sections in Chapter 6 for full details.
◆ Private residences or Greek housing in college towns: stovetop-only foods but otherwise normal.

Refrigerators

MMM Mini Fridge
◆ Price: §350
◆ Food Capacity: 80
◆ Need Effects: Fun 3 (Juggle Bottles or Play), Hunger 10

◆ Need Max: Fun up to 50 (Juggle Bottles or Play)

Its capacity is smaller than a traditional fridge, but it fits under countertops. Use it for cold, toaster oven, or microwave food (including the new Cup O' Ramen). It CANNOT be used to get baby bottles.

A freestanding minifridge without a counter serves as a prep surface, too, so keep it clear and Sims can prepare meals on it.

Wornable Fridge
◆ Price: $375
◆ Food Capacity: 200
◆ Need Effects: Fun 3 (Juggle Bottles or Play), Hunger 10
◆ Need Max: Fun up to 50 (Juggle Bottles or Play)

Electronics
Games

A-maz-ing Matey!
◆ Price: $1,050
◆ Need Effects: Fun 6 (Play), Fun 5 (Watch), Social (Watch)
◆ Need Max: Fun up to 90 (Watch)

Interactions:
◆ Play: Costs $1 per play. Gets more Fun for a win than a loss.
◆ Watch: Watchers get Fun. If multiple Sims are watching, they get double the Fun of a solo watcher plus Social.

Pimp Viking 3D Arcade Game
◆ Price: $1,050
◆ Need Effects: Fun 6 (Play), Fun 5 (Watch), Social (Watch)
◆ Need Max: Fun up to 90 (Watch)

Interactions:
◆ Play: Costs $1 per play. Gets more Fun for a win than a loss.
◆ Watch: Watchers get Fun. If multiple Sims are watching, they get double the Fun of a solo watcher plus Social.

Wrath of Sack Man Pinball
◆ Price: $1,750
◆ Need Effects: Fun 10 (Play), Fun 3 (Watch), Environment 2

Identical to standard pinball machines (see Chapter 5).

Lighting
Table Lamps

Flickering Mercenary Table Lamp
◆ Price: $195
◆ Need Effects: Environment 1

Floor Lamps

Circle of Light Friendship Lamp
◆ Price: $215
◆ Need Effects: Environment 1

Shining Knight Standing Lamp
◆ Price: $315
◆ Need Effects: Environment 2

Wall Lamps

Blinding Soldier Wall Lamp
◆ Price: $230
◆ Need Effects: Environment 1

Hanging Lamps

Orbs of Connectedness Ceiling Lamp
◆ Price: $180
◆ Need Effects: Environment 1

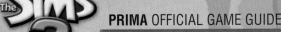

Hobbies
Creativity

Downbeat Kit

◆ Price: §2,500

◆ Skill: Creativity (slower if Performing)

◆ Need Effects: Fun 10 (Perform/Practice), Fun 4 (Watch), Fun 8 (Dance), Energy -2 (Dance), Social (Watch, Dance, Perform), Environment 3.

◆ Need Max: Fun up to 75 (Dance Solo) or 85 (Dance Together)

All interactions are the same as the Simbic Bisectaur Bass.

> **note**
>
> The Chimeway & Daughters Saloon Piano has been slightly modified from its function in the base game. It works essentially the same but now features the Perform and Joinable interactions.

Simbic Bisectaur Bass

◆ Price: §1,800

◆ Skill: Creativity (slower if Performing)

◆ Need Effects: Fun 10 (Perform/Practice), Fun 4 (Watch), Fun 8 (Dance), Energy -2 (Dance), Social (Watch, Dance, Perform), Environment 2.

◆ Need Max: Fun up to 75 (Dance Solo) or 85 (Dance Together)

Interactions:

◆ Practice: Sim plays (Country, Rock, or Jazz), has Fun, and builds Creativity. All practicing Sims play by themselves, not in unison. Sim's Creativity skill determines how well they play and how watchers react.

◆ Perform: Sim puts out a tip jar and plays (Country, Rock, or Jazz). If there are other instruments in the same room, other Sims can join in by clicking on the already-performing Sim. Sims get Creativity skill, Fun, and Social. If other Sims put tips in the tip jar, Sim earns money when they stop playing and empties the jar. Sim's Creativity skill determines how well they play and how watchers will react. Is available on community lots in regular neighborhoods but won't build Creativity.

◆ Dance: Click on instrument when another Sim is playing it and Sim dances to the music. Gives Fun and, if other Sims Dance Together, Social.

◆ Watch: Gives Fun and, if more than one Sim is watching, Social.

Superflux Über UV Guitar

◆ Price: §2,500

◆ Skill: Creativity (slower if Performing)

◆ Need Effects: Fun 10 (Perform/Practice), Fun 4 (Watch), Fun 8 (Dance), Energy -2 (Dance), Social (Watch, Dance, Perform), Environment 3.

◆ Need Max: Fun up to 75 (Dance Solo) or 85 (Dance Together)

All interactions are the same as the Simbic Bisectaur Bass.

Knowledge

Dahlen Library Bookcases

◆ Price: §700

◆ Skill: Cooking (Study), Mechanical (Study), Cooking (Study), Cleaning (Study)

◆ Need Effects: Fun 1 (Read or Read To), Fun 1 (Be Read To), Comfort 1 (Write in Diary), Fun 1 (Write in Diary)

◆ Need Max: Fun up to 75 (Read/Read To/Be Read To)

Interactions:

◆ Same as standard bookshelves. All bookcases now feature the College menu that allows for the new Research interaction. This joinable interaction builds Social and increases class performance. The more Sims that join (up to four), the faster the class performance increase. More than four Sims can join, but there's no additional speed benefit (though extra Sims provide insurance against Sims who drop out due to Mood or Needs). Research is, like other bookshelf interactions, also available from any unreturned book.

Exercise

Exerto Free Press Exercise Machine

◆ Price: §900

◆ Skill: Body (Work Out)

◆ Need Effects: Fun 1 (Work Out, Active only), Hygiene -4 (Work Out), Environment 2

◆ Need Max: Fun up to 90

Interactions:

◆ All interactions same as standard exercise equipment.

◆ Be Personal Trainer: If another Sim is using equipment, a Sim with higher Body skill can offer personal training services for money. Click on exercise machine to start job; training Sim earns money by the minute, and Sim on machine gets faster Body skill. The Sim on the machine can also click on any other playable Sim with higher Body skill and ask them to be their Personal Trainer (doesn't cost money).

Exerto Butterfly Exercise Machine

- ◆ Price: §900
- ◆ Skill: Body (Work Out)
- ◆ Need Effects: Fun 1 (Work Out, Active only), Hygiene -4 (Work Out), Environment 2
- ◆ Need Max: Fun up to 90

Interactions:

◆ See Exerto Free Press Exercise Machine, above

Exerto Leg Extension Exercise Machine

- ◆ Price: §900
- ◆ Skill: Body (Work Out)
- ◆ Need Effects: Fun 1 (Work Out, Active only), Hygiene -4 (Work Out), Environment 2
- ◆ Need Max: Fun up to 90

Interactions:

◆ See Exerto Free Press Exercise Machine, above

Fearless Flyin' 4000 Treadmill

- ◆ Price: §2,250
- ◆ Skill: Body (Run)
- ◆ Need Effects: Fun 5 (Run, Active only), Hygiene -4 (Run), Environment 2
- ◆ Need Max: Fun up to 60

Interactions:

◆ See Exerto Free Press Exercise Machine, above

Recreation

Corner Pocket Pool Table

- ◆ Price: §1,800
- ◆ Skill: Pool (Hidden)
- ◆ Need Effects: Fun 10 (Play), Fun 3 (Watch), Social (Group Play, Watch)
- ◆ Need Max: Fun up to 60 (Watch)

POOL SKILL

Every moment a Sim spends playing pool (either solo or against other players) or doing trick shots, the better at pool and trick shots they become. This is due to an invisible Pool skill that Sims acquire as they gain experience with the pool table. There is no way to view Pool skill.

Teen Sims who excel at pool are eligible for a pool scholarship. This is a good way to tell how good your teen Sim is and whether they'll have a chance to make consistent money hustling pool at college.

Interactions:

- ◆ **Play:** Sim can play alone for Fun. Up to three more Sims can join; earn Fun and Social. Builds Pool skill. Player with higher Pool skill wins; if equal, winner is random.
- ◆ **Join:** Joins game in progress. All players get Social in addition to Fun. Builds Pool skill.
- ◆ **Perform Trick Shot:** Sim chooses Xylophone or Cup trick shot, gets Fun. Quality of trick depends on hidden Pool skill. Builds Pool skill. Relationships with all watching Sims are boosted for a successful trick shot and reduced for unsuccessful trick shots.
- ◆ **Watch:** Gives Fun and Social.
- ◆ **Watch Trick Shots:** Relationship with Sim doing the trick shot increases if shot succeeds and decreases if shot fails.
- ◆ **Hustle:** Click on pool table while another Sim is playing solo or click on another Sim when your Sim is playing solo. Select a simolean amount for the game stakes. Sim with highest Pool skill wins; if both players are equal, winner is random. If your Sim offered the Hustle, the vanquished Sim reduces Daily Relationship with winner. Not available after game has begun; to change a regular game to a Hustle, cancel the game in progress or wait until it ends naturally and then Hustle.

tip

Hustling pool earns about the same amount of money per hour as working other campus jobs (Cafeteria, Personal Trainer, etc.).

tip

When hustling, play against Sims your Sim doesn't know or need as friends, since winning reduces Daily Relationship.

Miscellaneous

Dressers

note

Dressers now contain every career outfit any playable Sim in the household has ever worn. These can be changed into or designated as your Sim's Everyday outfit.

Groovy Dresser by Keen Co.
◆ Price: §425
◆ Need Effects: Environment 4

Interactions:
◆ Same as standard dressers.

Fusty Hors D'oeuvres Gym Lockers
◆ Price: §700
◆ Need Effects: Environment 4

Interactions:
◆ Same as standard dressers.

Party

Fruit Punch Barrel
◆ Price: §145
◆ Need Effects: Hunger 1 (Drink), Bladder -1 (Drink), Fun 6 (Drink from Tap)

> **note**
>
> If there's a Sports Party going on, Sims are especially attracted to the Fruit Punch Barrel.

Interactions:
◆ Have a Drink: Child or older can use to satisfy Hunger and deplete Bladder. When finished, Sims place cup on a surface or on the floor (depending on Neat/Sloppy), or randomly crush it on their forehead (teen and older only).
◆ Drink from Tap: Child or older can drink directly from the tap. Satisfies Fun and Hunger, depletes Bladder.

Stack-O-Flames Bonfire
◆ Price: §245
◆ Need Effects: Fun, Hygiene -2 (Clean Up), Environment 10

> **note**
>
> Bonfire is not a normal burning object. It must be located outside but can't ever ignite nearby objects or Sims.

Interactions:
◆ Light Fire: Teen or older can ignite bonfire. Fire spreads and slowly consumes woodpile. Sims cheer or hang out around it for Fun and Social. Burns for three hours.
◆ Join: Child and older Sims will gather around the fire and interact. Feeds Social and Fun.
◆ Roast Marshmallows: Satisfies Fun. Cooking skill dictates whether Sim's marshmallow ignites.
◆ Tell Stories: Satisfies Fun.
◆ Bonfire Dance: Click on another Sim and, if relationship is high enough, Sims does a special dance around the fire. Increases Social and Daily Relationship.
◆ Clean Up: After fire is spent, it becomes an ash pile (reduces Environment). Cleaning it eliminates the mess but reduces cleaner's Hygiene.

White Rabbit Nirvana Blower
◆ Price: §1,720
◆ Need Effects: Comfort 6, Fun 8, Social

Interactions:
◆ Blow Bubbles: Child or older Sims can use to increase Fun and Comfort. Sims will float while Blowing Bubbles. If multiple Sims Blow Bubbles, all get Social with Group Talk. Up to four Sims can join and blow at a time. Each station produces its own color bubbles.

> **note**
>
> If four Sims are using the Bubble Blower, the color of the bubbles depends on the personalities of the blowers. If all four have:
> ◆ exactly 5 Charisma: blue
> ◆ exactly 8 Playful: green
> ◆ more than 5 Charisma and 8 Playful: blue and green

Miscellaneous

Skimmer Securities Ceiling Sprinkler

◆ Price: §245

◆ Need Effects: Fun 3 (Prank)

Automatically triggered by fires in the same room and puts out any fire within sprinkler range without involving the Fire Department. The speedy response of this device reduces the damage from fires but creates a big mess to clean up. Place one in kitchens and near fireplaces. Can only be placed over covered floors.

Interactions:

◆ Pull Prank: Teens or older can hold a lighter under the sprinkler to set it off. Satisfies Fun but creates a big puddle (reducing Environment). Standing in the spray reduces Fun, Comfort, Hygiene, and Energy. Can, very rarely, occur autonomously.

Personal Inventory Objects

The Sims™ 2 University introduces Sims' first personal inventory objects: the Cozmo MP3 Player, the Noyin 2680 Cellular Phone, and the LeTournament Decahedron XS Handheld Game.

Purchasing each object unlocks a menu of self-interactions. If two Sims both have handheld games, they can play each other via social interaction.

Purchase these objects from the Sellafone Gadget Kiosk. These vending machines exist solely on community lots (in neighborhoods or college towns).

Only teens or older can purchase personal objects, but they can buy a LeTournament Decahedron XS Handheld Game and give it to a child via the Give Handheld social interaction. Others can thereafter play handheld games versus the child (for Fun and Social).

NOYIN 2680 Cellular Phone

◆ Price: §149

◆ Need Effects: Fun 5 (Text Message, Talk), Social (Talk, Text Message)

◆ Need Max: Fun up to 90 (Text Message)

note

Due to spectrum sharing issues between the nascent NOYIN mobile telephone company and the local phone service providers, there can often be interference between the cordless phones Sims use at home and their cellular phones. Often, only one or the other can be used at a time.

Interactions:

◆ Text Message: Satisfies Fun and Social. No Daily Relationship increase since message is between Sim and an unknown recipient.

◆ Call: Features the same menus as a home telephone but options differ depending on whether the Sim is on his home lot or on a community lot (i.e., can't initiate a party or order delivery). They can, however, get and make personal calls from other Sims to increase Social, Fun, and Daily Relationship with the other Sim.

Cozmo MP3 Player

◆ Price: §195

◆ Need Effects: Fun 7

◆ Need Max: Fun up to 75

note

All MP3 Player interactions are self-interactions, activated by clicking on the active Sim.

Interactions:

◆ Listen: Young adults or older satisfy Fun. Switches on to last music channel selected.

◆ Switch To: Choose among different musical genres: Techno, Salsa, Pop, Metal, Hip Hop, R & B, Jazz.

LeTournament Decahedron XS
◆ Price: §245
◆ Need Effects: Fun

Interactions:

◆ Play...Handheld: This interaction, found under the Play menu if the Sim owns an XS, allows the Sim to satisfy Fun by themselves.

◆ Play...Handheld (vs. other Sim): Click on a different Sim who owns a handheld game and choose this interaction to satisfy Fun and Social and build Daily Relationship. The other Sim will always accept.

note

All Townie Sims have handheld games.

Reward Objects
Aspiration Reward Objects

Genuine Buck's Famous Counterfeiting Machine
◆ Price: 27,750 Reward points
◆ Used by: young adult or older

tip

Put a sprinkler above a counterfeit machine. They get really hot.

Interactions:

◆ Counterfeit Simoleans: Teens or older can turn crank. Earns money until interaction is cancelled or until Sim is booted by Needs or Mood. There's a random chance of the friction of the machine starting a fire. There's also a random chance that the police will show up, fine your Sim $2,000, and confiscate the Counterfeiting Machine.

◆ Get Cash: After your Sim's turned the machine's crank for a while, collect the product and add it to his funds by clicking on the machine again and selecting "Get Cash."

Career Reward Objects
See Chapter 7.

Communal Lot Only
Appliances

Impresso Espress-o-Matic
- Price: §1,495
- Need Effects: Hunger 1, Energy 4, Bladder -1, Fun 1 (Drink)
- Need Max: Fun up to 50

Interactions:
- Order Coffee: Order coffee from NPC Barista in exchange for §5. Satisfies Energy but depletes Bladder.
- Work as Barista: Young adult or older can replace the NPC Barista at the machine (interact with machine or barista NPC) and serve any Sims who order coffee. Earn simoleans for time spent working job, awarded when you cancel interaction.

Electronics

Sellafone Gadget Kiosk
- Price: §2,500
- Need Effects: Fun 4, Environment 7
- Need Max: Fun up to 80

Interactions:
- Buy: Teen or older Sim can purchase personal objects (handheld game, cell phone, or MP3 player).

---

note

Using the kiosk does not, in itself, give Fun. The Fun rating for this object is based on the Fun derived from the objects bought from it.

Miscellaneous

Way Fluid Island Bar
- Price: §1,850
- Need Effects: Fun 3
- Need Max: Fun up to 80

note

If you place identical bars side by side, they'll connect.

Interactions:
- Order Drink: Order a Blended (§15) or Poured (§10) drink from NPC Bartender. Drinking satisfies Fun.
- Tend Bar: Young adult or older can replace the NPC Bartender at the machine and serve any Sims who order drinks. Earn simoleans for time spent working job, awarded when you cancel interaction.

Chapter 9
New Socials

This chapter outlines the new social interactions, when they're available, under what conditions they are accepted, what the outcomes are, and more. Most of these new interactions are available to Sims in the neighborhoods, but some are limited to Sims in, or who've been to, college.

New socials like Hang Out sum up what's great about college.

SIM-TO-SIM INTERACTIONS
Entertain Interactions
Bust-A-Move

◆ Who: teen/young adult/adult/elder to teen/young adult/adult/elder

SOCIAL INTERACTION DIRECTORY

Social Interactions: Availability, Autonomous Personalities, and Social/Daily/Lifetime Effects

Interaction	Menu	Availability Daily A to B Above	Availability Daily A to B Below	And/Or	Availability Lifetime A to B Above	Availability Lifetime A to B Below	Crush	Love or Go Steady	Autonomous Personality	User Directed
Bonfire Dance	Bonfire	-30	100	Or	-20	100	—	—	—	Yes
Bust-a-Move!	Entertain	15	100	And	5	100	—	—	Active	Yes
Freestyle Join	Entertain	25	100	Or	15	100	—	—	Outgoing	Yes
Handheld	Play	20	100	Or	10	100	—	—	—	Yes
Hang Out	Talk	10	100	Or	5	100	—	—	Outgoing	Yes
Introduce	Talk	35	100	And	20	100	—	—	Not Autonomous	Yes
Joy Buzzer	Prank	-100	100	And	-100	100	—	—	Mean	Yes
Kicky Bag	Play	15	100	Or	5	100	—	—	—	Yes
Pillow Fight	Play	40	100	Or	25	100	—	—	Playful	Yes
School Cheer	Entertain	5	100	Or	5	100	—	—	Outgoing	Yes
Secret Handshake	Entertain	-100	100	Or	-100	100	—	—	Outgoing	Yes
Ventrilo-Fart	Prank	-100	100	And	-100	100	—	—	Sloppy	Yes
Water Balloon	Prank	-100	100	And	-100	100	—	—	Playful	Yes
Wolf Whistle	Flirt	-15	50	And	-15	40	Sets	Sets	Sloppy	Yes

note

Only available to Sims with Dancing skill 6 or better.

Practice dancing and your Sims can entertain their friends with their fly moves.

Accepted if Sim B's:

1. Daily >25, or,

2. Daily -25–25 and Lifetime >10, or,

3. Daily -25–25, Lifetime <10, and Playful/Serious >6, or,

4. Daily -25–25, Lifetime <10, Playful/Serious <6, and Dancing >9

School Cheer

◆ Who: young adult/adult/elder to young adult/adult/elder

Accepted if Sim Bs:

1. Is at or went to college and Daily >5, or,

2. Did not go to college and Daily >15 and Playful/Serious >0, or,

3. Did not go to college and Playful/Serious 0 and Daily >45

note

If Sim B went to college, he joins in the cheering. If he didn't, he reacts with approval but doesn't cheer along.

Autonomous	If Accept, A's Social	If Accept, A's Daily	If Accept, A's Lifetime	If Accept, B's Social	If Accept, B's Daily	If Accept, B's Lifetime	If Reject, A's Social	If Reject, A's Daily	If Reject, A's Lifetime	If Reject, B's Social	If Reject, B's Daily	If Reject, B's Lifetime
Yes	20	5	1	20	5	1	-10	-4	-1	-10	-4	-1
Yes	18	9	2	18	9	2	-5	-5	-2	-5	-5	-2
Yes	Variable	Variable	Variable	Variable	Variable	Variable	Variable	Variable	Variable	Variable	Variable	Variable
No	0	4	0	0	4	0	-5	-2	0	-5	-2	0
Yes	Variable	Variable	Variable	Variable	Variable	Variable	Variable	Variable	Variable	Variable	Variable	Variable
No	16	13	5	16	13	5	-5	-3	-1	-5	-3	-1
Yes	18	4	0	16	4	0	—	—	—	—	—	—
Yes	10	1	0	10	1	0	0	-4	0	0	-4	0
Yes	Variable	Variable	Variable	Variable	Variable	Variable	-8	-5	-1	-2	-5	-2
Yes	12	4	0	12	4	0	-3	-2	0	-3	-2	0
Yes	20	5	1	20	5	1	-10	-4	-2	-10	-4	-2
Yes	18	4	0	16	4	0	—	—	—	—	—	—
Yes	18	4	0	16	4	0	—	—	—	—	—	—
Yes	14	4	1	14	4	1	-8	-3	-1	0	-6	-2

Join Freestyle

Who can freestyle? Sims can freestyle!

♦ Who: teen/young adult/adult/elder to teen/young adult/adult/elder

note

Up to four Sims can join, and other Sims can watch for Fun. Observers will cheer or boo based on Daily Relationship with participants. The higher a Sim's Charisma, the better the Sim will Freestyle.

Accepted if Sim B's:

1. Daily >25, or,

2. Daily -5–25 and Lifetime >10, or,

3. Daily -5–25, Lifetime <10, and Creativity >7, or,

4. Daily -5–25, Lifetime <10, Creativity <7, and Playful/Serious >9

note

Sims get +1 Daily for each change of turn.

Flirt Interactions

Wolf Whistle

He's got a thing for Mascots and isn't afraid to show it.

♦ Who: young adult/adult/elder to young adult/adult/elder

Accepted if Sim B's:

1. Mood >-20, Daily >30, and Lifetime >20, or,

2. Mood positive, Daily >30, Lifetime <20, or Playful/Serious >6, or,

3. Mood positive, Daily >30, Lifetime <20, Playful/Serious <6, and Nice/Grouchy >6, or,

4. Mood >20, Daily >30, Lifetime <20, oPlayful/Serious <6, and Nice/Grouchy <6, or,

5. Mood positive, Daily 20–29, and Outgoing/Shy >6.

Play Interactions

Secret Handshake

♦ Who: young adult/adult/elder to young adult/adult/elder and is member of Secret Society

Accepted if Sim B's:

1. A member of the Secret Society or was while in college and Daily >-20

Pillow Fight

Few better ways to blow off steam than a no-holds-barred pillow fight.

♦ Who: teen/young adult/adult/elder to teen/young adult/adult/elder

Accepted if Sim B's:

1. Daily >45, or,

2. Daily -5–45 and Lifetime >35, or,

3. Daily -5–45, Lifetime <35, and Active/Lazy >9, or,

4. Daily -5–45, Lifetime <35, Active/Lazy <9, and Playful >9

note

Daily Relationship increases 1 point with each hit. Pillow Fight increases Fun but reduces Energy and Hygiene.

Kicky Bag

A hot game of Kicky Bag helps Sims get to know each other quickly and have some Fun.

◆ Who: teen/young adult/adult/elder to teen/young adult/adult/elder

Accepted if Sim B's:

1. Daily >20, or,
2. Daily <20 and Lifetime >10, or,
3. Daily <20, Lifetime <10, and Active >7, or,
4. Daily <20, Lifetime <10, Active <7, and Playful >8, or,
5. Daily <20, Lifetime <10, Active <7, Playful <8, and Outgoing >9

> **note**
>
> Kicky Bag is joinable and gains Fun but depletes Energy in addition to Social and Daily.

Play Handheld

◆ Who: child/teen/young adult/adult/elder to child/teen/young adult/adult/elder. Both Sims must have LeTournament Decahedron XS Handheld Game (all Townie Sims have one).

If two friends have handheld games, they can play together for even more Fun.

Always accepted.

> **note**
>
> Accepting gives initial Daily and Lifetime boost. Play gains Fun and Social increases with time (+75 per hour).

Prank Interactions

Pranks can't be rejected, but Sim B's reaction depends on his Mood, Personality, and Lifetime Relationship with Sim A.

Sim B's Reaction to Pranks

Daily Relationship to A	Mood	Personality	Reaction
High	Bad	Grouchy	Shake Head
High	Bad	Nice	Smile
High	Good	Serious	Laugh Strong
High	Good	Playful	Prank Back
Low	Good	Mean	Poke
Low	Good	Nice	Light Cry
Low	Bad	Mean	Shove
Low	Bad	Nice	Heavy Cry

> **note**
>
> When a pranked Sim pranks back, the prank he chooses is dictated by personality, specifically his levels in Nice/Grouchy, Playful/Serious, and Neat/Sloppy. Whichever of the three is his the highest controls his return prank:
>
> ◆ Grouchy: Joy Buzzer
> ◆ Playful: Water Balloon
> ◆ Sloppy: Ventrilo-fart
>
> If two or more of these traits are equal, the Sim will choose randomly.

Joy Buzzer

Shock your Mascot, amuse your friends. Or the other way around.

◆ Who: teen/young adult/adult/elder to teen/young adult/adult/elder

◆ Prank Back and Laugh if: Lifetime >15, Mood positive, and Playful/Serious >5.

◆ Smile if: Lifetime >15, Mood positive, Playful/Serious <5 or Lifetime >15, Mood negative, and Nice/Grouchy >6.

◆ Shake Head if: Lifetime >15, Mood negative, and Nice/Grouchy <6.

◆ Light Cry if: Lifetime <15, Mood positive, and Nice/Grouchy >4.

◆ Poke if: Lifetime <15, Mood positive, and Nice/Grouchy <4.

◆ Heavy Cry if: Lifetime <15, Mood negative, and Nice/Grouchy >4.

◆ Shove if: Lifetime <15, Mood negative, and Nice/Grouchy <4.

Ventrilo-Fart

◆ Who: teen/young adult/adult/elder to teen/young adult/adult/elder

◆ Prank Back and Laugh if: Lifetime >15, Mood positive, and Neat/Sloppy >5.

◆ Smile if: Lifetime >15, Mood positive, Neat/Sloppy <5 or Lifetime >15, Mood negative, and Nice/Grouchy >6.

◆ Shake Head if: Lifetime >15, Mood negative, and Nice/Grouchy <6.

◆ Light Cry if: Lifetime <15, Mood positive, and Nice/Grouchy >4.

◆ Poke if: Lifetime <15, Mood positive, and Nice/Grouchy <4.

◆ Heavy Cry if: Lifetime <15, Mood negative, and Nice/Grouchy >4.

◆ Shove if: Lifetime <15, Mood negative, and Nice/Grouchy <4.

Water Balloon

This is gonna be messy, but funny.

◆ Who: teen/young adult/adult/elder to teen/young adult/adult/elder

◆ Prank Back and Laugh if: Lifetime >15, Mood positive, and Playful/Serious >5.

◆ Smile if: Lifetime >15, Mood positive, Playful/Serious <5 or Lifetime >15, Mood negative, and Nice/Grouchy >6.

◆ Shake Head if: Lifetime >15, Mood negative, and Nice/Grouchy <6.

◆ Light Cry if: Lifetime <15, Mood positive, and Nice/Grouchy >4.

◆ Poke if: Lifetime <15, Mood positive, and Nice/Grouchy <4.

◆ Heavy Cry if: Lifetime <15, Mood negative, and Nice/Grouchy >4.

◆ Shove if: Lifetime <15, Mood negative, and Nice/Grouchy <4.

Talk Interactions
Introduce

Use Introduce to help one Sim get to know another.

◆ Who: child/teen/young adult/adult/elder to child/teen/young adult/adult/elder

note

Offer to introduce Sim B to a Sim currently on the lot ("Sim C"). Sim B and C get a higher initial boost than if they'd met normally.

College graduates keep this interaction for life after they graduate.

Accepted if Sim B's:

1. Lifetime >20 and Daily >35, or,
2. Lifetime >20, Daily <35, and Nice/Grouchy >3, or,
3. Lifetime <20, Daily >35, and Nice/Grouchy >5, or,
4. Lifetime <20, Daily <35, and Nice/Grouchy >9

Hang Out

◆ Who: teen/young adult to teen/young adult

Always accepted. Up to six Sims can join with Hang Out. It follows the standard Talk model of volleying interests back and forth with Daily Relationship and Social Need points resulting from each volley. See Chapter 1 for details.

Talk about Major

◆ Who: young adult to young adult (when both Sims have same major)

Talking about their majors actually increases Sims' class performance.

Always accepted.

Ask for Tutoring

◆ Young adult to elder (Professor for A's major)
Always accepted.

Miscellaneous

Eurokiss

◆ Who: teen/young adult/adult/elder to teen/young adult/adult/elder

This greet is done in place of "Wave" if the Sims share a Daily Relationship between 30 and 50.

Influence to...

◆ Who: toddler/child/teen/young adult/adult/elder to toddler/child/teen/young adult/adult/elder

Accepted if Sim B's:

1. Daily and Lifetime >0

OBJECT-BASED INTERACTIONS

Bonfire Dance

◆ Who: child/teen/young adult/adult/elder to child/teen/young adult/adult/elder

There's something about burning furniture that helps Sims get in touch with their primal side.

Accepted if Sim A is interacting with a Stack-O-Flames Bonfire and Sim B's:

1. Daily >5

Chapter 10
New NPCs

College is the best time to cross paths with people you'd never meet back home. There are plenty of folks to meet in every college town, many of them the kind of classic characters one expects to encounter in institutions of higher learning. This chapter introduces you to all of the new nonplayer characters (NPCs) who come your way in *The Sims™ 2 University*.

> **note**
>
> All the new NPCs are Social NPCs, meaning they can be interacted with, befriended, and even romantically entangled. Young adult Sims can't marry, but they can get engaged. After graduation, their betrothed will be moved as an adult (or elder if they're already an elder) to the Sim's neighborhood. They can then be invited over and wedded/joined.

BARISTA

Baristas man the new industrial espresso bar object; there's an Impresso Espress-o-Matic, you'll find a Barista standing behind it. These coffee servers are tireless and apparently drinking straight from the caffeinated nozzle of the machine, because they're on the job twenty-four hours a day.

Since the Impresso Espress-o-Matic is only available on community lots (neighborhood and college town), these are the only places you encounter Baristas.

Sims can replace the Baristas at their job to earn a little money; click on either the machine or the

Barista and your Sim takes the helm of the coffee bean express. The relieved Barista becomes a standard visitor, wandering the lot, tending to Needs, and socializing until your Sim relinquishes the job.

BARTENDER

The Bartender goes wherever the Way Fluid Island Bar goes. Available only on neighborhood and college town community lots, Way Fluid Island Bar is staffed at all hours by these indefatigable mixologists.

Sims can replace the Bartender at his or her job to earn a little money; click on either the bar or the Bartender and your Sim takes control of the industrial-strength blender. The relieved Bartender becomes a standard visitor, wandering the lot, tending to Needs, and socializing until your Sim relinquishes the job.

> **note**
>
> This NPC Bartender is different from the Bartender who can be hired by telephone. That bartender costs your Sims money and will only work if there's a normal bar on the lot. The new Bartender is tethered to the Way Fluid Island Bar object and appears wherever it is. Your Sims only pay this NPC if they order a drink.

CAFETERIA WORKER

The Cafeteria Worker (male or female elder) labors wherever there's a ShinyTyme Cooktop. Though the cooktop itself can be placed on

either residential or community lots in neighborhoods or college towns, it's only tended by the Cafeteria Worker in college town dorm or community lots.

note

For full details on the food provided by the Cafeteria Worker, see the "Eating at College" section in Chapter 6.

The Cafeteria Worker's shift is 4 a.m. to midnight. During this shift, the Cafeteria Worker cooks a constant supply of mealtime-appropriate group meals and cleans up dishes and food containers in the immediate area. While the Cafeteria Worker is on the job, no other Sim can use the cooktop (or get anything out of the fridge that requires use of the cooktop unless there's another cooking appliance on the lot or unless they take the Cafeteria Worker's job.

note

The Cafeteria Worker only cleans up dishes and trash if there's a dishwasher or trash can/trash compactor, respectively, in the same room.

Sims can replace the Cafeteria Worker at his or her job to earn a little money; click on either the cooktop or the Cafeteria Worker and your Sim takes control of the kitchen. The relieved Cafeteria Worker becomes a standard visitor, wandering the lot, tending to Needs, and socializing until your Sim relinquishes the job.

CHEERLEADER

Cheerleaders (female young adults) visit college lots periodically to whip up school spirit. Most of the time, they are normal visitors, but they frequently do Flirt interactions and perform the School Cheer social (if the recipient of this cheer is very Outgoing, they'll cheer back). Other Sims gather to watch and cheer or boo—depending on Nice/Grouchy. You may also direct your Sims to watch a cheerleader for Fun.

COACH

The Coach (male or female elder) occasionally appears on lots to get students into shape. He or she acts generally as a visitor but frequently yells at and lectures Sims and forces them to work out (developing Body skill). If the unfortunate targets of the Coach's wrath are too low in Energy to work out, they'll cry.

Coaches are particularly drawn to Sims with low fitness, so constant badgering by the Coach might mean your Sims need to cut out the Chinese food.

EVIL MASCOT

The Evil Mascot (male young adult) from a rival college (home of "The Thunderin' Udders") occasionally visits residential and community lots in college towns. He sports an off-putting personality (Nice/Grouchy 0, Neat/Sloppy 0, Outgoing/Shy 10, Playful/Serious 10, Active/Lazy 0) and likes to:

◆ Flirt
◆ Irritate
◆ Do Pranks
◆ Pillow Fight
◆ Set Off Sprinklers
◆ Put Soap in Fountains
◆ Drink from Juice Barrels

Here we see an enraged Cheerleader engaged in a life-or-death struggle with an Evil Mascot.

If the Mascot or Cheerleader are on the lot, they likely attack the Evil Mascot. Given the Evil Mascot's low Body skill (0 vs. the Cheerleader/Mascot's 10), the hometown NPC *almost always* wins, and the Evil Mascot departs the lot in shame. There's a very small chance the Evil Mascot will win, but it doesn't happen often.

MASCOT

Your Sims' college's mascot (male young adult) arrives periodically to stir up school spirit. Functionally, he's identical to the Cheerleader (see above) but wears a funnier suit.

PROFESSORS

Professors (male or female elders) can be invited and befriended and will drop by when one of the playable Sims on the lot meets them. Your Sims may, of course, socialize with any professors

they meet, but the real benefits come from getting to know the profs in your Sim's current major.

note

The all-important in-major professors are announced on the first day your Sim goes to class in his or her major (or undeclared if it's the first day of school and your Sim doesn't declare first). Write down the professors' names because there's no way to distinguish them from other professors your Sim has already met.

Building Daily and Lifetime Relationships with professors associated with your Sim's major earns Class Performance points, as does the Ask for Tutoring interaction. WooHooing with professors is even more academically lucrative.

STREAKER

Randomly invades, pixilated and rapturously happy. He or she generally runs around and, well, streaks, occasionally doing a little streaker dance.

Streakers are more likely to show up when there's a party underway. They only appear in college towns and only when there are no Sims younger than young adults on the lot.

Streakers will revert to their clothes if you engage them in any kind of interaction.

Chapter 11
Build Mode Additions

Build mode in *The Sims™ 2 University* has become even more powerful with the addition of five new features and abilities. This chapter describes how to utilize each of them.

CONNECTING COLUMNS

For beautiful archways and more elaborate supported structures, builders can now make connecting columns. Found in Build mode under "Miscellaneous" and the "Connecting Column Arches" submenu, use this collection of five columns individually or in conjunction to create automatically connecting archways.

To make an arch, place one column from the Connecting Column Arches submenu.

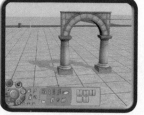

Then, place a second IDENTICAL column TWO TILES in any perpendicular direction (diagonals aren't allowed). The arch forms and previews automatically when the correct spacing is achieved.

Place additional identical columns to generate more arches. Several different configurations are possible.

Sims recognize these archways as passable and will walk under them. They do not, however, count as doors and don't, therefore, delineate a "room" for Environment scoring purposes.

MULTISTORY COLUMNS

Multistory columns function exactly as regular columns in terms of spacing and how much they can support. Unlike traditional columns, however, they can support floors two or three stories above ground.

Previously, to extend columns, you had to build one, put a single floor tile on it, and place the second column on top—effective but inelegant.

Now balconies or larger upper floors can be supported without so much fuss and considerably more style.

There are two kinds each of two-story and three-story columns, each with four Design mode variations. They are located under the Miscellaneous menu under "Multistory Columns."

MULTISTORY DOORS AND ARCHES

First there were multistory windows. Now there are multistory doors!

Under the Doors menu in the new Multistory Doors and Arches menu, there is one two-story door and one two-story arch, each with six Design mode variations.

Multistory doors and arches require a wall three-tiles long and two stories high.

SMART FENCES

Many fences are now "smart fences"—they automatically space out posts in long, straight runs. It also places posts at the fence's ends and anywhere it intersects with another smart fence.

> **note**
>
> There's no special menu for smart fences; the fences that need the ability have it and the ones that don't, do not.

This feature is automatic and applies to many (but not all) fences in the catalog; namely, those that look more realistic with more widely spaced posts.

The fence in the foreground uses the new smart fence system. The one in the background doesn't.

BUILD WALL ON WALL

It is now possible to build a wall directly atop other walls without having to lay down floor tiles for support.

To build wall on wall, go up one floor and start dragging from the top of any wall segment. Upper-story walls must have support and cannot overhang at all.

NEW BUILD MODE OBJECTS

Object	Purchase Price	Initial Depreciation	Daily Depreciation	Depreciation Limit
Colonial Column Plus—Three-Story, from Brace Yourself! Designs	§750	§30	§20	§80
Colonial Column Plus—Two-Story, from Brace Yourself! Designs	§450	§30	§20	§80
Colonial Connecting Column Arches from Brace Yourself! Designs	§200	§0	§0	§0
Creeping Ivy Trellis	§170	§25	§17	§68
Daniel the Lionhearted Arch	§455	§0	§0	§0
Daniel the Lionhearted Door	§480	§0	§0	§0
Hey Nonny No Arch	§1,010	§56	§37	§150
Hey Nonny No Door	§1,110	§56	§37	§150
High Society Connecting Column Arches	§230	§0	§0	§0
High Society Pillar Plus—Three-Story	§850	§30	§20	§80
High Society Pillar Plus—Two-Story	§500	§30	§20	§80
Myne Door	§140	§15	§10	§40
Out of the Dark Ages Window	§110	§16	§11	§44
Peace and Love Window	§120	§16	§11	§44
Portal of Peace Archway	§150	§0	§0	§0
Portal of Peace	§135	§0	§0	§0
Romanesque Column in Concrete with Lattice Belting, by Rich R. Son	§170	§21	§14	§58
Romanesque Column in Concrete, by Rich R. Son	§155	§21	§14	§58
Romanesque Column in Red Stone, by Rich R. Son	§185	§21	§14	§58
Romanesque Connecting Column Arches in Concrete, by Rich R. Son	§170	§0	§0	§0
Romanesque Connecting Column Arches in Red Brick and Concrete, by Rich R. Son	§155	§0	§0	§0
Romanesque Connecting Column Arches in Red Stone, by Rich R. Son	§185	§0	§0	§0

Chapter 12
College Town Mode and Creating Custom Colleges

The Sims™ 2 University comes with three thoroughly fleshed out and vibrant colleges, but there's no reason you can't change them or make your own from scratch. This chapter outlines the tools available for modifying existing college towns and building new ones. We even provide the super-secret cheats to alter the otherwise inalterable dorm lots.

ANATOMY OF COLLEGE TOWN

College towns function as separate neighborhoods from your Sims' base neighborhoods. The Sims in it can come from the base neighborhood and will return to it when they graduate.

Actually, any college town is a template that can be associated with any or all base neighborhoods with each incarnation existing entirely separate from every other. If you have three base neighborhoods, for example, there can be three Sim State Universities, each with totally different student bodies.

Within college towns, there are five different kinds of lots:

◆ Dorms: Can only be placed pre-made from the Lots and Houses Bin in the Specialty Lots panel. Can't be visited by taxi. Officially, you can't make your own dorms and can't significantly edit them once placed. Unofficially? We'll get to that later.

◆ Private Residences: Exactly like residential lots in the base neighborhoods. Can't be visited by taxi. Can be converted into Greek houses.

◆ Greek houses: Can't be placed in College Town view. Created by placing/constructing a private residence, moving in a household, and converting it to Greek status via the Apply for Charter interaction on the telephone. Can't be visited by taxi.

◆ Community lots: Built and function exactly like base neighborhood community lots. Can be visited by taxi.

◆ Secret Society lots: One per college town can only be placed pre-made from Lots and Houses Bin in the Specialty Lots panel. Can only be visited by members and only by special limo called via phone.

EDITING A COLLEGE TOWN

College towns can be substantially, but not entirely, edited from the College Town view. Here's a helpful list of what you *can* do:

◆ Add, move, or delete decorations. There are several new decorations that fit nicely into any university.

◆ Place unoccupied houses from the Lots and Houses Bin to serve as private residences or future Greek houses. These may include custom content houses.

◆ Place pre-made and unalterable dorms from the Specialty Lots panel in the Lots and Houses Bin. These can be moved or returned to the Lots and Houses Bin.

◆ Place pre-made Secret Society lots from the Specialty Lots panel in the Lots and Houses Bin. Once placed, they disappear and can't be moved. All unused Secret Society lots in the Lots and Houses bin also disappear. You can edit these

lots in Buy and Build modes, but only when visiting them with a playable Sim.

- Place and edit pre-made community lots. These may also include custom content lots.
- Place empty lots and specify whether they're residential or community.
- Build private residences or community lots from scratch.
- Create or modify dorms with cheats discussed later in this chapter.

CREATING A NEW COLLEGE TOWN TEMPLATE

Many of the steps for creating a new college town are identical to the procedures for base neighborhoods. See Chapter 25.

The College Chooser's Create College button is where to begin.

To begin the process, access the College Chooser and scroll through the available colleges to find the Create College button.

The Create College tool contains all unassociated templates, including the pre-made college towns. To add a new template, press the Create Custom College button below the Template Colleges list.

In the Create Custom College tool, choose a terrain file to form the canvas for your new college.

Next, press the Create Custom College button below the Template list.

note

College towns can use the same terrain files as base neighborhoods. Several of these were installed with your game but new ones can be created via the tools in SIMCITY™ 4.

Choose a terrain file on which to build your campus.

Finally, enter the name of your new college town, create a description of your college, and decide whether the terrain will be green and lush or beige and desert scrub.

Name the college town and choose its terrain.

The College template is now listed in the Create College tool. You can associate it with neighborhoods of your choice. First, however, add the critical structures for college life.

From then on, you can associate your custom college with ANY home neighborhood.

COLLEGE ESSENTIALS

There are no hard rules as to what should go in a college town, but there are several elements that probably *should* be present. Some, if missing, will make game elements unavailable.

A good college should have:

◆ Dorms of various capacities.

◆ Some private homes in a range of cost.

◆ At least one Greek house. No Greek house elements are available without one.

◆ A Secret Society lot. No Secret Society elements are available without one.

◆ Community lots, including a gymnasium, library, coffee shop, nightclub (with bar and live music), campus center and/or quad (outdoor space), and shops.

SPECIALTY LOTS

Two kinds of lots populate the Specialty Lots panel: dorms and Secret Society lots.

Dorms

Choose from 10 pre-made dorms of various sizes and capacities.

Pre-Made Dorms

	Lot Size	Rooms
	2 x 3	5
	3 x 2	6
	2 x 3	8
	3 x 3	8
	3 x 3	9
	3 x 2	10
	3 x 2	12
	3 x 3	14
	3 x 3	15
	2 x 3	16

Secret Society Lots

There are three Secret Society lot models available in the Specialty Lots panel. Each is used in one of the three built-in college towns and features a powerful selection of career and Aspiration reward objects to which college town Sims normally have no or limited access.

Secret Society lots are the opposite of dorm lots: you *can* freely use the Build and Buy modes (when you have a Sim visit the lot) to alter and save the lot. You *can't*, however, move it or access it from the college town view in any way.

There can only be one Secret Society lot in any college town, and it is (once placed) invisible. Thus, there's no way to either move it or replace it with a different Secret Society lot.

You can, however (as noted above), decide *which* of the three pre-made Secret Society lots you want in your custom colleges, place them initially wherever you wish, and later enter them with a playable Sim to alter them in Build and/or Buy mode.

Secret Society Lot 1

- Career skill objects: SensoTwitch Lie Finder (Creativity)
- Other career objects: Laganaphyllis Simnovorii, Dr. Vu's Automated Cosmetic Surgeon, Resurrect-O-Nomitron, Luminous Pro Antique Camera
- Aspiration reward objects: Genuine Buck's Famous Counterfeiting Machine
- Appears in: Académie Le Tour ("Volauvent Society")

Secret Society Lot 2

- Career skill objects: Execuputter (Charisma), SensoTwitch Lie Finder (Creativity)

- Other career objects: Laganaphyllis Simnovorii, Luminous Pro Antique Camera, Resurrect-O-Nomitron
- Aspiration reward objects: Genuine Buck's Famous Counterfeiting Machine (x2), Money Tree, Electric and Enigmatic Energizer
- Appears in: Sim State University ("Landgrabb Society")

Secret Society Lot 3

- Career skill objects: AquaGreen Hydroponic Garden (Creativity), Trauma-Time "Incision Precision" Surgical Training Station (Mechanical), Simsanto Inc. Biotech Station (Logic)
- Other career objects: Laganaphyllis Simnovorii, Genuine Buck's Famous Counterfeiting Machine
- Aspiration reward objects: None
- Appears in: La Fiesta Tech ("LFT Society")

THE DORM CHEAT: EDITING AND BUILDING DORMS

Free creation and modification of dorms is not permitted—unless you have the cheats that make it possible.

Dorm Doors should always face out from the room.

This, for example, is wrong.

Whether you're modifying or creating dorms, it's imperative that you observe the following rules when working with dorms or they *do not* function properly:

A door to the bathroom may seem practical, but it defeats any attempts to lock the dorm door.

◆ Dorm doors *must* always face out.

◆ Dorm rooms should not have more than one dorm door leading into them.

◆ Dorm rooms with dorm doors that share a bathroom do not lock properly.

◆ Don't change the zoning of your lot after you move in Sims.

A dorm isn't a dorm without this food-service cooktop. Remember the counter islands or the Cafeteria Worker won't have anywhere to place the finished food.

Every dorm *must* contain the following objects:

◆ ShinyTyme Cooktop

◆ Counter islands

◆ Dishwasher or sink in the same room as the ShinyTyme Cooktop

◆ Garbage can

◆ Lights

◆ Phone (at least one)

◆ Sprinkler

Modifying Existing Dorms

To alter an exiting dorm:

1. Place any dorm template from the Specialty Lot catalog or enter a placed dorm.

2. Enter the lot, open the cheat window (Ctrl Shift C) and type **boolprop dormspecific-toolsdisabled false** to unlock Build and Buy mode.

3. Make your desired changes.

4. Save and exit to college town.

Making Dorm Templates from Scratch

To make your own dorms:

1. Start by placing any size residential lot in a blank neighborhood.

2. Enter the lot and build your desired "dorm."

3. Open up the cheat window and type **changelotzoning dorm**. This will rezone your lot as a dorm.

4. Save and exit to college town.

Making a New Dorm for the Specialty Lot Catalog

The previous methods only affect dorms placed in the college town. These altered dorms can't, for example, be placed in any other college towns. To do that, you must get them into the Specialty Lots Bin.

1. From the College Town view, move your new dorm into the lot catalog.

2. Find the file you just modified (In \My Documents\ EA Games\The Sims 2\LotCatalog and find the newest lot by sorting under "date modified").

3. Copy that file into The Sims™ 2 > TSData > Res > LotTemplates and rename Anything_Permanent.package (adding the _Permanent.package part makes the file "infinitely" placeable.)

4. Exit and reload the game.

5. That new dorm template will now appear in your Specialty lot catalog in college towns.

Chapter 13
Campus Tour and the Student Bodies

The Sims™ 2 University comes with three elaborately designed college towns where your Sims can learn about literature, life, and love. Each campus has its own character and facilities and some unique personalities.

> ### note
>
> Each Neighborhood can have one or more colleges linked to it. Every college has a student bin. Student bin contains households. The same households appear in the student bin of every college linked to a common neighborhood, no matter how or in what college the household is created.

This chapter outlines all the structures on campus, including dorms, private residences, Greek houses, Secret Society clubhouses, and community lots.

For community lots, we list the lot's attractions, including what skill can be built there, what money-making opportunities are offered by its objects, and what stores or services are available.

> ### note
>
> When a lot features a computer, you can use these objects for several functions: Fun, Social, Creative skill (write novel), Hack Grades, Write Term Paper, etc.

ACADÉMIE LE TOUR

Community Lots

- ◆ Academy Gym: Body skill, swimming pool, food service
- ◆ Academy Park: Public grill
- ◆ Campus Boutiques: Electronics kiosk, clothing store, magazine rack
- ◆ Kings Music Hall: Creativity skill, band instruments, public grill, Logic skill
- ◆ Le Tour Student Center: Barista, bookcases, electronics kiosk, food service, Logic skill, pool tables
- ◆ Library D'Livre: Bookcases, computers, public grill
- ◆ Little Fallorayne Amphitheatre: Creative skill, band instruments, Barista, public grill
- ◆ Loungerama Leisureland: Bar, pool tables, Creative skill, band instruments, public grill
- ◆ Romara Coffee Shop: Barista, bookcases, public grill
- ◆ Waffleway Shoppes: Electronics kiosk, video game rack, grocery store

Dorms

◆ Lam Plaza Dormitory: 6 Rooms
  ◆ Caseroff Dormitory: 8 Rooms
  ◆ Romara Dorms: 9 Rooms
  ◆ Mille House Dorms: 10 Rooms
  ◆ Boggs Hall Dorms: 12 Rooms

Private Residences

  ◆ 1 Danish Drive: §2,607
  ◆ 6 Danish Drive: §4,114
  ◆ 9 Danish Drive: §4,112
  ◆ 30 Bundt Way: §4,453
  ◆ 46 Focaccia Place: §2,544
  ◆ 20 Croissant Court: §3,366
  ◆ 35 Croissant Court: §3,356
  ◆ 40 Croissant Court: §3,356
  ◆ 122 Baklava Boulevard: §4,025
  ◆ 132 Baklava Boulevard: §4,042
  ◆ 142 Baklava Boulevard: §4,155
  ◆ Chancellor's Hacienda: §11,505

Greek Houses

None

Secret Society Lot

◆ Volauvent Society (Secret Society Lot 1)

Moved-In Sims

Friends (4 Danish Drive)

  ◆ Mitch Indie: Freshman, Drama
  ◆ Max Flexor: Freshman, Physics

O'Feefe (25 Bundt Way)

  ◆ Delilah O'Feefe: Freshman, Art

Sharpe (58 Focaccia Place)

  ◆ Roxie Sharpe: Sophomore, Psychology
  ◆ Jonah Powers: Sophomore, Philosophy
  ◆ Edwin Sharpe: Freshman, Mathematics

Student Bin

Biggs

♦ Maria Biggs: Freshman, Biology

First Year

♦ Phineas Furley: Freshman, Political Science
♦ Ellen Frost: Freshman, Economics
♦ Chaz Whippler: Freshman, Literature

Students

♦ Emily Lee: Freshman, History
♦ Tom Freshe: Freshman, Economics

LA FIESTA TECH

Community Lots

♦ 51st Street Gym: Body skill, clothing store, food service, magazine rack
♦ Cacti Café: Logic skill, Barista, magazine rack
♦ College Corner Market: Barista, grocery store
♦ Fiesta Swim Center: Swimming pool, Barista, pool tables, Body skill
♦ LFT Student Union: Food service, pool tables, Logic skill, bookshelves, Barista, video game rack, magazine rack
♦ Mirage Shopping Center: Electronics kiosk, video game rack, Barista, bookshelves, magazine rack, grocery store, clothing store
♦ Shallow Valley Library: bookshelves
♦ The Plaza: Logic skill, Barista, public grill
♦ The Wasteland Lounge: Creativity skill, band instruments, bar

Dorms

♦ Oasis Dormitory: 5 rooms
♦ Desert Dormitory: 8 rooms
♦ Canyon Commons Dorms: 9 rooms
♦ Fiesta Hall: 16 rooms

Private Residences

◆ 12 Land Lane: §2,285
◆ 15 Land Lane: §2,247
◆ 16 Land Lane: §2,285
◆ 50 Dusty Drive: §2,153

◆ 54 Dusty Drive: §2,153
◆ 57 Dusty Drive: §2,153
◆ 58 Dusty Drive: §2,153
◆ 59 Dusty Drive: §2,153

Greek Houses

◆ Oresha-Hoh-Var House
◆ Tri-Fruhm House

Secret Society Lot

◆ LFT Society (Secret Society Lot 3)

Moved-In Sims
Fraternity (Oresha-Hoh-Var House)

◆ Guy Wrightley: Sophomore, Literature
◆ Matthew Hart: Freshman, Economics
◆ Mickey Dosser: Freshman, Undeclared (Probation)

Sorority (Tri-Fruhm House)

◆ DJ Verse: Freshman, Literature
◆ Jessie Pilferson: Freshman, Psychology
◆ Monica Bratford: Sophomore, Art
◆ Sarah Love: Freshman, Biology

Shifting Paradymes (116 Aridestra Drive)

◆ Gunnar Roque: Junior, History
◆ Jasmine Rai: Freshman, History
◆ Zoe Zimmerman: Freshman, History

Worthington (134 Aridestra Drive)

◆ Francis J. Worthington III: Freshman, Economics

Student Bin
Davis

◆ Almeric Davis: Freshman, Undeclared
◆ Aldric Davis: Freshman, Physics

Student Housing

- William Williamson: Freshman, Economics
- Blossom Moonbeam: Freshman, Biology
- Klara Von der Stien: Freshman, Politics

Terrano

- Stella Terrano: Freshman, Physics

SIM STATE UNIVERSITY
Community Lots

- 452–498 University Way: Electronics kiosk, bar, magazine rack, video game rack, public grill, grocery store, computers, pool tables
- Campus Coffee House: Barista, magazine rack, public grill

- Campus Gym: Body skill, food service, clothing store
- Campus Lounge: Bar, Creativity skill, band instruments, Barista, bookshelves, computer, public grill
- Central Quad: Public grill, Barista, swimming pool
- Chestnut Park: Public grill
- Old Sim State Tower: Public grill
- Sim State Library: Bookshelves, magazine rack, computers, public grill
- Sim State Tower: Public grill
- Student Union: Food service, electronics kiosk, bookshelves, computers, pool tables
- University Way Shops: Magazine rack, clothing store, electronics kiosk, pool table, Logic skill, public grill, Barista

Dorms

- Pinenut Plaza Dorms: 8 rooms
- Landgrabb House Dorms: 9 rooms
- Sim State Dormitory: 14 rooms

Private Residences

- 124 Almond Road: §2,478
- 132 Almond Road: §2,516
- 138 Almond Road: §2,483
- 80 Crumplebottom Drive: §7,594
- 120 Crumplebottom Drive: §6,476
- 10 Peanut Street: §4,045
- 15 Peanut Street: §3,928
- 25 Peanut Street: §3,963
- 30 Peanut Street: §4,044

Greek Houses

- Urele-Oresha-Cham Fraternity
- Tri-Var Sorority

Secret Society Lot

- Landgrabb Society (Secret Society Lot 2)

Moved-In Sims

Bright (20 Peanut Street)

- Martin Ruben: Freshman, Mathematics
- Jane Stacks: Junior, Physics
- Allegra Gorey: Freshman, Art

Tri-Var Sorority (Tri-Var House)

- Tiffany Sampson: Freshman, Literature
- Brittany Upsnott: Sophomore, Drama
- Heather Huffington: Freshman, Drama

Frat Brothers (Urele-Oresha-Cham House)

- Ashley Pitts: Sophomore, Mathematics
- Joshua Ruben: Freshman, Undeclared

- Kevin Beare: Freshman, Psychology
- Castor Nova: Freshman, Philosophy

Student Bin

Freshman

- Sam Thomas: Psychology
- Jared Starchild: Art
- Ty Bubbler: Philosophy

Phoenix

- Jimmy Phoenix: Freshman, History

Swain

- Erik Swain: Freshman, Art

Part 2

The Sims™ 2 Basics

This part is for the newcomers or the veterans who want to learn from the ground up. All the information in these two chapters appears in much greater detail elsewhere in this book, so veterans won't miss much if they skip right to Part 3.

For everyone else, however, to avoid being overwhelmed by this complicated world, it's best to start with the outline of basic concepts and starting strategies contained in this primer.

Chapter 14

Getting to Know The Sims™ 2

Yes, yes, all these facts and figures, what, wheres, and howfors are grand and all, you say, but how do you play *The Sims™ 2*? Good question.

First, however, a disclaimer. There are many ways to play *The Sims™ 2*, some by design and some only by the ingenuity of the community of players. Some players use it not as a game but as a palette for story-telling and their own creativity. This book addresses those approaches too but is, by necessity, grounded in the way the game is "meant" to be played.

The Sims™ 2 is, above all else, a time-management game. The more efficiently your Sims behave, the more opportunities they have for success. Everything in the game's structure revolves around this point (however subtly):

♦ The more quickly and efficiently you can meet your Sims' Needs, the less time they have to spend on them. The less spent on Needs, the more time they have for other things.

♦ Advancing in a career track brings more money, which brings objects that fill Needs more efficiently. It also can bring a lighter work schedule with fewer days and shorter hours.

♦ Skills allow Sims to do things more quickly and advance in their career.

♦ Satisfying Wants and avoiding Fears allows Sims to have a perpetual good Mood (a very efficient state to be in), gives them helpful reward objects, and keeps them from doing time-wasting behaviors that come with low Aspiration score.

The key challenge is to engineer your Sims' world to allow them to behave both efficiently and autonomously. The amount of intervention Sims require is a good measure of player success. That said, getting to that state is a big challenge and requires a deep understanding of the forces at play.

The latter parts of this book will help you to that understanding. For now, however, to bare basics.

> **note**
>
> This book is not intended to replace the manual that came with your game and, in fact, makes every effort to avoid repeating things explained in that volume. Any repetition is only for the sake of clarity and emphasis.

MODES

Which modes are available to you depends on where you are in the game. There are two views: Neighborhood view and Lot view.

Neighborhood View

Neighborhood view overlooks the entire neighborhood and all its lots from on high.

There are four modes in Neighborhood view:

♦ Families: Contains the Sim Bin (families created but not moved into any lot), the Move Family button to transfer families from the Sim Bin into a lot, and most importantly, the Create New Family button. This last transports you into the Create-A-Sim and Create-A-Family tools where new Sims and families are assembled.

♦ Lots and Houses: Contains the Empty Lots templates (for beginning new construction) and the Lots and Houses Bin in which you'll find constructed empty homes ready to be moved into the neighborhood and any occupied homes (Sims included) that you've saved or downloaded from elsewhere.

♦ Decorations: Place neighborhood decorations to customize what you see in Neighborhood view.

Neighborhood view is where Sims are moved into and out of houses and where you select which household to control.

◆ Neighborhood Story: Contains the tools needed to tell the story of a neighborhood in general. With each lot as a part of the cast of characters, the goings on can be assembled into a massive overarching epic.

The neighborhood is a given Sim's entire universe. Nothing exists to her outside her neighborhood. If something she needs can't be found in the neighborhood, it'd be a good idea to build whatever it is.

Lot View

Lot view is where Sims' lives are led, and where lots and houses are modified, constructed, landscaped, and populated with objects.

When inside a lot, the modes are geared to controlling individual Sims or altering/developing the lot.

◆ Live mode: Live mode is where the game itself is played; the clock runs only in Live mode. Here Sims can be directed (with the game moving or paused) to interact with each other or objects on their lots. Objects can't be moved, rotated, or deleted in Live mode.

◆ Buy mode: Buy mode is where all non-architectural objects are bought and sold. Objects may be moved, rotated, or sold in Buy mode but only Buy mode objects may be purchased.

◆ Build mode: Build mode is how houses and their environs are constructed and expanded. All objects can be moved, rotated, or sold in Build Mode but only Build mode objects may be purchased.

◆ Story mode: Snapshots taken on the lot are assembled here to tell the story of what's occurred on a lot. Every picture can be selected and arranged in any order and may be annotated with text. A lot's story can be uploaded to *TheSims2.com* to share with the world.

Story mode is where snapshots can be presented to tell the story of a household.

FUNDAMENTAL TERMINOLOGY

Many terms and concepts are tossed around in the game itself and this guide, but not all of them are as crystal clear as those deeply familiar with the game believe them to be.

Needs

Needs are a Sim's fundamental physical and emotional requirements for day-to-day life. Needs include the need for nourishment (Hunger), rest and emotional security (Comfort), going to the bathroom (Bladder), sleep (Energy), entertainment (Fun), interaction with other Sims (Social), personal cleanliness (Hygiene), cleanliness and beauty of surroundings (Environment).

With the exception of Environment, all Needs decay over time, can be reduced faster when doing certain things (e.g., cleaning a toilet speeds the depletion of the Hygiene Need), and are

113

satisfied by interacting with objects and (sometimes) other Sims.

Sims are largely able to take care of their own Needs (far more than before), but they often need help. How you lay out their home and where you place objects impacts how efficient Sims will be at meeting their own Needs. The less efficient the set-up, the more intervention they'll require.

The cumulative state of a Sim's Needs dictates his overall Mood.

Be mindful of your Sims' Needs, especially when sending them off to work or trying to engage them with skill or Fun objects. A low Need level can, by itself, cause problems. Furthermore, many Needs, if unfed, can be problematic: low Hunger can cause death; low Energy makes Sims pass out; low Bladder causes accidents that lower Hygiene, make a mess, and possibly realize a Fear; and low Hygiene repels other Sims.

Mood

Mood is, generally, the collective effect of all a Sim's Needs (except Energy and any age-based exclusions). The lower a Sim's Needs, the lower her overall Mood.

A Sim in a bad mood shows it in the "Plumbob" over his head and in his refusal to work on his skills.

> **note**
>
> Some Needs don't appear during some ages. Babies and toddlers don't have Comfort Need, they aren't affected by the level of their Bladder Need (because they wear diapers), and they (along with children) don't react to the tidiness of their Environment. These things play no role, therefore, in the determination of their Mood.

Mood affects a Sim's performance at work and school, his ability to interact socially, and his willingness to build skills and have fun.

Maximize mood by keeping all Needs high or being extraordinarily successful in the Sim's Aspiration. If Aspiration score is very high, the Sim will be in a persistent good Mood regardless of her Needs.

Aspiration, Wants, and Fears

Aspiration is a Sim's life goal. When Sims are young (toddler or child), their only overarching goal is to Grow Up. When they become teens, however, you must choose an Aspiration for them that will stay with them until they die.

If something the Sim Wants comes to pass, his Aspiration score rises. If something he Fears is visited upon him, Aspiration score drops.

> **note**
>
> Wants and Fears can be driven by other forces too, but Aspiration is the primary engine.

The chosen Aspiration (or Grow Up for youngsters) primarily affects what the Sim Wants and Fears. This in turn guides the choices that must be made for that Sims' life. Pursuing an Aspiration can determine what career a Sim should follow or if she should stay at home and take care of family. Aspirations can influence whether

a Sim should get married or have children or if he should spend his time collecting lovers or friends.

The Wants and Fears panel is always stocked with the top things a Sim desires or dreads.

Forcing a Sim to act contrary to her Aspiration leads inevitably to the realization of Fears and eventual negative behavior due to Aspirational failure. For example, directing a Romance Sim to marry may realize one of her biggest Fears, and getting her to have a baby could drive her utterly mad. She can be made to do these things, but her life becomes far more challenging to play.

Aspiration score when a Sim becomes an Elder directly affects how long the rest of her life will last. The score when she dies dictates the amount of death benefit surviving loved ones will receive.

Skills

Sims can develop seven basic skills over their lives: Cooking, Mechanical, Charisma, Body, Logic, Creativity, and Cleaning. Most skills help a Sim advance in her career while others make her better at workaday tasks or eliminate the need to hire professional services. Some skills even impact how well a Sim can fight or play games.

Skills are developed by interacting with special skill objects, studying books on certain skills, and practical learning from repairing, cleaning, and cooking. Faster skill development comes from special reward objects bestowed when a Sim reaches the middle levels of her career track. These objects also enable skilled Sims to teach other Sims the skill at a faster rate.

Interests

Interests are what Sims discuss when they chat. The more interested a Sim is in a topic of conversation, the more often he'll talk about it and the more engaged he'll be if the other Sim does. Mutual Interest in a topic is required for effective and lengthy talking interactions.

When Sims talk, the thought bubbles above their heads indicate what interest they're discussing.

A Sim's own Interests are randomly generated at birth or creation and can be altered only by reading a magazine (purchased on Community Lots) tied to that Interest or by having another Sim perform a Share Interests interaction.

Memories

Sims get Memories for major events in their lives. Memories can be positive or negative. Memories serve as a history of major events but also as potential topics of conversation.

Any Sim that hears about a Memory can then talk about it with another Sim and pass the topic of that Memory on to yet another Sim.

Fitness

Sims have three levels of physical Fitness: Fit, Neutral, or Fat. Fitness is lost when a Sim eats food when Hunger is 100 percent satisfied. This can happen if he tops out his Hunger while eating a plate of food (Sims always finish what they're served), so don't instruct your Sim to eat when he's anywhere near full or he will eventually get Fat.

Sims also eat when full if they're very Lazy because they're more likely to eat directly from the refrigerator. Regardless of personality, adult and elder Sims with low Aspiration score are also more likely to pig out at the fridge beyond their full Hunger satisfaction.

Higher levels of Fitness can be regained by working out in front of the TV or stereo, in the swimming pool, or on a piece of exercise equipment.

Relationship Scores

The relationship of one Sim to another is measured by their Relationship scores. There are two kinds of Relationship scores; both are interrelated and very important.

Daily Relationship is how well the Sims are relating in the short term. It's a very volatile score that decays quickly if the Sims spend time apart. Social interactions tend to affect Daily score most.

Lifetime Relationship is the long-term measurement of a relationship. Some social interactions feed it too, but only in small amounts. Most of its ability to grow or drop is tied to the state of Daily Relationship. Anytime Daily is high, it pulls Lifetime slowly upward. If Daily is low, it drags Lifetime slowly down.

It's important to understand that relationships go both ways, and two Sims likely have different Relationship scores toward each other. As such, looking at your Sim's own score toward another Sim won't tell you what she thinks of your Sim or whether she'll accept a social interaction. It's what the other Sim feels that matters there.

Personality

Personality is a collection of five traits that every Sim possesses to a greater or lesser degree. Every Sim is somewhere on the continuum between:

- Neat and Sloppy
- Outgoing and Shy
- Active and Lazy
- Serious and Playful
- Nice and Grouchy

Sims either get their Personality from the setting you chose when you created them or from their parents if the Sim was born in the game. Personality traits can be changed if an older Sim Encourages a younger family member.

Social Interactions

Social interactions are how two Sims relate. A Sim must meet an interaction's availability requirements before the interaction appears in his Socials menu. For the interaction to be accepted by another Sim, *he or she* must meet the interactions acceptance requirements. Often whether the other Sim will accept is unknowable (if you can't control the Sim and see his Relationship scores, for example).

Interacting socially builds (or destroys) relationships.

Whether or not an interaction is accepted dictates what will happen to both Sims' Daily and Lifetime Relationships and Social Needs. Generally, Social Need is increased by any interaction, whether it's rejected or accepted, but Daily and Lifetime Relationship scores are usually increased by acceptance and decreased by rejection.

Some interactions require both Sims to be interacting with the same object. For example, two Sims can cuddle only if both are already sitting on a sofa.

Relationship Types

Certain Relationship scores and interactions create special relationships:

- Friend: Daily Relationship 50
- Best Friend: Lifetime Relationship 50
- Crush: Daily Relationship 70 and one romantic interaction
- Love: Lifetime Relationship 70 and one romantic interaction
- Going Steady (teens only): Daily Relationship 70 and Propose Go Steady interaction
- Engaged: In love and Propose Engagement interaction
- Married/Joined: In love and Propose Marriage interaction
- Enemy: Either Daily or Lifetime Relationship -50

Careers

Sims may choose from several career tracks. Every career track features jobs for adults (10 levels) or teens and elders (3 levels). An elder may stay in his adult career track as long as he wants but can only *enter* an elder track once he becomes an elder. Teens who reach the top of their career track get a leg up in the same adult track.

Career promotions depend on the acquisition of three specific skills (each job level has a required minimum in each skill), the number of friends a Sim's household possesses, and the Sim's average Mood when she arrives at work.

High-end jobs often feature really cool vehicles.

Higher jobs give higher pay and sometimes shorter hours and shorter workdays.

School

Children and teens attend school five days a week. Grades are based on attendance, completion of homework, and average Mood when they leave for school.

Food Chain

One of the most time consuming Needs to fulfill is Hunger. To maximize efficiency, therefore, what the Sim eats must be as nourishing as possible in the minimum number of servings (the more satisfying it is, the fewer portions it takes to be "full") and be prepared in the least amount of time.

Playing this food game requires a smoothly organized kitchen, high-end cooking appliances and countertops, and high Cooking skill.

Community Lots

Community Lots are special lots in a neighborhood. No Sims live there, but any can visit via a free taxi ride. Summon a taxi using a household's telephone.

Most Community Lots contain stores or places for Sims to have fun and mingle with others. Sims may purchase clothing, video/computer games, and magazines on Community Lots.

Time does not pass when Sims are on a Community Lot, so they return the same time they left no matter how long they stay. The length of stay is usually limited only by a Sim's need for sleep; Energy is the only Need that can't be fed on a Community Lot.

SUMMARY

These are the basic concepts and challenges in *The Sims™ 2*. With this foundation, the detailed chapters in Parts 3 and 4 should be much more enlightening.

The next chapter offers advice on how to get started with a new Sim, shedding light on where to go and what to do.

Chapter 15
Getting Started

The Sims 2 is an accessible game, but it can seem so freeform that beginners often find themselves unsure what to do first. This chapter describes everything you should do to start playing and help you grasp the gist of the game as quickly as possible.

DO THE TUTORIALS

Even if you don't read the manual (which you should, though perhaps not until you've played a bit to get the feel), it's a good idea to do the excellent tutorials that come with the game.

Launch tutorials in the Choose a Neighborhood menu.

These tutorials are pretty basic, but they acclimate you to the controls (something no book can offer) and the rhythms of the game.

PLAY THE HOUSE

Each of the three neighborhoods has a number of populated houses in which certain events are about to occur. These houses serve several purposes, but one of the less obvious is that each is a largely unguided tutorial in some of the game's newest features and most important elements.

For walkthroughs on how to accomplish the intended goals of these houses, see Chapter 16.

CHOOSE A NEIGHBORHOOD

Three heavily populated neighborhoods ship with *The Sims 2*: Pleasantview, Strangetown, and Veronaville. Each has several varied households, many full-service Community Lots, and a couple dozen nonresident Townies with whom to mingle and marry.

It really doesn't matter which you play, as they each have all the neighbor Sims you could ever need to get started and many fantastic empty houses. Plus there are a slew of other lots in the Lot Bin to install anywhere in any neighborhood you wish.

There is no bad choice.

CHOOSING A HOUSE

Any of the houses in any neighborhood provide an interesting beginner's experience. As a general rule, avoid houses with lots of Sims and, if possible, any younger Sims until you have some experience; they can be overwhelming.

Houses with lots of Sims can be very hard to handle until you've gotten your feet wet. Save that for tomorrow.

tip

The premade families can be played by beginners but perhaps not as a first family. Get your feet wet on a simpler situation and then try these houses for more than their tutorial purposes (see above).

Playing these houses at length teaches how various important objects work, how houses should be laid out, how the pace of a day feels, and other extremely fundamental concepts. For a good introduction try:

◆ Pleasantview: Lothario, Caliente, Goth

◆ Strangetown: Specter

◆ Veronaville: Monty

All neighborhoods have a few families in the Sim Bin that can be moved into unfurnished houses. They lack the benefit of having an already assembled household, but several are good combinations of Sims for beginners. The Burbs of Pleasantview, the Singles or Loners (Loner, actually) of Strangetown, and Bianca Monty of Veronaville are all good starts.

The next step for absolute beginners and even moderately experienced *The Sims* veterans should be to make a simple family and move them in. That takes us to Create-A-Sim.

CREATE-A-SIM

Create-A-Sim is where you sculpt a Sim's appearance and Personality and choose an Aspiration.

For your first family, go with the most basic and traditional start: two adults whom you intend to eventually join in holy union.

tip

These Sims can be of either opposite or same gender; it doesn't make any difference to their future together.

For simplicity's sake, either randomly generate your first Sims or choose them out of the Sim Bin.

Take some time to tinker with appearance or take them as is.

Next, jump straight to panel 6 of the tool and choose an Aspiration for each Sim. The easiest combination for a traditional career and children (suburban life) is to have one Fortune and one Family Sim (it doesn't matter which is which). There are other good combinations, but we'll leave that for later experimentation.

As for Personality, click on the various Zodiac signs to bring up a preset of Personality traits. That's a quick way into the game but let's be a bit more strategic.

Personality can influence how quickly Sims gain levels in certain skills. Thus, Sims should look for careers that require the skills they learn at higher rates. Conversely, a Sim's Personality can be designed for success in a specific career.

Since a Family Sim is eventually likely to stay home to take care of household duties, it's best to make him extremely Neat; he'll learn Cleaning skill faster, clean autonomously more often, and get Fun from cleaning.

tip

With a Fortune Sim in the house, discretionary income is needed to buy stuff to fulfill her acquisitional Wants, so hiring a Maid could be a bad decision. Better to have a stay-at-home super cleaner.

A stay-at-home Sim with a working Fortune Sim spouse will probably do all the friend making the other Sim needs for promotions, so it's extremely valuable to spend his remaining Personality points in Outgoing/ Shy (10 points) and Nice/ Grouchy (5).

This is a solid, though hardly the only, combination for Sims who need friends.

With a very Neat Family Sim at home, you're free to make the Fortune Sim extremely Sloppy.

A Fortune Sim is best suited for certain careers, one of which is Business. Given the skills required, a good profile for a Business Sim is Outgoing/Shy 10, Playful/Serious 10, and Nice/Grouchy 5. The extremely Outgoing and Playful Personalities empowers the Sim to learn Creativity and Charisma at double speed. As a side benefit of the high Creativity, it enables her to spend days off painting very valuable paintings and writing novels (a major Want for Fortune Sims).

With everything set, add both Sims to the family and use the Family Relationships tool. So you can experience how a relationship blooms from nothing to true love, make them roomies.

BUYING AND FURNISHING A HOME

The next big decision is where to live. You have §20,000 to start with, so a small house will do just fine as long as it has two bedrooms. Look for a place for about §12,500.

Empty houses usually come with basic appliances and plumbing fixtures. Don't be afraid to rearrange or return them if they're not what you want.

With the remaining funds, purchase:

- 2 Caress of Teak Beds (§900): both in same room so one alarm clock can serve both
- 4 Tea Party in Teak Dining Chairs (§400)
- 1 Durable Value Sofa (§250)
- 5 Krampft Industries Value Counter (§700)
- 1 NuMica Allinall Card Table (§95)
- 1 Crazy 8 Table (§65): for the alarm clock
- 1 Retratech "Office Pal" Economy Desk (§80)
- 1 Reflective Glass Mirror (§100)
- 1 Sewage Brothers Resteze Toilet (§300)
- 1 Clean Water Shower System (§625)
- 1 Superlative Sink by "The Greatest Designer Alive" (§250): insert in counter top
- 1 Dialectric ReadyPrep Range (§400)
- 1 Brand Name "EconoCool" Refrigerator (§600)
- 1 Extra Pep Coffeemaker (§85)
- 1 XLR8R2 Food Processor (§220)

- 1 Gagmia Simore "RefuseNik" Trash Compactor (§375)
- 1 Wishy-Washer from Brandname LX (§550)
- 1 Trottco 27" MultiVid IV Television (§500)
- 1 Moneywell Computer (§1,000): can return after finding jobs
- 1 Compact Stereo by Lo-Fi Audio (§99)
- 1 Get Up! Alarm Clock (§30)
- 1 SmokeSentry SmokeSniffer 3000 (§50)
- 1 SimLine Wall Phone (§75)
- 1 SimSafety V Burglar Alarm (§250)
- 1 Independent Expressions Inc. Easel (§350)
- 1 CinderBooks by Retratech (§200)
- 1 Anti-Quaint-Ed Ltd. Ed. Armoire (§250)

note

The astute will notice that this adds up to more than §20,000. That's because the cheapest houses usually include all of the basic bathroom and kitchen fixtures in their sale price. Without these items the houses actually come in around §10,000. The basic items are included in the list for completeness sake.

KITCHEN LAYOUT

How a kitchen is laid out can affect the efficiency of food preparation.

A properly laid out kitchen should permit a Sim to go from refrigerator to counter to stove to dining room in a relatively straight line.

1. Cooking begins with the refrigerator, so put it on one end of the kitchen, farthest away from the dining area.

2. Lay two countertops between the fridge and the stove.

3. Drop a food processor on either of the two countertops, leaving the other one vacant. Because many foods are prepared without the food processor, there needs to be a clear counter for prep by hand.

4. Place the stove next to the second countertop.

5. Locate remaining countertops as needed for serving cooked food, depositing dirty dishes, or using as backup prep area (the more the better) and use one for situating the in-counter sink.

6. Install the dishwasher and trash compactor under countertops as near as possible to the dining area. Be sure Sims can approach both appliances from more than one direction to avoid traffic jams or interference with cooking Sims.

7. Hang the smoke detector on any wall near the stove.

The goal is to let Sims go through the cooking process with as few physical steps as possible. Putting an open countertop and a food processor between the fridge and the stove puts a mixing and chopping "station" in the next logical place after the food is taken from the fridge. From the final prep station, the stove should be as few steps away as possible.

Ideally, the stove should be on the side closest to the dining area so food may be taken from it to the table with minimal effort.

GETTING A JOB

On this first day, the newspaper arrives at 10 a.m. (it's usually at 9). Use it and/or the computer to find jobs for both roomies.

The computer has more job listings than the newspaper.

For the Fortune Sim, hold out for the Business career. This will likely satisfy a small Want for that Sim and get her in a track that fits her Personality and Aspiration.

Though the Family Sim is built to be a homemaker, there's no reason not to put him to work immediately, earning money until domestic responsibilities mount. The best track for temporary work is the Military career. It doesn't require much in the way of skill through level 4, requires no friends until level 6, and is consistently among the highest in weekly pay for low-level jobs.

tip

Unless you wish to keep it around, sell the computer and desk once both Sims are employed.

MAKING FRIENDS

There's no job-related need for friends at this early juncture, but it never hurts to start.

The key relationship to build is the one between the roomies.

Still, when the welcome wagon (a somewhat random collection of three Sims) arrives around noon, greet them, then kick them off the lot, and then invite them over for a one-on-one interaction.

MAILS AND BILLS

The mail won't come on the first day, but be ready to look for the flag on the mailbox every few days thereafter. These are the household bills.

Bills must be paid promptly or the Repo Man will come calling.

When bills come, interact with the mailbox to remove them. When the Sim lays them down on the nearest surface, interact with the bills to pay them and walk them back to the mailbox.

TENDING TO WANTS

In addition to all the other things Sims should be working on while they're at home, make an effort to satisfy any easily achievable Wants that appear in their Wants panel. If one looks a bit more difficult, consider locking it to keep it in the panel.

At this early stage, most Aspirations appear quite general, even random. As the Sim moves in the direction suggested by his Aspiration, however, Wants and Fears become more specific to it.

If your Sims Want something, make it happen. You'll soon have very happy Sims on your hands.

Constant satisfaction of Needs raises Aspiration score, amasses Aspiration Reward Points, and opens the way to other Wants that can't appear until a more basic Want is achieved.

TENDING TO NEEDS

You generally may let the Sims monitor their own Needs, but check in on them occasionally.

Dedicate the Family Sim's efforts on the first day to getting a few points in Cooking skill so he can make respectable meals without causing fires. This increases both Sims' ability to satisfy Hunger.

Be sure to get them to sleep in plenty of time for work, and set the alarm clock before sending them to bed.

ENGINEERING ROMANCE

One day is not enough to get these two Sims to the altar but you can start.

Daily Relationship should be approaching, if not exceeding, Friend level (Daily 50) and could be near Crush level (70) if you were focused. Over the next few days, keep Daily high and it will pull Lifetime up toward it.

Once Lifetime begins to grow and there's a Crush and Love, more intense (but risky) socials arise. These can have larger direct effects on Lifetime Relationship score, so they can accelerate a wedding day.

When, in a few days, both the Sim's Daily and Lifetime are above 75 (and Mood is positive), propose Engagement. When both scores are over 80, throw a

wedding party and propose Marriage/Joining either directly on the other Sim or on the wedding arch object for the full nuptial experience.

SUMMARY

A lot can be done in the first day, but only if you know what's in store for your Sims. With this guide, you'll be off to a good start with a household that should teach a lot about both old and new gameplay elements.

Raising young Sims is no longer just an extra challenge, its one of the driving forces of the game. Survival of the species by some means should be the primary goal. It all starts with one wee baby.

Get these two Sims to reproduce and guide them through the rest of their life span. Then see what the offspring can do to improve on their parent's efforts. And so on, forever and ever.

Part 3

Creating Neighborhoods, Families, and Sims

Neighborhoods, Families, and Sims are the concentric circles of the Sim universe. Every Sim is part of a family and every family is part of a neighborhood. Conversely, a neighborhood is the whole world to the families within it, and the family is the most important part of a Sims world.

Still, there's one facet of this game that's smaller than any Sim: a Sim's own genetics. This fundamental stuff of life will be the driving force behind every decision you make and it's expression in generation after generation will be your reward.

This part introduces you to the structure of neighborhood in general and the inhabitants of the three that came with your game in particular. Next, an exploration of the Sim genome. Finally, a detailed exploration of the forces you'll unleash when you plug a Personality and Aspiration into the hollow shell of a Sim in Create-A-Sim.

Chapter 16
Welcome to the Neighborhood

Entering the game, the first of many choices confronts you: Which neighborhood?

A neighborhood is the community in which your Sims will live. They can have no connection to anything outside it, so families cannot span multiple neighborhoods. Fortunately, each neighborhood is chock full of interesting neighbors; non-neighbor "Townies"; service personnel with whom Sims may become well acquainted; and Community Lots where Sims from all over the neighborhood convene and shop. Everything your Sim needs can be found in the neighborhood. Plus, there's ample open real estate, so feel free to move in dozens of new families.

This chapter uncovers the world of possibilities to be found in your Sims' neighborhoods and what awaits you in the neighborhoods already at your disposal.

NEIGHBORHOOD COMPOSITION

Neighborhoods consist of an underlying terrain, a network of roads, residential lots with vacant and occupied houses, Community Lots for neighborhood Sims' shopping and socializing pleasure, and moving and stationary props that give the neighborhood its character and living feel.

Entering an unoccupied residential lot or any Community Lot from the Neighborhood view (via the Lots and Houses mode) enables you to tinker with any structures and objects upon it. These adjustments don't cost anything now but will add to the purchase price of any residential lots.

Neighborhoods feel like living, breathing things, alive with movements and realistic touches.

Pop in to look around or make adjustments to the lot via Lots and Houses mode.

Entering an occupied lot permits you to play any Sims in the household.

Lot Information

Much of what you need to know is in a lot's information box.

Each lot has an information box. For residential lots the box presents, in various panes, the household's occupants (posed in accordance with their relationships and Aspiration scores), lot name and wealth, any descriptive text you or the lot creator wish to include, arrows displaying the connections between the lot and others in the neighborhood, and the Aspiration and Aspiration level of each occupant.

Community Lots display their name and any descriptive text.

Packaging lots to a saved file or to the Internet is easy via the Package Lot button on the info box.

PRIMA OFFICIAL GAME GUIDE

Saved families are stored in the Family Bin. From this pane, you may also enter the Create-A-Family tool.

note

Every lot information box also includes a button for uploading the lot to THESIMS2.COM or to a file on your hard drive. The lot, its house, all its objects, and the family within it (minus any relationships outside the lot) can be packaged en masse to share with others.

Even from Neighborhood view, it's easy to see much of what this lot has to offer.

Much can be learned about a lot just by zooming in on it. For example, a close look at a Community Lot can determine whether it has an outdoor pool or hot tub.

ESTABLISHED NEIGHBORHOODS

The Sims 2 comes with three fully fleshed out and meticulously designed neighborhoods full of Sims for your amusement. You may use these neighborhoods to play with the pre-configured families, move a family of your own design into an empty house, add a house and/or a new lot to the neighborhood and move in a family, or even build your own neighborhood from scratch.

note

Building houses and creating neighborhoods are covered in detail in Chapters 31 and 35, respectively.

This chapter addresses the easiest route, taking parts already in the game and using them as your canvas. Included with each of the game's new neighborhoods are:

- A neighborhood story for your perusal. Find out more about Story mode in Chapter 32.
- Families in furnished houses with neighborhood-wide relationships. These families have fully fleshed out stories and have lived rich lives before you even meet them. They all have major events about to occur, so playing these houses as designed (at first) teaches you a lot about *The Sims 2*'s features and strategy.
- Pre-built families in the Family Bin: These Sims are not yet installed in houses, but may have histories with and connections to Sims already living in the neighborhood. You can install these families into any house that they can afford in the neighborhood.
- Pre-built but vacant houses: Many houses in the neighborhood are available for sale in all price ranges. Most have the essential kitchen and bathroom objects but are otherwise unfurnished.
- Pre-built lots with houses in the Lots and Houses Bin: The architectural designers at Maxis have supplied a beautiful array of unoccupied, unfurnished homes for all budgets. Drag them onto any open space adjacent to a road (the underlying lot is included with the house).
- Pre-configured lots: Underlying every house is a lot. If you're going to build your own house,

you must first lay down an empty lot in the appropriate size. Note that the size of the lot factors into the cost of the house. On the other hand, the larger the lot, the lower the cost per tile, so a large lot might be worthwhile.

The Lots and Houses menu is the storage space for any lots (both occupied and vacant) that haven't been moved into any neighborhood.

CUSTOM CONTENT

Another alternative to building families and lots yourself is the vast world of custom content that awaits you on the internet and among your fellow *The Sims 2* players.

With varying degrees of difficulty, you can import entirely new neighborhoods, occupied and unoccupied lots, families (in occupied houses), individual Sims, neighborhood terrain, and completely new stories for existing neighborhoods.

This rich world of user and Maxis-designed custom content is covered in detail in Chapter 35.

PLAYING THE PRE-BUILT FAMILIES

Whichever avenue you wish to take into the game, it's very educational (and quite entertaining) take some time with each neighborhood's families. Popping into them in the right order and knowing what is scheduled to happen in each lot makes for a very enlightening introduction to *The Sims 2*.

Though these houses are set up to have a few scheduled events and to teach a few more advanced concepts than the tutorials, those can be ignored. If you prefer, just take the lots and play them how you like. Note, however, that once they've been played

a bit and saved, their orchestrated state will be gone and the "walkthroughs" below won't apply unless you reinstall the neighborhood by hand.

Each neighborhood section below lists the recommended order of houses. Some necessary events in some houses interfere with the events scheduled to occur in others, so it's important to do them in the right order or play them without saving.

Pleasantview

Recommended order:

1. Lothario	3. Caliente	5. Dreamer
2. Goth	4. Broke	6. Pleasant

Lothario

- ◆ Resident(s): Don Lothario
- ◆ Difficulty: Easy
- ◆ Central Character: Don

The hot tub is where Don makes all the magic happen.

1. Use the phone to call Nina Caliente and invite her over. She accepts, fulfilling one of Don's Wants.

2. Clean up all trash piles in the house. Don resists due to his Sloppy personality but complies. This increases Environment score.

3. For future cleanliness, use the phone to hire Don a Maid.

4. When the Maid arrives, she tidies up anything.

5. Greet Nina at the door.

6. Make drinks at the bar on the second level.

7. Get into the hot tub or join Nina if she's in already.

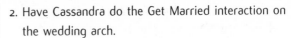

8. Do the Cuddle interaction on Nina, followed by the WooHoo interaction. Everyone's happy! This fulfills one of Don's major Wants and his Aspiration score climbs into Platinum territory.

9. Don's Power Want is to WooHoo with three Sims. If you look in his Memories (Simology panel) he's already had one. Nina makes two. The final step is to say goodbye to Nina and invite her sister Dina for a visit. Have a little lunch and call her on the phone; if she asks to bring a friend, say no (it's going to be Nina, and that would be awkward).

10. Greet Dina, but don't go for the gold just yet. A check of the Relationship panel shows that Don's not yet in love with Dina. Do a few romantic interactions until the Relationship scores rise a bit and you see red hearts floating above *Don's* head.

11. Coax Dina into the hot tub, cuddle, and WooHoo. That makes three and fulfills one of Don's Power Wants.

Goth

- Resident(s): Mortimer, Cassandra, and Alexander Goth
- Difficulty: Easy
- Central Character: Cassandra

Is Don really marriage material? Cassandra's going to find out.

1. Don and Cassandra are here and almost over the top in their relationship. Have Cassandra plant a kiss and a few other high-level romantic interactions on Don.

2. Have Cassandra do the Get Married interaction on the wedding arch.

3. If Don's Relationship score toward Cassandra (which you can't see) is high enough, and his mood is right, he'll either accept the marriage or leave poor Cassandra at the altar. If he accepts, Don moves in with all his money and takes the Goth name. If he rejects, Cassandra goes into Aspiration failure and requires a visit from the Sim Shrink.

Rush to the altar and things don't work out so well for Cassandra.

> **note**
>
> Stick around the lot late enough and you'll see quite a lot of ghosts.

Caliente

- Resident(s): Nina and Dina Caliente
- Difficulty: Medium
- Central Character: Dina

1. Dina wants to marry a rich Sim. Fortunately, the one she's in love with comes calling. Send her down to greet Mortimer Goth.

Mortimer's ripe for the picking. Dina just needs to make the first move, and probably the second.

Nina thinks about her sister's marriage and scans the paper for a place of her own.

2. Take the initiative and have Dina propose engagement to Mortimer.

3. Next, get married and fulfill Dina's Power Want to marry a rich Sim. Mortimer moves in with his extremely ample wealth and (if you choose) his family in tow. If he comes alone, he brings 10 percent of his household worth. If he brings his whole household, every penny comes over.

4. Nina sees it's time to move out; have her use the newspaper by the front walk to find her own place.

note

Wait until late at night and a burglar visits the house too. Dina takes an Aspiration hit if he takes an object, because that's one of her Fears.

To prevent him from taking anything, buy a burglar alarm and put it near the front door before he arrives.

Broke

◆ Resident(s): Brandi, Dustin, and Beau Broke
◆ Difficulty: Medium
◆ Central Character: Brandi

Teaching Beau to walk and potty train is demanding, but it feeds both Sims' Wants and, in turn, their Aspiration scores.

A first kiss over the pinball machine is a pretty big deal.

1. Brandi has one troublesome son but the other is still new enough to save. Start by teaching him to walk; he's almost there so it should only take a couple of interactions. They both get a Memory and a big Want fulfilled. Beau is in Platinum Aspiration.

2. Next, click on the potty in the bathroom to teach him to use the potty. This takes several interactions and emptyings. The process is slowed a bit by Brandi's Day 1 pregnancy symptoms. Beau may need a nap before completing this training.

3. Later, Dustin comes home from school with his girlfriend Angela and some mediocre grades. Brandi autonomously lectures him, reducing their relationship.

4. Dustin and Angela have a very tight relationship but haven't had their first kiss; tell Dustin what to do. This satisfies a big Want for Dustin and his Aspiration rises to Platinum. Instruct Dustin to say goodbye to Angela.

5. Soon, Beau wakes from his nap; finish the potty training and both mom and son get big Wants satisfied.

6. At 6 o'clock, the first warning comes that Beau is ready to grow up. Because his Aspiration score should be Platinum, grow him up now and he fulfills the Grow Up Well Want.

7. Buy a Cake and have Brandi interact with it for Beau. Congrats: Beau's now a child and a lot easier to take care of.

Dreamer

◆ Resident(s): Darren and Dirk Dreamer
◆ Difficulty: Easy
◆ Central Character: Darren

1. Send Darren upstairs to his easel to complete a regular painting with the Paint interaction.

2. When the painting's done, sell it.

3. Next, use the easel again to paint either a Still Life or a Portrait and follow the onscreen instructions.

Darren needs time in front of his easel to pay the two piles of bills downstairs.

4. Complete the chosen custom painting over the evening and (most likely) into the next day.

5. When it's done, sell it too.

6. With the money from the paintings, pay the two stacks of bills on the first floor.

note

It's difficult to paint high-end art without having to feed Needs a few times in the process. This is part of the challenge of being a "professional" artist. It's especially hard to maintain Social and Comfort and work on painting because it's done alone and standing up.

Pleasant

◆ Resident(s): Daniel, Mary Sue, Lilith, and Angela Pleasant

◆ Difficulty: Medium

◆ Central Character: Daniel

Daniel's fateful decision and some very bad timing lead to familial discord.

Everybody deals with it in his or her own way.

1. Mary Sue and the twins leave the house for the day, leaving Daniel alone.

2. At 10, the Maid ("Kaylynn") arrives and begins her work. A quick check of Daniel's Relationship panel shows he's has a little thing going with the Maid.

3. Sure enough, when she's done with the house, she asks if she can hang around. Say yes.

4. Send Daniel to relax on the bed and invite the Maid to join him.

5. Around this time, a career chance card comes up for Mary Sue. No matter what you choose, the answer is negative and results in her coming home early.

6. Just as Mary Sue gets home from work and the twins arrive from school, direct Daniel to offer the WooHoo interaction to Kaylynn. She accepts.

7. Daniel and Mary Sue get bad Memories, Mary Sue acts out jealousy behavior (trashing relationships with both Daniel and Kaylynn), and the girls react in their own ways.

Strangeville

Recommended order:

1. Curious   3. Beaker   5. Grunt
2. Specter   4. Smith

Curious

◆ Resident(s): Vidcund, Pascal, and Lazlo Curious

◆ Difficulty: Easy

◆ Central Character: Vidcund

1. Pascal is in his third day of an alien pregnancy. He'll deliver later today.

For the Curious boys, that telescope is a ticket to the stars and, surprisingly, family life.

2. Send Vidcund to one of the expensive telescopes on the roof where he's abducted.

3. Vidcund is returned a few hours later. He too is pregnant with an alien baby (as male abductees always are).

4. Soon, Pascal delivers his baby. All supplies and objects for the baby are already in the house.

5. You may, if you like, direct Pascal to hire a Nanny via the phone.

6. For further Want fulfillment, direct Pascal to make friends with the visiting Nervous, and Lazlo to watch the Yummy channel to max out his Cooking skill.

Specter

◆ Resident(s): Olive Specter and Ophelia Nigmos

◆ Difficulty: Easy

◆ Central Character: Olive

Olive wants to retire to enjoy her old age but it turns out she only gets to live two more days. Make them count and she'll pass on happily into the afterworld.

1. Olive wants to retire, so send her to the phone to call work. Select Retire and her working life is done, and she's satisfied a really big Want.

2. After dark, the ghosts start to come out. Their color reflects the way they died. Most of them seem to be service NPCs...Hmmm. They scare the family and haunt the toys on the lot. Deleting tombstones removes the ghosts from the lot.

3. Ophelia wants to go out with her boyfriend Johnny Smith. Have her ask Olive after Olive retires and she'll likely say yes. Call Johnny (using the Call > Go Out phone menu) and he comes by to pick her up.

4. Two days later, Olive dies of old age. The higher you get her Aspiration score before then, the more likely she'll die happily (there'll be hula dancers) and the more inheritance will come to her only child: Nervous Subject. It's probably too late for Ophelia, her niece, to build sufficient Lifetime Relationship to get her own bit of the death benefit.

Beaker

◆ Resident(s): Circe and Loki Beaker and Nervous Subject

◆ Difficulty: Easy

◆ Central Character: Circe

Circe heads off to work as Nervous suffers a little breakdown from the roaches in the kitchen. Maybe he shouldn't stuff his face at the fridge so much.

1. Circe wants to get promoted, so feed all her Needs in the time until the carpool leaves. Wait until about 20 minutes before the time Circe is to start work to maximize her Need feeding time. At 8:40, send her to the car.

2. Nervous's low Aspiration makes him engage in self-destructive or Desperation behavior: in

this case, stuffing his face at the refrigerator. This, in turn, brings out the roaches.

3. The roach infestation is the final straw for Nervous, who goes into total Aspiration failure and needs an intervention from the Sim Shrink.

4. When he's all better, direct him to call the Exterminator to get rid of the roaches.

5. Have Nervous call Pascal Curious on the phone to talk. This should be enough to get their relationship into Friendship and satisfy one of Nervous's Wants. That improves his Aspiration score for now.

6. When Circe returns from work, she should have that promotion.

Smith

- Resident(s): Pollination Technician #9, Jenny, Johnny, and Jill Smith
- Difficulty: Medium
- Central Character: Johnny

Blow out the candles, Johnny, it's your big day and there's still time to save this party.

1. Johnny is on his transition day from teen to adult. Get him on the phone to invite everyone to the party.

2. Fire up the stereo as the guests arrive. Johnny has a Want for a good party, so it'll have to score well.

3. Tank Grunt arrives, uninvited, to crash.

4. Direct Johnny to blow out the candles on the cake that's already in the house. His age transitions into an adult.

5. Johnny's Aspiration score was high so he has a Grow Up Well Memory, raising his score even higher. If the party is successful, he gets a Good Party Memory too. Aspiration points accrue for both.

Grunt

- Resident(s): Tank, Buzz, Rip, and Buck Grunt
- Difficulty: Easy
- Central Character: Tank

Buzz likes spending time running his home like a boot camp.

Tank wants to impress his father, so get him in the Military career track and top out his grades by getting him to school on time.

1. Tank wants to follow in his father's footsteps by entering the Military track. Send him to the computer and get him the job he wants.

2. Buzz and Tank want Tank to get an A+ report card, so make sure he gets to school the next day (Monday).

3. Spend this day off with Buzz training the kids. Direct him to offer lessons to them on the obstacle course.

4. The next day, make sure Tank gets to school. When he returns, he and his dad will have something to be proud of.

Veronaville

Recommended order:

1. Capp   2. Monty   3. Summerdream

Capp

- ◆ Resident(s): Consort, Tybalt, Juliette, and Hermia Capp
- ◆ Difficulty: Easy
- ◆ Central Character: Juliette

Star crossed lovers have it so rough. No sooner are they going steady than the old man is reading poor Romeo the riot act. No good can come of this.

1. While Consort is lounging on the sofa in the living room, Juliette should take the opportunity to ask Romeo to go steady. Do it fast and he'll accept.

2. This brings Consort out of the house and into Romeo's face with a very stern lecture that reduces their Relationship score and sends Romeo off the lot.

Monty

- ◆ Resident(s): Romeo, Mercutio, Patrizio, and Isabella Monty
- ◆ Difficulty: Easy
- ◆ Central Character: Romeo

1. Romeo wants to get serious with Juliette. Inviting her is one of his Wants; making out with her is one of his Power Wants. Call her on the phone and she asks if she can bring a friend; it'll be Tybalt.

2. When they arrive, Romeo should immediately make out with Juliette.

3. Mercutio insults Juliette then fights Tybalt.

4. Mercutio loses (one of his Power Fears) and Tybalt leaves, but not before kicking the flamingo.

Back at Romeo's house, things get steamier between the young lovers and their families take it out on each other.

Summerdream

- ◆ Resident(s): Puck, Titania, Oberon, and Bottom Summerdream
- ◆ Difficulty: Easy
- ◆ Central Character: Puck

Plant one on the lovely Hermia for a stirring first kiss. Then, give the older generation some happiness too by getting them engaged and married (they're ready).

1. Puck is ready for his first kiss from Hermia. Direct him to it without delay and she accepts. This fulfills a Power Want and pushes Puck into Platinum Aspiration.

2. Meanwhile Oberon should propose engagement to Titania. She accepts. Love is really in the air! Why wait? Get one of them to propose marriage too. It's a party after all and there's a wedding arch on in the yard.

Chapter 17
Create-A-Sim and Genetics

A Sim's appearance is an extremely complex package of subtle facial features, coloring, eye shapes, hair, clothing, and more. What's inside them too is a varied web of Personality traits, Aspiration, and Interests. Putting all these things together and seeing how they persist into future generations is a matter of utilizing the tools available to you and understanding the mysterious Sim genome.

This chapter walks you though the interplay of the game's various ways of making and changing Sims and provides a useful overview of how Sim genetics work.

SIM CREATION

Sims in *The Sims 2* are created in three ways:

- In the Create-A-Sim tool that's part of the Create New Family system
- In the external *The Sims 2 Body Shop* utility that came with your game
- In "the wild" of the game itself when two Sims create a new life

Create New Family

The Create New Family system is launched from Neighborhood view, under the Families menu (or press F1 by default). Click on the Create New Family button and you're on your way.

This system has two aspects:

- The Create-A-Sim tool lets you assemble parts and generate Personality for a Sim that will be part of the family.
- The Family Relationships tool is where a family is assembled and their initial relationships established.

Enter the Create New Family mode in the Neighborhood view and press Create New Family to get started.

Create-A-Sim

In the Create New Family mode, enter the Create-A-Sim tool by pressing the Create-A-Sim button and choosing if you want to make a Sim from parts or generate one from the genetic material of two Sims. To do the latter, there must be a "breeding pair" (two adult Sims of opposite genders) already saved into the family.

Click on the Create-A-Sim button to choose whether to Create-A-Sim or Make a Child.

note

Babies can't be made in Create-A-Sim; toddler is the youngest possible age. Babies can be made only in the more traditional ways.

First, however, give the family a name in the flashing orange box.

Next, give the Sim a name and start designing him or her to your liking. There are many ways to go about this.

The Randomize button generates a completely random Sim of the specified gender and age. Press the button as many times as you like until one suits you.

The main Create-A-Sim interface shows the total results of your work.

The Sim Bin holds complete Sims made by you or Maxis, and any other Sims you've downloaded. Just add a name and Aspiration and you're ready to go.

The Choose Existing Sim area (a.k.a. "The Sim Bin") holds any fully designed (in appearance only, that is) Sims made by Maxis or brought in/designed by you in *The Sims™ 2 Body Shop* (see below). The Sim Bin contains all existing Sims of the specified age and gender. Choose one and adjust him as necessary.

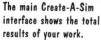

Any Sims marked with the "*" Custom Content icon were either created in THE SIMS™ 2 BODY SHOP or imported into the game.

Once there's a Sim in front of the mirror, you may do with him what you will. The six main panels to the Create-A-Sim tool each alter a specific aspect of the Sim's appearance or Personality:

Panel 1: Name, gender, age, color, and Fitness (Thin or Fat only). Also the Randomize and Sim Bin buttons.

Panel 2: Head. Choose from several heads of the chosen age/gender/skin tone. Essentially, a subset of the heads in the Sim Bin, sorted by age/gender/ skin tone. Save heads into collections for each age/gender/ skin tone to highlight favorites and narrow options for players who download a lot of custom Sims.

Panel 3: Hair and face. Alter the Sim's hair color and style and adjust facial aspects of their full face, brow, eyes, nose, mouth, and jaw and chin.

Panel 4: Makeup, facial hair, and glasses. Adjust makeup, costume makeup, glasses, eyebrows, stubble, and beard and mustache. The latter two are grayed out for females.

Panel 5: Clothing. Mix and match outfits for the Sim's Everyday, Formal, Undies, PJs, Swimwear, and Athletic selections. These will be all he owns until he buys new clothes at a store (see "Changing Appearance Later," following).

Panel 6: Personality and Aspiration. Consult Chapters 18 and 21 before choosing.

note

Clothing items can be assembled in collections that can be shared.

Highlight a clothing option and click on **Add to Collection**. Collections can be built around any theme or no theme at all, but they're basically a player-created subset of all available clothing.

See Chapter 35 for how to share these collections.

In Create New Family, finished Sims await their portrait and entry into the Neighborhood.

Once everything is set, Accept the Sim and she's added to the Create New Family mode. Add as many Sims (up to eight) as you like into the family.

HAIR AND FACIAL TOOLS

There's a very powerful but not entirely obvious feature in panel 3 in Create-A-Sim. For any of the five facial region or full-face changes (but not hair), there are two rows of examples (or "archetypes") at the top of the panel. Right-clicking on one of them morphs your Sim's feature(s) one-tenth of the way toward the pictured facial archetype. Left-clicking switches to the facial archetype in one big step (with a cute little bounce at the end of this drastic alteration).

Want to be just a bit more like one of the archetypes? Right-click a couple of times and the feature or full face shifts subtly in that direction.

If there's a breeding pair (two adults of opposite gender) in the family, you may use Create-A-Sim to Make a Child.

Make a Child

Make a Child is a special interface that enables the on-the-fly blending of two Sim's genetic material to create an entire new Sim of any age or gender. Within the tool, you may specify which two Sims should be the parents.

Make a Child is a laboratory to visualize how two Sims' genes could mix. You may create a Sim of any age or relationship to the two Sims who contribute their genetics.

Click on the Make a Child button as many times as you like to mix the chosen "parents." Alter their age and gender to see what they'd look like at different times or as a different sex. When the desired appearance, gender, and age are set, click Accept Sim and the scene moves to the normal Create-A-Sim interface.

Note that in using Make a Child, you are not creating any family relationship between the genetic pair and the "offspring." You can, in fact, produce an elder Sim (who'd be older than her "parents") by this method.

tip

If you want to create adult siblings but don't want the elder parents in the family, create the elders first, use Make a Child for each sibling, and delete the elders. The result is a group of Sims genetically created by same two Sims but with no actually existing parents.

Link them up by the Family Relationships tool and you're ready to go.

Once a genetically created child is in place in Create-A-Sim, you can still change anything you wish, including everything generated in Make a Child.

The biggest difference between creating a Sim this way versus in-game reproduction is that here the Sim's Personality is not genetically created. It's set instead to a random Zodiac sign and can be adjusted at will.

Create-A-Family

All Sims designed in Create-A-Sim for this family appear in the Create-A-Family mode. Arrayed before a portrait studio backdrop, they wait patiently for all members of their future household to arrive.

Once you have every desired Sim in the family, it's time to decide how everyone's connected.

Family Relationships

Before completing a family, decide how they're related to each other in the Family Relationships tool.

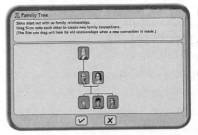

Use the Family Relationships tool to pre-establish who relates to whom. Be aware that there isn't total freedom to relate two Sims; some things must be saved for the game.

note

If no relationship is chosen, Sims are deemed roomies.

Young Sims of the same or similar ages (i.e. teen to child or toddler, toddler to child and teen, and child to teen and toddler) can be either roomies or siblings.

Adults and adults or elders and elders can be set to roomies, siblings, or spouses. Adults and elders may not be spouses in this tool but may in the game.

If an intergenerational marriage is desired, leave the eventual spouses as roomies and create the family. Once they're moved into a lot, get romance going and the two Sims may marry each other if they choose.

Older (adult or elder) Sims can be established as either a parent or roomie to a younger Sim.

The Family Relationships tool doesn't allow total freedom to set any relationships you can imagine. Some must simply be achieved in the game itself. For example:

◆ Teens or younger may not be children of elders.

◆ Elders and adults can't be spouses.

◆ Single parents can be set, but only in game can a child be the biological offspring of one parent but not the other (stepparent).

As a general rule, if there's a relationship that can't be made here, set up the Sims as roommates. Once in the game, they may reside in the same house and develop the relationship or be split into different houses by having one (or more) household Sim leave via the Find Own Place interaction in the newspaper or computer.

Finally, there must be at least one adult or elder in a family created in this tool or the family cannot be finished. In the game, however, children and toddlers can be under the care of only a teen. Thus, if that situation is intended, move the adult/elder Sim out of the house at the first opportunity.

You can't make families without an elder or adult. But you can always kick them out later.

When all Sims are added and all relationships set, click Accept Family. You're returned to the Neighborhood, where you may move your new family into a lot or reenter Create New Family and work on another household.

Once Accept Family is pressed, the household as it is then constituted and the members of it can never be altered in Create-A-Sim. They can, as you'll see below, be changed in other ways but not so fundamentally as in Create-A-Sim.

Nor can they be duplicated for use in other families or as a template for any other new Sim. If you want to preserve your Sim appearances in a way that lets you eternally reedit them or build new Sims based on them (or an army of evil genetic clones), the Sim's appearance should instead be forged in the external THE SIMS™ 2 BODY SHOP utility. See "THE SIMS™ 2 BODY SHOP" below and in Chapter 34.

When they move into a lot, Sims have initial Relationship scores toward each other based on their relationship in the family tree. The actual scores are random within the ranges below:

Only spouses have Love, Crush, Friend, or Best Friend set at move-in. That must be achieved naturally for all others.

Initial Household Relationship Scores

RELATIONSHIP	DAILY	LIFETIME
Spouse to spouse	70–90	70–80
Roommate to roommate	10–45	0–20
Child to parent	20–49	20–49
Parent to child	30–60	30–60
Grandparent to grandchild	30–60	30–60
Grandchild to grandparent	10–40	10–40
Cousin to cousin	1–49	1–49
Uncle/aunt to nephew	1–49	1–49
Nephew to uncle/aunt	1–49	1–49
Sibling to sibling	-10–49	1–49

THE SIMS™ 2 BODY SHOP

The external *The Sims™ 2 Body Shop* utility is on your hard drive along with the game. It is very similar to Create-A-Sim, but it empowers both the sharing and preserving of individual Sims. From this tool, Sims may be cloned, redesigned, or assembled from scratch.

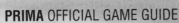
Sims created in *The Sims™ 2 Body Shop* appear in Create-A-Sim's Sim Bin. Custom skin tones engineered via *The Sims™ 2 Body Shop*'s Create Parts section can be chosen via the Custom Content icon on the Skin Tone line of panel 1 of Create-A-Sim.

For full detail, see Chapter 34 and the *The Sims™ 2 Body Shop* manuals and tutorials available on TheSims2.com.

If you want your Sim design work to be preserved, do all your appearance designing in THE SIMS™ 2 BODY SHOP, not Create-A-Sim. Everything gets imported automatically when you load Create-A-Sim.

In-Game Sim Creation

Though the name for this means of creating Sims is a bit stuffy and obtuse, the process appears to be a great deal of fun for all involved.

Whether a new Sim is created in a bed, a hot tub, a clothing booth, in the netherworld of adoption, or by alien abduction, all newborn Sims are created by the forces of Sim genetic code.

Sim genetics are based on four different systems controlling different parts of the Sim:

- Eye and hair color
- Facial features
- Skin tone
- Personality

Human beings are based on a complex genetic system in which traits are inherited from mother or father. Sims are, to that extent, the same, but certain elements follow a different inheritance system.

One bit of extremely simplified genetics first. For every trait, humans get one gene from one parent and one from the other. These pairs of genes are called "alleles."

While you wait, all the genetic operations discussed here are being speedily crunched.

Which gene the child actually displays (or, in the lingo of genetics, "expresses") is determined by a reasonably simple system that we'll address in a moment. No matter which gene the Sim actually expresses, however, he always carries the non-expressed gene that can, in the right combinations with a future mate, express in his own child. This is how a child can have different hair color than either parent.

For Sims, this system carries over to a greater or lesser extent depending on the trait.

Let's examine each trait to see how it works:

Eye and Hair Color

Eye and hair color reflect the closest thing to real-world human genetics.

Traits (e.g., blue eyes, brown hair, etc.) are either dominant or recessive. If a child gets one of each, the dominant always become the child's trait. If the child gets two recessive or two dominant traits, the choice between them is a random 50 percent.

There are four Maxis hair colors, and each is either dominant or recessive:

- Brown: Dominant
- Blonde: Recessive
- Black: Dominant
- Red: Recessive

There are five Maxis eye colors:

- Brown: Dominant
- Blue: Recessive
- Dark blue: Dominant
- Green: Recessive
- Gray: Recessive

When a Sim is created in Create-A-Sim, all Sims are "homogeneous" (carrying a matched pair of the identical gene). For example, a brown-haired Sim made in Create-A-Sim carries the same gene on both sides (brown/brown).

In reproduction, however, somewhat real-world genetics come into play. Let's say the child is the offspring of two Create-A-Sim–made parents, one with brown eyes (brown/brown) and one with blue (blue/blue). The child's eye color allele would look like this: brown/blue. Because dominant genes always rule over recessive, the child would have brown eyes.

If both sides of the Create-A-Sim alleles were the same dominance (both parents had blue eyes or both had brown eyes), the child would always have the same eye color as her parents.

Further down the generational trail, however, Sims will have parents who carry two different traits ("heterogeneous" alleles). In this case, from each parent, the child will have some combination of the four possibilities. If Dad is brown/blonde and Mom is blonde/red, child could have:

1. brown/blonde: Expresses brown (dominant)
2. brown/red: Expresses brown (dominant)
3. blonde/red: Expresses blonde or red (50 percent chance)
4. blonde/blonde: Expresses blonde (homogeneous)

No matter what the child expresses, he always carries both halves of the allele. When, therefore, the brown/red Sim mates with a red/red Sim, there's a 50 percent chance the child will have red hair.

Custom Content Hair and Eyes

Custom content eyes and hair (created by other users rather than by Maxis) are sometimes dominant. They may be expressed when paired with a recessive color or even a Maxis dominant color. Purple hair, therefore, sometimes wins out over, for example, blonde or brown but stands a 50-50 chance against any other custom content color.

> **note**
>
> Custom content hair appears only for the gender for which it was created. A male child of a female with custom content hair cannot express his mother's hair color and falls back on the other color in his allele. If that too is a female custom content color, he expresses the original hair color upon which his mother's custom content color was created.

Skin Tone

Skin tone works on similar principles. There are four Maxis skin tones from light to dark (let's call them "S1, S2, S3, and S4").

Just as with hair and eyes, Sims carry one skin tone gene from each parent (for Create-A-Sim Sims, it'll be the same on both sides). Unlike with hair and eyes, however, there is no dominance in skin tone: the choice of which tone to pass on is random.

The resulting child, therefore, ends up with two skin tone genes, one from each parent. If those genes are the same, the child will have that skin tone (e.g., if she gets S2 and S2, she'll be S2).

If, however, the tones are different, the child can randomly express any skin tone in between the two. For example, if a Sim receives S2 and S4 from his parents, he can be S2, S3, or S4. When he reproduces, however, he passes on *either* S2 or S4 to his child.

Custom Content and Skin Tone

Custom content is trickier when it comes to skin tone. It's effectively a fifth skin tone. Because, however, it's not one of the original four, there can't be a range between, for example, S2 and the custom tone.

For example: Dad is S4/Orange and Mom is S1/S3. The child could be:

◆ S1/Orange: 50 percent chance of either
◆ S3/Orange: 50 percent chance of either
◆ S1/S4: S1, S2, S3, or S4
◆ S3/S4: S3 or S4

Facial Features

Facial features don't follow the human genetic pattern at all. Sims' faces are divided into five regions:

◆ Brow   ◆ Mouth   ◆ Eyes
◆ Jaw   ◆ Nose

Every Sim actually has 12 faces: one for each age for both genders. They only, however, show the six faces of their gender as they grow up, though the hidden six faces of the opposite gender are written into the Sim's genes. When a Sim is born, therefore, the six faces for her lifetime are simultaneously created along with six other faces she can pass on genetically.

When a Sim is made in Create-A-Sim, each region of his face is randomly labeled dominant or recessive. Gender, however, makes certain features more likely to be dominant than recessive.

Dominance Probability for Facial Features

FEATURE	MALE	FEMALE
Brow	66%	50%
Eyes	50%	66%
Nose	66%	50%
Mouth	50%	66%
Jaw	66%	50%

The offspring of any coupling receives each gender-specific region from a blending of his mother's and father's male faces. In what proportion they blend, however is a function of dominance.

If only one is dominant, the child has a 66 percent chance of inheriting the dominant feature. If both sides for a region are dominant or both sides recessive, the inheritance is random.

The facial regions are then blended randomly, with the inherited region having a heavier influence. When the genetically created child herself reproduces, her features retain their dominance or recessiveness based on what she received. She also carries with her both the male and female versions of her own face, which are used to create her own child.

Custom Content and Facial Features

Because there is no truly custom content for facial features, all facial genetics work the same no matter where the Sim came from.

Personality

A Sim's Personality is also inherited. For each Personality trait, the child receives the trait's point assignment from his father, his mother, or at random.

Unlike a Create-A-Sim Sim, a genetically created Sim can have up to 35 (but no less than 25) Personality points distributed between the five traits.

Children created in-game can be born with more than 25 total Personality points.

Traits are assigned in random order. If, before setting all traits, the total points equal 35, all subsequent traits are set to zero.

If, once all five traits have been set, the total number of Personality points is less than 25, points will be randomly added to any low traits until the total number is 25.

Alien Genetics

Alien genetics are a special situation. When an alien baby is born, parented by alien abduction, she will not show alien facial structure right away. Sims will show any alien facial structure they carry genetically as soon as they become toddlers. Babies have a human baby structure, although they will still be green and have a greater than 50 percent chance of having alien eye color. The face expresses later due to the mystery of alien DNA. There's also a slightly less than 50 percent chance that the baby will have alien eye color; thus it's likely that the child will be all alien with her father's eyes.

Alien babies always look VERY alien but may have their father's eye color.

> **note**
>
> The Maxis-made alien features, skin tone, and eye color are not accessible in Create-A-Sim or THE SIMS™ 2 BODY SHOP.

Once an alien-abduction-born Sim reproduces, standard genetics rules apply and all of his alien features are treated as dominant.

> **note**
>
> Fitness and Interests are not inherited. All children are born with neutral Fitness and random Interests.

CHANGING APPEARANCE LATER

Once a Sim is living in a neighborhood, you may still change her appearance. If there's a mirror on the lot, you may do the Change Appearance interaction. Though the essential shape of the Sim's head and her genetic code will remain unchanged, you may alter:

- Hair color or style
- Makeup
- Glasses
- Costume makeup
- Facial hair (eyebrows, stubble, or beard) shape and color.

You can give your Sim a whole new look, but these changes are only cosmetic. Genetics are forever.

These changes are superficial, however, and have no impact on the Sim's genetics. The hair color genes he passes on are the same, even if he later sports a new color.

Change clothing by purchasing new outfits at Community Lot clothing stores and selecting them from any dresser on the Sims' lot using the Plan Outfit system.

Chapter 18
Simology

Simology is the study of what makes Sims tick. Well, it could be. Really, though, it's a collection of four elements that make up who your Sim is: Personality, Interests, Fitness, and Memories. Each has myriad influences on various parts of *The Sims 2*; knowing how they work and the consequences of the choices you've made are essential to a successful Sim life.

This chapter unravels the interplay of the Simology elements and many other parts of the game. Included here is but a taste of the intricate connections underlying this quiet little world.

PERSONALITY

Personality is the first panel under Simology. It displays the Sim's Zodiac sign and her level in each of the five Personality traits.

The very core of your Sim's being is her Personality. It drives countless things she does in her daily life. Here are but a few of the things Personality can affect:

Skill Acquisition Speed

Some skills are learned more quickly (up to twice as fast) by Sims with certain Personality traits. The more points a Sim has in a trait, the less time it takes to gain a point in that skill.

Most skills have an aligned Personality trait that makes the skill easier to learn:

- Body: Active
- Charisma: Outgoing
- Cleaning: Neat
- Cooking: None
- Creativity: Playful
- Logic: Serious
- Mechanical: None

Only a Sim of the specified Personality extreme will see any difference in skill speed. A Sim with Active/Lazy of 0–5 will, for example, increase Body skill at the normal rate while a Sim of Active/Lazy 6–10 will do it faster (increasing the more Active they are). Among Active Sims, the increase is gradual; a 6 will see a slight increase while a 10 will work at double the normal rate.

Need Decay Rate

Some Personality traits alter the rate at which Needs decay. In other words, they shorten or lengthen how long a Sim can go without satisfying a specific Need.

- Hunger: Active decays faster; Lazy decays slower
- Bladder: None
- Energy: Lazy decays faster; Active decays slower
- Hygiene: Sloppy decays faster; Neat decays slower
- Fun: Playful decays faster; Serious decays slower
- Social: Outgoing decays faster; Shy decays slower
- Comfort: Lazy decays faster; Active decays slower

In each case, a neutral Sim (5 points) decays at the standard rate, while those above and below her decay faster or slower. The farther from neutral, the greater the effect.

Teens must spend far more time doing Fun things because of their faster decay rate.

For example, a teen Sim with Playful/Serious 5 loses 170 Fun per day. With Playful/Serious of 0, he loses more slowly (120 per day). Playful/Serious of 7 loses faster (190 per day), but Playful/Serious 10 loses even faster (220 per day).

> **note**
>
> Decay in each Need is different for each age group, but the Personality-based patterns are constant. In other words, Playful Sims of all ages decay Fun faster in every age.

Career Affinities

Some Personality traits make a Sim more likely to succeed in certain careers. Each career focuses on three skills that must be developed for the Sim to advance. If a Sim's Personality allows her to build those skills more easily, she'll advance more quickly in any career that requires the skill.

A Sim with extreme scores in one or more of Personality traits has an easier time in these careers:

- Science: Serious, Neat
- Medical: Serious, Neat
- Business: Serious or Playful, Outgoing
- Criminal: Active, Playful
- Athletic: Active, Outgoing
- Culinary: Serious or Playful
- Law Enforcement: Serious, Active, Neat
- Military: Active, Outgoing
- Politics: Serious or Playful, Outgoing
- Slacker: Outgoing, Playful

> **note**
>
> Some careers benefit from conflicting traits (e.g., Culinary has both Serious and Playful). Obviously, a Sim may only be one or the other, so any score other than neutral provides some advantage in the career.
>
> This conflict makes Culinary a difficult career because only one of its three skills can be accelerated (Cooking has no corresponding trait).

Other Effects

Personality impacts many parts of a Sim's life:

- Whether they accept certain social interactions.
- What they do when left to their own devices.
- Whether they clean up after themselves or others.
- Whether special object interactions are available.
- Whether they cheat at games or steal other Sims' garden gnomes.
- How good they are at telling jokes.
- Whether they get in a hot tub in the buff.
- Which Sims they get along with and with which they clash.
- Changing Personality settings dictates how they behave in the Create-A-Sim shop.
- How comfortable they are doing certain interactions and how much time they waste showing you their displeasure.
- What your Sim does when left to their own decisions.
- What things they want to buy when their Mood is low.
- Which Aspiration best suits them.
- Which "universal" Fears your Sim harbors, e.g., fire, Bladder failure, getting Fat.
- Whether they get Fat autonomously.

PERSONALITY TRAITS

A Sim's Personality is the sum of five traits. These traits are expressed in terms of their extremes:

- Neat/Sloppy
- Outgoing/Shy
- Active/Lazy
- Playful/Serious
- Nice/Grouchy

Each trait has 10 settings; zero points represents the "negative" extreme and 10 points represents the "positive." The more toward one extreme or the other a Sim leans, the more often he'll autonomously behave in accordance with that extreme. For example, a Sim with Nice/Grouchy of 8 exhibits sweet and helpful behavior toward other Sims, Nice/Grouchy of 5 will be neutral, and a Sim of Nice/Grouchy 2 will be very surly indeed. The higher or lower the number, the more frequently these behaviors occur.

Grouchy Sims tend more toward Irritate and Attack interactions.

Personality is more than a Sim's autonomous mindset. It also affects which interactions a user-directed Sim will accept.

> ### note
>
> The term "negative" is a bit of a misnomer regarding Personality traits. Being Serious, for example, might be just what you want in your Sim, because she'll tend toward reading, find gregarious Sims insufferable, and learn Logic very quickly. This doesn't cripple her socially in any way; she can make friends and find love too, although perhaps not with extremely Playful Sims.

Assigning Personality points, however, requires choices. Every Sim has only 25 Personality points that can be distributed between these five traits. Unless you construct a perfectly balanced Sim with five points in each trait, you must put one trait in the negative to get another in the positive.

Strategically, this means that you must make decisions about what you want your Sim to be. If you want a social butterfly with Outgoing 10, you may have to make him a total slob or extremely lazy. Understanding the consequences of these choices is what this section is all about.

Neat/Sloppy

- Modify Need Decay: Hygiene (Neat: Slower/ Sloppy: Faster)
- Speeds Skill: Cleaning (Neat)
- Career Tilt (Neat): Medical, Science, Law Enforcement

Neat Sims LOVE to clean!

Neat Sims (6–10) pick up after themselves and others. Sloppy Sims (0–4) rarely put anything away, make messes whenever possible, and don't clean up things left by others.

Neutral Sims (5) show weak tendencies toward both extremes.

- Hygiene decays much faster for Sloppy Sims than for Neat ones, meaning they require more showers/baths to keep their Mood high.
- Neat Sims increase Cleaning skill much faster than Sloppy ones. As such, much of the time a Neat Sim "wastes" cleaning things is offset by his impressive speed at doing it, the Fun he

receives, and further acquisition of skill (cleaning things actually bestows Cleaning skill).

- Because of their acumen at Cleaning skill, Neat Sims advance faster in Law Enforcement, Medical, and Science careers.

- The Sloppier a Sim is, the faster she *creates* messes. For example, a very Sloppy Sim can foul a shower with a few uses, while a Neat Sim's shower won't need cleaning for several uses. They're also messier in the kitchen.

- Neat Sims get Fun from cleaning while Sloppy Sims lose Fun when forced to tidy.

- Sloppy Sims autonomously eat out of the trash and may autonomously eat food that has attracted flies (whereas a Neat Sim would never consider it). This can result in illness but does provide a cheap and quick Hunger satisfaction source (see Chapter 21).

- Neat parents clean a toddler's high chair after the toddler is removed.

- Sloppy children leave toys out of the toy box (and be resistant if directed to put them away) while Neat children autonomously put their toys away.

- Sloppy Sims (Neat/Sloppy <6) with very low Hygiene autonomously give themselves a sponge bath in any sink if a shower or tub isn't available and their Hygiene is low enough.

- Sloppy Sims gobble their food, causing Neat Sims nearby to react.

Outgoing/Shy

- Modify Need Decay: Social (Outgoing: Faster/Shy: Slower)
- Speeds Skill: Charisma (Outgoing)
- Career Tilt (Outgoing): Business, Politics, Athletic, Military, Slacker

Outgoing Sims (6–10) thrive on social interaction; the more other Sims around the better. Shy Sims don't like to attract attention to themselves and are visibly uncomfortable with it even if they actually like the interest. Because, on the other hand, Shy Sims (0–4) require less social interaction, they can spend more time in seclusion, working on skills or fulfilling their Aspirations. Neutral Outgoing/Shy Sims (5) have neither the benefits nor drawbacks of either extreme, which is not a desirable setting for any purpose.

Outgoing Sims aren't uptight about their pixelization.

- Outgoing Sims crave social interaction, so their Social motive decays at an accelerated rate. Shy Sims need less contact and their Social Need decays at a slower rate.

- If a high Outgoing Sim gets into a hot tub, she enters in the pixilated buff.

- Outgoing Sims talk to garden statuary.

- Shy Sims have several special animations when accepting or rejecting some particularly (to them) racy interactions.

- Outgoing Sims who are naked sometimes forget to put their clothes back on, even in the event of a fire.

- If a Sim uses a telescope to spy on an Outgoing neighbor, that neighbor will come over and lecture your Sim.

- Outgoing Sims have more animated conversations.

- If a Chat concerns a Memory, Outgoing Sims are more interested in the subject than Shy Sims.

- Outgoing Sims are more likely to autonomously Brag about their good Memories.

- When dancing solo, Shy Sims dance a bit more reservedly.

- If a fight occurs in a room, a Shy Sim will flee the room.

PRIMA OFFICIAL GAME GUIDE

- An extremely Outgoing male Sim with very low Bladder Need can autonomously relieve himself on a bush (decreases local Environment and Sim's own Hygiene).

Active/Lazy

- Modify Need Decay: Hunger (Active: Faster/ Lazy: Slower), Energy (Lazy: Faster/Active: Slower), Comfort (Lazy: Faster/Active: Slower)
- Speeds Skill: Body (Active)
- Career Tilt (Active): Criminal, Athletic, Law Enforcement, Military

Active Sims (6–10) have the undeniable benefit of needing less sleep and less time sitting, but they require a lot more visits to the feed bag. For the more physical professions, Active Sims build Body skill at a higher rate.

Because their metabolisms run so fast, Active Sims must eat constantly but don't need to sleep as much.

Neutral Sims (5) show weak tendencies toward both extremes.

Lazy Sims (0–4) actually require less food than others but must sit, nap, and sleep more frequently.

- Active Sims can run to any location on a lot; all other Sims can run only if the destination is very far away.
- There's a random chance that a Lazy Sim will turn off her alarm clock, go back to sleep, and miss work.
- Lazy Sims are more likely to autonomously get a snack from the refrigerator when they're already full. This, in turn, results in low Fitness.

- Active Sims tend toward Fun activities and objects that are more physical while Lazy Sims tend toward the sedentary.
- An extremely Lazy male Sim with very low Bladder Need can autonomously relieve himself on a bush (decreases local Environment and Sim's own Hygiene).

Playful/Serious

- Modify Need Decay: Fun (Playful: Faster/ Serious: Slower)
- Speeds Skill: Creativity (Playful), Logic (Serious)
- Career Tilt (Serious): Science, Medical, Law Enforcement, Business, Politics, Culinary
- Career Tilt (Playful): Criminal, Slacker, Business, Politics, Culinary

Double the juggling, double the Fun.

Playful Sims (6–10) can find Fun in the oddest places where no other Sim can, but they need a heck of a lot more of it than their Serious counterparts. They are extremely well-suited for creative endeavors.

Neutral Sims (5) show weak tendencies toward both extremes.

Serious Sims (0–4) can go longer between Fun activities and are naturally attracted to quieter, more cerebral activities (reading, playing chess, etc.). Serious is the only "negative" trait that speeds the learning of a skill; Serious Sims are very adept at Logic.

- Fun decays faster for Playful. Serious Sims decay more slowly, requiring only occasional Fun interactions.
- Playful Sims can skip to places rather than simply walking.

◆ Playful Sims have some special fun with the garden gnome.

Nice/Grouchy

◆ Modify Need Decay: None
◆ Speeds Skill: None
◆ Career Tilt: None

Nice Sims (6–10) are very considerate toward the feelings of others, autonomously engaging in social interactions that benefit both parties.

Grouchy Sims (0–4), on the other hand, bring down almost any relationship if left to their own devices. When autonomously interacting, they are drawn to Fight and Irritate interactions that reduce the other Sim's Relationship scores and even Social need. Sometimes Grouchy Sims even derive a positive benefit (Social, Relationship, or Fun) from being mean to others.

Nice/Grouchy is also a major factor in the acceptance of many social interactions. Which way a Sim tilts can change the difficulty of relationship building, but not fatally so.

Strategically, Nice/Grouchy is not a factor in either skills or career, so it's a theoretically expendable trait. That doesn't, however, mean that it should be set to zero; Grouchy Sims can do a lot of damage to hard-won relationships. Unless a surly Sim is what you want, never set Nice/Grouchy below 5.

◆ Grouchy are more likely than Nice to accept an Argue interaction. They receive a boost to Social from an argument while Nice Sims get a small loss.

◆ Grouchy Sims are more likely to autonomously spy on a neighbor when using a telescope.

◆ Grouchy Sims watching other Sims compete will more likely taunt the contestants, while a Nice Sim will cheer.

◆ Grouchy Sims walking by your house may steal your garden gnome. If they're really Grouchy, they'll do it even if your Sim is standing nearby.

◆ Grouchy Sims walking by your property may kick over your garbage can.

Zodiac Signs

Every Sim sports one of the 12 astrological signs. Each star sign represents a set of Personality settings that approximate the real-world astrological character of the sign.

> **note**
>
> A Sim's astrological sign has nothing to do with his birthday, but is rather a reflection of his Personality settings.
>
> Hence twins may have different signs despite their identical birthdates.

> **note**
>
> A Sim's Zodiac sign can be set in panel 6 in Create-A-Sim and viewed in-game in the Simology panel under Personality (above the Personality bars). Pointing to the Zodiac symbol offers a description of the Sim's overall Personality.

As you change each Personality trait, the Sim's sign changes to show into which astrological profile she fits. It also works the other way; change the sign and all Personality traits change to the settings below:

In Create-A-Sim, click on a Zodiac sign to bring up a Personality preset or fiddle with the traits and see what star sign you end up with.

Personality Presets by Zodiac Sign

Zodiac Sign	Neat	Outgoing	Active	Playful	Nice
Aries	5	8	6	3	3
Taurus	5	5	3	8	4
Gemini	4	7	8	3	3
Cancer	6	3	6	4	6
Leo	4	10	4	4	3
Virgo	9	2	6	3	5
Libra	2	8	2	6	7
Scorpio	6	5	8	3	3
Sagittarius	2	3	9	7	4
Capricorn	7	4	1	8	5
Aquarius	4	4	4	7	6
Pisces	5	3	7	3	7

These values are the default for each sign but they aren't precise; you can tweak them up to a point without changing the sign. Extreme changes eventually cause the sign to shift.

Sims may befriend and fall in love with anyone but, due to inherent differences in Personality types, some combinations are harder or easier than others. Keep the affinities/aversions below in mind to discover who's a more likely friend and who will pose an interesting challenge.

Zodiac Sign Compatibility

Zodiac Sign	Attracted to	Repelled by
Aries	Gemini/Taurus	Cancer/Libra
Taurus	Aries/Libra	Virgo/Cancer
Gemini	Pisces/Virgo	Capricorn/Aries
Cancer	Taurus/Scorpio	Gemini/Aries
Leo	Sagittarius/Cancer	Capricorn/Gemini
Virgo	Aquarius/Sagittarius	Leo/Taurus
Libra	Virgo/Cancer	Pieces/Scorpio
Scorpio	Pieces/Leo	Libra/Aquarius
Sagittarius	Pisces/Capricorn	Libra/Scorpio
Capricorn	Aquarius/Taurus	Leo/Gemini
Aquarius	Capricorn/Sagittarius	Scorpio/Virgo
Pisces	Scorpio/Gemini	Leo/Aries

Changing Personality

Personality can be changed, but it's difficult without a solid multi-generational family. An older blood-related Sim may use an "Encourage" social interaction on a younger Sim to add or subtract points to the younger Sim's Personality traits.

note

Being older means being in a higher age stage. It does not refer to how long the Sim has been alive. Thus, an adult one day away from becoming an elder cannot Encourage another adult no matter how much "younger" the other adult is.

Encourage socials and alter a younger Sim's Personality traits. The older and more extreme in a trait the encouraging Sim is, the faster the change occurs.

note

Encourage is not available if the younger Sim is already at 10 for a positive trait or 0 for a negative trait.

Unlike Interests, below, altering one Person-ality trait does not change another; a heavily Encouraged Sim could eventually have 10 points in every trait.

To perform an Encourage social, the older Sim must have a 7 or higher (if the Encourage trait is positive) or 3 or lower (if it's negative). The other Sim can accept or reject the interaction based on Mood and Relationship.

Depending on what trait you wish to Encourage, the older Sim will:

◆ Niceness: Friendly hug

◆ Grouchiness: Annoy

◆ Seriousness: Nag

◆ Playfulness: Red hands

◆ Neatness: Preen

◆ Sloppiness: Belch

◆ Activeness: Squats and stretches

◆ Laziness: Sit

◆ Outgoingness: Joke

◆ Shyness: Make diary entry

The power of the influence depends on many things:

◆ Age Difference: The greater the age gap between the Sims, the stronger the effect. Thus, an elder can more effectively Encourage a teen than an adult can.

◆ Daily Relationship: The greater the Daily Relationship, the more influence Encouragement will have.

◆ Strength of Personality: The higher or lower an older Sim is in a trait, the more effective her Encouragement. A Playful/Serious 10 Sim has more impact Encouraging Playfulness than a Playful/Serious 7.

With the influence at maximum strength (an elder with 10 in the chosen Personality trait and Daily Relationship 100 Encouraging a child), a Sim gains a full Personality point in about two interactions. An average situation requires three or four interactions while a weak one may need as many as five.

INTERESTS

Upon either creation or birth, Sims are randomly assigned a slate of "Interests" that guide them in conversation. There are 18 possible Interests:

◆ Animals   ◆ Food   ◆ Sci-Fi

◆ Crime   ◆ Health   ◆ Sports

◆ Culture   ◆ Money   ◆ Toys

◆ Entertainment   ◆ Paranormal   ◆ Travel

◆ Environment   ◆ Politics   ◆ Weather

◆ Fashion   ◆ School   ◆ Work

Interests are displayed in the second of the three Simology panels.

Upon creation, Interest points are randomly distributed among the 18 Interests. An Interest can be assigned 0–10 points; 0 indicates no interest, 5 moderate interest, and 10 intense interest.

Interest in Conversation

The number of points in an Interest dictates how likely the topic is to arise in a Chat initiated by your Sim. The choice of topic in a given conversation is random, but the higher an Interest's level, the more likely it is to be picked.

When your Sim's on the receiving end of a conversation, Interest level in the other Sim's chosen topic determines how likely your Sim is to continue the conversation (if Interest is high) or end it (Interest low).

Interests drive Chat interactions as displayed in the conversation icons.

tip

Determining Interests doesn't have to be a guessing game. Unless the other Sim is a Townie (an exclusively computer-controlled Sim who doesn't reside on any neighborhood lot) or an NPC (i.e. a maid, gardener, etc. whose Interests and Personality are randomly generated), you can enter a Sim's lot, check out his Interests, and switch back to the Sim you want to control. When the other Sim comes calling, you'll know what he likes to talk about.

If a topic is clearly not going over well (the other Sim is reacting negatively), change the topic by clicking on your own Sim and choosing Change Topic. At the first opportunity, your Sim introduces a new topic for the other Sim to accept or reject.

Click on the controlled Sim to change her topic at the next conversational switch.

The key strategy in conversation is determining what another Sim's Interests are. This is done by a process of trial-and-error; several conversations reveal which topics appeal and which do not. Then, in all future conversations with that Sim, use Change Topic to force your Sim to discuss an Interest the other Sim is known to like.

note

Micromanaging conversations between Sims of divergent Interests requires more supervision than those between more like-minded Sims. It might be wise, then, to build major relationships only with Sims whose Interests are similar to your Sim's; this permits longer and better conversations with no intervention from you.

If, however, a meeting of differing minds is what you want, you can always try changing your or the other Sim's levels of Interest in a given topic.

Changing Interests

Just because you can't set Interests doesn't mean they can't be changed. There are, in fact, two ways to alter Interest levels: Magazines and the Share Interests interaction.

Keep in mind, though, that raising one Interest causes another randomly chosen Interest to drop.

Magazines

Change Interests most easily by purchasing and reading magazines. Spending enough time reading the correct publications increases your Sim's Interest level in that topic. Because, however, the number of Interest points is finite, adding an Interest point in one topic decreases Interest level in another randomly chosen topic.

Magazines are available at most Community Lots.

The Share Interests interaction is an alternative to Chatting that affects the other Sim's Interest levels.

Magazines are available from Magazine Racks in a neighborhood's Community Lots. Click on the Magazine Rack, choose Buy, and select the magazine that corresponds to the Interest you desire to change:

◆ The Superstar Report: Entertainment/ Fashion/Sports

◆ Beyond Belief: Sci-Fi/Paranormal/Health

◆ Young Sim Magazine: Toys/Animals/School

◆ Rat Race: Work/Money/Crime

◆ Highbrow Review: Politics/Culture/Environment

◆ Mode:Live: Food/Travel/Weather

Sims automatically bring magazines back from Community Lots and deposit them as useable objects in their own home. Any Sim in the house may then use the magazine to affect her Interest levels by clicking on the magazine and choosing which of the three topics you'd like to change. After reading for several minutes, the Sim learns enough to add to her Interest in the topic.

Talk > Share Interests

Reading magazines changes your Sim's Interests, but the Share Interests interaction can be used to change other Sim.

> **note**
>
> For details on this interaction, see Chapter 24.

If the interaction is accepted, your Sim chooses a topic of high Interest to himself, and a lengthy conversation begins. At the end, the other Sim receives a one-point increase in her Interest in that topic (and a likewise reduction in one other).

> **note**
>
> If you later enter the other Sim's lot, you'll find her Interest permanently changed by the Share Interests interaction.

FITNESS

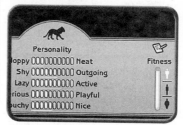

Fitness level is accessible on the Personality panel or just by looking at your Sim.

Every child, teen, adult, and elder Sim has one of three Fitness levels:

◆ Fit   ◆ Neutral   ◆ Fat

Every new Sim is generated as Neutral unless you specified Fat in the Create-A-Sim process. You cannot create a Fit Sim; the Fit state can only be earned in-game by working out.

> **note**
>
> A Sim created as Fat can be trimmed up into a Fit Sim (as can a Sim who achieved his girth the longer way) with lots of exercise.

A Sim can become less or more Fit depending on their actions.

Losing Fitness

Fitness is reduced by consuming any Hunger satisfying thing (food, drinks, coffee, dessert, etc.) when the Hunger Need is already *completely satisfied*.

Every consumable is assigned "Fitness points" that subtract from the Sim's current Fitness. Whenever a Sim consumes something on an already "full stomach," these points are deducted from Fitness. If Fitness falls below the threshold for the next state (from Fit to Neutral or Neutral to Fat), the Sim's appearance visibly changes to show the drop in Fitness.

Generally, your Sim only eats or drinks when her Hunger Need is low, but overeating can occur autonomously. Active Sims are vaguely tempted to get a snack from the refrigerator when they're fully satisfied, but Lazy Sims hear the call of the cookie even more. This is another important reason why Lazy Sims require a bit more supervision than Active ones.

Sims in Aspirational distress (Aspiration score below zero but above the failure line) autonomously overeat as a result of their low Aspiration score. Unhappy and Fat is no way to go through life.

Gaining Fitness

Fitness is gained by exercising. Specifically this means:

- Work out by clicking on the TV (teens, adults, and elders)
- Use the weight bench (teens, adults, and elders)

- Swimming in pools (children, teens, adults, and elders)
- Play Tag or Play Cops and Robbers (children)

Too Fat? Get on the weight bench.

Each of these activities adds points to Fitness. When the Sim amasses enough points to move into the next stage of Fitness, her appearance visibly changes.

MEMORIES

Memories are a record of major events in a Sim's life. Whenever one of these big moments happen, a Memory is added to the Memories panel to show what the Memory is, which other Sims were involved, and whether the Memory was positive or negative.

Memories are, however, more than a historical chronicle. Memories can be witnessed by other Sims, talked about in conversation, and passed to other Sims who will, in turn, discuss them. Sometimes, these discussions aren't pleasant for the Sim who holds the Memory.

Memories are revealed in the Memories panel under Simology.

Positive vs. Negative

Memories are either positive or negative. A positive Memory sports a green background and a negative one shows a red background.

Certain interactions use only one kind or the other. If a Sim Brags, for example, he'll only choose one of his good Memories; no one touts his failures. Likewise, Gossip only uses bad Memories (about Sims not part of the conversation).

Memory Strength and Decay

Memories come with a strength; the more significant the Memory, the greater the strength. Strong Memories are more likely to be discussed and stay with your Sim for a longer time, extending their lives as conversational topics.

> **note**
>
> Memories that have decayed to zero still appear in the Memories panel, but they won't ever come up in conversation again.

Over a Memory's life-span, its strength decays until it reaches zero. The length of time this process takes depends on the Memory's strength; weak Memories disappear quickly while strong ones persist for some time.

Power Memories

Power Memories arise from the accomplishment of so-called Power Wants and Fears (see Chapter 21). Like the Power Wants and Fears, they are highlighted by a starburst on their icon's background.

These Memories are special because they're extremely strong, have very long life-spans, and never decay completely to zero. Thus, long after the event, a Power Memory arising from it can still be talked about (though very infrequently).

Recent Memories

Strong recent Memories, both positive and negative, affect your Sim's behavior for a while.

You may notice him thinking about the event (flashing its icon in a thought bubble). If the Memory is pleasant, he'll smile or giggle. If it's unpleasant, he'll frown or (if the Memory is very bad) stop and cry.

After a break-in, this Sim is an emotional wreck over the Memory.

> **note**
>
> Autonomous crying over a bad Memory is a small time waste. Guard against bad events for efficiency's sake if nothing else.

Memories vs. Memory Markers

An important distinction must be made between Memories and Memory Markers.

Memories are only granted to Sims who participated in a significant event or, in rare instances, who are important to the event (i.e. a grandmother will get a Memory of her granddaughter's wedding even if she wasn't present). Only Memories appear in the Memory panel.

> **note**
>
> Memory Markers can trigger jealousy. If a third party Sim witnesses another Sim cheating on his significant other, she gets a Memory Marker for it.
>
> If, by happenstance, the third-party Sim talks about the Memory Marker with the cheating Sim's love, the cheated on Sim will react as if she witnessed the betrayal (see "Cheating and Jealousy," Chapter 25).

Memory Markers don't appear visibly in the game but are passed between Sims when a Memory is either witnessed or spoken about. To witness a Memory, an uninvolved Sim must be in close proximity to the event.

Social interactions are the most common vehicles for passing Markers. If the Sim who directly had the Memory speaks about it to another Sim, that Sim gains a Marker for that Memory.

The Marker allows the Sim to use the Memory of another Sim as a conversational topic with other Sims. The third Sim would then have the Marker that he could then pass or use with the original Sim.

Like the Memories that give rise to them, Markers have a strength and a duration, but they're only a percentage of the original Memory. Most Markers eventually diminish and drop out as conversational topics but Markers for Power Memories endure (albeit minimally) forever.

Memories and Social Interactions

Memories, like Interests, can be conversational topics or the trigger for several autonomous interactions. When a Sim accepts a social interaction that involves a Memory, she gets the Marker for any Memory being discussed.

> **note**
>
> Full details on these interactions can be found in Chapter 24.

Each of these interactions rely on a Memory or Marker:

♦ Gossip: Negative Markers are discussed negatively between two Sims about the Sim who has the Memory.

♦ Tell Secret: Same as Gossip but between children.

♦ Tease: Negative Markers are discussed negatively with the Sim who holds the original Memory.

♦ Console: Negative Markers are discussed positively with the Sim who holds the original Memory.

♦ Congratulate: Positive Markers are discussed positively with the Sim who has the original Memory.

♦ Talk: Positive or negative Memories or Markers are used as conversational topics similarly to Interests. The details of this system are discussed in Chapter 24.

♦ Brag: Positive Memories are discussed in a positive way by the Sim who holds the Memory to another Sim. If the other Sim doesn't already have the Marker for that Memory, she gets it as a result of the Brag.

Choosing Memories and Markers

Memories are chosen for interaction based on their strength. A Sim always randomly chooses between her top three strongest Memories when discussing her own Memories. Therefore, recent strong Memories arise more often.

With Markers, the Sim's Lifetime Relationship with the Memory's original owner influences the decision:

♦ Negative Interactions: The more negative the Lifetime Relationship, the more likely the Marker is to be used.

♦ Positive Interactions: The more positive the Lifetime Relationship, the more likely the Marker is to be used.

♦ Neutral Interactions (i.e. Talk): If the Marker refers to a negative Memory, it's more likely to arise if there's a negative Lifetime Relationship with the owner of the Memory. If, on the other hand, it's positive, the converse is true.

Memories and Dreams

Memories can color or haunt a Sim's dreams if they're strong enough. You see the icon pop up while your Sim is asleep if the Memory has infiltrated her dream world.

Part 4

It's A Lot Like Life

The chapters in this part open up the clockwork that makes *The Sims 2* go. All the game's major systems and subjects are described here in ways that everyone can use for strategic advantage and to understand why things happen the way they do.

Grasping this information pays dividends again and again, and gives a profound glimpse into the richness and complexity of the world you're entering. It also offers the knowledge required to unleash your creative energies and play the game in a way no one ever could have predicted.

Chapter 19

The Six Ages of Sims: Playing the Generation Game

Sims don't live forever.

Much in this book is useful, some of it a bit obtuse, but useful and powerful nevertheless. None of it, however, is as fundamentally important as this simple truth that bears repeating: Sims don't live forever.

Why is this important? Because Sims only have so much time to do what they (or you) want to do with their lives. If they want to conquer their career, they won't have time for much else in their adult lives. Balancing career and family becomes a greater challenge because tending to one costs a finite and inconceivably valuable currency: time.

The realization of the value of time profoundly changes the way *The Sims 2* is played. Every phase of life must, thus, be maximized to offer the richest and most numerous opportunities. The Sim that lives most efficiently is the one who'll accomplish all his goals and leave his offspring the most formidably equipped to conquer their world.

To do this, you must understand the six ages of Sims and how to milk them for everything they're worth.

You must also learn the rhythms and demands of the multigenerational game and how the actions and successes (or failures) of one generation affect the next. This chapter explains it all and whets the appetite for the chapters that follow.

LIVING THROUGH THE AGES

Sims live through six ages, spending a number of days in each stage:

- Babies: 3 days
- Toddlers: 4 days
- Children: 8 days
- Teens: 15 days
- Adults: 29 days
- Elders: 9 to 31 days

Elder's time is uncertain due to the randomness of death and the life-extending powers of Aspirational success. Thus, in the end, deft use of time in younger ages earns the most valuable thing of all: more time.

Age Transitions

The transition from one age to the next is a very important strategic opportunity. Know how they work and they'll work for you.

Two days before the scheduled end of a Sim's current age, the impending birthday is announced. From this point on, the Sim can grow up, or "age transition," any time (up to two days early) in two or three ways:

- Do the Grow Up self-interaction (for children, teens, and adults).
- Do the Blow Out Candles interaction on a birthday cake object.
- Wait until 7 p.m. on the age transition day when the transition happens automatically.

Adult (Becomes an Elder in 20 days)

Keep track of impending age transitions with the Age Meter below the active Sim's portrait.

Which way you choose can impact how "well" the Sim grows up which, in turn, dictates what kind of Memory the Sim will have. The Memory and the quality of the birthday can fulfill one or more Wants and Fears of the Sim and those who love her.

When to Age Transition

Generally, Sims should milk as much time out of their ages as possible, transitioning only on the scheduled day. There are, however, good reasons to do it sooner.

Adam's birthday is only a day away. It seems like only yesterday that the little bundle of joy came into this world. Oh, how quickly they grow up.

Babies should transition as soon as possible.

Very young Sims can be a challenge to take care of, so you may want to transition them into more self-sufficient children at the earliest opportunity. With babies this is almost always fine because there isn't much babies can do with their time until they're toddlers.

Once toddlerhood is reached, however, they have some very important things to learn that can affect their future careers and their lifelong Aspiration scores. Reaching these goals takes time and may be difficult to achieve in the mere four days of the toddler age.

If a Sim Wants to grow up well but is in danger of falling out of positive Aspiration score, consider age transitioning as soon as possible.

Still, there is often a good reason to advance a birthday. When Sims near an age transition, they may either Want or Fear the change depending on their Aspiration Scores and if this Want/Fear is rather high scoring. If, for example, Sims have positive but low Aspiration scores two days shy of their birthday, it might be a good strategy to age transition before the score has a chance to decay and the Want changes to a Fear.

By advancing a birthday, however, your Sim is losing those days forever; they aren't tacked onto the next age. You must decide if any benefits of aging early are worth the sacrifice.

Extending Age Transition

More often, an age needs to be longer, not shorter. For this, there's the Elixir of Life Aspiration reward object (see Chapter 21). If used successfully, it delays an age transition by three days per dosage with a maximum of five doses. If it fails, however, it advances the big moment by three days.

If you need the time, however, to raise Aspiration score or go further in a career, using this magic liquid might be just the ticket.

tip

Using the Elixir of Life to buy time to raise Aspiration score is only smart if you need the time to get from Gold to Platinum. If a Sim takes the potion with Green Aspiration score, there's a 50-50 chance of advancing three days. Using the Elixir any lower than Green is a huge gamble; it's nearly guaranteed to fail.

Babies

- Age Span: 3 Days
- Goals: None
- Needs: Hunger, Bladder, Energy, Fun, Social, Hygiene
- Most Important Need(s): Social, Hunger because the Social Worker will take a baby away if these go into failure
- Least Important Need(s): Bladder, Fun

Babies consume a lot of time and can't be directed. Don't worry; they'll be toddlers soon.

Babies are the shortest and most limited age. They aren't controllable and their Needs can't be viewed. Their Mood is, however, visible in the background color of their portrait along the left edge of the screen. The only Needs they can satisfy for themselves are Energy and Bladder; nodding off on the floor if no one places them in the crib and going to the bathroom in their diaper.

> **note**
>
> **Though it may feel odd, it's ok to leave babies on the floor. No one will step on them and it gives them a chance to take in the world around them.**

Babies require a crib for sleeping (unless you want them snoozing on the cold ground) but no other mandatory objects. A changing table satisfies more Hygiene than a simple diaper change and it also gives the baby Comfort.

Feed babies by getting a bottle from the refrigerator.

The changing table makes diaper changes (mandatory with babies) much more efficient.

Babies need only be babies for a full day, after which they get notice of an upcoming birthday. Because their age span is so short, they alone receive only one day's notice of the impending birthday.

There's little reason to delay the transition from baby to toddler. Because, however, babies can't be directed, the only way to grow up early is to use the birthday cake object; a teen/adult/elder Sim must interact with the cake for the baby.

Other baby characteristics:

◆ Babies lack Environment and Comfort Needs.

◆ Hygiene primarily comes from diaper changes. Changes via changing table give extra Hygiene plus Comfort.

◆ Babies may be bathed in a sink for full Hygiene satisfaction.

◆ Bladder can't be tended to but simply fails regularly into the diaper. Dirty diaper then becomes a Hygiene issue but Bladder will be fully satisfied.

◆ When babies are in Need distress, they cry with increasing intensity and frequency.

◆ Babies need to sleep about twice a day.

◆ Babies need diaper changes about three times a day.

◆ If Social or Hunger fail, the Social Worker will permanently remove the baby and all other babies, toddlers, and children from the household.

◆ Babies don't get sick.

    ◆ Babies are fireproof and can't die by any cause.

Toddlers

◆ Age Span: 4 Days

◆ Goals: Learn to Talk, Learn to Walk, Potty Train, Begin skill learning (Charisma, Logic, and Creativity only), build relationships with family members, and get Aspiration score as high as possible for gameplay advantages

◆ Needs: Hunger, Bladder, Energy, Fun, Social, Hygiene

◆ Most Important Need(s): Social, Hunger

◆ Least Important Need(s): Hygiene, Bladder

The toddler high chair offers Comfort while eating and enables serving toddler mush.

The toddler age is the first time newly born Sims can be player-controlled. They are mobile and primitively able to express themselves and can be directed into limited interactions. Their Motives, Mood, skills, relationships, Simology, Aspiration scores (Grow Up), and Wants and Needs can all be viewed.

There are several things, however, that toddlers can't do. They can't climb stairs, so they need to be carried. They can't feed themselves, though they will drink from a bottle left on the floor, even if it's spoiled.

It's important for toddlers and their families to tend to the tot's education in these three skills, though they're not essential to function in life (all children begin their phase of life knowing how to talk, walk, and use the toilet). Generally, they offer several opportunities for both the toddlers and those around them to satisfy several valuable Wants. For grown-ups, these opportunities help keep them successful in their Aspiration (even if they're not Family Aspiration Sims) and let them spend less time caring for the toddler's more basic Needs (no more diapers). For the toddlers, having all three skills virtually guarantees them a strong Aspiration score when they transitions to childhood, allowing them to want, rather than fear, growing up.

Get to work on skills now, and this toddler will be a teaching machine during the elder years.

In addition to the three toddler skills, toddlers can develop Charisma, Creativity, and Logic through use of skill training toys. A few skill points now means less time spent skill building when time is more precious.

> **note**
>
> Starting concerted skill building as a toddler helps Sims max out several skills. This level of skill mastery will make them greater skill teachers to the generations that follow.

> **tip**
>
> Children are limited in Charisma building because they can't use mirrors. They can build Charisma only if someone in the house has a Business or Politics career reward objects. For a Sim to have a head start in that skill, focus on it in the toddler days.

Equip the home with a potty chair and teach them to use it.

A crib is needed for sleeping and a changing table enhances Hygiene derived from diaper changes. A high chair enables toddlers to eat toddler mush instead of just bottles. A potty chair is required for potty training and the toddler will use it autonomously once trained.

A few other features to ponder:

♦ Toddlers need to sleep twice per day.

♦ Toddlers who haven't been potty trained need changing about two times per day.

♦ When a meal is served from the kitchen, a bowl of toddler mush is served to any toddler sitting in a high chair.

♦ Toddlers lack Environment and Comfort Needs.

◆ Hygiene primarily comes from diaper changes. Changes via changing table give extra Hygiene.

◆ Toddlers may be bathed in bathtub or shower tub for extra Hygiene satisfaction.

◆ Bladder, when the toddler's not potty trained, can't be tended to but simply fails regularly into the diaper. The dirty diaper then becomes a Hygiene issue and Bladder is fully satisfied.

◆ When toddlers are in Need distress, they, like older Sims, show thought balloons but also indicate the degree of their distress by progressively crying, whining, and tantruming.

◆ If Social or Hunger fail, the Social Worker will permanently remove toddlers and all other babies, toddlers, and children from the household.

◆ A toddler lagging in her Aspiration will exhibit Immaturity behaviors (e.g. playing in the toilet or in puddles, and throwing tantrums).

◆ Toddlers don't earn nor can they use Aspiration reward objects. They are, however, collecting Reward points with every Want fulfilled and can use these points when they become a teen.

◆ Though toddlers can fulfill their own Needs, they can get others to do it for them by using Ask For interactions (either autonomously or by direction). A toddler can ask to be fed, diaper changed, read to, or given attention.

◆ Toddlers are fireproof and can't die from any cause.

Children

◆ Age Span: 8 Days

◆ Goals: Learn to Study, get good grades, make friends, build skills, and get Aspiration as high as possible for gameplay advantages

◆ Needs: Hunger, Bladder, Energy, Fun, Social, Hygiene, Comfort

◆ Most Important Need(s): Social, Hunger, Fun

◆ Least Important Need(s): Comfort, Bladder

Getting on the school bus is the Sim child's job. Attendance is just as important (if not more so) for grades than for job performance.

Childhood is marked primarily by the Sim's entering school. Five days a week, Sims must begin the routine of getting up, maximizing their Needs and getting to the curb on time. Poor performance in this new task means low Aspiration score and potential removal by the Social Worker.

Childhood is also the first phase with real self-sufficiency. Children can tend to all their own Needs, though their access to food is somewhat limited: they may get a snack from the refrigerator, order pizza, or make a muffin in the toy oven but are at the mercy of older Sims for truly satisfying meals.

Skills become even more important, though still optional, during childhood. Children can train in all skills but may get Charisma only from the two Charisma-training career reward objects (from the Business and Politics career tracks). Cooking is problematic because children can't use kitchen appliances, but they can study Cooking from the bookshelf or use the toy oven for more hands-on learning.

Getting help with homework teaches children to study, halving the time it takes to do homework.

More important than these basic skills is one that's more directly relevant to a child's daily life: learning to study. Having an older Sim help him or her with his or her homework teaches him or her to study. Once children learns this skill, they can do homework alone much faster, leaving more time for other things.

Children may also receive help in life being taught a skill on a career reward object by a Sim with higher skill. They may also have their Personality traits altered by being Encouraged by older Sims. The older the Sims and more extreme their Personalities, the faster change can be made.

Children are somewhat limited in their social interactions. In many cases (such as Attack), they can do the same interactions as older Sims but only with other children.

Friends are very important to children. They can befriend Sims of their age or older but may invite only other children or non-household blood relatives via the phone. On the computer, children may chat only with other children.

Children can use most objects adults can use, but having toys around the house is always a plus.

Lots of toys give children more options for autonomous Fun.

Other features of childhood:

◆ Children with very bad grades will be taken away by the Social Worker.

◆ Children need to sleep and bathe once per day and must eat two or three times per day (including the meal they theoretically consume at school).

◆ Children have no Environment Need.

◆ Children may use bathtubs or showers for Hygiene satisfaction.

◆ When children are in Need distress, they show thought balloons.

◆ If Social or Hunger fail, the Social Worker will permanently remove the child and all other babies, toddlers, and children from the household.

◆ Children lagging in their Aspiration will exhibit Immaturity behaviors.

◆ Children don't earn nor can they use Aspiration reward objects. They are, however, collecting Reward points with every Want fulfilled and can use these points when they become a teen.

◆ Children can't clean or repair but can learn both Cleaning and Mechanical from the bookshelf.

◆ Children can't use fireplaces, bars, hot tubs, or coffee/espresso machines and cannot use some career reward objects independently.

◆ Children can hire services and order pizza and groceries for the household.

◆ Children can die, though only from disease, drowning, or fire. Rather than starving to death, children in Hunger failure are taken away by the Social Worker.

Teens

◆ Age Span: 15 Days

◆ Goals: Depend on Aspiration, get a head start in career track, do well in school, get Aspiration as high as possible for gameplay advantages

◆ Needs: All

◆ Most Important Need(s): Social, Hunger, Fun

◆ Least Important Need(s): Energy, Comfort

Industrious teens can get an after-school job to help with family finances and get a leg up in an adult career.

Teenage days are the time to begin preparing for adult life but also to have a whole lot of fun.

Every adult career track has a three-level teen career track. Reaching level 3 in these tracks allows a teen to begin his adult career at level 2. Getting into private school allows him to skip the first level of any teen career and begin at level 2.

Teens of any Aspiration want to get a taste of amore.

Romance becomes important for the first time. Teens can develop Crushes (Daily Relationship score 70) and enter committed relationships (Go Steady: Have a Crush and acceptance of the Propose interaction) and fall in Love (Lifetime 70). Teens may engage in romance only with other teens.

Teens become more responsible and can fully care for babies and toddlers, teach basic toddler skills, and encourage children in Personality traits. They can teach children to study and can help with homework.

School for teens is shorter than for children, leaving them time for afternoon jobs.

- Teens with bad grades must quit their jobs and can't get new ones until grades improve.
- Teens need to sleep and bathe once per day and must eat three times per day (including the meal they theoretically consume at school).
- Teens may use bathtubs or showers for Hygiene satisfaction.
- When teens are in Need distress, they display and experience it identically to adults and elders.
- Teens lagging in their Aspirations will exhibit Immaturity behaviors despite (unlike children and toddlers) having specific Aspirations.
- Teens can learn all skills from all skill objects.
- Teens can use all objects just as adults and elders.
- Teen romantic interactions are limited to flirts, kisses, and hugs.

- Teens with low Daily and Lifetime Relationships with *all* household Sims will run away. If not found, they'll come back the day before their transition to adult.
- Teens can ask for permission to go out or can sneak out for a night in the big city with a friend.
- Teen career chance cards feature a choice that will either grant a reward or impose a penalty.
- Teens can die of anything except, of course, old age.

Adults

- Age Span: 29 Days
- Goals: Depend on Aspiration, succeed in career track, get Aspiration score as high as possible for gameplay advantages and age transition to elder
- Needs: All
- Most Important Need(s): Hunger
- Least Important Need(s): Fun

The adult age is, by and large, the classic *The Sims* gameplay. Sims must go to work in a good Mood, develop skills to help in job promotion and daily living, make friends, fall in love, perhaps get married/joined and have children.

Adult motives are mostly equal in weight but they do lose Hygiene faster than any other group and Hunger second only to teens.

The adult career tracks have 10 levels and require coming to work in a good Mood, development in three skills, and a number of household friends. If the adults were in level 3 of a teen career before they grew up, they'll start in the adult version of the same career track at level 2.

The increased demand of a career means adults must spend more time skill building.

Career is important, but adults' primary occupation should be fulfilling their Wants. High Aspiration is the ticket to productivity and longevity.

A Sim's Aspiration score is very important. Many of the things adults do require a good Mood, and very high Aspiration score provides that. More importantly, however, an adult's Aspiration score at the moment he or she becomes an elder affects how long his or her elder age will last. Sub-zero Aspiration score subtracts up to two days and high score can add up to 10 days. The precise timing of this age transition is, therefore pretty important. If he or she is within two days and has very high Aspiration score (Platinum if possible), he or she should consider transitioning early (after the two-day birthday warning) to get the most out of his or her elder years.

The romantic game really gets going in the adult years. Adults can fall in love, cohabitate, get engaged, get married/joined, and have kids or just have unrestrained romantic fun with anyone they meet.

Other features of adult life:

- Adults need to sleep and bathe once per day and must eat three times per day (including the meal they theoretically consume at work).
- Adults may use bathtubs, sinks, or showers for Hygiene satisfaction.
- Adults lagging in their Aspirations exhibit Desperation behaviors in general and specific ones tied to their chosen Aspirations.
- Adults can learn all skills from all skill objects.
- Adults can use all objects that aren't restricted to babies, children, or toddlers.
- Adults can die of anything except, of course, old age.

Elders

- Age Span: 9–31 Days
- Goals: Depend on Aspiration, retire, work on career, enter elder career track to enhance income, encourage traits in and teach skills to younger Sims, collect pension, maximize Aspiration score to increase death benefit for loved ones
- Needs: All
- Most Important Need(s): Comfort, Bladder
- Least Important Need(s): Hunger, Fun

The most important feature of the elder age is that its length is unknown (elders' age is shown, for the first time, in terms of days alive, not days remaining). Elders live 10 days by default but that's altered by two factors:

- A random lifetime increase of 1–10 additional days.
- A bonus based on Aspiration score at elder transition. If bottom Red -2, top Red 0, Green 3, Gold 7, and Platinum 10.

Elder motives are unbalanced with Comfort and Bladder becoming paramount.

Sims are not required to retire when they become elders but they may want to so they are available to help younger family members. Elders can use their elder time to further increase their job level and raise their pension amount when they do retire. Be careful about working full time too far into the elder age; you don't know when the day of reckoning will be. It'd be a shame if a Sim worked too long and died on his or her retirement day.

Being an elder doesn't have to mean a Sim has to stop working.

The elder career tracks are the same as the teen tracks. Elder careers are meant to provide extra income on top of whatever pension the elder received from her adult career. The shorter work schedules permit elders to earn more money and spend more time at home. Their levels in their adult career tracks, however, have no impact on where they start in any elder track (including the one from which they retired).

Elders should continue to work on their Aspirations so those who survive them may be financially better off.

Elder Aspiration score is still important because the score on the day Sims die dictates how much of a death benefit goes to their families and anyone with whom they had a high long-term relationship. Because death by old age is out of your control, the only way to assure large inheritance is to keep the elder's Aspiration score as high as possible after his or her eighth elder day.

Romance doesn't end when a Sim's hair turns gray. Romantically, there's no difference between elders and adults. They can still fall in love with adult or elder Sims, create relationships, get married/ joined, and have more children (elder male with adult female only).

Other characteristics of the golden years:

- Elders need to sleep and bathe once per day and must eat three times per day (including the meal they theoretically consume at work).

- Elders may use bathtubs, sinks, or showers for Hygiene satisfaction.

- Elders take twice the amount of time to satisfy their Bladders than any other age.

- Elders lagging in their Aspirations exhibit Desperation behaviors in general and specific ones tied to their chosen Aspirations.

- Elders can learn all skills from all skill objects.

- Elders can use all objects that aren't restricted to babies, children, or toddlers.

- An elder married/joined couple that was married/joined while they were adults can have a special Anniversary Party.

- Elders have the most impact when encouraging children in their Personality traits.

- Elders can die of anything.

PLAYING THE GENERATION GAME

As suggested above, playing the generational game is about maximizing three things:

1. Life-span   2. Income   3. Influence

Life-span

A Sim's most important asset is time. Even when Sims used to live forever, their every day focus was about living efficiently and economically. Well, now it's still important but matters far more than the day-to-day issues of eating satisfying food or shortening shower times.

What it's about now is what some philosophers say it's about for all of us too: making the most of whatever time is given to us.

Taking the long view of life makes building skills and teaching the youngsters a noble endeavor.

In *The Sims 2*, there's a simple formula for living a long life: Aspiration success. Your choice of a Sim's Aspiration and understanding of what it requires strategically is critical to positioning him or her for this crucial opportunity. Realize his or her Wants, avoid his or her Fears, and guide him or her into a life that makes doing both as smooth as possible.

Income

Despite the loftier visions of Aspiration, the frank need for income and high quality stuff is still hardwired into Sim DNA. Money makes this world go around too, so it's only natural that much effort be expended in the pursuit of economic opportunity.

In *The Sims 2*, however, the goal is more than just having money for the here and now. It's constructing the next generation to be even more successful and become so with less effort.

For most Sims, advancing in a career eases life for everyone in the house, because more money means a better-running home.

Deny it if you want, but a financially comfortable existence makes life much easier.

Influence

Influence is the convergence of both life-span and income, where success in those areas join to determine how much a Sim's efforts in life will assist those who come after him or her.

Much of an elder's time should be spent doing Encourage and Teach interactions with younger Sims.

As noted above, elders are the most powerful influence on younger Sims. They exert the most force on altering a younger Sim's Personality, they have the longest time to develop skills that ease younger Sims' acquisition of those skills, and they have the free time to spend bestowing the benefits of their well-lived life.

That last point is the tricky one. How much free time Sims have (and, therefore, how much influence they can exert) is dependent on (you guessed it): life-span and income. The longer Sims are in the world, the more time they have to influence younger Sims and the more income they've earned, the less time they will need to work during their most influential years.

THE BOTTOM LINE

Playing with an eye toward what your Sims can offer their future progeny affects every aspect of play. With that as the goal, feeding your Sim's Wants can become an obsession that pays off in spades. Getting him or her the skills he or she needs when he or she is young so he or she can enjoy his or her adult and elderhood takes on a thrilling urgency. Propelling him or her up the career ladder becomes more a matter of pride and financial success as a quest for happiness and future freedom.

Look into those red eyes; your Sims do it all for him.

Immerse yourself in the information in the following chapters to grasp the interactions of the game's complex systems. You won't be able to keep it all humming all the time, but it isn't difficult to use this knowledge to your advantage. Internalize it and a world of creative possibilities opens, offering constant new goals to achieve and increasing standards of success against which to measure your Sims' lives.

Chapter 20

Every Sim is driven, at the most fundamental level, by his or her common physical and psychological *Needs*. This chapter examines how those Needs function, how to most efficiently satisfy them, and how to enable Sims to take care of them autonomously.

Taken together, the level of a Sim's Needs dictates his overall *Mood*.

Mood and Needs drive and impact several important elements of the game including:

◆ A Sim's performance at work or grade at school is largely dictated by his Mood when he leaves the lot.

◆ The acceptance of social interactions depends on Mood and Needs.

◆ Mood and Needs affect a Sim's willingness to build skills.

◆ Mood and Needs affect a Sim's willingness to use Fun objects.

◆ Mood and Needs affect a Sim's willingness to Encourage or teach other Sims.

◆ Certain special behaviors and interactions are triggered by the level of individual Needs or overall Mood.

◆ Many Wants and Fears arise based on Mood.

◆ Visitors stay only as long as they can fulfill certain Needs.

◆ Time management depends largely on your Sims' ability to quickly and efficiently tend to their Needs.

This chapter examines each of the eight Needs, how they're satisfied and depleted, and how to deal with them most efficiently. It also discusses the mechanics of the most elaborate elements of the Need game: food preparation.

A NOTE FOR THE SIMS™ 1.0 VETERANS

Those of you who've dealt with Sims before will notice a major difference in how Needs are managed. Sims can actually take care of themselves.

In the original game, dealing with Needs was *the* major part of the game. Because totally self-sufficient Sims don't make for demanding and skillful gameplay, *The Sims 1* Sims would randomly choose between their top four most important tasks. Frequently, this meant they didn't deal with their most pressing Needs, forcing you to intervene on their behalf. Such unwise autonomous choices are only rarely the case in *The Sims 2*.

Now, Sims always autonomously choose their most pressing task. You may not like the order or timing they choose to take care of their Needs, but they *will* do it.

As a result, Sims are much smarter in their autonomous life, allowing you to pay more attention to their more life-altering tasks: their Aspirations (see Chapter 21).

NEEDS DEFINED

Every Sim has eight basic Needs:

◆ Hunger   ◆ Fun

◆ Comfort   ◆ Social

◆ Bladder   ◆ Hygiene

◆ Energy   ◆ Environment

Not all ages have all Needs. The following ages have only the listed Needs:

◆ Babies: Hunger, Energy, Bladder, Hygiene, Fun, Social

◆ Toddlers: Hunger, Energy, Bladder, Hygiene, Fun, Social

◆ Children: Hunger, Bladder, Energy, Hygiene, Social, Fun, Comfort

◆ Teens, Adults, and Elders: Hunger, Bladder, Energy, Hygiene, Social, Fun, Comfort, Environment

The Needs panel shows all the Sim's current Need levels and which direction they're moving. The vertical Mood bar, to the left, displays the Sim's overall Mood.

The Needs Panel

Needs are measured on a scale of -100 (fully depleted) to +100 (fully satisfied). In the middle is zero.

> **note**
>
> The numbers mentioned in this chapter and others that describe the level of a Need or Mood are not seen in the actual game, but should provide a guide to where on the meter the numbers would be. For example, if a Need is at zero, the meter is dead center (50 percent full). If it's at -50, it'll be 25 percent full. If it's at +50, it'll be at 75 percent full.

Needs are shown in the Needs panel. Under each Need is a horizontal bar. When a bar is filled with green, the Need is fully satisfied (+100). When it's in the middle (part green/part yellow), the Need is partially satisfied. When the bar is mostly red and part yellow, the Need is said to be "in distress" (around -60 to -80). When the bar is all red, the Need is in "failure" (-100).

When a Need is changing, arrows appear at one end of the bar or the other. If they're on the right side and green, the Need is being satisfied by whatever the Sim is doing. If they're on the left and red, the Need is decaying. The number of triangles indicates the speed of the change; three triangles mean a fast change and one indicates a gradual change.

MOOD

Sims' overall sense of well-being is reflected in their Mood. Mood, in turn, is the sum effect of all Needs (except Energy and, for babies and toddlers, Bladder).

Mood (without regard for any of the individual Needs) dictates which social interactions will be accepted, whether a Sim will look for a job or develop his skills, how well a Sim is doing at work, and whether he's eligible for a job promotion.

Not all the Needs impact Mood to the same extent. The level of each Need dictates how much it affects overall Mood. If, for example, Hunger is just below fully satisfied, it affects Mood just a little. If it's in the middle, it affects Mood more, but at only a minimal level. Once Hunger gets very low, however, its effect is multiplied several times, growing stronger as the Need creeps lower.

The Mood Meter

Mood is reflected in the crystal, or "Plumbob" over the active Sim's head. Green is good and red is bad.

Mood is shown both by the Mood Meter (on the Needs panel) and in the crystal (called the "Plumbob") that floats above an active Sim's head. Green is good and red is bad.

> **note**
>
> If a Sim is particularly successful in the pursuit of her Aspiration, her Mood Meter and crystal turn shimmering, platinum white. In this state of success (called "Platinum" level) a Sim is in a constant, bulletproof good Mood regardless of her individual Need levels. This frees her up to do many things without having to micro-manage her various Needs. Sims in this state must still attend to these Needs, and low Bodily Needs (Hunger, Energy, or Bladder) still kick them out of some activities, but the level of their overall Mood will not be an impediment to any activity that relies upon it.
>
> See Chapter 21 for more detail on Platinum Aspiration score.

NEED DECAY

All Needs (except Environment) decay over time. If left unsatisfied, they'll eventually drop to their lowest value (-100).

Elders must sit down more often because their Comfort Need decays more quickly. The decay rates of all Needs vary by age.

The speed of this decay dictates how often a Sim has to tend to a Need and is influenced by several factors:

◆ Personality: Many Needs are tied to certain Personality traits that accelerate (if at one extreme) or slow (if at the other) decay. A Sim with 10 Active/Lazy decays Hunger the fastest, 5 is normal, and 0 is slowest.

◆ Age: Each age has its own rate of decay in each of its Needs. Elders, for example, decay Comfort more quickly, meaning they have to take breaks of sitting or relaxing more often. Children and teens decay Fun faster, and must engage in Fun activities more often.

◆ Sleep: Many Needs decay at a slower rate or not at all when a Sim is asleep. Energy, and sometimes Comfort, replenish during sleep.

◆ Objects and Interactions: Many objects or interactions speed the decay of a certain Need or Needs.

note

Each factor of decay (age, Personality, etc.) adds to all others. Thus, a very Active teen decays Hunger faster than any other Sim.

DISTRESS AND FAILURE

When Needs get very low, they enter two stages: distress and then failure.

Distress

For adult Sims, Need distress occurs in two stages: at -60 and -80. At -60, Sims gesture about their dwindling Need and display blue thought bubbles indicating the Need that's getting low.

Adults in Need distress try to alert you to their situation. If it's come to this, there might be a reason the Sim hasn't already satisfied his own Need.

note

Unless you're actively preventing a Sim from fulfilling her Needs and she has access to the objects she requires, you shouldn't normally see Need distress. If you do, the Sim will probably care for the Need without your direction. Sims are a bit smarter about these things now.

If a Need is below -80, the Sim indicates his trouble in jagged red "scream" bubbles, gestures more frequently, and calls for your help.

note

Sims with low Energy, Hunger, Fun (skill only), Comfort (if not seated for the activity), or Bladder (regardless of overall Mood), automatically exit out of or refuse to enter skill or Fun objects, wake from sleep, and refuse to look for a job.

Other Needs don't have this effect, though they bring down overall Mood as they decline. Low Mood causes some of the same kickouts as Energy, Hunger, Fun, Comfort, or Bladder distress.

Babies don't use thought/scream balloons but rather cry to indicate Need distress.

Toddlers and children do use thought/scream balloons to indicate distress but also use different kinds of vocal clues. The level of their crying indicates the degree of the distress:

◆ -60: Cry   ◆ -70: Whine   ◆ -80: Tantrum

> **note**
>
> If the toddler's in someone's arms, she tantrums at all levels of distress.

Failure

Failure occurs when a Need reaches -100. What happens then depends largely on the age of the Sim and the specific Need.

HUNGER

Hunger is the physical need for food and drink.

Depletion

Hunger depletes at a steady rate all day, though it slows when the Sim is asleep. The speed of Hunger depletion depends also on age and Personality.

> **note**
>
> Pregnant Sims suffer accelerated Hunger decay while pregnant. Thus, they need to eat more often. This may be puzzling on the first day of pregnancy before the Sim begins "showing." Increased Hunger decay is a very good sign of being great with child.

Hunger can also be depleted by social interactions. For example, a session of WooHoo or Trying for Baby make a Sim pretty peckish.

Satisfaction

Hunger is satisfied by eating food or drinking liquid. The more "satisfying" a meal, the more Hunger it refills. The more Hunger is fulfilled, the fewer servings Sims need to become full, and the less time they must spend eating.

> **note**
>
> For all the minute details on making the most satisfying food, see "The Food Game" later in this chapter.

Personality

Active Sims lose Hunger faster than other Sims. The more Active they are (more Personality points they have in Active/Lazy), the faster Hunger depletes.

Ages

From fastest to slowest, the rate of Hunger decay by age:

1. Teen   4. Baby
2. Adult   5. Child
3. Toddler   6. Elder

The faster the decay, the more often they must eat.

Mood Impact

Hunger has a low impact on Mood when it's high or even moderate. As the Need descends into negative territory, Hunger's impact on Mood grows quickly. By the time it nears failure, Hunger has more impact on Mood than any other Need.

Thus, a satisfied Sim doesn't give much thought at all to having a full stomach but he cares plenty when it starts to growl.

If Hunger declines too low, Sims either exit or refuse to use skill building or Fun objects even if Mood is still positive.

Distress and Failure

When Hunger gets low, Sims wave and gesture to indicate their condition. Hunger icons appear above their heads.

For any Sim beyond childhood, starvation means death.

If Sims are prevented from eating and Hunger reaches -100, they go into Need failure. In the case of Hunger, this means different things for different ages.

For elders, adults, and teens, it means...death. Dying of Hunger, however, takes a while after the Need reaches rock bottom, but getting your Sim a hearty meal should be job one.

For babies, toddlers, and children, the instant failure occurs, the Social Worker comes and takes away *all* babies, toddlers, and children (even if only one is in Hunger failure).

> **note**
>
> Children, teens, adults, and elders need to eat about three times per day (including the meal they presumably eat while at work), though it can be less if the food they're eating is from a highly skilled cook.

COMFORT

Comfort is the physical need to get off your feet and the emotional need to feel safe, well, and cared for.

Depletion

Comfort is steadily depleted every minute a Sim is not sitting, reclining, or lying down. Like Energy, Comfort is satisfied when the Sim is sleeping anywhere but the floor.

Comfort is also decreased by doing certain activities. For example:

- Sleeping on the floor
- Standing
- Dancing
- Working out (TV or stereo)
- Being electrocuted
- Using exercise equipment

Satisfaction

Comfort is satisfied by sitting, reclining, using comfortable objects, and engaging in comforting activities.

- Sleeping or relaxing a bed
- Doing anything on a sofa
- Sitting or reclining in chairs
- Sitting in high chair
- Using hot tub
- Taking a bath or bubble bath
- Using an expensive toilet
- Looking into a fireplace
- Snuggling with a stuffed animal (Children)
- Stargazing on the grass (not with the telescope)
- Watch clouds

> **note**
>
> The main difference between a shower and a bath is that the bath provides Comfort in addition to Hygiene; hence the higher price of bathtub with the identical Hygiene of a cheaper shower. Even more Comfort can be squeezed out a bathtub if a Sim takes a bubble bath (though Hygiene fills more slowly).

Bubble baths take a long time, but they do wonders for Comfort.

Any Comfort object or interaction has a speed of satisfaction and a cap; the more expensive an object, the faster it satisfies Comfort and the higher it can possibly climb.

> **note**
>
> If a child or teen attends private school instead of public, he returns home with his Comfort higher than when he left (it's the opposite for public school).
>
> Likewise, if a Sim has a desk job rather than a more physical occupation, she'll come home with increased Comfort.

Personality

Lazy Sims lose Comfort faster than other Sims. The Lazier they are (fewer Personality points they have in Active/Lazy), the faster Comfort depletes.

Ages

From fastest to slowest, the rate of Comfort depletion by age:

1. Elder   3. Teen
2. Adult   4. Child

> **note**
>
> Babies and toddlers don't need Comfort.

The faster the decay, the more often Sims must seek Comfort.

Mood Impact

Like Hunger, Comfort has no exaggerated effect on Mood until it gets very low. Unlike Hunger, however, this moment comes only after Comfort drops just shy of halfway into the red zone. As it drops farther and eventually empties, however, its effects are increasingly multiplied.

At its lowest point, Comfort has its greatest influence on Mood, though it's still considerably less than for extremely low Hunger.

Comfort can knock a Sim out of skill building if the Sim is standing for the activity.

Distress and Failure

Sims in Comfort distress wave and signal with a comfy chair thought bubble and look generally uncomfortable (stretching, fighting back pain).

There is no failure state for Comfort, Sims just waste a lot of time telling you how uncomfortable they are. Plus, their Mood will be thoroughly tanked until you allow them to sit.

BLADDER

Bladder is the physical need to use a toilet.

Depletion

Bladder decreases steadily all the time, albeit more slowly when a Sim is sleeping.

Depletion can be accelerated if a Sim eats food or drinks a liquid (especially coffee and espresso).

Satisfaction

For child, teen, adult, and elder Sims, Bladder can be satisfied anywhere, but there's only one way that doesn't simultaneously cause a total depletion of Hygiene: a toilet. All toilets fulfill the Bladder Need at the same rate but more expensive ones also give Comfort.

Why is that Sloppy Sim's Bladder Need being satisfied while she's in the shower? Never mind, don't ask.

Extremely Sloppy Sims are Bladder multitaskers; they use their shower time to satisfy Bladder as well (though it's slower than using a toilet). Think of that what you will but it is efficient.

note

The only other thing on which Sims can relieve them-
selves is a shrub. This can be done only by very
Outgoing and very Lazy Sims, and only when their
Bladder Need is very low.

Finally, elders must spend longer on the toilet
than any other age; they get Bladder satisfaction at
half the rate of everyone else.

When all else fails,
an Outgoing and Lazy
Sim will utilize a
nearby shrub.

Personality

All Personalities have identical Bladder motives.

Ages

From fastest to slowest, the rate of Bladder depletion
by age:

1. Elder   3. Baby   5. Adult
2. Toddler   4. Teen   6. Child

The faster the decay, the more often they must
relieve themselves.

Mood Impact

Bladder has no heightened effect on Mood until it
gets very low. At that point, its effect becomes
quickly and profoundly serious.

Babies and toddlers suffer no Mood impact based
on the level of their Bladder Need. It simply doesn't
factor in. The only purpose to their Bladder Need is
to control how often their diaper must be changed.

If Bladder declines too low, Sims either exit or
refuse to use skill building or Fun objects even if
Mood is still positive.

Distress and Failure

Around the time Bladder begins to seriously affect
Mood, Sims start to show their distress by waving
and displaying toilet thought balloons.

How very mortifying!
Plus, thanks to the
Hygiene drop, he now
stinks. That ruins a
Sim's cool image.

At -100, failure occurs and the Sim wets himself.
This completely refills the Bladder Need, but also deci-
mates the Hygiene Need. A Sim who's gone through
Bladder failure won't need a toilet until Bladder
decays again, but he'll need a bath or shower.

When Bladder failure occurs, nearby Sims either
laugh (if Grouchy) or are disgusted (if Neat). Also,
Sims get a short-lasting Memory of the event (Sims
who witnessed it get a Memory Marker that they can
talk about to other Sims).

For some Sims (particularly if they're Shy or have
Popularity or Teen Grow Up Aspirations), it's likely
that Bladder failure is a Fear that will bring down
Aspiration score.

When Bladder fails on toddlers and babies, they
wet their diapers, Bladder restores to full, and
Hygiene drops.

note

Once a toddler is potty trained, she still won't care if
Bladder fails but she can autonomously use the potty
chair before failure, saving other Sims the labor of
diaper changing.

ENERGY

Energy is the basic physical need for sleep and rest.

Depletion

Every waking moment, Sims use Energy, though the rate varies by age and Personality.

> **note**
>
> Baby and toddler Sims need to sleep about twice per day. All other Sims need to sleep only once.

Energy is depleted more quickly when Sims engage in physically demanding activities. Physical objects/activities include:

- Work Out (self interaction or via TV)
- Yoga (self interaction)
- Dancing
- Trimming Shrubs
- Pulling Weeds
- Change Diaper on Changing Table
- Extinguish Fire
- WooHoo/Try for Baby
- Teach to Walk
- Potty Chair
- Bake with Toy Oven

> **note**
>
> Pregnant Sims suffer accelerated Energy decay until the baby is born. Thus, they need sleep more often.
>
> This may be puzzling on the first day of pregnancy before the Sim begins "showing." Increased Energy decay is a very good sign of being great with child.

> **note**
>
> If using any of these objects or doing any of these interactions drops the Sim's Energy too low, he'll automatically exit.

Satisfaction

There's nothing like a good night's sleep. The more expensive the bed, the less time Sims must spend unconscious.

When Sims sleep, the Energy Need is refilled at a rate defined by what they're sleeping on:

- Couch or Recliner: Naps on couches and recliners refill Energy, but at a slower rate than beds. They are also, unlike beds, capped with a maximum Energy restoration. The speed of and caps on Energy restoration generally rise with the cost of the couch or recliner.
- Bed: Beds are the primary engine for fulfilling Sim's Energy Need. They tend to fill Energy faster than other furniture and fill the Need to its top. The speed with which a bed restores Energy is generally tied to its expense, and the difference can be dramatic.
- The Floor or Standing: If a Sim can't get to a bed, couch, or recliner before her Energy need fails, she'll fall asleep on the ground. Not surprisingly, the ground provides very, very slow Energy satisfaction. Give her a few minutes to recharge, wake her up, and get her into a real bed.

Money spent on a bed is simoleans well-spent. A cheap bed provides full rest in about nine game hours, a medium bed requires seven and a half hours, and an expensive bed needs only six hours.

tip

Some Sims (particularly Popularity and Active Sims) have a Fear of passing out, so failing to meet their Energy need can have the added penalty of reducing their Aspiration score.

There are a couple of less obvious ways to gain Energy:

◆ Drinking Coffee or Espresso: Both strong brown brews add a fixed amount of Energy but take time to drink and cause Bladder motive to deplete (more so for espresso than for coffee).

◆ Eating candy factory Mess: Toddlers can gain Energy by eating from the puddles left by low-skill Sims using the candy factory career reward object (See Chapter 23).

Personality

Lazy Sims lose Energy faster than other Sims. The Lazier they are (fewer Personality points they have in Active/Lazy), the faster Energy depletes.

Ages

From fastest to slowest, the rate of Energy depletion by age:

1. Toddler   3. Child   5. Adult
2. Baby   4. Elder   6. Teen

The faster the decay, the more often they must sleep.

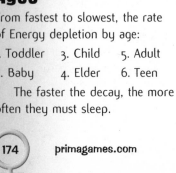

Mood Impact

Energy has no effect on a Sim's overall Mood. Therefore, for job performance, it doesn't matter how high Energy is when the Sim goes to work; if it's too low, however, he'll collapse on the sidewalk when he returns home. Teen Sims who have afternoon jobs should be well rested when they leave for school or they may not have enough Energy to refill their other needs and catch their ride to work.

If Energy declines too low, Sims either exit or refuse to use skill building or Fun objects even if Mood is still positive.

Distress and Failure

Sims in Energy distress wave and gesture and show food thought balloons. This behavior wastes time.

It isn't just toddlers who can fall asleep anywhere. Get any Sim tired enough and he'll collapse on the ground.

When Energy reaches rock bottom, elder, adult, teen, child, and toddler Sims instantly fall asleep on the ground or where they're standing (depending if there's anywhere to collapse). Passed out Sims can't be revived until they gain sufficient Energy to get to a bed (about five game minutes).

If there isn't room to collapse, he'll fall asleep standing up. After a few moments, the Sim can be awakened by clicking on him and selecting Wake Up. Take the opportunity to get him to a bed.

Babies and toddlers in Energy failure simply fall asleep wherever they are.

4   prima   oster tight f   collapse p.

FUN

Fun is the psychological need for amusement and relaxation.

Depletion

Fun decays steadily while a Sim is awake. No decay occurs during sleep.

Fun can, albeit rarely, be further decreased by certain unequivocally not-fun occurrences: homework, electrocution, burning, being struck by lightning. No surprises there, really.

Satisfaction

Fun is satisfied by engaging in any interaction with a Fun rating. The higher the rating, the more Fun it imparts. This rating is typically a measure both of the speed of satisfaction and the maximum to which Fun will rise.

> ### tip
> You know a Fun object has a maximum limit if the meter stops filling even if the Sim is still doing the activity.

A very expensive Fun object, for example, gives Fun quickly all the way up to 100. Less pricey diversions might get a Sim to max Fun but do it very slowly, or they work quickly but only raise Fun to a fixed level. And still others might offer a fixed dose of Fun but one that allows the Sim to go back for additional doses until Fun hits maximum.

> ### note
> A Sim's Personality (whether she's more Playful or more Serious) has nothing to do with how much Fun she gets out of an interaction. But it does affect which interactions Sims are attracted to when acting autonomously. If left to his own devices, a Serious Sim will pull a book off the shelf before he'll turn on the TV. This Fun attraction is a function of a system called "advertisement," which is covered in detail in Chapter 33.
> Directing a Serious Sim to watch TV, however, gives him whatever Fun the TV offers, regardless of Personality.

Games, especially ones that other Sims can watch, make for great Fun.

Fun can be had from interactions with both objects and other Sims. In the latter case, many social interactions (in addition to Relationship and Social Need benefits) also give Fun. See Chapter 24 for full details.

> ### FUN SOCIALS, SOME EXAMPLES
> ◆ All "Play..." interactions
> ◆ WooHoo/Try for Baby
> ◆ Dance Together
> ◆ Play with Baby

Still, it's nice to have a little Fun by yourself sometimes.

Fun can also be had from watching other Sims engaged in a Fun activity.

Personality

Playful Sims lose Fun faster than other Sims. The more Playful they are (10 Personality points in Playful/Serious), the faster Fun depletes.

> **note**
>
> Neat Sims receive Fun from Cleaning while Sloppy Sims lose Fun.

> **note**
>
> Playful Sims (Playful/Serious >5) need about two hours of Fun per day, while Serious require only about an hour to be fully satisfied.

Ages

From fastest to slowest, the rate of Fun depletion by age:

1. Child
2. Teen
3. Adult
4. Toddler
5. Elder
6. Baby

The faster the decay, the more often they must have Fun.

Mood Impact

Fun has its greatest impact on Mood when it's very high (about 50 to 100) or very low (about -50 to -100). Your Sim will never be in a top notch Mood unless his Fun is totally satisfied, but only truly bored Sims allow a lack of Fun to dampen their otherwise positive Mood.

Fun will, by itself, knock a Sim out of skill building if it gets too low. Less dire levels of the Fun Need can indirectly have the same effect if they lower Mood below zero.

Distress and Failure

Sims without Fun gesture, complain, and show TV thought bubbles, all of which waste time. They're also likely to be in a pretty sour overall Mood.

There is no failure state for Fun; the effects of distress simply worsen. If the Sim is a baby or toddler, Fun failure results in crying and tantruming (respectively).

SOCIAL

Social is the psychological need to interact with other Sims.

Depletion

Any time Sims aren't directly interacting with another Sim, Social is decaying at a steady rate.

Social is also reduced by negative social interactions. If the outcome of an interaction (mostly rejected ones but some positive too) is negative, it'll probably reduce Social.

> **note**
>
> Complete listings of all social interactions, including outcomes, appear in Chapter 24.

Satisfaction

Social is satisfied by having positive social interactions. In most such interactions, both sides receive some increase in the Social Need. In some interactions, there can be an increase for one side and a decrease for the other.

There are more ways to interact, however, than face-to-face. Sims can: talk on the phone, chat over a computer, or (if they're truly desperate) socialize with the Social Bunny.

> **note**
>
> All forms of social interaction are covered in Chapter 24, and the Social Bunny is introduced in Chapter 26.

Playing with babies and toddlers gives them the Social interaction they need. Ignore them and they'll be taken away.

Babies can't initiate their own interactions, but they require socializing too. They depend on others to engage them, so don't neglect the infants.

There's also Social satisfaction to be had in teaching or Encouraging another Sim or helping a student do homework.

When Sims join an activity (e.g., talking, watching TV, etc.), that activity usually gains a Social benefit for all involved. Thus, playing darts alone increases Fun, while doing it with more Sims yields both Fun and Social.

Personality

Outgoing Sims lose Social faster than other Sims. The more Outgoing they are (the more Personality points they have in Outgoing/Shy), the faster Social depletes.

note

Shy Sims need about an hour of Social per day (on top of what they get at work) while Outgoing Sims need about two hours of non-job-related interaction.

Ages

From fastest to slowest, the rate of Social depletion by age:

1. Teen   3. Adult   5. Child
2. Elder   4. Toddler   6. Baby

Mood Impact

Like Fun, Social has its strongest influence on Mood when it's very high and very low. Also as with Fun,

Social's baseline impact on Mood is higher than for the physical Needs; Social's "normal" effect is twice that of the other Needs. This means when all Needs are high, Social and Fun are actually the strongest determinants of Mood.

Distress and Failure

Sims in Social distress wave and gesture and show socializing thought bubbles. These displays waste time and reduce efficiency. Really low Social is also a serious drag on Mood.

For adults, elders, and teens, there is no failure state for Social, but something significant does happen when it reaches -100. When Social hits rock bottom, the Social Bunny arrives. This creature, visible only to the Sim for whom it came, increases Social just by being on the lot and can also be the recipient of any but romantic interactions. The Social Bunny departs when the Social Need restores to zero.

The Social Bunny can get any Sim out of the doldrums. Go ahead, give the giant, plush, one-eyed bunny a hug.

For babies, toddlers, and children, a total decay of the Social Need is a sign of serious neglect. As such, when their Social fails, the Social Worker comes and permanently removes all babies/toddlers/children from the lot.

HYGIENE

Hygiene is the physical need to feel clean.

Depletion

If a Sim is awake, he's gradually losing Hygiene. When sleeping, this rate is slowed but not stopped.

Many activities accelerate the loss of Hygiene, especially ones involving physical exertion (using any exercise object, trimming hedges, pulling weeds, cleaning, doing yoga, working out in front of the TV, etc.), performing WooHoo or Trying for Baby, changing a diaper, or dealing with inherently dirty things (Sloppy Sims picking things out of the trash).

Sweatin' to the tunes takes a toll on a Sim's Hygiene.

Getting puked on by a baby or toddler can (not surprisingly) reduce the pukee's Hygiene. As for the baby or toddler, wearing a soiled diaper causes Hygiene to crash. Toddlers sitting in an unclean high chair also suffer accelerated Hygiene decay.

> **note**
>
> Teens with consistently low Hygiene get zits. Teens get zits if their five-day Hygiene average drops below 50. Acne can be remedied by using the Apply Acne Cream interaction in mirrors. Zits go away in about a day and don't come back for at least five more days.

> **note**
>
> If a toddler plays in the toilet, Hygiene decreases faster.

Satisfaction

Hygiene is satisfied by several objects, depending somewhat on age.

For children, teens, adults, and elders, Hygiene is primarily gained from showers and bathtubs. Tubs provide slower Hygiene than showers but provide simultaneous Comfort. Combination shower/ tubs have slightly faster Hygiene satisfaction. Hot tubs have even slower Hygiene satisfaction but also provide Comfort, Fun, and Social.

> **note**
>
> Sims can autonomously take a sponge bath in any sink but only if their Neat/Sloppy is below 6 and current Hygiene is less than -50.

Children use only bathtubs or shower/tubs, but are otherwise identical to their elders in the way they restore Hygiene.

Toddlers and babies gain most of their Hygiene satisfaction from having their diaper changed. Changing a diaper on a changing table has an even higher Hygiene max. To gain even more Hygiene for a toddler or baby, teens, adults, or elders can bathe them. Babies may be bathed only in a sink and toddlers only in a bathtub or shower/tub.

Personality

Sloppy Sims lose Hygiene faster than other Sims. The Sloppier they are (o Personality points in Neat/ Sloppy), the faster Hygiene depletes.

Ages

From fastest to slowest, the rate of Hygiene depletion by age:

1. Adult   4. Elder
2. Child   5. Toddler
3. Teen   6. Baby

The faster the decay, the more often they must bathe.

Mood Impact

Hygiene doesn't begin to seriously affect Mood until it reaches -40. At this point, its impact quickly multiplies (though not as much as the other physical Needs).

Hygiene does not, by itself, knock a Sim out of skill building except to the extent that it may lower Mood below zero.

Distress and Failure

When a Sim's Hygiene is in distress, he emits a green stink cloud and nearby Sims (Neat/Sloppy 5–10) react to the odor.

The shower thought bubbles and the cloud of green stink should be a clue that Hygiene is just a bit low.

Low Hygiene doesn't directly affect Sims' ability to work on skills (unless it brings Mood down below medium), but it does make it difficult to interact socially. Also, all the gesturing wastes valuable time.

There is no failure state for Hygiene; your Sim is just in a pretty bad Mood, stinks to high heaven, and is unable to interact fully or (if Mood is low enough) have Fun or work on skills.

Babies and toddlers cry or tantrum (respectively) intermittently.

ENVIRONMENT

Environment is the psychological need for order and cleanliness in one's surroundings. This Need is unique in both the way it works and how it influences Mood.

The Environment Need doesn't decay like other motives. Rather, it exists as a score in a given location that pushes the Environment Need of any nearby Sim either up or down.

In this room, Environment is very high.

Here, however, among the dirty dishes, it's very low.

Generally, Environment score is based on the quality and cleanliness of each room, though the amount of light and whether the Sim is indoors or out creates more localized effects.

note

Indoors, a "room" is defined as a place enclosed by walls with access only via doors or archways. If two spaces are connected by a gap in the wall rather than a door or archway, the two spaces together form a single "room" for Environment score purposes.

Calculating Environment Score

Environment score defines where a Sim's Environment Need will be set when she is in that room.

Two elements make up Environment score:

◆ The "niceness" of the room
◆ The presence of any messes

The final score is determined by subtracting messiness from niceness. Which things influence these elements provide the strategy behind Environment score.

note

Environment score scales to the size of the room. Thus, it takes more total Environment score (and money) to top out a large room than a small one.

Niceness

Niceness reflects four elements:

◆ Purchase price of objects in the room

◆ Purchase price of flooring

◆ Purchase price of wallpaper

◆ Amount of natural and artificial light

Each of these elements has only a partial impact on Environment. The bulk of the score comes from objects but the rest comes from sizeable allotments for each of the rest.

In other words, a room packed with expensive objects but no light sources, wall coverings, or floor coverings offers only about 60 percent full Environment score.

Objects

The combined purchase prices of all objects in a room dictate the first portion of the niceness calculation.

Every object is assigned a "niceness" factor that raises Environment score in the room in which it's placed.

note

Every object has a niceness factor, but the factor is minimal for ordinary objects. Only the more expensive and decorative objects have really significant Environment scores.

Each object in the room contributes its niceness to the room's overall Environment score.

note

Given the strong but limited effect of objects on Environment score, there always comes a point when spending money on decorative objects shows no further increase in Environment score. The precise simolean amount of this point rises with the size of the room.

If, therefore, you're trying to improve Environment score and adding a new object doesn't show any effect, consider returning it and instead upgrading the lighting, flooring, or wall covering.

The cost of an object largely determines how much effect it will have on Environment, but decorative objects have a far greater effect per simolean spent.

Wall and Floor Covering

The plywood floors and sheetrock walls that you put up in Build mode contribute nothing to Environment score. This leaves two massive chunks of niceness empty, making a full score impossible.

The quality (read: purchase prices) of the coverings you place on walls and floors determine how much these two elements add to niceness. The more expensive they are, the more they'll contribute.

Uncovered walls and floors are brutal on Environment score. Work-in-progress chic is so last year.

note

Each of these elements is scored as an average for the room. Thus, if a room is mostly expensive wallpaper with some sections of the cheap stuff, top score won't be possible.

Lighting

Unlike the other elements, lighting is not a function of the entire room. It is, instead, the amount of light in a specific location. Thus, a dark corner of a very high-scored room will have a lower score than the rest.

Every light source has an area that it illuminates and an amount of light it casts. A light improves niceness within the area it illuminates; the more light it casts, the more it adds to niceness.

tip

Because lights affect only the area within their illumination, place skill building objects or places where socializing happens (e.g., the couch in front of the TV) near windows and very bright lights. The higher the Environment score in those crucial locations, the longer a Sim can keep up his Mood.

During the day, light is provided by windows and glass doors (the more glass a door has, the more light it permits). At night, fixtures placed in Buy mode provide illumination. To maximize Environment score, consider the lighting during both times of day.

tip

Floodlights are always preferable to spot lights because they illuminate a larger area of the room.

Only the most expensive lights (§300 and up) have an additional effect on Environment because they're also nice to look at. This effect is room-wide, like any other beautiful object.

Messiness

Niceness is, however, only part of the Environment equation. What separates overall Environment score from niceness is the element of messiness.

A messy object in the room deducts a fixed amount from Environment score everywhere in the room. Messy objects hold down Environment score until they are cleaned or removed.

Messy objects include:

- Dirty dishes
- Trash piles
- Spoiled food
- Soiled objects (dirty sinks, toilets, countertops)
- Unmade beds
- Puddles
- Old newspapers
- Books left out
- Ash piles
- Dead fish in the aquarium
- Full trash cans or compactors
- Kicked over trash cans (outside)
- Uncovered wall sections
- Uncovered floor sections
- Weeds (outside)
- Roaches (alive or dead)
- Dirty aquarium
- Unwatered or overwatered plants (outside)
- Broken objects
- Flies (in addition to dirty object's messiness)
- Green stink cloud from dirty objects (in addition to dirty object's messiness)

note

Messiness can be a result of noise too; a ringing alarm clock pulls down Environment score in its room until it's turned off.

Dirty objects detract from Environment only if they're *visibly* dirty. Thus, an object may show a "Clean" interaction before it actually begins to bring down Environment.

Flies and Roaches

Flies and roaches appear in Sims' homes in response to certain messes. Each is dealt with differently.

Flies appear above dirty dishes, spoiled food, or trash piles (including full trash cans or compactors) after a few hours. They create an additional Environment reduction beyond the dirty object itself.

Flies and green stink mean these plates are shredding this room's Environment score.

To get rid of flies, clean up the object that attracted them.

> **note**
>
> If there are a lot of flies in a Sim's house, they can converge into a huge super swarm that can literally kill a teen, adult, or elder Sim. See "Death by Flies," Chapter 29.

Roaches are attracted only to piles of trash but, unlike flies, they take on a life of their own even if the trash is subsequently cleaned up. Roaches can be killed only by spraying them (an interaction available on the roaches themselves) or by calling an Exterminator (see "Exterminator," Chapter 26).

Roaches can also cause disease (see "Disease," Chapter 29).

Many Sims (particularly Family and Fortune Sims with Neat Personalities) fear seeing roaches (or "vermin"). Witnessing a roaming swarm of roaches brings down their Aspiration score if the Fear is high enough on the list.

Even dead roaches bring down Environment score. They must be cleaned up to neutralize their effect.

Environment Outdoors

The game considers any outdoor space as one big "room" for Environment score purposes. Still, it functions differently than for interior rooms.

Adorn the walk to work with high Environment score items to send Sims off in the best possible Mood.

Whereas in interior rooms, the Environment score is the same room-wide (except for the effect of lighting), outside Environment is entirely localized. Thus, a pile of trash in the front yard is too far away to affect Environment in the back yard. Likewise, a beautiful tree in the back yard won't improve Environment score in a barren front yard.

When considering Environment score outside, therefore, focus on areas where Mood matters. If lots of socializing happens around the back patio, make sure it's surrounded by well-tended flowers, trees, statues, and plenty of outdoor lighting (for nighttime).

Even more important is the front walkway and sidewalk: the route your Sim takes to work or school. Because a Sim's Mood at the moment he gets in the car is what counts for job performance, you want the Environment contribution to Mood to be as high as possible. Thus, focus outside decorations and foliage around the route from the front door to the sidewalk. The boost this provides could be the difference between promotion and stagnation.

Personality

Environment affects all Personality types equally.

Ages

Babies, toddlers, and children don't have an Environment need. The state of their surroundings has absolutely no effect on them.

Otherwise, Environment affects all other ages alike.

Mood Impact

Environment is the least Mood-influencing of all the Needs (other than Energy, of course). Like Fun and Social, it exerts greater effect when it's very high or very low.

Distress and Failure

When a Sim suffers Environment distress, he gestures and flashes a broom-and-dustpan thought balloon. This wastes time, and the effect of low Environment somewhat depresses overall Mood.

There is no failure state for Environment, but gesturing becomes more frequent.

NEEDS AT WORK

Every job and school has a distinctive effect on a Sims Mood. When the Sim is off the lot at a job or school, her Mood when she returns will be altered by this effect. Thus a Sim with a physical job returns home with a large deduction from Energy. Some of these effects are positive too; Sims with desk jobs return home with higher Comfort. Most jobs, except really solitary ones (security guard) increase Social.

See the tables in Chapter 23 for the specifics.

THE FOOD GAME: HOW TO MAXIMIZE HUNGER SATISFACTION

Food is pretty important to your Sims, and not just because the lack of it causes an awful demise. Eating food satisfies your Sims Hunger Need.

Hunger is a powerful Need, severely impacting Mood if allowed to drop too low. How to keep this all-important Need efficiently satisfied is one of the game's major challenges.

A lovely serving of lobster thermidor is just the thing for efficient Hunger satisfaction.

The goal for food should be for it to give maximum Hunger satisfaction in the minimum time. More Hunger satisfaction per plate of food means fewer plates of food per meal to get full. The better equipped and designed the kitchen and the more highly trained the Sim doing the cooking, the faster food can be prepared and the more quickly anyone eating the food can fill his Hunger Need (really good food only requires one portion).

Clearly, focusing on food is an extremely effective way to provide your Sim more free time to do the important stuff like climb to the top of his career or fulfill his Wants.

Meal Times

The kinds of foods available are different depending on the time of day:

◆ Breakfast: 2:00 a.m.–10:30 a.m.

◆ Lunch: 10:30 a.m.–4:30 p.m.

◆ Dinner: 4:30 p.m.–2:00 a.m.

note

Snacks are available any time of day.

Each meal has its own set of possible foods. Some (e.g., hamburgers) can be made at either lunch or dinner, but these are an exception.

Foods By Meal Time

Breakfast	Lunch	Dinner
Instant Meal	Instant Meal	Instant Meal
Cereal	Chef's Salad	Chef's Salad
Pancakes	Lunch meat Sandwich	TV Dinner
Omelets	Grilled Cheese	Spaghetti
Toaster Pastry	Hamburgers	Salmon
Chips	Hot Dogs	Pork Chop
Cookies	Chili Con Carne	Mac and Cheese
Juice	Chips	Lobster Thermidor
	Cookies	Hamburgers
	Juice	Hot Dogs
	Gelatin	Grilled Ribs
	Layer Cake	Turkey
	Baked Alaska	Chips
		Cookies
		Juice
		Gelatin
		Layer Cake
		Baked Alaska

The Food Chain

> **note**
>
> Children can learn Cooking skill and provide edible food by baking muffins in the toy oven.

Food can come from three sources: your Sims' own kitchen, pizza ordered over the phone, or from grills on Community Lots. The most important of these, however, is the kitchen.

> **note**
>
> Actually, Sloppy Sims have a fourth source of nourishment: they can eat out of trash cans. It's not very satisfying and can cause illness, but it is free.

To make food at home as satisfying as possible, several factors come into play. Each element adds to the resulting food's total Hunger satisfaction:

◆ **Countertops:** The better the countertops, the more satisfying any food that's prepared on them.

◆ **Food Processor:** For food that requires chopping, a food processor is used instead of the counter to provide even more Hunger satisfaction.

◆ **Cooking Appliance:** The better the cooking appliance, the more satisfying the food cooked on it. Stoves can cook all foods except ribs and hot dogs, which can be made only on the grill. Toaster ovens and microwaves can prepare only a few foods and don't contribute much food satisfaction.

◆ **Cooking Skill:** Cooking skill dictates what kind of foods a Sim can cook and what cooking techniques they can employ. The more difficult the food and challenging the cooking method, the more satisfying the food.

> **note**
>
> Food cooked on grills is inherently less satisfying because it doesn't benefit from the preparation stage's contribution to food points.

Home cooked food comes in five varieties:

◆ **Ready to Eat Meals:** Require no preparation or cooking

◆ **Cold Foods:** Require only preparation

◆ **Grilled Food:** Require cooking but no preparation and are only cooked on an outdoor grill

◆ Cooked Foods: Require both preparation and cooking

◆ Desserts: Require preparation, and sometimes cooking

The Refrigerator

No matter what kind of food you want, everything must come out of a refrigerator. Without this basic appliance, your Sim must live on nothing but delivered pizza—yummy but expensive.

> ### note
> So important is the refrigerator that it can't be stolen by a burglar.

Refrigerators

Fridge	Capacity	Cost
Brand Name "EconoCool" Refrigerator	200	§600
Ciao Time Bovinia Refrigerator Model BRRR	300	§1,500

If ready to eat meals are all you want, the refrigerator is all that's needed. These snack foods, however, offer very little Hunger satisfaction.

Food Preparation

For more satisfying food, you need a food preparation area. Preparation always requires a counter, and Sims choose the closest and nicest counter available (a tabletop won't do). The nicer (and, by the way, more expensive) the counter, the more satisfying the food prepared on it.

Ideally, leave two countertops between the refrigerator and the stove: one for manual preparation and one for a food processor. Keep dirty dishes off the open countertops or there won't be anywhere to prepare food.

If your kitchen has a food processor, preparation is a bit different. When a food requires chopping as part of its preparation, Sims will use a food processor. This appliance adds more Hunger satisfaction to the food than all but the best countertops. Foods that don't require chopping, such as pancakes, still need a clean countertop for preparation.

Preparation Surfaces/Appliances

Object	Food Points	Prep Time	Cost	Environment Score
Krampft Industries Value Counter	15	Slow	§140	0
Counter Culture "Surface"	20	Medium	§200	0
Catamaran Kitchen Island	20	Medium	§210	0
XLR8R2 Food Processor	20	Medium	§220	0
Epikouros "Sleek Cuisine" Counter	25	Fast	§325	0
Epikouros "Sleek Cuisine" Island	20	Medium	§335	0
Chiclettina "Fjord" Kitchen Counter	20	Medium	§490	0
Chiclettina "Archipelago" Kitchen Island	25	Fast	§500	0
Club Room Countertop	25	Fast	§600	0
Club Distress Butcher's Block	25	Fast	§610	0
Chiclettina "Sardinia" Kitchen Counter	25	Fast	§780	2
Chiclettina "Sardinia" Kitchen Island	25	Fast	§790	2
Chez Moi French Country Counters	25	Fast	§800	0
Counter Cooking Conundrum	25	Fast	§810	2

Cooking Appliances

Cooked foods are the most completely satisfying. To make them, however, your Sims need a cooking appliance.

Which cooking appliance Sims use dictates how much Hunger satisfaction is contributed to the food and determines what kinds of foods can be cooked.

> ### COOKING ON COMMUNITY LOT GRILLS
> Community Lot grills are free and can produce both hot dogs and hamburgers (depending on the cook's skill). Community grills can't cause fires and food never fails.

Grills

◆ Foods: Hot dogs, hamburgers, grilled ribs

Locate grills outside or else they'll cause a fire. They're the only appliance that can cook hot dogs or grilled ribs. If you're trying to economize, buy just a refrigerator and a grill for all your food needs. It won't produce as satisfying foods as a complete kitchen, but it does the job when money's tight.

note

Because there are no grilled breakfast foods, grills can't be used until lunchtime.

Toaster Oven

◆ Foods: Toaster pastry, grilled cheese, salmon, pork chop, TV dinner

Toaster ovens are very limited in the foods they can cook and add very little in the way of Hunger satisfaction.

Microwave

◆ Foods: TV dinner

The microwave offers as much Hunger satisfaction as the basic stove but can make only one relatively unsatisfying food. On the upside, it will never cause a fire.

tip

If you don't expect any Sim in the house to learn how to cook, do cooking in the microwave. Otherwise, you could have daily calls to the fire department.

Stoves

◆ Foods: All except hot dogs and grilled ribs

Stoves, especially the more expensive ones, are where the great food is made. They can produce almost any kind of cooked food by every cooking method. The more expensive stove adds 10 times the Hunger satisfaction of the toaster oven and basic stove and five times that of the microwave.

Cooking Appliances

COOKING APPLIANCE	FOOD POINTS	COST
TechTonic Touch Toaster Oven	100	§100
The Grillinator "BigBQ"	50	§210
Brand Name Zip Zap Microwave	100	§250
Brand Name MetalKettle	100	§299
Dialectric ReadyPrep Range	50	§400
Ciao Time "Mondo Fuego" Gas Stove	100	§650
Elegant Chef FlameBay Gas Range	150	§900
Shiny Things, Inc. Grandiose Grill	150	§1,100

Cooking Skill

Cooking is one of the seven basic skills (see Chapter 22). Cooking skill is learned in several ways:

◆ Bookshelves: Study Cooking skill from a book.

◆ Learn by doing: Cooking foods teaches experience and technique; every time a Sim cooks, he's learning Cooking skill.

◆ Watching TV: Watching the Yummy channel on TV offers a decent increase in Cooking skill.

Skill adds to the Hunger satisfaction of food in two indirect ways.

The more they cook, the better they cook. Cooking skill comes from both books and hands-on cooking.

Foods Options

Sims with no Cooking skill can only make a few basic (and relatively unsatisfying foods). With every increase in skill, more nourishing foods are unlocked.

The greater the skill, the more cooking options there'll be.

Increases in skill also permit Sims to make their known foods in new ways that further add to Hunger satisfaction. For example, a pork chop fried on the stovetop is less satisfying than one that's been fry/baked. In other words, a more skilled Sim can make a more nourishing version of some foods than a less skilled Sim.

Unlocked Foods By Cooking Skill Level

Cooking Skill	Anytime	Breakfast	Lunch	Dinner	Dessert
0	Juice, Chips, Cookies, Instant Meal	Cereal, Toaster Pastry	Lunch meat Sandwiches, Hot Dogs	TV Dinner, Mac and Cheese, Hot Dogs	Gelatin
1				Spaghetti	
2			Grilled Cheese		
3		Pancakes	Hamburgers, Chef's Salad	Hamburgers, Chef's Salad	
4		Omelets	Chili Con Carne		
5				Pork Chop	
6				Salmon, Turkey	Layer Cake
7				Grilled Ribs	
8					Baked Alaska
9					
10				Lobster Thermidor	

Finally, Cooking skill speeds preparation time. When a Sim learns a new food, he prepares it slowly. At the next skill level, he prepares that food more quickly. Finally, at two skill levels after a food's introduction, he prepares and cooks it with optimum efficiency.

Desserts

There are three levels of dessert, each available only at lunch or dinner:

◆ Gelatin: Skill 0   ◆ Baked Alaska: Skill 8

◆ Layer Cake: Skill 6

As with cooked foods, Cooking skill speeds the preparation of each dessert and increases its Hunger satisfaction.

Cooking Failure

Every meal carries a chance of cooking failure.

Even good cooks mess up sometimes. Ruined food is edible but loses all of its score enhancements.

When a food is first unlocked, it carries a 20 percent chance of failure. At one skill level later, the chance drops to 10 percent. Two skill levels higher, the chance falls to its final level of 5 percent. Thus, no matter how experienced a Sim is with a given food, there's always at least a 5 percent chance of ruining it.

> **note**
>
> Because lobster thermidor is introduced at Cooking skill 10, a Sim never has the chance to gain two more skill levels. Thus, even a fully experienced chef still ruins lobster thermidor 20 percent of the time.

Ruined food can be consumed but is stripped of most of its Hunger satisfaction. Any additions to food points from preparation or cooking are eliminated, leaving only the food's base Hunger satisfaction.

Cooking failure also carries a 20 percent chance of fire.

> **caution**
>
> If you have Free Will turned off, there's a major cooking hazard you must avoid. If, after putting food in the oven, you cancel the Sim's cooking interaction, she'll leave the food in the stove and forget about it. To prevent it burning and possibly igniting a fire, you must direct her to remove the food from the oven.
>
> This also happens if you direct the Sim to do something else while the food is cooking unattended.

Spoilage

Once a food is served, it is good and edible for about six hours. Any food, including partially prepared meals and opened pizza boxes, left out for more than six hours will spoil.

> **note**
>
> A few foods have spoilage times other than six hours:
> Cereal: 4 hours
> Gelatin: 24 hours
> Instant Meal: 12 hours

Once food is spoiled, its Hunger satisfaction drops to its base amount and it'll be surrounded by flies and emit a green "stinky" cloud. Spoiled food brings down Environment score (see "Environment," above) and, if eaten, can cause illness (See Chapter 29).

Sims autonomously eat spoiled food only if there is no other food source in the house. Leave them no options, however, and they'll eat fly-infested food.

> **note**
>
> If there is too much spoiled food around the house, the flies can come together to devour one of your Sims. For more on Death by Flies, see Chapter 29.

If you direct a Sim to eat a plate of spoiled food, he won't refuse. Be careful about which plates you instruct Sims to eat or they could end up with food poisoning.

Food Economics

Food costs simoleans and food wasted is money frittered away. While the main part of the food game is time efficiency, there's an economic side too.

Food Cost

A refrigerator is not really stocked with food, it's stocked with food points (200 for the cheap fridge and 300 for the expensive). A food point costs exactly two simoleans.

Every kind of food has a price tag per serving. The higher the Hunger satisfaction of the food, the greater the cost. Every time you extract a serving of a food, its cost is deducted from the refrigerator's stock.

note

Food efficiency is a measure of how to get the most Hunger satisfaction in the shortest time. The most nutritious food may not be the most efficient if it takes a long time to eat. Thus, Food efficiency allows you to see which foods at each cooking level give the most bang for the buck.

For example, a chef's salad and chili con carne take the same amount of time to eat but the chili gives more Hunger satisfaction in the same amount of time.

Note that Food efficiency is based only on the foods' base scores; anything added by other cooking methods, prep areas, and cooking appliances adds to this. Grilled items, therefore, are not as efficient as they appear because no prep points get added to them. Thus, grilled ribs and lobster thermidor have the same efficiency but the lobster inevitably ends up a better investment.

Food Cost and Efficiency

Food	§ Have	§ Serve	§ Per Served Helping	Hunger Efficiency
Baked Alaska	§6	§24	§4	75%
Cake, Layer	§5	§20	§3	75%
Cereal	§4	§16	§3	63%
Chef's Salad	§5	§20	§3	63%
Chili Con Carne	§6	§24	§4	75%
Gelatin	§4	§16	§3	63%
Grilled Cheese	§5	§20	§3	75%
Hamburgers	§6	§24	§4	75%
Hot Dogs	§5	§20	§3	75%
Instant Meal	§3	§12	§2	50%
Juice Can/Cookies/Chips	§3	N/A	N/A	50%
Lobster Thermidor	§8	§32	§5	100%
Lunch meat Sandwiches	§4	§16	§3	63%
Mac and Cheese	§5	§20	§3	75%
Muffin (Toy Oven)	§2	N/A	N/A	50%
Omelets	§5	§20	§3	75%
Pancakes	§5	§20	§3	75%
Pizza	N/A	§40	§5	100%
Pork Chop	§7	§28	§5	88%
Ribs, Grilled	N/A	§28	§5	100%
Salmon	§7	§28	§5	88%
Spaghetti	§5	§20	§3	75%
Toaster Pastries	§4	§16	§3	63%
Toddler Mush	§6	N/A	N/A	75%
Turkey	N/A	§28	§5	88%
TV Dinner	§4	§16	§3	83%

Having vs. Serving

Instructing your Sim to "Have" a meal commands her to make a single serving of the food. If your Sim lives alone, she should always Have a meal unless she has company.

note

Some foods only come in single servings: chips, cookies, juice, or TV dinners.

Others can only be "Served" (multiple servings): grilled ribs and turkey.

Alternatively, Sims may "Serve" most foods. Serving yields six helpings of the food. This may seem like a lot, but there's a hidden savings: the cost of a Served meal is only four times that of a single meal. Thus, the cost per meal is lower. If you're feeding company or a family, or your Sim is so hungry he'll need several servings, Serve meals. Served meals save money and take the same amount of time to prep as a single serving.

Ordering Food

When your refrigerator runs out of food (stock at 0 or too low to purchase any single helping of any food), order some more. You can't prepare a meal until the fridge is restocked.

note

Monitor your food stock by using the Check Food Supplies interaction on the fridge. You won't get advance warning of a shortage until it's too late. Food always seems to run out just as you're making dinner for the private school headmaster or before a big party.

note

You can order food in three ways:

◆ Delivery over the phone

◆ Delivery over a computer

◆ By visiting Community Lots

The first two methods include a §50 delivery fee for the convenience of door-to-door service. Going to the Community Lot is free.

Delivery

If you have groceries delivered, the truck arrives at your Sims' door shortly after the call regardless of the time of day. The driver rings the doorbell and waits for someone to accept delivery and pay the bill.

If no one accepts, he leaves the food at the door (extracting money for the bill automatically).

Going Shopping

If you want to pick out your groceries yourself (and do some other shopping and socializing on the same trip), you can use the phone to call a cab to a Community Lot.

Most Community Lots feature food stands where food can be purchased in exactly the same way as by delivery but without the delivery fee. To buy food, interact with the food stand or case and specify how much food you wish to purchase (up to your refrigerator's maximum).

When your Sim arrives home from the Community Lot, she carries the food bags straight to the fridge.

Pizza

There's another way to get food for your family but it has nothing to do with the kitchen. All you need is a phone.

Any child, teen, adult, or elder can call to order pizza delivery any time of day.

Pizza arrives at the front door within minutes. As with groceries, someone must accept the delivery or the pizza guy/gal will leave the box by the door.

Mmmmm...pizza. Sims can live on it, but they'll go broke doing so.

> **note**
>
> Thanks to breakthroughs in space-age pizza box design, unaccepted pizza never spoils. You can create a large stock of ready-on-demand food by letting pizza boxes pile up by the door. Hungry? Go to the porch and snag a pizza...the sunshine even keeps it warm!

Pizzas come with eight servings, each with a fair amount of Hunger satisfaction. Still, at §40 per pie, the cost (§5) and Hunger satisfaction (50) per serving are less appealing than cooked food.

Chapter 21

Aspirations, Wants, and Fears

Sims are so much more than just the sum of their physical and psychological needs. Any Sim sociologist would tell you (it isn't a career track yet, but you never know) that what really makes life worth living for Sims is getting what they *want*. Conversely, what makes life so treacherous is realizing their deepest *fears*.

And what Sims want (and what they fear) is pretty rich and complex. Much of it is a matter of Personality, but most will be in some way directed by one overarching factor: their life's goal, or Aspiration.

This chapter introduces you to the world of Sims' higher callings: Wants, Fears, Aspirations, and how the whole complex web shapes a Sim's life.

GAME IMPACT

Satisfying your Sims' Wants, preventing realization of their Fears, and fulfilling their Aspirations significantly affects many aspects of *The Sims 2*.

note

As with every part of THE SIMS 2, you must be aware that time is limited; Sims don't live forever anymore. There's only so much time before a Sim becomes an elder for them to amass enough Aspiration points to live a longer life. Miss too many opportunities and you'll doom your Sim to unhappiness and deprive his progeny of his potentially powerful influence.

◆ Sims with high Aspiration scores (many Wants satisfied and few Fears realized), exhibit special behaviors to show their command of life.

◆ When Aspiration score is really high, Sims are constantly in a good Mood. This means they perform well at work, accept most social interactions, and skill build and have Fun longer, no matter what the levels of their individual Needs.

◆ When Aspiration is low, Sims exhibit destructive behavior that wastes time, damages relationships, and frustrates their ability to meet their Needs. When Aspiration is really low, elder and adult Sims suffer a dramatic but temporary breakdown.

◆ A Sim's Aspiration score at the moment she ages from adult to elder dictates how much longer she'll live. Unsuccessful Sims die sooner while successful ones live longer to pass on their wisdom, contribute to the household income, babysit for free, and ease life for the younger generations.

◆ A Sim's Aspiration score when he dies of old age affects the size of his estate. The higher his Aspiration, the greater the inheritance for those left behind.

The crux of the Aspiration challenge is to carve out sufficient time to meet Wants and avoid Fears by making all other parts of your Sims' lives (Need fulfillment, cooking, cleaning, skill building, socializing, and career climbing) as efficient as possible. Your Sims are counting on you to help them get what they want (they won't specifically pursue a Want on their own but may do so coincidentally), and engineer their world to protect them from what they fear.

note

If a different approach appeals to you, you can make it your mission to visit every horrible Fear upon your Sims to make them all jagged wrecks on the rocky shores of life. It's your call.

WANTS AND FEARS

A "Want" is an experience the Sim sees as positive and desirable. A "Fear" is an experience the Sim sees as negative and undesirable. An experience that's a Want for one Sim can be a Fear for another.

PRIMA OFFICIAL GAME GUIDE

The Wants and Fears panel shows the Sim's Aspiration, her Aspiration score, her top four Wants, and her top three Fears.

At any given moment, every toddler, child, teen, adult, and elder Sim may have dozens of Wants and Fears, but the Wants and Fears panel only shows the top four Wants and the top three Fears. The displayed Wants and Fears are the only ones that matter for Aspiration scoring.

Wants can be as simple as the desire to try a new food or buy a TV or talk to a family member, or be as complex as a quest to completely master a skill or get very physical with several Sims.

Fears can be just as simple or just as remote. They can even be unavoidable or just seem so. Sims can fear being rejected for a social interaction, losing a job, having a fire, or the death of a loved one.

The goal is to do everything in your power to help your Sim get many of the displayed Wants and avoid the displayed Fears. The more difficult the Want/ Fear, the longer or more work it will take; some Wants can take several days and skilled planning to achieve.

How Wants and Fears Are Chosen

If you tried to understand the way the seven Wants and Fears are chosen, your brain might implode. It's really complicated.

There are, however, a few basic principles.

The Universe of Wants and Fears

There are usually more active Wants and Fears than appear on the Wants and Fears panel. Behind the scenes, they're competing for the coveted top four (or, for Fears, top three) positions and pop into the Wants/Fears panel.

note

This vying for position among Wants and Fears is very similar to the concept of interaction advertising (see Chapter 33) that dictates the choices Sims make among the various interactions available to them.

Want/Fear advertising and interaction advertising are, however, different in that the interactions are advertising themselves TO SIMS while Wants/Fears are calling out to the Wants/ Fears panel. In other words: Sims don't respond to Wants/Fears. You must do that for them.

Wants and Fears are defined by to whom they appeal and in what amount. How important a Want/Fear is to a Sim depends on the Sim's:

- Age group
- Aspiration
- Current Aspiration score
- Mood
- Personality
- Relationship to a given Sim

note

A good example of a Personality-based Fear is the fear of seeing vermin (roaches). If a Sim is particularly Neat, she'll fear seeing roaches regardless of her Aspiration.

Seeing roaches can be a pretty traumatic experience for a Neat Sim.

Just because a Want or Fear isn't in the panel doesn't mean you can't unknowingly realize it. You may, in fact, be doing this constantly and never know it. There won't be any score for these successes but many of these Wants open the path to even more important Wants that *will* show in the panel. Had you not cleared the weaker undisplayed Want, you never would have gotten the higher one.

However, if a Want/Fear drops off the panel, that may not mean it's gone for good. It may just mean that a stronger Want/Fear has come to the fore. When it's satisfied or a weaker one drops away, the original one can return. The problem is that you can't know; it's better to treat every significant Want/Fear like gold and tend to it promptly.

Want/Fears Panel Refreshing

When the Want/Fear panel refreshes, it rolls like a slot machine.

Any time the panel is refreshed, any Wants/Fears that drop out of the top four give way to more pressing Wants/Fears. The Want/Fear panel refreshes when:

♦ A Want or Fear is either achieved or rendered impossible or meaningless by intervening events. (In this case only the affected Want/Fear is refreshed, not the entire panel.)

♦ A Sim wakes from a sleep of three hours or more
♦ Any Sim on the lot transitions to a new age
♦ A baby is born on the lot (regular or alien)
♦ Any loss of a family member
♦ Social Worker takes children
♦ Death in household
♦ Move out
♦ Break up
♦ Gain of or change in a family member
♦ Adoption
♦ Come home from work/school
♦ Becoming pregnant
♦ Returning from an alien abduction
♦ Teaching a toddler something (walk, talk, potty training), as other people may have wanted to teach him
♦ Three times a day when the food selection on the fridge changes between breakfast, lunch, and dinner
♦ Coming back from a Community Lot

"Aging Out"

The instant a Want or Fear is triggered, it begins a countdown to its own demise. As a Want/Fear ages, its strength diminishes, rendering it less able to remain in the panel. Eventually, it ages out completely.

Once a Want/Fear is completely aged out, any subsequent Wants or Fears that relied on it as a prerequisite will evaporate. Unless the original Want/Fear returns, the opportunity to achieve it and any beyond it is gone for the rest of a Sim's life.

Not every Want/Fear has the same life-span but, generally, the longer it takes to achieve

and the more important it is to the Sim's overall Aspiration, the longer it persists and the more slowly it tails off.

Once a Want/Fear ages out, it won't come back unless a new version of the Want/Fear is later triggered. For really important Wants/Fears, such resurrection is rare.

Note that a Want/Fear's dropping off the panel doesn't mean it's completely aged out yet. It just means that four Wants or three Fears can out-shout it in its diminished state.

note

A Want/Fear that's aged out can remain in the panel if it's been locked. What's more, you still get a score for it if you achieve it. The Wants/ Fears to which it led, however, are still gone.

Dropping off the panel means that you won't get a score for the Want/Fear even if you achieve it later. The lesson: If a Want/Fear is important to you, either lock it (see "Locking Want/Fears" below) or get to work making it happen. If an important Want/Fear has been on the panel long enough to age out, you weren't making enough of an effort to achieve it.

Locking Wants/Fears

If you spot a Want/Fear that you really want to achieve, consider locking it. Locking a Want/Fear (by right-clicking on it) exempts the Want/Fear from panel refreshment. The lock even keeps the Want/Fear on the panel once it's aged out and all of its subsequent Wants/Fears have died off.

Locking a Want or Fear keeps it in the panel as long as the lock is applied or until the Want or Fear is realized.

Only one Want or Fear may be locked at a time.

Though it may seem like a good idea, locking can create invisible but damaging situations. Locking a Want/Fear that appears important may block out an even more important Want/Fear.

For example, a Family Sim gets the best Aspiration scores from family-related experiences. You can put her in a career and she'll want to advance, though not with any real enthusiasm. Career-related Wants take the fore only as long as the Sim is young and hasn't found a promising mate yet. At this moment, it might be a good idea to lock the Sim's Want for a promotion. The moment she meets someone, however, her Wants will be all about falling in love, then engagement, then marriage, and then children. To her, a career promotion is no longer important. Thanks to the lock, however, that career Want is still clogging up a slot in the Wants panel. If four very important Wants are clamoring for attention and promising big scores, one of them (and any based on it) may never appear because of the locked career Want.

Before you lock a Want/Fear make sure you understand the general course of the Sim's Aspiration and Personality so you may judge what's truly important to that Sim in particular.

Want/Fears and Where They Lead

Wants and Fears are progressive. In other words, accomplishing one often opens paths to a higher-level Wants or Fears. It's impossible to get to the second tier Want or Fears without first realizing the most basic ones. For example:

◆ A Knowledge Aspiration Sim enters a random career (let's say Slacker) without much thought to what careers fit best with his Aspiration.

◆ Once he reaches level 2 in that career (or any career other than Science or Medicine), two Wants arise: to enter the Science career and to enter the Medical career.

◆ Once he switches to one of these "preferred" careers, the Want to get into the other of the two

drops off due to irrelevance. Were the Sim to switch again and advance to level 2 in something other than Medical or Science, these twin Wants would arise anew.

◆ Once he reaches level 3 in a preferred career, he has a taste for career success and a new Want will arise: To reach the top of the career he's in.

◆ With the achievement of level 4 in his career, he's become emotionally invested in it and two new Fears ascend: being demoted and being fired.

◆ If, on the other hand, the Sim stays in the Slacker career (for example), the Wants to get into Medicine or Science remain in the panel but become weaker over time. Eventually, they become so weak that they drop off the panel. Finally, they age out and the desire never arises again. Likewise, the desire to reach the top of those careers has become forever unavailable. A major scoring opportunity was missed.

One of the crucial skills is discerning which low-level Wants lead to something bigger and which are temporary and lead nowhere. Again, it's all about experience and understanding each Aspiration. A low-scoring desire to buy something, for example, can pop up for a Sim in any Aspiration for a variety of reasons. Chances are, it won't lead to any higher scoring Wants and can be comfortably ignored or easily fulfilled. If, however, the Sim is a Fortune Aspiration Sim, buying several increasingly expensive objects leads to greater and greater Aspiration point payoffs.

Fortune Sims want to buy stuff. When they get it, they want to buy more expensive stuff. You're going to need a lot of money to make a Fortune Sim happy.

note

Sometimes it's not a good idea to give your Sims what they want. For example, when things go badly at work, most Sims want to quit their job. If there aren't many strong Wants on the panel, this one can appear. Weigh, however, the damage caused by quitting over leaving this particular rash Want unsatisfied.

Want and Fear Scoring

note

If a Want or Fear has a starburst symbol, it's a "Power" Want or Fear. These provide the biggest scoring opportunity and may take a while to achieve.

Power Wants and Fears make big changes in Aspiration score.

Every Want or Fear has an individual score (typically ranging from 500 to 30,000) that's generally tied to how much effort, time, or money it requires to achieve. Score is shown if you point at the Want/Fear.

Power Wants/Fears are Wants/Fears that are central to the Sims' Aspiration and are very hard to achieve or extremely destructive. In fact, Power Wants are all the higher scoring Wants in each of the following catagories. Power Wants/Fears are highlighted by a starburst in the icon's background and are worth a tremendous number of points. "Impossible" Wants are the most difficult of all wants and ones that few players can achieve. They are Power Wants with extremely high requirements. As such they're the highest scoring. Normally, even having a chance at these Wants requires the longest possible

life-span (having, therefore, high Aspiration when going from adult to elder) and liberal use of the correct reward objects (see "Reward Objects," below).

A mere list doesn't do justice to the variety of Wants and Fears awaiting your Sims, but these are the most common general types (in order of score potential):

◆ Eating Interactions: The desire to try new foods or eat a favorite food.

◆ Social interactions: The desire to perform an interaction with anyone or with a specific Sim. The more difficult the interaction, the greater the score. Romance, Family, and Popularity Sims may have some high-scoring opportunities with interactions.

◆ Object purchases: The desire to purchase objects. The more expensive the object, the greater the score. If the object replaces one you already have, return the old one to soften the financial blow.

◆ Skill building: The desire to advance in a given skill. The higher the level, the greater the payoff.

◆ Career advancement: The desire to get and be promoted in a career.

◆ Relationship creation: The desire to achieve a kind of relationship with any or a specific Sim. The more difficult the relationship, the more points it offers.

> **note**
>
> If you buy an object to satisfy a Want, returning it too quickly results in a loss of Aspiration score. Fortunately, this period only lasts 25 game hours; after that, you can return it without losing Aspiration score (but you'll be out a bit for the initial depreciation).

> **note**
>
> When Sims feel low (Mood -20 to 20), they tend to want to buy things, depending on age and Personality. Teens, for example, regardless of Aspiration want to buy a phone (if Outgoing), a game (if Shy), entertainment (if Playful), a stereo (if Active), or a TV (if Lazy). Children want an entertainment object (if Lazy or Playful), a telescope (if Shy or Serious), a toy (if Shy or Playful), or a game (if Outgoing or Playful). Adults want to buy stuff too, but that's influenced heavily by their Aspirations.

ASPIRATIONS

Aspirations are goals that make Sims' lives meaningful. They provide direction to the Sims' Wants and Fears and give your Sim something to strive for over the course of her life.

These Aspirations profoundly (though not exclusively) shape a Sim's Wants and Fears and deeply impact how a Sim is played. It's not possible (or even helpful) to know every Want and Fear a Sim of a given Aspiration will have, but it's extremely illuminating to grasp the general bent of each Aspiration so you may anticipate, prioritize, and strategize effectively.

The Six Aspirations

Elder, adult, and teen Sims can aspire to six goals:

◆ Family   ◆ Popularity
◆ Fortune   ◆ Romance
◆ Knowledge   ◆ Growing up
                    (toddler and child)

> **note**
>
> Grow Up is the sixth Aspiration, but it is not one Sims can choose and is only available to toddlers and children.

Choose a Sim's Aspiration in Create-A-Sim or when he becomes a teenager.

tip

For the Wants and Fears game in THE SIMS 2, a Sim living alone is very difficult to play successfully. It can be done, but it takes very careful planning.

One further Aspiration drives only toddlers and children, but the Aspiration's Wants and Fears differ for each age:

◆ Growing Up

Toddlers and children just want to Grow Up.

note

Babies don't have the Grow Up Aspiration. They lack the foresight, let's say, to aspire beyond the next diaper or bottle.

Growing Up
Toddler

◆ Sample Wants: Learn to talk, walk, and be potty-trained, be talked to, played with, snuggled, read to, tickled, and learn Charisma, Logic, or Creativity skills
◆ Sample Fears: Fire, family break up, vomit (if Neat), see a ghost, have a party (if Shy), family death

The Growing Up Aspiration is shared by toddlers and children but how it manifests itself in each age is distinct.

For toddlers, growing up means getting pleasurable social interactions (tickled, snuggled, talked to) from people they know and learning the three basic toddler skills: talking, walking, and potty training.

Ultimately, like children, toddlers want to grow up well (if their Aspiration score is high enough) or fear growing up (if Aspiration score is low).

Most toddler Wants and Fears are pretty low scoring, but the scale of their Aspiration is pretty small: 250 points goes a long way for a toddler.

Child

◆ Sample Wants: Learn to study, get an A+ report card, get best friends, win games or fights, invite Sims over, build skills, play games with family
◆ Sample Fears: Death of others, losing games or fights, losing best friends, having invitations rejected, having a party (if Shy), Bladder failure (if Shy), be kissed by a grandparent (if Grouchy), be lectured (if Shy), clean something up (if Sloppy), get a D report card, see a ghost (if Serious), Energy failure (if Active)

Growing Up for children is a bit more complicated and requires far more to be a success.

Children's Wants and Fears tend to revolve around making friends, doing well at school, winning games with other children, spending time with best friends, and (naturally) growing up well (if Aspiration score is high).

Because they're just starting school, they also have Wants and Fears related to their grades and are keen to be taught how to do homework.

Family

- ◆ Preferred Careers: None
- ◆ Skill Bent: Cooking and Cleaning
- ◆ Sample Power Wants: Get Engaged, Get Married, Have a Baby, Teach to Walk, Teach to Talk, Potty Train, Teach to Study, Get a Grandchild
- ◆ Sample Wants: Gain skill in cooking and cleaning, interact with family, fall in love, get engaged, marry/join, have lots of children, remarry if widowed or left, romantic interactions with loved Sims, encourage Personality traits in their children/grandchildren
- ◆ Sample Fears: Be rejected for interactions with family, fire, break-up of family, rejected first kisses, family death, being unmarried/unjoined and/or childless as an elder, going to work in a negative Mood, be sick, burn food, see vermin, or fight with a relative

Family Sims are happiest at the center of a large family.

A Sim with the Family Aspiration dedicates his life to the enrichment and expansion of his family. A Family Sim wants to fall in love, get engaged, marry, and have children. Once he has children, he wants to have more children, wants them to learn all they can, and wants to be the one to teach them. He also wants his relatives to succeed, to encourage his children and grandchildren, and to have constant interactions with family members (particularly their own spouses and offspring).

> **note**
>
> Family is the only Aspiration that perfectly aligns with another Aspiration (Grow Up). Several of the Wants important to a Family Sim are identical to the Wants of toddlers and children. This provides many of the relatively rare opportunities to satisfy two Sims' Wants with one interaction.

Family Sims fear the failure, loss, or death of their loved ones. They fear being cheated on and the arrival of the Social Worker (see Chapter 26).

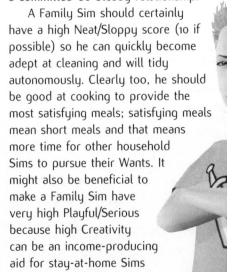

A Family Sim would rather read to his child than go to work.

A Family Sim has no particular career ambitions but will want to advance in a career if put in one. It won't, however, be a high priority Want.

A teen Sim with this Aspiration yearns to be in a committed Go Steady relationship.

A Family Sim should certainly have a high Neat/Sloppy score (10 if possible) so he can quickly become adept at cleaning and will tidy autonomously. Clearly too, he should be good at cooking to provide the most satisfying meals; satisfying meals mean short meals and that means more time for other household Sims to pursue their Wants. It might also be beneficial to make a Family Sim have very high Playful/Serious because high Creativity can be an income-producing aid for stay-at-home Sims (painting or writing a novel).

When a Family Sim's Aspiration score is low, she'll crave her basic Wants even more intensely. Being below zero in Aspiration score triggers very strong Wants to marry, have a child, go steady, or have a grandchild (depending on age). Unlike the normal desires for these things, these "Desperation" Wants aren't directed toward any Sim in particular and don't follow the normal chain of events toward childbirth. For example, a desperate Family Sim wants to have a child even if she's not married; an "Aspirationally healthy" Sim would not.

Otherwise, if there are traits you want to encourage in the Family Sim's offspring, make the Family Sim as extreme as possible in the chosen trait. If you want the future generation to be Outgoing, give the parent 10 points in Outgoing/ Shy so she may encourage more effectively.

Though it adds to family income, time spent pursuing writing or painting detracts from a Family Sim's ability to fulfill his Aspiration.

Fortune

- Preferred Careers: Business, Athletic, Criminal, and Medical
- Skill Bent: Creativity and whatever needed to advance career
- Sample Power Wants: Be an Overachiever, Big Bonus, Marry a Rich Sim, Earn §50,000
- Sample Wants: Personally earn increasing amounts of money, build skills needed for work, home upgrades, purchase art, get bonuses and promotions, buy expensive items, hire service Sims, marry or join rich, sell a great novel or painting
- Sample Fears: The Repo Man, burglary, selling lousy novel or painting, fire, missing carpool, being fired

Fortune Sims are all about the simoleans. Anything that doesn't involve the acquisition of money or stuff is not really on their radar.

Fortune Sims need time to reach the top of their careers.

Career is more important for this Aspiration than any other; Fortune Sims are the only Sims who won't sacrifice career success for other Wants.

The easiest marriage to manage is a Fortune and a stay-at-home Family Sim.

The first thing is to get her into the right careers: Athletic, Criminal, Medical, or Business.

Because they'll need lots of extra money, Fortune Sims want to sell novels and paintings. Give them Creativity skill and the objects they need (computers and easels, respectively) to produce these extra income-producing pursuits. They want to earn money somehow every day.

Spend days off producing great works of art—not because they're beautiful, of course, but because they make more cash.

Fortune Sims make the best earners and are well-paired with Family Sims. Anything that takes a Fortune Sim away from work or job-related skill building is a waste of their time, so having someone to handle everything else is a boon.

note

When his Aspiration score is failing, a Fortune Sim clamors for promotions, earning money, selling a great painting or novel, and (especially) marrying a rich Sim (depending on his Personality).

Unlike other Sims who have buying Wants for major life transitions or when their Mood is low, Fortune Sims want to acquire stuff all the time and always in ever increasing degrees of magnitude. This can be very difficult economically, so be sure to sell your old stuff to minimize the expense.

Personality for a Fortune Sim should be geared to her career. She should be very Sloppy (unless Medical is her field) because Personality points can be better used elsewhere. For the creation of valuable paintings and novels, Fortune Sims should always have high Playful/Serious to maximize their Creativity. Creativity can do double duty if you limit your Fortune Sim to the Criminal and Business fields that also require this skill. A Fortune Sim can, but probably shouldn't, be Lazy; a Lazy Sim wants to quit his job when his Mood is bad and this would be damaging to a Fortune Sim.

tip

Making a Fortune Sim Sloppy means she makes messes faster. This provides a Family Sim living with her plenty of opportunity to learn Cleaning skill by mopping up after the messy Fortune Sim. It may not sound like it, but this is a benefit to the Family Sim. Right, Mom and Dad?

Knowledge

- ◆ Preferred Careers: Science, Medicine
- ◆ Skill Bent: All
- ◆ Sample Power Wants: Learn to Study, Get an A+ Report Card, Maximize a Skill, Meet Aliens, See a Ghost, Maximize All Skills, Be Saved from Death
- ◆ General Wants: Learn to cook, be or have loved ones abducted by aliens, learn and maximize skills, see ghosts, or repair things
- ◆ General Fears: Lose a point of skill, see vermin, burn food, be sick, fire

Most of a Knowledge Sim's time should be geared toward gaining skills.

The Knowledge Sim wants experiences that involve learning, even if the lessons are some of life's darker ones.

tip

If you're going to have a Sim living alone, Knowledge is the best Aspiration.

Skill building is a major preoccupation of Knowledge Sims, and they get their best Aspiration scoring from maxing out several, and eventually all, their skills. Knowledge Sims want skills even if they have no career. They really want to know how to repair things, especially if they're Serious, and how to cook every kind of food.

A "near death experience" is one in which the Sim experiences something that can kill him but doesn't. For example, the Sim is electrocuted but his motives are so high that he survives.

Knowledge Sims also want to experience the truly bizarre. They hanker to see the ghosts of Sims, be abducted by aliens (several times if possible), and be saved from death.

Keep peering through the expensive telescope and maybe, just maybe, the Knowledge Sim will get her dearest wish. Hello aliens!

note

Being Saved from Death is a very complex and risky undertaking. First, the Sim who desires this experience must stage his own death in a way that permits others to bargain with the Reaper (i.e. it can't be in the pool). Second, there must be someone present with whom he has a strong relationship to challenge the Reaper. Third, he must be lucky enough to have his partner (preferably a Popularity Sim) win his life back. That's a lot to leave to fate, but the Knowledge Sim thinks it's worth it.

When they have a low Mood, Knowledge Sims want to buy items that feed their thirst for knowledge: bookcases and telescopes.

note

If a Knowledge Sim's Aspiration score is failing, she very hungrily desires to have a near death experience or max out a skill.

Most Fears revolve around losing skill points.

Knowledge Sims are attracted to the Medical and Science professions but want to quit or stay home from work to pursue their general love of learning. Knowledge Sims make some of the most content stay-at-home Sims, especially if there are no children. Their desire for all skills means they learn three skills mostly by doing: Cooking, Cleaning, and Mechanical. It helps (for Cleaning at least) if they're very Neat.

A good Personality profile for a Knowledge Sim is 10 Neat/Sloppy, 10 or 0 in Playful/Serious, 5 in Nice/Grouchy, and (if Playful/Serious is 0) 10 in Outgoing/Shy or Active/Lazy. This gives them accelerated learning in three skills.

Popularity

- Preferred Careers: Politics, Military, and Athletic
- Skill Bent: Charisma
- Power Wants: Have a Great Party, Have Several Best Friends, Sell a Masterpiece, Win Fight
- General Wants: Make best friends, have successful parties, meet new Sims, sneak out (if teen), entertain other Sims, make drinks, hire a Bartender, gain Charisma skill, dance, do Appreciate interactions, win games
- General Fears: Being rejected for social interactions, making enemies, deaths or loss of friends, have an invitation rejected, throw a bad party, Bladder failure, receive Irritate interactions, get Fat, see the Social Bunny, be booed, smell bad, or lose games

Popularity Sims crave companionship and collect friends like trading cards.

Popularity Sims want notoriety and to be liked. Their Wants/ Fears, therefore, revolve around making and keeping as many best friends as possible and throwing successful parties. They particularly want to beat the Reaper to save another Sim's life (making them a great roommate for a Knowledge Sim).

> **tip**
>
> Popularity Sims make great uncles for younger Sims.

Their career ambitions fit their desire for fame. Politics, Military, and Athletic careers meet this need.

A Popularity Sim is also good to have as a stay-at-home Sim, especially if the working Sim has a career that requires lots of friends (e.g., Slacker, Politics, Law Enforcement). The Popularity Sim already spends much of his time making friends, so having enough for a career is no extra work. They match up well with Fortune Sims and make good roommates for Romance (because jealousy won't make their Wants conflict) or Knowledge Sims.

> **note**
>
> When Popularity Sims' Aspiration score begins to fail, they have powerful desires to beat the Reaper, buy magazines to change their Interests, have several best friends, and have a party.

Popularity Sims want to get the party started and keep it going.

Popularity Sims' Fears tend to be about having bad parties and the death or loss of friends. One of their biggest Fears is losing a challenge to the Reaper. This makes their desire to challenge death a very risky one; the positive payoff is massive, but the negative is disastrous.

Personality traits for Popularity Sims should center on those that help them make friends, develop Charisma, and succeed in one of the Aspiration's favored careers. They should certainly have 10 Outgoing/ Shy and probably 10 Nice/ Grouchy. Beyond that, it depends on career choice. If they stay at home, a high Neat/Sloppy score is helpful.

Romance

- ◆ Preferred Careers: Slacker
- ◆ Skill Bent: Creativity, Charisma
- ◆ Power Wants: Have First Kiss, WooHoo, Have Two Loves at Once, WooHoo with Three Different Sims
- ◆ General Wants: Fall in love; WooHoo; WooHoo in public; having romantic interactions accepted; buying a fireplace, double bed, sofa or hot tub; meet new Sims (especially if they have a child); get Fit (if Active)
- ◆ Sample Fears: Having romantic or talking interactions rejected, going steady, engagement, marriage/joining, having children, Hygiene or Bladder failure (if Neat), Energy failure (if Active), go to work in a negative Mood (if Lazy), get Fat (if Active)

Romance Sims are all about romantic conquest and want nothing to do with anything smacking of commitment or children. Their biggest desires involve experiencing love and making "WooHoo" with as many Sims as possible before they die. They're even happier if they can maintain more than one love at once.

> **tip**
>
> Without a doubt, the worst marriage pairing is Romance and Family because many of their highest scoring Wants and Fears are in direct conflict.

Their Fears involve being rejected in romantic interactions. They save their greatest Fears, however, for the conventions of family life. They deeply fear engagement, marriage, and having children. If you force them into these tracks, their Aspiration score may drop irretrievably low. To make matters worse, once married, they eventually have a powerful desire to meet someone new. They are, to say the least, not a good match for Family Sims.

The Love Tub makes courting several Sims MUCH easier.

---

note

Logistically, the hardest part of playing a Romance Sim is avoiding jealousy. Doing this means going to great lengths to keep lovers from being in the same room or even on the same lot. The more intricate a Romance Sim's web of paramours becomes, the harder it becomes to fulfill her greatest Wants.

A teen Romance Sim spends all of her energy wanting to have romantic interactions (especially Make Out) with as many other Sims as possible.

After a romantic interaction with a new Sim, Romance Sims want to buy objects that facilitate amour: double beds, fireplace, hot tubs, etc.

Romance Sims don't mind work but the only *specific* career they desire is the Slacker career. They're comfortable being jobless but fear the commitments that would allow them to live the unemployed life. Popularity Sims make good room-mates for them, however, because of their different but similarly met goals. A Popularity Sim wants friends while a Romance Sim wants lovers. Because these two relationships aren't incompatible and don't

lead to jealousy, one third-party Sim can satisfy the Wants of both a Romance and a Popularity Sim in one visit. He can be the Romance Sim's lover and the Popularity Sim's friend without causing any static.

Jealousy is a major pitfall for Romance Sims.

Personality-wise, a Romance Sim should be very high in the traits that facilitate Romance: Outgoing and Nice. For success in the Slacker career, very high in Outgoing and Playful helps speed skill development.

Universal Wants and Fears

Many Wants and Fears have nothing to do with Aspiration. These can be driven by several factors, but most commonly by Personality.

Universal Wants and Fears can be about buying things, the death of loved ones, common misfortunes (fire, robbery, vermin, illness, getting Fat, Energy or Bladder failure), and the ups and downs of work.

If Sims are demoted at work, they want to quit or stay home. If they stay home a lot, they want to switch to the Slacker career track.

---

note

Interestingly, there's a universal fear (for all but Family Sims) of having more than four children. For all but the most rabid Family Sims, three seems to be the limit.

Making and eating food are small but important elements in the Aspirations game.

Some of the more interesting universal Wants have to do with making and eating good food. Pursuing this track offers many extra opportunities to add to Aspiration score but also requires commitment to maximizing Cooking skill. All Sims benefit from this course (except that it takes them away from their core Aspiration) but a stay-at-home Sim benefits the most and has the most time to make it happen. Pursuing this course also leads to a desire to enter the Culinary career and to buy better kitchen objects.

ASPIRATION METER

note

There's a difference between Aspiration points and Reward points. Both are earned and lost when a Want/Fears are realized but the similarity ends there.

Aspirations points drive the Aspirations Meter and dictate how successful your Sim is in his Aspiration. Wants push it up and Fears push it down. Aspiration decay also drives the Aspiration Meter down.

Reward points are added to each Sim's fund for buying the special Aspiration reward objects. Fears can deduct from this pot but decay doesn't.

The Aspiration Meter displays how your Sim is doing in the pursuit of her Aspiration. The higher the level, the more successful your Sim currently is.

The Aspirations Meter is a funny looking device (a top-heavy hourglass), but its every feature communicates important information.

The narrow point about two-thirds down is zero. Below is negative and above is positive.

Positive Aspiration range is divided into four sectors. The first two sectors are "Green." The third sector is "Gold." The final and highest level is "Platinum."

When Aspiration score is positive in the first two tiers, the bar is green. In the third sector, it appears gold. When it's really positive (Platinum), it turns white.

A Sim's chosen Aspiration is displayed above his Aspiration Meter. The Sim's level of Aspiration success is shown by the meter's level and color.

Negative Aspiration range is cut into two parts: distress and failure. Whenever Aspiration score is below zero, the meter will show red.

The larger a section of the meter is, the more points it requires to fill it. Thus, going from Green to Gold takes very few points while going from Gold to Platinum takes considerably more.

Aspiration Meter and Ages

The number of Aspiration points from zero to the top and bottom of the scale varies by Sim age. In other words, a toddler requires very few points to fill her Aspiration Meter while an elder requires a tremendous number.

Note the Aspiration Meter before aging from teen to adult.

And now, after the change. The Sim's score didn't change, but the scale of the meter did.

Thus, scoring a Want of, for example, 500 points is a huge jump for a toddler but only slightly moves an adult's meter.

When Sims age, the scale of this meter shifts to the new age. The result is that a Sim's Aspiration score shifts toward zero (positive score dropping and negative score rising) when he ages.

> **note**
>
> The point capacity of the Aspiration meter grows with each age. This is why score drops when a Sim age transitions. The 5,000 points that nearly filled a child's meter fills just over half of a teen's meter. Point capacity for each age is:
>
> - Toddler: 3,000 pts
> - Child: 6,000 pts
> - Teen: 9,000 pts
> - Adult: 12,000 pts
> - Elder: 15,000 pts
>
> For every age, however, the percentage of total points in each sector of the meter is:
>
> - 35 percent (Platinum)
> - 25 percent (Gold)
> - 20 percent (Top Green)
> - 10 percent (Bottom Green)
> - 5 percent (Top Red)
> - 5 percent (Bottom Red)

It's easy to be alarmed by this sudden change, but it's not a reflection of your Sim's success, just a consequence of moving to a new stage in life. It takes more for an older Sim to consider herself a success.

REWARD POINTS

Every achieved Want and Fear also contributes its score to a Sim's Reward point total.

> **note**
>
> The Reward points total can be viewed under Rewards in main interface. The panel shows the available rewards (in full color), unavailable rewards (grayed out), and the individual Sim's total Reward points.

Reward points and the objects they purchase display in the Rewards panel.

Wants add to the pot of Reward points and Fears deduct from it.

Note that the Aspiration reward objects are (with one exception) limited use items. They may seem "cheap," but you'll likely have to buy several of the same kind over a Sim's lifetime.

ASPIRATION DECAY

Aspiration score decays hourly while a Sim is awake. No decay occurs while your Sim sleeps.

The higher the level of Aspiration, the more it decays each hour. Thus, it's easy to maintain low to moderate Aspiration score, but staying Platinum requires constant attention. Here's the time it takes to decay through each segment of the meter:

- 8 hours (plat)
- 16 hours (gold)
- 32 hours (top green)
- 32 hours (bottom green)
- 32 hours (top red)
- 0 (bottom red: no decay)

If you completely stop fulfilling Wants for an extended time, decay will reduce your score below zero, stopping one sector shy of Aspiration failure. At that point, one good Fear will send your Sim over the brink.

THE HIGHS AND LOWS OF ASPIRATION

The rewards of success are many and the penalties are severe. Even low levels of success or failure can have dramatic impact on your Sims' daily lives.

The payoff and pitfalls of very high (Platinum) or very low (failure) Aspiration are critical.

Aspiration Moniker

The levels of accomplishment in each Aspiration have their own titles that indicate the level of success. These differ based on Aspiration and age.

Grow Up

Aspiration Level	Moniker, Toddler	Moniker, Child
Distress—Moderate to Severe	Rotten Rugrat	Neglected Nightmare
Distress—Low to Moderate	Hectic Handful	Bothersome Brat
Green—Low	Diaper-Filler	Typical Tyke
Green—High	Little Wonder	Gifted Kid
Gold Pre-Schooler	Precocious	Wonder Boy/Girl
Platinum	Miracle Mite	Child Prodigy

Teen Monikers by Aspiration

Aspiration Level	Romance	Popularity	Fortune	Family	Knowledge
Distress—Moderate to Severe	Lonely Loser	Abject Reject	Pitiful Parasite	Family Flunk-Out	Dense Dunce
Distress—Low to Moderate	Wallflower	Maladjusted Misfit	Tapped-Out Teen	Bad Seed	Addled Adolescent
Green—Low	Hormonal Hurricane	One of the Gang	Mini-miser	Routine Relative	Solid Student
Green—High	Hottie	Stylin' Scenester	Early Bird	Good Son/Darling Daughter	Smarty Pants
Gold	Total Babe	Mr./Ms. Popularity	Junior Achiever	Pride and Joy	Whiz Kid
Platinum	Major Heart-throb	Teen Idol	Future Financier	Shining Example	Young Genius

Adult Monikers by Aspiration

Aspiration Level	Romance	Popularity	Fortune	Family	Knowledge
Distress—Moderate to Severe	Total Turn-Off	Wretched Outcast	Penniless Peon	Black Sheep	Incredible Ignoramus
Distress—Low to Moderate	Cold Fish	Left-Out Loner	No-Account Nickel Monkey	Brood Bungler	Silly Goose
Green—Low	Hopeless Romantic	Man/Woman-about-town	Bacon Bringer	Solid Provider	Brainstretcher
Green—High	Lusty Lover	Real Somebody	Big Cheese	Good Influence	Free Thinker
Gold	Love Machine	Noted Notable	Cash Machine	Role Model	Impressive Intellect
Platinum	Don Juan/Femme Fatale	Local Hero/Heroine	Moolah Mogul	Family Rock	Savant Supreme

Elder Monikers by Aspiration

Aspiration Level	Romance	Popularity	Fortune	Family	Knowledge
Distress—Moderate to Severe	Burned-out Cinder	Forgotten Fogie	Doddering Deadbeat	Creepy Crank/Crone	Senile Simpleton
Distress—Low to Moderate	Dirty Old Man/Woman	Has-been	Spent Spendthrift	Grumpy Gramps/Grams	Decaying Dullard
Green—Low	Old Flame	Aging Acquaintance	Creaky Cash-Bringer	Sweet Old Coot	Well-Read Whitehair
Green—High	Sexy Senior	Long-time Luminary	Affluent Ancient	Sire/Matron	Mature Mastermind
Gold	Silver Fox	Gray Eminence	Fat Cat	Matriarch/Patriarch	Wizened Wise One
Platinum	Fiery Fossil	Senior Socialite	Towering Tycoon	Town Father/Mother	Senior Sage

Aspiration Rewards

Reward points can be redeemed for any of nine Aspiration reward objects. These objects are designed to assist in advancing your Sim's Aspiration; though sometimes in indirect ways.

> **note**
>
> Money Tree income adds to the household budget but also counts toward the harvesting Sim's individual personal lifetime income (important for certain Wants).

Pasteur's HomoGenius Smart Milk

> **note**
>
> Five bottles of Smart Milk should easily ensure a toddler can walk, talk, and use the potty before his age transition.

> **note**
>
> Aspiration reward objects can be moved by entering Build mode and moving them like any other object. When an object is used up, it remains on the lot with no available interactions. To remove it, enter Buy mode and drag it onto the Buy mode panel as if returning it. You won't, however, receive any money or Reward points for the transaction even if there are uses left in the object.

One feature common to all Aspiration reward objects is their tendency to fail if the user's Aspiration is too low at the time. Thus, an Aspiration reward object only helps those who are successful already.

- Platinum: Guaranteed success
- Gold: Guaranteed success
- Green: 50 percent chance of success
- Red: 20 percent chance of success

Money Tree

- Used By: Teen/adult/elder
- Reward Point Cost: 3,000
- Uses/Time Limit: Unlimited but must water regularly
- Success: If regularly watered and harvested, Money Tree should require as much care time (watering every six hours) and pay as much (§40 per harvest) as a low-level job.
- Failure: If Aspiration score is low, only §1 per harvest. If it's not watered frequently, plant will die and must be discarded.

The Money Tree

Pasteur's HomoGenius Smart Milk

- Used By: Adult
- Reward Point Cost: 7,500
- Uses/Time Limit: 5 uses
- Success: For three hours, toddler who drinks Smart Milk learns to talk, walk, potty train and other skills at an accelerated rate.
- Failure: Bottle turns red. Toddler spits up and loses a random skill point. Based on Aspiration score of adult who prepares Smart Milk.

Cool Shades

Cool Shades

- Used By: Teen/adult/elder
- Reward Point Cost: 10,000
- Uses/Time Limit: 5 uses

- Success: First social interaction a Sim does with Cool Shades on has amplified effect, whether it's positive or negative.
- Failure: None

Noodlesoother

Noodlesoother

- Used By: Teen/adult/elder
- Reward Point Cost: 5,000
- Uses/Time Limit: 24 hours. Green lights on front of helmet indicate time remaining.
- Success: Sim's overall Mood is boosted by 50 points. While wearing the helmet, however, all Needs decay at an accelerated rate. Eventually, the benefit of the Mood boost is outweighed by the drag on Needs.
- Failure: Sim's Energy drops to -100 and Sim passes out. All other Needs severely lowered. When Sim awakens, he automatically removes the helmet.

The Eclectic and Enigmatic Energizer

The Eclectic and
Enigmatic Energizer

- Used By: Teen/adult/elder
- Reward Point Cost: 14,000
- Uses/Time Limit: 5 uses

- Success: 750 points randomly added to all Needs
- Failure: 750 points randomly subtracted to all Needs. Can't kill a Sim.

Thinking Cap

Thinking Cap

- Used By: Teen/adult/elder
- Reward Point Cost: 16,000
- Uses/Time Limit: 24 hours
- Success: Skill building rate doubled. Works in Teach/Help interactions too. If both Sims in Teach/Help are teen or older, both can wear Thinking Caps and effect is cumulative. Speeds up toddler training if teacher is wearing Thinking Cap.
- Failure: Energy drops to zero (Sim passes out) and Sim loses one random skill point.

SimVac

SimVac

- Used By: Teen/adult/elder
- Reward Point Cost: 17,500
- Uses/Time Limit: 5 uses
- Success: Sim specifies another Sim (teen, adult, or elder), chooses whether he wants to transfer Aspiration or skill points and applies the vacuum to the chosen Sim. One skill point or 3,000 Aspiration points per use. Relationship reduction for both parties and can remove love or a crush.

◆ Failure: Aspiration or skill points go from user of the vacuum to the other Sim and user takes a severe hit to Needs. Relationship reduction for both parties and can remove love or a crush.

Love Tub

Love Tub

> **note**
>
> The candles should last long enough to complete five socials.

◆ Used By: Teen/adult/elder
◆ Reward Point Cost: 20,000
◆ Uses/Time Limit: Four hours. When candles burn out, object's special powers are spent but the Sim can keep a very nice and fully functional hot tub.
◆ Success: Between two Sims in the tub, acceptance requirements are lowered and relationship outcomes are increased. Upshot: makes Sims much more accepting of romantic advances.
◆ Failure: None

> **note**
>
> When the Love Tub is spent, it becomes a regular hot tub with Comfort (6) and Fun (7).

Elixir of Life

Elixir of Life

◆ Used By: Teen/adult/elder
◆ Reward Point Cost: 30,580
◆ Uses/Time Limit: 5 uses
◆ Success: Upcoming age transition or death by old age is pushed back three days. If Sim is within the first three days of her current age range, she won't be pushed back into the previous age but rather held at her birthday for five days.
◆ Failure: Sim's age pushed forward three days. If within three days of age transition or death by old age, the Sim will age or die immediately.

Platinum Aspiration

If Aspiration rises into the upper portion of the Aspiration meter, your Sim will be lovin' life. So much so, in fact, that she'll be in a perfect Mood no matter what her individual Needs. You still have to tend to falling Needs (eat, sleep, bathe, toilet, etc.) to keep from suffering Needs failures, but they don't impact overall Mood.

When your Sims enter this state of Platinum Aspiration, his Mood Meter glows white and the Aspirations Meter does the same.

A Sim with very high Aspiration score sports a Platinum Plumbob.

> **note**
>
> From the highest level of Platinum Aspiration, a Sim drops out of the Platinum region (losing her constant good Mood) in about eight game hours if she satisfies no further Wants.

The strategic benefits of reaching this state should be obvious. A Sim in a perfect good Mood will:

- Accept any social interaction that requires only high Mood
- Improve his job performance/school grades every time he goes to work or school
- Work at skill-developing objects longer

Every good thing, however, must come to an end. Once a Sim achieves Platinum Aspiration score, decay quickly drags it down. Because higher Aspiration score decays fastest, staying in the Platinum level requires constant accomplishment of Wants.

> **tip**
>
> Just because a Sim's in a good Mood doesn't mean he'll accept ANY social interaction. Mood is usually but one condition for acceptance. Check the tables in Chapter 24 for others.)

> **tip**
>
> By locking big, but nearly achieved Wants, you can have them ready when you need to be in the perfect Mood won with Platinum Aspiration. For example, just before you head off to work, put in the last bit of skill training that achieves the next skill level. If the push is enough to raise the Sim into Platinum territory, she'll dramatically improve her job performance.

Utilizing this state is a great challenge, not just because it's hard to keep, but because the Aspiration Meter only goes so high. Achieving big Wants when the meter is at or near the top is a waste of Aspiration points. Sure, you get the Reward points, but the Aspiration points do nothing to keep you in the Platinum zone. Locking Wants at strategic moments is, therefore, one of the more important skills you can learn. It takes practice, but knowing when is the right time to score a Want is as important as achieving it.

Inheritance

A Sim's Aspiration score at the time of death partially dictates the amount of inheritance his family and friends will receive.

For family members, this amount depends on the kind of family connection and the deceased's Aspiration score. Lifetime Relationship with the deceased dictates what percentage of the potential inheritance the survivor will receive.

For friends, inheritance depends on Aspiration score and the friend's Lifetime Relationship score with the deceased at the time of death.

Inheritance Amounts Based on Aspiration Score

Relationship to Deceased	High Aspiration	Medium Aspiration	Low Aspiration
Spouse	§20,000	§10,000	§5,000
Children	§10,000	§5,000	§2,500
Grandchildren	§2,500	§1,250	§625
Friend, Lifetime Relationship 75–100	§1,000	§500	§250
Friend, Lifetime Relationship 50–74	§500	§250	§125

Thus, a spouse of a medium Aspiration Sim who had a Lifetime Relationship score of 90 receives an inheritance of §9,000. A friend of a high Aspiration Sim with Lifetime Relationship of 85 would get §850.

For family members in particular, it matters quite a bit what an elder's Aspiration score is on the day she passes away.

> **note**
>
> Inheritance has nothing whatsoever to do with the household value or the deceased Sim's personal lifetime income. It is, therefore, more like a death benefit than an actual inheritance.

Aspiration Distress and Failure

When Aspiration score goes below zero but still above the failure line, a Sim is in "Aspirational Distress." At the failure line, a Sim is in "Aspirational Failure."

In these states, Sims experience heightened Wants and exhibit autonomous behaviors that waste time, disrupt sleep, cost money, reduce Fitness, damage relationships, and create disorder. The worse the Aspiration score, the worse these behaviors become.

When Aspirations are getting low, Sims signal to get you to notice.

Elders and adults exhibit even more severe behaviors when in failure and will suffer complete breakdowns if score reaches bottom.

For children, toddlers, and teens, these behaviors are called "Immaturity." For elders, adults, and teens, they're called "Desperation."

note

When a Sim is exhibiting Immaturity or Desperation, his thought balloons periodically show his Aspiration icon in one of three states: Blue (mild), Red (moderate), and Red in a jagged scream balloon (severe).

note

Sims insert these behaviors into their queue directly after their current action, jumping ahead of all other interactions. The only way to get out of them is to manually cancel the interaction by clicking on its icon in the queue. Once you insert any other interaction behind an Immaturity/Desperation interaction, however, it can no longer be cancelled.

Desperation Wants

When a Sim is failing in her Aspiration, several Wants appear that represent her despair. Usually these Wants reflect the Aspiration's core desires.

Desperation Wants are extremely helpful because they tend to advertise very highly and offer heavy scores that can quickly get a Sim back in the green.

Immaturity

Children and toddlers have a single Aspiration: Grow Up. When they are failing in this Aspiration and realizing too many of their Fears, they behave immaturely. Usually, this behavior is destructive to the household and distracting to the older Sims in the family and can actually worsen their Aspirational situation.

Toddlers' Immaturity behavior includes playing in the toilet.

These behaviors range from mild to severe. The lower the Aspiration score, the more severe the behaviors, the longer they last, and the more frequently they occur. For example, a child with a slightly negative score infrequently exhibits mild behaviors. With a worse score, she more frequently does both mild and moderate behaviors. With a really low or rock bottom score, she exhibits all three behaviors very frequently.

An immature teen will bounce on the sofa.

Immaturity behaviors are:

Immaturity Behaviors

Immaturity Behavior	Type	Immaturity Behavior	Type
Annoy: Noogie	Mild	Kick Tombstone	Moderate
Annoy: Nyah/Nyah	Mild	Splash Puddle	Moderate
Belch	Mild	Stomp Diaper	Moderate
Cry (Toddler only)	Mild	Stomp Flowers	Moderate
Fart	Mild	Tantrum Mild	Moderate
Gross Out	Mild	Trashcan: Kick over Trash	Moderate
Jump on Couch	Mild	Urn: Smash	Moderate
Swing on Fridge Door	Mild	Cry (toddler only)	Severe
Play in Toilet	Mild	Fight: Attack	Severe
Cry (toddler only)	Moderate	Fight: Poke	Severe
Dollhouse: Smash	Moderate	Fight: Shove	Severe
Easel: Ruin Painting	Moderate	Fight: Slap	Severe
Kick Flamingo	Moderate	Tantrum Strong (child/toddler only)	Severe
Kick Gnome	Moderate		

Desperation

note

Though teens have specific Aspirations like adults and elders, they still exhibit Immaturity behaviors like children and toddlers, don't have Aspiration-specific behaviors, and don't suffer breakdowns if in Aspiration failure.

Adults exhibit Desperation by stuffing their face at the fridge....

Elder and adult Sims in negative Aspirational territory autonomously display "Desperation" behaviors. These become more frequent and last longer as score worsens toward the failure line. When they drop into moderate Desperation, new behaviors emerge, the

worst of which are specific to their Aspiration. When they finally hit bottom, adult and elder Sims will suffer a total breakdown, become temporarily undirectable, and need a visit from the Sim Shrink.

◆ When in mild Desperation (from 0 to the first line), Sims autonomously perform mild behaviors with increasing frequency and duration.

◆ When in moderate Desperation (from first line down to near bottom), they exhibit the mild behaviors with alarming frequency and duration, do Aspiration-specific time-wasting behaviors (with increasing frequency and duration), and (when very close to severe Desperation) have crying breakdowns.

◆ When Desperation fails, they break down completely. In this state, they sit on the floor and babble and won't accept direction, interact with other Sims or objects, or accept any interactions. Other Sims react to the Sim like he's loco. In the end, Sim is increased by one Aspiration level: still in the red but not barking mad either.

Elder/Adult Desperation Behaviors

Interaction	Aspiration	Severity	Description
Worry	All	Mild/Moderate	Sim stands and wrings hands and mumbles to self.
Crying	All	Moderate (near severe)	Sim stops and sobs for a long time.
Flour Sack Baby	Family	Severe	Sim pulls out and cuddles a flour sack marked up to look like a baby.
Panhandle	Fortune	Severe	Sim begs for money from passing Sims.
Professor Von Ball	Knowledge	Severe	Sim has an intellectual discussion with a ball wearing a mortar board.
Cup Stick Buddy	Popularity	Severe	Sim has a lively conversation with a paper cup decorated with a drawn-on face.
Sponge Mop Lover	Romance	Severe	Sim puts a paper plate face on the sponge mop and whispers sweet nothings to it.

...or, if things are really grim, going more than a bit over the edge.

BIRTHDAYS AND ASPIRATIONS

Two days before an age transition, you receive a message reminding you of the coming event. This is also a major strategic opportunity.

If a Sim has a high Aspiration score on her birthday, she'll have a Want to Grow Up. This gives an extra boost to Aspiration score when the transition occurs.

If, on the other hand, the Sim has low Aspiration score as his transition approaches, he'll have a Fear of Growing Up. This deducts points at the crucial moment.

Use this system to your advantage. The important thing to know is that once you see the birthday reminder, the Sim can be directed to Grow Up anytime you choose. If she has high Aspiration at that point, there's no reason not to throw the party immediately.

If, on the other hand, score is low enough that the Fear of Growing Up appears, you have only two days to remedy the situation. In this case, focus on satisfying Wants and put off the transition as long as possible (it happens automatically at 7 p.m. on the final day). See Chapter 25 for the mechanics of birthdays.

> ## tip
>
> If you need more time to change Aspiration score so the Sim wants to Grow Up rather than fearing it, the Elixir of Life Aspiration reward object can help. It's risky though. If successful, the transition is delayed by three days. If unsuccessful, the transition is pushed forward three days (forcing the age transition if within three days of it). Because any Sim for whom you'd try this must have low Aspiration (or else why bother?), the odds of the Elixir failing will be very high.

ASPIRATION AND FUTURE GENERATIONS

Much of this chapter deals with matching a Sim's Personality traits to the Aspiration you want him to assume. This is only possible, however, with the first generation of Sims you produce in Create-A-Sim. Once genetics take over, the personalities of future Sims are out of your control.

You can still, of course, choose his Aspiration when he reaches the teen age, but the process of assigning an Aspiration must be the reverse of what's described above. Rather than molding the Personality to fit the Aspiration, pick the Aspiration to fit the Personality.

What makes this challenging is that offspring won't fit perfectly into an Aspiration's most strategically advantageous mold. It takes far more skill to make a genetically created Sim successful than one you custom built for success.

On the other hand, genetically created Sims may have the advantage of having a well-established and successful home with a good family and nice objects and a steady income. All these things make satisfying Wants a whole lot easier.

The same goes for finding a mate. It's entirely possible that love will bloom between two Sims whose Aspirations are in conflict. You can wait for the better Sim to come along but that could waste valuable time.

Take the lessons of this chapter and use them creatively. Imagine how they work in other unforeseen situations. This is the secret to dynastic Sim success.

Chapter 22

Whether Sims are climbing the career ladder, staying home to raise a family, or living a life of self-improvement, they need skills. Acquiring them effectively and efficiently in a Sim's now limited life-span, however, can be one of the game's great challenges.

Skills can impact many things:

- To advance in any career, Sims must highly develop three defined skills. Career advancement increases your Sim's income, increases the amount of his retirement pension, gives him better work hours, and provides fulfillment of career-related Wants.
- The Wants of many Sims are tied to the acquisition of a skill or all skills. Aspiration points increase with each skill level and pay off big time if the skill is maximized.
- Some Sims have a Fear of losing a skill point, thus reducing Aspiration score.
- Some skills provide the opportunity for extra income.
- Doing certain activities with high or low skill can elicit reactions from nearby Sims.
- Some skills make household chores faster and easier.
- Skills play a role in the acceptance of some social interactions.
- Skills determine who will win a fight or many physical games and how well a Sim can dive.
- Some special abilities are unlocked by advancing in certain skills.
- Hidden skills can hold some surprises.
- High household skills lessen the need for hired help.

- Skills dictate how safe it is for a Sim to use certain objects.

This chapter introduces you to the seven basic skills, three toddler skills, one school-related skill, and three hidden skills, and details how they impact your Sims' everyday lives and entire lifetimes.

KINDS OF SKILLS

Seven basic skills appear in the Skills and Career panel. Basic skills affect many aspects of the game, including career and homemaking. The basic skills are:

- Cooking
- Logic
- Mechanical
- Creativity
- Charisma
- Cleaning
- Body

These basic skills can be built by child, teen, adult, or elder Sims though children need special objects for some. Toddlers can only build Logic, Charisma, and Creativity and only with toys designed for skill development.

> **note**
>
> Over the course of a Sim's life, she should, with considerable effort, totally master three to five skills. With the help of the Thinking Cap reward object, she could even master all seven.

Toddlers have three life skills that they can learn with the help of an adult:

- Learn to Talk
- Learn to Walk
- Potty Train

Children and teens have an additional skill of Learn to Study. Failure to master this skill means their homework throughout their school years will take twice as long.

Finally, there are three hidden skills:

- Dancing
- Yoga
- Meditation

Each hidden skill is learned by doing it and enables the Sim to execute progressively more difficult moves. They don't, with one exception, have much impact on the rest of the game.

SKILL BUILDING

Each basic skill is broken down into 10 increasingly difficult levels. Each level takes longer to master than the one before. For example, it should take a Sim one Sim hour to earn the first level of any skill. The 10th level of that skill should require 12 hours.

For the three toddler-only skills and Learn to Study, there is only one level of skill. When the meter is full, the skill is mastered. The rate of training, however, increases as the skill builds. Thus, a toddler just starting out builds skill slowly, but speeds up as he learns; the second half of the meter fills much faster than the first.

The Skill Meter

The Skill Meter over the Sim's head indicates progress toward the next level of the skill.

Progress in each skill level is displayed in the Skill Meter that appears above the Sim's head while skill building. This meter fills, from bottom to top, as the Sim trains in the current skill level. When the meter reaches the top, the Sim graduates to the next level and begins working on the following level. The meter resets to empty and the process begins anew (more slowly with each more difficult level).

note

If you stop skill building in the middle of a level, the Sim's progress in that level is preserved the next time she returns to build.

SKILLS AND ASPIRATIONS

Skills play a prominent role in the Aspirations game. Sims of all Aspirations want to gain skill levels, though some desire it more intensely and often than others. The higher the skill level, the more points the Want will bestow.

Skill increases appear frequently as Wants.

Eventually, some Sims want to get to the top of a skill or (in the case of Knowledge Sims) maximize all skills. The big payoffs for these Wants reflect how difficult a feat that is.

Intimately understanding the course of each Aspiration will guide you in how much to engage your Sims in skill building; for some Aspirations, it's central and for others, it's a minor pursuit.

SKILLS AND CAREERS

As detailed in Chapter 23, Sims need skills for their careers. Each career requires development in three skills. With each level of the career, the skill requirements increase.

tip

When choosing a career, consider how many of the career's required skills can be learned faster thanks to your Sim's Personality. Having at least one skill match the Sim's Personality substantially aids career advancement.

The Skills and Careers panel shows the required skill levels for the Sim's next job level.

Career Tracks, Featured Skills, and Helper Personalities

CAREER TRACK	SKILL 1 (PERS.)	SKILL 2 (PERS.)	SKILL 3 (PERS.)
Athletic	Body (Active)	Mechanical (None)	Charisma (Outgoing)
Business	Logic (Serious)	Creativity (Playful)	Charisma (Outgoing)
Criminal	Body (Active)	Creativity (Playful)	Mechanical (None)
Culinary	Logic (Serious)	Creativity (Playful)	Cooking (None)
Law Enforcement	Logic (Serious)	Body (Active)	Cleaning (Neat)
Medical	Logic (Serious)	Mechanical (None)	Cleaning (Neat)
Military	Body (Active)	Mechanical (None)	Charisma (Outgoing)
Politics	Logic (Serious)	Creativity (Playful)	Charisma (Outgoing)
Science	Logic (Serious)	Cooking (None)	Cleaning (Neat)
Slacker	Creativity (Playful)	Mechanical (None)	Charisma (Outgoing)

BASIC SKILLS
How Basic Skills Are Learned

Every basic skill can be learned in one or two ways: by interacting with objects and/or, for a few skills, by doing the thing for which the skill trains ("practical skill building").

Object Interaction

Many objects impart skill building with certain interactions. Object skill building is the most common and effective method. The amount of skill building an interaction gives depends on the object. Learning Cooking by watching the Yummy Channel, for example, gives slower skill building than Studying Cooking with a bookshelf.

Objects with a skill building interactions are the primary source of skill acquisition.

Some special objects, earned by progressing through a specific career track, offer somewhat accelerated skill building speeds. See "Career Reward Objects," below.

Practical Skill Building

Three skills offer skill building while performing the skill itself: Cooking, Mechanical, and Cleaning. Whenever a Sim cooks a meal, fixes an object, or cleans a mess, she's increasing her acumen in the skill. This increase is marked by the Skill Meter over the Sim's head.

Cleaning begets cleaning. The more Sims clean, the better they are at it.

Practical skill training is equal in speed to object-based training, but the activities themselves don't last indefinitely. A Sim can sit and study for as long as his Needs and Mood allow but cleaning the toilet or cooking a meal lasts only a short time, after which skill building is over.

In two primary ways, however, practical skill building is preferable to object-based:

◆ **Efficiency:** Sims have to either clean or repair things themselves or pay someone to do these things for them. Learning a skill practically means they're getting the job done and improving a skill at the same time, without having to expend money. On the flip side, they're expending something more valuable than money: time. This is, therefore, only an advantage if you intended the Sim to learn these skills anyway.

◆ **Always Available:** As described below, Sims can't skill build with objects if Mood or certain Needs are too low. They can still get skill from cooking and cleaning (but not repairing) no matter what their Mood or Needs. On the other hand, there isn't always something to clean or someone to feed.

As noted below (See "Skills and Personality"), another major difference between practical and object-based skill building arises when a Sloppy Sim gains practical Cleaning skill. The lower the Neat/Sloppy score, the more slowly she learns Cleaning. This can be as low as one-third the rate that a Neat/Sloppy 10 Sim would.

> **note**
>
> Kids in private school with good grades get skill points as rewards (instead of money).

Speeding Skill Building

Three things accelerate skill building:

◆ Personality traits
◆ Using career reward objects
◆ Teaching by older Sims
◆ Thinking Cap Aspiration reward object

Skills and Personality

Many basic skills are learned (whether using an object or learning by doing) more easily by Sims of a certain Personality trait. The more extreme the Sim is in the trait, the faster he learns the aligned skill.

The skill/Personality alliances are:

◆ Cooking: None   ◆ Logic: Serious
◆ Mechanical: None   ◆ Creativity: Playful
◆ Charisma: Outgoing   ◆ Cleaning: Neat
◆ Body: Active

A Sim with an extreme Personality trait (e.g. 10 points in Active) trains at double the normal speed.

In each case, skill speed increases with every point toward the aligned skill. Thus, a Sim with Outgoing/Shy of 0–5 would take a game hour to get her first level of Charisma skill and one with Outgoing/Shy 10 would take only 30 game minutes. A Sim with 7 Outgoing/Shy would not gain full speed but would still do better than a neutral or Shy Sim: about 48 minutes.

There is one exception to this system: Sloppy Sims and practical Cleaning skill. In most cases, a Sim of the opposite Personality extreme trains at the same normal rate as a neutral Sim (5 points). In the case of practical Cleaning skill only, a Sloppy Sim (Neat/Sloppy 0–4), the fewer points in Neat/Sloppy, the more slowly he'll learn to clean. To gain the first level of Cleaning skill, for example, an extremely Sloppy Sim (Neat/Sloppy 0) would take about 90 minutes.

Career Reward Objects

Each career track has a unique career reward object that is granted once a Sim in that track reaches some specified level. These objects offer skill building in one skill at a somewhat faster speed than Buy mode skill objects.

A single Sim on a career reward object builds skill faster than a normal Buy mode skill object.

Teaching

With the help of special career reward objects, any Sim with points in a skill can teach a Sim with fewer points in that same skill.

When an older Sim teaches a younger Sim via a career reward object, the younger Sim gets faster skill building.

The Thinking Cap reward object further increases skill building.

note

For toddler teaching, having the adult in the Thinking Cap and the toddler drinking Smart Milk (see below and Chapter 21) dramatically shortens the time required.

The Thinking Cap is a limited time object and should be used only by Sims with high to very high Aspiration scores. Use by low Aspiration Sims causes failure of the Thinking Cap and loss of a skill point.

note

The more-experienced Sim can offer lessons to someone, or the less-experienced Sim can ask for lessons. Acceptance is based on Mood.

Lessons double the learning Sim's rate of skill building above accelerations for Personality trait and the Thinking Cap. All increases to skill development speed are, therefore, cumulative.

Thinking Cap

The Thinking Cap is an Aspiration reward object (see Chapter 21) that doubles the speed of skill building. This boost is on top of any increase from both lessons and Personality. Thus a Sim with 10 in the aligned Personality trait being taught by a Sim who's maxed out the skill and wearing the Thinking Cap will learn at a dizzying speed.

Both teacher and pupil in a teaching interaction can wear the Thinking Cap to fully boost the skill building effect. When teaching a toddler to walk, talk, and use the potty, or when teaching a child to study, the process is sped by the teacher (only) wearing the Thinking Cap.

Skill Kickout

Sims may build skills only when they're in a good Mood and their core bodily Needs are reasonably satisfied.

Sims will leave or refuse to use a skill object if their Mood or certain core Needs are too low.

If Mood drops below zero, regardless of individual Need levels, a Sim will refuse to do object-based skill building and will immediately cease skill building if already engaged with a skill building object.

Even if Mood is above zero, five individual core Needs can, by themselves, forestall or end skill building:

◆ Energy   ◆ Bladder
◆ Hunger   ◆ Fun
◆ Comfort (if Sim isn't sitting to work on skill)

Other than these, no other Need automatically bumps a Sim out of skill building. If the other Needs are low enough, however, they quickly reduce Mood to negative.

It's important to note that practical skill building in Cooking and Cleaning (but not Mechanical) is not affected by Motive or Need level. A Sim gains skill building from practical avenues even if Mood is rock bottom and Needs are dwindling. It may not be the best choice of actions when Bladder is about to bottom out, but Sims will clean and learn Cleaning skill if you tell them to.

Skill Loss

Skill levels can be lost in several, mostly random, ways.

Throughout life, Sims receive random "chance cards" that present the Sim with a choice. Many penalize an incorrect answer with a reduction in a skill level. See "Chance Cards" in Chapter 23. To avoid skill loss this way, simply press the "Ignore" button; you won't get the potential pay off but you also avoid the possible penalties.

Using a Thinking Cap with low Aspiration score usually results in lost skill points.

Sims can also lose skill points through unwise use of reward objects (see "Reward Objects," Chapter 21). When many of these objects fail, they cause several mishaps, including a reduction in skill levels. These effects are random but are nearly guaranteed to happen if the Sim uses the reward object when his Aspiration score is too low. To avoid skill loss in this way, use Aspiration reward objects only when Aspiration score is Gold level or higher.

Electrocution, along with the possibility of death, carries a reduction in a random skill. To avoid this reduction, don't repair electronic objects unless the Sim has very high Mechanical skill.

Finally, a Sim can have skill point "sucked" out of her if another Sim uses the SimVac Aspiration Reward Object on her. Because this object can only be user directed (not autonomous), this will never happen unless you command it.

Basic Skills and Toddlers

Toddlers can use only certain objects to build skills. Thus, they can only develop Charisma, Logic, and Creativity.

Some toys act as skill objects for toddlers.

Skills Detailed
Cooking Skill

- Personality Acceleration: None
- Careers Used In: Science, Culinary
- Objects: Bookshelves (Study...), TV (watching Yummy Channel), Rip Co. Little Baker Oven (children only), Schokolade 890 Chocolate Manufacturing Facility (Culinary reward)
- Interactions: Cooking

Cooking skill is learned on the bookshelf or while cooking.

Cooking influences how quickly a Sim can cook and how nourishing (in terms of Hunger satisfaction) the meals he creates will be. It also determines the odds of a Sim starting a cooking fire (the lower the skill, the greater the chances).

tip

A Sim with no Cooking skill using any cooking appliance other than a microwave often starts a fire when she tries to cook. Be sure to have a smoke alarm somewhere in the same room as the stove.

Watching the Yummy Channel on TV imparts Cooking skill too.

Cooking skill is reflected in food quality in two ways. First, increasingly satisfying foods are available once a Sim reaches a certain level of skill (see Chapter 20). Second, after a food is unlocked, the Sim learns a new, more difficult, and more satisfying way to cook it with each of the next two skill levels. Once a new food is introduced, the Sim's chances of ruining the meal decline with each of the next two skill levels.

For example, salmon is unlocked at Level 6. At this level, the Sim can prepare it only with the most basic technique and the chance of ruining it is 20 percent. With level 7, the next, more satisfying technique is unlocked (the same food carries more Hunger satisfaction than at level 6) and chances of ruining decline to 10 percent. Finally, at level 8, the most satisfying way to make salmon is unlocked and the Sim ruins it only 5 percent of the time.

note

No cook, no matter how skilled, will master a food 100 percent of the time. Even the most accomplished chef screws up a meal he's mastered five percent of the time. In the case of lobster thermidor (introduced at Level 10), the chances of ruining are always 20 percent because there are no subsequent Cooking levels for the Sim to master. It's just a risky dish, but very satisfying.

High Cooking skill Sims' better food gets reactions from other Sims nearby. If they're close enough to smell the culinary creations, they react very positively.

tip

If you're attempting to get a young Sim into private school, one of the requirements is to cook a nice meal for the school's headmaster. To score well on the dinner, the meal must be cooked by a Sim with at least Cooking skill level 5.

Mechanical

- Personality Acceleration: None
- Careers Used In: Criminal, Military, Athletic, Slacker
- Objects: All bookshelves (Study...), piano (Tune), TraumaTime "Incision Precision" Surgical Training Station (Medical reward)
- Practical: Repair any broken object

Mechanical skill dramatically speeds the time required to repair broken objects and decreases the chance of electrocution when repairing electronic objects.

Mechanical skill is learned from fixing things, but don't let him work on electronics until he has high skill.

---
note

When repairing an object, the Repair Meter (which looks very similar) covers the Skill Meter. The meter you see, therefore, is not reflecting progression to a new skill but rather the progress of the repair itself.

---
note

For details on object breakage and repair, see Chapter 28.

Mechanical can be learned using the Study interaction on any bookshelf or by repairing any broken object. When the Sim is low in Mechanical skill, repairs take a very long time and the Sim gives up frequently (requiring you to reactive the interaction). On the upside, he's learning Mechanical skill the entire time.

If a house includes a stay-at-home Sim and a Fortune Aspiration Sim at work, learning Mechanical is very valuable because it preserves money otherwise spent on Repairmen for the Fortune Sim's constant acquisitional Wants.

---
note

Children can't die of electrocution.

Mechanical skill also factors into Sims' acumen at pinball (along with Body) and darts.

Charisma

◆ Personality Acceleration: Outgoing
◆ Careers Used In: Business, Military, Politics, Athletic, Slacker
◆ Objects: All mirrors (Practice Speech, Practice Romance), Execuputter (Business reward), Enterprise Office Concepts Bushmaster Tele-Prompter (Politics reward), Rip Co. Wobbly Wabbit Head (toddler only)
◆ Practical: N/A

Charisma is primarily useful for careers that require it and is learned by practicing speeches or romance into any mirror. Children learn Charisma only by using one of the Charisma-granting career reward objects.

Toddlers can build Charisma only via the Rip Co. Wobbly Wabbit Head toy.

Charisma is mostly learned from mirrors.

Charisma is because it plays a role in a few social interactions. The higher a Sim's Charisma, the more likely other Sims will laugh at their jokes and dirty jokes.

Body

◆ Personality Acceleration: Active
◆ Careers Used In: Athletic, Military, Criminal, Law Enforcement
◆ Objects: Exerto 5000 Multipress Exercise Machine, Exerto Punching Bag (Athletic reward), Exerto Selfflog Obstacle Course (Military reward), work out (any TV or stereo), swimming pool
◆ Practical: Yoga

Body skill comes from several exercise devices.

Body is one of the most important skills because it impacts so many little things (too many to list here). It's most prominently important as a career skill, but there's more.

It also comes from swimming and doing yoga.

To name a few, Body skill affects which Sim wins in a fight, how hard she hits in Punch U Punch Me games, how well she dives off a diving board or plays pinball (along with Mechanical skill), whether she'll break an alarm clock by smashing it.

Build body skill by using exercise equipment, swimming in a swimming pool, or working out to the TV or any stereo. Children only gain it from swimming or using obstacle course and punching bag career rewards.

note

Building Body skill also helps maintain Fitness level (see "Fitness," Chapter 18).

Body skill is also built by doing yoga. Yoga is a self interaction that appears (somewhat circularly)

only once a Sim has developed Body to Level 3. Thereafter, Do Yoga becomes available on that Sim as a self-interaction.

note

Yoga is also a hidden skill (see below) so a Sim doing it is actually building both Yoga and Body skill simultaneously. The meter you see above the Sim's head, however, reflects only the progress of Body skill.

Logic

◆ Personality Acceleration: Serious
◆ Careers Used In: Business, Law Enforcement, Medical, Politics, Science, Culinary
◆ Objects: Astrowonder Telescope (Stargaze, night only), Farstar e3 Telescope (Stargaze, night only), Grand Parlour Chess Table (Practice or Play), King for a Day Outdoor Chess Table (Practice), Magical Mystery's "Shape, Rattle & Roll" (toddler only), Prints Charming Fingerprinting Scanner (Law Enforcement reward), Simsanto Inc. Biotech Station (Science reward)
◆ Practical: N/A

Logic is important primarily as a career skill.

Logic is developed using several objects. Both telescopes give Logic. Chess is an excellent way to simultaneously have Fun and build Logic; Sims get Social too if they play against another person.

Learn logic from looking through telescopes.

Another source of Logic, the chess board, also gives Fun and (if playing against another Sim) Social.

Toddlers can build Logic too, via the Magical Mystery's "Shape, Rattle & Roll" peg box toy.

Sims who've achieved Logic level 3 can perform a rather handy self-interaction: Meditation. While meditating, they can freeze their Needs and Mood indefinitely.

Creativity

◆ Personality Acceleration: Playful

◆ Careers Used In: Business, Criminal, Politics, Slacker, Culinary

◆ Objects: Moneywell Computer (Write Novel), Little Sister WD15 (Write Novel), Chimeway & Daughters Saloon Piano (Play), Independent Expressions Inc. Easel (Practice Painting), Rip Co. Xylophone (toddlers only), SensoTwitch Lie Finder (Criminal reward), AquaGreen Hydroponic Garden (Slacker reward)

◆ Practical: N/A

Painting and playing music impart Creativity.

Creativity is important in several careers but it has other applications as well, some of them financially beneficial.

Painting on an easel teaches Creativity, but you can sell the paintings the Sim produces either directly (by clicking on the painting) or returned in Buy mode. The greater the Sim's Creativity, the higher the painting's sale price.

note

You can also hang Sim-made paintings on the wall. Paintings created by high Creativity Sims (4–10) appreciate in value. Hang onto them long enough and their sale price will increase significantly.

Toiling away at the computer gives you a sellable novel and steady increases in Creativity.

Sims can also write novels on their computer; the greater the Sim's Creativity, the better the novel. When the book is finished, the Sim is offered a sale price based on her Creativity.

A Sim's performance of music is also affected by his Creativity. Low Creativity Sims just bang away on the piano while high Creativity Sims play lovely music. Nearby Sims react to music's quality.

Toddlers can also build Creativity with the Rip Co. Xylophone. The more skill they have, the better they play.

Cleaning

- Personality Acceleration: Neat
- Careers Used In: Law Enforcement, Medical, Science
- Objects: All bookshelves (Study...)
- Practical: Cleaning any object

Cleaning is a very important skill for Sims in careers that call for it and those who don't want to hire a Maid.

Very highly trained Cleaning Sims "ultra-clean" everything. You can tell by the bubbles.

The better a Sim is at cleaning, the faster she'll perform cleaning tasks. Faster cleaning means more free time for other things.

note

High Cleaning skill doesn't make a Sloppy Sim clean more often, it just makes him clean faster. If you want a Sloppy Sim with high Cleaning skill to tidy up after himself, you must direct him to the messes.

When a Sim is *very* good at Cleaning (level 9 or 10 Neatness) she cleans things "ultra-clean." Ultra-cleaned objects are actually cleaned beyond 100 percent clean, meaning they take somewhat longer to get dirty again. Sparkling bubbles come from a high Cleaning skill Sim when she's ultra-cleaning something. This is very handy when the high Cleaning Sim lives with a very Sloppy Sim who makes things dirty faster.

note

Not surprisingly, Neat Sims are the best candidates for Cleaning skill because they clean autonomously and learn the skill faster.

SPECIAL TODDLER SKILLS

Toddlers can get an early start on three of the basic skills with the help of some toddler-only educational toys:

- Creativity: Rip Co. Xylophone
- Charisma: Rip Co. Wobbly Wabbit Head
- Logic: Magical Mystery's "Shape, Rattle & Roll"

Training in these skills increases the chances that the toddler will top out skills as an adult or elder.

More important for toddlers' immediate Wants/Fears are three special toddler skills:

- Learn to Talk
- Learn to Walk
- Potty Train

Each of these special skills is taught when a teen, adult, or elder interacts with the toddler (or the potty chair) and chooses the appropriate interaction. Toddlers can't initiate the training of these skills.

Learn to Talk and Learn to Walk take time and don't require any object. Queue up several repetitions of the interaction and continue until toddler or teacher can't go on.

note

Learn to Walk and Learn to Talk don't require any special objects, but Potty Train requires the potty chair object.

Toddler skills are important because they represent every toddler's highest scoring Wants. Failing to achieve these skills guarantees the toddler a low Aspiration score and a Fear of Growing Up. This gives him a decided disadvantage when he becomes a child.

These skills are not required for the toddler to become a child and the child version of the Sim will be in no way, other than low Aspiration, crippled by not having learned to do them while a toddler.

The challenge, therefore, is to accomplish all three goals during the very limited time that the Sim is a toddler.

Potty Train with the help of the potty chair object.

The chances of success are dramatically increased if the child is fed "Smart Milk" from a special Aspiration reward object (Pasteur's HomoGenius Smart Milk). This doubles the rate at which the toddler learns the special toddler skills.

tip

If the teen, adult, or elder teaching a toddler to walk, talk, or use the potty wears a Thinking Cap reward object, it further speeds the toddler's skill acquisition.

Smart Milk is essential if you want a toddler to get all three toddler skills and build some points in the standard skills.

Be careful with Smart Milk, however, because it can fail if the teen, adult, or elder preparing the milk uses it when her Aspiration score is low. Failure creates red bottles that make the toddler throw up and lose a random skill point. If the grown-up pulls out a red bottle, cancel the interaction before the bad milk is given to the toddler.

Don't drink the red Smart Milk!

note

The toddler's Aspiration score has no bearing on whether Smart Milk will work or not.

There are several benefits to having a toddler trained in talking, walking, and using the potty:

- Aspiration score: The toddler's Aspiration score will be sky high with the successful learning of the toddler skills. If the toddler is taught by a Family Sim, his Aspiration score will be lofty too, because teaching a toddler to talk, walk, and use the potty are major Wants.

- No more diapers: Once a toddler is potty trained, teens, adults, and elders won't have to change diapers. The toddler will autonomously use the potty chair object.

- Talking toddler: Once a toddler learns to talk, she gets a Want to be talked to. This provides further Aspiration scoring opportunities.

LEARN TO STUDY

Once a Sim becomes a child, he can Learn to Study. This skill allows him to complete his homework much faster, leaving him time for other pursuits, and aids in improving his grades.

note

Learn to Study can be done by children or teens but may only be completed once. After that, they have all the skill they need to do their homework.

To Learn to Study, either the child/teen or a teen, adult, or elder who has learned how to study can select any homework object and either ask for or offer help. If accepted, the pair convenes and works through the homework until the homework is complete.

The progress bar in Learn to Study refers to the completion of the homework. Progress on Learn to Study is invisible but it takes one full homework assignment.

Learning to study takes one full homework assignment with help. If the teaching Sim began helping with partially complete homework, it'll take part of another homework assignment to finish, get the Memory/Want fulfillment, and learn the skill.

note

The Skill Meter over the child/teen's head indicates progress with the homework item itself, not in the Learn to Study process.

Once the student has learned to study, she can independently complete her homework much faster.

HIDDEN SKILLS

Three hidden skills can be their own reward:

◆ Dancing ◆ Yoga ◆ Meditation

Dancing

The more Sims dance, the better they dance, but they only improve by dancing TOGETHER.

Dancing skill is earned invisibly whenever a Sim dances with another Sim (solo dancing doesn't count). As they dance, Sims are earning Dancing points that enable them to pull off increasingly impressive steps and moves.

The more a Sim dances with other Sims, the better his dancing will be. There is no Skill Meter for dancing, so you only know a Sim is improving by watching him strut his stuff.

Yoga

Sims with Body skill of three or higher gain the self-interaction "Do Yoga." This skill builds Body skill (à la Work Out) but also builds Yoga skill.

Increased Yoga skill allows a Sim to perform progressively more difficult positions.

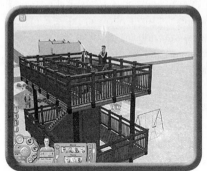

Yoga is a totally self-sufficient (no object required) way to build Body, increase Fitness, and learn cooler yoga poses.

Meditation

Sims with Logic skill of three or higher gain the self-interaction "Meditate."

The longer a Sim meditates, the more Meditation points she amasses. After several collective hours of meditation, the Sim gains a new ability: floating while meditating.

Meditation is a powerful weapon, allowing Sims to freeze their motives indefinitely. And, again, it looks pretty cool.

note

The two changes in Meditation ability are signaled by flashes of purple light from the Sim's body. That must be what inner peace looks like.

After several more hours, the Sim can tele-port around the lot while meditating (click on a location and select Teleport Here).

There is more to meditation, however, than just cool tricks; it's actually a strategically fabulous tool. While meditating, a Sim's Needs and Mood freeze indefinitely.

This is very handy when a Sim needs to be in a good Mood for an event that won't occur for a while. For example, a Sim who goes to work at 9 and leaves plenty of time to build up all his Needs can walk to the curb and meditate to freeze his good Mood until the carpool arrives. When the car pulls up, he can stop meditating and go to work in a great mood that should increase his job performance.

Teleportation's useful because it's faster than walking and can be done while Mood is still frozen. Thus, the work-bound Sim can Meditate in his house, teleport to the curb, and go to work without losing any of his good Mood on the way.

Chapter 23

Careers and School

So, what do *you* do? It's the classic question that just goes to show that everyone's character is, fairly or not, defined by how he or she earns a living. It's no different for Sims: their career choice is a huge decision and one that impacts their lives in myriad ways.

> ## note
>
> In the broadened universe of THE SIMS 2, the available choices of occupation are profoundly expanded—not in terms of the number of careers (though there are plenty of them), but in terms of the options life presents them beyond the traditional career tracks. The advent of Aspirations gives Sims (except Fortune Sims who are completely committed to career) something beyond the next promotion to strive for.

This chapter introduces you to the working world of *The Sims 2*, explains how it functions, and lays out all the occupational choices for adults, teens, and elders. We'll also discuss the ins-and-outs of primary, secondary, and private education.

CAREER

The largest chunk of a Sim's life takes place during a Sims' "earning years": teen through elder. To say that career isn't a major consideration during these ages is to deny the character and life-style defining power of work. Learning to play the career game is absolutely essential if Sims are to have a reasonably efficient and successful life.

That is not to say that every Sim *must* have a career; not so. The stay-at-home life is richer and

more rewarding than ever, thanks to Aspirations, and a few money-earning ventures allow creative Sims to eke out the life of a starving artist.

Generally, however, it's an undeniable truth that every house must have at least one high-level bread-winner. Without a regular and substantial income:

◆ Bills won't get paid

◆ The refrigerator will be empty

◆ Environment score will be hopelessly mediocre

◆ Hired help or trips to Community Lots will be unaffordable

As such, have a look at the mechanics of the working life.

Getting a Job

Sims find job listings in two sources: the newspaper and the computer.

The computer is your best source for jobs, especially if the Sim already has lots of skill points and friends.

Each day, the newspaper is delivered to the Sims' front walk. Select "Find Job" and you're presented with *three* job openings. The computer offers more variety, serving up *five* job openings a day.

When a Sim with few skills or friends enters a new career track, he starts at level 1 (unless he's a teen and in private school in which case he begins at level 2 of a teen career). If, however, the Sim has developed skills and friends, the jobs offered *on the computer only* will be higher:

◆ If the Sim's skills and number of friends qualify her for a position up to level 6, she'll be offered a job two levels below the one for which she's qualified. For example, if the Sim is qualified for a level 6 job, the job listing will be for level 4 in that career.

♦ If the Sim is qualified for a level 7 or higher job, she'll always be offered the level 6 job.

If a Sim's been fired from a track, he can get back into the career track based on this system too. Sims fired at level 5 and still qualified for the job would reenter at level 3. If performance is good, he'll quickly regain his former position.

> **note**
>
> All jobs in the newspaper are always level 1 positions.

The newspaper offers only three jobs and always at level 1.

When teens become adults, they automatically switch to the adult version of the same career track. Where they begin depends on their level in the teen career:

♦ Teen No Job: Adult Level 1
♦ Teen Level 1: Adult Level 1
♦ Teen Level 2: Adult Level 1
♦ Teen Level 3: Adult Level 2

Career Structure

The career structure features two kinds of careers: adult careers and teen/elder careers. They differ, but both kinds have basic features that define how and when the job is done and what impact it will have on a Sim's life.

Skill Requirements

Every career features *three* skills that must be developed in order to climb the ladder.

Build the right three skills to advance in careers.

With every job level, the skill requirements may increase, requiring the Sim to meet all the skill thresholds before even being eligible for promotion.

> **note**
>
> If, in losing a skill point, a Sim falls below the skill requirements for a job, she won't be demoted. All that matters is what skills the Sim had on the day she was promoted. Of course, she won't be eligible for promotion to the NEXT job until she earns back the lost point(s) and tackles any required by the higher level.

Friends Requirement

Many jobs require, as a condition for promotion, that a Sim have a certain number of family friends. What this means, though, isn't as clear as it seems.

> **note**
>
> The friend count on the Skills and Career panel is displayed a bit differently than in the original THE SIMS. It now shows the current number of family friends, then the number NEEDED for promotion. If you already have enough friends for the promotion, this number shows as "0."

Friends for job promotion purposes are shown in the Skills and Career panel. The top number is how many friends the household has and the bottom is how many this Sim needs for promotion.

For promotion purposes, a "friend" is any non-household Friend (Daily 50) or Best Friend (Lifetime 50) of any member of the Sim's household. Thus, in a two Sim family in which both Sims are best friends to each other:

◆ Sim A has 3 friends, including Sim B
◆ Sim B has 2 friends, including Sim A

For Sim's B's promotion eligibility, he has three friends: his own non-household friend and Sim A's two non-household friends.

note

If a Sim is friends with a blood relative who does not live in the household, that relative counts as a friend for job purposes. They are members of the Sim's "family" (as in "blood relation") but not part of the Sim's "family" (as in "a Sim who lives on the same lot").

Thus, it's a very powerful strategy to have a stay-at-home Sim do most of the friend-making work for the working Sim. This frees the working Sim to develop her skills and keep her Needs high when she goes to work.

note

As with skill requirements, falling below the friend requirement for a Sim's current job won't result in demotion, but further promotion will be impossible until the friend count is up to the next job's demands.

tip

If a Sim is otherwise eligible for promotion but is a friend short, here are a couple of tricks:

1. If Daily Relationship score is just a few points shy with a Sim, leave some time to talk to her on the phone before work. If the friend's relationship is with a non-working Sim, have that Sim hold the conversation while the working Sim is getting ready for work.

2. If the relationship needs more than a few points work, more drastic measures are required. Save and exit the lot about an hour before the carpool arrives. Next, load the lot of a family friend with whom someone in the first lot is reasonably close to Daily Relationship 50, and have that Sim invite over the Sim from the first lot. Interact until friend status is achieved (with some cushion to allow for decay), save and exit the lot, and return to the original lot. You'll find the lot just as you left it, except the family friend count is one higher.

3. If more than one friend is needed, call a taxi well before it's time to go to work and go to a Community Lot. Spend as much time as you can there, making as many friends as possible and return to the lot. The Sim arrives home only a bit later than he left (time works strangely in the Sims' world) with their friend count suitably adjusted.

Hours

Jobs vary in their hours (both the start and quitting times and number of hours per shift), though teen/elder jobs never begin before 3 p.m.

Use the time between the carpool's arrival and work start time for skill building, Want satisfaction, or Need cushioning. The vehicle waits until the top of the hour.

note

Carpools arrive one hour before the job's start time and wait (honking annoyingly) until the exact start time. Sims return home 10 minutes after quitting time.

Generally, higher-level jobs require fewer hours than lower level jobs.

Workdays Per Week/Days Off

No job requires more than five days per week, but many (especially top-tier jobs) demand less. More days off means more time for skill building and Want satisfaction.

Daily Salary/Weekly Average

With each higher job level, daily salary increases. For jobs with fewer than five shifts per week, it's helpful to compare the weekly average rather than the daily.

Needs Effects

Sims' Needs don't stand still while they're at work. When Sims return home, their Need levels at their departure time are adjusted by fixed amounts.

> **note**
>
> If a Sim's Energy or Bladder is near failure when he leaves for work, it's possible that the at-work Need adjustment will cause him to go into Need failure upon his return. Send him to work too tired and he'll come home and pass out on the sidewalk.

Every job decreases Energy of course (none, sadly, permit napping on the job); more physical jobs decrease Energy more.

Not all Needs are, however, diminished at work. Some jobs increase Fun and particularly cushy ones increase Comfort. All jobs, except the most solitary (e.g., Security Guard or Dishwasher), increase Social.

Paid Time Off

For every shift worked of every job at every level, Sims earn paid vacation time (0.15 days per shift). When enough vacation time is accumulated (about seven shifts), Sims earn a paid day off (shown in the Skills and Career panel).

Paid time off means the Sim can skip the carpool and, without calling in sick, be paid her usual daily salary, and receive no decrease in job performance.

> **MATERNITY/PATERNITY LEAVE**
>
> When a Sim (female or alien-impregnated male) is pregnant he or she receives extra time off from work.
>
> The second and third day of pregnancy simply become days off; the carpool doesn't come but the Sim is paid for the day.
>
> After the child is born, leave works just like regular paid time off. The carpool does come but Sims may ignore it and get paid for the day. There's no requirement that they actually take all or any of the days; they can instead save the time for later as long as someone's at home to take care of the newborn.

Promotion

Each day a Sim goes to work, there's a random chance he'll be promoted to the next level, but whether a promotion's available and the Sims odds of getting it depend on several factors.

> **note**
>
> If you have the skills and friends required, a Sim can be promoted on the first day on the job if Mood is high. First day promotion is guaranteed if Mood is very high.

Skills and Friends

As described above, to be eligible for promotion, a Sim must meet the next level's skill and friends requirements. If she lacks these, there is no chance of promotion.

> **note**
>
> In the Skills and Career panel, needed skill levels are highlighted by a blue glow on the indicator for the level. Friends are shown by the second of the two friend numbers (the first is the number of friends you have), showing how many you need to be eligible for promotion (e.g. "+2").

Job Performance

Find the Job Performance indicator in the Skills and Career panel. The halfway point is considered zero and the line of demarcation between "good" performance and "bad." Job performance ranges from -100 to 100.

Team Mascot	Cooking
$125	Mechanical
3 pm to 6 pm	Charisma
S M T W T F S	Body
Vacation Days: 0	Logic
	Creativity
	Cleaning

The vertical Job Performance meter shows the current state of a Sim's performance. Below the halfway mark, performance is negative.

The other variable in promotion is job performance. The higher it is, the greater the odds of promotion. High job performance isn't a guarantee of promotion, but it tilts the odds in the Sim's favor.

Presuming a Sim has the skill and friend requirements for promotion, going to work three days in a row with high Mood guarantees promotion.

Job performance is a cumulative measure of two things:

◆ Sims' Mood when they leave for work
◆ Attendance

A Sim's Mood each day either adds or detracts from job performance. The higher his Mood when he gets in the car, the more his job performance will rise.

Specifically, job performance changes by one-half the Sim's Mood when she departs for work. For example, if job performance is +40 and the Sim goes to work with Mood +80, job performance will rise 40 points to +80. If, on the other hand, Mood is -10, job performance will drop to +35.

None of these numbers are visible in the game, but you can judge their proportions by looking at the Job Performance indicator and Mood meter.

Job performance only increases when the Sim goes to work; taking a paid day off or calling in sick leaves the rating unchanged.

Promotion Bonus

On the happy day when a Sim rises to a new job level, she receives her daily salary for the old job plus a promotion bonus of twice the daily salary of the new job level.

It is possible to get promoted without possessing the skill and friend requirements or even having good job performance. Some chance cards have as their reward a one-level promotion.

Demotion

There are two ways to get demoted in a job:

◆ Poor job performance
◆ Chance cards

Poor Job Performance

If job performance drops too low, the Sim gets demoted to the next lowest level. If, however, on his first day back, the Sim has all requirements and goes to work in a very good Mood, he's guaranteed promotion to the previous level.

Chance Cards

Some chance cards have as their penalty the loss of a job level. This is unfortunate but sometimes life, even Sim life, isn't fair.

Chance cards present an opportunity to gamble on your Sim's career. There's no right answer, but the question can be simply ignored.

Getting Fired

If job performance drops to -100 or she misses two days in a row without calling in sick, she'll be fired.

Teens who have low grades (D+ or lower) will also be fired from their jobs.

Calling in Sick

A Sim can call in sick on a work day any time before work starts or for one hour after (before the missed work call comes). Calling in sick means that the Sim won't lose any job performance or have to expend any paid time off. He won't be paid for the day, but he won't be penalized either.

If a Sim is faking sick, he better giggle quietly.

If a Sim actually is sick (See Chapter 29), calling in sick will always be accepted.

If the Sim isn't sick when he calls in sick, his lie will be accepted if job performance is above +50. If it's below +50, the excuse will be rejected and he'll be penalized with a missed day.

Chance Cards

Chance cards are occasional opportunities to gamble on an elder, adult, or teen Sim's career. You may either play the card or click on the Ignore button.

In a chance card, you're presented with a scenario and given the choice of two solutions. Which answer earns the reward is randomly generated, so there's no "correct" answer every time.

note

OK, it's not pure luck. Chance cards are statistically weighted a bit so the safest or morally "good" answer is usually, but not always, the correct one. This is still a pretty subjective standard, so you might want to just consider the whole thing hopelessly and blissfully random.

If your choice is the "right" choice for this card, the Sim receives a bonus, a promotion, or a rise in skill level. Penalties for wrong answers range from the loss of a skill points to a one-level demotion to dismissal. A Sim should see about four to five chance cards over the course of a lifetime.

note

The higher the Sim is in a career, the more rewarding or damaging a chance card can be. School chance cards are a bit different. No choice is involved; they're just random rewards.

Career Reward Objects

Every career track has a career reward object bestowed upon the Sim when she reaches the object's designated job level. Upon promotion to that level, the object becomes available in the Reward panel.

tip

If both Sims in a teaching situation are wearing Thinking Cap Aspiration reward objects, the younger Sim will learn even faster. Be sure both Sims have at least Gold Aspiration score or the Thinking Cap will likely fail.

The 10 reward objects are special accelerated skill objects with several very interesting interactions (see Chapter 28). They're especially useful in training less-skilled Sims in the object's specialty skill. Sims being taught via the reward object learn the skill at an extremely high rate.

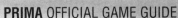

Reward objects such as this surgical dummy train skills quickly and allow Sims to teach the skill to others.

The level at which each object is awarded differs for each career:

Reward Objects

CAREER	OBJECT	LEVEL AWARDED	SKILL TAUGHT
Business	Execuputter	5	Charisma
Law Enforcement	Prints Charming Fingerprinting Scanner	6	Cleaning
Criminal	SensoTwitch Lie Finder	4	Mechanical
Medical	TraumaTime "Incision Precision" Surgical Training Station	4	Mechanical
Military	Exerto Selfflog Obstacle Course	4	Body
Politics	Enterprise Office Concepts Bushmaster Tele-Prompter	5	Charisma
Athletic	Exerto Punching Bag	5	Body
Science	Simsanto Inc. Biotech Station	6	Creativity
Slacker	AquaGreen Hydroponic Garden	5	Creativity
Culinary	Schokolade 890 Chocolate Manufacturing Facility	6	Cooking

Jobs by Career Level

Adult Careers

Adult careers can be held by adults or elders, but elders must already be in an adult career track when they transition from adult to elder.

There are 10 adult careers from which to choose, each with 10 job levels.

	CAREER	JOB NAME	LOGIC	BODY	CREATIVITY	MECHANICAL	CHARISMA	COOKING	CLEANING	FRIENDS	HOURS
Level 1 Careers	Athletic	Team Mascot	0	0	0	0	0	0	0	0	3p–9p
	Business	Mailroom Technician	0	0	0	0	0	0	0	0	9a–3p
	Criminal	Pickpocket	0	0	0	0	0	0	0	0	11a–5p
	Culinary	Dishwasher	0	0	0	0	0	0	0	0	2p–10p
	Law Enforcement	Security Guard	0	0	0	0	0	0	0	0	8p–2a
	Medical	Emergency Medical Technician	0	0	0	0	0	0	0	0	8a–2p
	Military	Recruit	0	0	0	0	0	0	0	0	7a–1p
	Politics	Campaign Worker	0	0	0	0	0	0	0	0	9a–6p
	Science	Test Subject	0	0	0	0	0	0	0	0	11a–5p
	Slacker	Golf Caddy	0	0	0	0	0	0	0	0	5a–10a

Days Off	# Work Days	Daily Salary	Weekly Average	Energy	Bladder	Hygiene	Social	Hunger	Fun	Comfort
Mon & Thu	5	§154	§770	-48	-48	-60	0	-60	18	-60
Sun & Fri	5	§168	§840	-48	-48	-18	24	-24	-18	-48
Mon & Thu	5	§196	§980	-48	0	-60	-30	-60	30	-30
Mon & Fri	5	§126	§630	-64	-40	-80	-32	-80	-24	-24
Mon & Fri	5	§336	§1,680	-48	-60	-6	-30	-12	-6	-6
Mon & Sat	5	§280	§1,400	-48	-48	-18	24	-24	-18	-48
Mon & Wed	5	§350	§1,750	-60	-30	-60	0	-60	-30	-30
Mon & Wed	5	§308	§1,540	-72	-72	-27	36	-36	-27	-72
Sun & Fri	5	§217	§1,085	-48	-30	-60	-24	-60	-12	-42
Mon & Sat	5	§126	§630	-40	-40	-15	20	-20	-15	-40

Level 2 Careers

Career	Job Name	Logic	Body	Creativity	Mechanical	Charisma	Cooking	Cleaning	Friends	Hours
Athletic	Minor Leaguer	0	1	0	0	0	0	0	0	9a–3p
Business	Executive Assistant	0	0	0	0	1	0	0	0	9a–4p
Criminal	Bagman	0	0	0	0	0	0	0	0	5p–1a
Culinary	Drive Through Clerk	0	0	0	0	0	0	0	0	5p–9p
Law Enforcement	Cadet	0	1	0	0	0	0	0	0	9a–3p
Medical	Paramedic	0	0	0	0	0	0	1	0	8p–2a
Military	Elite Forces	0	0	0	0	0	0	0	0	7a–1p
Politics	Intern	0	0	0	0	0	0	0	0	9a–3p
Science	Lab Assistant	0	0	0	0	0	1	1	0	4p–10p
Slacker	Gas Station Attendant	0	0	0	0	0	0	0	0	10p–3a

Level 3 Careers

Career	Job Name	Logic	Body	Creativity	Mechanical	Charisma	Cooking	Cleaning	Friends	Hours
Athletic	Rookie	0	2	0	0	0	0	0	0	9a–3p
Business	Field Sales Rep	0	0	0	0	2	0	0	0	9a–4p
Criminal	Bookie	0	0	1	0	0	0	0	0	11a–6p
Culinary	Fast Food Shift Manager	0	0	1	0	0	0	0	0	5p–10p
Law Enforcement	Patrol Officer	0	2	0	0	0	0	0	0	3p–11p
Medical	Nurse	1	0	0	0	0	0	2	0	7a–2p
Military	Drill Instructor	0	1	0	1	0	0	0	0	7a–1p
Politics	Lobbyist	0	0	0	0	0	0	0	0	8a–2p
Science	Field Researcher	1	0	0	0	0	1	3	0	9a–3p
Slacker	Convenience Store Clerk	0	0	0	1	0	0	0	0	9a–3p

Level 4 Careers

Career	Job Name	Logic	Body	Creativity	Mechanical	Charisma	Cooking	Cleaning	Friends	Hours
Athletic	Starter	0	3	0	0	1	0	0	1	9a–3p
Business	Junior Executive	0	0	1	0	2	0	0	1	9a–4p
Criminal	Con Artist	0	0	3	0	0	0	0	1	9a–3p
Culinary	Host/Hostess	1	0	2	0	0	0	0	1	10a–4p
Law Enforcement	Desk Sgt	1	2	0	0	0	0	0	1	9a–3p
Medical	Intern	2	0	0	2	0	0	4	1	9a–6p
Military	Junior Officer	0	1	0	2	1	0	0	0	7a–1p
Politics	Campaign Manager	1	0	1	0	0	0	0	1	8a–5p
Science	Science Teacher	1	0	0	0	0	2	5	1	8a–3p
Slacker	Record Store Clerk	0	0	0	1	1	0	0	0	10a–3p

Days Off	# Work Days	Daily Salary	Weekly Average	Energy	Bladder	Hygiene	Social	Hunger	Fun	Comfort
Tue & Thu	5	§238	§1,190	-48	-48	-60	0	-42	18	-48
Mon & Sat	5	§252	§1,260	-56	-56	-21	28	-28	-21	-56
Mon & Wed	5	§280	§1,400	-64	0	-80	-16	-56	24	-24
Mon & Wed	5	§168	§840	-32	-16	-40	4	-28	-4	-20
Mon & Sat	5	§448	§2,240	-48	-30	-60	24	-42	18	-60
Wed & Fri	5	§385	§1,925	-48	-48	-18	24	-24	-18	-48
Wed & Fri	5	§455	§2,275	-48	-30	-60	0	-42	-18	-24
Sun & Fri	5	§420	§2,100	-48	-48	-18	24	-24	-18	-48
Mon & Sat	5	§322	§1,610	-36	-42	-30	12	-42	12	12
Mon & Thu	5	§154	§770	-40	-40	-15	20	-20	-15	-40

Days Off	# Work Days	Daily Salary	Weekly Average	Energy	Bladder	Hygiene	Social	Hunger	Fun	Comfort
Tue & Wed	5	§322	§1,610	-48	-48	-48	0	-36	30	-48
Tue & Thu	5	§350	§1,750	-56	-56	-21	28	-28	-21	-56
Tue & Wed	5	§385	§1,925	-56	-35	-56	28	-42	35	35
Wed & Thu	5	§182	§910	-40	-30	-40	20	-30	15	15
Wed & Fri	5	§552	§2,760	-64	0	-64	80	-48	8	-64
Mon & Thu	5	§476	§2,380	-56	-56	-21	28	-28	-21	-56
Mon & Tue	5	§560	§2,800	-48	-30	-24	0	-36	30	-18
Sun & Sat	5	§504	§2,520	-48	-48	-18	24	-24	-18	-48
Wed & Fri	5	§448	§2,240	-48	-36	-48	-18	-36	18	-24
Mon & Tue	5	§210	§1,050	-48	-48	-18	24	-24	-18	-48

Days Off	# Work Days	Daily Salary	Weekly Average	Energy	Bladder	Hygiene	Social	Hunger	Fun	Comfort
Tue & Thu	5	§420	§2,100	-48	-48	-18	0	-24	30	-24
Wed & Sun	5	§448	§2,240	-56	-56	-21	35	-28	-21	-28
Sun & Sat	5	§490	§2,450	-36	-18	-6	60	-24	30	36
Mon & Tue	5	§242	§1,210	-48	-30	-12	30	-24	18	-12
Sun & Sat	5	§616	§3,080	-30	-36	-18	30	-24	30	-18
Tue & Fri	5	§574	§2,870	-81	-72	-27	45	-36	-27	-45
Sun & Sat	5	§630	§3,150	-48	-36	-18	0	-24	18	18
Tue & Wed	5	§602	§3,010	-64	-64	-24	40	-32	-24	-32
Sun & Sat	5	§525	§2,625	-56	-42	-14	35	-28	35	42
Tue & Thu	5	§252	§1,260	-40	-40	-15	25	-20	-15	-20

Level 5 Careers

CAREER	JOB NAME	LOGIC	BODY	CREATIVITY	MECHANICAL	CHARISMA	COOKING	CLEANING	FRIENDS	HOURS
Athletic	All Star	0	6	0	0	2	0	0	2	9a–3p
Business	Executive	2	0	1	0	4	0	0	1	8a–3p
Criminal	Getaway Driver	0	1	4	2	0	0	0	2	10p–6a
Culinary	Waiter/Waitress	3	0	2	0	0	0	0	2	2p–7p
Law Enforcement	Vice Squad	1	3	0	0	0	0	0	2	10a–4p
Medical	Resident	3	0	0	3	0	0	5	2	6p–1a
Military	Counter Intelligence	0	4	0	2	2	0	0	0	8a–2p
Politics	City Council Member	2	0	2	0	2	0	0	2	9a–3p
Science	Project leader	2	0	0	0	0	3	6	2	10a–5p
Slacker	Party D.J.	0	0	1	1	2	0	0	2	11p–4a

Level 6 Careers

CAREER	JOB NAME	LOGIC	BODY	CREATIVITY	MECHANICAL	CHARISMA	COOKING	CLEANING	FRIENDS	HOURS
Athletic	MVP	0	8	0	1	3	0	0	3	9a–3p
Business	Senior Manager	3	0	3	0	4	0	0	2	8a–3p
Criminal	Bank Robber	0	2	5	4	0	0	0	3	3p–11p
Culinary	Prep Cook	3	0	2	0	0	3	0	2	9a–3p
Law Enforcement	Detective	4	3	0	0	0	0	2	3	9a–3p
Medical	General Practitioner	4	0	0	4	0	0	6	3	10a–6p
Military	Flight Officer	0	5	0	4	3	0	0	1	9a–3p
Politics	State Assemblyperson	3	0	2	0	4	0	0	3	9a–4p
Science	Inventor	4	0	0	0	0	4	6	3	10a–7p
Slacker	Projectionist	0	0	1	3	2	0	0	4	6p–1a

Level 7 Careers

CAREER	JOB NAME	LOGIC	BODY	CREATIVITY	MECHANICAL	CHARISMA	COOKING	CLEANING	FRIENDS	HOURS
Athletic	Superstar	0	10	0	2	4	0	0	4	9a–4p
Business	Vice President	4	0	3	0	5	0	0	1	8a–4p
Criminal	Cat Burglar	0	5	7	4	0	0	0	3	9p–3a
Culinary	Sous Chef	4	0	4	0	0	4	0	3	2p–9p
Law Enforcement	Lieutenant	5	4	0	0	0	0	4	5	9a–3p
Medical	Specialist	5	0	0	7	0	0	7	4	10a–4p
Military	Senior Officer	0	6	0	5	3	0	0	3	8a–2p
Politics	Congressperson	4	0	3	0	6	0	0	5	9a–3p
Science	Scholar	5	0	0	0	0	5	7	3	8a–1p
Slacker	Home Video Editor	0	0	2	4	2	0	0	5	11a–5p

Days Off	# Work Days	Daily Salary	Weekly Average	Energy	Bladder	Hygiene	Social	Hunger	Fun	Comfort
Tue & Wed	5	§539	§2,695	-36	-48	-48	0	-24	36	-12
Sun & Sat	5	§560	§2,800	-42	-56	-14	35	-28	-14	-14
Sun & Sat	5	§595	§2,975	-48	-40	-64	-24	-32	16	64
Tue & Wed	5	§308	§1,540	-45	-25	-25	35	-25	30	-40
Tue & Wed	5	§686	§3,430	-36	-30	-30	30	-24	36	-30
Wed & Thu	5	§672	§3,360	-42	-56	-14	35	-28	-14	-35
Wed & Thu	5	§700	§3,500	-36	-36	-12	0	-24	48	-12
Sun & Sat	5	§679	§3,395	-36	-48	-12	30	-24	-12	-12
Mon & Thu	5	§630	§3,150	-42	-28	-28	35	-28	42	42
Tue, Wed, Thu	4	§385	§1,540	-30	-40	-10	25	-20	10	-10

Days Off	# Work Days	Daily Salary	Weekly Average	Energy	Bladder	Hygiene	Social	Hunger	Fun	Comfort
Tue, Wed, Thu	4	§893	§3,572	-24	-48	-30	0	-30	18	-12
Sun & Sat	5	§728	§3,640	-42	-56	-14	35	-28	-14	-14
Sun & Sat	5	§742	§3,710	-32	-40	-40	-40	-40	24	-64
Mon & Tue	5	§469	§2,345	-36	-30	-54	-6	3	18	-30
Mon & Tue	5	§756	§3,780	-24	0	-24	30	-30	18	-24
Sun & Sat	5	§770	§3,850	-48	-64	-16	40	-32	-16	-16
Sun & Sat	5	§770	§3,850	-24	-6	-30	0	-30	18	18
Sun & Sat	5	§756	§3,780	-42	-56	-14	35	-28	-14	-14
Tue & Thu	5	§756	§3,780	-36	-36	-9	-27	-45	99	54
Wed & Thu	5	§392	§1,960	-42	-56	-14	35	-28	-14	-14

Days Off	# Work Days	Daily Salary	Weekly Average	Energy	Bladder	Hygiene	Social	Hunger	Fun	Comfort
Tue, Wed, Thu	4	§1,190	§4,760	-35	-56	-28	0	-28	28	-7
Sun & Sat	5	§924	§4,620	-40	-64	-16	48	-32	-8	-8
Tue & Thu	5	§896	§4,480	-30	-6	-24	-42	-24	36	-48
Tue & Thu	5	§812	§4,060	-42	-21	-49	21	3	28	-21
Sun & Sat	5	§826	§4,130	-30	-30	-24	36	-24	24	-24
Sun & Sat	5	§875	§4,375	-30	-48	-12	36	-24	-6	-6
Sun & Sat	5	§812	§4,060	-30	-18	-24	0	-24	24	18
Sun & Sat	5	§840	§4,200	-30	-48	-12	36	-24	-6	-6
Sun & Sat	5	§896	§4,480	-25	-20	-10	30	-20	20	20
Tue, Wed, Thu	4	§613	§2,452	-30	-48	-12	36	-24	-6	-6

Level 8 Careers

Career	Job Name	Logic	Body	Creativity	Mechanical	Charisma	Cooking	Cleaning	Friends	Hours
Athletic	Assistant Coach	0	10	0	4	5	0	0	5	9a–2p
Business	President	6	0	4	0	5	0	0	1	8a–4p
Criminal	Counterfeiter	0	6	7	7	0	0	0	4	9a–3p
Culinary	Executive Chef	6	0	5	0	0	5	0	4	9a–3p
Law Enforcement	SWAT Team Leader	6	5	0	0	0	0	6	6	11a–6p
Medical	Surgeon	7	0	0	9	0	0	8	5	10a–4p
Military	Commander	0	7	0	5	5	0	0	4	9a–3p
Politics	Judge	7	0	3	0	8	0	0	6	10a–2p
Science	Top Secret Researcher	8	0	0	0	0	6	7	3	10a–3p
Slacker	Freelance Photographer	0	0	3	4	3	0	0	7	2p–7p

Level 9 Careers

Career	Job Name	Logic	Body	Creativity	Mechanical	Charisma	Cooking	Cleaning	Friends	Hours
Athletic	Coach	0	10	0	7	7	0	0	6	9a–3p
Business	CEO	7	0	6	0	6	0	0	1	9a–4p
Criminal	Smuggler	0	7	9	7	0	0	0	5	2a–8a
Culinary	Restaurateur	7	0	7	0	0	8	0	6	2p–10p
Law Enforcement	Police Chief	9	7	0	0	0	0	7	8	8a–4p
Medical	Medical Researcher	8	0	0	0	0	0	9	7	11a–6p
Military	Astronaut	0	10	0	6	5	0	0	5	9a–3p
Politics	Senator	8	0	5	0	9	0	0	8	9a–6p
Science	Theorist	9	0	0	0	0	7	9	5	10a–2p
Slacker	Freelance Web Designer	0	0	4	4	4	0	0	10	10a–3p

Level 10 Careers

Career	Job Name	Logic	Body	Creativity	Mechanical	Charisma	Cooking	Cleaning	Friends	Hours
Athletic	Hall of Famer	0	10	0	7	10	0	0	8	11a–5p
Business	Business Tycoon	9	0	7	0	8	0	0	1	10a–4p
Criminal	Criminal Mastermind	0	8	10	10	0	0	0	7	5p–11p
Culinary	Celebrity Chef	8	0	10	0	0	10	0	7	3p–8p
Law Enforcement	Captain Hero	9	10	0	0	0	0	8	10	10a–4p
Medical	Chief of Staff	10	0	0	0	0	0	10	9	9a–4p
Military	General	0	10	0	8	7	0	0	6	10a–4p
Politics	Mayor	10	0	7	0	10	0	0	10	10a–4p
Science	Mad Scientist	10	0	0	0	0	9	10	8	10p–2a
Slacker	Professional Party Guest	0	0	5	4	5	0	0	13	10p–2a

Days Off	# Work Days	Daily Salary	Weekly Average	Energy	Bladder	Hygiene	Social	Hunger	Fun	Comfort
Tue, Wed, Thu	4	§1,488	§5,952	-25	-40	-35	0	-35	5	-15
Tue, Sat, & Sun	4	§1,400	§5,600	-40	-64	-16	48	-32	8	0
Sun & Sat	5	§1,064	§5,320	-30	-36	-42	-36	-42	18	48
Tue, Wed, Thu	4	§1,208	§4,832	-30	-36	-24	36	3	42	-12
Sun & Sat	5	§875	§4,375	-35	-28	-49	42	-49	42	-49
Sun & Sat	5	§980	§4,900	-30	-48	-12	36	-24	6	-6
Sun & Sat	5	§840	§4,200	-30	0	-18	0	-42	6	42
Sat, Sun, Wed	4	§1,138	§4,552	-20	-32	-8	0	-16	4	20
Tue & Thu	5	§1,036	§5,180	-25	-20	-10	-15	-35	40	35
Tue, Wed, Thu	4	§788	§3,152	-25	-40	-10	30	-20	5	0

Days Off	# Work Days	Daily Salary	Weekly Average	Energy	Bladder	Hygiene	Social	Hunger	Fun	Comfort
Tue, Wed, Thu	4	§1,750	§7,000	-24	-48	-12	0	-24	18	12
Wed, Sat, Sun	4	§1,663	§6,652	-28	-56	-14	42	-28	7	7
Mon, Tue, Wed	4	§1,575	§6,300	-60	-48	-12	36	-24	18	42
Mon, Tue, Wed	4	§1,330	§5,320	-40	-32	-16	64	3	40	-8
Sun & Mon	5	§910	§4,550	-32	-56	-16	56	-32	56	-16
Fri, Sat, Sun	4	§1,356	§5,424	-28	-56	-14	-7	-28	7	21
Sat, Sun, Mon	4	§1,094	§4,376	-24	-6	-12	0	-24	60	-30
Sat, Sun, Mon	4	§1,225	§4,900	-36	-72	-18	54	-36	27	27
Sun, Mon, Sat	4	§1,522	§6,088	-16	-24	-8	24	-16	12	24
Fri, Sat, Sun, Mon	3	§933	§2,799	-20	-40	-10	30	-20	5	5

Days Off	# Work Days	Daily Salary	Weekly Average	Energy	Bladder	Hygiene	Social	Hunger	Fun	Comfort
Fri, Sat, Sun, Mon	3	§3,033	§9,099	-24	-48	-12	0	-24	12	12
Fri, Sat, Sun	4	§2,100	§8,400	-24	-48	-12	48	-24	12	12
Sun, Mon, Wed	4	§1,925	§7,700	-24	-30	-12	-30	-24	36	48
Fri, Sat, Sun, Mon	3	§2,170	§6,510	-20	-20	-10	50	2	45	15
Tue, Wed, Thu	4	§1,225	§4,900	-24	0	-12	48	-3	54	-12
Sat, Sun, Mon	4	§1,488	§5,952	-28	-56	-14	56	-28	14	14
Fri, Sat, Sun	4	§1,138	§4,552	-24	-42	-12	0	-24	12	30
Fri, Sat, Sun	4	§1,313	§5,252	-24	-48	-12	48	-24	30	30
Sun, Mon, Fri, Sat	3	§2,333	§6,999	-16	-12	-28	8	-16	28	12
Mon, Tue, Wed, Thu	3	§1,400	§4,200	-16	-32	-8	32	-16	8	8

Teen/Elder Careers

Teen/elder careers can be held by teens or elders (after they retire from their adult career).

Some Sims believe that working in their elder years gives them dignity.

The same 10 career tracks offer jobs to teens and elders. These jobs, however, have only three levels, require fewer hours, pay less, and demand lower levels of skill and friends than adult jobs.

	Career	Job Name	Logic	Body	Creativity	Mechanical	Charisma	Cooking	Cleaning	Friends	Hours
Level 1 Teen/Elder Jobs	Athletic	Waterperson	0	0	0	0	0	0	0	0	3p–6p
	Business	Gofer	0	0	0	0	0	0	0	0	3p–6p
	Criminal	Street Hawker	0	0	0	0	0	0	0	0	3p–6p
	Culinary	Dishwasher	0	0	0	0	0	0	0	0	3p–6p
	Law Enforcement	School Crossing Guard	0	0	0	0	0	0	0	0	3p–6p
	Medical	Nursing Home Attendant	0	0	0	0	0	0	0	0	3p–6p
	Military	Paintball Attendant	0	0	0	0	0	0	0	0	3p–6p
	Politics	Door to Door Poller	0	0	0	0	0	0	0	0	5p–9p
	Science	Lab Glass Scrubber	0	0	0	0	0	0	0	0	3p–6p
	Slacker	Golf Caddy	0	0	0	0	0	0	0	0	3p–6p

	Career	Job Name	Logic	Body	Creativity	Mechanical	Charisma	Cooking	Cleaning	Friends	Hours
Level 2 Teen/Elder Jobs	Athletic	Locker Room Attendant	0	1	0	1	0	0	0	1	3p–6p
	Business	Mailroom Technician	1	0	0	0	0	0	0	2	3p–6p
	Criminal	Numbers Runner	0	0	1	0	0	0	0	1	3p–6p
	Culinary	Drive Through Clerk	0	0	0	0	0	1	0	1	5p–9p
	Law Enforcement	Parking Lot Attendant	1	1	0	0	0	0	0	1	6p–9p
	Medical	Orderly	0	0	0	0	0	0	1	1	3p–6p
	Military	Recruit Training Corps	0	0	0	0	1	0	0	1	6p–10p
	Politics	Campaign Worker	0	0	0	0	1	0	0	2	3p–6p
	Science	Test Subject	1	0	0	0	0	0	0	1	3p–6p
	Slacker	Gas Station Attendant	0	0	0	1	0	0	0	2	3p–6p

Teens enrolled in private school enter any new career track at level 2. If they already have a level 1 job before getting into private school, however, they aren't automatically elevated to level 2 by a change of school.

Elders who retire from a career track and then get an elder job in the same career track don't get any level bonus. They will, however, likely advance quickly because they already have all skill levels required for promotion.

Days Off	# Work Days	Daily Salary	Weekly Average	Energy	Bladder	Hygiene	Social	Hunger	Fun	Comfort
Sun & Fri	5	§97	§485	-31	-25	-9	13	-16	-13	-31
Sun & Fri	5	§52	§260	-31	-25	-9	13	-16	-13	-31
Mon & Thu	5	§50	§250	-31	-25	-9	13	-16	-13	-31
Mon & Fri	5	§63	§315	-31	-25	-9	13	-16	-13	-31
Sun & Sat	5	§45	§225	-31	-25	-9	13	-16	-13	-31
Mon & Wed	5	§65	§325	-31	-25	-9	13	-16	-13	-31
Mon & Sat	5	§57	§285	-31	-25	-9	13	-16	-13	-31
Mon & Thu	5	§53	§265	-42	-33	-13	17	-21	-17	-42
Sun & Fri	5	§64	§320	-31	-25	-9	13	-16	-13	-31
Mon & Sat	5	§45	§225	-31	-25	-9	13	-16	-13	-31

Days Off	# Work Days	Daily Salary	Weekly Average	Energy	Bladder	Hygiene	Social	Hunger	Fun	Comfort
Mon & Sat	5	§110	§550	-24	-24	-9	12	-12	-9	-24
Mon & Sat	5	§76	§380	-24	-24	-9	12	-12	-9	-24
Mon & Wed	5	§62	§310	-15	-18	-12	12	-18	9	-6
Mon & Wed	5	§84	§420	-32	-20	-40	-16	-40	-12	-12
Tue & Thu	5	§75	§375	-15	-15	-15	-15	-15	-15	-15
Sun & Wed	5	§87	§435	-24	-24	-21	12	-12	-9	-24
Mon & Wed	5	§77	§385	-24	-24	-60	12	-20	-20	-28
Wed & Sun	5	§72	§360	-27	-18	-18	15	-18	-12	-24
Mon & Sat	5	§105	§525	-21	-21	-6	-9	-21	-21	-18
Mon & Thu	5	§71	§355	-24	-24	-9	12	-12	-9	-24

	Career	Job Name	Logic	Body	Creativity	Mechanical	Charisma	Cooking	Cleaning	Friends	Hours
Level 3 Teen/Elder Jobs	Athletic	Team Mascot	0	2	0	2	1	0	0	0	3p–6p
	Business	Executive Assistant	1	0	1	0	1	0	0	6	3p–7p
	Criminal	Pickpocket	0	1	2	1	0	0	0	1	3p–6p
	Culinary	Fast Food Shift Manager	1	0	1	0	0	1	0	4	5p–10p
	Law Enforcement	Security Guard	1	2	0	0	0	0	0	3	9p–1a
	Medical	Emergency Medical Technician	0	0	0	2	0	0	2	3	7p–10p
	Military	Recruit	0	1	0	0	1	0	0	2	3p–6p
	Politics	Intern	1	0	1	0	1	0	0	4	3p–6p
	Science	Lab Asst	1	0	0	0	0	1	1	2	3p–6p
	Slacker	Convenience Store Clerk	0	0	1	1	1	0	0	4	5p–9p

Retirement and Pension

Once a Sim becomes an elder, he can retire from his adult career track any time by calling work on the telephone and selecting "Retire."

There's no mandatory retirement, but you'd want to direct a Sim to do this if you wanted him to have more free time to help or baby-sit younger Sims or work on his Aspiration score so he could finish his life in good Aspirational shape.

Retired Sims get a daily pension of one-half their weekly salary when they retire. This amount is paid in seven parts every day of the week. They also receive a day's pay for each vacation day they had when they retired.

Pension is payable for the rest of the Sim's life, even if he subsequently gets an elder job.

Stay-At-Home Careers

There are several ways to make money that don't involve leaving the house. Unfortunately, the pay isn't that great, so these pursuits are only sufficient as supplemental income or for Sims living at subsistence level.

Most promisingly, highly Creative Sims can make paintings on easels and write novels on computers

and sell the product. The higher the Sim's Creativity skill, the more the item will fetch.

Slogging away on a novel for several days promises a handsome payoff for high Creativity Sims.

> **note**
>
> When paintings are done, they have a Sell interaction. Use this to sell the painting, or you can "return" it in Buy mode as you would any other object. Keeping a painting is also an option because it will appreciate over time and be worth more in the future. For the very patient, waiting until the artist Sim dies dramatically ups the value of the painting. Stockpile a Sim's high-value paintings and sell them upon her death for a big dose of income.

The downside to these methods is that they take several hours or even days to complete. A novel, for example, takes 30 game hours.

Days Off	# Work Days	Daily Salary	Weekly Average	Energy	Bladder	Hygiene	Social	Hunger	Fun	Comfort
Sun & Mon	5	§125	§625	-24	-24	-9	12	-12	-9	-24
Sun & Sat	5	§98	§490	-32	-32	-12	16	-16	-12	-32
Wed & Thu	5	§105	§525	-36	-15	-24	-24	-27	-18	-21
Wed & Thu	5	§91	§455	-40	-20	-50	5	-29	-5	-25
Mon & Tue	5	§125	§625	-24	-28	-16	-16	-20	-12	-24
Tue & Thu	5	§125	§625	-24	-24	-24	12	-12	-27	-24
Sun & Wed	5	§100	§500	-30	-15	-30	3	-30	-15	-15
Sun & Sat	5	§112	§560	-24	-24	-9	12	-12	-9	-24
Sun & Sat	5	§115	§575	-24	-15	-30	-12	-30	-6	-21
Mon & Tue	5	§96	§480	-32	-32	-12	16	-16	-12	-32

There are several other income-producing objects, but many of them are rewards granted by advancement in a career track. Thus, the only way a stay-at-home Sim could have them is if he left the career track after getting the reward or if it was earned by another member of the household. These objects can't be bought in Buy mode.

The Money Tree produces small amounts forever, but only if it's watered diligently.

Other income producing objects are:

◆ The Money Tree: This Aspiration reward object sprouts cash that can be harvested. It stays alive as long as it's watered regularly. The amount of income it produces and the time required to keep it producing at maximum efficiency are roughly equivalent to a low-level career track job.

◆ AquaGreen Hydroponic Garden: Sell successfully grown plants.

◆ Simsanto Inc. Biotech Station: Sell successfully completed medicines.

◆ Schokolade 890 Chocolate Manufacturing Facility: Sell successfully completed candy.

SCHOOL

Children and teens must attend school and maintain at least moderately good grades. The better a child performs in school, the higher her Aspiration score and the more rewards she'll receive.

Sims begin school automatically in public school.

Making sure your wee and tween Sims have the best possible education means knowing how they're graded.

Grades

Grades are shown in the Skills and Career panel just as job performance is for working Sims.

Every fresh-out-of-Create-A-Sim child or teen and any child on his first day of school begins with a grade of C. Where it goes from there is influenced by three things:

◆ Attendance ◆ Homework ◆ Mood

Attendance

Just getting on the bus keeps grades steady. Missing it is where the trouble starts.

Children and teens must attend school five days a week (Monday through Friday), though their hours differ:

◆ Children: 9 a.m.–3 p.m.
◆ Teens: 9 a.m.–1 p.m.

Attending school does not raise grades, but missing it lowers them. Every missed day means a reduction of one letter grade.

Homework

Though it reduces Fun, do homework every day if you want Sims to have top-notch grades.

Every day, students bring home homework (a colored book-shaped object) and deposit it somewhere on the lot. If there are multiple students on the lot, each homework is labeled with the owner's name.

> **note**
>
> If the Sim is Playful, she'll place homework on the floor. Otherwise, it goes on a desk or table if there's space available.

Completing all homework objects (none of that Sim's homework objects left on the lot when Sim goes to school) raises the Sim's grade by one letter on the next school day.

> **note**
>
> Homework can be moved, but only in Buy mode. It cannot, however, be deleted.

Failing to do homework for two days results in a one-letter-grade reduction. This is tracked by the number of homework objects on the lot. If there's one homework on the lot when the Sim goes to school, his grade will be unchanged. Two or more homework objects on the lot mean a one-letter-grade reduction.

Mood

The student's Mood fine-tunes the grade earned by attendance and doing homework. If the Sim goes to school with high Mood, her grade will have a "+" appended to it. For each day she leaves in a low Mood, she gets a "-" tacked on.

Many Wants are triggered by having an A+; nothing less will do.

Doing Homework

As discussed in Chapter 22, homework is done by using the object's Do Homework interaction.

Homework takes time, as displayed in the progress bar over the student's head. This time can be shortened if the student asks for help from another household Sim who's in a sufficiently good Mood.

Asking for help teaches young Sims to study.

When first starting out in school, students should always ask for help with homework. Not only does it speed the completion of the homework, but it's part of the process of learning to study. A Sim who's learned to study gets a Memory of the event, probably gets a high-scoring Want satisfied, and can do homework even faster in the future.

It usually takes one day's worth of homework to completely learn to study.

note

Sims' progress in learning to study isn't itself observable; the progress bar refers to the homework at hand, not the process of learning to study. If the older Sim began helping at the start of the day's homework and stayed through the end, the progress of the homework and learn to study will be the same. Once the Sim has learned to study, a Memory marks the achievement; look in the Simology>Memory panel to confirm.

tip

Ideally, Sims should ask for help from Family Aspiration Sims because this often satisfies the Family Sim's Wants too.

Report Cards

Every day, students bring home a report card, reflecting the Sim's current grade.

Good students boast about their report cards to anyone who'll listen.

Arriving home with this object triggers several things:

note

Teens with a Knowledge Aspiration take a bigger gain or hit for good or bad grades. Their Want of good grades or Fear of bad grades is more likely to appear in the panel and carry much higher scores than for teens of other Aspirations.

◆ Very good grades or very bad grades create a Memory viewable in the Sim's Memories panel; this can be talked about by the Sim as a chat topic.

◆ The Sim reacts based on the quality of the grade and Aspiration score (immature Sims will rip up a bad report card).

◆ If grades are very high, the Sim will show off the report card to any household members on the lot.

Grade Rewards and Chance Cards

During each school age (child and teen), any day a student has an A or better grade, there's a random chance he'll get money from grandparents as a reward.

note

To get the grandparent award, the Sim needn't actually have a living grandparent. Only one student per day can get this card and it can only happen once per age.

Students can also get one school chance card per age (once as a child and once as a teen). If the student is in public school, she'll get cash. If she's in private school, she'll get an increase in skill level. The chances of getting a skill level reward are higher if the Sim has at least two points in several different skills.

Unlike career chance cards (which teens can also get if they have a job), school chance cards don't involve a choice and can only give a reward.

Bad Grades

There are serious consequences if a Sim isn't doing well in school:

- ◆ A teen with C- or lower is prohibited from getting a job.
- ◆ If child's grade reaches F, he must raise the grade by the next school day or he'll be permanently removed from the lot by the Social Worker.
- ◆ If teen's grade reaches F, she'll be fired from her job.
- ◆ If a Sim other than the failing student answers the phone to receive a grade warning, he gets a Memory of it.
- ◆ Adults who receive a grade warning phone call lecture the failing student (possibly realizing a Fear of lecturing, reducing the student's Aspiration score).

Needs at School

Just as with jobs, Sims' Needs change by a fixed amount during the time they're at school:

School Type	Bladder	Comfort	Energy	Fun	Hunger	Hygiene	Social
Private School	-200	50	-175	-200	-300	-50	125
Public School	-200	-75	-175	-300	-300	-100	50

Private School

Sims can switch from public school to private school. The rewards are significant, but the admissions process is demanding.

> ### note
> Private school doesn't actually cost money.

Private school differs from public school in that:
- ◆ Private school students starting a teen career track begin at level 2.

- ◆ Hours for teens are from 9 a.m.–1 p.m. Children get out at the standard 3 p.m.
- ◆ Performance rewards for Sims in private school are skill increases rather than money.
- ◆ Spending the day at private school has less of an effect on Sims' Needs. Thus, they return home less depleted than if they were in public school and more prepared to start an after-school job. Comfort is actually replenished instead of depleted by going to private school.
- ◆ Private school students wear special uniforms.

Getting into Private School— The Headmaster Scenario

To get students into private school, families must do two things:
- ◆ There must be at least one child on the lot with C or better grades.
- ◆ Sims must have the school's headmaster for a dinner party and sufficiently impress him/her.

Any child or older Sim on a lot with at least one C-or-better student can summon the headmaster via the Invite Headmaster interaction on the telephone (if no one has sufficient grades, the headmaster will decline). If the call is placed before 5 p.m., the headmaster will arrive at 5 p.m. If it's after 5 p.m., the headmaster will come the next day.

Greet the headmaster before 6 p.m.

When the headmaster arrives, he must be greeted within one hour (by 6 p.m.) or he'll leave. Greeting him initiates the scenario; you have *six hours* to impress him. Doing this requires three tasks:

- Serve good food
- Give tour
- Schmooze

Scoring

Each of these three tasks earns points toward the winning score of 100 points. In each case, the more points scored in each area, the fewer required for the other two.

> ### tip
>
> It may help to buy some objects just for the headmaster scenario (e.g. hot tubs, art objects, etc.); return them before midnight for a full refund.

Serve Good Food

Good food is an important part of the meal, so it helps to have an accomplished chef in the family.

To maximize this element, a meal should be prepared successfully by a Sim with Cooking skill of five or higher. The higher the chef's Cooking skill, the more points the meal will earn.

Ruined meals, regardless of the chef's skill, will not score well. Leave time for mishaps and start over if the Sim ruins a meal.

When the food is served, click on the headmaster, choose "Entertain" and select "Call for Dinner." This tells the headmaster to have a serving and results in the final food score.

Give Tour

This element is based on the Environ-ment of every room shown on the tour (including, possibly, outside). Verify that the house is clean and do what you can afford to boost Environment score in every room before the headmaster's arrival. The tour ends when you choose "End Tour" or the total score for the tour reaches 40.

If Environment score is high in a room, the headmaster gets VERY excited.

To score this element, click on the headmaster and choose "Entertain," then "Give Tour." Next, direct the Sim giving the tour to the highest Environment score room; the headmaster will follow. Next, click on the head-master and select "Show Room." The headmaster gives a score based on the room's Environment score and this is added to tour points. Then, move to more high Environment rooms and repeat the process. If you've shown every room

in the house (including the outside) without reaching 40 or more tour points, click on the headmaster and choose "End Tour." This closes tour points scoring.

tip

Remember that outdoor Environment score is localized, so take the headmaster to a place where the score is high (near a tree, statue, flowerbed, outdoor light, etc.). Observe your own Sim's Environment score to pick the right spot and don't show the headmaster the room until you've found it.

Indoors, position the tour leader near light fixtures before showing the room. Proximity to a light source boosts Environment score.

Schmoozing

Chat up the headmaster and, if he engages with a group Fun object, get as many Sims as possible to join him. The more Daily Relationship he amasses with household Sims, the better the schmooze score.

The family's ability to socially interact with the headmaster is reflected in the schmooze score. Every time any family Sim raises the headmaster's Daily Relationship score, points are added to the schmooze score.

Bonus Scoring

A few interactions provide extra scoring opportunities:

◆ Get in the hot tub
◆ Drink coffee
◆ Have drinks from bar

Getting the headmaster to have a cup of coffee, drink juice from the bar, or get in the hot tub can help your cause.

If household Sims do any of these interactions, the headmaster should follow suit (as long as he's not engaged in something else). Each bonus scores 10 extra points, but can only be scored once. Successful bonus scoring opportunities show up in the Scenario Status panel, for example: "Headmaster in the Hot Tub: +10."

Winning the Scenario

When you amass (by whatever combination) 100 points, the scenario ends and the headmaster informs you that the family's been accepted. Any student in the family with a C or better grade will go to private school on the next school day.

If time runs out before 100 points are earned, the headmaster somewhat snootily, informs the family that they don't make the cut. You may invite him back the next day to try again.

Chapter 24
Social Interactions

The Sims who live alone and friendless are pretty creepy; they leave their houses only to pick up the mail, open the door only enough to go in and out, and claim they spend time with a giant one-eyed gregarious rabbit. For the rest of the population, however, socializing is a crucially important activity.

note

Kidding aside, it's possible to be a very happy loner in THE SIMS 2. Social Need satisfaction can be gained from the Chat interaction on a computer or regular visits from the Social Bunny.

Every Sim, regardless of Personality or Aspiration, needs good relationships with other Sims to have a successful career and a rich life. Thanks to the challenges of Personality and the demands of Wants and Fears, socializing is harder for some Sims than others. Everyone can, however, succeed as long as you help.

This chapter details, to the finest degree, the mechanisms of the social interaction system: how relationships are formed, under what conditions each and every social interaction appears and what the outcomes can be, and how each outcome is determined.

EFFECTS OF SOCIALIZING

Interacting with other Sims is imperative for several reasons:

1. Careers: Higher levels of each career require a Sim to have a minimum number of family friends. Without the requisite number, a Sim can be promoted only so far. Career limitation means less income, less ability to purchase objects that better fulfill her Needs, less time to build skill and satisfy Wants.

2. Social Interactions: The most rewarding interactions require highly positive Daily and Lifetime Relationship levels before they become available.

3. Aspirations: Several Wants are based on a Sims' meeting and having relationships with a number of other Sims. Satisfying the basic Wants of this type open up higher-level and higher scoring Wants. Some Aspirations demand a great deal of socializing while some require very, very little.

RELATIONSHIP SCORES

The Relationship panel shows a Sim's relationship toward everyone he knows. What you can't see here is how those Sims feel toward your Sim.

A Sim has some kind of relationship toward every Sim he's met; it can be positive, negative, or neutral (zero). Every positive interaction between two Sims increases the Relationship score of each, and most (but not all) negative interactions decrease the Relationship score. Higher-level relationships (friends, best friends, crushes, loves, etc.) require very high Relationship scores.

The first time your Sim meets a previously unfamiliar Sim, that Sim's picture appears in your Sim's Relationships panel and remains there until the Sim dies or is removed from the neighborhood.

Everything you need to know about your Sim's relationship with this Sim can be found in the Relationship panel:

◆ Daily Relationship Score: Your Sim's current feelings toward the other Sim.

◆ Lifetime Relationship Score: Your Sim's cumulative feelings toward the other Sim.

PRIMA OFFICIAL GAME GUIDE

◆ Family Icon: Found in the lower right corner of Sim's Relationship panel portrait. Indicates whether a Sim is either a blood relation or family by direct marriage (i.e. husband or wife). This includes extended family members living on other lots in the neighborhood.

◆ Relationship Types: Icons indicate the kind of relationship your Sim has toward the other Sim.

> **note**
>
> Relationships can be filtered by Family Only, Friends Only, Household Only, and All. Note that friends who are not family and don't live in your Sim's house show up only in the All sort.

Relationships, A Two-Way Street

It's crucially important to understand that a Relationship score indicates *only* how *your* Sim feels about the other Sim, not the other way around. It's possible (probable actually) that the other Sim won't have the exact same score toward your Sim.

Juliet's relationship with her brother Tybalt is a mildly negative Daily Relationship and a strong, Friend-worthy Lifetime Relationship.

Tybalt has the identical Daily Relationship but only half the Lifetime.

> **note**
>
> It's impossible to know precisely what a nonresident Sim's relationship is toward your Sim. Even if you pop into the other Sim's lot and check the numbers, there's no guarantee they'll be the same when they come a-callin' at your Sim's lot.
>
> It's important, therefore, to be observant. You can only be sure, for example, that another Sim loves your Sim if you see the telltale hearts (the red kind) floating above their heads after an initial romantic interaction that causes them to fall in love.

This difference in how two Sims feel about each other is especially important in judging how interactions will work out. Keep in mind that, generally, your Sim's relationship numbers impact whether the interaction is available at all, while the receiving Sim's relationship numbers impact whether the interaction is accepted. Success in interactions, therefore, has nothing to do with the numbers for *your Sim*.

Daily vs. Lifetime Relationship Scores

There are actually two distinct but related Relationship scores for every Sim: Daily Relationship and Lifetime Relationship.

Daily Relationship is on the top and Lifetime is on the bottom.

Daily Relationship is a much more volatile number that represents recent history between your Sim and the other Sim. Daily is dramatically impacted by social interactions and by long periods of separation (see "Decay and Normalization," below).

Lifetime Relationship is a more stable figure that represents the entire course of two Sims' interactions. Unlike Daily Relationship, Lifetime isn't directly impacted by all social interactions; when it is, the change is only about one to three points.

The distinction between Daily and Lifetime is important because relationship types are based upon one or the other. For example, Friendship requires an easier-to-achieve high Daily Relationship score while Best Friends demands a more difficult high Lifetime Relationship score. Even the most Outgoing Sim would have a hard time making a Best Friend in a single encounter but should be able to make a Friend in about 4–5 Sim hours (less for Outgoing).

Not only does the Daily vs. Lifetime distinction make the more intense relationships harder to achieve, but it also makes the more superficial ones more likely to disappear. Relationships based on Daily can't withstand much neglect; a few days is usually enough to drop a borderline relationship's score below the relationship's threshold.

Finally, the distinction matters because availability and acceptance of social interactions often depends on one or both kinds of Relationship scores. Because high Daily Relationship can come pretty quickly and a high Lifetime score takes a while to achieve, interactions dependent on a high Lifetime aren't immediately available. What's more, once available, they won't be accepted until the Lifetime score rises high enough.

Decay and Normalization of Relationship Scores

When two Sims aren't interacting, their relationship is still changing. Some changes are positive and some are negative but they are driven by two forces: decay and normalization.

Decay

Relationship decay affects Daily Relationship, changing it by *two points per day* (at 4 p.m.) until it reaches zero. Thus, a positive relationship declines by two points per day until it reaches zero and a negative relationship improves by two points per day until it reaches zero.

Keep relationships steady with an occasional phone call.

tip

A regular phone call can keep a relationship, at the very least, steady by providing more positive Daily Relationship points than decay takes away. An hour's worth of interaction every five days is enough to maintain a relationship.

Decay can only be overcome by daily interaction (of more than two points, obviously).

Keep in mind that decay directly affects only *Daily* Relationship. Lifetime Relationship scores are indirectly impacted by decay through a process called "normalization."

note

Decay and normalization occur between household Sims and all their relationships (both ways), and between all non-household Sims simultaneously visiting the lot. They do not, however, occur between two non-household Sims when one of them is on the lot and the other isn't.

For example, if X and her spouse Y are visiting A and B's lot, decay and normalization are occurring between A and B, A/B and Y, A/B and X, and X and Y. If Y leaves the lot or X visits alone, NO DECAY AND NORMALIZATION takes place between X and Y.

Normalization

Normalization is the tendency of Daily and Lifetime to slowly converge until they're equal. Every eight game hours, Lifetime Relationship score changes by three points toward the Daily score. Thus, if Daily is higher, Lifetime increases by three and, if it's lower, Lifetime decreases by three. When the two numbers meet, normalization stops.

This change is in addition to the Daily decay of minus two per day.

It's because of normalization that a single bad day won't severely damage a strong Lifetime relationship. Allow it to stay low, however, and it will eventually drag Lifetime down. Likewise, a series of really good days will gradually pull Lifetime up; this is how serious relationships are built.

An Example

◆ Sim A has a Daily/Lifetime score toward Sim B of 60/55.

◆ Sim A and Sim B have a fight. Daily drops to 46.

◆ Every eight hours, Lifetime drops by three points. In 24 game hours, therefore, both scores will be 46.

◆ After 24 hours, however, Daily decays by two points, lowering it to 44.

◆ Due to normalization, these numbers level off at 44 eight hours later.

◆ With no further interaction, both scores will drop by two points a day until they reach zero (in this case 22 days).

note

To give you a sense of what it takes to create a Love relationship, consider that it will take Lifetime relationship eight days to reach 70 through the action of normalization alone. Interactions that directly feed Lifetime relationship accelerate this advance, but the lesson stands fast: Love takes time.

TYPES OF RELATIONSHIPS

Several different kinds of relationships can exist between two Sims.

Relationship types impact several things:

◆ How Sims autonomously react to one another.

◆ What interactions are available.

◆ The number of friends a Sim has is a requirement for many career promotions.

◆ Several Wants/Fears are triggered and fulfilled by the existence of relationship types.

Family

Family relationships are established in the Create-A-Family system or through marriage/joining and childbirth/adoption.

The full extent of family relationships is shown in the family tree.

A Sim will recognize as family any Sim to which she's related by blood or by direct marriage/joining. In other words, spouses will be family to each other but the spouse-by-marriage won't be family to anyone in her husband's family except her own offspring.

note

The blood relationship requirement has a potential side effect. If they're appropriate ages (both teen, both adult, or one elder one adult), an uncle/aunt and a niece/nephew could interact romantically. What will the family say!?

Score-Based Relationships

All other relationships are a function of Relationship score. Many require other factors or actions, but all share a reliance on Daily and/or Lifetime Relationship score.

Enemy

- ◆ Who: Child/teen/adult/elder
- ◆ Relationship Score Threshold: -50 Daily or Lifetime for both
- ◆ Reciprocal: No
- ◆ Required Interaction: None
- ◆ Break Requirement: Both Daily and Lifetime rise above -50 for both

Friend

- ◆ Who: Toddler/child/teen/adult/elder
- ◆ Relationship Score Threshold: Daily 50 or above
- ◆ Reciprocal: Yes
- ◆ Required Interaction: None
- ◆ Break Requirement: Daily drops below 50

Best Friend

- ◆ Who: Toddler/child/teen/adult/elder
- ◆ Relationship Score Threshold: Lifetime 50 or above
- ◆ Reciprocal: Yes
- ◆ Required Interaction: None
- ◆ Break Requirement: Lifetime drops below 50 for both

Crush

- ◆ Who: Teen/adult/elder
- ◆ Relationship Score Threshold: Daily 70 or above
- ◆ Reciprocal: No
- ◆ Required Interaction: Romantic interaction
- ◆ Break Requirement: Daily falls below 70 and there's a direct Daily Relationship score loss from the other Sim

Go Steady

- ◆ Who: Teen
- ◆ Relationship Score Threshold: None
- ◆ Reciprocal: Must be accepted
- ◆ Required Interaction: Crush must exist, Propose > Go Steady must be done and accepted
- ◆ Break Requirement: Break Up interaction

Love

Sweet Love is born in this young lady.

- ◆ Who: Teen/adult/elder
- ◆ Relationship Score Threshold: Lifetime above 70
- ◆ Reciprocal: No
- ◆ Required Interaction: Romantic interaction
- ◆ Break Requirement: Lifetime falls below 70 and there's a direct Lifetime Relationship score loss from the other Sim

Engaged

- ◆ Who: Adult/elder
- ◆ Relationship Score Threshold: None
- ◆ Reciprocal: Must be accepted
- ◆ Required Interaction: Propose > Engagement must be done and accepted
- ◆ Break Requirement: Break Up interaction

Married/Joined

- ◆ Who: Adult/elder
- ◆ Relationship Score Threshold: None
- ◆ Reciprocal: Must be accepted

- Required Interaction: Engaged must already exist and Propose > Marriage interaction must be done and accepted
- Break Requirement: Break Up Interaction

Marriage can be achieved either directly on the other Sim or via the special wedding arch object.

Romantic Interactions

Romantic interactions are socials that, if accepted, cause a Crush or Love to be born. If the appropriate Relationship score has reached the requisite threshold, doing one of these interactions seals the deal for *both* Sims (if their Daily or Lifetime scores are high enough), regardless of the other Sim's gender.

From a little flirt, a Crush is born.

If you don't want Love or a Crush to form, therefore, don't do romantic interactions; they are the difference between an intense friendship and a love connection.

Romantic interactions are:

- Caress
- Charm

- Goose (can set Love only because Crush is prerequisite)
- Hit On
- Hold Hands
- Leap into Arms (can set Love only because Crush is prerequisite)
- Make Out (can set Love only because Crush is prerequisite)
- Peck
- Romantic Hug
- Romantic Kiss
- Smooch (can set Love only because Crush is prerequisite)
- Squeeze (can set Love only because Crush is prerequisite)
- Suggestion
- Sweet Talk
- Tender Kiss
- Up Arm Kiss

Crush and Love, unlike friendship, can be a one-way street. If your Sim has a Daily of 60 but the other Sim has a Daily of 48 and you perform Charm, your Sim will develop a Crush while the other will not.

OPPORTUNITIES TO INTERACT

There are many, many ways to meet Sims and maintain relationships.

Household Sims

It's very important to maintain relationships with members of the household; they're almost always around, and you can see both sides of the interactions. This means you can strategically choose interactions you know will be accepted and will benefit both sides.

Note, however, that friendships with household Sims do not count toward friends needed for career promotions. Only friendships with Sims outside the household matter for that purpose.

Keep things friendly in the family, if for no other reason, to keep up the Social Need.

On the upside, the external friendships of any family member count for all members. If John has two friends and his wife, Cindy, has three (with different Sims), then John has five for career promotion purposes.

Walkbys and Dropbys

Each day, four or more Sims (whom, if possible, your Sims don't yet know) will stroll by the house, pause for a few game minutes (possibly reading your newspaper if you've left it out), and move on. If you greet these Sims, they'll become visitors who'll stay for as long as you meet their Needs or until you ask them to leave.

Folks out on a walk are always happy to be asked in.

note

Sloppy walkby Sims may rifle through your garbage can while Grouchy Sims may kick it over.

These will be Sims from the neighborhood or Sims called "Townies," Sims who live just outside the neighborhood but who pop up around town.

note

Townies are discussed in detail in Chapter 28.

Each day, a randomly chosen Sim with a relationship with one child, teen, adult, or elder in the household has a 15 percent chance of dropping by uninvited.

Telephone, Invite

You may, during "decent hours" (8 a.m.–12 midnight) use the telephone to call any neighborhood Sim and invite him over. Whether he accepts depends on a rather complex set of issues, but it boils down to the other Sim's Daily and Lifetime Relationships with your Sim and a random factor. In general, though, if it's not during the other Sim's work hours and not in the middle of the night, a Daily relationship above 20 and a Lifetime Relationship above 5 yields a guaranteed yes. It's possible to get an acceptance below this level but it's less likely.

A telephone invitation is the sure way to get a Sim in the home for serious socializing. Otherwise, you're leaving it to chance.

Acceptance also depends on the other Sim's work schedule; if he's away from home, he can't answer.

note

Sims can call other Sims only if they too have a telephone or if they are Townies.

Calling too late at night or too early in the morning (before 7 a.m.) or after 12 midnight will get you an automatic rejection, a surly response, and a reduction in Daily Relationship.

If the invitation is accepted, the other Sim pops by and rings the bell about half a game hour later.

There is a random chance (25 percent) the other Sim will ask to bring a friend along; your Sim has the option to allow the friend to come or not. If you reject the invitee's friend, the invitee still comes. Adults and elders may also bring elders, adults, teens, or children but never toddlers or babies. There's a 20 percent chance the companion will be the adult or elder's spouse or fiancé; if there's no fiancé or spouse, she may bring a child.

If the visitor is a child, there's a 20 percent chance he'll bring a mutual friend: the friend with the best combined Relationship score with your Sim and the invitee.

Elders, adults, and teens may invite children, teens, adults, or elders while children may invite only other children. Invited children may bring along an adult or elder.

> **note**
>
> No walkbys or dropbys occur on the move in day. This day is for the welcome wagon (see below).

Bring Friends Home

Working Sims may randomly bring another Sim home from work (25 percent chance) and school-age Sims may take home a classmate. Such Sims don't need to be greeted to make them visitors.

Telephone, Talk

Sims stroll around the house socializing cordless style.

Sims can call any Sims they know (who has a telephone) and talk without inviting them over.

> **note**
>
> Because phones are cordless, Sims wander around the house while they yammer on the phone.

This conversation satisfies the Social Need and adds to Daily Relationship. The conversation goes on just like a Talk interaction, with Sims handing the speaking role back and forth and deciding whether to continue based on their interest in the other Sim's chosen topic.

Non-household Sims also call your Sims to talk. If the Sim they're calling for doesn't answer, they'll ask if another Sim is available.

Chatting on Computer

Sims can use the computer to Chat with other Sims that they may or may not know.

Chatting on computer offers Sims Social and can randomly result in the other Sim being invited over.

A Sim never has to have anyone over or leave the house to keep up their Social Need. That can be done by computer but that, by itself, won't build relationships.

> **note**
>
> Children may Chat only with other children.

E-Mail

Sending and receiving e-mail can gain your Sim either Social or Daily Relationship boosts. Sims may send e-mail to any Sim they know (except household

members) who also has a computer. Sent e-mail causes a rise in Daily for both Sims.

Sims may also randomly receive e-mail and gets a bit of Social multiplied by the number of incoming messages.

Community Lots

Community Lots are social target-rich environments. They are typically full of neighborhood and Townie Sims with whom your Sim may interact. Sims starved for Social can have it for the price of a cab ride to a Community Lot.

Community Lots are great places to add lots of Sims to the relationship panel. Then your Sim can call his new acquaintance when he returns home.

See Chapter 29 for more on Community Lots.

Talking to the Help

Chatting with the Maid can lead heaven knows where.

Sims can meet and socialize with the Sims who provide services. Maids, Newspaper Delivery, Police, Burglars, Firefighters, Nannies, Gardeners, etc. can also become friends if you take the time to introduce your Sims to them. Keep things going well and you can even marry them.

The Welcome Wagon

On a family's first day on a new lot, three visitors (neighbors or Townies) drop by at noon. This welcome wagon is made up of Sims with no relationship to anyone in the household. Neighbor Sims will likely come from the closest nearby lot.

To get you started, a trio of neighbors drops by on a Sim family's first day in a house.

The welcome wagon visitors must be greeted within 50 minutes or they'll leave.

If the household is a single adult or elder Sim, the welcome wagon will consist of two non-related Sims of the opposite gender and one of the same gender.

If the household has more than one member, the visitors are more likely to be pulled from the same household.

The Social Bunny

Even if interactions with the Social Bunny are on the ugly side, they ARE increasing this Sim's Social Need.

The Social Bunny is the last resort of the lonely Sim. When Social Need bottoms out, the Social Bunny appears, visible only to the lonely Sim. The desperate Sim gets Social while the Bunny

is on the lot and may perform almost any interaction (except romantic ones) with the Bunny to raise her Social Need faster. Once Social is restored above zero, the Bunny disappears as mysteriously as it arrived.

More on the Social Bunny can be found in Chapter 26.

SOCIAL INTERACTION MECHANICS

Social interactions (mostly all) follow a basic pattern. Each interaction involves two Sims: the Sim who initiated ("Sim A") and the Sim who is receiving the interaction ("Sim B").

In any interaction, the Sim you control is Sim A and the Sim on whom you click for the interaction is Sim B.

When A clicks on B, the only interactions that appear are the ones that are "available." Availability depends entirely on *Sim A's* characteristics and his relationship with B and whether A and B's age groups are permissible for the interaction (e.g., no romantic interactions with children). In other words, whether A can do an interaction has absolutely nothing to do

with how B will react to it. Availability normally involves a specified range of Daily and/or Lifetime Relationship scores of A toward B and perhaps some other factors (whether A is in love with B or if B is family).

note

In fact, it's quite likely that interactions will be available BEFORE there's a chance of them being accepted. Don't be too hasty about trying out shiny new interactions unless you crave rejection.

Once Sim A executes the interaction, B may either accept or reject it. This decision is based entirely (with a few small exceptions) on *Sim B's* characteristics and relationship toward A. Acceptance factors can be B's Daily and/or Lifetime relationship, Personality levels, Mood, or skills.

note

Because you most often won't know the values of Sim B's relationship toward your Sim, using successful interactions is a matter of trial and error. A few strategically chosen interactions can narrow down the range and allow you to make informed decisions.

When dealing with Sims in the same household, on the other hand, you can always switch to the other Sim to see everything you need to know about whether they'll accept.

Whether B accepts dictates what happens next. Each interaction has different outcomes for each Sim depending on whether B accepted or rejected. These outcomes are most often changes to Daily Relationship and Social Need but can also directly change Lifetime

Relationship (but usually only by a few points). Other outcomes can include the creation of a Crush or Love relationship.

VISITOR BEHAVIOR

When a Sim is invited into your Sims' home, she becomes a visitor. This role precisely defines what she can and cannot do on your lot.

A non-household Sim becomes a visitor when greeted by a resident.

Initial Needs

Visitors arrive with their Needs set within a defined range. Crucial to their happy and lengthy stay is your ability to provide opportunities for them to fulfill these Needs. When they arrive, their Needs are randomly set within the ranges below:

- Energy: 100
- Comfort: 50
- Hunger: 25–50
- Hygiene: 20–80
- Bladder: 15–85
- Social: -25–50
- Fun: 10–40

Visitor Dos and Don'ts

- Visitors DO NOT do anything that spends your Sims' money.
- Visitors DO NOT clean.
- Visitors DO attempt to fulfill their Fun, Social, Hunger, Comfort, and Bladder.
- Visitors DO leave if any Need falls below -60.

- Visitors DO leave in three hours if there's no functioning way to feed their Fun, Bladder, Social, and Comfort.
- Visitors DO stay for at least seven hours if you have functioning objects to feed their Fun, Bladder, Social, and Comfort.
- Visitors DO leave at 2 a.m. unless they've been invited to stay the night.
- Visitors DO leave in three hours if there's no food.
- Visitors DO autonomously socialize when they arrive.
- Visitors DON'T reject Join requests when they first arrive.

Visitor Need Satisfaction

Ample food, switched on sources of Fun, someone to talk to, a working bathroom, and a place to sit are all necessary to keep visitors around for the long haul.

Visitors will be forced to leave if any of their Needs drop too low (below -60). You must, therefore, provide facilities to permit them to satisfy these Needs autonomously. The problem is, they can't freely use all objects in your Sims' home. Working around these limitations is the key to successful hosting of visitors.

PRIMA OFFICIAL GAME GUIDE

note

Just because you provide the means for visitors to fill their Needs doesn't mean they can use them. If, for example, a visitor Need is near minimum and another Sim is blocking or using the only available object, he has no choice but to leave. This happens most often when there aren't enough places to sit.

Fun

Visitors may not turn on Fun objects but may freely use them autonomously. For example, they can watch a TV that's already on and can even change the channel, but they can't turn it on themselves. They may Join joinable objects but only if another Sim (resident or another visitor) is already using it.

When visitors come, be sure that stereos and TVs are switched on.

Hunger

Visitors can't use the refrigerator but will partake of served meals just as a resident would. They'll even clean up after themselves after they've eaten if they're Neat.

Keep fresh food out and available by Serving a meal. If any visitors exhibit Hunger distress thought bubbles, whip up some more quick.

note

Visitors can't repair or clean anything in the house, though they will put their own dish in the dishwasher or sink if they're Neat.

Energy

Energy is the most difficult Need for visitors. They can't use sofas or beds to replenish Energy, so they won't be allowed to sleep.

Caffeine is the only way visitors get Energy.

The only way to give your visitors Energy is to own an espresso machine and have a resident Sim occasionally Serve espresso. This leaves two cups of hot caffeinated brew out and available to visitors; be ready for a bathroom stampede!

A visitor can be invited to Stay the Night (from the Propose menu). If she accepts (her Daily toward your Sim is greater than 45 and Lifetime is greater than 25 and her Mood is also above 25), she becomes able to sleep, nap, or lounge on beds, sofas, recliners until she leaves the next day.

Comfort

Visitors may sit in any chairs or sofas to replenish their Comfort Needs. They may not, however, use beds.

Have plenty of easily accessible chairs.

Social

Don't ignore your guests; they've come to satisfy their Social Needs too. Interacting with household Sims and other visitors allows them to keep this Need fulfilled.

Hygiene

Visitors can't use sinks, tubs, or showers to fulfill Hygiene. There's nothing you can do to help them here.

Visitors invited to Stay the Night can use these objects to replenish their Hygiene.

Bladder

Visitors may freely use toilets to satisfy their Bladder Needs.

Make sure bathrooms are accessible when visitors are on the lot. If they can't get to the bathroom, visitors won't stay as long.

Visitor Departure

Visitors leave the lot for several reasons:

◆ If they haven't been greeted in a reasonable amount of time.

◆ If any of their Needs drop too low.

◆ If it's too late at night (2 a.m.). If asked to Stay the Night, however, they remain. Child guests are picked up by an adult/elder at 8 p.m.

◆ If asked to leave by any household Sim.

SOCIAL INTERACTION DIRECTORY

There are two kinds of Sim-to-Sim interactions: basic and object-assisted.

Basic interactions occur when a Sim interacts directly with another Sim. In other words, if both Sims are standing and you click on the other Sim.

Object-assisted interactions can be done only when both Sims are using the same specific object. For example, Cuddle may be performed only if both Sims are on the same bed or sofa. These interactions are listed in their own section below.

> **note**
>
> The interactions below are mostly organized by the menus in which they appear when you click on another Sim. If an interaction doesn't appear when you click on another Sim, it's because it's not available yet. Consult the directory for each interaction's availability conditions.
>
> Toddler and baby interactions can appear under certain menus but also at the main menu level. For this reason, they're each listed in their own section though you never see menus titled "toddler" or "baby."

> **note**
>
> When an availability condition includes a number in parenthesis, this indicates differing availability for members of the same household or blood relatives (outside parenthesis) on one side and everyone else (in the parenthesis) on the other side.

Social Interactions: Availability, Autonomous Personalities, and Social/Daily/Lifetime Effects

Interaction	Menu	Availability Daily A to B Above	Availability Daily A to B Below	And/Or	Availability Lifetime A to B Above	Availability Lifetime A to B Below	Crush	Love or Go Steady	Autonomous Personality	User Directed
Admire	Appreciate	0	100	And	0	100	—	—	Outgoing	Yes
Annoy	Irritate	-45	-1	Or	-30	-1	—	—	Mean	Yes
Apologize	Appreciate	-100	-20	And	-100	100	—	—	Nice	Yes
Argue	Irritate	-100	100	Or	-100 (15)	100	—	—	Mean	Yes
Ask to Go Out	Teen	-100	100	Or	-100	100	—	—	Not Autonomous	Yes
Ask to Leave	Ask to Leave	-100	100	Or	-100	100	—	—	Not Autonomous	Yes
Ask to Teach/ be Taught	Ask to Teach	-100	-100	Or	-100	100	—	—	Not Autonomous	Yes
Attack	Fight	-100	-65	Or	-100	-65	—	—	Active	Yes
Attention	Ask For	-100 (0)	100	And	-100 (0)	100	—	—	Active	Yes
Backrub	Appreciate	40	100	And	15	100	—	—	Playful	Yes
Brag	Talk	0	50	Or	10	50	—	—	Outgoing	Yes
Break Up	Break Up	-100	45	And	-100	45	—	—	Not Autonomous	Yes
Call Over	Call Over	-100	100	Or	-100	100	—	—	Not Autonomous	Yes
Caress	Flirt	65	100	And	40	100	Sets	Sets	Playful	Yes
Change Diaper	Ask For	-100 (0)	100	Or	-100 (0)	100	—	—	Nice	Yes
Change Diaper	Social baby	-100 (20)	100	And	-100 (10)	100	—	—	Active	Yes
Change Diaper	Social toddler	-100 (20)	100	And	-100 (10)	100	—	—	Neat	Yes
Charm	Flirt	15	70	And	5	70	Sets	Sets	Nice	Yes
Chat	Talk	-100	100	Or	-100	100	—	—	None	Yes
Cheer Up	Appreciate	20	100	And	20	100	—	—	Nice	Yes
Congratulate About	Memory	25	100	Or	25	100	—	—	Serious	No
Console	Memory	50	100	And	35	100	—	—	Nice	No
Cops and Robbers	Play	0	100	Or	10	100	—	—	Playful	Yes
Cuddle	Bed	35	100	And	25	100	Sets	Sets	Not Autonomous	Yes
Cuddle	Hot Tub	35	100	And	25	100	Sets	Sets	Not Autonomous	Yes
Cuddle	Love Tub	-5	100	And	-15	100	Sets	Sets	Not Autonomous	Yes
Cuddle	Sofa	35	100	And	25	100	Sets	Sets	Not Autonomous	Yes
Cuddle Baby	Social baby	-100 (0)	100	And	-100 (0)	100	—	—	Nice	Yes
Dance Together	Dance	-10	100	Or	-10	100	—	—	Outgoing	Yes
Dirty Joke	Entertain	55	100	And	35	100	—	—	Playful	Yes
Encourage	Encourage	-100	100	Or	-100	100	—	—	Not Autonomous	Yes

Autonomous	If Accept, A's Social	If Accept, A's Daily	If Accept, A's Lifetime	If Accept, B's Social	If Accept, B's Daily	If Accept, B's Lifetime	If Reject, A's Social	If Reject, A's Daily	If Reject, A's Lifetime	If Reject, B's Social	If Reject, B's Daily	If Reject, B's Lifetime
Yes	10	5	1	22	4	2	0	-10	-1	0	-7	-2
Yes	0	0	0	0	0	0	4	-4	-1	-3	-10	-1
Yes	16	10	0	16	10	0	0	0	0	0	0	0
Yes	16	-7	-2	0	-9	-2	4	-6	-1	-2	-4	-1
No	10	8	0	16	10	0	0	-8	-1	0	-2	0
No	0	0	0	0	0	0	0	0	0	0	0	0
No	14	6	0	20	13	0	-4	-4	0	-4	-4	0
Yes	24	-7	-10	-8	-11	-10	-8	-11	-10	24	-7	-10
Yes	14	5	0	20	13	0	-4	-4	0	-4	-4	0
Yes	14	4	2	20	6	3	0	-7	-2	0	-10	-3
Yes	14	6	0	20	4	0	0	-5	0	0	-5	0
No	0	-20	-20	0	-50	-30	0	0	0	0	0	0
No	0	0	0	0	0	0	0	0	0	0	0	0
Yes	22	10	2	24	11	2	-5	-10	-3	-3	-10	-2
Yes	14	6	0	20	13	0	-4	-4	0	-4	-4	0
Yes	14	6	0	20	13	0	0	0	0	0	0	0
Yes	14	6	0	20	13	0	-4	-4	0	-4	-4	0
Yes	14	4	1	16	5	1	0	-4	-1	0	-6	0
Yes	Variable	Variable	Variable	Variable	Variable	Variable	Variable	Variable	Variable	Variable	Variable	Variable
Yes	16	6	1	30	8	2	0	-10	-1	0	-5	-1
Yes	8	5	1	8	5	1	0	0	0	0	0	0
Yes	8	5	1	8	5	1	0	0	0	0	0	0
Yes	24	6	0	24	6	0	0	-5	0	0	-5	0
No	20	6	2	20	10	2	0	-10	-3	0	-10	-2
No	20	6	2	20	10	2	0	-10	-3	0	-10	-2
No	20	6	2	20	10	2	0	-10	-3	0	-10	-2
No	20	6	2	20	10	2	0	-10	-3	0	-10	-2
Yes	20	4	1	40	4	1	0	0	0	0	0	0
Yes	10	6	0	10	8	0	-2	-3	0	-2	-2	0
Yes	18	6	1	20	6	1	4	-8	-2	0	-12	-1
No	14	6	0	20	13	0	-4	-4	0	-4	-4	0

Social Interactions: Availability, Autonomous Personalities, and Social/Daily/Lifetime Effects continued

Interaction	Menu	Availability Daily A to B Above	Availability Daily A to B Below	And/Or	Availability Lifetime A to B Above	Availability Lifetime A to B Below	Crush	Love or Go Steady	Autonomous Personality	User Directed
Engagement	Propose	75	100	And	70	100	—	Required	Not Autonomous	Yes
Family Kiss	Kiss	-100	100	And	0	100	Not allowed	Not allowed	Nice	Yes
Family Kiss	Social toddler	-50 (—)	100	And	0 (—)	100	Not allowed	Not allowed	Nice	Yes
First Kiss	Kiss	50	100	And	25	100	Sets	Sets	Not Autonomous	Yes
Food	Ask For	-100 (0)	100	Or	-100 (0)	100	—	—	Active	Yes
Friendly Hug	Hug	10	100	Or	10	100	—	—	Serious	Yes
Go Steady	Propose	70	100	And	25	100	Required	—	Not Autonomous	Yes
Goose	Flirt	75	100	And	55	100	Required	Sets	Playful	Yes
Gossip	Talk	30	100	Or	35	100	—	—	Mean	Yes
Groom	Appreciate	50	100	And	25	100	—	—	Neat	Yes
Gross Out	Irritate	-100	-5	Or	-100	-5	—	—	Sloppy	Yes
Hit On	Flirt	45	80	And	25	80	Sets	Sets	Mean	Yes
Hold Hands	Flirt	55	100	And	30	100	Sets	Sets	Nice	Yes
Insult	Irritate	-60	-5	Or	-45	-5	—	—	Mean	Yes
Joke	Entertain	-10	100	Or	-5	100	—	—	Playful	Yes
Leap into Arms	Hug	55	100	And	35	100	Required	Sets	Active	Yes
Make Out	Bed	80	100	And	50	100	Required	Sets	Not Autonomous	Yes
Make Out	Hot Tub	80	100	And	50	100	Required	Sets	Not Autonomous	Yes
Make Out	Love Tub	40	100	And	20	100	Required	Sets	Not Autonomous	Yes
Make Out	Sofa	80	100	And	50	100	Required	Sets	Not Autonomous	Yes
Make Out	Kiss	80	100	And	50	100	Required	Sets	Outgoing	Yes
Marriage (Join)	Propose	75	100	And	70	100	—	Required	Not Autonomous	Yes
Mary Mack	Play	15	100	Or	15	100	—	—	Lazy	Yes
Massage	Hot Tub	55	100	And	30	100	—	—	Not Autonomous	Yes
Massage	Love Tub	15	100	And	0	100	—	—	Not Autonomous	Yes
Move In	Propose	60	100	And	45	100	—	—	Not Autonomous	Yes
Nag	Irritate	-100	100	And	25	100	—	—	Outgoing	Yes
Noogie	Irritate	-25	50	And	-10	50	—	—	Playful	Yes
Peck	Hot Tub	40	100	And	20	100	Sets	Sets	Not Autonomous	Yes
Peck	Love Tub	0	100	And	-15	100	Sets	Sets	Not Autonomous	Yes
Peck	Sofa	40	100	And	20	100	Sets	Sets	Not Autonomous	Yes
Peck	Kiss	40	100	And	20	100	Sets	Sets	Nice	Yes

Autonomous	If Accept, A's Social	If Accept, A's Daily	If Accept, A's Lifetime	If Accept, B's Social	If Accept, B's Daily	If Accept, B's Lifetime	If Reject, A's Social	If Reject, A's Daily	If Reject, A's Lifetime	If Reject, B's Social	If Reject, B's Daily	If Reject, B's Lifetime
No	100	6	3	100	9	3	-30	-15	-5	-4	-8	-4
Yes	18	5	1	20	6	1	0	-4	0	0	-5	0
Yes	18	5	1	20	6	1	0	-4	0	0	-5	0
No	70	15	3	70	13	2	0	-15	-5	0	-10	-3
Yes	14	6	0	20	13	0	-4	-4	0	-4	-4	0
Yes	16	5	1	16	6	1	0	-5	-1	0	-5	-1
No	30	6	3	30	9	3	-4	-10	-5	-4	-4	-4
Yes	20	11	1	14	10	1	-2	-9	-2	-6	-11	-3
Yes	24	9	0	24	9	0	0	-7	0	0	-6	0
Yes	4	3	0	4	0	3	0	0	0	0	0	0
Yes	24	6	0	24	6	0	6	-5	0	-4	-5	0
Yes	18	8	1	14	9	1	4	-8	-1	0	-10	-2
Yes	20	9	1	20	10	1	-4	-9	-2	-3	-8	-2
Yes	16	-8	-1	-7	-14	-2	10	-10	-1	-7	-14	-2
Yes	14	4	0	14	4	0	0	-4	0	0	-4	0
Yes	20	11	2	16	13	2	0	-15	-4	0	-10	-2
No	30	19	4	30	19	4	8	-15	-4	0	-15	-4
No	30	19	4	30	19	4	8	-15	-4	0	-15	-4
No	30	19	4	30	19	4	8	-15	-4	0	-15	-4
No	30	19	4	30	19	4	8	-15	-4	0	-15	-4
Yes	30	19	4	30	19	4	8	-15	-4	0	-15	-4
No	100	6	3	100	6	3	-100	-100	-85	-50	-50	-20
Yes	30	8	0	30	8	0	0	-6	0	0	-7	0
No	14	4	2	20	6	3	0	-7	-2	0	-10	-3
No	14	4	2	20	6	3	0	-7	-2	0	-10	-3
No	40	6	3	40	6	3	-4	-10	-5	-4	-4	-4
Yes	0	0	0	0	0	0	6	-4	0	-8	-8	-1
Yes	14	6	1	6	-5	0	0	0	0	0	0	0
No	14	8	1	14	8	1	8	-6	-1	0	-6	-1
No	14	8	1	14	8	1	8	-6	-1	0	-6	-1
No	14	8	1	14	8	1	8	-6	-1	0	-6	-1
Yes	14	8	1	14	8	1	8	-6	-1	0	-6	-1

Social Interactions: Availability, Autonomous Personalities, and Social/Daily/Lifetime Effects continued

Interaction	Menu	Availability Daily A to B Above	Availability Daily A to B Below	And/Or	Availability Lifetime A to B Above	Availability Lifetime A to B Below	Crush	Love or Go Steady	Autonomous Personality	User Directed
Play With	Social baby	-100 (0)	100	And	-100 (0)	100	—	—	Playful	Yes
Poke	Fight	-100	-15	Or	-100	-20	—	—	Mean	Yes
Punch U Punch Me	Play	45	100	Or	35	100	—	—	Mean	Yes
Read To	Ask For	-50 (25)	100	And	-50 (15)	100	—	—	Serious	No
Read To	Social toddler	-50 (25)	100	And	-50 (15)	100	—	—	Outgoing	Yes
Red Hands	Play	35	100	Or	25	100	—	—	Active	Yes
Romantic Kiss	Sofa	60	100	And	35	100	Sets	Sets	Not Autonomous	Yes
Romantic Hug	Hug	35	100	And	25	100	Sets	Sets	Outgoing	Yes
Romantic Kiss	Kiss	60	100	And	35	100	Sets	Sets	Outgoing	Yes
Rub Belly	Baby	60	100	Or	50	100	—	—	Serious	Yes
Serenade	Flirt	70	100	And	60	100	Required	Required	Outgoing	Yes
Share Interests	Talk	35	100	Or	20	100	—	—	Not Autonomous	Yes
Shoo from Room	Shoo	-100	100	Or	-100	100	—	—	Not Autonomous	Yes
Shove	Fight	-100	-25	Or	-100	-30	—	—	Outgoing	Yes
Slap	Fight	-100	-40	Or	-100	-40	—	—	Serious	Yes
Smooch	Kiss	70	100	And	40	100	Required	Sets	Playful	Yes
Snuggle	Social toddler	-50 (—)	100	And	0 (—)	100	—	—	Nice	Yes
Snuggle	Sofa	35	100	Or	30	100	Required	Required	Not Autonomous	Yes
Splash	Hot Tub	20	100	Or	15	100	—	—	Not Autonomous	Yes
Splash	Love Tub	-20	100	Or	-25	100	—	—	Not Autonomous	Yes
Squeeze	Hug	70	100	And	55	100	Required	Sets	Playful	Yes
Stay the Night	Propose	55	100	And	40	100	—	—	Not Autonomous	Yes
Suggestion	Flirt	25	70	And	15	70	Sets	Sets	Playful	Yes
Sweet Talk	Flirt	35	80	And	20	80	Sets	Sets	Outgoing	Yes
Tag	Play	-25	100	Or	5	100	—	—	Active	Yes
Talk To	Social baby	-100 (-100)	100	And	-100 (-100)	100	—	—	Playful	Yes
Talk To	Social toddler	-50 (-50)	100	And	-50 (-50)	100	—	—	Outgoing	Yes
Talk to Belly	Baby	15	100	Or	25	100	—	—	Playful	Yes
Teach to Use Potty	Social toddler	-100 (—)	100	And	-100 (—)	100	—	—	Not Autonomous	Yes
Teach to Talk	Social toddler	25 (—)	100	And	15 (—)	100	—	—	Not Autonomous	Yes
Teach to Walk	Social toddler	25 (—)	100	And	15 (—)	100	—	—	Not Autonomous	Yes
Tease	Memory	-100	10	Or	-100	10	—	—	Mean	No

Autonomous	If Accept, A's Social	If Accept, A's Daily	If Accept, A's Lifetime	If Accept, B's Social	If Accept, B's Daily	If Accept, B's Lifetime	If Reject, A's Social	If Reject, A's Daily	If Reject, A's Lifetime	If Reject, B's Social	If Reject, B's Daily	If Reject, B's Lifetime
Yes	20	4	3	2	25	1	0	0	0	0	0	0
Yes	6	0	0	-6	-8	-2	10	-8	-2	10	-7	-2
Yes	28	8	0	28	8	0	0	-5	0	0	-5	0
No	14	6	0	20	13	0	-4	-4	0	-4	-4	0
Yes	14	6	2	20	6	3	-4	-4	0	-4	-4	0
Yes	24	6	0	24	6	0	0	-7	0	0	-5	0
No	24	16	3	26	16	3	8	-13	-3	0	-13	-4
Yes	20	6	2	20	10	2	0	-10	-3	0	-10	-2
Yes	24	16	3	26	16	3	8	-13	-3	0	-13	-4
Yes	20	11	3	32	13	3	-10	-12	-3	0	-10	-3
Yes	28	13	2	30	15	2	-6	-12	-3	0	-10	-3
No	6	0	0	6	0	0	-3	-3	0	-3	-3	0
No	14	6	0	20	13	0	-4	-4	0	-4	-4	0
Yes	8	0	0	-8	-9	-3	10	-7	-1	14	-8	-3
Yes	10	0	0	-15	-10	-5	14	-5	-3	30	-7	-3
Yes	22	13	2	20	11	2	0	-11	-2	0	-12	-3
Yes	20	6	2	20	10	2	0	-10	-3	0	-10	-2
No	24	8	2	24	10	2	0	-10	-2	0	-10	-2
No	12	5	0	14	8	0	0	-4	0	0	-8	-1
No	12	5	0	14	5	0	0	-5	0	0	-5	0
Yes	20	6	2	20	10	2	0	-10	-2	0	-10	-2
No	14	6	0	20	13	0	-4	-4	0	-4	-4	0
Yes	16	5	1	16	6	1	0	-5	-1	0	-7	-1
Yes	18	6	1	18	8	1	0	-7	-1	0	-8	-1
Yes	20	6	0	20	6	0	0	-5	0	0	-5	0
Yes	16	5	2	16	10	2	-5	-2	-1	5	1	2
Yes	14	6	2	20	6	3	-4	-4	0	-4	-4	0
Yes	20	6	2	28	8	2	-10	-8	-2	0	-10	-3
No	0	6	0	0	13	0	0	-4	0	0	-4	0
No	14	6	0	20	13	0	-4	-4	0	-4	-4	0
No	14	6	0	20	13	0	-4	-4	0	-4	-4	0
Yes	14	6	1	10	6	1	-5	-4	-1	4	-10	-1

Social Interactions: Availability, Autonomous Personalities, and Social/Daily/Lifetime Effects continued

Interaction	Menu	Availability Daily A to B Above	Availability Daily A to B Below	And/Or	Availability Lifetime A to B Above	Availability Lifetime A to B Below	Crush	Love or Go Steady	Autonomous Personality	User Directed
Tell Secret	Talk	60	100	Or	60	100	—	—	Mean	Yes
Tender Kiss	Bed	50	100	And	25	100	Sets	Sets	Not Autonomous	Yes
Tender Kiss	Hot Tub	50	100	And	25	100	Sets	Sets	Not Autonomous	Yes
Tender Kiss	Love Tub	10	100	And	-10	100	Sets	Sets	Not Autonomous	Yes
Tender Kiss	Kiss	50	100	And	25	100	Sets	Sets	Nice	Yes
Tickle	Play	20	100	Or	15	100	—	—	Playful	Yes
Tickle	Social toddler	20 (10)	100	And	15 (0)	100	—	—	Playful	Yes
Toss in Air	Social toddler	-50 (25)	100	And	-50 (10)	100	—	—	Active	Yes
Up Arm Kiss	Kiss	55	100	And	30	100	Sets	Sets	Playful	Yes
WooHoo/Try for Baby	Bed	85	100	And	65	100	Required	Required	Not Autonomous	Yes
WooHoo/Try for Baby	Hot Tub	85	100	And	65	100	Required	Required	Not Autonomous	Yes
WooHoo/Try for Baby	Love Tub	45	100	And	25	100	Required	Required	Not Autonomous	Yes
WooHoo/Try for Baby	Booth	-100	100	Or	-100	100	Required	Required	Not Autonomous	Yes

SIM-TO-SIM INTERACTIONS

Appreciate Interactions

Admire

◆ Who: Adult/elder to adult/elder or teen to teen

Accepted if Sim B's:

1. Daily >5 and Mood >10, or,
2. Daily <5 and Lifetime positive.

Apologize

◆ Who: Child/teen/adult/elder to child/teen/adult/elder

Always accepted.

Backrub

◆ Who: Adult/elder to adult/elder or teen to teen

Accepted if Sim B's:

1. Mood positive and Daily >45, or,
2. Mood positive and Lifetime >25.

Cheer Up

◆ Who: Teen/adult/elder to child/teen/adult/elder

Accepted if Sim B's:

1. Lifetime >25 and Daily >25, or,
2. Lifetime >25, Daily <25, and Nice/Grouchy >2, or,
3. Lifetime <25, Daily >35, and Nice/Grouchy >4.

Groom

◆ Who: Adult/elder to child

Always accepted.

Autonomous	If Accept, A's Social	If Accept, A's Daily	If Accept, A's Lifetime	If Accept, B's Social	If Accept, B's Daily	If Accept, B's Lifetime	If Reject, A's Social	If Reject, A's Daily	If Reject, A's Lifetime	If Reject, B's Social	If Reject, B's Daily	If Reject, B's Lifetime
Yes	24	9	0	24	9	0	0	-7	0	0	-6	0
No	18	10	2	16	10	2	8	-8	-2	0	-8	-2
No	18	10	2	16	10	2	8	-8	-2	0	-8	-2
No	18	10	2	16	10	2	8	-8	-2	0	-8	-2
Yes	18	10	2	16	10	2	8	-8	-2	0	-8	-2
Yes	16	5	0	16	5	0	0	-5	-1	0	-6	-1
Yes	16	5	0	16	5	0	0	-5	-1	0	-8	-2
Yes	14	6	2	20	13	2	0	-10	-3	0	-10	-2
Yes	20	11	1	24	11	2	8	-10	-1	0	-10	-1
No	50	9	1	30	9	1	-5	-6	-1	-45	-6	-1
No	50	13	8	50	13	8	0	-12	-5	0	-15	-5
No	50	13	8	50	13	8	0	-12	-5	0	-15	-5
No	50	13	8	50	13	8	0	-12	-5	0	-15	-5

> **note**
>
> Availability requires that child's Hygiene be below 90. Interaction satisfies 30 Hygiene.

Baby
Rub Belly

◆ Who: Child/teen/adult/elder to adult (visibly pregnant)

Accepted if Sim B's:

1. Lifetime >60 and Mood positive, or,
2. Lifetime <60 and Daily >75.

Talk to Belly

◆ Who: Child/teen/adult/elder to adult (visibly pregnant)

Accepted if Sim B's:

1. Lifetime >35 and Mood positive, or,
2. Lifetime <35 and Daily is >50.

Entertain Interactions
Joke

◆ Who: Child/teen/adult/elder to child/teen/adult/elder

> **note**
>
> The "funniness" of the joke is assured if Sim A has Charisma of 5 or more, B has Daily >15 and Playful/Serious of 5 or more, and B's Mood is above 30 (or even slightly negative so long as A's Playful and Charisma are BOTH above 5). Each factor adds to the joke's funniness. Finally, a random number either adds or subtracts to funniness. If the joke is funny enough, the social will be accepted.

Accepted if: Joke has final funniness rating of 6 or more.

1. Joke begins with 2 points.
2. If B's Daily >15, +3 funny.

3. If A's Charisma >4 and B's Mood >-30 or if A's Charisma <4 and B's Mood >20, +2 funny.

4. If B's Playful/Serious >4 and B's Mood >-20 or if B's Playful/Serious <4 and Mood >30, +2 funny.

5. Random addition or subtraction of -1 to 2 further funny points.

Dirty Joke

◆ Who: Teen/adult/elder to teen/adult/elder

Dirty Joke functions the same as Joke except its appearance requires a much closer and established relationship. Also, B's Daily must be above 65 to get its funny enhancement.

Accepted if: Joke has final funniness rating of 6 or more.

1. Joke begins with 2 funny points.

2. If B's Daily >65, +3 funny.

3. If A's Charisma >4 and B's Mood >-30 or if A's Charisma <4 and B's Mood >20, +2 funny.

4. If B's Playful/Serious >4 and B's Mood >-20 or if B's Playful/Serious <4 and Mood >30, +2 funny.

5. Random addition of subtraction of -1 to 2 further funny points.

Fight Interactions

note

If a parent (adult or elder) witnesses his offspring (any age) initiating a Fight social, he'll lecture her. This results in a Daily reduction for parent and progeny.

Poke

◆ Who: Adult/elder to adult/elder or teen to teen or child to child

In this case, Sim B always receives the interaction; whether he accepts or rejects determines whether he

fights back. The Grouchier Sim B is, the more likely he is to give a poke in return. If the social is rejected, Sim B instead walks away dejected.

Accepted if Sim B's:

1. Lifetime >15, Mood positive, and Nice/Grouchy >2, or,

2. Lifetime >15, Mood negative, and Nice/Grouchy >5, or,

3. Lifetime <15, Mood positive, and Nice/Grouchy >4, or,

4. Lifetime <15, Mood negative, and Nice/Grouchy >7.

Shove

◆ Who: Adult/elder to adult/elder or teen to teen or child to child

In this case, Sim B always receives the interaction; whether she accepts or rejects determines whether she fights back. The Grouchier Sim B is, the more likely she is to give a shove in return. If the social is rejected, Sim B instead walks away dejected.

Accepted if Sim B's:

1. Lifetime >20, Mood positive, and Nice/Grouchy >2, or,

2. Lifetime >20, Mood negative, and Nice/Grouchy >5, or,

3. Lifetime <20, Mood positive, and Nice/Grouchy >5, or,

4. Lifetime <20, B's Mood negative and B's Nice/Grouchy >9.

Slap

◆ Who: Adult/elder to adult/elder or teen to teen or child to child

In this case, Sim B always receives the interaction; whether he accepts or rejects determines whether he fights back. The Grouchier Sim B is, the more likely he is to give a slap in return. If the social is rejected, Sim B instead walks away dejected.

Accepted if Sim B's:

1. Lifetime >25, Mood positive, and Nice/Grouchy >2, or,

2. Lifetime >25, Mood negative, and Nice/Grouchy >6, or,

3. Lifetime <25, Mood positive, and Nice/Grouchy >5, or,

4. Lifetime <25, Mood negative, and Nice/Grouchy >9.

Attack

◆ Who: Adult/elder to adult/elder or teen to teen or child to child

◆ Winner Outcome A: Social +12, Daily -7, Lifetime -10

◆ Winner Outcome B: Social +12, Daily -7, Lifetime -10

◆ Loser Outcome A: Social -8, Daily -11, Lifetime -10

◆ Loser Outcome B: Social -8, Daily -11, Lifetime -10

The winner is determined by comparing both Sims' Body skill, regardless of who initiated the attack. If one Sim's Body skill is 7 or more points greater than the other's, the higher Sim will always win. If the gap is less than 7, either Sim could win, though the more physical Sim will win most often.

> ### note
>
> Sims involved in an attack receive a Memory of the event as do any observers. This means that the attack can be raised as a conversational topic.
>
> If both Sims have identical Body skills, neither will receive a Memory, regardless of the outcome.

Nearby Sims either flee the room (if Shy) or gather around to watch the rumble. While watching, Nice Sims will look dismayed, as will a parent of any Nice/Grouchy rating if her offspring is one of the combatants. All non-parental Sims either cheer or boo depending on their relationship to the victor. After the fight, any parents of the combatants will lecture their offspring (causing Daily loss to both parent and progeny).

Flirt Interactions
Charm

◆ Who: Adult/elder to adult/elder or teen to teen

Accepted if Sim B's:

1. Mood >-20, Lifetime >10, Nice/Grouchy >6, and Daily >10, or,

2. Mood >-20, Lifetime >10, Nice/Grouchy <6, and Daily >20, or,

3. Mood >-20, Lifetime <10, Outgoing/Shy >6, and Daily >20, or,

4. Mood >-20, Lifetime <10, Outgoing/Shy <6, and Daily >30.

Suggestion

◆ Who: Adult/elder to adult/elder or teen to teen

Accepted if Sim B's:

1. Mood >-20, Daily >35, Lifetime >25, or,

2. Mood positive, Daily >35, Lifetime <25, and Playful/Serious >6, or,

3. Mood positive, Daily >35, Lifetime <25, Playful/Serious <6, and Nice/Grouchy >6, or,

4. Mood >20, Daily >35, Lifetime <25, Playful/Serious <6, and Nice/Grouchy <6, or,

5. Mood positive, Daily 26–35, Outgoing/Shy >6.

Sweet Talk

◆ Who: Adult/elder to adult/elder or teen to teen

Accepted if Sim B's:

1. Mood >-20, Lifetime >25, and Daily >45, or,

2. Mood >-20, Lifetime >25, Daily 36–45, and Nice/Grouchy >8, or,

3. Mood >-20, Lifetime >25, Daily 36–45, Nice/Grouchy <8, and Outgoing/Shy >8, or,

4. Mood >-20, Lifetime <25, Nice/Grouchy >8, and Daily >35, or,

5. Mood >-20, Lifetime <25, Nice/Grouchy <8, and Outgoing/Shy >8, Daily >35.

Hit On

◆ Who: Adult/elder to adult/elder or teen to teen

Accepted if Sim B's:

1. Mood >-10 and Daily >65, or,
2. Mood >-10, Daily 56–65 and Lifetime >30, or,
3. Mood positive, Daily 56–65, Lifetime <30, and Outgoing/Shy >5, or,
4. Mood >20, Daily 56–65, Lifetime <30, and Outgoing/Shy <5, or,
5. Mood >20, Daily <55, and Outgoing/Shy >6.

Hold Hands

◆ Who: Adult/elder to adult/elder or teen to teen

Accepted if Sim B's:

1. Mood >-40, Daily >65 and Lifetime >35, or,
2. Mood >10, Daily >65, Lifetime <35, Nice/Grouchy >5, or,
3. Mood >-40, Daily <65, and Lifetime >50.

Caress

◆ Who: Adult/elder to adult/elder

Accepted if Sim B's:

1. Mood positive, Daily >70 and Lifetime >55, or,
2. Mood >20, Daily >70, Lifetime <55, and Playful/Serious >7, or,
3. Mood >20, Daily >70, Lifetime <55, Playful/Serious <7, and Nice/Grouchy >7,
4. Mood >20, Daily <70, Outgoing/Shy >7, and Lifetime >35

Serenade

◆ Who: Adult/elder to adult/elder

Accepted if Sim B's:

1. Mood positive and Lifetime >75, or,
2. Mood positive, Lifetime <75, and Daily >80, or,
3. Mood positive, Lifetime <75, and Daily 71–80, and Nice/Grouchy >6, or,
4. Mood negative and Lifetime >85, or,
5. Mood negative, Lifetime <85, and Daily >95.

Goose

◆ Who: Adult/elder to adult/elder or teen to teen

Accepted if Sim B's:

1. Mood positive, Daily >80 and Lifetime >65, or,
2. Mood positive, Daily >90, and Lifetime <65, or,
3. Mood positive, Daily 81–90, Lifetime <65, and Outgoing/Playful >6, or,
4. Mood >20, Daily 81–90, Lifetime <65, and Outgoing/Playful <6, or,
5. Mood positive, Daily 76–80, and Outgoing/Shy >8.

Hug Interactions

Friendly Hug

◆ Who: Child/teen/adult/elder to child/teen/adult/elder

Accepted if Sim B's:

1. Crush on A and Mood >-15, or,
2. Loves A and Mood >-35, or,
3. Lifetime >15 and Mood > positive, or,
4. Lifetime <15 and Mood >90.

Romantic Hug

◆ Who: Adult/elder to adult/elder and teen to teen

Accepted if Sim B's:

1. Crush on A and Mood >-20, or,

2. Loves A and Mood >-30, or,

3. Lifetime >30, Daily >35, and Mood >-10, or,

4. Lifetime >30, Daily <35, and Mood >10, or,

5. Lifetime <30, Daily >50, Mood >10.

Leap into Arms

◆ Who: Adult/elder to adult/elder

Accepted if Sim B's:

1. Crush on A and Mood >-35, or,

2. Loves A and Mood >-15, or,

3. Lifetime >45 and Mood >10, or,

4. Lifetime <45 and Mood 100.

Squeeze

◆ Who: Adult/elder to adult/elder or teen to teen

Accepted if Sim B's:

1. Crush on A and Mood >-5, or,

2. Loves A and Mood >-15, or,

3. Lifetime >60 and Mood >20, or,

4. Lifetime <60 and Mood >90.

Irritate Socials

Argue

◆ Who: Teen/adult/elder to teen/adult/elder

◆ Accepted Outcome A and B: Depends on level of Interest in each topic. Both Sims lose Daily. Sim A gains some Social. When A is finished, B takes over the talking role.

◆ Rejected Outcome A and B: Both lose Daily. Interaction ends after first volley usually because A chose a topic about which B feels a similar level of Interest; in other words, there's really nothing to argue about.

Nag

◆ Who: Teen/adult/elder to teen/adult/elder

Insult

◆ Who: Teen/adult/elder to teen/adult/elder

Accepted if Sim B's:

1. Lifetime >30, Mood positive, Nice/Grouchy >3, or,

2. Lifetime >30, Mood negative, Nice/Grouchy >5, or,

3. Lifetime <30, Mood positive, Nice/Grouchy >4, or,

4. Lifetime <30, Mood negative, Nice/Grouchy >6.

Acceptance/Rejection does not change whether the insult is delivered, only what happens next. If it's accepted, B walks away and cries. If rejected, B defiantly stands his ground.

If parents see their offspring perform Insult, they will lecture them resulting in a further Daily and Lifetime loss for both parent and child.

Annoy/Nyah-Nyah

◆ Who: Teen/adult/elder to teen/adult/elder (as "Annoy") or child to child (as "Nyah-Nyah").

Noogie

◆ Who: Teen to child/teen

Gross Out

◆ Who: Teen/adult/elder to teen/adult/elder or child to child

Accepted if Sim B's:

1. Lifetime >10, Playful/Serious >7, and Neat/Sloppy <5, or,

2. Lifetime >10, Playful/Serious <7, and Neat/Sloppy <3, or,

3. Lifetime <10, Playful/Serious >5, and Neat/Sloppy <3, or,

4. Lifetime <10, Playful/Serious <5, and Neat/Sloppy <1.

Kiss Interactions

Family Kiss

◆ Who: Child/teen/adult/elder to toddler/child/teen/adult/elder

Accepted if Sim B's:

1. Lifetime >30 and Mood >-25, or,
2. Lifetime <30 and Mood >25.

Peck

◆ Who: Adult/elder to adult/elder or teen to teen

Accepted if Sim B's:

1. Daily >50 and Mood positive, or,
2. Daily >50, Mood -19 to 0, and Lifetime >30, or,
3. Daily <50, Lifetime >30, and Mood positive.

Tender Kiss

◆ Who: Adult/elder to adult/elder or teen to teen

Accepted if Sim B's:

1. Daily >60 and Mood positive, or,
2. Daily >60, Mood -19—0, and Lifetime >35, or,
3. Daily <60, Lifetime >35, and Mood positive.

First Kiss

◆ Who: Adult/elder to adult/elder or teen to teen

Accepted if Sim B's:

1. Outgoing >5, Mood >20, and Daily >45, or,
2. Outgoing >5, Mood >20, Daily <45, and Lifetime >35, or,
3. Outgoing >5, Mood <20, and Lifetime >45, or,
4. Outgoing <5, Mood >40, and Daily >50, or,
5. Outgoing <5, Mood >40, Daily <50, and Lifetime >40, or,
6. Outgoing <5, Mood <40, Lifetime >45.

Only available until Sim A has a successful First Kiss.

A snapshot of this moment is taken automatically and put in the Snapshot Bin.

Up Arm Kiss

◆ Who: Adult/elder to adult/elder

Accepted if Sim B's:

1. Daily >65 and Mood positive, or,
2. Daily >65, Mood -19 to 0, and Lifetime >45,
3. Daily <65, Lifetime >45, and Mood positive.

Romantic Kiss

◆ Who: Adult/elder to adult/elder

Accepted if Sim B's:

1. Daily >70 and Mood positive, or,
2. Daily >70, Mood -19 to 0, and Lifetime >50,
3. Daily <70, Lifetime >50, and Mood positive.

Smooch

◆ Who: Adult/elder to adult/elder or teen to teen

Accepted if Sim B's:

1. Crush on A, Daily >80 and Mood positive, or,
2. Crush on A, Daily >80, Mood -19 to 0, and Lifetime >55,
3. Crush on A, Daily <80, Lifetime >55, and Mood positive.

Make Out

◆ Who: Adult/elder to adult/elder or teen to teen

Accepted if Sim B's:

1. in Love with A and Mood > positive, or,
2. has a Crush on A and Mood >20.

Play Interactions

Play interactions always result in a small amount of Fun for both parties. Generally, accepting yields both Social and Daily gains for each Sim and rejecting is limited (in all but one case) to a drop in Daily; only Tickling because of its somewhat intrusive nature, has any effect on Lifetime.

Tag

◆ Who: Child to child

Accepted if Sim B's:

1. Daily >10, or,

2. Daily <10 and Lifetime >5, or,

3. Daily <10, Lifetime <5, and Active/Lazy >8, or,

4. Daily <10, Lifetime <5, Active/Lazy <8, and Playful >8.

Tag must be played outside. Up to three Sims can Join the Tag game once it's underway (for a total of five Sims) by clicking on any currently playing Sim. The game continues for each Sim until his Fun motive is fulfilled or until only one player remains.

While playing Tag, Sims lose Energy faster.

Cops and Robbers

◆ Who: Child to child

Accepted if Sim B's:

1. Daily >15, or,

2. Daily <15 and Lifetime >10, or,

3. Daily <15, Lifetime <10, and Playful/Serious >9, or,

4. Daily <15, Lifetime <10, Playful/Serious <9, and Active/Lazy >9.

Cops and Robbers can be played inside or out but only by two Sims. The game continues for each Sim until her Fun motive is fulfilled or until only one player remains.

Mary Mack

◆ Who: Child to child

Accepted if Sim B's:

1. Daily >20, or,

2. Daily <20 and Playful/Serious >9, or,

3. Daily <20, Playful/Serious <9, and Lifetime >20.

Sims will play for a few rounds and stop. Must be repeated to entirely fulfill Fun.

Tickle

◆ Who: Teen/adult/elder to child/teen/adult/elder

Accepted if Sim B's:

1. Daily >25, or,

2. Daily <25 and Lifetime >20, or,

3. Daily <25, Lifetime <20, and Active/Lazy >9, or,

4. Daily <25, Lifetime <20, Active/Lazy <9, and Playful/Serious >9.

Red Hands

◆ Who: Child/teen/adult/elder to child/teen/adult/elder

Accepted if Sim B's:

1. Daily >40, or,

2. Daily <40 and Playful/Serious >8, or,

3. Daily <40, Playful/Serious <8, and Lifetime >30.

Success in the game depends upon a comparison of Body skill. Game repeats a fixed number of times and stops regardless of Fun fulfillment.

Punch U Punch Me

◆ Who: Teen/adult/elder to teen/adult/elder or child to child

Accepted if Sim B's:

1. Daily >50, or,

2. Daily <50 and Lifetime >40, or,

3. Daily <50, Lifetime <40, and Active/Lazy >9, or,

4. Daily <50, Lifetime <40, Active/Lazy <9, and Playful/Serious >9.

Success on each punch is random depending on Body skill. After five attempts or one successful punch, roles switch. The game continues until max Fun is fulfilled.

A Grouchy Sim may sometimes throw a stronger than normal punch. If it lands, the other Sim will quit the game and both parties will experience a small reduction in Daily.

Propose
Move In
◆ Who: Adult/elder to adult/elder

Accepted if Sim B's:

1. Lifetime >60, Daily >70, Mood positive, or,
2. Lifetime 51–60, Nice/Grouchy >9, and Mood >10, or,
3. Lifetime >60, Daily <70, Nice/Grouchy >7, and Mood >10, or,

Stay the Night
◆ Who: Adult/elder to adult/elder

Accepted if Sim B's:

1. Lifetime >35, Daily >45, Mood >25, or,
2. Lifetime 26–35, Outgoing/Shy >7, Lifetime >25, Daily >15, and Mood >-20, or,
3. Lifetime >35, Daily <45, Outgoing/Shy >6, Daily >15, and Mood >-20, or,
4. Lifetime >35, Daily >45, Mood <25, Outgoing/Shy >5, Lifetime >25, Daily >15, and Mood >-20.

Go Steady
◆ Who: Teen to teen

Accepted if Sim B's:

1. Lifetime >40, Daily >30, and Mood >40, or,
2. Lifetime 21–40, Nice/Grouchy >9, and Mood positive, or,

3. Lifetime >40, Daily <30, Nice/Grouchy >7, and Mood positive, or,
4. Lifetime >40, Daily >30, Mood 0–40, and Nice/Grouchy >6.

Marriage/Join
◆ Who: Adult/elder to adult/elder

Accepted if Sim B's:

1. Lifetime >80, Daily >80, and Mood >5, or,
2. Lifetime 76–80, Nice/Grouchy >9, and Mood >15, or,
3. Lifetime >80, Daily <80, Nice/Grouchy >7, and Mood >15.

Engagement
◆ Who: Adult/elder to adult/elder

Accepted if Sim B's:

1. Lifetime >75, Daily >75, and Mood >0, or,
2. Lifetime <75, Nice/Grouchy >9, and Mood >10, or,
3. Lifetime >75, Daily <75, Nice/Grouchy >7, and Mood >10.

Baby and Toddler Socials
Change Diaper
◆ Who: Teen/adult/elder to baby/toddler

Accepted (toddler only) if Sim B's:

1. a blood relative to or in same household as A, or,
2. not a blood relative to or in same household as A and Neat >5, and Mood positive, or,
3. not a blood relative to or in same household as A and Neat <5, and Mood >30.

Social and Hygiene increases are greater if the changing table object is used (See Chapter 28).

Talk to Baby
◆ Who: Child/teen/adult/elder to baby

Cuddle

♦ Who: Teen/adult/elder to baby

Play with Baby

♦ Who: Teen/adult/elder to baby

Talk to Toddler

♦ Who: Child/teen/adult/elder to toddler

Accepted if Sim B's:

1. a blood relative to or in same household as A, and Outgoing/Shy >3, and Mood >-70, or,

2. a blood relative to or in same household as A, Outgoing/Shy <3, and Mood >-60, or,

3. not a blood relative to or in same household as A, Outgoing/Shy >4, and Mood >-20, or,

4. not a blood relative to or in same household as A, Outgoing/Shy <4, and Mood positive.

Toss in Air

♦ Who: Teen/adult/elder to toddler

Accepted if Sim B's:

1. a blood relative to or in same household as A, and Playful/Serious >3, and Mood >-70, or,

2. a blood relative to or in same household as A, Playful/Serious <3, and Mood >-60, or,

3. not a blood relative to or in same household as A, Playful/Serious >5, and Mood >10, or,

4. not a blood relative to or in same household as A, Playful/Serious <5, and Mood >30.

There is a random chance (which rises with the toddler's level of Hunger satisfaction) that the toddler will throw up during this interaction. If this happens, Sim A's Hygiene will plunge. Can be initiated from floor or held positions.

Tickle

♦ Who: Child/teen/adult/elder to toddler

Accepted if Sim B's:

1. a blood relative to or in same household as A, and Playful/Serious >3, and Mood >-70, or,

2. a blood relative to or in same household as A, Playful/Serious <3, and Mood >-60, or,

3. not a blood relative to or in same household as A, Playful/Serious >3, and Mood >20, or,

4. not a blood relative to or in same household as A, Playful/Serious <3, and Mood >50.

Snuggle Toddler

♦ Who: Teen/adult/elder to toddler

Accepted if Sim B's:

1. a blood relative to or in same household as A, and Nice/Grouchy >3, and Mood >-70, or,

2. a blood relative to or in same household as A, Nice/Grouchy <3, and Mood >-60, or,

3. not a blood relative to or in same household as A, Nice/Grouchy >5, and Mood >20, or,

4. not a blood relative to or in same household as A, Nice/Grouchy <5, and Mood >40.

Family Kiss (Toddler)

♦ Who: Child/teen/adult/elder to toddler

Accepted if Sim B's:

1. a blood relative to or in same household as A, and Nice/Grouchy >3, and Mood >-70, or,

2. a blood relative to or in same household as A, Nice/Grouchy <3, and Mood >-40, or,

3. not a blood relative to or in same household as A, Nice/Grouchy >5, and Mood >20, or,

4. not a blood relative to or in same household as A, Nice/Grouchy <5, and Mood >40.

Teach to Talk

♦ Who: Teen/adult/elder to toddler

Accepted if Sim B's:

1. a blood relative to or in same household as A, and Outgoing/Shy >3, and Mood positive, or,

2. a blood relative to or in same household as A, Outgoing/Shy <3, and Mood >20.

Progress bar appears above toddler, who learns slowly at first and faster as bar rises.

Teach to Walk

◆ Who: Teen/adult/elder to toddler

Accepted if Sim B's:

1. a blood relative to or in same household as A, and Outgoing/Shy >3, and Mood positive, or,

2. a blood relative to or in same household as A, Outgoing/Shy <3, and Mood >20.

Progress bar appears above toddler, who learns slowly at first and faster as bar rises.

Teach to Use Potty

◆ Who: Teen/adult/elder to toddler

Accepted if Sim B's:

1. a blood relative to or in same household as A, and Neat/Sloppy >3, and Mood positive, or,

2. a blood relative to or in same household as A, Neat/Sloppy <3, and Mood >20.

Progress bar appears above toddler, who learns slowly at first and faster as bar rises.

Ask for and Educational Interactions
Ask for Attention

◆ Who: Toddler to teen/adult/elder

Accepted if Sim B's:

1. the Nanny, or,

2. a blood relative to A and Nice/Grouchy >2, and Mood >-50, or,

3. a blood relative to A and Nice/Grouchy <2, and Mood >-25, or,

4. not a blood relative to A, Lifetime >5, and Nice/Grouchy >2, Mood >40, or,

5. not a blood relative to A, Lifetime >5, and Nice/Grouchy <2, Mood >-25, or,

6. not a blood relative to A, Lifetime <5, Nice/Grouchy >4, and Mood > positive, or,

7. not a blood relative to A, Lifetime <5, Nice/Grouchy <4, and Mood >20.

Ask for Diaper Change

◆ Who: Toddler to teen/adult/elder

Accepted if Sim B's:

1. the Nanny, or,

2. a blood relative to A and Nice/Grouchy >3, and Mood > positive, or,

3. a blood relative to A and Nice/Grouchy <3, and Mood >25, or,

4. not blood relative to A, Lifetime >5, and Nice/Grouchy >3, Mood positive, or,

5. not blood relative to A, Lifetime >5, and Nice/Grouchy <3, Mood >25, or,

6. not blood relative to A, Lifetime <5, Nice/Grouchy >4, and Mood >25, or,

7. not blood relative to A, Lifetime <5, Nice/Grouchy <4, and Mood >40.

Ask for Food

◆ Who: Toddler to teen/adult/elder

Accepted if Sim B's:

1. the Nanny, or,

2. a blood relative to A and Nice/Grouchy >3, and Mood >-75, or,

3. a blood relative to A and Nice/Grouchy <3, and Mood >-50

4. not blood relative to A, Lifetime >5, and Nice/Grouchy >3, Mood -75, or

5. not blood relative to A, Lifetime >5, and Nice/Grouchy <3, Mood >-50, or,

6. not blood relative to A, Lifetime ‹5, Nice/Grouchy ›4, and Mood ›-25, or,

7. not blood relative to A, Lifetime ‹5, Nice/Grouchy ‹4, and Mood › positive.

Ask for Read to

◆ Who: Toddler or child to teen/adult/elder

Accepted if Sim B's:

1. the Nanny, or,

2. a blood relative to A and Nice/Grouchy ›3, and Mood ›-25, or,

3. Is a blood relative to A and Nice/Grouchy ‹3, and Mood › positive

4. not blood relative to A, Lifetime ›5, and Nice/Grouchy ›3, Mood -25, or,

5. not blood relative to A, Lifetime ›5, and Nice/Grouchy ‹3, Mood › positive, or,

6. not blood relative to A, Lifetime ‹5, Nice/Grouchy ›4, and Mood ›25, or,

7. not blood relative to A, Lifetime ‹5, Nice/Grouchy ‹4, and Mood ›40.

Ask to Go Out

◆ Who: Teen to adult/elder

Accepted if Sim B's:

1. Daily ›20, Lifetime ›30, Nice/Grouchy ›7, and Mood ›-50, or,

2. Daily ›20, Lifetime ›30, Nice/Grouchy ‹7, and Mood positive, or,

3. Daily ›20, Lifetime ‹30, Nice/Grouchy ›7, and Mood ›50, or,

4. Daily ›20, Lifetime ‹30, Nice/Grouchy ‹7, Mood ›90.

Ask to be Taught/Offer to Teach

◆ Who: Child or teen to teen/adult/elder or teen/adult/elder to teen or child; can only teach a lower age range

Accepted if Sim B's:

1. Daily and Mood positive.

Encourage

◆ Who: Teen/adult/elder to child/teen/adult; can only teach a lower age range

Accepted if Sim B's:

1. Mood positive and Lifetime ›20, or,

2. Mood positive, Lifetime ‹20, and Daily ›50.

Talk Interactions
Chat

◆ Who: Child/teen/adult/elder to child/teen/adult/elder

Chatting is a back and forth interaction based on both Sims' interests. A conversation begins with Sim A.

> **note**
>
> View Interests in the Simology panel under "Interests."

1. Sim A picks one of her own Interests. The higher her level of Interest in the topic, the more likely it will be chosen and the more animated A will be in discussing it. Shy Sims behave less enthusiastically regardless of Interest level. Each Interest contains five topics that Sim A will discuss; the icon for each appears above Sim A's head. If Sim A is very Interested in the topic or is very Outgoing, she may do special animations connected with each topic.

2. While Sim A is talking, Sim B is listening. His level of Interest in the chosen topic dictates how animated he is in listening.

3. When Sim A finishes, Sim B decides whether to continue the conversation based on his Interest level in Sim's A's topic; the higher the Interest, the more likely to accept and continue.

4. If accepted, Sim A gets +2 or +4 Daily (depending on level of Interest) and both get some Social. Then, Sim B chooses a topic to discuss. He can choose from among his own Interests but the choice is heavily weighted toward Sim A's

initial topic. The conversation can continue for six of these changes of speaker (A will be last to speak).

5. If rejected, A gets -1 Daily and both get some Social. Sim B indicates via icons his disinterest in A's topic and ends the conversation.

note

The more alike two Sims are in their Interests, the longer the conversation is likely to last.

During a conversation, a Sim's autonomous choice of topic can be overridden by manually choosing a topic. Do this by clicking on the speaking Sim and choosing "Change Topic." The top 12 topics are displayed; find the remaining four under the "More" button.

Memories can also be used as Chat topics in lieu of Interests. The "strength" of the Memory serves as the "Interest level" of the Memory as a topic and commands whether and how often it's chosen. Additionally, the longer a Memory has existed, the less likely it is to be chosen.

note

When a Sim is using a Memory as a topic, icons of the Sim whose Memory it is (unless Memory is the speaker's own) appear as conversational icons along with the icon for the Memory.

Interest level in a Memory is affected by several other factors:

1. If Sim B doesn't know the Sim whose Memory is being discussed, or if he does know her but Lifetime with her is 0, his Interest in the Memory topic is set at medium.

2. If Sim B is Shy, his interest in discussing a Memory is reduced. Likewise, if he's Outgoing, it is increased.

3. If a Memory is negative, Sim B's Interest level depends on his Lifetime with the Sim whose Memory is being discussed; the worse the Lifetime, the higher the Interest.

4. If a Memory is positive, Sim B's Interest level depends on his Lifetime with the Sim whose Memory is being discussed; the better the Lifetime, the higher the Interest.

note

When Sims participate in Chats about a Memory Marker, the Marker is added to their Memories (if they don't already have it). This allows them to use the topic in discussion in the future.

Brag

◆ Who: Child/teen/adult/elder to child/teen/adult/elder

Accepted if Sim B's:

1. Lifetime >15, Daily >15, and Nice/Grouchy >4, or,

2. Lifetime >15, Daily >15, Nice/Grouchy <4, and Mood >0, or,

3. Lifetime >15, Daily <15, and Nice/Grouchy >5, or,

4. Lifetime <15, Daily >30, and Nice/Grouchy >5, or,

5. Lifetime <15, Daily >30, Nice/Grouchy <5, and Mood >10, or,

6. Lifetime <15, Daily <30, and Mood >90.

A Sim chooses one of her own positive Memories to Brag about.

Gossip

◆ Who: Teen/adult/elder to teen/ adult/elder

Accepted if Sim B's:

1. Daily >15, or,

2. Daily <15 and Nice/Grouchy >7, and Lifetime >10, or,

4. Daily <15, Nice/Grouchy >7, Lifetime <10, and Mood >-10.

Sim A chooses a negative Memory Marker about another Sim as conversational topic. The Memory must be one that neither belongs to nor involves B in any way.

Tell Secret

◆ Who: Child to child

Accepted if Sim B's:

1. friends with Sim A.

Sim A chooses a negative Memory Marker about another child Sim as conversational topic. The Memory must be one that neither belongs to nor involves B in any way.

Share Interests

◆ Who: Child/teen/adult/elder to child/teen/adult/elder

Accepted if Sim B's:

1. Lifetime >25, Daily >45, or,

2. Lifetime >25, Daily <45, and Nice/Grouchy >3, or,

3. Lifetime <25, Daily >45, and Nice/Grouchy >5, or,

4. Lifetime <25, Daily <45, and Nice/Grouchy >9.

Sim A chooses a high-level Interest just as in Chat.

If accepted, A talks about the Interest, one of its five topics at a time. At the end of three topics, B has his level of the chosen Interest increased by one.

> **note**
>
> Recall that when an Interest is increased, some other (random) Interest decreases as well.

If rejected, B listens to the first topic and then ends the conversation. No change occurs in B's Interests.

Miscellaneous Interactions
Ask to Leave/Ask Everyone to Leave

◆ Who: Adult/elder to child/teen/adult/elder, child/teen to child/teen

Ask Everyone to Leave dismisses all visitors from the lot in one interaction.

Break Up

◆ Who: Adult/elder to adult/elder or teen to teen

If Sims Breaking Up were Married, Sim B immediately (after she's done crying) moves out by leaving the lot. She is removed from the family and is again available to start a new life as a single Sim in the Neighborhood's Family Bin. Once she finds a new place, A and B can interact again.

Call Over

◆ Who: Teen/adult/elder to teen/adult/elder, child to child

Can be done from standing or seated position. Call Over tends to override any other activities Sim B has queued up, causing Sim B to eliminate all other actions and come over immediately to A. If A moves after Call Over, B goes to Sim A's previous location.

Accepted if Sim B's:

1. Mood >-5 and Daily >5, or,

2. Mood <-5 and Daily >30.

Dance Together

◆ Object(s): Any Stereo

◆ Who: Teen/adult/elder to teen/adult/elder

Accepted if Sim B's:

1. Daily >20.

Greet/Greet Everyone

◆ Who: Child/teen/adult/elder to child/teen/adult/elder

Greeting a passerby turns her into a visitor.
A visitor is an autonomous Sim with whom your Sims may interact and who has limited freedom to use the objects on your lot.

How a Sim is individually greeted is a matter of Daily and the type of relationship:

◆ Shake Hands: Daily -20 to 20 for both Sims

◆ Kiss Romantic: Teen/adult/elder, Crush or Love for both Sims

◆ Friendly Hug: Daily >70 for both Sims

◆ Secret Handshake: Daily 50–70

◆ Cold Greet: Daily <-40

◆ Nod: Daily -40 to -30

◆ Wave: Daily >30

Say Goodbye/Say Goodbye to Everyone

◆ Who: Child/teen/adult/elder to child/teen/adult/elder

Ask everyone to leave forces all visitors off lot in one interaction.

How Sims say goodbye one-on-one depends on their Daily and the kind of relationship:

◆ Shake Hands: Daily -20 to 20 for both Sims

◆ Kiss Romantic: Teen/adult/elder, Crush or Love for both Sims

◆ Friendly Hug: Daily >70 for both Sims

◆ Cold Greet: Daily <-40

◆ Nod: Daily -40 to -30

◆ Wave: Daily >30

Shoo from Room

◆ Who: Child/teen/adult/elder to child/teen/adult/elder

Autonomous Memory Socials

These interactions cannot be player-initiated but happen instead only autonomously.

Tease

◆ Who: Child/teen/adult/elder to child/teen/adult/elder where Sim A has a Marker about one of Sim B's negative Memories

Accepted if Sim B's:

1. Lifetime >15, Daily >35, and Nice/Grouchy >2, or,

2. Lifetime >15, Daily <35, and Nice/Grouchy >3, or,

3. Lifetime <15, Daily >15, and Nice/Grouchy >4, or,

4. Lifetime <15, Daily <15, and Nice/Grouchy >5.

Sims with negative Memories can be teased by Grouchy Sims who've obtained a Marker about Sim B's Memory.

Congratulate

◆ Who: Child/teen/adult/elder to child/teen/adult/elder where Sim A has a Marker about one of Sim B's positive Memories

Serious Sims autonomously congratulate a Sim with a positive Memory if the Nice Sim has obtained a Marker about the Memory.

Accepted if Sim B's:

1. Lifetime >15 and Daily >35, or,

2. Lifetime >15, Daily <35, and Nice/Grouchy >1, or,

3. Lifetime ‹15, Daily ›15, and Nice/Grouchy ›2, or,

4. Lifetime ‹15, Daily ‹15, and Nice/Grouchy ›3.

Console

◆ Who: Child/teen/adult/elder to child/teen/adult/elder where Sim A has a Marker about one of Sim B's negative Memories

Nice Sims autonomously console Sims who have negative Memories if the Nice Sim has received a Marker about the Memory.

Accepted if Sim B's:

1. Lifetime ›15 and Daily ›35, or,

2. Lifetime ›15, Daily ‹35, and Nice/Grouchy ›4,

3. Lifetime ‹15, Daily ›15, and Nice/Grouchy ›6,

4. Lifetime ‹15, Daily ‹15, and Nice/Grouchy ›8.

OBJECT BASED INTERACTIONS

Several interactions arise out of two Sims sharing an object. Most, it probably won't surprise you to hear, are romantic. Some, *very* romantic! These appear only when Sim A and Sim B are both interacting with an appropriate object and all other requirements are met.

> **note**
>
> Some object-based interactions are the same as other non-object-based interactions (e.g. Tender Kiss) but the relationship requirements and effects are different.

◆ Beds: All bed interactions must begin with either one Sim doing the Relax interaction and asking the other to Join or with both Sims Relaxing.

◆ Hot Tub/Love Tub: Both Sims must be in the hot tub. In some cases, they must be the only two Sims in the tub.

◆ Sofa: All Sofa interactions must start with the Cuddle interaction before others become available.

◆ Clothing Booth: One Sim must be in the clothing booth before the interaction becomes available.

◆ Stereo: One Sim must be dancing solo at the stereo.

Snuggle

◆ Objects: Sofa

◆ Who: Child to teen/adult/elder

Accepted if Sim B's:

1. a blood relative to A and Mood -70–0

2. a blood relative to A, Mood ›0, and Nice ›2

3. not blood relative to A, Mood ›0, and Nice ›4

Cuddle

◆ Objects: Bed, Hot Tub, Love Tub, Sofa

◆ Who: Adult/elder to adult/elder or teen to teen

Accepted if Sim B's:

1. Daily ›45, or,

2. Daily ‹45, Nice/Grouchy ›7, Lifetime ›35, and Mood ›50.

WooHoo/Try for Baby

◆ Objects: Bed, Hot Tub, Love Tub, Clothes Booth

◆ Who: Adult/elder to adult/elder

Accepted if Sim B's:

1. Mood ›15 and Lifetime ›65, or,

2. Mood ›15, Lifetime ‹65, and Daily ›85, or,

3. Mood ›15, Lifetime ‹65, Daily 51–85, Outgoing/Shy ›8, or,

4. Mood <15 and Lifetime >70, or,

5. Mood <15 and Lifetime <70, and Daily >90.

Kiss, Tender

- ◆ Objects: Hot Tub, Love Tub
- ◆ Who: Adult/elder to adult/elder or teen to teen

Accepted if Sim B's:

1. Daily >60 and Mood positive, or,

2. Daily >60, Mood -19 to 0, and Lifetime >35, or,

3. Daily <60, Lifetime >35, and Mood positive.

Kiss, Make Out

- ◆ Objects: Bed, Hot Tub, Love Tub, Sofa
- ◆ Who: Adult/elder to adult/elder or teen to teen (in Hot Tub, Love Tub, or Sofa only)

Accepted if Sim B's:

1. in Love with A and Mood > positive, or,

2. has a Crush on A and Mood >20.

Kiss, Peck

- ◆ Objects: Hot Tub, Love Tub, Sofa
- ◆ Who: Adult/elder to adult/elder or teen to teen

Accepted if Sim B's:

1. Daily >50 and Mood positive, or,

2. Daily >50, Mood -19 to 0, and Lifetime >30, or,

3. Daily <50, Lifetime >30, and Mood positive.

Kiss, Romantic

- ◆ Objects: Sofa
- ◆ Who: Adult/elder to adult/elder or teen to teen

Accepted if Sim B's:

1. Daily >70 and Mood positive, or,

2. Daily >70, Mood -19 to 0, and Lifetime >50, or,

3. Daily <70, Lifetime >50, and Mood positive.

Massage

- ◆ Objects: Hot Tub, Love Tub
- ◆ Who: Adult/elder to adult/elder or teen to teen

Accepted if Sim B's Mood >-10, and:

1. Outgoing/Shy >5 and Lifetime >50, or,

2. Outgoing/Shy >5, Lifetime <50, and Playful/Serious >8, or,

3. Outgoing/Shy >5, Lifetime <50, Playful/Serious <8, and Daily >60, or,

4. Outgoing/Shy <5 and Daily >70.

Splash

- ◆ Objects: Hot Tub, Love Tub
- ◆ Who: Adult/elder to adult/elder or teen to teen

Accepted if Sim B's:

1. Daily >25, or

2. Daily <25 and Lifetime >20, or,

3. Daily <25, Lifetime <20, and Playful/Serious >9, or,

4. Daily <25, Lifetime <20, Playful/Serious <9, and Mood >70.

Chapter 25

All Sims, not just Family Sims, are dependent on their families. Family life is the foundation of almost everything your Sim does. This chapter introduces you to the complexities of the modern, multigenerational Sim family, including how Sims come together, celebrate, prosper, procreate, fail, and divide.

"FAMILY" VS. "FAMILY"

The first thing to clarify is what "family" means. In *The Sims 2*, it has two meanings.

"Family" refers to the residents of a lot (as in the "Create-A-Family" tool). Sims in a Family need not be related, though they will, by virtue of being generated and assembled in Create-A-Family, all have the same last name.

note

Once a Family is created and saved in a lot, it's possible to have Sims in the same Family with different last names. Any Sims who come to live on the lot as roommates, for instance, keep their last name.

Perhaps the clearer way to think of this meaning of Family is "household."

Family, as used in this guide, generally refers to any Sims marked with this family icon.

More important is the concept of "family," which precisely means any Sim who gets the family icon in the Relationship panel. Specifically, this goes to any *blood relative* or a non-blood relative by direct

marriage (a.k.a. a spouse). Technically speaking, therefore, an uncle-by-marriage is not "family."

A NOTE ON GENDER PREFERENCE

There is no gender limitation on any romantic interaction or relationship; any Sim can fall in love with any other Sim of appropriate age regardless of gender. Sims will, however, display autonomous gender preference.

Who Sims choose to romance autonomously is shaped by what you direct them to do. If the bulk of a Sim's player-directed romantic interactions have been toward the opposite sex, the Sim will autonomously gravitate to the opposite sex. If the lion's share has been toward Sims of the same sex, autonomy will direct them to Sims of the same gender. The directives you issue can change this preference if the balance tips from one side to the other.

FAMILY RELATIONSHIPS

Sims in a household can be connected any number of ways. They can be just roommates, siblings, spouses, parents and children, grandparents, cousins, aunts, and uncles.

Elaborate family trees show the complexities of Sim family life.

Many interactions can be performed or will autonomously be done only by blood family members or (non-blood) household members.

THE ARC OF A LOVE AFFAIR

The road to lifelong happiness, or just fleeting but intense intimacy, begins with that special feeling of amore but moves from there to increasing levels of commitment. Getting to the altar, however, takes some development.

Crushes and Love

There are two kinds of romantic relationship: Crush and Love. As detailed in Chapter 24, Crush is based on Daily Relationship score and Love on Lifetime Relationship (greater than 70 in either case).

---
note

When a Sim has a crush, she'll autonomously choose that Sim for socializing and do low-level Flirt interactions.

Crush and Love are serious steps with many profound consequences, so there must be an affirmative step to generate the relationship. For Sims, it's the performance of a romantic interaction. Don't do romantic interactions if you don't want romance (and all that comes with it) to bloom.

Given the more immediate and volatile nature of Crushes, they are easier to achieve; it should take no more than two days of normal socializing (with interruptions for Needs and Career) to get a Crush.

Love is more stable and better able to withstand change and, as such, it takes longer to reach. Love can be won in about three days of normal socializing.

Pink hearts mean Crush but red hearts mean L-O-V-E, Love!

---
note

For full details on how Crushes and Love are created, see Chapter 24.

Love and Crushes are broken if the appropriate relationship score drops below 70 *and* one Sim does an interaction that directly reduces that score. Love and Crush can't, therefore, break merely because of decay/normalization.

Go Steady

Teens can't get married, but they can enter committed relationships. Teen Sims with a Crush and the proper relationship and Mood requirements, can propose going steady to another Sim.

When you're young, going steady is as committed as you get. Still, pretty sweet.

If the other Sim does not meet the requirements, the go steady proposal will be rejected, the proposing Sim will receive a negative Memory, and the relationship will take a hard hit to both Daily and Lifetime scores.

Going steady can be broken only by using the Break Up interaction.

Move In

Any Sim, even one with non-romantic relationship, can be invited to move in if there's a strong relationship.

Once the proposal is accepted, the other Sim becomes part of the household but keeps his last name. As for their finances and other considerations, see "Moving In" below.

Engagement

Sims in love who have very high Daily and Lifetime Relationship scores with another Sim may propose

engagement. Once engaged, the proposee Sim wears a ring symbolizing the commitment.

If the other Sim does not meet these requirements, the engagement will be rejected, the proposing Sim receives a negative Memory, and the relationship will take a hard hit to both Daily and Lifetime scores.

Engagement is a necessary step to getting married or joined.

Engagement can only be broken by the Break Up interaction (see "Breaking Up" below).

Marriage/Joining

> **note**
>
> If Sims are of opposite genders, it's called "marriage" and if the same gender, it's called "joining."

> **note**
>
> If a household already contains eight Sims, a marriage/ joining cannot occur on the lot. It must occur on the lot of the other member of the couple or both members must move into a new lot before the marriage can take place.
>
> If the non-resident Sim to be married is pregnant, he/she counts as two Sims. She can't, therefore, be married on a lot that already has seven Sims because the birth will take the household over the eight-Sim limit.

For the complete wedding experience, propose marriage via the wedding arch object.

Sims who are engaged and who have very high Daily and Lifetime Relationship scores with another Sim may get married/joined. This may be done two ways: by clicking on the other Sim and selecting Propose › Marriage/Joining or by buying the Trellisor Wedding Arch from Buy mode and interacting with it.

> **note**
>
> The mechanics of a wedding arch wedding are discussed below.

In either case, the other Sim will accept if she meets the relationship score and Mood requirements.

If the other Sim does not meet the requirements, the engagement will be rejected, the proposing Sim will receive a negative Memory, and the relationship will take a devastating hit to both Daily and Lifetime scores.

After the marriage/joining, both Sims wear wedding bands. The married/joined couple's last name becomes that of the Sim who proposed the engagement. The new spouse moves into the household where the marriage/joining took place.

Marriage can only be broken by the Break Up interaction (see "Breaking Up" below).

> **tip**
>
> A High relationship score between Sims ensures that, should the marriage be rejected, the relationship will not end.

MOVING IN

When a Sim moves into a household either by Move In proposal or marriage/joining, several things occur.

If the new Sim lives alone, his entire household worth comes with him to the new house. If the Sim is an NPC (see Chapter 26), a random amount (§1,000–§10,000) is brought as her net worth.

> **note**
>
> NPCs brought to live on the lot come in unemployed (there is no Maid career track) but retain their uniforms as a clothing options.

Life is, however, rarely so simple. Usually, there are other family members to consider.

When a Sim is invited to move in or marries into a household, you can choose whom he brings with him. If you elect to bring the entire family, they contribute their entire net worth (including the value of their old house) to the new household.

Moving Sims don't automatically bring their offspring. If the moving Sim has a child, toddler, or baby in the old household, you can leave the minor behind if a teen, adult, or elder remains with them. Households are limited, however, to eight Sims, so it's possible that not all members of another lot can be moved. If a Sim is pregnant she counts as two Sims for move-in purposes.

Unless an entire household moves into the lot, the moving Sim(s) brings 10 percent of the old household's funds. The wealth of the old household, however, is not reduced.

MOVING OUT AND BREAKING UP

Not every relationship works out. Even platonic roommates must occasionally go their separate ways. How Sims part company is as important as how they get together.

Moving Out

An adult or elder Sim can move out of the household voluntary by using the Find Own Place interaction in the newspaper or computer. He may then choose whom (if anyone) in the household he'd like to bring along.

Moving out can be a big step but, when the time is right, the best one.

All other Sims bid the departing Sim adieu as he walks out the door and into a waiting cab. He reappears in the neighborhood's Family Bin and can be moved into any empty lot. He gets §20,000 to start his new life and keeps all his skills and Memories and any relationships as of the time he left the lot.

If the moving out Sim is leaving any baby, toddler, or child Sims behind, there must be one teen, adult, or elder remaining on the lot.

note

Married/joined Sims can separate without divorcing by moving out in this way. Moving out doesn't change the relationship at all, just places one of the couple in another lot.

Sims can be invited back if they meet the Move In relationship requirements with a member of their former home.

Breaking Up

Breaking up committed relationships is a serious matter, especially if they share a lot or have offspring. This interaction is the same for going steady, engagement, or married/joined.

Getting dumped is never easy, but in this case, he deserves it.

The Sim initiating the break up must have a negative to moderately positive (-100—45) Daily and Lifetime Relationship with the potential dumpee. In other words, the relationship must be on the skids already.

note

If the relationship score isn't low enough, but you want a Sim to break up, do something heinous like kiss another Sim in front of the Sims partner; that should sufficiently trash the relationship. Then switch to the other Sim and do the Break Up interaction.

If the relationship has decayed to these levels, the Break Up interaction becomes available. Once initiated, the interaction is always accepted and can't be cancelled.

Both parties take a massive Daily and Lifetime Relationship hit (though Social remains unchanged). If they're married/joined, the dumped Sim leaves the lot immediately (she does not have the option of bringing anyone with her) and is removed from the family.

The dumped Sim is deposited in the Sim Bin and can be moved into any uninhabited lot. She leaves with §20,000 in the bank but the value of the departed lot remains unchanged.

JEALOUSY AND CHEATING

Sims love to love but they can't abide betrayal. Unfortunately some Sims just can't stay loyal to one Sim. Such is the complex web of jealousy and cheating. Knowing how it works makes getting away with it much easier.

Cheating

Any Sim who's in love, crush, engaged, or married/joined who does a romantic interaction with another Sim is cheating. If the cheating Sim's beloved is unaware of the transgression, the cheatee gets an Affair Memory and there's no effect on their other romantic relationship.

Jealousy

If a Sim is in a love, crush, engaged, or married/joined relationship with another Sim, doing any romantic interaction with some other Sim when the beloved is in the same room (even if not in sight) or doing WooHoo with another Sim when the beloved is *anywhere on the lot* triggers jealousy.

Infidelity can be extremely hard on everyone, especially the innocent party and the children.

Jealousy has several effects:

◆ Big reductions in Daily and Lifetime Relationship scores.

◆ Caught Cheating Memory for the cheater and Caught Lover Cheating Memory for the cheatee.

◆ If relationship numbers of the couple are low enough, they lose crush and/or love status but not engagement or spousal status. In other words, jealousy can't cause a break up but can cause a couple to fall out of love.

◆ If the cheater Fears getting caught and the innocent partner Fears catching his partner Cheating, they both take massive hits to their Aspiration scores.

Jealousy is always directed toward the Sim who initiated the romantic interaction and the one who accepted it, and the effects are always more severe against the Sim with whom the jealous Sim shares a relationship. If the receiver rejected the advance, she's spared the effects of jealousy.

For example, A and B are in love:

◆ If A attempts a romantic social with C (regardless of whether C accepts), B will slap A, Lifetime and Daily Relationships between B and A will be radically reduced, A gets a Caught Cheating Memory, B gets a Caught Lover Cheating Memory.

◆ If C accepts the interaction, C will get slapped too and have drastic (but smaller) reductions to Lifetime and Daily Relationship with B.

◆ If, instead, C attempts a romantic interaction with A and A rejects, B will slap and lose relationship points with C but not A.

Witnessing Cheating

If relatives of the cheated-on Sim are in the room (for most romantic interactions) or on the lot (if there's WooHoo), they'll witness the cheating and lecture the cheating Sim. If the witness is the cheating Sim's offspring, he'll cry.

Witnesses also get a Memory Marker of the infidelity. If, by chance, this Marker arises as a conversational topic between the witness and the (heretofore) ignorant cheated-on Sim, this conversation triggers the jealousy response as if the cheated-on Sim had been there himself.

CHILDBIRTH AND ADOPTION

Sure you can genetically engineer a child in Create-A-Sim, but the real magic happens when the life your Sims lead and the choices they make produce a little bundle of joy.

There are two ways to add offspring to a family:

◆ Adoption   ◆ Childbirth

Adoption

Any adult or elder Sims (even single ones) can adopt by using the telephone (Call... > Service > Adoption Service).

Adoption begins at the phone.

The Adoption request will be approved immediately if:

◆ Family funds exceed §3,000

◆ Calling Sim does not have a Memory of having a baby, toddler, or child taken away by the Social Worker.

◆ Family size is less than 8.

The new family member is delivered at 10 a.m. the next day.

tip

Be sure to take the delivery day off work or the Social Worker can't turn over the child.

Ideally, arrange for the event to occur on one of your Sims' scheduled days off. There's maternity/paternity leave for adoptions.

The Social Worker comes for a good reason for a change. Meet your new family member.

When the Social Worker arrives, decide what age the new family member should be: baby, toddler, or child.

note

The child you get in an adoption will be either a randomly generated child of the appropriate age or a child previously removed from another family in the neighborhood.

All other aspects (name, personality, interests, appearance) of the child are out of your control. The child does, however, automatically take the household's last name.

note

The members of the household get an Adoption Memory.

All adopted Sims arrive with Daily Relationship of 25 and Lifetime of 0 toward all members of the household.

From this point on, raising an adopted child is identical to any other offspring.

Pregnancy

Only two events can cause pregnancy:

◆ Sims of opposite genders doing the Try for Baby interaction
◆ Alien abduction

Try for Baby

Sims may perform the Try for Baby interaction only via a few particularly conducive objects:

◆ Beds
◆ Hot tubs
◆ Clothing booths (Community Lot only)

This kiddies, is how babies are made. Well, it's one way.

If the interaction is accepted, there's a chance of conception depending on where it was done (60 percent if in a bed, 25 percent if in a hot tub, and 50 percent if in a clothing booth). The only evidence of success, however, is a vague musical cue of a lullaby shortly after the interaction; it's easy to miss.

Alien Abduction

If Sims use the Stargaze interaction with the expensive telescope (Farstar e3 Telescope) at night, there is a chance they'll be abducted by aliens. Abducted Sims are returned to the lot three hours later.

The chances are pretty small, but if aliens take this guy for a ride, start saving for a crib.

If the abductee is a male adult, he always returns from the ordeal impregnated with an alien baby.

Other than the "mother" being male, alien pregnancies are identical to normal ones.

The Three Trimesters

Pregnancy lasts three days, each representing a trimester of pregnancy.

Day 1

A sure sign of pregnancy

The first day of a pregnancy, everything seems normal. There is a chance, however, that the Sim will spontaneously throw up. When idling, pregnant Sims might appear queasy.

Throwing up in the toilet severely messes up the commode. The bathroom needs frequent cleaning during this first day.

Pregnant Sims' Needs undergo a subtle but noticeable change; both Energy, Bladder, and Hunger decay are accelerated, requiring the Sim to sleep and eat more often.

Day 2

In the second trimester, the Sim's "delicate condition" becomes unmistakable.

Hunger, Bladder, and Energy continue to decay faster than normal.

The Sim will be a bit more irritable and it will be harder to increase and easier to decrease his/her relationship score toward other Sims. All positive relationship changes for social interaction with the pregnant Sim are decreased by 25 percent and all negative changes are increased by 25 percent.

On day 2, the pregnancy begins to show.

At some point, the Sim becomes visibly pregnant, begins wearing a maternity outfit, and is notified that he/she has the day off from work (with pay). The carpool does not come.

note

For this day and the next, other Sims may do the Rub Belly and Talk to Belly interactions with the pregnant Sim.

For the remainder of the pregnancy, the Sim cannot go to a Community Lot.

Day 3

On the final day of pregnancy, all of the day 2 changes continue. Hunger, Bladder, and Energy still decay faster and relationship changes are still toned down.

Big belly means today's the day!

The Sim appears hugely pregnant and waddles noticeably.

Day 3 pregnant Sims are prohibited from using many objects (e.g. hot tubs) and cannot perform many social interactions. They also can't (to name a few) dive, fight (except argue), use the swing set, or be abducted by aliens. They can't Try for Baby (obviously) but they can WooHoo (though getting sufficient Mood for this high-end interaction may be challenging).

Delivery

At some point on day 3, the Sim goes into labor. Other Sims on the lot gather around and the delivery cinematic plays.

The game pauses briefly while the new baby's genetics are generated.

In a moment, poof! You have a new genetically unique family member. If the baby is the product of an alien abduction, she might sport obvious alien features but should also have her father's eye color.

Naming the baby is permanent, so give it some thought.

Finally, the new baby may be named. Decide carefully as this name cannot ever be changed.

Twins

Twins randomly occur 10 percent of the time. Twins from married parents won't always be the same gender (which one is a toss up).

In the event of twins, the first birth occurs as described above except when the time for naming arrives. The first baby gets handed off and the second is born without the birth cinematic. After the second twin is born, two naming boxes permit you to name both babies.

TEENAGE ISSUES

Two special situations make having a teenager particularly challenging: running away and going out/sneaking out.

Runaway

If a teen has a bad relationship with her household (Daily and Lifetime below -20 with *all* household Sims), the teen announces that she's running away and leaves the lot.

If, within 24 hours, a household Sim calls the police to report the teen missing, she'll be returned the next day.

Runaway teens just need a little love. Get them back and shower them with positive attention or they'll bolt again.

If the police are called more than 24 hours after the teen ran away, there's a 50 percent chance she'll be found and returned.

When the teen returns, she won't run away again for one day. If, after one day, all relationships are still below the threshold, she will run away again. Use the day of return to improve the relationship.

If a teen isn't found or the police are never called, the teen always returns in time for her transition to adulthood.

Go Out/Sneak Out

Teens like to have fun away from home, but they don't necessarily wait for permission to go out on the town.

A teen may either ask an older household Sim for permission to go out, or sneak out via the telephone.

Going Out with Permission

A teen may ask an older household Sim for permission to go out. The older Sim accepts or rejects based on his Daily and Lifetime Relationships with the teen, his Nice/Grouchy Personality, and his Mood.

Permission to go out is what good teens get. Is Ophelia a good teen? Didn't think so.

If the older Sim approves, the Go Out interaction is unlocked on the phone (regardless of the time of day). The teen may call any teen friend; acceptance is based on their Relationship score. If the other teen accepts the invitation, she'll come at 8 p.m.

Four hours later, the teen returns with Fun and Social increased and Energy and Hunger decreased.

note

The teen driving for a Go Out or Sneak Out interaction shows up in a car linked to the Sim with the highest career level in her household.

Sneaking Out

Teens may go out without permission if they sneak out.

After 10 p.m., the Sneak Out interaction becomes available on the telephone. The teen may call any other teen he knows; acceptance or rejection is based on their Relationship score.

Sneaking out requires some stealth and planning. Send the grown-ups to bed before 1 a.m. or keep them busy in another room.

The other teen arrives at 1 a.m. and waits for one hour. To go out, the teen must get out of the house without any older Sims spotting him. If caught, he gets a reduction in Social and Relationship score with the Sim who caught him and a bad Memory of being caught. He may also take an Aspiration hit if he Feared getting caught. Try to make sure all the grown-ups are asleep before sneaking out.

If he's successful, the teen jumps in the car and leaves the lot. While gone, his Fun and Social motives skyrocket and his Energy and Hunger decrease.

At 4 a.m., the teen returns to the lot and attempts to get back into the house undetected. Getting caught means reductions in Relationship score with the Sim who caught him and a bad Memory.

There's a random chance the teen will be brought home in a police car and receive all the punishments of getting caught.

PARTIES

Parties are a huge part of family life. All of life's big moments call for parties, but sometimes it's just a good way to have fun or satisfy a Sim's Wants.

Initiating a Party

All parties begin with picking up the telephone and selecting the Throw Party interaction.

Kinds of Parties

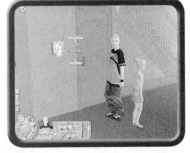

Choose your party.

There are four kinds of parties:

◆ House Party: Always available.
◆ Birthday: Available only if a household Sim has a birthday in two or fewer days.
◆ Wedding: Available only if a Sim on the lot is engaged.
◆ Anniversary: Available only if there are two elders in the household who were married when they were adults. Late in life marriages don't qualify for an Anniversary party because such Sims are still giddy newlyweds.

The kind of party you throw impacts what is expected to occur at the party and how it will be scored. See "Party Scoring," later in this chapter.

Invitations

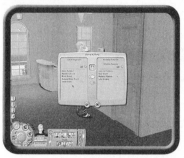

Inviting guests is no guarantee they'll come, so try to invite at least a few Sims with whom your Sim has a strong relationship.

Once you pick what kind of party to throw, it's time to invite the guests. A list appears with the names of every Sim with whom the Sim making the call is familiar. Select which Sims you want to invite off the list, up to the maximum shown.

note

Party guest maximums are dictated by your computer's processing and memory power. The slower the processor and lower the RAM, the fewer guests can attend.

Just because you invite a guest doesn't mean he'll show. The higher the guest's Daily Relationship with the person doing the inviting, the more likely he is to attend.

tip

Assign the Sim with the highest relationships to the largest number of Sims to make the invitation call. This increases the odds of having a well-attended party.

The number of Sims in attendance isn't crucial just so long as *someone* shows. If no one accepts, the Party score takes a massive decline.

Party Objects

Many objects might be useful for a successful party.

They look festive (and increase Environment). Need they do more?

Party decorations are not required, but they do enhance Environment score, thus allowing visitors to stay longer. Balloons pop at the end of the party and must be cleaned up.

note

Remember all non-food items can be purchased for a party and returned for a full refund before midnight of the same day.

Having a constant supply of food is essential for a five-hour party. Fail to keep it flowing and the guests won't make it to the end, greatly reducing the party score. Either keep one Sim cooking or buy the Whatay Buffet object.

Sims gathered around Fun objects are a pretty good sign of a successful party.

Because party success is based on the amount of positive socializing, get as many group Fun objects as possible on the lot. These fulfill guests' Fun Need and generate social interaction among Sims participating and watching. Good group Fun objects include:

◆ Hot tubs

◆ It's MYSHUNO! (The Fabulously Zany Party Game)

◆ Maxis Game Simulator

◆ Any television

◆ Any stereo

◆ Burled Wood Dartboard

◆ Any pinball machine

◆ Swing Kidz Deluxe Swing Set (several joined together)

◆ Any bar

For Wedding and Birthday parties, you can buy special objects (the wedding arch and birthday cake, respectively). They're not mandatory, but using them to initiate the blessed event while the appropriate party is in progress triggers otherwise unavailable cinematic events.

Party Scoring

Parties are scored based on the amount of socializing among attendees.

When the first guest arrives, the party begins and continues for the next five hours. Every 15 minutes, the net change in everyone's collective Daily Relationship scores is marked and compared to the previous amount. If there's an increase, the Party score rises. If it falls, so too does the Party score.

The number of people at a party affects how the score is calculated. Small parties (those with two or three guests) are scaled (by two-fifths and three-fifths, respectively) because it's too easy to get a

high score with fewer guests. With four or more guests, score is based on the total number of Daily Relationship points gained divided by the number of people on the lot.

Party Success Levels

There are six levels of party success (three positive and three negative):

◆ A Roof-Raiser

◆ A Good Time

◆ Not Bad

◆ A Snoozer

◆ A Real Dud

◆ A Total Disaster

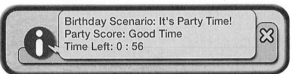

Birthday Scenario: It's Party Time!
Party Score: Good Time
Time Left: 0 : 56

The Party score lets you know how things are going. Don't worry if the score is low at the beginning of a party, but get things going before the end.

The higher the score, the better the party.

Attendance and Party Score

If no invited guests show up to the party, the festivities (if you can call them that) go on as planned. The total snubbing, however, causes a major reduction in Party score.

The same is true if all invited guests leave before the party is complete.

Thus, a successful party requires that you meet the Needs of all visitors (see "Visitor Behavior," Chapter 24). If visitors can't satisfy Hunger, Bladder, Comfort, Fun, Social, and Energy (via coffee or espresso only), their stay will be shortened.

Special Event Parties

Birthday and Wedding parties have an extra scoring element that can trash the party.

If the party's main event doesn't occur as the party's end nears, a massive deduction is taken from Party score.

Thus, no matter how festive the party, a Wedding with no marriage/joining or a Birthday party with no age transition will be a failure.

> ### note
>
> Though it seems like a special event party, the Anniversary party has no central event that must occur. Functionally, it's the same as a House Party except guests come in Formal attire.

Party Final Score

When time runs out, the final social interaction measurement is made and the outcome of the party is declared. If the Party score is one of the three positive verdicts, the Sim who initiated the party gets a positive party Memory. If the Party score is negative, the Sim gets a negative party Memory.

This Memory can fulfill Wants or Fears in household Sims, so party success can be very important. Keep an eye on all household Sims' Wants/Fears panel to see how much they have riding on the party.

> ### note
>
> Not all Sims like parties. If they're particularly Shy, for instance, they Fear having a party. They might, therefore, be better off getting married or having an age transition quietly at home.
>
> This doesn't mean, however, that a Shy Popularity Sim is doomed; all Popularity Sims, even Shy ones, Want parties.

Cops

The police may come to break up a party if all the following conditions are met:

- If the time is after 11 p.m.
- If more than four visitors are on the lot
- If there's a turned-on stereo on the lot

Every minute after 11 p.m., there's a chance the police could show and break up the party. When the party is broken up, the last measured score is the final score for the party. If the party is a Birthday or Wedding party, much depends on when the police arrive. If they arrive before the wedding or age transition occurs, the party simply ends with its last measured score and no penalty for the lack of the party's central event.

Special Event Parties

As discussed above, there are two special event parties: Birthday and Wedding parties.

Birthday Party

The Birthday party invitation becomes available on the telephone two-days before any Sim's scheduled age transition. Throwing this party provides an extra opportunity to improve a Sim's Aspiration score by giving her a special good Birthday party Memory.

Birthday parties have only one essential element: someone has to grow up during the party.

PRIMA OFFICIAL GAME GUIDE

For the party to be successful, the Sim must age transition during the party. Thus, she must click on the cake and select "Blow Out Candles," do the "Grow Up" self-interaction, or grow up autonomously at 7 p.m. Any means fulfills the Party scoring requirement.

No special objects are necessary for a Birthday party but growing up via the cake during a party serves up an otherwise unavailable cinematic and provides a ready-made dessert for guests to consume together and chat over.

note

For full details on age transitions, see "Age Transitions," Chapter 19.

When the age transition occurs (by whatever means), the age transitioning Sim goes to the cake (if any) and the party gathers around him.

Weddings

A Wedding party is held to communally celebrate the joining of two Sims and, as with Birthdays, provide an extra opportunity to affect the Sims' Aspiration scores by having a successful party (if they harbor this Want). There are also some other benefits.

When the invitation goes out to a Wedding party, the guests arrive in their Formal clothing.

The party goes along like any other until the marriage/ joining itself occurs in either of two ways.

First, one Sim can simply do the Propose > Marriage/Joining interaction on the Sim to whom he's engaged.

You can get married just fine without the wedding arch; it just won't be as formal.

Second, if the wedding arch object is placed on the lot, one of the engaged Sims can click on *it* to initiate the marriage/joining ceremony. If a Wedding party is underway, using the wedding arch causes several things to happen:

◆ An otherwise unavailable cinematic of either the successful or unsuccessful wedding plays.
◆ If chairs are placed around the arch, wedding guests will fill them before the ceremony. Otherwise, they'll simply gather around the arch.

note

If the toasting set object is on the lot, guests may autonomously toast to the newlyweds.

Whether the actual marriage/joining event happens is crucial to a Wedding Party score. If it doesn't happen before the end of the party or if the marriage is rejected (left at the altar), the party score drops precipitously.

Once the party is over and the marriage/joining is successfully completed, the final reason to have the party arrives: the honeymoon. The newlyweds are whisked away by a limo for a few hours of post-nuptial honeymoon bliss. When they return, they're aglow with a substantial Mood boost, ready to resume the grind of normal life. Marriages/ joinings not celebrated with a Wedding party do not get a honeymoon.

Chapter 26

NPCs

The world of *The Sims 2* is full of Sims who don't live in the neighborhood. That is, they can't be found or played on any existing lot. These folks are called "Non-Player Character" Sims or "NPCs."

There are three kinds of NPC Sims:

◆ Social NPCs ◆ Non-Social NPCs ◆ Townies

There is also one additional and very important NPC: the Social Bunny. Most Sims don't think it exists, but lonely Sims still believe.

This chapter introduces you to all the game's NPCs and explains how and with which your Sims may interact.

SOCIAL NPCS

Social NPCs are Sims that exist primarily to perform services or tasks. With richer lives and personalities, many more NPCs can now socialize and be your Sims' friends and lovers.

Chatting with "the help" is actually a great way to expand a Sim's base of friends and provide interesting new people to invite into the household.

When no or little relationship yet exists, you can do a few basic interactions:

◆ Talk > Chat

◆ Talk > Gossip: With higher Relationship Score (Daily 30 or Lifetime 35).

◆ Talk > Brag: Disappears once Daily and Lifetime Relationship increases above 50.

◆ Flirt: Flirt interactions become progressively available as Relationship Scores increase. Flirt is not available with Community Lot salespeople.

After a Sim is introduced to a specific Social NPC, he appears in the Sim's Relationship panel. Several things can now happen: he can be called on the phone, sent e-mail, invited to parties or a Community Lot, and he can even become a "regular" service provider (as detailed below).

Once a relationship with an NPC has begun to really grow, the social possibilities expand considerably. See "Interacting with Social NPCs," later in this chapter.

Social NPCs come in two flavors:

◆ Service NPCs ◆ Autonomous NPCs

Service NPCs

Service NPCs are Sims you call when you need something. In each case, they're reached via telephone and charge by the hour. Service NPCs include:

◆ Bartender ◆ Maid
◆ Exterminator ◆ Nanny
◆ Gardener ◆ Repairman (or -woman)

Hiring Service NPCs

All Service NPCs are hired via the Services menu on a telephone. Depending on the time of day, the NPC comes over either about 30 minutes after the call or first thing (after 9 a.m. except for the Maid who comes at 10 a.m.) the next morning.

note

Service NPCs' responses on the phone tell you when they'll come but, for NPCs with limited hours, you can presume that calls made late in the day will be answered immediately, but the service person won't come until the next morning.

Services are summoned by telephone.

The particular Sim that arrives at the house will be one of six randomly selected and could be either male or female. If the calling Sim has previously interacted with any service Sims of that kind, the one with whom she has the highest Lifetime Relationship score will come.

> **note**
>
> Nannies are always female and elder.

NPC Fees

All Service NPCs charge a base fee per visit (§5–§10) plus an hourly rate (§5–§50 per hour).

If they arrive and find nothing that needs to be done (if house is clean for Maid or contains no broken items for Repairman), they charge the base fee and leave.

Household Sims are not charged for time spent socializing *after* work is done.

If, when an NPC is finished and ready to be paid, the household funds are insufficient to pay the bill, the Service NPC will remove objects with depreciated value collectively equal to the amount of the bill. He also terminates any recurring service and can't be rehired for two days.

Hours

Each Service NPC has hours in which she can work. Some leave at a specific time and some only stay for a maximum number of hours regardless of the time of day.

NPCs with a specific start time can come the same day only if their work hours allow it; if not, they promise to come first thing the next day. See the listings below for each kind of NPC's hours and work restrictions.

If his quitting time arrives and he hasn't completed his job, he leaves the work unfinished.

Some Service NPCs (e.g., Bartenders, Nannies) can come any time of day, as needed, and have no specific quitting time.

Recurring vs. One-Time Services

Nannies work whenever the Sim who called them is away from the house, or on a one-shot basis.

Some Service NPCs are hired once to come on a regular basis (Maids, Gardeners) while other are hired for a single visit (Repairmen, Exterminators, Bartenders). The Nanny can be hired for either kind of work.

Service Interactions

In addition to the usual Social NPC interactions, service NPCs have several other basic interactions related to their work:

> **note**
>
> Tip is also available on Autonomous Social NPCs (see following page).

A tip is a fast but costly way to build a relationship with an NPC.

◆ Tip: Gives NPC extra money (§1, §5, §10, §25, §100) in exchange for a proportional amount of Daily Relationship and Social Need. May only be done by teen, adult, and elder Sims.

◆ End Services/Fire: Ends a recurring service. Appears as "End Services" if relationship with NPC is positive, "Fire" if it's negative. End Services adds to Daily Relationship, Fire deducts from it.

◆ Shoo: Commands NPC to leave current room or move out of Sim's path.

◆ Dismiss: Sends the NPC away for the day only.

tip

NPCs can be interrupted from their work any time with these interactions but they're still "on the clock." Excessive on-the-job interactions extend their work times and thus increase the expense of the visit and possibly force them to leave the job unfinished. Therefore, wait for them to finish before socializing.

A Service NPC can't do any other interactions until his job is done. When he finishes his job, what he does next depends on the relationship. If Lifetime Relationship is low, he announces that the work is complete and waits around to give you a chance to engage him socially. If Lifetime Relationship is high, he offers to hang out; accept and he becomes a visitor. Interaction must be initiated before the NPC charges for his service. Once the charge is made, he's unavailable for interaction.

Bartender

A Bartender

◆ Call Hours: Any time
◆ Shift: 6 hours (can be dismissed sooner)
◆ Fee: §10 per visit, §15 per hour
◆ Service: One Time

The Bartender can be called to make and serve drinks from a bar object. She also works the crowd with a tray of six drinks.

note

You can hire the Bartender without a bar on your lot, but she'll refuse to work and charge you §10 for the call.

Because parties can be held any time, Bartenders can be summoned any time of the night or day, and they stay on the lot for six hours after their arrival. This helps party guests feed their Fun and Hunger Needs, though it might create a line to the bathroom.

Exterminator

An Exterminator

◆ Call Hours: 9 a.m. to 5 p.m.
◆ Shift: Unlimited, until all roaches are killed
◆ Fee: §10 per visit plus §50 per hour
◆ Service: One Time

The Exterminator comes when called whether there are roaches in the household or not; if not, he'll charge §10 and depart.

note

Sims can spray roaches themselves, but it's not nearly as efficient as hiring the Exterminator.

The Exterminator wanders around the house, spraying any roaches until they're dead, but he won't clean up the piles of roach carcasses. He stays as many hours as necessary to completely eradicate the bugs.

After the Exterminator departs, Sims must clean up the dead roaches to fully restore the damage done to Environment score.

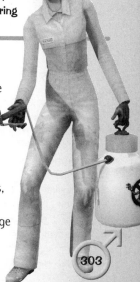

Gardener

♦ Call Hours: 9 a.m. to 6 p.m.
♦ Shift: Until finished or up to eight hours
♦ Fee: §5 per visit, §10 per hour
♦ Service: Recurring, three days per week

A Gardener

The Gardener comes when called, waters flowers, pulls weeds, and trims shrubs. She works until there's nothing left to do, or calls it a day after eight hours.

Maid

♦ Call Hours: 10 a.m. to 5 p.m.
♦ Shift: Until finished or no later than 5 p.m.
♦ Fee: §5 per visit and §10 per hour
♦ Service: Recurring, daily

A Maid

The Maid is summoned by phone and comes every day to clean all messes in the house.

note

Consider carefully the cost of having a house full of Sloppy Sims. Even a small house takes at least a few hours to clean, so you're looking at a minimum of §220 per week for a Maid (probably much more). Consider also that you have to work around myriad messes in between the Maid's visits. You might want to reconsider the tried-and-true The Sims strategy of making everyone Sloppy and hiring someone to clean up. A Neat Sim with 10 Cleaning is more effective and costs nothing, plus he builds skill as he cleans.

He or she arrives at 10 a.m. and departs when everything's clean. If any uncleaned messes remain at 5 p.m., the Maid leaves them uncleaned. On the first day of service and during call hours, the Maid comes 30 minutes after the call and stays until 5.

If there's nothing on the lot to clean, the Maid charges §10 and departs.

Nanny

♦ Call Hours: Anytime
♦ Shift: Eight hours or as long as needed
♦ Fee: §10 per visit and §15 per hour
♦ Service: One Time or Recurring (anytime all teen, adult, elder Sims are at work)

A Nanny

Nannies are summoned by phone and come to take care of babies, toddlers, and children. She feeds and changes babies and toddlers, plays with them, and makes food as needed (she's a very good cook). In baby/toddler care, she autonomously uses the changing table, crib, and high chair. She cleans up after the children and herself, and will clean in general if there's nothing else to do.

Unlike other Service NPCs, Sims have a choice of what kind of Nanny service they require.

They can choose a one-time service in which the Nanny arrives 30 minutes later and stays for an eight-hour shift; if no teen, adult, or elder is home at the end of her shift, she stays until someone arrives.

note

If a family contains only child-age kids, the Nanny won't stay while they're at school. Thus, if parent works 9 a.m. to 6 p.m. and school goes from 9 a.m. to 3 p.m., Nanny comes from 3 p.m. to 6 p.m.

Alternately, the Nanny can be hired indefinitely to come whenever the caller must be off the lot for work or school and any babies, toddlers, and children are at home. She automatically tracks the caller's work schedule (even if his hours change) and arrives in advance of the caller's departure.

> **tip**
>
> Whoever calls the Nanny dictates when the caretaker will come. If parents work differing hours, consider having the earlier-departing adult call the Nanny. Thus, the later-starting adult can work on Skills or Wants or socialize rather than taking care of the minors.

Even if an adult, elder, or teen Sim is home but the calling Sim is not, the Nanny stays until the calling Sim returns or eight hours has passed, unless the Dismiss interaction is done.

Repairman (or Repairwoman)

A Repairman

- Call Hours: 9 a.m. to 5 p.m.
- Shift: As long as it takes to complete all repairs
- Fee: §10 per visit and §50 per hour
- Service: One Time

The Repairman (or -woman) is summoned by phone and arrives about 30 minutes later. He or she repairs all broken objects on the lot, staying until everything is fixed.

> **note**
>
> The Repairman has very high Mechanical skill but still can be electrocuted. This singes but doesn't kill the Repairman and can start a fire.

If the Repairman arrives and there's nothing to fix on the lot, he charges §10 and leaves.

> **tip**
>
> Given the massive expense of the repairman, it pays to have a household Sim highly trained in Mechanical skill if career, essential skill building, and Wants/Fears time permits.

Autonomous NPCs

Autonomous NPCs are like service NPCs but their visits are triggered more by events than by a service they provide. When they do provide services, they're not paid hourly like Service NPCs.

As with Service NPCs, many Autonomous NPCs can be interacted with and tipped to establish a relationship.

You can't really control when these NPCs visit a household, but take the opportunity when they do.

Autonomous Social NPCs include:

- Burglar
- Community Lot Salespeople
- Delivery People
- Firefighters
- Mail Carrier
- Paper Delivery
- Police

Burglar

A Burglar

The Burglar comes to Sims homes on random nights and tries to pilfer some of the family's most valuable objects.

The Burglar may not seem like marriage or friendship material, but you never know. The only way to begin a relationship with him or her, however, is to engage in a bit of skullduggery and lawlessness.

After a Burglar is apprehended, he's put in the back of the police car. Then, the cop comes inside to talk to your Sims and make herself available for social interaction. Click on the police car door to find the "Open Rear Door" interaction, and release the Burglar. You may then interact with him before he runs off the lot, adding him to the Relationship panel. In the future, the Burglar is just like any other acquaintance who can be invited, visit, befriended, and even married.

note

If a Burglar is brought into the family, he leaves most of his life of crime behind him; as with all Social NPCs, he enters the household unemployed.

Community Lot Salespeople

When on a Community Lot, all stores are manned by NPC Salespeople; their job is to ring up the sale. You can perform basic social interactions with Salespeople, but only when no interaction is in progress.

Community Lot Sales-people have one quirk

A Salesperson

compared to other Social NPCs: you can't flirt with them on the Community Lot. Invite them to a Sim's home, however, and anything goes.

Delivery People

◆ Hours: Anytime

◆ Fee: Pizza (§40), Groceries (§50 plus cost of groceries)

Pizza and groceries are brought by Delivery People.

A Delivery Person

If household funds are insufficient to pay the Delivery Person, she takes the equivalent value in household objects.

Firefighters

Firefighters come when called either via the phone or automatically by a ringing smoke detector object.

When they arrive, they busy themselves putting out all fires and briefly wait to be spoken to or tipped. They can't be interrupted while extinguishing the blaze.

A Firefighter

note

Unless you want to pay the §500 fine for false fire alarms, you have to wait until a fire occurs naturally to become acquainted with a Firefighter.

Mail Carrier

The Mail Carrier comes Tuesday and Thursday mornings (at 10 a.m.) to deliver bills to the household mailbox. He also comes the following day after the bill payment goes into the mailbox (except for Sunday).

A Mail Carrier

Newspaper Delivery

The Newspaper Carrier comes every day at 7 a.m. to bring the day's paper.

A Newspaper Carrier

note

On the first day on the lot, the newspaper arrives at 9 a.m.

If there isn't a free tile near the mailbox, the Newspaper Carrier will complain, refuse to make the delivery, and leave the lot. He'll also refuse to deliver if there are already three unrecycled papers on the lot.

Police

A Police Officer

Police come when called either via the phone or automatically by a ringing burglar alarm object. They may also come to break up parties or if they need to bring home a teen who's snuck out.

When the cop arrives, he'll busy himself apprehending the Burglar. If he wins the fight, he'll take the Burglar to the squad car and return to the house to reassure the household and present compensation for lost objects or a reward if nothing was stolen. If he loses the fight with the Burglar, he'll stand around dejected for a time and then leave.

He can't be interrupted while apprehending the Burglar.

note

Unless you want to pay the §500 fine for false alarms, you have to wait until a robbery occurs naturally, a teen is returned, or a party gets out of hand to become acquainted with a Police Officer.

Interacting With Social NPCs

When a Social NPC is on a Sim's lot or your Sim is on a Community Lot, unfamiliar Service and Autonomous NPCs have several basic interactions:

◆ Talk > Chat

◆ Talk > Brag

◆ Tip (except Community Lot Salespeople)

As Relationship scores toward the NPC grow, other basic interactions arise:

◆ Talk > Gossip

◆ Flirt (rising in intensity as relationship climbs)

Service NPCs linger for a while. This is your chance to engage them in social interaction.

If the relationship with a NPC is low or nonexistent, she offers the opportunity for interaction by hovering wordlessly for 10–20 minutes (basic service interactions only). Once engaged, she stays as long as interaction goes on. Unlike visitors, however, if you leave her alone, she'll depart.

If an NPC has a high enough Daily and Lifetime Relationship (Daily 30, Lifetime 20) with your Sim and vice versa, NPCs ask to hang around. If you accept, they become standard visitors (see "Visitor Behavior," Chapter 24).

When they're finished, Service NPCs inform you of the charge. Once that happens, the opportunity for interaction ends.

Once the NPC is a visitor, she behaves just like any other, staying as long as her Needs are being fulfilled, and departing no later than 2 a.m.

Marrying/Joining or Cohabitating with NPCs

Relationships with NPCs can reach the pinnacle of socializing: marriage/joining. It's true: one day a simple Maid and the next, husband to the most powerful politician in SimCity.

These rags-to-riches tales are yours to make, but only if you cultivate relationships with NPCs just as intensely as with any other Sim. In this way, NPC Sims are really just like any other non-household Sim with a few small exceptions:

♦ Career: When an NPC moves in or marries/joins into a household, his former career is over. He enters the home unemployed with no skills.

♦ Aspiration: When an NPC moves or marries/joins into a household, she gets a randomly generated Aspiration. There's no way to know what this will be until the Sim comes under your control. Townie Sims, by contrast, have Wants/Fears and Aspirations even before they move in.

NPCs who join a household bring with them random wealth of §1,000—§10,000.

NON-SOCIAL NPCS

Some Sims you just can't engage no matter how much you want to. These Non-Social NPCs are vital parts of life, but are unable to interact beyond their duties:

♦ Reaper   ♦ Drivers
♦ Repo Man   ♦ Sim Shrink
♦ Social Worker

Grim Reaper

Death itself isn't much of a social butterfly; he's all about the job. When a Sim dies, the Reaper appears, stands near the dead Sim, ushers him off the mortal coil, and replaces his lifeless body with a tombstone or urn.

> ### note
>
> If no living Sims are on the lot when the Reaper comes to claim someone, there's a random chance he'll use the bathroom, make himself a drink at the bar, or watch a little TV before departing.

The Grim Reaper

The only interaction the living may have with the Reaper is to plead with him to spare the dead Sim's life. The better the challenger's relationship with the deceased, the better his or her chances in this random contest.

Find full details about death and the Reaper in Chapter 29.

Repo Man

The Repo Man

Almost as dreaded as Reaper, the Repo Man is one of the most unwelcome figures in SimCity. He doesn't talk much, but happily goes about his business of squeezing blood from the turnips of Sims who haven't paid their bills on time.

If a bill remains unpaid three days after delivery, you receive a warning that it's past due. If no payment is made in the next 24 hours, the bills explode and the Repo Man is dispatched, arriving sometime on the fourth day.

When the Repo Man arrives, Buy mode gets disabled. He goes through the house (even into inaccessible places if need be) choosing objects by their depreciated value to pay the debt. Once he's sucked up the equivalent value of the unpaid bills, he departs.

> ### note
>
> Sims mourn the loss of their objects to the Repo Man in the same way as loss by burglary.

Social Worker

The Social Worker isn't always a bearer of bad tidings, but she isn't one of the more welcome guests. Generally, she only appears to remove babies, toddlers, and children from the lot when some kind of neglect has occurred:

The Social Worker

◆ She takes all the family's babies, toddlers, and children if Hunger of any fails.
◆ She takes all the family's babies, toddlers, and children if the Social of any fails.
◆ She takes any babies, toddlers, and children left on lot without a teen, adult, elder, or Nanny.
◆ She takes any child whose grades fall to F.

Removal warnings are issued when a baby, toddler, or child's Hunger or Social drops below -50.

The Social Worker can reach removable offspring even if they're inaccessible.

note

Removed babies, toddlers, and children go into a random collection of adoptable kids.

Sims can't be directed to interact with the Social Worker.

The Social Worker has one positive function: delivering adopted children. See Chapter 25 for details.

Drivers

The Drivers of cabs, buses, cars, etc. exist only to transport your Sims. They can't exit the vehicle or interact in any way.

A Driver

Sim Shrink

The Sim Shrink arrives automatically as the last resort of a Sim in Aspiration failure. Such a Sim collapses into a frantic, disturbed, and uncontrollable state when his Aspiration meter reaches rock bottom.

The Sim Shrink

The Sim Shrink drops from the sky and performs a lengthy therapy on the desperate Sim. At the end, the Sim returns to normal functionality but still with dangerously low Aspiration score; he'll need some Wants satisfied to avoid another visit from the Shrink.

Sims may not be directed to interact with the Shrink. In fact, no Sim other than the Shrink's patient can see the good doctor.

TOWNIES

The Community Lots are lousy with Townies, each quite befriendable and marriage-worthy.

Townies are Sims that don't live in any house in the neighborhood and can't be player-controlled until they're either married/joined or invited to move into a family.

note

Where's Bella Goth? Pleasantview's most famous missing person is actually a Townie in Strangetown.

They do appear as walkbys in front of neighborhood households and on the Community Lots. Once met, they can be called on the phone or e-mailed. In essence, they provide additional Sims for socialization and an even more varied gene pool.

Townies are fully realized Sims with Personalities, skills, jobs (teen, adult, and elder), Aspiration scores, and Needs. They are all single.

At any time, there will be 30 Townies (half male and half female):

◆ 17 Adults

◆ 8 Teens

◆ 5 Children

Townies don't age, per se, but they are replaced whenever the Townie pool dips below 25 randomly generated Townies. If adult or elder Townies move into a household, however, they begin to age normally.

As with Social NPCs, Townies can be married/joined or invited to move in. They bring with them a random amount of simoleans between §1,000 and §10,000. Unlike Social NPCs, however, they have a defined career track and level and pick up their work schedule as soon as they arrive.

SOCIAL BUNNY

The Social Bunny is a very special NPC that comes when the Social Need of a teen, adult, or elder fails. It drops from the sky to provide companionship to lonely Sim, and stays until her Social Need is positive. When a Sim leaves the lot, the Social Bunny goes too, but it returns with the Sim if Social is still at failure level when she returns.

The Social Bunny is the last refuge of the lonely Sim. Try to get more than one on the lot and watch the fireworks.

The Social Bunny follows the Sim for whom it came from room to room. Its mere presence on the lot feeds the particular Sim's Social motive, but it also can be the recipient of any non-romantic social interaction.

The Bunny is visible only to the Sim for whom it arrived; switch control to another Sim and the Bunny disappears. When a Sim interacts with the Bunny, nearby Sims react as if the Sim is crazy.

Every Sim in Social failure get his own Social Bunny in one of three randomly selected colors: blue, yellow, and pink. Color dictates how the Bunnies interact *with each other* when not engaged with their Sim:

◆ Bunnies of the same color do Fight, Irritate, and Play interactions.

◆ Bunnies of different colors do Entertain, Appreciate, and Play interactions.

◆ Blue and Pink Bunnies interacting with each other do Romantic interactions.

Chapter 27
Community Lots

Community Lots are nonresidential destinations in Sims' neighborhoods where Sims can do a little shopping and interact with copious other Sims.

But that's not all. You can construct your own Community Lots and make destinations your neighborhood Sims will be clamoring to visit.

This chapter introduces you to the draw of Community Lots, how to best utilize them, and some tips on setting up your own.

GETTING TO A COMMUNITY LOT

To get to a Community Lot, pick up the phone and use the Call...menu to select "Transportation."

The transportation option on the phone brings the taxi to Community Lots.

You may choose to call the taxi (to get a ride solely for the calling Sim and any others in the household) or invite another Sim first.

Invitations may be extended only to one Sim acquainted with the caller. As with invitations to visit, invited Sims are more likely to accept the higher their relationship is with the caller. The calling Sim then hangs up and places a second call to the taxi.

Invite a Sim's lover to a Community Lot with a clothing store and the shop's booths can be a venue for a bit of romantic audacity.

---
tip

The invited Sim will be at the chosen destination when you arrive. Inviting a Sim to a Community Lot is a good way to make sure you get some social time with a specific Sim while having lots of other Sims around for new connections.

Invitations to Community Lots are essential, in fact, if your goal is to have a little romantic fun in public (wink, wink) with a non-household Sim. For public WooHoo (a major Want for Romance Sims), invite a Sim with whom your Sim has a strong romantic relationship and meet at a lot with a clothing store. Have one Sim enter a booth to try on clothes and have the other Sim click use the WooHoo (or Try for Baby) interaction on the booth itself. Nearby Sims will cheer your cheekiness.

In either case, when the Sim calls for the taxi, she must choose who in the household will go. If only the caller, choose the caller's name. If all other present members of the household will be going too, choose "Multiple Sims."

Shortly after you call for a taxi, the vehicle pulls up to the house. Depending on your choice, the entire household or just the calling Sim will pile into the cab.

---
note

Going to and from the Community Lot is free. In fact, it's a cheaper way to buy groceries than ordering via phone or computer.

In this special community lot view, all community lots are highlighted for easy location. They are the only lots that can be entered.

The final step is to chose which Community Lot from the Neighborhood view. Community Lots are highlighted with a blue outline.

WHO'S AT THE COMMUNITY LOT

The Community Lots can be populated by:

- The Sims who rode in the taxi to the lot
- Random Sims from the neighborhood
- Random Townies
- Sims invited to meet your Sims at the lot
- Salespeople

> **note**
>
> The actual number of Sims on a Community Lot beyond the accompanying members of the caller's household and the salespeople is dictated by your computer's performance. The slower the processor and lower the RAM, the fewer Sims will appear.

Community lots are busiest in the middle of the day.

There can be up to seven Townies wandering the lot at any given time, though there'll be more in the middle of the day than during the night.

> **note**
>
> If only one Sim from a lot goes to the Community Lot, it's possible one or more of the randomly selected, computer-controlled neighborhood Sims will be members of their household. These Sims won't, however, spend any household money while on the Community Lot; only Sims under your control may do that.

SATISFYING NEEDS AT COMMUNITY LOTS

Community Lots should always have facilities for satisfying Sims' Needs. The only Need they can't fulfill is Energy, thus forcing even the most gregarious Sim to go home for some rest.

Always know where the public toilet is. It can be a long run on a big lot.

Needs can be fed at:

- Energy: No facilities
- Comfort: Benches, chairs, etc.
- Bladder: Public bathrooms
- Social: Other Sims
- Fun: Pinball machines, dartboards, chess boards, televisions, etc.
- Hygiene: Sinks, showers, tubs, changing tables
- Environment: Everywhere

> **note**
>
> Keep in mind that Neat Sims with low Mood may have a Fear of using public toilets. Taking them to Community Lots, therefore, can pose challenges.

High Cooking skill Sims should be the ones to man the community grills.

The Community grills are self-service but they're free. They can produce both hot dogs and hamburgers and the satisfaction derived from them depends a bit on the Cooking skill of the Sim making the meal.

WHAT TO DO AT COMMUNITY LOTS

There are several uses for Community Lots. Primary among them, however, are shopping and socializing.

> ### note
>
> Two skills can be built while on Community Lots. Cooking on the grills grants a bit of Cooking skill. More significantly, swimming in pools grants Body skill. Because Sims return to their home lot two hours after departing, no matter how long they spend on the Community Lot (see "Time and Community Lots," below), building Body in public is extremely time efficient.

Shopping

Stores provide alternatives to shopping at home or goods Sims can't get anywhere else.

Depending on the design of the Community Lot, there are many possible places to shop. Sims can purchase:

- Clothing
- Video/Computer Games
- Magazines
- Groceries

Clothing

Clothing stores consist of various racks of clothes from which Sims may buy new outfits in any of their six clothing categories.

Sims may try on outfits to see how they look if there's a clothing booth in the store, and they may purchase any outfits they fancy.

Clothing purchased at a cash register becomes available in any dresser back at your Sim's home lot. Any Sim in the household may don the outfit (every dresser contains infinite copies). If the lot lacks a dresser, however, purchased clothes can't be worn until you buy one.

Clothing purchases are available to any Sim in the household of the correct age and gender.

> ### note
>
> As mentioned previously, clothing booths have an alternative function: a venue for public WooHoo.

Sims may buy clothing for other ages and genders, though they may try on clothes only for their own.

Clothing prices depend on the class of clothing:

- Everyday: §200
- Swimwear: §150
- Formal: §400
- Undies: §50
- PJs: §75
- Gym Clothes: §100

Magazines

Sims may purchase magazines to influence their Interest level in various topics (see "Interest" in Chapter 18).

Magazines are used to change your Sims' interests. Buy a few and keep them around the house.

Magazines are exclusively bought from magazine rack objects on Community Lots. When the Sims arrive home, they place any purchased magazines on an available surface where any household Sim may interact with them.

All magazines cost §15.

Video/Computer Games

Any computer or the Maxis Game Simulator object can share video games purchased from video game racks on Community Lots. Buying these objects provides greater variety in the games Sims may choose from.

When the Sim returns home from the Community Lot, any computer or the Maxis Game Simulator will have a selection of all games the Sim has purchased. There are no functional differences between the games; it just gives life some variety.

This kind of variety costs §95 per game.

Groceries

Groceries can be purchased from any grocery stand on a Community Lot. The buying process is identical to purchasing over the phone or by computer, but there is no §50 delivery fee when buying directly from the store.

Groceries from the store are the same as delivered food but without the hefty delivery fee.

When the Sim returns home, he carries his bag of groceries to the refrigerator and restocks it.

Groceries cost §2 per unit of food.

THINGS SIMS CAN'T DO ON COMMUNITY LOTS

Sims on Community Lots can't:

◆ Satisfy Energy Need

◆ Age transition

◆ Get married

◆ Go to a Community Lot if pregnant

◆ Die

LEAVING COMMUNITY LOTS

When it's time to go to another Community Lot or go home, or when your Sims' Energy Need is about to bottom out, call a taxi with the public phone (every Community Lot has them).

When it's time to go, locate the public phone on the community lot.

When the cab comes, elect to go home or to another lot.

TIME AND COMMUNITY LOTS

Time passes a bit unusually when Sims are on a Community Lot. No matter how much time the Sim spends at the Community Lot, he always returns about two hours from the time he departed.

Due to this time anomaly, spending time socializing on the Community Lots is actually far more time efficient than doing it at home. The same is true for fulfilling Wants and building Body skill (if there's a pool). Who says you can't cheat time?

EXISTING COMMUNITY LOTS

Each of the three original neighborhoods (Pleasantview, Strangetown, and Veronaville) has a variety of Community Lots to explore. Each has its own character and selection of services:

Pleasantview

◆ Woodland Park: Lovely suburban park with central lake, chess boards, swingsets, grills, lots of benches

◆ 250 Main Street (Pleasantview Community Center): Swimming pool, hot tub, groceries, chess boards, grills, swingsets

◆ 290 Main Street: Groceries, magazines, video games, grill, pinball

◆ 330 Main Street: Clothing boutique, swingsets

Strangetown

◆ 88 Road to Nowhere: Groceries, clothing, magazines, video games, grill

◆ 94 Road to Nowhere (Strangetown Spa): Swimming pool, hot tub, groceries, grill

Veronaville

◆ 5 Pentameter Parkway: Groceries and magazines

◆ 431 Globe Street: Video games, pinball, magazines

◆ Veronaville Market: Bar, groceries, chessboards, grill

BUILDING YOUR OWN COMMUNITY LOT

If the Community Lots provided with *The Sims 2* aren't quite to your liking, or you just yearn to build your own commercial or recreational paradise, the tools are at your disposal. You can construct your own Community Lot.

note

Get details on setting up lots and using Build mode in your game's manual and in this book in Chapter 31.

Start by laying down an empty lot (a big one) and choosing "Community" as the lot type. Name the lot and begin building.

A big lot is best for community lots so there's room for expansion.

note

Don't forget to input a description of your Community Lot into the lot's information box.

Study the objects and facilities available for Community Lots and see where the imagination wanders. Regardless of your lot's function, however, all lots should have few things.

◆ Public toilets

◆ Community grills

◆ Several objects that provide Fun, especially if they offer group interaction

◆ Sinks, showers, tubs

◆ High Comfort seating for at least 10 Sims

A hot tub (it's so powerful, it should be everywhere)

Lots of lighting and decorations for high Environment score

Swingsets and changing tables for the little ones

Remember, there are no budgetary constraints on a Community Lot, because no one needs to purchase it. When it comes to décor and Motive satisfaction, spare no expense if you want Sims to stay until their Energy Need sends them home.

Community Lot-Only Objects

Several objects can be bought only for use on a Community Lot. For full details on these objects, see "Community Lot Objects" in Chapter 28.

- ClothesHorse Display Rack
- CounterRevolution Commercial Counter
- Countertop Game Display from Group Interaction LTD
- Deluxe Magazine Rack
- Empress's New Clothes Rack
- Enterprise Office Freestanding Game Rack
- Exceptionally Expensive Clothing Collator
- Food Shrine Commercial Display Freezer
- Food Temple Commercial Display Freezer
- GazeEase "Stow 'N' Show" Produce Bin
- Imperial Plumbing Pole-Air Freezer Bin
- Llamark Electronic Cash Register
- Neukum Systems "Art of Darkness" Heavy Metal Wall Speaker

- Neukum Systems "Bubblegum Sugar" Pop Wall Speaker
- Neukum Systems "En Fuego" Salsa Wall Speaker
- Neukum Systems "Glo Stik" Techno Wall Speaker
- Neukum Systems "The Badunkadunk" Hip Hop Wall Speaker
- Neukum Systems "The Cold Train" R&B Wall Speaker
- Old Boys Club Commercial Counter
- Old Fashioned Change Room
- Produce Market Shingle
- 'Right Away' Community Trash-Can
- SCTC Universal Public Phone
- Sewage Brothers Resteze Urinal
- SimCity SynapseSnapper Industrial Sign
- SimSentry Clothing Booth
- The Great Dress Rack
- VeggiStuf Produce Bin
- Wear's the Sale? Shop Sign

Packaging the Lot

Package a lot from its information box to share it with friends, back it up for safekeeping, or upload to TheSims2.com.

Community Lots can be packaged like any other lot (see Chapter 35). A packaged lot can be shared among The Sims 2 players or uploaded to TheSims2.com.

Chapter 28

Objects

Despite their higher Aspirations, Sims are still material creatures; they do love their objects.

This chapter describes the use, abuse, disuse, and refuse of objects in *The Sims 2*. We discuss the economics of objects, how and why they break and get dirty, what happens after you buy them, and how much they'll cost you down the road. As the final treat, behold the most detailed object catalog ever published for a *The Sims* game, detailing every household, community lot, aspiration reward, and career reward objects.

BUY MODE

Buy mode is where most (but not all) objects are acquired. Entering Buy mode pauses the simulation and enables movement, rotation, addition, duplication, redesign, and removal of objects.

> **note**
>
> Build mode has several objects too. Those are discussed in Chapter 31.

Purchasing and Return

When an object is dropped into a lot, it is purchased and the price is deducted from household funds. Once it's in the lot, the object can be moved (with the Hand tool) to any legal location.

Try to place an object in an illegal position and the error message should tell you precisely where the object should be put.

If you reconsider a purchase before leaving Buy mode, you can nullify it by pressing Undo ([Z] by default) or simply selling it (for full value).

Items dragged onto the Buy mode panel are resold for their current depreciated (or, if art, appreciated) value.

Objects are "returned" or "sold" by dragging them with the Hand tool onto the Buy mode panel at the bottom of the screen. The panel displays the object's current value (see "Depreciation/Appreciation," below); if you've just purchased it, the value will still be the purchase price. To complete the return, left-click again or press [Delete].

tip

Objects take a huge hit of depreciation at midnight on the day they're purchased. Thus, until then, they can be returned for full value. Need a hot tub for that big party? Buy it, use it, and return it by midnight and get every simolean back.

This is also an excellent trick when job searching. Buy a computer, search job listings, get a job, and return the computer. It don't cost NOTHIN'!

Design Alternatives

Many items have design variations that provide greater customization and personalization.

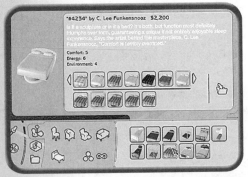

Many objects have substantial variation in the object's appearance. Design changes are free at the time of purchase. Click on a variation to see how it'll look.

Left-click on an object in the catalog to see its description and all design variations; left-click on a variation to change the model. When you find a look you like, the object with the chosen design will be ready to place. There is no extra cost for design alternatives when buying from the catalog.

Once an object is on the lot, it can be redesigned to any of these variations by using the Design tool (see following page), but it'll cost §15.

Multiple Objects

Drop commonly batch purchased items like chairs, and another identical version pops onto the Hand tool.

Some objects are commonly bought in bunches (e.g., chairs, lights, etc.). Such objects automatically replicate themselves for easy purchasing; buy one and a new one appears on the Hand tool, ready to purchase with a single click. To exit multiple purchasing, press Esc.

The Buy Mode Panel

The Buy mode panel has many useful tools for your shopping pleasure.

The Hand Tool

Use the Hand tool to pick up, move, and rotate objects in the lot and drag them out to be sold/returned.

The Eyedropper

The Eyedropper offers easy duplication and identification of objects already on the lot.

The Eyedropper tool duplicates any object, switches the catalog to the object's listing and displays the name of the chosen object.

Point at an object to reveal its name and click on it to create a duplicate, ready for purchase. The Buy mode panel jumps directly to the object's function sort page.

Design Tool

Existing objects can be redesigned for a mere §15.

The Design tool can change any purchased object into any of its available design variations. Unlike choosing a design before purchase, however, using the Design tool costs §15 per change.

Day/Night Toggle

Day and night can be switched in Buy mode with the Day/Night toggle. Time of day in Live mode is unchanged by this control.

Use the Day/Night toggle to see how lights look in their intended conditions.

This is very helpful when placing lights around the lot. Returning to Live mode switches day and night back to normal.

Undo/Redo

The Undo button undoes the last action taken in Buy (and Build) mode. The last 100 actions are stored in the memory, so you can go pretty far back.

Redo reverses the process, restoring an undone action. Doing something new after undoing, however, erases any of the subsequent actions and disables redo.

Redo memory is preserved when switching between Buy and Build mode but is cleared when you enter Live mode.

Top Down View

Top down view is perfect for designing the perfect arrangement of a room.

Seeing the scene directly from top down can be helpful in laying out objects. This button toggles between the top down and normal views.

Sorts

Objects are sorted in multiple ways for easy location.

Objects are sorted by function or by room.

In residential lots, the object catalog is sorted by either function or room. The object directory below

follows the function sort but the object table displays alphabetically and lists all sorts in which an object can be found.

In Community Lots, objects are sorted by special Community Lot function sorts; one object may appear in several sorts. Use the object table if you need help locating these items.

note

Objects available in both the residential and Community Lot catalogs are listed under the residential directory in this chapter. Community Lot—only items are detailed later in the chapter.

Collections

Collections are groupings of Buy and Build mode objects and Build mode elements (e.g., floor or wall coverings) built around a theme. They act, effectively, as customizable object sorts.

Collections are customizable object sorts based around any organizing principle.

Several Collections ship with your game but you can make your own or import Collections assembled by another player. See "Collections," Chapter 35 for full details.

OBJECT EXIT CONDITIONS

Sims intelligently refuse to use or stop using objects that no longer serve their purposes, but only if certain Need levels are reached. These conditions depend on what kind of object it is.

Sims' willingness to skill build, have Fun, and remain in certain interactions depends on either Mood or several specific Need levels.

Skill Objects

A Sim will exit or refuse to use a skill object when any of the following drop below the listed value:

- ◆ Mood: 0
- ◆ Energy: -80
- ◆ Fun: -80
- ◆ Comfort: -70
- ◆ Bladder: -75

Fun Objects

Different conditions apply whether the Sim is currently above an object's maximum Fun amount.

If the Sim has not yet reached the object's maximum Fun, he'll be kicked out when any of the following drop below the listed value:

- ◆ Hunger: -80
- ◆ Energy: -80
- ◆ Bladder: -85
- ◆ Comfort: -90

note

Exit conditions for Fun also depend on whether the Sim is a visitor. Because you can't control visitors, suffice to say that their exit conditions are stricter than for residents, and they exit sooner if their Needs drop. Take good care of your visitors.

If the Sim has surpassed the Fun maximum for the object, the rules depend on how she began using the object. If you directed her to use it, she'll be kicked out when any of the following drop below the listed value:

- Hunger: 0
- Social: 0
- Bladder: 0
- Hygiene: 0
- Energy: -70
- Comfort: 0

If she chose to do the action autonomously, she'll be kicked out when any of the following drop below the listed value:

- Hunger: 35
- Social: 35
- Bladder: 35
- Hygiene: 35
- Energy: -70
- Comfort: 20

Comfort Objects

A Sim will exit it any Comfort-giving object (except chairs) under certain conditions.

note

None of the Comfort exit conditions kick a Sim out if the Need is below the kick-out point but rising due to the Comfort object itself or some other object nearby. For instance, if the Sim is sitting on a sofa watching TV, he won't be kicked out for below-minimum Fun as long as the Fun level is rising.

If maximum Comfort hasn't yet been reached, the Sim will exit when any of the following drop below the listed value:

- Hunger: -80
- Energy: -80
- Bladder: -85

If maximum Comfort has been surpassed, the rules depend on how she began using the object. If you directed her to use it, she'll be kicked out when any of the following drop below the listed value:

- Hunger: -60
- Social: -50
- Bladder: -80
- Hygiene: -70
- Energy: -90
- Fun: -50

If she chose to do the action autonomously, she'll be kicked out when any of the following drop below the listed value:

- Hunger: 35
- Social: 35
- Bladder: 35
- Hygiene: 35
- Energy: -70
- Fun: 35

Need Failure

Sims exit *any* object if Hunger, Energy, or Bladder fail (-100).

APPRECIATION/DEPRECIATION

Objects either drop (depreciate) or rise (appreciate) in value over time. Which direction an object's value goes depends on what it is.

The longer objects reside in a lot, the less resale value they'll have. This TV originally cost §400.

When an object is sold/returned, its current value (minus depreciation and plus appreciation, if any) is the sale price.

Buy Mode Depreciation

Most objects depreciate in value starting at midnight on the day they're purchased. Each item features three depreciation factors:

- Initial Depreciation: Depreciation taken after midnight on the day of purchase. This is the largest depreciation drop, usually 15 percent.
- Daily Depreciation: Depreciation taken at midnight each subsequent day. Usually 10 percent.

◆ Depreciation Limit: Minimum value for an object after depreciation. Once an object depreciates to this level, no further depreciation occurs. Usually 40 percent.

note

The only Buy mode objects that don't depreciate in this manner are the grandfather clock, paintings, and sculptures.

Depreciation factors are shown in the Object table later in this chapter.

Art Object Depreciation/ Appreciation

Art objects (paintings and sculptures) don't depreciate in the same manner. They, instead, randomly appreciate and depreciate each day: there's a 50-50 chance that the painting will either appreciate or depreciate by an amount dictated by the object's current value:

◆ If less than §100, depreciates/appreciates §2.

◆ If more than §100 but less than §1,000, depreciates/ appreciates §15.

◆ If more than §1,000, depreciates/appreciates §50.

In general, art should gradually increase in value.

Sim-Created Art

Easel created paintings don't depreciate. Rather, they appreciate every two days for Sims with Creativity 8 or higher.

Once a Sim with Creativity 8 or higher dies, his paintings become much more valuable. Upon death, all paintings the Sim created while alive double in value and the rate of appreciation accelerates to every day.

Hang onto that; it could be worth a lot some day.

An easel painting still on the easel can be depreciated or increased in value if a Sim does the Ruin Painting interaction. If the ruining Sim has high Creativity, her attempt to ruin the painting will actually increase its value.

BILLS

Every three days, the property tax bill arrives at a Sim's home via the mailbox. The amount of bills is calculated as:

◆ §6 for every §1,000 worth of Buy mode objects

◆ §4 for every §1,000 Build mode objects (e.g., fireplaces, columns, fences, etc.)

Flag up means bills have arrived.

Thus, a small house will have bills of around §150–§200 per cycle, a moderate house should have around §200–§350 per cycle, and a large house will have about §500 or more.

Bills arrive at the mailbox. Paying them requires two interactions. First, an interaction on the mailbox removes the bills and places them on a surface on the lot (or on the ground). Second, an interaction on the bill deducts its amount from household funds and deposits the payment in the mailbox. The mail carrier picks them up the next day (except Sunday).

tip

Put a cheap end table right near the mailbox and make sure it stays clear. Sims will autonomously deposit bills on it rather than leaving them on the ground or bringing them all the way inside. It's easier, thus to get the bills and pay them at once and you can always find them.

When bills exceed the amount of family funds, Sims can't pay the bill; no partial payments are allowed.

Past due bills begin to change color over time. Red means you better see to them soon.

You needn't pay bills the day they arrive (though doing so may aid the forgetful), but they must be paid within four days. Bills are color-coded based on age:

- 1 day after delivery: Bills turn yellow
- 2 days after delivery: Bills turn orange
- 3 days after delivery: Bills turn red
- 4 days after delivery: Bills explode. Repo Man's comin'!

When bills are four days past due, they explode (making it too late to pay them) and the Repo Man is sent to the household.

note

Keep in mind that bills keep coming every three days, so where there's a seriously past due bill, there's another bill festering somewhere on the lot.

The Repo Man (as described in Chapter 26) will take objects the depreciated value of which is roughly equal to the past due bill.

CLEAN AND DIRTY STATES

Many objects require cleaning. How often they must be cleaned depends on the Neat/Sloppy personalities of the Sims using them.

note

In most cases, being Neat/Sloppy 10 versus Neat/Sloppy 0 means things stay clean about two days longer. Moderate Neat/Sloppy makes about one day's difference.

Objects that need regular cleaning include:

- Toilets
- Sinks
- Showers
- Tubs
- Stoves
- Countertops
- Aquariums
- High Chairs

An object can be a little dirty without affecting Environment score, but it begins to take a toll once it becomes *visibly* dirty. Before this happens, however, the Clean interaction becomes available and advertises itself to Neat Sims.

Thus, if there's a Neat Sim in the house with time to do cleaning, objects shouldn't become visibly dirty.

Watch a Sloppy Sim cook or shower and you'll see why things get dirty faster when he uses them.

> ### note
> Cleaning an object restores it to its fully clean state, effectively resetting the clock on its dirtiness. Cleaning also builds Cleaning skill.

Objects cleaned by very Neat Sims take longer to get dirty.

If a Sim is Neat (Neat/Sloppy 8 or higher), she'll actually clean the object beyond its fully clean state, making it take longer to get dirty. The higher the Neat/Sloppy, the further clean the object will be.

Time required to clean an object depends on the degree of dirtiness and the Cleaning skill of the Sim doing the cleaning.

BREAKABILITY AND REPAIR

After the first 24 hours after purchase, many objects have a random chance of breaking after an interaction is complete.

> ### note
> Breakability increases as the object ages. Generally, however, a breakable object can be expected to break three times over a Sim's adult/elder life.
>
> The value of an object, however, has no effect on its breakability, but it can affect how long the object takes (and, thus, how much it costs) to repair.

If an object sits unused for a long time, it has a higher chance of breaking when a Sim uses it.

Repairing

What happens when an object breaks depends on what kind of object it is.

> ### note
> Broken objects can be sold in Buy mode. For very old objects, this might make more sense than paying for a repair since breakage probability rises with age. A broken object sells for one-half its original sale price.

Most objects are repairable. When these break, they display some kind of broken visual state (e.g., sparking or leaking). If the broken object is unusable when broken, the only available interaction will be Repair.

Repairs can be done by any teen/adult/elder household Sim or by a hired Repairman. The Repairman costs money but he/she is very skilled, completing repairs quickly and safely. Do-it-yourself

Sims can repair for free, but their speed, success, and risk of electrocution depend on their Mechanical skill level.

In general, the length of time a repair takes is governed by the Sim's Mechanical skill, the kind of object it is, and the price of the object. Electronics take the most time while plumbing objects take the least; the more expensive the object, the longer time to repair.

This WAS a dollhouse. Now it's garbage. Throw it out; it's pulling down Environment score.

Some breakable objects, however, cannot be repaired. They instead crumble into a debris pile that brings down Environment score and should be cleaned up. Such objects include:

◆ Soma "Wall-Eye" Large Screen Flat-Panel Television

◆ Will Lloyd Wright Dollhouse

◆ Urns and Tombstones

Plumbing

Plumbing objects, unlike most others, are usable when broken but cause puddles and floods. Broken toilets, showers, and tubs leak on each use, and sinks spray water continuously whether used or not. Leaked water, in turn, reduces Environment score.

Repairing and Mechanical Skill

Repairing an object increases a Sim's Mechanical skill, turning any broken object into a Mechanical skill object.

Note, however, that the progress bar above the Sim's head is the status of the repair, not the development of skill. Skill progress is visible only when studying Mechanical from books.

Electronics

Electronic objects (e.g., TVs, computers, etc.) are unusable when broken and carry a significant risk of electrocution and fire during repair.

A Sim with low Mechanical skill or a Sim of any Mechanical skill standing in a puddle will likely be electrocuted (possibly to death) when repairing an electronic object.

The higher the Mechanical skill, the less likely the chance of electrocution (though no one's completely safe). Even the Repairman can be electrocuted, though he usually survives.

Object	Price 1	Price 2	Price 3	Price 4	Category
Bella Squared	$1,000	$0	$0	$0	Decorative
Bibliofile Bookcase	$400	$40	$40	$60	Hobbies
Black Lacquer Bar Counter	$60	$60	$60	$60	Miscellaneous
Blazin' Buckaroos Lantern	$50	$150	$100	$400	Lighting
Blue Sky Bonsai Tree	$50	$7	$5	$20	Decorative
Blue Suede Chair	$99	$9	$9	$20	Comfort
Bon Appetit Dining Chair	$611	$91	$91	$39	Comfort
Bowl of Plastic Fruit	$1,100	$165	$61	$244	Decorative
Bowl of Plastic Fruit	$150	$110	$110	$480	Appliances
Brand Name "EconoCool" Refrigerator	$600	$22	$15	$60	Appliances
Brand Name MetalKettle	$299	$44	$29	$100	Appliances
Brand Name Zip Zap Microwave	$250	$37	$25	$19	Plumbing
Bubble-Up "Soaking Zone" Hot Tub	$6,500	$975	$650	$2,600	Plumbing
Burled Wood Dartboard	$180	$27	$18	$72	Hobbies
Burnished Blaze Torchiere	$89	$29	$19	$79	Lighting
Candy Coated Sofa	$450	$67	$157	$180	Comfort
Caress of Teak Bed	$1,570	$235	$21	$84	Comfort
Catamaran Kitchen Island	$210	$31	$21	$320	Surfaces
Centerpieces Coffee Table	$370	$55	$37	$48	Surfaces
Chabadii "Yet Another" Coffee Table	$290	$43	$29	$16	Surfaces
Chabadii Chabudsky	$265	$39	$26	$106	Surfaces
Cheap Eazzzzze Morrissey Double Bed	$450	$67	$45	$180	Comfort
Cheap Eazzzzze Puffy Recliner	$515	$77	$51	$206	Comfort
Chesterstick Cherry Dresser	$2,125	$318	$212	$850	Miscellaneous
Chez Chaise	$900	$135	$90	$772	Comfort
Chez Moi French Country Counters	$800	$20	$80	$320	Surfaces
Chez Moi French Country Counters	$800	$20	$80	$320	Surfaces
Chiclettina "Archipelago" Kitchen Island	$500	$75	$50	$200	Surfaces
Chiclettina "Fjord" Kitchen Counter	$490	$73	$49	$196	Surfaces
Chiclettina "Fjord" Kitchen Counter	$490	$73	$49	$196	Surfaces
Chiclettina "Sardinia" Kitchen Counter	$780	$78	$79	$312	Surfaces
hiclettina "Sardinia" Kitchen Island	$790	$118	$79	$316	Surfaces
Chiclettina Execudrone Desk	$1,000	$150	$100	$400	Surfaces
Chimeway & Daughters Saloon Piano	$3,500	$525	$350	$1,400	Hobbies
Chinese Opera Mask by Old Face	$150	$0	$0	$0	Decorative

Table continues on page 329

Object Directory

Object	Price	Initial Depreciation	Daily Depreciation	Depreciation Limit	Hunger	Comfort	Hygiene	Bladder	Energy	Fun	Environment	Cleaning	Study	Charisma	Creativity	Body	Logic	Mechanical	Cooking	Function	Kids	Study	Dining Room	Outside	Living Room	Bathroom	Bedroom	Kitchen	Miscellaneous	Street	Outdoor	Shopping	Food
#4234 by C. Lee Funkensmooz	$2,200	$330	$220	$880	0	0	0	0	0	0	4									Comfort					X		X						X
? = (C*II)?	$470	$70	$47	$188	0	5	0	0	6	0	—									Comfort					X							X	
12th Century Song Dynasty Sculpted Vase	$4,000	$0	$0	$0	0	0	0	0	0	0	10									Decorative			X		X				X			X	
4 by 4 Designer Chandelier	$20	$18	$12	$48	0	0	0	0	0	0	2									Lighting	X	X	X		X				X				
Absolutely Nothing Special	$85	$12	$8	$34	0	0	0	0	0	0	—									Decorative		X	X		X				X			X	
Ad-a-Quaint Barstool	$285	$42	$28	$56	0	6	0	0	0	0	1									Comfort			X		X			X	X			X	
Ad-a-Quaint Coffee Table	$140	$21	$14	$14	0	0	0	0	0	0	—									Surfaces			X		X				X			X	
Almost Deco Wall Sconce	$184	$27	$18	$73	0	0	0	0	0	0	1									Lighting	X	X	X		X	X	X	X	X			X	
Aluminium Privacy Blinds by P. King Tom Trading Co.	$80	$12	$8	$32	0	0	0	0	0	0	—									Decorative		X	X		X	X	X		X				
Ancient Transport Urn Sculpture	$500	$0	$0	$0	0	0	0	0	0	0	2									Decorative		X	X		X				X			X	
Antebellum Wall Lamp	$360	$54	$36	$144	0	0	0	0	0	0	4									Lighting		X	X		X	X	X		X				
Ltd. Ed. Armoire	$250	$37	$25	$100	0	0	0	0	0	0	—									Miscellaneous		X	X		X				X			X	
Anti-Quaint-Ed	$165	$24	$16	$52	0	0	0	0	0	0	2									Decorative		X	X		X				X			X	
Antique Lace Curtains	$155	$23	$15	$66	0	0	0	0	0	0	2									Lighting		X	X		X	X	X		X				
Antique Metal Sconce	$400	$60	$40	$160	0	0	0	0	0	0	—									Miscellaneous				X					X		X		
Antonio's Prize-Winning Wedding Cake	$100	$15	$10	$40	0	0	0	0	0	0	—									Lighting					X				X			X	
Anytime Candles	$400	$45	$30	$160	0	0	0	0	0	0	3									Decorative		X	X		X	X	X		X				
Apple of the Eye	$300	$0	$0	$120	0	0	0	0	0	0	10									Decorative					X				X				
AquaBox Five-Gallon Aquarium	$0	$0	$10	$0	0	0	0	0	0	4	10				X					Decorative				X							X		
AquaGreen Hydroponic Garden	$1,100	$165	$0	$440	0	0	0	0	0	0	2									Plumbing		X	X			X			X		X	X	
AquaPlus Shower Stall	$2,000	$0	$0	$0	0	0	0	0	0	0	5									Career Rewards	X								X				
Arghist Soldier	$629	$94	$62	$251	0	7	0	0	0	0	—									Comfort		X	X		X	X			X			X	
Armchair by Club Design	$550	$82	$55	$220	0	0	0	0	2	4	2						X			Hobbies					X				X				
Astrowonder Telescope	$600	$90	$60	$240	0	0	0	0	0	3	—									Miscellaneous		X	X	X	X			X	X			X	
Bachman Busbar	$700	$0	$0	$0	0	8	0	0	2	0	2									Decorative		X	X		X				X			X	
Bangpae Yeon from Simporters, Ltd.	$1,250	$187	$125	$500	0	9	0	0	0	0	1									Comfort					X	X			X			X	
Barococo Loveseat by MiRE	$1,500	$225	$150	$600	0	8	0	2	0	0	2									Comfort		X	X		X	X			X			X	
Barococo Sofa by MiRE	$75	$3	$2	$10	0	0	0	0	0	0	—									Lighting			X	X	X						X	X	
Basically Bare Bulb from Electric Lighting	$800	$120	$80	$320	0	8	0	2	0	2	2									Comfort		X	X		X	X	X	X	X			X	
Be There Designs "Bazaar Sofa"	$1,200	$180	$120	$480	0	5	0	0	6	2	4									Comfort					X		X					X	
Bed by St. Ajeque Reproductions	$1,200	$180	$120	$480	0	5	0	0	6	0	4									Comfort					X		X					X	

Item	Price	Initial Depr.	Daily Depr.	Depr. Limit	Category
Contempto Penn Station Side Chair	$310	$46	$31	$124	Comfort
Cool Shades	$0	$0	$0	$0	Aspiration Rewards
Cornerstone "Sentinel" End Table	$250	$37	$25	$100	Surfaces
Cornerstone Victoriana Velvet Drapes	$250	$37	$25	$100	Decorative
Counter Cooking Conundrum	$200	$30	$20	$80	Surfaces
Counter Culture "Surface"	$200	$30	$20	$80	Surfaces
Counter Culture "Surface"	$540	$81	$54	$216	Surfaces
Counter Productive Work Surface	$200	$30	$20	$80	Surfaces
Counter/Revolution Commercial Counter	$750	$112	$75	$300	Surfaces
Countertop Game Display from Group Interaction LTD.	$3,500	$525	$350	$1,400	Miscellaneous
Country Comfort Corner Table	$110	$16	$11	$44	Surfaces
Courtly Sleeper Day Dreamer	$700	$105	$70	$280	Comfort
Cowboy's Caboose Chair	$385	$57	$38	$154	Comfort
Cozy Colonial End Table	$400	$60	$40	$160	Surfaces
Craftmeister Booknook	$250	$37	$25	$100	Hobbies
Craftmeister's Pine Bed	$300	$45	$30	$120	Comfort
Crazy 8 Table	$65	$9	$6	$26	Surfaces
Curvaceous Colonial End Table	$430	$64	$43	$172	Surfaces
CyberChronometer Alarm Clock	$60	$9	$6	$24	Electronics
Dangling Daylight Ceiling Lamp	$145	$21	$14	$58	Lighting
Decorative House Armoire	$550	$82	$55	$220	Decorative
Deluxe Magazine Rack	$2,500	$375	$250	$1,000	Miscellaneous
Deluxe Veil of Dreams	$150	$22	$15	$60	Decorative
Dialectric Ready/Prep Range	$400	$60	$40	$160	Appliances
Diamondback by Desert Designs	$900	$135	$90	$360	Comfort
Discourse Dining Table	$650	$97	$65	$260	Surfaces
Double-Helix Designer Bookshelf	$1,200	$180	$120	$480	Hobbies
Doublewide Tieback Curtains	$35	$5	$3	$14	Decorative
Dreams of a Gifted Mind	$880	$132	$88	$352	Decorative
Durable Value Sofa	$250	$37	$25	$100	Comfort
Durably Plush Teddy Bear	$49	$7	$4	$19	Miscellaneous
Dynasty "Enlightenment" Lamp	$95	$14	$9	$38	Lighting

Table continues on page 331

Object Directory continued

Column groups: **Price and Depreciation** (Price, Initial Depreciation, Daily Depreciation, Depreciation Limit) · **Needs** (Hunger, Comfort, Hygiene, Bladder, Energy, Fun, Environment) · **Skills** (Cleaning, Study, Charisma, Creativity, Body, Logic, Mechanical, Cooking) · **Function** · **Room Sort** (Kids, Study, Dining Room, Outside, Living Room, Bathroom, Bedroom, Kitchen) · **Community Sort** (Miscellaneous, Street, Outdoor, Shopping, Food)

Object	Price	Init. Dep.	Daily Dep.	Dep. Limit	Hun	Com	Hyg	Bla	Ene	Fun	Env	Clean	Study	Charis	Creat	Body	Logic	Mech	Cook	Function	Kids	Study	Dining	Outside	Living	Bath	Bed	Kitchen	Misc	Street	Outdoor	Shop	Food
Chinese Riddle Lantern "Mondo Fuego"	$175	$26	$17	$70	0	0	0	0	0	0	0									Lighting					X	X	X	X	X			X	
Ciao Time "Mondo Fuego" Gas Stove	$650	$97	$65	$260	0	0	0	0	0	0	0								X	Appliances								X	X			X	
Ciao Time Bovinia Refrigerator Model BRRR	$1,500	$225	$150	$600	4	0	0	0	0	0	0							X		Appliances								X	X			X	
Ciao Time Espresso Machine	$450	$67	$45	$180	0	0	0	-1	4	3	0									Appliances			X					X	X			X	
Cinderbooks by Retratech	$200	$30	$20	$80	0	0	0	0	0	0	0		X							Hobbies	X	X			X		X		X			X	
City Dweller "Dims"	$70	$10	$7	$28	0	0	0	0	0	0	0									Lighting				X	X		X		X	X	X		
Civic Idol by Adora Wall Arts	$50	$0	$0	$0	0	0	0	0	0	0	2									Decorative				X	X				X	X	X	X	
Clean Water Shower System	$525	$78	$52	$210	0	0	8	0	0	0	0									Plumbing						X			X				
Clotheshorse Display Rack	$3,000	$450	$300	$1,200	0	0	0	0	0	0	0	X								Miscellaneous				X		X	X		X		X	X	
Club Distress Avignon Rectangular Coffee Table	$240	$36	$24	$96	0	0	0	0	0	0	0									Surfaces					X				X				
Club Distress Butcher's Block	$610	$91	$61	$244	0	0	0	0	0	0	0									Surfaces								X	X				
Club Distress Square Coffee Table	$155	$23	$15	$62	0	0	0	0	0	0	0									Surfaces					X				X				
Club Distress Wall Mirror	$580	$87	$58	$232	0	0	0	0	0	0	3			X						Decorative					X	X	X		X				
Club Room Countertop	$600	$90	$60	$240	0	0	0	0	0	0	0									Surfaces						X		X	X				
Club Room Countertop	$600	$90	$60	$240	0	0	0	0	0	0	0									Surfaces						X		X	X				
Collage in Black and White	$300	$0	$0	$0	0	0	0	0	0	0	3									Decorative		X	X		X		X		X			X	
Colonial Bathtub by Imperial Plumbing Works	$1,800	$270	$180	$720	0	8	8	0	0	0	0									Plumbing						X			X				
Colonial ComboClean by Imperial Plumbing Works	$2,200	$330	$220	$880	0	0	10	8	0	0	0									Plumbing						X			X				
Colonial Ironwood Bed	$3,000	$450	$300	$1,200	0	7	0	0	6	0	3									Comfort							X		X				
Coloratura by Chrome Concepts	$1,500	$225	$150	$600	0	6	0	0	0	0	2									Comfort					X				X				
Coming Up Roses Loveseat by OakTowne	$220	$33	$22	$88	0	6	0	0	0	0	5									Comfort					X				X				
Compact Stereo by Lo-Fi Audio	$99	$14	$9	$39	0	0	0	0	0	7	0					X				Electronics		X			X		X		X				
Contempto Adirondack Chair	$400	$60	$40	$160	0	6	0	0	0	0	3									Comfort				X					X		X		
Contempto Adirondack End Table	$80	$12	$8	$32	0	0	0	0	0	0	0									Surfaces				X	X				X		X		
Contempto Adirondack Loveseat	$450	$67	$45	$180	0	7	0	0	0	0	0									Comfort				X					X		X		
Contempto Good Livin' Chair	$80	$12	$8	$32	0	4	0	0	0	0	0									Comfort				X	X				X		X	X	
Contempto Outdoor Living Lounge	$420	$63	$42	$168	0	6	0	0	0	0	0									Comfort			X	X	X				X		X	X	

Item				Category
FLATWOOD Dining Table by Isseya	$450	$67	$45	$180	Surfaces
Flight-Away Model Plane	$250	$0	$0	$0	Decorative
Floor-Length Tieback Curtains	$335	$50	$33	$134	Decorative
Floral Fancy Hanging Lamp	$445	$66	$44	$78	Lighting
Floral Fantasy Sofa by OakTowne	$360	$54	$36	$160	Comfort
Floral Sink	$330	$49	$33	$32	Plumbing
Food Shrine Commercial Display Freezer	5,000	$750	$500	$2,000	Appliances
Food Temple Commercial Display Freezer	$5,000	$750	$500	$2,000	Appliances
Founding Fathers Electric Lamp	$235	$35	$23	$94	Lighting
Frost de Fleur Bud Vase	$30	$4	$3	$12	Decorative
Fruitless Fig Tree	$333	$49	$33	$133	Decorative
Fun-Kadelic Frequency Stereo SystemÅ from Kauiker Inc.	$375	$56	$37	$150	Electronics
Futunesque Fantasy Sofa	$180	$27	$18	$72	Comfort
Gagnia Simore "RefuseNik" Trash Compactor	$375	$56	$37	$50	Appliances
Garden Fresh Pedestal Sink	$355	$53	$35	$42	Plumbing
Garden Glow Spotlight	$35	$5	$3	$4	Lighting
GazeEase "Stow 'N' Show" Produce Bin	$3,000	$450	$300	$1,200	Surfaces
GentleGlow Table Lamp	$120	$18	$12	$48	Lighting
Get Up! Alarm Clock	$30	$4	$3	$12	Electronics
Glitteri & Co. Trieste End Table	$310	$46	$31	$24	Surfaces
Grand Parlour Chess Table	$500	$75	$50	$200	Hobbies
Ha-hye-tal Mask	$3,000	$0	$0	$0	Decorative
Handle and Spout	$2,500	$0	$0	$0	Plumbing
Here and There Thing	$280	$42	$28	$112	Decorative
Home Office Desk by Quaint Design	$220	$33	$22	$88	Surfaces
Hosta La Vista	$80	$13	$9	$36	Decorative
Hydronomic CleanSheen Basin	$410	$61	$41	$164	Plumbing
Ilistara Lamp	$80	$12	$8	$32	Lighting
Illuminating Angles by Newt Yo	$250	$37	$25	$100	Lighting
Immobile Chimes Mobile in Steel	$1,500	$0	$0	$0	Decorative
Imperial Lyon Basin	$640	$96	$64	$256	Plumbing
Imperial Plumbing Pole-Air Freezer Bin	$3,000	$450	$300	$1,200	Appliances
Imperial Plumbing Works Tivoli Basin	$580	$84	$56	$224	Plumbing

Table continues on page 333

Object Directory continued

Object	Price	Initial Depreciation	Daily Depreciation	Depreciation Limit	Hunger	Comfort	Hygiene	Bladder	Energy	Fun	Environment	Cleaning	Study	Charisma	Creativity	Body	Logic	Mechanical	Cooking	Function	Kids	Study	Dining Room	Outside	Living Room	Bathroom	Bedroom	Kitchen	Misc.	Street	Outdoor	Shopping	Food
Dynasty Armoire	$560	$84	$56	$224	0	0	0	0	0	0	2									Miscellaneous							X		X			X	X
Dynasty Dining Chair	$415	$62	$41	$166	0	5	0	0	0	0	2									Comfort			X					X				X	X
Dynasty Dresser 2	$900	$135	$90	$360	0	0	0	0	0	0	2									Miscellaneous							X					X	X
Election Day Retro Space-Age Action Pinball	$1,750	$262	$175	$700	0	0	0	0	0	10	0									Electronics					X				X			X	
Elegant Chef FlameBay Gas Range	$900	$135	$90	$360	10	0	0	0	0	0	1									Appliances								X					X
Elixir of Life	$0	$0	$0	$0	0	0	0	0	0	0	0									Aspiration Rewards													
Empress's New Clothes Rack	$5,000	$750	$500	$2,000	0	0	0	0	0	0	0									Miscellaneous							X					X	
End-to-End Table	$135	$20	$13	$54	0	0	0	0	0	0	1									Surfaces					X		X		X			X	
Engineered Angst Full-Color Poster	$40	$0	$0	$0	0	0	0	0	0	0	2									Decorative		X										X	
Engineered Angst Poster in Red	$40	$0	$0	$0	0	0	0	0	0	0	2									Decorative		X										X	
Enterprise Office Concepts Bushmaster Tele-Prompter	$0	$0	$0	$0	0	0	0	0	0	0	0			X						Career Rewards		X											
Enterprise Office Freestanding Game Rack	$4,000	$600	$400	$1,600	0	0	0	0	0	10	2									Miscellaneous	X				X				X			X	
ErgoSupreme Dining Chair	$325	$48	$32	$130	0	7	0	0	0	0	2									Comfort			X					X				X	X
Exceptionally Expensive Clothing Collator	$5,000	$750	$500	$2,000	0	0	0	0	0	0	0									Miscellaneous		X					X					X	
Execucutter	$1,000	$150	$100	$400	0	0	0	0	0	0	0									Career Rewards		X											
Epikouros "Sleek Cuisine" Counter	$335	$50	$33	$134	0	0	0	0	0	0	2									Surfaces								X					X
Epikouros "Sleek Cuisine" Island	$0	$0	$0	$0	0	0	0	0	0	0	3									Surfaces								X	X				X
Exerto 5000 Multipress	$1,400	$210	$140	$560	0	0	0	0	0	0	0					X				Career Rewards									X				
Exerto Punching Bag	$0	$0	$0	$0	0	0	0	0	0	4	0					X				Hobbies									X		X		
Exercise Machine	$0	$0	$0	$0	0	0	0	0	0	4	0					X				Career Rewards									X				
Exerto Selffig Obstacle Course	$0	$0	$0	$0	0	0	0	0	3	6	0					X				Decorative				X							X		
Exotic (Non)Screen from Simports, Ltd.	$900	$135	$90	$360	0	0	0	0	0	6	2									Decorative					X				X			X	
Exotic Reflections Mirror	$340	$51	$34	$136	0	0	0	0	0	0	0			X						Decorative						X	X					X	
Exploding Dragon Dining Table	$755	$113	$75	$302	0	0	0	0	0	0	1									Surfaces			X									X	X
Extra Pep Coffeemaker	$85	$12	$8	$34	0	0	0	0	0	0	0						X			Appliances								X	X				X
Falling Fern	$111	$16	$11	$44	0	0	0	0	0	0	2									Decorative				X	X				X			X	X
Fancifully Fuzzy Fern	$70	$10	$7	$28	0	0	0	0	0	0	1									Decorative				X	X				X		X	X	X
Farstar e3 Telescope	$2,100	$315	$210	$840	0	0	0	0	0	10	0						X			Hobbies				X							X	X	
Filigree Facebowl by Imperial Plumbing Works	$610	$91	$61	$244	0	0	6	-1	0	0	2									Plumbing						X						X	X

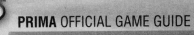

Object	Price	Initial Depreciation	Daily Depreciation	Depreciation Limit	Category
Lunatech Amber Ceiling Lamp	$220	$33	$22	$88	Lighting
Lunatech B17/6	$135	$20	$13	$54	Lighting
Lunatech Spare Fixture in "Crimson Light"	$45	$6	$4	$18	Lighting
Lunatech Spare Fixture in "Grass"	$45	$6	$4	$18	Lighting
Lunatech Spare Fixture in "Ocean"	$45	$6	$4	$18	Lighting
Luxiary "Ample King" Dining Table	$850	$127	$85	$340	Surfaces
Luxiary King Armchair	$1,200	$180	$120	$480	Comfort
Luxuriare Loveseat	$900	$135	$90	$360	Comfort
Magical Mystery's "Shape, Rattle & Roll"	$30	$4	$3	$12	Miscellaneous
Manor House Paree Dining Table	$900	$135	$90	$360	Surfaces
Manor House Multi-Mirror	$160	$24	$16	$64	Decorative
Maxis' Game Simulator	$1,080	$162	$108	$432	Electronics
Mentionable Porcelain Toilet	$560	$84	$56	$224	Plumbing
MeroKkan End Table	$210	$31	$21	$84	Surfaces
MeroKkan Loveseat	$500	$75	$50	$200	Comfort
Milana Royale Dining Table	$850	$127	$85	$340	Surfaces
Moderniste Dining Chair	$200	$30	$20	$80	Comfort
Modular Image Full-length Mirror	$150	$22	$15	$60	Decorative
Money Tree	$0	$0	$0	$0	Aspiration Rewards
Moneywell Computer	$1,000	$150	$100	$400	Electronics
Moar is More Coffee Table	$225	$33	$22	$90	Surfaces
Mr. Bearlybutts	$365	$54	$36	$146	Comfort
Musee Public "Collection Sculpture"	$200	$30	$20	$80	Decorative
Mystic Life "Flower Vase"	$150	$22	$15	$60	Decorative
Narcisco Rubbish Bin	$45	$6	$4	$18	Miscellaneous
Neon Flamingo	$75	$0	$4	$0	Decorative
Neukum Systems "Art of Darkness" Heavy Metal Wall Speaker	$400	$60	$40	$160	Electronics
Neukum Systems "Bubblegum Sugar" Pop Wall Speaker	$400	$60	$40	$160	Electronics
Neukum Systems "En Fuego" Salsa Wall Speaker	$400	$60	$40	$160	Electronics
Neukum Systems "Glo Stik" Techno Wall Speaker	$400	$60	$40	$160	Electronics
Neukum Systems "The Badunkadunk" Hip Hop Wall Speaker	$400	$60	$40	$160	Electronics

Table continues on page 335

Object Directory continued

Object	Price	Initial Depreciation	Daily Depreciation	Depreciation Limit	Hunger	Comfort	Hygiene	Bladder	Energy	Fun	Environment	Cleaning	Study	Charisma	Creativity	Body	Logic	Mechanical	Cooking	Function	Kids	Study	Dining Room	Outside	Living Room	Bathroom	Bedroom	Kitchen	Miscellaneous	Street	Outdoor	Shopping	Food
In the Beginning	$600	$0	$0	$0	0	0	0	0	0	0	4									Decorative		X			X		X					X	X
Independent Expressions Inc. Easel	$350	$52	$35	$140	0	0	0	0	0	0	0				X					Hobbies		X			X						X	X	
Inverted Vertigo, Cover Art	$80	$0	$0	$0	0	0	0	0	0	0	1									Decorative	X				X		X					X	
It's MYSHUNO! (The Fabulously Zany Party Game)	$870	$130	$87	$348	0	0	0	0	0	10	0									Hobbies					X	X						X	
Juniper Bonsai Tree	$60	$0	$0	$0	0	0	0	0	0	0	2									Decorative				X			X				X		
Keister Kompanion Barstool	$120	$18	$12	$48	0	3	0	0	0	0	0									Comfort			X		X			X				X	X
Kick BackYard Loungechair by Survivall	$185	$27	$18	$74	0	4	0	0	0	0	0									Comfort				X	X						X		
King for a Day Outdoor Chess Table	$130	$19	$13	$52	0	0	0	0	0	7	0						X			Hobbies				X	X						X		
Korean Keumungo	$399	$59	$39	$159	0	0	0	0	0	4	2				X					Decorative					X		X					X	
Kozy Kitsch Gnome	$80	$0	$0	$0	0	0	0	0	0	0	1									Decorative				X							X		
Krampft Industries "Hubbalubba Economy" Bathtub	$700	$105	$70	$280	0	4	5	0	0	0	0									Plumbing						X						X	
Krampft Industries Value Counter	$140	$21	$14	$56	0	0	0	0	0	0	0									Surfaces													
Lamp on the Half Shell	$90	$13	$9	$36	0	0	0	0	0	0	1									Lighting			X	X	X	X	X	X				X	X
Lap of Luxury Sofa	$1,700	$255	$170	$880	0	10	0	0	2	0	3									Comfort			X		X		X					X	
Legno's Modern Chandelier	$190	$28	$19	$76	0	0	0	0	0	0	2									Lighting		X	X	X	X	X	X	X				X	X
Light Effects Ceiling Lamp	$65	$9	$6	$26	0	0	0	0	0	0	1									Lighting		X	X	X	X	X		X				X	X
Light Orbiter Floor Lamp	$250	$37	$25	$100	0	0	0	0	0	0	1									Lighting			X	X	X	X	X	X				X	X
Little House Lantern	$80	$12	$8	$32	0	0	0	0	0	0	1									Lighting			X	X	X	X	X	X			X	X	X
Little Sister, W015	$2,800	$420	$280	$1,120	0	0	0	0	0	0	0									Electronics					X	X	X					X	
Llamark Electronic Cash Register	$2,015	$330	$201	$882	0	0	0	0	0	0	0									Electronics				X					X		X		
Loft Curtains by Sparse and Fine	$195	$29	$19	$78	0	0	0	0	0	0	2									Decorative		X	X	X	X		X	X			X	X	X
London's Famous Birthday Cake	$30	$4	$3	$12	0	0	0	0	0	0	0									Miscellaneous										X		X	X
Look Upon the Orient Mirror	$370	$55	$37	$148	0	0	0	0	0	0	2			X						Decorative	X		X		X		X	X			X	X	X
Love Tub	$0	$0	$0	$0	0	6	0	0	2	7	0									Aspiration Rewards				X	X	X	X				X	X	
Loveseat by Club Distress	$750	$112	$75	$300	0	8	0	0	2	1	2		X							Comfort			X		X	X	X	X				X	X
Lunatech "GaulleVanizer" Wall Sconce	$85	$12	$8	$34	0	0	0	0	0	0	1									Lighting		X	X		X	X	X	X				X	X
Lunatech "Lighten Up" Lighting Fixture	$75	$11	$7	$30	0	0	0	0	0	0	1									Lighting			X		X	X	X	X				X	X

Poisonous Forest (In Love with a Curse)	$5,500	$0	$0	$0	0	0	0	0	0	0	10									Decorative		X	X		X		X		X			X	
Polychromed Seating Surface With Cushion	$375	$56	$37	$150	0	5	0	0	0	0	0									Comfort			X									X	X
Poppin' Party Balloon Centerpiece	$7	$5	$20	0	0	0	0	0	0	0	0									Miscellaneous	X		X					X	X				
Porcelain Oval Mirror	$200	$30	$20	$80	0	0	0	0	0	0	1			X						Decorative					X	X	X					X	
PrevenTek Luminlight Streetlamp	$439	$65	$43	$175	0	0	0	0	0	0	2									Lighting				X						X	X		
PrevenTek Tri-Luminlight Streetlamp	$600	$90	$60	$240	0	0	0	0	0	0	3									Lighting				X						X	X		
Prints Charming Fingerprinting Scanner	$0	$0	$0	$0	0	0	0	0	0	4	0	X								Career Rewards													
Prisoner of Azkalamp	$35	$5	$3	$14	0	0	0	0	0	0	1									Lighting			X	X	X	X	X		X			X	
Produce Market Shingle	$99	$14	$9	$39	0	0	0	0	0	0	0									Decorative									X	X	X	X	X
Qadim Bauble Lamp	$150	$22	$15	$60	0	0	0	0	0	0	1									Lighting	X				X		X		X			X	
Queen Anne Coffee Table	$470	$70	$47	$180	0	0	0	0	0	0	0									Surfaces		X			X				X				
Rainy Day Main Street	$350	$0	$0	$0	0	0	0	0	0	0	3									Decorative		X	X		X		X					X	X
Rave Against the Machine Nightclub Lamp	$350	$52	$35	$140	0	0	0	0	0	0	2									Lighting		X	X		X		X		X			X	
Recycled Relaxer	$250	$37	$25	$100	0	5	0	0	0	0	0									Comfort					X				X			X	
Red vs. Blue Oil Portrait	$120	$0	$0	$0	0	0	0	0	0	0	1									Decorative		X	X		X		X					X	
Reflective Glass Mirror	$100	$15	$10	$40	0	0	0	0	0	0	1			X						Decorative					X	X	X		X			X	
Regulars Only Barstool	$650	$97	$65	$260	0	6	0	0	0	0	0									Comfort					X			X	X			X	
Renaissance Bookcase by Literary Designs	$950	$142	$95	$380	0	0	0	0	0	1	2	X						X	X	Hobbies		X			X		X						
ResiStall Astro Divider 7	$700	$105	$70	$280	0	10	0	10	0	0	0									Plumbing						X						X	X
Retratech "Office Pal" Economy Desk	$80	$12	$8	$32	0	0	0	0	0	0	0									Surfaces		X							X				
Retratech Padded Egg Chair	$150	$22	$15	$60	0	3	0	0	0	0	0									Comfort		X	X									X	X
Retro Lounge "High Liquidity" Juice Bar	$800	$120	$80	$320	0	0	0	0	0	3	0									Miscellaneous			X		X			X					
'Right Away' Community Trash-Can	$75	$11	$7	$30	0	0	0	0	0	0	0									Miscellaneous									X	X	X		
Rip Co. Little Baker Oven	$100	$15	$10	$40	0	0	0	0	0	1	0								X	Miscellaneous	X												
Rip Co. Toy Bin	$55	$8	$5	$22	0	0	0	0	0	7	0									Miscellaneous	X												
Rip Co. Wobbly Wabbit Head	$35	$5	$3	$14	0	0	0	0	0	10	0			X						Miscellaneous	X												
Rip Co. Xylophone	$40	$6	$4	$16	0	0	0	0	0	4	0				X					Miscellaneous	X												
Rob R. Barron " Nouveau" Wardrobe	$1,000	$150	$100	$400	0	0	0	0	0	0	3									Miscellaneous							X						
Rolling Hills by H. Sean	$400	$0	$0	$0	0	0	0	0	0	0	3									Decorative		X	X		X		X		X				X
Rubber Tree Plant	$165	$24	$16	$66	0	0	0	0	0	0	1									Decorative			X	X	X			X	X		X	X	X
Sanitation Station Baby Changing Table	$400	$60	$40	$160	0	0	10	0	0	0	0									Miscellaneous	X								X				
Satinistics Loveseat	150	$22	$15	$60	0	5	0	0	2	0	0									Comfort					X				X				
Schokolade 890 Chocolate Manufacturing Facility	$0	$0	$0	$0	0	0	0	0	0	1	0								X	Career Rewards													

Table continues on page 337

Object Directory (continued)

Object	Price	Initial Depreciation	Daily Depreciation	Depreciation Limit	Hunger	Comfort	Hygiene	Bladder	Energy	Fun	Environment	Cleaning	Study	Charisma	Creativity	Body	Logic	Mechanical	Cooking	Function	Kids	Study	Dining Room	Outside	Living Room	Bathroom	Bedroom	Kitchen	Misc.	Street	Outdoor	Shopping	Food
Neukum Systems "The Cold Train" RGB Wall Speaker	$400	$60	$40	$160	0	0	0	0	0	2	0									Electronics		X			X		X		X		X	X	X
Neukum Systems Wall Speaker	$60	$40	$40	$160	0	0	0	0	0	2	2									Electronics		X			X		X					X	X
No-Fuss Ficus	$400	$0	$0	$0	0	0	0	0	0	0	7									Decorative	X	X	X	X	X		X	X	X		X	X	X
Noodlesoother	$300	$0	$0	$0	0	0	0	0	0	0	2									Aspiration Rewards		X			X		X					X	
Novellas Nouveau Bookcase	$800	$120	$80	$320	0	3	0	0	0	0	2									Hobbies	X	X			X		X					X	
NuMica Allinall Card Table	$95	$14	$9	$38	0	6	0	0	0	4	0	X				X		X	X	Surfaces	X	X	X	X	X			X	X		X	X	X
Oaktowne Dining Chair	$615	$92	$61	$246	0	6	0	0	0	0	2									Comfort			X	X	X			X			X	X	
Oaktowne East Side Dining Chair	$250	$37	$25	$100	0	3	0	0	0	1	7									Comfort	X	X	X		X		X	X	X		X	X	X
Obviously Modern Wall Mirror	$399	$59	$39	$159	0	0	0	0	0	0	2			X						Decorative		X			X	X	X					X	
Oil "Fantasy Scape"	$690	$103	$69	$276	0	0	0	0	0	4	10									Decorative		X		X	X	X	X				X		
Ol' Grandfather Clock	$3,500	$525	$350	$1,400	0	0	0	0	0	2	3									Decorative	X	X	X	X	X		X					X	
Old Boys Club Commercial Counter	$710	$106	$71	$284	0	0	0	0	0	3	2								X	Surfaces								X					X
Old Fashioned Change Room	$690	$0	$0	$0	0	0	0	0	0	0	0									Miscellaneous									X			X	
Olive Peynter's City SkyScape	$4,000	$0	$0	$0	0	0	0	0	0	0	10									Decorative	X	X			X		X					X	
On A Pedestal by Yucan Byall	$5,000	$0	$0	$0	0	5	0	0	0	0	2									Decorative	X	X			X			X	X			X	X
Open-Wall Wall Fan	$3,500	$0	$0	$0	0	0	0	0	0	0	2							X		Decorative	X	X			X	X	X	X				X	
Organic Material's Barstool	$700	$105	$70	$280	0	7	0	0	0	0	0					X				Comfort			X	X	X	X	X	X	X		X		X
Outdoor Ergo Ergonomic Chair by Gudtner-Ebadi Furnishings	$320	$48	$32	$128	0	5	0	0	2	0	2									Comfort				X						X	X		X
Paper Moon Ceiling Light	$300	$45	$30	$120	0	0	0	0	0	0	0									Lighting		X			X	X	X		X			X	X
Park Plates Mini Outdoor Dining Table	$15	$7	$11	$46	0	0	0	0	0	0	0									Surfaces				X						X	X		X
Pasteur's HomoGenius Smart Milk	$0	$0	$0	$0	0	0	0	0	0	0	0									Aspiration Rewards								X					
PatioPlastics Dining Chair	$80	$12	$8	$32	0	2	0	0	0	0	0									Comfort			X	X	X		X	X	X	X	X		X
Peace of Garbage Can	$30	$4	$3	$12	0	0	0	0	0	0	0									Miscellaneous									X		X		
Piece of Quiet Park Bench	$500	$75	$50	$200	0	8	0	0	0	0	0									Comfort				X	X	X	X			X			
PINEGULTCHER Outdoor Minitable	$220	$33	$22	$88	0	0	0	0	0	0	0									Surfaces			X	X	X	X	X	X	X	X	X	X	X
Pix-Arm Drafting Lamp	$30	$4	$3	$12	0	0	0	0	0	0	0									Lighting	X	X	X		X		X		X		X	X	
Plasticity NodePod by Yoko Onasis	$500	$75	$50	$200	0	6	0	0	2	0	1									Comfort					X		X		X			X	

SmokeSentry SmokeSniffer 3000	§50	§7	§5	§20	0	0	0	0	0	0	0									Electronics	X	X	X	X	X		X	X					
Social Climbing Ivy Floor Lamp	§105	§15	§10	§42	0	0	0	0	0	0	1									Lighting		X	X		X		X		X			X	
Social Climbing Ivy Table Lamp	§79	§11	§7	§31	0	0	0	0	0	0	1									Lighting	X	X	X		X		X		X				
Sofa by Club Distress	§1,450	§217	§145	§580	0	8	0	0	2	0	2									Comfort					X							X	
Sofa of Substance	§1,625	§243	§162	§650	0	10	0	0	2	0	2									Comfort					X							X	
Soma "Wall-Eye" Large Screen Flat-Panel Television	§8,000	§1,200	§800	§3,200	0	0	0	0	0	10	7					X			X	Electronics					X		X		X				
Soma 44" PancakeTek Television	§3,500	§525	§350	§1,400	0	0	0	0	0	8	3					X			X	Electronics					X		X		X				
Soma AudioGeek TK421 Tower System	§2,550	§382	§255	§1,020	0	0	0	0	0	10	2					X				Electronics		X			X		X						
Spherical Splendor	§225	§0	§0	§0	0	0	0	0	0	0	2									Decorative	X		X		X	X	X					X	X
St. Ajoque Reproductions "See Plus" Mirror	§750	§112	§75	§300	0	0	0	0	0	0	4			X						Decorative					X	X	X					X	
Stark Inspiration Chair	§800	§120	§80	§200	0	7	0	0	0	0	2									Comfort		X										X	X
Stewart Mourning Café Curtains	§97	§14	§9	§38	0	0	0	0	0	0	1									Decorative						X	X	X	X			X	
Stiff by Superfluous Seating	§750	§112	§75	§300	0	6	0	0	0	0	2									Comfort					X			X	X			X	
Studio Bakonmi Deluxe Chair	§680	§102	§68	§272	0	8	0	0	0	0	0									Comfort					X				X			X	
Studio Bakonmi Deluxe Lounge	§830	§124	§83	§332	0	8	0	0	0	0	2									Comfort					X				X			X	
Studio Bakonmi Deluxe Loveseat	§1,100	§165	§110	§440	0	8	0	0	2	0	0									Comfort					X							X	
Sunflowers	§45	§6	§4	§18	0	0	0	0	0	0	1									Decorative				X	X	X		X	X			X	X
Superlative Sink by "The Greatest Designer Alive"	§250	§37	§25	§100	0	0	5	0	0	0	0									Plumbing						X		X	X			X	X
Suspense	§475	§0	§0	§0	0	0	0	0	0	0	4									Decorative		X	X		X		X					X	X
Su-Tove Armoire	§1,200	§180	§120	§480	0	0	0	0	0	0	3									Miscellaneous							X						
Sweet Tooth Survivor Pinball	§1,750	§262	§175	§700	0	0	0	0	0	10	2									Electronics					X				X				
Swing Kidz Deluxe Swing Set	§450	§67	§45	§180	0	0	0	0	0	7	0									Miscellaneous	X			X							X		
Tablablanca from Simporters, Ltd.	§690	§103	§69	§276	0	0	0	0	0	0	0									Surfaces			X										X
Tea Party in Teak	§100	§15	§10	§40	0	3	0	0	0	0	0									Comfort		X	X					X				X	X
TechTonic Touch Toaster Oven	§100	§15	§10	§40	1	0	0	0	0	0	0									Appliances								X					
Tempered Tea Table	§221	§33	§22	§88	0	0	0	0	0	0	0									Surfaces		X			X				X				
The "Gold-end" Ratio Table	§190	§28	§19	§76	0	0	0	0	0	0	0									Surfaces					X		X					X	
The "Spike Light"	§150	§22	§15	§60	0	0	0	0	0	0	1									Lighting				X					X		X		
The Black and White "Bare" Bath	§900	§135	§90	§360	0	6	6	0	0	0	2									Plumbing						X			X				
The Eclectic and Enigmatic Energizer	§0	§0	§0	§0	1	1	1	1	1	1	9									Aspiration Rewards													

Table continues on page 339

Object Directory continued

Object	Price	Initial Depreciation	Daily Depreciation	Depreciation Limit	Hunger	Comfort	Hygiene	Bladder	Energy	Fun	Environment	Cleaning	Study	Charisma	Creativity	Body	Logic	Mechanical	Cooking	Function	Kids	Study	Dining Room	Outside	Living Room	Bathroom	Bedroom	Kitchen	Miscellaneous	Street	Outdoor	Shopping	Food
ScienStone "Dramatic" Coffee Table	$340	$51	$34	$136																Surfaces					X							X	
Scraps Ranch "CafeMate" Coffee Table	$90	$13	$9	$36																Surfaces		X	X		X			X	X			X	X
SCTC Universal Public Phone	$550	$82	$55	$220																Electronics		X			X		X	X	X	X	X	X	X
Searing Indifference Wall Poster	$50	$0	$0	$0							1									Decorative					X		X		X			X	
Seatris by Ima Hack	$1,220	$183	$122	$488		8			2											Comfort					X								
Secure Sentinel Post Lamp	$185	$27	$18	$74							2									Lighting				X					X	X	X	X	
SensiTwitch Lie Finder Rewards	$950	$0	$0	$0																Career					X							X	
Serenity Sitter	$800	$120	$80	$320		8														Comfort					X								
Sewage Brothers Resteze Toilet	$300	$45	$30	$120			5	10												Plumbing						X						X	
Sewage Brothers Resteze Urinal	$400	$60	$40	$160				10												Plumbing						X							
Shiny Things Inc. Whisp-Aire Dishwasher	$950	$142	$95	$380																Appliances								X	X			X	X
Shiny Things, Inc. Grandiose Grill	$1,100	$165	$110	$440	10															Appliances				X				X			X	X	X
Shocking Pink Flamingo	$12	$1	$1	$4						4	3									Decorative				X					X	X	X	X	
Shoji Table Lantern	$175	$26	$17	$70							1									Lighting					X		X		X			X	
Sill-Length Tieback Curtains	$300	$45	$30	$120							3									Decorative	X				X		X		X			X	
SimCity at Night	$425	$63	$42	$170						4	3				X					Decorative	X	X	X		X				X	X	X	X	X
SimCity SynapseSnapper Industrial Sign	$99	$14	$9	$39							1									Decorative				X					X		X		
SimLine Table Phone	$50	$7	$5	$20																Electronics					X			X				X	X
SimLine Wall Phone	$75	$11	$7	$30																Electronics					X			X				X	X
Simple Sink from Krampft Industries	$275	$41	$27	$110																Plumbing						X		X	X			X	
Simple Sit Chair	$200	$30	$20	$80		3					1									Comfort	X		X		X				X			X	
Simple Structure End Table	$60	$9	$6	$24																Surfaces		X			X		X		X			X	
Simple Tub from Krampft Industries	$1,500	$225	$150	$600		3	8													Plumbing						X			X			X	
Simply Spindle Coffee Table	$40	$6	$4	$16																Surfaces	X				X				X			X	
SimSafety V Burglar Alarm	$250	$37	$25	$100																Electronics	X	X	X		X		X	X	X			X	
Simsanto Inc. Biotech Station	$0	$0	$0	$0						4							X			Career Rewards		X					X						
SimVac	$370	$55	$37	$148							10									Miscellaneous									X			X	
SimSentry Clothing Booth	$0	$0	$0	$0																Aspiration Rewards													

Item	Price	Category
Transcendence by Joan Schnitzel	$800	Decorative
Traumatime "Incision Precision" Surgical Training Station	$0	Career Rewards
Trellisar Wedding Arch	$800	Miscellaneous
Tri-Tip Table	$155	Surfaces
Trottco 27" Multivid IV Television	$500	Electronics
Tulip Light from Luxiary	$900	Lighting
Ultra Funky Curtain Clothes	$70	Decorative
VaporWare Submergence Spa	$8,500	Plumbing
VeggiStuf Produce Bin	$300	Appliances
Veil of Dreams	$70	Decorative
Victor Victorian Pedestal Sink	$300	Plumbing
Vision Mirrors "Past Reflections"	$1,100	Decorative
VroomMaster 4000	$149	Miscellaneous
Waterfall	$35	Decorative
Wall Flowers Sconce	$149	Lighting
Way-Back Recliner	$99	Comfort
Wear's the Sale? Shop Sign	$510	Miscellaneous
Werkbunnst Stonewood Dresser	$790	Miscellaneous
Werkbunnst/Shuttlecraft Recliner	$300	Comfort
Whatay Buffet	$300	Surfaces
Whodunit? Table Lamp	$180	Lighting
Will Lloyd Wright Dollhouse	$650	Miscellaneous
Winter Blossoms	$550	Decorative
Wishy-Washer from Brandname LX	$200	Appliances
Wooden Post n' Lamp	$220	Lighting
XLR8R2 Food Processor	$400	Appliances
Zecutime Cityside Loveseat	$550	Comfort
Zecutime Cityside Sofa	$335	Comfort
Zecutine Social Chair	$350	Comfort
Zenu Meditation Sleeper	$350	Comfort

Object Directory (continued)

Column groups: **Price and Depreciation** (Price, Initial Depreciation, Daily Depreciation, Depreciation Limit) · **Needs** (Hunger, Comfort, Hygiene, Bladder, Energy, Fun, Environment) · **Skills** (Cleaning, Study, Charisma, Creativity, Body, Logic, Mechanical, Cooking) · **Function** · **Room Sort** (Kids, Study, Dining Room, Outside, Living Room, Bathroom, Bedroom, Kitchen) · **Community Sort** (Miscellaneous, Street, Outdoor, Shopping, Food)

Object	Price	Init. Dep.	Daily Dep.	Dep. Limit	Hun	Com	Hyg	Bla	Ene	Fun	Env	Charisma	Function	Kids	Study	Dining	Outside	Living	Bath	Bedroom	Kitchen	Misc	Street	Outdoor	Shopping	Food
The Fourth Element Wall Hanging	$5,000	$0	$0	$0	0	0	0	0	0	0	8		Decorative		X	X		X		X	X	X			X	
The Glassic Chair	$320	$92	$92	$368	0	2	0	0	0	0	2		Comfort			X		X				X			X	X
The Great Dress Rack	$3,000	$450	$300	$1,200	0	0	0	0	0	0	0		Miscellaneous					X		X		X			X	
The "Grillinator "BigBQ"	$920	$138	$92	$368	—	0	0	0	0	0	0		Appliances			X	X	X			X			X	X	X
The Inner Light	$210	$31	$21	$84	0	0	0	0	0	0	1		Lighting		X	X		X		X	X	X			X	
The Kinder Kuddler	$50	$7	$5	$20	0	0	0	0	12	0	0		Miscellaneous	X						X		X			X	
The Kinder Kontainer	$200	$30	$20	$80	0	0	0	0	0	0	0		Miscellaneous	X	X			X		X		X			X	
The Lady On Red	$275	$41	$27	$110	0	0	0	0	0	0	2		Decorative		X	X		X				X			X	
The Lone Daisy	$80	$0	$0	$0	0	0	0	0	0	0	1		Decorative			X			X		X	X			X	X
The Meaning of Fruit	$285	$0	$0	$0	0	0	0	0	0	0	5		Decorative			X					X	X			X	X
The Measure of a Sim Wooden Model	$1,500	$0	$0	$0	0	0	0	0	0	0	7		Decorative		X			X				X				
Monster Under My Bed by Little Timmy	$100	$15	$10	$40	0	0	0	0	0	0	1		Decorative	X						X		X			X	
My-Chi Sculpture Form	$2,500	$0	$0	$0	0	0	0	0	0	0	2		Decorative				X	X				X		X		
Nofowle Armchair	$2,600	$390	$260	$1,040	0	7	0	0	4	0	0		Comfort		X			X		X		X			X	
Old-timer Recliner	$155	$23	$15	$62	0	6	0	0	4	0	0		Comfort					X		X		X			X	
Simulated Succulent	$650	$97	$65	$316	0	0	0	0	0	0	5		Decorative			X	X	X	X	X	X	X		X	X	
Slim System, by Jim Slimboy	$60	$24	$16	$64	0	0	0	0	0	0	0		Comfort					X		X		X			X	
Soma "Sleep Well" Talking Table	$1,050	$157	$105	$420	0	4	0	0	6	0	10		Surfaces		X	X		X	X	X		X			X	X
Thinking Cap	$0	$0	$0	$0	0	0	0	0	0	0	1		Aspiration Rewards													
Watt is it Table Lamp	$35	$5	$3	$14	0	0	0	0	0	0	0		Lighting		X	X		X	X	X	X	X		X	X	
Thrice As Nice Floor Lamp by Lumpen Lumeniat	$100	$15	$10	$40	0	0	0	0	0	0	1		Lighting		X	X		X	X	X	X	X		X	X	
Tibetan Desk	$670	$100	$67	$268	0	0	0	0	0	0	0		Surfaces		X			X		X		X			X	
Tinkle Trainer 6000 Potty Chair	$70	$10	$7	$28	0	4	0	10	0	0	0		Comfort	X					X						X	
Titania Vineyards 1914 Toasting Set	$350	$52	$35	$140	0	0	0	0	0	0	2		Miscellaneous			X		X			X	X			X	X
Torcher "Luminescence" Sconce	$202	$30	$20	$80	0	0	0	0	0	0	2		Lighting		X	X		X	X	X	X	X		X	X	
Torcher Clamshell Wall Sconce	$75	$11	$7	$30	0	0	0	0	0	0	1		Lighting		X	X		X	X	X	X	X		X	X	
Tornado Torch Floor Lamp	$330	$49	$33	$132	0	0	0	0	0	0	2		Lighting		X	X		X	X	X	X	X		X	X	
Total Mirror	$303	$45	$30	$121	0	0	0	0	0	0	2	X	Miscellaneous					X	X	X		X			X	
Touch of Teak Bed	$1,800	$270	$180	$720	0	9	0	0	8	0	3		Comfort							X		X			X	
Touch of Teak Plymouth Armoire	$812	$121	$81	$324	0	0	0	0	0	0	2		Miscellaneous							X		X			X	

The Need effects numbers in this directory go into more detail than the figures in the in-game catalog, breaking down Need effects (where possible) by interaction. For example, the catalog Comfort rating for loveseats and sofas is actually for the Lounge interaction, not the Sit interaction (which has a lower rating than posted). The number in the in-game catalog is always whatever is the highest scoring interaction for the object and Need regardless of whether it's the most common use.

These ratings are a somewhat subjective reflection of an object's rate of Need satisfaction or amount of one-time satisfaction.

Also, many objects have Need maximums. These numbers are the point at which the Need simply stops fulfilling. Often, the Sim will be booted from the interaction when the Need reaches the object's max. Fun and Comfort objects allow a Sim to continue past these maximums but only under conditions described above (see "Exit Conditions," above). If no maximum is listed, the interaction can satisfy it all the way to 100.

Comfort

Comfort objects offer Sims places to sit but also provide Comfort, Energy, and a venue for socializing.

Dining Chairs

Dining chairs can be placed anywhere but are primarily intended for dining tables and desks.

PatioPlastics Dining Chair
- ◆ Price: §80
- ◆ Need Effects: Comfort 2

Tea Party in Teak
- ◆ Price: §100
- ◆ Need Effects: Comfort 3

Retratech Padded Egg Chair
- ◆ Price: §150
- ◆ Need Effects: Comfort 3

Simple Sit Chair
- ◆ Price: §200
- ◆ Need Effects: Comfort 3

OakTowne East Side Dining Chair
- ◆ Price: §250
- ◆ Need Effects: Comfort 3

Contempto Penn Station Side Chair
- ◆ Price: §310
- ◆ Need Effects: Comfort 4

Zecutime Social Chair

◆ Price: §335

◆ Need Effects: Comfort 4

Polychromed Seating Surface With Cushion

◆ Price: §375

◆ Need Effects: Comfort 5

Cowboy's Caboose Chair

◆ Price: §385

◆ Need Effects: Comfort 5

Dynasty Dining Chair

◆ Price: §415

◆ Need Effects: Comfort 5

Plasticity NodePod by Yoko Onasis

◆ Price: §500

◆ Need Effects: Comfort 6

OakTowne Dining Chair

◆ Price: §615

◆ Need Effects: Comfort 6

Moderniste Dining Chair

◆ Price: §720

◆ Need Effects: Comfort 6, Environment 2

Stark Inspiration Chair

◆ Price: §800

◆ Need Effects: Comfort 7, Environment 2

Diamondback by Desert Designs

◆ Price: §900

◆ Need Effects: Comfort 7, Environment 2

ErgoSupreme Dining Chair

◆ Price: §1,000

◆ Need Effects: Comfort 7, Environment 2

Bon Appetit Dining Chair

◆ Price: §1,100

◆ Need Effects: Comfort 7, Environment 2

Living Chairs

Living chairs are essentially couches for one, built more for comfort than for function. Fortunately, they offer Comfort in spades.

Unlike dining chairs, living chairs can't be scooted and, thus, can't be used at dining tables or desks.

It's best to place these right next to a bookcase or in front of the TV.

Contempto Good Livin' Chair
- Price: §80
- Need Effects: 4

The Nofowle Armchair
- Price: §155
- Need Effects: Comfort 5

Recycled Relaxer
- Price: §250
- Need Effects: Comfort 5

Mr. Bearlybutts
- Price: §365
- Need Effects: Comfort 5

Contempto Adirondack Chair
- Price: §400
- Need Effects: Comfort 6

Blue Suede Chair
- Price: §611
- Need Effects: Comfort 7

Armchair by Club Design
- Price: §629
- Need Effects: Comfort 7

Studio Bakonmi Deluxe Chair
- Price: §680
- Need Effects: Comfort 8

Serenity Sitter
- Price: §900
- Need Effects: Comfort 8, Environment 2

Studio Bakonmi Deluxe Lounge
- Price: §830
- Need Effects: Comfort 8, Environment 2

The Classic Chair
- Price: §920
- Need Effects: Comfort 9, Environment 2

Luxiary King Armchair
- Price: §1,200
- Need Effects: Comfort 9, Environment 2

Recliners

Recliners are similar to living chairs in their offer of Comfort; recliners of a given Comfort score are usually a bit more expensive than a similarly satisfying living chair. They offer the extra benefit of being a valid place to sleep but consume much more space.

Recliners offer two interactions:

◆ Sit: Satisfies Comfort

◆ Nap: Satisfies Energy and Comfort, not available when Energy fully satisfied

Kick BackYard Loungechair by Survivall

◆ Price: $130

◆ Need Effects: Comfort 4, Energy 1 (Nap)

◆ Need Max: Energy up to 20 (Nap)

Way-Back Recliner

◆ Price: $149

◆ Need Effects: Comfort 5, Energy 1 (Nap)

◆ Need Max: Energy up to 25 (Nap)

Contempto Outdoor Living Lounge

◆ Price: $420

◆ Need Effects: Comfort 6, Energy 2 (Nap)

◆ Need Max: Energy up to 40 (Nap)

? = (C ^ 11)?

◆ Price: $470

◆ Need Effects: Comfort 6, Energy 2 (Nap)

◆ Need Max: Energy up to 40 (Nap)

Cheap Eazzzzze Puffy Recliner

◆ Price: $515

◆ Need Effects: Comfort 7, Energy 2 (Nap)

◆ Need Max: Energy up to 50 (Nap)

The Old-Timer Recliner

◆ Price: $650

◆ Need Effects: Comfort 7, Energy 2 (Nap)

◆ Need Max: Energy up to 70 (Nap)

Werkbunnst/Shuttlecraft Recliner

◆ Price: $790

◆ Need Effects: Comfort 7, Energy 2 (Nap), Environment 2

◆ Need Max: Energy up to 67 (Nap)

Chez Chaise

◆ Price: $900

◆ Need Effects: Comfort 8, Energy 2 (Nap), Environment 2

◆ Need Max: Energy up to 80 (Nap)

Sofas & Loveseats

Sofas can give Comfort, Energy, or Fun. They're also a venue for group talk and have several object-assisted Sim-to-Sim interactions (e.g., Cuddle, Make Out, etc.)

Sofas seat three Sims and loveseats seat two.

---

note

Object-assisted interactions are ones that two Sims can do if they're both engaged with the same of object of a particular kind. For example, to cuddle, both Sims must be using the same sofa or bed.

All sofas have the following interactions:

◆ Sit: Satisfies Comfort

◆ Lounge: Satisfies Comfort faster, but can't do other things (talk, watch TV, etc.)

◆ Nap: Satisfies Energy

◆ Play: Satisfies Fun

Satinistics Loveseat

◆ Price: $150

◆ Need Effects: Comfort 4 (Sit), Comfort 5 (Lounge), Energy 2 (Nap), Fun 4 (Play)

◆ Need Max: Energy up to 20 (Nap)

Futonesque Fantasy Sofa
◆ Price: $180
◆ Need Effects: Comfort 4 (Sit), Comfort 5 (Lounge), Energy 2 (Nap), Fun 4 (Play)
◆ Need Max: Energy up to 20 (Nap)

Coming Up Roses Loveseat by OakTowne
◆ Price: $220
◆ Need Effects: Comfort 5 (Sit), Comfort 6 (Lounge), Energy 2 (Nap), Fun 4 (Play)
◆ Need Max: Energy up to 20 (Nap)

Durable Value Sofa
◆ Price: $250
◆ Need Effects: Comfort 5 (Sit), Comfort 6 (Lounge), Energy 2 (Nap), Fun 4 (Play)
◆ Need Max: Energy up to 20 (Nap)

Floral Fantasy Sofa by OakTowne
◆ Price: $360
◆ Need Effects: Comfort 5 (Sit), Comfort 6 (Lounge), Energy 2 (Nap), Fun 4 (Play)
◆ Need Max: Energy up to 20 (Nap)

Zecutime Cityside Loveseat
◆ Price: $400
◆ Need Effects: Comfort 6 (Sit), Comfort 7 (Lounge), Energy 2 (Nap), Fun 4 (Play)
◆ Need Max: Energy up to 40 (Nap)

Contempto Adirondack Loveseat
◆ Price: $450
◆ Need Effects: Comfort 6 (Sit), Comfort 7 (Lounge), Energy 2 (Nap), Fun 4 (Play)
◆ Need Max: Energy up to 40 (Nap)

Merokkan Loveseat
◆ Price: $500
◆ Need Effects: Comfort 7 (Sit/Nap), Comfort 7 (Lounge), Energy 2 (Nap), Fun 4 (Play)
◆ Need Max: Energy up to 50 (Nap)

Zecutime Cityside Sofa
◆ Price: $550
◆ Need Effects: Comfort 7 (Sit/Nap), Comfort 7 (Lounge), Energy 2 (Nap), Fun 4 (Play)
◆ Need Max: Energy up to 40 (Nap)

Loveseat by Club Distress
◆ Price: $750
◆ Need Effects: Comfort 7 (Sit/Nap), Comfort 8 (Lounge), Energy 2 (Nap), Fun 4 (Play)
◆ Need Max: Energy up to 70 (Nap)

Be There Designs "Bazaar Sofa"
◆ Price: $800
◆ Need Effects: Comfort 7 (Sit/Nap), Comfort 8 (Lounge), Energy 2 (Nap), Fun 4 (Play)
◆ Need Max: Energy up to 50 (Nap)

Luxuriare Loveseat
◆ Price: $900
◆ Need Effects: Comfort 8 (Sit/Nap), Comfort 9 (Lounge), Energy 2 (Nap), Fun 4 (Play)
◆ Need Max: Energy up to 70 (Nap)

Studio Bakonmi Deluxe Loveseat
◆ Price: $770
◆ Need Effects: Comfort 7 (Sit/Nap), Comfort 8 (Lounge), Energy 2 (Nap), Fun 4 (Play)
◆ Need Max: Energy up to 67 (Nap)

Seatris by Ima Hack
◆ Price: $1,220
◆ Need Effects: Comfort 7 (Sit/Nap), Comfort 8 (Lounge), Energy 2 (Nap), Fun 4 (Play)
◆ Need Max: Energy up to 69 (Nap)

Baroccoco Loveseat by MIRE
◆ Price: $1,250
◆ Need Effects: Comfort 8 (Sit/Nap), Comfort 8 (Lounge), Energy 2 (Nap), Fun 4 (Play)
◆ Need Max: Energy up to 80 (Nap)

Sofa by Club Distress
◆ Price: $1,450
◆ Need Effects: Comfort 7 (Sit/Nap), Comfort 8 (Lounge), Energy 2 (Nap), Fun 4 (Play), Environment 2
◆ Need Max: Energy up to 70 (Nap)

Baroccoco Sofa by MiRE

- Price: §1,500
- Need Effects: Comfort 9 (Sit/Nap), Comfort 9 (Lounge), Energy 2 (Nap), Fun 4 (Play), Environment 2
- Need Max: Energy up to 80 (Nap)

Candy Coated Sofa

- Price: §1,570
- Need Effects: Comfort 9 (Sit/Nap), Comfort 10 (Lounge), Energy 2 (Nap), Fun 4 (Play), Environment 2
- Need Max: Energy up to 82 (Nap)

Sofa of Substance

- Price: §1,625
- Need Effects: Comfort 9 (Sit/Nap), Comfort 10 (Lounge), Energy 2 (Nap), Fun 4 (Play), Environment 2
- Need Max: Energy up to 90 (Nap)

Lap of Luxury Sofa

- Price: §1,700
- Need Effects: Comfort 9 (Sit/Nap), Comfort 10 (Lounge), Energy 2 (Nap), Fun 4 (Play), Environment 2
- Need Max: Energy up to 90 (Nap)

Beds

Though Sims can sleep in other places, beds are the primary vehicle for efficient, restful sleep. Sleeping on beds provides simultaneous Energy and Comfort. Other interactions allow satisfaction of just Comfort, increasing of Environment (making bed), and as a conduit for several *very* important object-assisted Sim-to-Sim interactions (e.g., WooHoo, Try for Baby).

> ### note
> Sims remember in which bed and on which side of a double bed they sleep on after a few repetitions of the same bed/side. Be consistent and your Sim will be too.

Bed interactions include:

- Sleep in Pajamas/Sleep in Underwear: Satisfies both Comfort and Energy
- Relax: Satisfies Comfort; initial interaction for object-assisted interactions
- Make Bed: Reduces messiness and, thus, increases Environment
- Jump: Satisfies Fun (Autonomous immaturity only)

Craftmeister's Pine Bed

- Price: §300
- Need Effects: Comfort 1, Energy 2, Fun 2 (Jump)
- Need Max: Fun up to 60 (Jump)

Cheap Eazzzzze Morrissey Double Bed

- Price: §450
- Need Effects: Comfort 1, Energy 2, Fun 2 (Jump)
- Need Max: Fun up to 70 (Jump)

Caress of Teak Bed

- Price: §450
- Need Effects: Comfort 3, Energy 3, Fun 2 (Jump)
- Need Max: Fun up to 70 (Jump)

Courtly Sleeper Day Dreamer

- Price: §700
- Need Effects: Comfort 3, Energy 3, Fun 2 (Jump), Environment 2
- Need Max: Fun up to 70 (Jump)

Zenu Meditation Sleeper

- Price: §950
- Need Effects: Comfort 4, Energy 4, Fun 2 (Jump), Environment 2
- Need Max: Fun up to 80 (Jump)

The Slim System, by Jim Slimboy

◆ Price: $1,050

◆ Need Effects: Comfort 4, Energy 4, Fun 2 (Jump), Environment 2

◆ Need Max: Fun up to 80 (Jump)

Bed by St. Ajoque Reproductions

◆ Price: $1,200

◆ Need Effects: Comfort 5, Energy 6, Fun 2 (Jump), Environment 2

◆ Need Max: Fun up to 80 (Jump)

Touch of Teak Bed

◆ Price: $1,800

◆ Need Effects: Comfort 4, Energy 4, Fun 2 (Jump), Environment 3

◆ Need Max: Fun up to 80 (Jump)

#4234 by C. Lee Funkensnooz

◆ Price: $2,200

◆ Need Effects: Comfort 5, Energy 6, Fun 2 (Jump), Environment 4

◆ Need Max: Fun up to 80 (Jump)

The Soma "Sleep Well"

◆ Price: $2,600

◆ Need Effects: Comfort 6, Energy 6, Fun 2 (Jump), Environment 5

◆ Need Max: Fun up to 80 (Jump)

Colonial Ironwood Bed

◆ Price: $3,000

◆ Need Effects: Comfort 7, Energy 6, Fun 2 (Jump), Environment 5

◆ Need Max: Fun up to 80 (Jump)

Miscellaneous

Miscellaneous Comfort items include barstools (for use at kitchen islands or bars) and outdoor seating furniture (can be used indoors too).

All have the following interactions:

◆ Sit: Satisfies Comfort

◆ Nap: Park Bench only; satisfies Energy

◆ Lounge: Park Bench only; satisfies more Comfort than Sit but no object-assisted interactions.

◆ Play: Park Bench only; satisfies Fun

Keister Kompanion Barstool

◆ Price: $185

◆ Need Effects: Comfort 3

Ad-a-Quaint Barstool

◆ Price: $285

◆ Need Effects: Comfort 3

Outdoor Ergo Ergonomic Chair by Güdfoer-Ebadi Furnishings

◆ Price: $320

◆ Need Effects: Comfort 5

Piece of Quiet Park Bench

◆ Price: $500

◆ Need Effects: Comfort 7 (Sit), Comfort 8 (Lounge), Energy 2, Fun 4

◆ Need Max: Energy up to 50 (Nap)

Regulars Only Barstool

◆ Price: $650

◆ Need Effects: Comfort 6

Organic Material's Barstool
◆ Price: §700
◆ Need Effects: Comfort 7, Environment 2

Stiff by Superfluous Seating
◆ Price: §750
◆ Need Effects: Comfort 7, Environment 2

Surfaces

Surfaces encompass all kinds of tables, counters, and desks.

Counters

Counters are the only surfaces on which food can be prepared. If there isn't at least one available countertop without something on it, cooking will be impossible until an obstructing object is cleaned or removed.

> **note**
>
> Countertops have no Hunger satisfaction rating because they don't directly impact the satisfaction of Hunger. For that figure, see Chapter 20.

Counters automatically join adjacent countertops to make a continuous-looking object.

Some objects must be placed inside countertops: dishwashers, trash compactors, and insert sinks. Functionally, the counter's prep surface is unchanged by the presence of an under-counter appliance but a sink (which goes on top) prevents the preparation of food.

> **note**
>
> Unlike in the original THE SIMS, under-counter appliances MUST be inside a counter. They can't stand alone and act as a prep surface.

Kitchen islands can act as either prep or dining surfaces if barstools are placed on the side with the overhanging counter. Make sure this overhang is facing out of the kitchen if you want Sims to use this object properly.

Interactions include:

◆ Clean: Increases Environment and builds Cleaning skill. Only available when drops below fixed level of dirtiness.

> **note**
>
> Many counters have two seemingly identical listings in the Buy mode catalog. One is for a four-drawer unit and the other is for a drawer plus cabinet unit. There's no functional difference, but these add variety.

Krampft Industries Value Counter
◆ Price: §140

Counter Culture "Surface"
◆ Price: §200

Catamaran Kitchen Island
◆ Price: §210

Epikouros "Sleek Cuisine" Counter
◆ Price: §325

Epikouros "Sleek Cuisine" Island
◆ Price: §335

Chiclettina "Fjord" Kitchen Counter
◆ Price: §490

Chiclettina "Archipelago" Kitchen Island
◆ Price: §500

Club Room Countertop
◆ Price: §600

Club Distress Butcher's Block
◆ Price: §610

Chiclettina "Sardinia" Kitchen Counter
◆ Price: §780
◆ Need Effect: Environment 2

Chiclettina "Sardinia" Kitchen Island
◆ Price: §790
◆ Need Effect: Environment 2

Chez Moi French Country Counters
◆ Price: §800
◆ Need Effect: Environment 2

Counter Cooking Conundrum
◆ Price: §810
◆ Need Effect: Environment 2

Tables

Tables include all manner of dining surfaces. To sit at a table, there must be dining chairs around it; without chairs, Sims will use a table solely to dump dirty dishes and unread books.

Tables provide a place to sit and eat (the better the chairs, the more Comfort Sims get while dining), and can act as a venue for group talk. They can also double as a desk, hold a computer, or act as a serving table for special party foods (e.g., wedding or birthday cake).

Seating capacity varies from four to eight.

There are no interactions with dining tables.

NuMica Allinall Card Table
◆ Price: §95

PINEGULTCHER Outdoor Minitable
◆ Price: §220

The Talking Table
◆ Price: §275

FLATWÖUD Dining Table by Iseeya
◆ Price: §450

Tablablanca from Simporters, Ltd.
◆ Price: §690

Exploding Dragon Dining Table
◆ Price: §755
◆ Need Effects: Environment 2

Luxiary "Ample King" Dining Table
◆ Price: §850
◆ Need Effects: Environment 2

Milano Royale Dining Table
◆ Price: §900
◆ Need Effects: Environment 2

Manor House Paree Dining Table
◆ Price: §1,080
◆ Need Effects: Environment 2

Discourse Dining Table
◆ Price: §1,200
◆ Need Effects: Environment 2

End Tables

End tables act as surfaces for housing small objects (e.g., alarm clocks, table lamps, table phones, small potted plants and sculptures).

End tables have no interactions.

Crazy 8 Table
◆ Price: §65

Contempto Adirondack End Table
◆ Price: §90

Country Comfort Corner Table
◆ Price: §110

Tri-Tip Table
◆ Price: §155

The "Gold-end" Ratio Table
◆ Price: §190

Merokkan End Table
◆ Price: §210

Cornerstone "Sentinel" End Table
◆ Price: §250

Here and There Thing
◆ Price: §280

Gliteri & Co. Trieste End Table
◆ Price: §310

Curvaceous Colonial End Table
◆ Price: §430

Coffee Tables

Coffee tables, like end tables, are primarily receptacles for small objects (e.g., table telephone, compact stereo, video game console, small plants and statues).
Coffee tables have no interactions.

Simply Spindle Coffee Table
◆ Price: §40

Simple Structure End Table
◆ Price: §60

Scraps Ranch "CafeMate" Coffee Table
◆ Price: §90

End-to-End Table
◆ Price: §135

Ad-a-Quaint Coffee Table
◆ Price: §140

Club Distress Square Coffee Table
◆ Price: §155

Tempered Tea Table
◆ Price: §221

Moor is More Coffee Table
◆ Price: §225

Club Distress Avignon Rectangular Coffee Table
◆ Price: §240

Chabadii Chabudinky
◆ Price: §265

Chabadii "Yet Another" Coffee Table
◆ Price: §290

ScienStone "Dramatic" Coffee Table
◆ Price: §340

Centerpieces Coffee Table
- Price: $370

Cozy Colonial End Table
- Price: $400

Queen Anne Coffee Table
- Price: $470

Desks

Desks function as host to various tabletop objects including, but not limited to, computers. They can house table lamps, some small electronics, and small to medium statues as well as dirty plates, newspapers, books, and other messy objects.

Desks have no interactions.

Retratech "Office Pal" Economy Desk
- Price: $80

Home Office Desk by Quaint Design
- Price: $220

Tibetan Desk
- Price: $670

Counter Productive Work Surface
- Price: $750
- Need Effects: Environment 2

Chiclettina Execudrone Desk
- Price: $1,000
- Need Effects: Environment 2

Miscellaneous

This four-top dining table can be used inside too, but it's aesthetically designed to go outside.

Park Plates Mini Outdoor Dining Table
- Price: $115

Decorative

Decorative items are just that: decorative. The only Need they impact is Environment, though their effect can be profound (if you spend enough money).

Depending on their design, decorative objects can go in several places: on the floor, a countertop, a dining, coffee, or end table, a desk, the outdoor ground, the wall, or suspended from the ceiling.

note

All sculptures and paintings can appreciate in value over time. See "Art Object Depreciation/Appreciation," earlier in this chapter.

Plants

None of these plants need any water or maintenance and will live forever.

Plants have no interactions.

Frost de Fleur Bud Vase
- Price: $30
- Need Effects: Environment 1

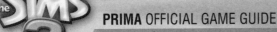

Sunflowers
- Price: §45
- Need Effects: Environment 1

Hosta La Vista
- Price: §90
- Need Effects: Environment 1

Blue Sky Bonsai Tree
- Price: §99
- Need Effects: Environment 1

Falling Fern
- Price: §111
- Need Effects: Environment 1

Juniper Bonsai Tree
- Price: §120
- Need Effects: Environment 1

Mystic Life "Flower Vase"
- Price: §150
- Need Effects: Environment 1

The Simulated Succulent
- Price: §160
- Need Effects: Environment 1

Rubber Tree Plant
- Price: §165
- Need Effects: Environment 1

Fancifully Fuzzy Fern
- Price: §170
- Need Effects: Environment 1

No-Fuss Ficus
- Price: §300
- Need Effects: Environment 2

Fruitless Fig Tree
- Price: §333
- Need Effects: Environment 2

Sculptures

Most sculptures only serve to be visually interesting and enhance Environment score. Some, however, have some very interesting hidden interactions.

Placement of sculptures vary by kind and size.

All sculptures have at least one interaction:

- View: Satisfies Fun

Shocking Pink Flamingo
- Price: §12
- Need Effects: Fun 4 (Kick), Fun 2 (View)
- Need Max: Fun up to 60 (View)

Must be placed outdoors.

Interactions:
- Kick: Satisfies Fun, may cause Flamingo to fall over. Autonomous if Mood is low. Sims also kick it over when viewing it if they don't like it.
- Stand up: Resets Flamingo upright.

Kozy Kitsch Gnome
- Price: §68
- Need Effects: Fun 4 (Kick), Fun 2 (View), Fun 1 (Play With), Fun 5 (Steal), Fun 2 (Steal Back), Environment 1
- Need Max: Fun up to 60 (View)

Must be placed outdoors.

Interactions:

◆ Kick: Satisfies Fun, may cause Gnome to fall over. Autonomous if Mood is low. Sims kick it over autonomously when viewing if they don't like the gnome.

◆ Stand up: Resets gnome upright.

◆ Play With: Satisfies Fun, Playful only.

◆ Gnome Buddy: Outgoing Sims may autonomously talk to the gnome.

◆ Steal: Grouchy Neighbors (not Townies) walking by the house may autonomously steal a gnome. If they leave the sidewalk and head toward the gnome, they're going to try to steal it. If a member of the household is near the gnome, the Neighbor will give up or, if they're really Grouchy, they'll steal it anyway. The thief gets Fun for a successful pilfering.

◆ Steal Back: If a member of a household whose gnome has been stolen appears on another lot as a walk by Neighbor and is Playful and Grouchy, she'll autonomously steal back the gnome. Rescuer gets Fun.

The Measure of a Sim Wooden Model

◆ Price: §100

◆ Need Effects: Fun 3 (View), Environment 1

◆ Need Max: Fun up to 95 (View)

Museé Public "Collection Sculpture"

◆ Price: §200

◆ Need Effects: Fun 3 (View), Environment 2

◆ Need Max: Fun up to 95 (View)

Flight-Away Model Plane

◆ Price: §250

◆ Need Effects: Fun 3 (View), Environment 2

◆ Need Max: Fun up to 95 (View)

Apple of the Eye

◆ Price: §400

◆ Need Effects: Fun 3 (View), Environment 3

◆ Need Max: Fun up to 95 (View)

Ancient Transport Urn Sculpture

◆ Price: §500

◆ Need Effects: Fun 3 (View), Environment 4

◆ Need Max: Fun up to 95 (View)

Immobile Chimes Mobile in Steel

◆ Price: §1,500

◆ Need Effects: Fun 3 (View), Environment 10

◆ Need Max: Fun up to 95 (View)

The My-Chi Sculpture Form

◆ Price: §2,500

◆ Need Effects: Fun 3 (View), Environment 10

◆ Need Max: Fun up to 95 (View)

12th Century Song Dynasty Sculpted Vase

◆ Price: §4,000

◆ Need Effects: Fun 3 (View), Environment 10

◆ Need Max: Fun up to 95 (View)

On A Pedestal by Yucan Byall

◆ Price: §5,000

◆ Need Effects: Fun 3 (View), Environment 10

◆ Need Max: Fun up to 95 (View)

Wall Hangings

Paintings are purely decorative objects, enhancing Environment score. They must hang on walls, but may be indoor or outdoor. They can't, however, hang on foundation (basements) or diagonal walls.

note

Any painting created by a household Sim on an easel can be hung on the household's walls. Like Buy mode paintings, these easel paintings fluctuate in value though they do have some extra elements that can enhance further (See "Art Object Depreciation/Appreciation"). The better the artist's Creativity, the higher an easel painting's Environment score.

All paintings have one interaction:

◆ View: Satisfies Fun

Waterfall

- Price: §35
- Need Effects: Fun 3 (View), Environment 1
- Need Max: Fun up to 95 (View)

The Monster Under My Bed by Little Timmy

- Price: §35
- Need Effects: Fun 3 (View), Environment 1
- Need Max: Fun up to 95 (View)

Dreams of a Gifted Mind

- Price: §35
- Need Effects: Fun 3 (View), Environment 1
- Need Max: Fun up to 95 (View)

Engineered Angst Full-Color Poster

- Price: §40
- Need Effects: Fun 3 (View), Environment 1
- Need Max: Fun up to 95 (View)

Engineered Angst Poster in Red

- Price: §40
- Need Effects: Fun 3 (View), Environment 1
- Need Max: Fun up to 95 (View)

Searing Indifference Wall Poster

- Price: §50
- Need Effects: Fun 3 (View), Environment 1
- Need Max: Fun up to 95 (View)

Civic Idol by Adora Wall Arts

- Price: §50
- Need Effects: Fun 3 (View), Environment 1
- Need Max: Fun up to 95 (View)

Inverted Vertigo, Cover Art

- Price: §60
- Need Effects: Fun 3 (View), Environment 1
- Need Max: Fun up to 95 (View)

Neon Flamingo

- Price: §75
- Need Effects: Fun 3 (View), Environment 1
- Need Max: Fun up to 95 (View)

Korean Keumungo

- Price: §80
- Need Effects: Fun 3 (View), Environment 1
- Need Max: Fun up to 95 (View)

Red vs. Blue Oil Portrait

- Price: §120
- Need Effects: Fun 3 (View), Environment 1
- Need Max: Fun up to 95 (View)

Chinese Opera Mask by Old Face

- Price: §150
- Need Effects: Fun 3 (View), Environment 1
- Need Max: Fun up to 95 (View)

The Lady On Red

- Price: §180
- Need Effects: Fun 3 (View), Environment 2
- Need Max: Fun up to 95 (View)

Spherical Splendor

- Price: §225
- Need Effects: Fun 3 (View), Environment 2
- Need Max: Fun up to 95 (View)

The Lone Daisy

- Price: §285
- Need Effects: Fun 3 (View), Environment 2
- Need Max: Fun up to 95 (View)

Collage in Black and White

- Price: §300
- Need Effects: Fun 3 (View), Environment 2
- Need Max: Fun up to 95 (View)

Rainy Day Main Street

◆ Price: §350

◆ Need Effects: Fun 3 (View), Environment 3

◆ Need Max: Fun up to 95 (View)

Rolling Hills by H. Sean

◆ Price: §400

◆ Need Effects: Fun 3 (View), Environment 3

◆ Need Max: Fun up to 95 (View)

SimCity at Night

◆ Price: §425

◆ Need Effects: Fun 3 (View), Environment 3

◆ Need Max: Fun up to 95 (View)

Suspense

◆ Price: §475

◆ Need Effects: Fun 3 (View), Environment 4

◆ Need Max: Fun up to 95 (View)

Oil "Fantasy Scape"

◆ Price: §500

◆ Need Effects: Fun 3 (View), Environment 4

◆ Need Max: Fun up to 95 (View)

In the Beginning

◆ Price: §600

◆ Need Effects: Fun 3 (View), Environment 4

◆ Need Max: Fun up to 95 (View)

Winter Blossoms

◆ Price: §650

◆ Need Effects: Fun 3 (View), Environment 5

◆ Need Max: Fun up to 95 (View)

Bangpae Yeon from Simporters, Ltd.

◆ Price: §700

◆ Need Effects: Fun 3 (View), Environment 5

◆ Need Max: Fun up to 95 (View)

Transcendence by Joan Schnitzel

◆ Price: §800

◆ Need Effects: Fun 3 (View), Environment 6

◆ Need Max: Fun up to 95 (View)

Bella Squared

◆ Price: §1,000

◆ Need Effects: Fun 3 (View), Environment 7

◆ Need Max: Fun up to 95 (View)

The Meaning of Fruit

◆ Price: §1,500

◆ Need Effects: Fun 3 (View), Environment 10

◆ Need Max: Fun up to 95 (View)

Arghist Soldier

◆ Price: §2,000

◆ Need Effects: Fun 3 (View), Environment 10

◆ Need Max: Fun up to 95 (View)

Handle and Spout

◆ Price: §2,500

◆ Need Effects: Fun 3 (View), Environment 10

◆ Need Max: Fun up to 95 (View)

Ha-hye-tal Mask

◆ Price: §3,000

◆ Need Effects: Fun 3 (View), Environment 10

◆ Need Max: Fun up to 95 (View)

Open-Wall Wall Fan

◆ Price: §3,500

◆ Need Effects: Fun 3 (View), Environment 10

◆ Need Max: Fun up to 95 (View)

Olive Peynter's City SkyScape

◆ Price: §4,000

◆ Need Effects: Fun 3 (View), Environment 10

◆ Need Max: Fun up to 95 (View)

The Fourth Element Wall Hanging

◆ Price: §5,000

◆ Need Effects: Fun 3 (View), Environment 10

◆ Need Max: Fun up to 95 (View)

Poisonous Forest (In Love with a Curse)

◆ Price: $5,500
◆ Need Effects: Fun 3 (View), Environment 10
◆ Need Max: Fun up to 95 (View)

Mirrors

Mirrors serve three purposes: decorative, skill building, and Hygiene satisfaction. Depending on the kind, each mirror must be placed on a wall or on the floor.

Mirrors have several interactions:

◆ Practice Speech/Practice Romance: Builds Charisma skill. Teen/adult/elder only.

◆ Gussy Up: Satisfies Hygiene. Neat will do this autonomously.

◆ Change Appearance: Opens interface that permits a Sim to change his hair color or style, makeup, glasses, costume makeup, color and shape of eyebrows, and color and shape of stubble and beards. See "Changing Appearance" in Chapter 17.

◆ Check Self Out: Teen only. Teens with consistently low Hygiene will notice Zits (see "Hygiene" in Chapter 20).

◆ Practice Kissing: Teens only if they have high Aspiration score.

Reflective Glass Mirror

◆ Price: $100
◆ Skill: Charisma (Practice Romance or Practice Speech)
◆ Need Effects: Hygiene 2 (Gussy Up), Environment 1
◆ Need Max: Hygiene up to 80 (Gussy Up)

Modular Image Full-length Mirror

◆ Price: $150
◆ Skill: Charisma (Practice Romance or Practice Speech)
◆ Need Effects: Fun 3 (View), Environment 1
◆ Need Max: Fun up to 95 (View)

Manor House Multi-Mirror

◆ Price: $160
◆ Skill: Charisma (Practice Romance or Practice Speech)
◆ Need Effects: Fun 3 (View), Environment 1
◆ Need Max: Fun up to 95 (View)

Porcelain Oval Mirror

◆ Price: $200
◆ Skill: Charisma (Practice Romance or Practice Speech)
◆ Need Effects: Fun 3 (View), Environment 1
◆ Need Max: Fun up to 95 (View)

Total Mirror

◆ Price: $303
◆ Skill: Charisma (Practice Romance or Practice Speech)
◆ Need Effects: Fun 3 (View), Environment 2
◆ Need Max: Fun up to 95 (View)

Exotic Reflections Mirror

◆ Price: $340
◆ Skill: Charisma (Practice Romance or Practice Speech)
◆ Need Effects: Fun 3 (View), Environment 2
◆ Need Max: Fun up to 95 (View)

Look Upon the Orient Mirror

◆ Price: $370
◆ Skill: Charisma (Practice Romance or Practice Speech)
◆ Need Effects: Fun 3 (View), Environment 2
◆ Need Max: Fun up to 95 (View)

Obviously Modern Wall Mirror

◆ Price: $399
◆ Skill: Charisma (Practice Romance or Practice Speech)
◆ Need Effects: Fun 3 (View), Environment 2
◆ Need Max: Fun up to 95 (View)

Club Distress Wall Mirror

- Price: §580
- Skill: Charisma (Practice Romance or Practice Speech)
- Need Effects: Fun 3 (View), Environment 3
- Need Max: Fun up to 95 (View)

St. Ajoque Reproductions "See Plus" Mirror

- Price: §750
- Skill: Charisma (Practice Romance or Practice Speech)
- Need Effects: Fun 3 (View), Environment 4
- Need Max: Fun up to 95 (View)

Vision Mirrors "Past Reflections"

- Price: §1,100
- Skill: Charisma (Practice Romance or Practice Speech)
- Need Effects: Fun 3 (View), Environment 6
- Need Max: Fun up to 95 (View)

Curtains

Curtains enhance Environment. They don't even need to be placed over windows. Try to match window and curtain size or you might get some unattractive combinations.

Aluminium Privacy Blinds by P. King Tom Trading Co.

- Price: §80
- Need Effects: Environment 1

Stewart Mourning Café Curtains

- Price: §97
- Need Effects: Environment 1

Veil of Dreams

- Price: §120
- Need Effects: Environment 1

Deluxe Veil of Dreams

- Price: §150
- Need Effects: Environment 2

Antique Lace Curtains

- Price: §165
- Need Effects: Environment 2

Ultra Funky Curtain Clothes

- Price: §170
- Need Effects: Environment 2

Loft Curtains by Sparse and Fine

- Price: §195
- Need Effects: Environment 2

Cornerstone Victoriana Velvet Drapes

- Price: §250
- Need Effects: Environment 2

Sill-Length Tieback Curtains

- Price: §300
- Need Effects: Environment 3

Floor-Length Tieback Curtains

- Price: §335
- Need Effects: Environment 3

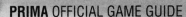

Doublewide Tieback Curtains

◆ Price: §400

◆ Need Effects: Environment 4

Miscellaneous

Anytime Candles

◆ Price: §100

◆ Need Effects: Fun 3 (View), Environment 1

◆ Need Max: Fun up to 95 (View)

Bowl of Plastic Fruit

◆ Price: §150

◆ Need Effects: Fun 3 (View), Environment 1

◆ Need Max: Fun up to 95 (View)

AquaBox Five-Gallon Aquarium

◆ Price: §300

◆ Skill: Cleaning (Clean Tank)

◆ Need Effects: Fun 10 (Watch), Fun 5 (Feed), Fun 4 (Restocking), Environment 1

◆ Need Max: Fun up to 70 (Watch) or 50 (Feed)

Interactions:

◆ Restock: Teens/adults/elders only. Satisfies Fun and puts fish in tank. Only available when tank is empty or when fish have died (removes dead fish and puts in new).

◆ Watch: Satisfies Fun

◆ Feed Fish: Satisfies Fun and adds food to tank. Fish must be fed once every 48 hours or they'll die. Feeding more often makes the tank dirtier.

◆ Clean: Teens/adults/elders only. Increases Environment score if tank is in visibly dirty state. Sloppy Sims make puddles when cleaning. The Maid will clean the tank if it's dirty. Builds Cleaning skill.

The aquarium is a very complicated and powerful object but it requires some care. When bought, it doesn't contain any fish; someone must do the Restock interaction that adds fish and costs §35. If no fish are put in, the tank is merely a lovely Environment enhancing object with no interactions.

Aquaria also emit light, further enhancing Environment score in their immediate area.

The tank becomes steadily dirty over time, coating the glass with green algae and progressively decreasing Environment score. Feeding adds extra dirtiness to the tank. If tank gets very dirty, fish will die.

If fish die, they independently reduce Environment score until removed.

Exotic (Non)Screen from Simports, Ltd.

◆ Price: §900

◆ Need Effects: Fun 3 (View), Environment 6

◆ Need Max: Fun up to 95 (View)

Ol' Grandfather Clock

◆ Price: §3,500

◆ Need Effects: Environment 3

◆ Skill: Mechanical (Maintain)

Interactions:

◆ Wind: Clock must be wound by a teen, adult, or elder every 72 hours or it will stop. If wound every 72 hours, the clock will chime every six hours.

◆ Maintain: Increases clock's value. Can only be done once every 10 days. Every time the Maintain interaction is done, the clock increases in value. Maintenance is not, however, required. While maintaining, Sims build Mechanical skill but risk breaking the clock. The lower Mechanical skill, the greater the chance the clock will break beyond repair.

tip

Don't let a Sim with less than 5 Mechanical maintain the clock.

Plumbing

Plumbing objects provide many essential interactions; if porcelain is involved, Plumbing is where you look.

Toilets

All toilets are created equal; some just have cushier seats. In other words, they all replenish Bladder at the same rate, but public and high-end models boast gaudy amounts of Comfort while a Sim is parked on the seat.

Toilets have the following interactions:

◆ Use: Satisfies Bladder. Also dirties toilet.

◆ Flush: Available only if toilet is "filled." Clears toilet of use thus upping Environment. Also lowers chance of toilet clogging because full toilets are more likely to break. Neat Sims flush autonomously.

- Clean: Available only if toilet is dirty and resets toilet to fully clean state. Increases Cleaning skill.
- Play: Immature Toddlers with low Fun autonomous only. Satisfies Fun but depletes Hygiene and makes puddles that lower Environment.
- Unclog: Fixes clogged toilet and builds Mechanical skill. The longer toilet goes without a flush, the greater the probability it will clog. Clogged toilets are usable.

Elders take twice as long to fulfill their Bladder Need than any other group.

Sewage Brothers Resteze Toilet

- Price: §300
- Skill: Cleaning (Clean), Mechanical (Unclog)
- Need Effects: Bladder 10 (Use), Fun 2 (Play), Hygiene -2 (Play), Hygiene -1 (Use, Clean, Unclog)
- Need Max: Fun up to 50

ResiStall Astro Divider 7

- Price: §700
- Skill: Cleaning (Clean), Mechanical (Unclog)
- Need Effects: Bladder 10 (Use), Comfort 10 (Use), Fun 2 (Play), Hygiene -2 (Play), Hygiene -1 (Use, Clean, Unclog)
- Need Max: Fun up to 50

Mentionable Porcelain Toilet

- Price: §950
- Skill: Cleaning (Clean), Mechanical (Unclog)
- Need Effects: Bladder 10 (Use), Comfort 10 (Use), Fun 2 (Play), Hygiene -2 (Play), Hygiene -1 (Use, Clean, Unclog)
- Need Max: Fun up to 50

Showers & Tubs

Showers, bathtubs, and shower tubs are the primary mechanisms for replenishing Hygiene. Up the line from cheapest to most expensive, several things vary: the time required to satisfy Hygiene, how much if any Comfort Sims receive, and impact on Environment.

Generally, showering is the fastest way to get clean. Bathing is slower but also offers Comfort.

Age also comes into play in the comparison of showers vs. tubs. Toddlers can only bathe in a bath.

note

Toddlers can't, themselves, interact with bathtubs or shower tubs; they must be bathed by a teen, adult, or elder.

Showers, tubs, and shower tubs can have the following interactions:

- Take Bath: Satisfies Hygiene and Comfort.
- Take Shower: Satisfies Hygiene. If Sim is Sloppy and in shower stall only, also satisfies Bladder (yes, that means what you think it means).
- Take Bubble Bath: Fills Hygiene and Comfort. Compared to regular bath, fills Hygiene slower and Comfort faster.
- Clean: Available only if shower or bath is dirty and resets it to fully clean state. Increases Cleaning skill.
- Repair: Fixes broken showers/bathtubs and builds Mechanical skill.
- Bathe Toddler: Satisfies toddler's Hygiene.
- Play: Autonomous Fun.

Clean Water Shower System

- Price: §650
- Skill: Cleaning (Clean), Mechanical (Repair)
- Need Effects: Hygiene 8 (Take a Shower), Bladder 1 (Take a Shower, Sloppy only)

Krampft Industries "HubbaTubba" Economy Bathtub

- Price: §700
- Skill: Cleaning (Clean), Mechanical (Repair)
- Need Effects: Hygiene 6 (Take a Bath), Comfort 4 (Take a Bath), Hygiene 5 (Take a Bubble Bath), Comfort 6 (Take a Bubble Bath), Hygiene 6 (Bathe Toddler), Fun 3 (Play), Environment 2

The Black and White "Bare" Bath

- Price: §900
- Skill: Cleaning (Clean), Mechanical (Repair)
- Need Effects: Hygiene 7 (Take a Bath), Comfort 6 (Take a Bath), Hygiene 6 (Take a Bubble Bath), Comfort 10 (Take a Bubble Bath), Hygiene 7 (Bathe Toddler), Fun 3 (Play), Environment 2

AquaPlus Shower Stall

- Price: §1,000
- Skill: Cleaning (Clean), Mechanical (Repair)
- Need Effects: Hygiene 7 (Take a Shower), Hygiene 6 (Take a Bath), Comfort 4 (Take a Bath), Hygiene 5 (Take a Bubble Bath), Comfort 6 (Take a Bubble Bath), Hygiene 6 (Bathe Toddler), Environment 2

Simple Tub from Krampft Industries

- Price: §1,500
- Skill: Cleaning (Clean), Mechanical (Repair)
- Need Effects: Hygiene 8 (Take a Bath), Comfort 8 (Take a Bath), Hygiene 7 (Take a Bubble Bath), Comfort 10 (Take a Bubble Bath), Hygiene 8 (Bathe Toddler), Fun 3 (Play), Environment 3

Coloratura by Chrome Concepts

- Price: §1,500
- Skill: Cleaning (Clean), Mechanical (Repair)
- Need Effects: Hygiene 10 (Take a Shower), Bladder 2 (Take a Shower, Sloppy only), Environment 3

Colonial Bathtub by Imperial Plumbing Works

- Price: §1,800
- Skill: Cleaning (Clean), Mechanical (Repair)
- Need Effects: Hygiene 8 (Take a Bath), Comfort 8 (Take a Bath), Hygiene 7 (Take a Bubble Bath), Comfort 10 (Take a Bubble Bath), Hygiene 8 (Bathe Toddler), Fun 3 (Play), Environment 3

Colonial ComboCleen by Imperial Plumbing Works

- Price: §2,200
- Skill: Cleaning (Clean), Mechanical (Repair)
- Need Effects: Hygiene 10 (Take a Shower), Hygiene 8 (Take a Bath), Comfort 8 (Take a Bath), Hygiene 7 (Take a Bubble Bath), Comfort 10 (Take a Bubble Bath), Hygiene 6 (Bathe Toddler), Fun 3 (Play), Environment 4

Sinks

Sinks are a minor tool for satisfying Hygiene, the only way to bathe a baby, a means of washing dishes, and way to get small doses of Hunger satisfaction.

There are two kinds of sinks:

- Pedestal: Freestanding, must be placed against wall
- Countertop: Inset in countertop object

Sinks include the following interactions:

- Get a Drink: Satisfies Hunger, depletes Bladder
- Wash Hands: Satisfies Hygiene
- Bathe Baby: Increases baby Hygiene
- Sponge Bath: Autonomous Only. If Sim's Neat/Sloppy is below 6 and Hygiene is less than -50, Sim may strip and take a sponge bath.
- Clean: Available only if sink is dirty. Resets it to fully clean state. Increases Cleaning skill.
- Repair: Fixes broken sinks and builds Mechanical skill.

> **note**
>
> There's no functional difference between sinks in bathrooms, kitchens, or anywhere else.

Superlative Sink by "The Greatest Designer Alive"

◆ Price: §250
◆ Type: Countertop
◆ Skill: Cleaning (Clean), Mechanical (Repair)
◆ Need Effects: Hygiene 5 (Wash), Hygiene 6 (Sponge Bath), Hunger 1 (Drink)
◆ Need Max: Hygiene up to 90 (Wash), Hygiene up to 25 (Sponge Bath), Hygiene up to 70 (Bathe Baby)

Simple Sink from Krampft Industries

◆ Price: §275
◆ Type: Pedestal
◆ Skill: Cleaning (Clean), Mechanical (Repair)
◆ Need Effects: Hygiene 5 (Wash), Hygiene 6 (Sponge Bath), Hunger 1 (Drink)
◆ Need Max: Hygiene up to 90 (Wash), Hygiene up to 25 (Sponge Bath), Hygiene up to 70 (Bathe Baby)

Floral Sink

◆ Price: §330
◆ Type: Countertop
◆ Skill: Cleaning (Clean), Mechanical (Repair)
◆ Need Effects: Hygiene 5 (Wash), Hygiene 7 (Sponge Bath), Hunger 1 (Drink)
◆ Need Max: Hygiene up to 90 (Wash), Hygiene up to 25 (Sponge Bath), Hygiene up to 70 (Bathe Baby)

Garden Fresh Pedestal Sink

◆ Price: §355
◆ Type: Pedestal
◆ Skill: Cleaning (Clean), Mechanical (Repair)
◆ Need Effects: Hygiene 5 (Wash), Hygiene 7 (Sponge Bath), Hunger 1 (Drink)
◆ Need Max: Hygiene up to 90 (Wash), Hygiene up to 25 (Sponge Bath), Hygiene up to 70 (Bathe Baby)

Hydronomic CleenSheen Basin

◆ Price: §410
◆ Type: Countertop
◆ Skill: Cleaning (Clean), Mechanical (Repair)
◆ Need Effects: Hygiene 6 (Wash), Hygiene 7 (Sponge Bath), Hunger 1 (Drink)
◆ Need Max: Hygiene up to 90 (Wash), Hygiene up to 25 (Sponge Bath), Hygiene up to 90 (Bathe Baby)

Imperial Plumbing Works Tivoli Basin

◆ Price: §560
◆ Type: Countertop
◆ Skill: Cleaning (Clean), Mechanical (Repair)
◆ Need Effects: Hygiene 6 (Wash), Hygiene 7 (Sponge Bath), Hunger 1 (Drink)
◆ Need Max: Hygiene up to 90 (Wash), Hygiene up to 25 (Sponge Bath), Hygiene up to 90 (Bathe Baby)

Filigree Facebowl by Imperial Plumbing Works

◆ Price: §610
◆ Type: Countertop
◆ Skill: Cleaning (Clean), Mechanical (Repair)
◆ Need Effects: Hygiene 6 (Wash), Hygiene 7 (Sponge Bath), Hunger 1 (Drink)
◆ Need Max: Hygiene up to 90 (Wash), Hygiene up to 25 (Sponge Bath), Hygiene up to 70 (Bathe Baby)

Imperial Lyon Basin

◆ Price: §640
◆ Type: Pedestal
◆ Skill: Cleaning (Clean), Mechanical (Repair)
◆ Need Effects: Hygiene 6 (Wash), Hygiene 7 (Sponge Bath), Hunger 1 (Drink)
◆ Need Max: Hygiene up to 90 (Wash), Hygiene up to 25 (Sponge Bath), Hygiene up to 70 (Bathe Baby)

Victor Victorian Pedestal Sink

◆ Price: §700
◆ Type: Pedestal
◆ Skill: Cleaning (Clean), Mechanical (Repair)
◆ Need Effects: Hygiene 6 (Wash), Hygiene 7 (Sponge Bath), Hunger 1 (Drink), Environment 2
◆ Need Max: Hygiene up to 90 (Wash), Hygiene up to 25 (Sponge Bath), Hygiene up to 70 (Bathe Baby)

Hot Tubs

The hot tubs are extremely powerful objects, especially when it comes to socializing. They simultaneously provide Hygiene, Comfort, and Fun. If there's more than one Sim in the tub, group talk and, thus, Social satisfaction, ensues.

Only teens, adults, and elders may use a hot tub, though any pregnant Sims are barred until after delivery. The tubs hold up to four Sims at once.

VaporWare Submergence Spa
- Price: $8,500
- Skill: Mechanical (Repair)
- Need Effects: Hygiene 5, Fun 7, Comfort 6, Environment 10
- Need Max: Fun up to 80, Hygiene up to 50

> **note**
>
> Extremely Outgoing Sims will get in the tub naked and will influence those entering after to do the same.

> **note**
>
> There's a third hot tub ("The Love Tub") but it can be acquired only as an Aspiration reward. After its special powers have expired, it reverts to being a regular hot tub. See "Aspiration Rewards," Chapter 21.

Sims may stay in the tub until all affected Needs are fulfilled or Hunger, Energy or Bladder get too low.

Hot tubs are also one of the three places in which adult or elder Sims can do WooHoo or Try for Baby (they must be cuddling first).

Interactions include:

- Get In: Enter empty hot tub.
- Join: Enter hot tub with at least one (but no more than three) Sims.
- Move: Moves Sim from one seat to another.
- Talk: Talk to a specific Sim.
- Repair: Fixes broken hot tubs and builds Mechanical skill.

Appliances

Appliances include everything your Sims need to cook food and dispose of a variety of messes. Some even provide a little pick-me-up for sagging Sims.

The functionality of most of these objects is discussed in the food preparation guide in Chapter 20.

Cooking

Cooking appliances are where cooked food gets, well, cooked. Cooking is the crucial final step in the preparation of extremely satisfying food.

Interactions include:

- Have Meal: Satisfies Hunger. Prepares one serving of specified food.
- Serve Meal: Satisfies Hunger. Prepares six servings of specified food.
- Grill: Grill only. Satisfies Hunger. Prepares six servings of a specified grill food.
- Clean: Satisfies Fun for Neat. Increases Cleaning skill and Environment score.

> **note**
>
> All "object-assisted" interactions require both Sims to be in the tub in adjacent seats. WooHoo and Try for Baby work only if there are no more than two Sims in the tub. WooHoo or Try for Baby in a hot tub can yield a special cinematic.

Bubble-Up "Soaking Zone" Hot Tub
- Price: $6,500
- Skill: Mechanical (Repair)
- Need Effects: Hygiene 5, Fun 7, Comfort 6, Environment 9
- Need Max: Fun up to 80, Hygiene up to 50

The Grillinator "BigBQ"
- Price: $210
- Need Effects: Hunger 1

Brand Name MetalKettle
◆ Price: §299
◆ Need Effects: Hunger 1

Dialectric ReadyPrep Range
◆ Price: §400
◆ Skill: Cleaning (Clean)
◆ Need Effects: Hunger 1

Ciao Time "Mondo Fuego" Gas Stove
◆ Price: §650
◆ Skill: Cleaning (Clean)
◆ Need Effects: Hunger 4

Elegant Chef FlameBay Gas Range
◆ Price: §900
◆ Skill: Cleaning (Clean)
◆ Need Effects: Hunger 10

Shiny Things, Inc. Grandiose Grill
◆ Price: §1,100
◆ Need Effects: Hunger 10

Refrigerators

Refrigerators are the starting point of the Sim food chain. The better the fridge, the higher quality the food that comes out of it, the greater its capacity, and the more it contributes to Environment.

Refrigerators have two different Fun interactions that can provide quick amusement for members of the household.

Interactions include:

◆ Have a Snack: Satisfies Hunger.
◆ Have Meal: Satisfies Hunger. A single serving of specified food.
◆ Serve Meal: Satisfies Hunger. Six servings of a specified food.
◆ Serve Dessert: Satisfies Hunger and Fun.
◆ Grill: Satisfies Hunger. Six servings of a specified grilled food. Requires grill on lot.
◆ Juggle Bottles: Satisfies Fun.
◆ Check Food Supplies: Not available when fridge is fully stocked.
◆ Play: Satisfies Fun. Autonomous only. Immature Sims swing on the refrigerator doors.

Brand Name "EconoCool" Refrigerator
◆ Price: §600
◆ Food Capacity: 200
◆ Need Effects: Fun 3 (Juggle Bottles or Play), Hunger 10
◆ Need Max: Fun up to 50 (Juggle Bottles or Play)

Ciao Time Bovinia Refrigerator Model BRRR
◆ Price: §1,500
◆ Food Capacity: 300
◆ Need Effects: Fun 3 (Juggle Bottles or Play), Environment 2, Hunger 10
◆ Need Max: Fun up to 50 (Juggle Bottles or Play)

Small Appliances

Small appliances fit on countertops.

Extra Pep Coffeemaker
◆ Price: §85
◆ Need Effects: Hunger 1, Bladder -1, Energy 3, Fun 1 (Juggle Mugs)
◆ Need Max: Fun up to 70 (Juggle Mugs)

(note)

Sims who drink too much coffee or espresso start to visibly shake.

Interactions:

◆ Make Coffee: Prepares eight servings. Instantaneous.

◆ Drink Coffee: Take and consume one cup. Satisfies Energy and Hunger and depletes Bladder. Must be made first. Each cup takes about thirty to forty minutes to consume.

◆ Juggle Mugs: Satisfies Fun.

(note)

When a Sim is juggling either coffee mugs or espresso cups, other Sims can click on the juggling Sim and choose Join Juggling.

TechTonic Touch Toaster Oven

◆ Price: $100

◆ Need Effects: Hunger 1

Interactions:

◆ Have Meal: Satisfies Hunger. Makes one serving of specified food.

XLR8R2 Food Processor

◆ Price: $220

◆ Need Effects: Hunger 2

No interactions. Speeds preparation of food.

Brand Name Zip Zap Microwave

◆ Price: $250

◆ Skill: Mechanical (Repair)

◆ Need Effects: Hunger 2

Interactions:

◆ Have Dinner: Dinner hours only. Satisfies Hunger. Makes one serving of TV Dinner. No other meals available.

Ciao Time Espresso Machine

◆ Price: $450

◆ Need Effects: Hunger 1, Bladder -1, Energy 4, Fun 3 (Juggle Mugs), Fun 1 (Serve or Have)

◆ Need Max: Fun up to 50 (Serve, Have, or Juggle Cups)

Interactions:

◆ Make Espresso: Satisfies Fun. Makes one serving. Sim takes a cup automatically when done. Preparation process takes slightly longer than coffee.

◆ Serve Espresso: Satisfies Fun. Makes two servings. Sim takes a cup automatically when done. Preparation process takes slightly longer than coffee.

◆ Take a Cup: Satisfies Energy and Hunger but accelerates Bladder depletion. Occurs automatically for first cup but can select interaction if a cup is waiting on the machine.

◆ Juggle Cups: Satisfies Fun.

(note)

Serving espresso and coffee are very important when you have visitors because there are no other ways for visitors to replenish Energy. They can take prepared servings but can't work the machine, so household Sims must actually prepare the beverages.

Large Appliances

Large appliances make many of life's more tedious chores bearable or at least quicker.

Gagmia Simore "RefuseNik" Trash Compactor

◆ Price: $375

◆ Skill: Mechanical (Repair)

Compactor is a large capacity trash can that tucks out of the way inside a countertop object.

Sims fill the unit autonomously or when directed to clean up a piece of trash.

Interactions:

◆ Empty: Available only if compactor contains trash. Sim takes a trash bag from the compactor and deposits it in the curbside trashcan. Can be done before compactor is full. If compactor is full, drawer sticks open lowering Environment. After eight hours, open drawer begins to stink, further lowering Environment.

◆ Repair: Fixes broken trash compactor and builds Mechanical skill.

Wishy-Washer from Brandname LX

◆ Price: §550

◆ Skill: Mechanical (Repair)

Dishwashers are much faster than washing dishes in the sink, increasing time efficiency. Household members, Maids, and visitors can put dishes in the dishwasher any time (even if it's running) and there's no need to unload (they magically return to their proper place). Must be installed inside a countertop object but not an island or counter with a sink.

This inexpensive dishwasher is noisy and will awaken Sims sleeping in the room.

Interactions:

◆ Repair: Fixes broken dishwasher and builds Mechanical skill.

Shiny Things Inc. Whisp-Aire Dishwasher

◆ Price: §950

◆ Skill: Mechanical (Repair)

See above.

This expensive dishwasher is quiet and won't awaken Sims sleeping in the room.

Electronics

Electronic items are primarily used for entertainment but many serve vital household functions too.

Entertainment

Entertainment objects serve up fun to Sims who use them and anyone who watches.

VroomMaster 4000

◆ Price: §149

◆ Need Effects: Fun 5 (Play), Fun 3 (Watch)

◆ Need Max: Fun up to 90 (Play) and 85 (Watch)

The VroomMaster toy can be used by one Sim, but others may autonomously watch the car as it zooms around the room (getting Fun as well). The car goes wherever it wants; it can't be directed (not by you at least).

Can be placed on any table or counter or on the floor.

Interactions:

◆ Play With: Satisfies Fun.

◆ Watch: Satisfies Fun. Autonomous only.

Maxis™ Game Simulator

◆ Price: §560

◆ Need Effects: Fun 9 (Play), Fun 9 (Watch)

◆ Need Max: Fun up to 90 (Play, adult) or 80 (Play, elder) and 90 (Watch)

◆ Group Activity

Actual Fun satisfaction is based on age:

◆ Child: 11 (extra, extra Fun)   ◆ Adult: 9

◆ Teen: 10   ◆ Elder: 8

Fun maximums are also age dependent: Elders top out at 80 Fun while adults last until 90. Teens and children have no max.

Winner is determined based on each Sim's Logic, Mood, and age; teens are usually the best players but usually it's the Sim with the highest Logic who prevails.

Additional games can be purchased from video game racks in Community Lots. All games, however, offer the same Fun to each age.

When a game is done, Neat Sims put the game away properly and others leave controllers where they sit.

Can be placed on a coffee table or the floor and must be near a TV.

Interactions:

◆ Play Game: Satisfies Fun.

◆ Join Play: Satisfies Fun and Social.

◆ Watch: Satisfies Fun and Social.

◆ Put Away Controllers: Increases Environment. Only available if controllers are not put away.

Sweet Tooth Survivor Pinball

◆ Price: §1,750

◆ Need Effects: Fun 10 (Play), Fun 3 (Watch), Environment 2

At end of game, Sim either wins or loses based, in part, on Sim's Mechanical and Body skills.

If player Joins, Sims take turns. Both get Social. Winner is random but usually the Sim with highest Body and/or Mechanical wins.

Interactions:

◆ Play: Satisfies Fun

◆ Join: Satisfies Fun and Social

Election Day Retro Space-Age Action Pinball

◆ Price: §1,750

◆ Need Effects: Fun 10 (Play), Fun 3 (Watch), Environment 2

See above.

TVs and Computers

TVs and computers are extremely important objects, providing hours of group Fun, myriad Social outlets, and several essential services.

Trottco 27" Mult7iVid IV Television

- Price: §500
- Skill: Cooking (Watch Yummy Channel), Body (Work Out), Mechanical (Repair)
- Need Effects: Fun 6 (varied by Sim's reaction to the channel), Energy -3, Comfort -3, Hygiene -7, (Work Out)
- Need Max: Depends on Sim's reaction to channel

TVs have several channels, changeable with the Change interaction on the TV. Ages prefer different channels as reflected in each age's Fun satisfaction speed and Fun maximum when watching the channel. The more they like a channel, the longer they'll watch. If they hate a channel, they'll exit sooner. Sims turning on a TV or joining it when no other Sims are watching will change to their age's preferred channel. There are four levels of reaction: Love, Like, Dislike, and Hate.

TV Channel Reactions By Age

Age	SBN	SimStation Dance	KidzTube	Yummy Channel
Toddler	Hate	Dislike	Love	Like
Child	Dislike	Like	Love	Hate
Teen	Like	Love	Hate	Dislike
Adult	Love	Hate	Dislike	Like
Elder	Like	Hate	Dislike	Love

tip

If mixed groups are watching TV, find a station they all feel reasonably favorable toward. There is no station, however, that every group likes, so compromises are essential.

TVs impart skills but at a lower rate than dedicated skill objects. Cooking skill is learned from the Yummy Channel and Body is gained by using the Work Out interaction on the TV itself.

Interactions:

- Turn On: Sim turns on TV to age-favored channel.
- Watch: Satisfies Fun. Watching can be done sitting in a seat, on the floor or standing.
- Turn Off: Sim turns off TV. Neat Sims will do this autonomously when done watching.
- Change Channel: See above.
- Join: Toddlers, children, teens, adults, and elders will join a Sim already watching TV. Social interaction ensues.
- Work Out: Sim dons workout clothes and does floor exercises to get Body skill.
- Repair: Builds Mechanical skill.

Moneywell Computer

- Price: §1,000
- Skill: Creativity (Write Novel), Mechanical (Repair)
- Need Effects: Fun 7 (Play, Watch, Chat), Social (Send/Receive e-mail, Chat)
- Need Max: Fun up to 75 (Chat), 90 (Play), 80 (Watch Play)

Must be placed on a desk or table with a dining chair in front.

Interactions:

- Play Game: Satisfies Fun. Playing games works identically to the Maxis™ Game Simulator and buying games from Community Lots makes them available on all computers too.
- Write Novel: Sim writes a novel, the quality and monetary value of which depends on Sim's Creativity. Writing novels builds Creativity skill and takes about 50 hours. Value of novel ranges from §2,000 for lousy novel to §3,500 for excellent novel.
- Send E-mail: Satisfies Fun. Sims can e-mail non-household Sims who they know and who have a computer. Gain Relationship score for sent e-mail.
- Receive E-mail: Satisfies Fun and Social (multiplied by number of e-mails received).
- Chat With: Satisfies Social. Chat with Sims who Sims may not know and who could be an NPC. Sometimes, other Sim ask to be invited over. Children may Chat only with other children.

◆ Find Job: Several job listings (many more than newspaper) appear on the computer, changing daily.

◆ Restock Groceries: Order groceries online just as over the telephone.

◆ Find Own Place: Initiates move out procedure (see Chapter 25).

◆ Repair: Builds Mechanical skill.

Little Sister, WD15

◆ Price: $2,800

◆ Skill: Creativity (Write Novel), Mechanical (Repair)

◆ Need Effects: Fun 7 (Play, Watch, Chat), Social (Send/Receive E-mail, Chat), Environment 3

◆ Need Max: Fun up to 75 (Chat), 90 (Play), 80 (Watch Play)

See Moneywell Computer, above. The only difference is Environment score.

Soma 44" PancakeTek Television

◆ Price: $3,500

◆ Skill: Cooking (Watch Yummy Channel), Body (Work Out), Mechanical (Repair)

◆ Need Effects: Fun 8 (varied by Sim's reaction to the channel), Energy -3, Comfort -3, Hygiene -7, (Work Out), Environment 3

◆ Need Max: Depends on Sim's reaction to channel

See Trottco 27" MultiVid IV Television, above.

Soma "Wall-Eye" Large Screen Flat-Panel Television

◆ Price: $8,000

◆ Skill: Cooking (Watch Yummy Channel), Body (Work Out)

◆ Need Effects: Fun 10 (varied by Sim's reaction to the channel), Energy -3, Comfort -3, Hygiene -7, (Work Out), Environment 7

◆ Need Max: Depends on Sim's reaction to channel

See Trottco 27" MultiVid IV Television, above.
Can't be repaired.

Audio

Audio objects enable two primary activities: dancing and working out.

The amount of Fun (satisfaction speed and maximum) derived from dancing increases with the quality of stereo. The high-end stereo also increases Environment.

Interactions:

◆ Turn On: Activates stereo.

◆ Switch To: Changes music channel. Channels include: Techno, Salsa, Pop, Metal, Hip Hop. Channels have no effect on Fun or the way Sims dance.

◆ Dance Solo: Satisfies Fun. Sim dances by herself. Multiple Sims can dance solo to stereo but no Social motive is gained. To dance together, Sims must do a Dance Together interaction on one another; high relationship Sims switch from Dance Solo to Dance Together autonomously. Alternately, high relationship Sims who are both dancing Solo will face and look at each other. Dance Solo does not build Dancing skill (see Chapter 22) and does not satisfy Social.

◆ Join: Satisfies Fun. Available on the stereo or a solo dancing Sim. Directs Sim to dance solo alongside others.

◆ Next Song: Changes to next song on music station.

◆ Work Out: Sim dons workout clothes and does floor exercises to get Body skill.

◆ Turn Off: Switches Stereo off.

◆ Listen to Music: Satisfies Fun. Available only when Sim is relaxing in bed and only when stereo is in same room as bed (no remote speakers).

◆ Repair: Builds Mechanical skill.

note

To dance together, click on intended dance partner and choose "Dance Together" (available only if music is playing nearby). If relationship is high enough, other Sim will accept. Increases Relationship scores and Social and can increase Dancing skill. For full details on dancing, see Chapter 24.

Compact Stereo by Lo-Fi Audio
- ◆ Price: §99
- ◆ Skill: Body (Work Out)
- ◆ Need Effects: Fun 7 (Dance together), Fun 5 (Dance Solo), Fun 3 (Listen to Music—in Bed), Energy -3, Comfort -3, Hygiene -7, (Work Out)
- ◆ Need Max: Fun up to 55 (Dance Solo) or 65 (Dance together) or 60 (Listen to Music).

Fun-Kadelic Frequency Stereo System from Kauker Inc.
- ◆ Price: §375
- ◆ Skill: Body (Work Out), Mechanical (Repair)
- ◆ Need Effects: Fun 9 (Dance Together), Fun 8 (Dance Solo), Fun 3 (Listen to Music—in Bed), Energy -3, Comfort -3, Hygiene -7, (Work Out)
- ◆ Need Max: Fun up to 75 (Dance Solo) or 85 (Dance together) or 60 (Listen to Music)

Neukum Systems Wall Speaker
- ◆ Price: §400

These speakers extend music produced by the closest stereo on the same floor. Normally, music is limited to the room with the stereo. With speakers arrayed around the lot, Sims can dance anywhere there's a speaker.

To dance to music from a remote speaker, click on the stereo itself and choose Dance Solo or click on another Sim near the speaker and pick Dance Together.

Working out can be done only near the stereo itself.

To operate the stereo itself (turn on, switch station, etc.), the Sim must walk to it.

Soma AudioGeek TK421 Tower System
- ◆ Price: §2,550
- ◆ Skill: Body (Work Out), Mechanical (Repair)
- ◆ Need Effects: Fun 10 (Dance Together), Fun 10 (Dance Solo), Fun 3 (Listen to Music—in Bed), Energy -3, Comfort -3, , Hygiene -7, (Work Out), Environment 2
- ◆ Need Max: 60 (Listen to Music)

Small Electronics

Get Up! Alarm Clock
- ◆ Price: §30

Can be placed on tall end tables and dining tables.

Interactions:
- ◆ Set Alarm: Set clock to ring every work or school day one hour before carpool arrives. Alarm will not sound if the Sim does not have a job or isn't in school. Wakes all Sims in the room, not just the one for whom the bell tolls.
- ◆ Unset Alarm: Available only if alarm's been set. Deactivates alarm until reset.
- ◆ Turn Off Ringing Alarm: Any child, teen, adult, or elder in the room will wake up and autonomously deactivate the alarm for the day. Does not "unset" alarm for the future. Can also be user directed. If Sim is Lazy, there's a random chance he'll turn off the alarm and go back to sleep. If his Mood is lower than -25, the Sim will instead smash the alarm clock; there's a chance of breaking the clock if the Sim has Body skill of five or more.
- ◆ Clean: If clock is smashed and broken, cleans up debris and throws in trash.

note

A ringing alarm clock in a room dramatically brings down Environment score.

SimLine Table Phone
- ◆ Price: §50
- ◆ All telephone interactions are covered throughout this book.

Must be placed on a table, counter, coffee table, or end table.

If the phone is put down away from the base and phone rings, phone can be answered by clicking on either the base or the remote handset.

SmokeSentry SmokeSniffer 3000
- ◆ Price: §50

Will sound and automatically (no interaction required) summon the fire department if a fire breaks out in the same room. Without this alarm, a Sim must be stopped from panicking and directed to call the fire department.

tip

The smoke alarm is essential if low Cooking skill Sims are using the kitchen, as fires tend to break out frequently.

Put one in any room that has a stove or a fireplace.

CyberChronometer Alarm Clock

◆ Price: §60

No functional difference to cheaper version. See Get Up! Alarm Clock, above.

SimLine Wall Phone

◆ Price: §75

Same as Sim Line Table Phone (above) but must be placed on a wall.

SimSafety V Burglar Alarm

◆ Price: §250

This wall-mounted alarm sounds and automatically summons the police if a burglar enters the room it's in. Puts burglar in panic mode, preventing him from taking any objects.

tip

Place the burglar alarm in any room with an exterior entrance that's accessible from the ground.

Lighting

Lighting makes houses look better inside and out during nighttime hours but is also a major factor in Environment score (see Chapter 20).

Every light has several interactions that govern how it operates:

◆ Turn On/Turn Off: Elect to turn on or off an individual light, all lights in the room, or all lights on the lot regardless of time of day.

◆ Auto-Lights: Deactivates or activates the Auto-lights feature for the individual light, all lights in the room, or all lights on the lot. This turns on lights after dark whenever a Sim enters the room.

Though these interactions must be done by an individual Sim, the Sim won't actually route to the light or stop whatever it is she's doing.

Table Lamps

Table lamps go on any kind of table, desk, or countertop.

Pix-Arm Drafting Lamp

◆ Price: §30

◆ Need Effects: Environment 1

The 'Watt is it' Table Lamp

◆ Price: §35

◆ Need Effects: Environment 1

Lunatech Spare Fixture in "Crimson Light"

◆ Price: §45

◆ Need Effects: Environment 1

Lunatech Spare Fixture in "Grass"

◆ Price: §45

◆ Need Effects: Environment 1

Lunatech Spare Fixture in "Ocean"

◆ Price: §45

◆ Need Effects: Environment 1

Social Climbing Ivy Table Lamp

◆ Price: §79

◆ Need Effects: Environment 1

PRIMA OFFICIAL GAME GUIDE

Ilistara Lamp
◆ Price: §80
◆ Need Effects: Environment 1

Absolutely Nothing Special
◆ Price: §85
◆ Need Effects: Environment 1

Dynasty "Enlightenment" Lamp
◆ Price: §95
◆ Need Effects: Environment 1

GentleGlow Table Lamp
◆ Price: §120
◆ Need Effects: Environment 1

Lunatech BCT/6
◆ Price: §135
◆ Need Effects: Environment 1

Shoji Table Lantern
◆ Price: §175
◆ Need Effects: Environment 1

The Inner Light
◆ Price: §200
◆ Need Effects: Environment 1

Founding Fathers Electric Lamp
◆ Price: §235
◆ Need Effects: Environment 1

Whodunnit? Table Lamp
◆ Price: §300
◆ Need Effects: Environment 2

Floor Lamps

Floor lamps go...we'll let you figure it out.

Thrice As Nice Floor Lamp by Lumpen Lumeniat
◆ Price: §100
◆ Need Effects: Environment 1

Social Climbing Ivy Floor Lamp
◆ Price: §105
◆ Need Effects: Environment 1

Burnished Blaze Torchiere
◆ Price: §199
◆ Need Effects: Environment 1

Light Orbiter Floor Lamp
◆ Price: §250
◆ Need Effects: Environment 1

Tulip Light from Luxiary
◆ Price: §300
◆ Need Effects: Environment 2

Tornado Torch Floor Lamp

◆ Price: §330

◆ Need Effects: Environment 2

Rave Against the Machine Nightclub Lamp

◆ Price: §350

◆ Need Effects: Environment 2

Wall Lamps

Wall lamps can go on any unoccupied bit of wall. They can be placed above low objects positioned against the wall (including counters).

Basically Bare Bulb from Electric Lighting

◆ Price: §25

◆ Need Effects: Environment 1

Prisoner of Azkalamp

◆ Price: §35

◆ Need Effects: Environment 1

Torcher Clamshell Wall Sconce

◆ Price: §75

◆ Need Effects: Environment 1

Lunatech "GaulleVanizer" Wall Sconce

◆ Price: §85

◆ Need Effects: Environment 1

Wall Flowers Sconce

◆ Price: §110

◆ Need Effects: Environment 1

Antique Metal Sconce

◆ Price: §155

◆ Need Effects: Environment 1

Almost Deco Wall Sconce

◆ Price: §184

◆ Need Effects: Environment 1

Torcher "Luminescence" Sconce

◆ Price: §202

◆ Need Effects: Environment 1

Illuminating Angles by Newt Vo

◆ Price: §250

◆ Need Effects: Environment 1

Antebellum Wall Lamp

◆ Price: §360

◆ Need Effects: Environment 2

Hanging Lamps

Hanging lamps dangle from the ceiling and, as such, can only be used indoors with flat roofs. They're more expensive than floor or table lamps but don't consume any floor space.

Light Effects Ceiling Lamp

◆ Price: §65

◆ Need Effects: Environment 1

Lunatech "Lighten Up" Lighting Fixture

◆ Price: §75

◆ Need Effects: Environment 1

PRIMA OFFICIAL GAME GUIDE

Lamp on the Half Shell
- Price: §90
- Need Effects: Environment 1

4 by 4 Designer Chandelier
- Price: §120
- Need Effects: Environment 1

Dangling Daylight Ceiling Lamp
- Price: §145
- Need Effects: Environment 1

Qadim Bauble Lamp
- Price: §150
- Need Effects: Environment 1

Chinese Riddle Lantern
- Price: §175
- Need Effects: Environment 1

Legno's Modern Chandelier
- Price: §190
- Need Effects: Environment 1

Lunatech Amber Ceiling Lamp
- Price: §220
- Need Effects: Environment 1

Paper Moon Ceiling Light
- Price: §300
- Need Effects: Environment 2

Floral Fancy Hanging Lamp
- Price: §445
- Need Effects: Environment 2

Outdoor Lamps

There's no requirement that these lights be placed outside. Several of them, however, must be placed on rail post or fence post.

Garden Glow Spotlight
- Price: §35
- Type: Floor or Ground
- Need Effects: Environment 1

Blazin' Buckaroos Lantern
- Price: §50
- Type: Post-mounted
- Need Effects: Environment 1

Little House Lantern
- Price: §90
- Type: Post-mounted
- Need Effects: Environment 1

The "Spike Light"
- Price: §150
- Type: Floor or Ground
- Need Effects: Environment 1

Secure Sentinel Post Lamp

◆ Price: §185

◆ Type: Post-mounted

◆ Need Effects: Environment 1

Miscellaneous Lamps

City Dweller 'Dims'

◆ Price: §70

◆ Need Effects: Environment 1

Wooden Post n' Lamp

◆ Price: §200

◆ Need Effects: Environment 1

Outdoor only.

PrevenTek Luminlight Streetlamp

◆ Price: §439

◆ Need Effects: Environment 2

Outdoor only.

PrevenTek Tri-Luminlight Streetlamp

◆ Price: §600

◆ Need Effects: Environment 3

Outdoor only.

Hobbies

Hobbies include both Fun and Skill development objects. Many, happily, do both.

Creativity

These items build Creativity skill.

Independent Expressions Inc. Easel

◆ Price: §350

◆ Skill: Creativity (Paint)

◆ Need Effects: Fun 5 (Paint), Fun 10 (Ruin Painting)

◆ Need Max: Fun up to 70 (Paint)

◆ Practice Painting/Paint: Satisfies Fun and builds Creativity Skill (at 75 percent of rate of other skill objects because the easel also produces income). "Practice Painting" becomes "Paint" when Sim reaches 5 Creativity. Sim paints a random image, the quality of which increases with Creativity skill.

◆ Paint Still Life: Satisfies Fun, builds Creativity skill. Once Sim reaches Creativity 5, he can paint a still life by selecting a location to paint. Sim paints the location exactly as framed and zoomed.

◆ Paint Portraits: Satisfies Fun, builds Creativity skill. Once Sim reaches Creativity 5, she can paint any Sim on the lot. The chosen Sim approaches the easel and waits. Frame the Sim just as for a still life and painter paints that Sim exactly as posed.

◆ Continue: Satisfies Fun, builds Creativity skill. If painting was left unfinished, the Sim who began the painting can pick up where he left off.

◆ Sell: When a painting is finished, use this interaction to sell it. Sale price depends on Creativity of artist (§0–§500 average). Once the Sim reaches Creativity 10, every painting produced adds hidden points to the value of her art. Extremely diligent painters can fetch up to the absolute maximum of §4,500 per painting. The same price can be had by selling the painting in Buy mode. A finished painting may also be hung on the wall by entering Buy mode and placing it on any empty wall section.

◆ Scrap This Painting: Eliminates a partially finished painting.

◆ Ruin Painting: Satisfies Fun. If the Sim is in a low Mood (0–5), there's a random chance that this interaction will be available. The Sim splatters paint on the canvas, preventing any further painting. If the splatterer has high Creativity skill, this actually increases the sale price of the painting. If splatterer's Creative skill is low, the painting is reduced to its current value. An immature Sim (see "Immaturity and Desperation," Chapter 21), can also autonomously splatter paint on an easel picture.

Chimeway & Daughters Saloon Piano

◆ Price: §3,500

◆ Skill: Creativity (Play), Mechanical (Tune)

◆ Need Effects: Fun 10 (Play), Fun 4 (Watch), Environment 3

Interactions:

◆ Play: Satisfies Fun and builds Creativity skill. Playing speed and quality increases with Creativity skill.

◆ Watch: Satisfies Fun. The more highly skilled the player, the faster watchers' Fun is satisfied. Observers will boo a bad player and cheer a good one, especially if they're Grouchy or Nice, respectively.

◆ Tune: Builds Mechanical Skill. The higher the tuner's skill, the more quickly it's done. Tuning needs to be done after several hours of playing.

Knowledge

Knowledge includes objects that build Logic but also skills that can be learned from books (Cooking, Cleaning, and Mechanical) and some of the more solitary and cerebral Fun objects.

All bookcases are identical in all but their appearance and effect on Environment. Interactions include:

◆ Read Book: Satisfies Fun.

◆ Read to...: Satisfies Fun for reader and child or toddler being read to. Available to teen, adult, and elder if there's a toddler or child on the lot. Menu specifies who to read to.

◆ Ask to be Read To: Same as Read to except initiated by child or toddler (autonomously only).

◆ Study...: Builds Cooking, Cleaning, or Mechanical skill.

◆ Write in Diary: Satisfies Fun and Comfort. Initiated on bookcase but Sim has diary on his person.

◆ Put Away All Books: Sim will find and return all books on the lot.

CinderBooks by Retratech

◆ Price: §200

◆ Skill: Cooking (Study), Mechanical (Study), Cleaning (Study)

◆ Need Effects: Fun 1 (Read or Read to), Fun 1 (Be Read to) Comfort 2 (Write in Diary), Fun 1 (Write in Diary)

◆ Need Max: Fun up to 75 (Read/Read to/Be Read to)

Craftmeister Booknook

◆ Price: §250

◆ Skill: Cooking (Study), Mechanical (Study), Cleaning (Study)

◆ Need Effects: Fun 1 (Read or Read to), Fun 1 (Be Read to) Comfort 1 (Write in Diary), Fun 1 (Write in Diary)

◆ Need Max: Fun up to 75 (Read/Read to/Be Read to)

BiblioFile Bookcase

◆ Price: §400

◆ Skill: Cooking (Study), Mechanical (Study), Cleaning (Study)

◆ Need Effects: Fun 1 (Read or Read to), Fun 1 (Be Read to) Comfort 1 (Write in Diary), Fun 1 (Write in Diary)

◆ Need Max: Fun up to 75 (Read/Read to/Be Read to)

Astrowonder Telescope

◆ Price: §550

◆ Skill: Logic (Stargaze)

◆ Need Effects: Fun 4 (Look Through/Stargaze)

◆ Need Max: Fun up to 80 (Look Through/Stargaze)

Interactions:

◆ Look Through: Satisfies Fun, increases Logic skill. During daylight hours only and indoors only if telescope is facing a window. Sim may peep on neighbor Sims, especially if the Sim is on the Grouchy end of Grouchy/Nice. The neighbor may come over and lecture spying Sim.

◆ Stargaze: Satisfies Fun, increases Logic skill. Same as Look Through but done at night.

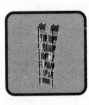

Double-Helix Designer Bookshelf

◆ Price: §650

◆ Skill: Cooking (Study), Mechanical (Study), Cleaning (Study)

◆ Need Effects: Fun 1 (Read or Read to), Fun 1 (Be Read to) Comfort 1 (Write in Diary), Fun 1 (Write in Diary)

◆ Need Max: Fun up to 75 (Read/Read to/Be Read to)

Novellas Nouveau Bookcase

- Price: $800
- Skill: Cooking (Study), Mechanical (Study), Cleaning (Study)
- Need Effects: Fun 1 (Read or Read to), Fun 1 (Be Read to) Comfort 1 (Write in Diary), Fun 1 (Write in Diary)

- Need Max: Fun up to 75 (Read/Read to/Be Read to)

Renaissance Bookcase by Literary Designs

- Price: $950
- Skill: Cooking (Study), Mechanical (Study), Cleaning (Study)
- Need Effects: Fun 1 (Read or Read to), Fun 1 (Be Read to) Comfort 1 (Write in Diary), Fun 1 (Write in Diary), Environment 2

- Need Max: Fun up to 75 (Read/Read to/Be Read to)

Farstar e3 Telescope

- Price: $2,100
- Skill: Logic (Look Through/Stargaze)
- Need Effects: Fun 10 (Look Through/Stargaze)
- Need Max: Fun up to 60 (Look Through/Stargaze)

All interactions same as Astrowonder Telescope.

With this telescope only, there's a low random chance of alien abduction when stargazing. See Chapter 29 for details on alien abduction.

Exercise

Exercise machines build Body skill.

Exerto 5000 Multipress Exercise Machine

- Price: $1,400
- Skill: Body (Work Out), Mechanical (Repair)
- Need Effects: Fun 3 (Active only)
- Need Max: Fun up to 90

Interactions:

- Work Out: Satisfies Fun for Active Sims only. Builds Body Skill. Increases Fitness level. Sim works out faster with fewer rests with higher Body Skill.
- Repair: Increases Mechanical skill.

Recreation

Buried Wood Dartboard

- Price: $180
- Need Effects: Fun 4 (Play), Fun 2 (Watch), Fun 1 (Cheat)
- Need Max: Fun up to 80 (Cheat and Watch)

note

Success at darts is based on a Sim's Mechanical skill.

Interactions:

- Play: Satisfies Fun. If Sims are watching, players receive Social too.
- Join: Satisfies Fun and Social. Joins Sim already playing.
- Watch: Satisfies Fun and Social. Watchers react based on Grouchy/Nice.
- Cheat: Satisfies Fun. If cheater caught, Daily relationship reduced.

King for a Day Outdoor Chess Table

- Price: $399
- Skill: Logic (Practice)
- Need Effects: Fun 7 (Play), Fun 3 (Watch), Fun 1 (Cheat), Fun 1 (Ruin)
- Need Max: Fun up to 80, Social up to 85

There must be at least one dining chair on a playing side of the board. For two Sims to play each other, there must be two chairs.

The "outdoor" chess table can be used anywhere.

Interactions:

- Practice: Satisfies Fun. Builds Logic skill.
- Ask to Join: Satisfies Fun and Social. Builds Logic skill. Available if one Sim is already practicing.
- Watch: Satisfies Fun.
- Cheat: Satisfies Fun. If cheater caught, Daily relationship reduced.

Ruin: Satisfies Fun, autonomous only (Immature).

Grand Parlour Chess Table

- ◆ Price: §500
- ◆ Skill: Logic (Practice)
- ◆ Need Effects: Fun 7 (Play), Fun 3 (Watch), Fun 1 (Cheat), Fun 1 (Ruin)
- ◆ Need Max: Fun up to 80, Social up to 85

Identical to King for a Day Outdoor Chess Table.

It's MYSHUNO! (The Fabulously Zany Party Game)

- ◆ Price: §870
- ◆ Need Effects: Fun 10 (depends on age and number of players), Social (by number of players)
- ◆ Need Max: Fun up to 80
- ◆ Group Activity

Interactions:

- ◆ Call: Satisfies Fun and Social. First player waits for others to join. If no one joins in 15 minutes, it becomes a practice game (see "Practice," below). If players are already waiting for a caller when Sim chooses Call, game starts. Elders get more Fun than other ages.
- ◆ Play: Satisfies Fun and Social. If first player, waits for others to join. If no one joins, Sim quits. If game starts, Caller calls out numbers and winner is first Sim with three matches. Elders get more Fun than other ages.
- ◆ Practice: Satisfies Fun (much less than real game). Sim plays alone. Elders get more Fun than other ages.

Miscellaneous

Objects that fit nowhere else: Dressers, children's stuff, and party objects.

Dressers

All dressers are functionally identical but vary in the amount of Environment they supply.

Interactions:

- ◆ Change Into: Changes into any outfits owned by any members of the house of the same age and gender. Choose by outfit type (e.g., Everyday, Formal, etc.) as defined in "Plan Outfit."
- ◆ Plan Outfit: Select which clothing items will be the default outfit for each outfit type. Once defined,

Sim always changes into the planned outfit for each situation.

- ◆ Dress for Work: Changes into Sims uniform for their specific career and job level.

Anti-Quaint-Ed Ltd. Ed. Armoire

- ◆ Price: §250

Werkbunnst Stonewood Dresser

- ◆ Price: §510
- ◆ Need Effects: Environment 2

Decorative House Armoire

- ◆ Price: §550
- ◆ Need Effects: Environment 2

Dynasty Armoire

- ◆ Price: §560
- ◆ Need Effects: Environment 2

Touch of Teak Plymouth Armoire

- ◆ Price: §812
- ◆ Need Effects: Environment 2

Dynasty Dresser 2

- ◆ Price: §900
- ◆ Need Effects: Environment 3

Rob R. Barron "Nouveau" Wardrobe
- ◆ Price: §1,000
- ◆ Need Effects: Environment 3

Su-Tove Armoire
- ◆ Price: §1,200
- ◆ Need Effects: Environment 3

Touch of Teak Tansu Dresser
- ◆ Price: §1,520
- ◆ Need Effects: Environment 4

Chesterstick Cherry Dresser
- ◆ Price: §2,125
- ◆ Need Effects: Environment 6

Children

Kids (children and toddlers, to be exact) require special objects for Fun and Skill building. It's not that they can't use *any* adult objects (though they are limited), but some are just more suited to their age. This menu also contains some extremely handy baby helpers.

Magical Mystery's "Shape, Rattle & Roll"
- ◆ Price: §30
- ◆ Skill: Logic (Play)
- ◆ Need Effects: Fun 6 (Play), Fun 2 (Play With), Social
- ◆ Need Max: Fun to 80 (Toddler) or 75 (Others)

Interactions:
- ◆ Play: Toddler only. Satisfies Fun, builds Logic.
- ◆ Play With: Child/teen/adult/elder. Satisfies Fun and Social.

Rip Co. Wobbly Wabbit Head
- ◆ Price: §35
- ◆ Skill: Charisma (Play)
- ◆ Need Effects: Fun 10 (Play, Play With), Social (Play With)
- ◆ Need Max: Fun up to 75

Interactions:
- ◆ Play: Toddler only. Satisfies Fun and builds Charisma.
- ◆ Play With: Child/teen/adult/elder. Satisfies Fun and Social.

Rip Co. Xylophone
- ◆ Price: §40
- ◆ Skill: Creativity
- ◆ Need Effects: Fun 4 (Play, Play With, Watch), Social (Play With, Watch)
- ◆ Need Max: Fun up to 70

Interactions:
- ◆ Play: Toddler only. Satisfies Fun and builds Creativity. Music improves with Creativity.
- ◆ Play With: Child/teen/adult/elder. Satisfies Fun and Social.
- ◆ Watch: Child/teen/adult/elder. Satisfies Fun and Social.

Durably Plush Teddy Bear
- ◆ Price: §49
- ◆ Need Effects: Comfort 3 (Carry, Play—child), Fun 10 (Play—child), Fun 8 (Play—toddler), Fun 9 (Talk Through), Social (Talk Through)
- ◆ Need Max: Fun up to 85 (toddler) or 90 (others)

Interactions:
- ◆ Carry: Children. Satisfies Fun and Comfort.
- ◆ Play: Children and toddlers. Satisfies Fun and Comfort.
- ◆ Talk Through To: Teen/adult/elder to any other Sim. Satisfies Fun and Social.

The Kinder Koddler
- ◆ Price: §50
- ◆ Skill: Cleaning (Clean)
- ◆ Need Effects: Comfort 2, Hygiene -1 (if dirty)
- ◆ Need Max: Comfort up to 70

note

If any of a toddler's Needs drop too low while in the chair, she'll cry, whine, or tantrum. If left in the chair too long and her Hunger or Social fails, the Social Worker comes and removes toddler from household.

Interactions:

◆ Place Toddler in Chair: Teen/adult/elder puts toddler in high chair. Toddlers can't do this themselves and can't get out. If high chair is dirty, it depletes Hygiene.

◆ Serve Toddler Food: Bring toddler a bowl of toddler mush from refrigerator. Autonomous if a meal is being served.

◆ Give Bottle to Toddler: Bring toddler a bottle from refrigerator.

◆ Clean Up Bowl/Bottle: Removes and disposes item from tray.

◆ Let Toddler Out: Removes toddler from chair and places him on ground. If remover is Neat, she'll clean the chair.

◆ Hold Toddler: Removes toddler from chair.

◆ Clean: Cleans dirty chair. Improves Environment and builds Cleaning skill.

Rip Co. Toy Bin

◆ Price: §55
◆ Need Effects: Fun 7
◆ Need Max: Fun up to 85

Interactions:

◆ Get Toys Out: Child/toddler/adult/elder. Take toy out of box and place on floor to make toy available to toddler.

◆ Join/Ask to Join: Child only. Click on other child playing with toys from box to join in play and group talk. Satisfies Fun and Social.

◆ Play With Toys: Child or walking toddler pulls toy from box and plays with it. Satisfies Fun.

◆ Play With: Toddler or child plays with toy already on the floor. Satisfies Fun.

◆ Put Away: Put individual toy away. Autonomous for Neat.

◆ Put Toys Away: Puts away all toys on lot. Autonomous for Neat.

Tinkle Trainer 6000 Potty Chair

◆ Price: §70
◆ Skill: Potty Training
◆ Need Effects: Bladder 10

Interactions:

◆ Potty Train Toddler: Teen/adult/elder. Teaches toddler to use potty. Gradual process, see Chapter 22. Depletes Energy and satisfies Social.

◆ Take to Potty: Teen/adult/elder. Available after complete potty training. Toddler always accepts. Depletes Energy and satisfies Social. Useful when toddler can't get to potty (i.e. up stairs).

◆ Use: Satisfies Bladder. Once potty trained, toddler can use potty without help.

◆ Empty: Increases Environment and makes potty useable (if full).

Rip Co. Little Baker Oven

◆ Price: §100
◆ Skill: Cooking
◆ Need Effects: Fun 1
◆ Need Max: Fun up to 75

Interactions:

◆ Bake: Children only. Satisfies Fun and builds Cooking skill. Muffin burning and quality depends on Cooking skill.

◆ Get Food: Children only. Removes muffin from oven. Muffin can be eaten.

Will Lloyd Wright Dollhouse

◆ Price: §180
◆ Need Effects: Fun 10 (Play—Toddler/child), Fun 4 (Play, teen/adult/elder), Fun 4 (Watch), Social
◆ Group Activity

Interactions:

◆ Play: Toddler/child only. Satisfies Fun.

◆ Join: Toddler/child/teen/adult/elder can join playing with child/toddler already playing. Satisfies Fun and Social.

◆ Watch: Teen/adult/elder can watch toddler/children playing. Satisfies Fun and Social.

◆ Smash: Destroys dollhouse, must be disposed of. Immature child or teen may do autonomously.

The Kinder Kontainer

◆ Price: §275
◆ Need Effects: Energy 12, Social (Tuck In)

Interactions:

◆ Put Baby/Toddler in Crib: Teen/adult/elder puts baby/toddler in crib. If baby/toddler Energy is very low, he will automatically go to sleep. If toddler Energy is high, she'll cry. If Energy low but above automatic

sleeping level but other motives are low, he will cry and shake bars (toddler).

◆ Tuck In Baby/Toddler: Teen/adult/elder only when baby/toddler is sleeping. Satisfies Social.

◆ Hold Baby/Toddler: Teen/adult/elder picks up baby/toddler.

◆ Let Baby/Toddler Out: Teen/adult/elder picks up baby/toddler and places her on the floor.

◆ Sneak Out: Walking toddlers shaking the crib may autonomously sneak out of the crib by themselves.

Sanitation Station Baby Changing Table
◆ Price: §400
◆ Need Effects: Hygiene 10
Interactions:
   ◆ Dress Baby/Toddler in Everyday/PJs: Teen/adult/elder changes baby/toddler into other outfit.
◆ Change Diaper: Teen/adult/elder changes baby/toddler's diaper. Baby/toddler gets Hygiene (more than changing without changing table)

Party

Parties are better with objects. Some objects are absolutely crucial to certain events.

London's Famous Birthday Cake
◆ Price: §30
Interactions:
   ◆ Blow Out: Available only to Sim with age transition within two days. Sim grows up. If there's a party too, cinematic runs.
◆ Help Baby/Toddler Blow Out: Available to teen/ elder/adult to help baby/toddler with age transition within two days. Otherwise identical to Blow Out.
◆ Grab a Plate: Once cake's been used for age transition, it becomes a food item.
◆ Clean Up: After cake's been used for age transition or after it spoils, it can be thrown away like any food.

Poppin' Party Balloon Centerpiece
◆ Price: §50

Whatay Buffet
◆ Price: §300
◆ Need Effects: Hunger 8
◆ Need Max:

Interactions:

◆ Serve Food: Stocks buffet's three stations (Turkey, Gelatin, Salad). Each station costs money to stock (§150 for Turkey and §75 for Salad and Gelatin).

◆ Grab a Plate: Satisfies Hunger. Choose which food to select.

◆ Clean Up: Removes all uneaten food. Buffet is ready for restocking.

Titania Vineyards 1914 Toasting Set
◆ Price: §350
◆ Need Effects: Fun 1, Hunger 1, Social

note

Toast may randomly be rejected based on relationship.

◆ Toast To: Teen/adult/elder only. Choose which teen/adult/elder Sim to toast to. All Sims on lot gather and toast. Satisfies Hunger and Fun. At Wedding party only, guests may autonomously toast newlyweds (who obligingly kiss).

◆ Toast With: Teen/adult/elder only. Choose which teen/adult/elder to share a private toast. Both Sims gather and toast. Satisfies Hunger, Fun, and Social.

◆ Dispose: Throw away toasting set.

Antonio's Prize-Winning Wedding Cake
◆ Price: §400
◆ Need Effects: Hunger 1
◆ Need Max:
◆ Group Activity
◆ Cut: Newlyweds only. The Sim not doing the cutting will be fed a piece of cake.
◆ Grab a Plate: Satisfies Hunger. Available once cake has been cut by newlyweds.
◆ Clean Up: Dispose of cake after cutting.

Bachman Busbar

◆ Price: $600

◆ Need Effects: Fun 3

◆ Need Max: Fun up to 50 (Juggle) or 80 (Make Drinks) or 50 (consume drinks) or 70—90 (Drink from Bottle, depends on Playful/Serious).

Bars also enable group talk when many Sims are engaged with them. Bars are also, thus, a source of Social Need satisfaction.

note

It makes no functional difference whether drinks are blended or poured.

Interactions:

◆ Drink from Bottle: Satisfies Hunger and Fun. Playful Sims get a higher maximum Fun than Serious.

◆ Make a Drink: Satisfies Fun. Prepares single drink.

◆ Make Drinks: Prepares multiple drinks.

◆ Juggle Tumblers: Satisfies Fun.

◆ Join: Satisfies Fun Join juggling.

note

Making the drinks at the bar is fun but just drinking them gives a bit of Fun too.

Retro Lounge "High Liquidity" Juice Bar

◆ Price: $800

◆ Need Effects: Fun 3

◆ Need Max: Fun up to 50 (Juggle) or 80 (Make Drinks) or 50 (consume drinks) or 70—90 (Drink from Bottle, depends on Playful/Serious).

See Bachman Busbar, above.

Trellisor Wedding Arch

◆ Price: $900

◆ Need Effects: Fun 1, Social

Required items to get the Wedding/Joining cinematic and partial requirement for the party to end in a honeymoon. See Chapter 25 for full details.

Interactions:

◆ Get Married/Joined: Satisfies Fun and Social. Triggers marriage/joining and accompanying cinematic.

Black Lacquer Bar Counter

◆ Price: $1,000

◆ Need Effects: Fun 3

◆ Need Max: Fun up to 50 (Juggle) or 80 (Make Drinks) or 50 (consume drinks) or 70—90 (Drink from Bottle, depends on Playful/Serious).

See Bachman Busbar, above.

Miscellaneous Miscellaneous

Peace of Garbage Can

◆ Price: $30

◆ Need Effects: Hunger 3 (Eat from Trash), Hygiene -2 (Eat from Trash), Hygiene -1 (Salvage)

Low capacity trash can. Must be emptied frequently.

Interactions:

◆ Salvage: Available to Sloppy Sims only. Adds simoleans but decreases Hygiene.

◆ Eat from Trash: Available to Sloppy Sims only (autonomous only). Satisfies Hunger but depletes Hygiene. Carries risk of illness.

◆ Empty: Take trash to outdoor can. Hygiene reduced when carrying trash bag.

Narcisco Rubbish Bin

◆ Price: $45

◆ Need Effects: Hunger 3 (Eat from Trash), Hygiene -2 (Eat from Trash), Hygiene -1 (Salvage)

Double the capacity of the cheap trash can.

See Peace of Garbage Can, above.

Swing Kidz Deluxe Swing Set

◆ Price: $450

◆ Need Effects: Fun 7 (Swing), Fun 4 (Push), Fun 5 (Chill), Social

◆ Need Max: Fun up to 70 (Push) or 80 (Chill)

note

Swing Sets connect when placed next to each other in the same orientation.

Interactions:

◆ Swing: Satisfies Fun. Satisfies Social if others are on swings or someone is pushing (group talk).

◆ Push: Only available if someone is swinging. Satisfies Fun and Social.

◆ Chill: Teens only. Satisfies Fun and, if others are Chilling, Social (group talk).

Community Lot—Only Objects

Many of the objects cataloged above are also available for designing your Community Lots. Some, however, are exclusive to these non-residential destinations.

Surfaces

Old Boys Club Commercial Counter

◆ Price: §710

◆ Need Effects: Environment 2

CounterRevolution Commercial Counter

◆ Price: § 750

◆ Need Effects: Environment 2

Decorative

Produce Market Shingle

◆ Price: §99

SimCity SynapseSnapper Industrial Sign

◆ Price: §99

Wear's the Sale? Shop Sign

◆ Price: §99

Plumbing

Sewage Brothers Resteze Urinal

◆ Price: §400

◆ Need Effects: Bladder 10

Interactions are the same as other toilets but can be used by males only. Additionally, urinals don't get dirty (so no cleaning is necessary) and can't be thrown up in. OK, too much information.

Appliances

GazeEase "Stow 'N' Show" Produce Bin

◆ Price: $3,000

◆ Need Effects: Fun 4, Environment 3

◆ Need Max: Fun up to 80

Imperial Plumbing Pole-Air Freezer Bin

◆ Price: $3,000

◆ Need Effects: Fun 4, Environment 3

◆ Need Max: Fun up to 80

VeggiStuf Produce Bin

◆ Price: $3,000

◆ Need Effects: Fun 4, Environment 3

◆ Need Max: Fun up to 80

Food Shrine Commercial Display Freezer

◆ Price: $3,000

◆ Need Effects: Fun 4, Environment 3

◆ Need Max: Fun up to 80

Food Temple Commercial Display Freezer

◆ Price: $3,000

◆ Need Effects: Fun 4, Environment 3

◆ Need Max: Fun up to 80

Electronics

Llamark Electronic Cash Register

◆ Price: $205

Neukum Systems Wall Speakers

◆ Price: $400

◆ Need Effects: Fun 2

These commercial grade speakers produce one kind of music and don't have to be connected to a stereo. They are color-coded to the precise musical genre:

◆ Black: "Art of Darkness" Heavy Metal Wall Speaker

◆ Blue: "Bubblegum Sugar" Pop Wall Speaker

◆ Green: "En Fuego" Salsa Wall Speaker

◆ Red: "Glo Stik" Techno Wall Speaker

◆ Yellow: "The Badunkadunk" Hip Hop Wall Speaker

◆ Brown: "The Cold Train" R&B Wall Speaker

SCTC Universal Public Phone

◆ Price: $550

Every lot comes with a public phone, the sole purpose of which is summoning taxis. Additional phones may be added for aesthetics or to reduce walking.

Miscellaneous

'Right Away' Community Trash-Can

◆ Price: $75

◆ Need Effects: Hunger 3 (Eat from Trash), Hygiene -2 (Eat from Trash), Hygiene -1 (Salvage)

Identical to outdoor trash can on residential lots. Bottomless.

Interactions:

◆ Eat from Trash: Available to Sloppy Sims only (autonomous only). Satisfies Hunger but depletes Hygiene. Carries risk of illness.

SimSentry Clothing Booth

◆ Price: $370

◆ Need Effects: Fun 4

◆ Need Max:

When Try On is chosen from a clothing rack, the Sim will go inside the nearest clothing booth to change.

Clothing booths have no interactions, per se, unless a Sim is inside trying on clothes:

◆ WooHoo/Try for Baby: Satisfies Fun and Social, depletes Hunger and Energy. See "Object Assisted Sim-to-Sim Interactions," Chapter 24.

Old Fashioned Change Room

◆ Price: $690

◆ Need Effects: Fun 4

See SimSentry Clothing Booth, above.

Deluxe Magazine Rack

◆ Price: $2,500

◆ Need Effects: Fun 4, Environment 7

◆ Need Max: Fun up to 80

Interactions:

◆ Buy: Satisfies Fun. Choose which magazine to buy based on the interests it alters.

ClothesHorse Display Rack

◆ Price: $3,000

◆ Need Effects: Fun 4, Environment 8

All clothes are available at all clothing racks.

note

In "Try On" and "Buy," an outfit already owned by a member of the Sim's household has a "dresser" icon on it.

Interactions:

◆ Browse: Satisfies Fun.

◆ Try On: Choose outfits for Sim to apply in the clothing booth. Only outfits for Sim's age and gender are shown. Choose an outfit and click "OK." If there's a mirror nearby, Sim will take a look.

◆ Buy: Teen/elder/adult. Can buy clothes for any age and gender. Put items in the shopping cart and, when finished, check out.

The Great Dress Rack

◆ Price: $3,000

◆ Need Effects: Fun 4, Environment 8

See ClothesHorse Display Rack, above.

Countertop Game Display from Group Interaction LTD.

◆ Price: $3,500

◆ Need Effects: Fun 4, Environment 9

◆ Need Max: Fun up to 80

Interactions:

◆ Buy: Satisfies Fun. Choose which game to be available in all video game consoles and computers in the household.

Enterprise Office Freestanding Game Rack

◆ Price: $4,000

◆ Need Effects: Fun 4, Environment 10

◆ Need Max: Fun up to 80

Interactions:

◆ Buy: Satisfies Fun. Choose which game to be available in all video game consoles and computers in the household.

Empress's New Clothes Rack

◆ Price: $5,000

◆ Need Effects: Fun 4, Environment 10

See ClothesHorse Display Rack, above.

Exceptionally Expensive Clothing Collator

◆ Price: $5,000

◆ Need Effects: Fun 4, Environment 10

See ClothesHorse Display Rack, above.

Aspiration Reward Objects

Aspiration reward objects are detailed in Chapter 21.

Career Reward Objects

Career reward objects are designed to be used alone or in an instructive mode with a more-experienced Sim teaching a less-experienced one.

When these objects are used alone, skill building is faster than for Buy mode skill building objects. Children using these objects alone, however, build skill at a slower rate than adults.

All career reward objects have the same basic interactions:

◆ Offer Lessons To: More experienced teen/adult/elder offers lessons to anyone less experienced in the object's skill.

◆ Ask Sim for Lessons: Less Experienced Sim asks Teen/Adult/Elder with more experience for lessons in the object's skill.

Selling a reward object won't yield any money because they have no resale value. Once sold, however, they must be re-earned by another Sim reaching the required career level.

SensoTwitch Lie Finder

◆ Career (Level): Criminal (4)
◆ Skill: Creativity, Mechanical (Repair)

Interactions:

◆ Practice Lying: Increases Creativity skill. Occasionally, Sim is caught lying and receives a completely harmless electrical shock.

AquaGreen Hydroponic Garden

◆ Career (Level): Slacker (5)
◆ Skill: Creativity
◆ Need Effects: Fun 4 (Tend)

Interactions:

◆ Plant: Plants seeds in pots. No interaction is possible for several hours until the plants have sprouted.

◆ Tend: Satisfies Fun and builds Creativity. Once plants sprout, the must be tended regularly to reach their full bloomed growth stage. If not tended enough, they'll wilt instead of growing into the next stage.

◆ Harvest: Plants, if properly tended will grow into tall, leafy plants that can be used as houseplants or sold in Buy mode. Harvesting empties the pots for a new planting.

Enterprise Office Concepts Bushmaster Tele-Prompter

◆ Career (Level): Politics (5)
◆ Skill: Charisma
◆ Need Effects: Fun 5 (Play), Fun 3 (Practice)

◆ Need Max: Fun up to 75 (Play), 90 (Listen), or 60 (Practice).

Interactions:

◆ Practice Speech: Satisfies Fun and increases Charisma skill.
◆ Play: Satisfies Fun. Child only.
◆ Listen: Satisfies Fun.

Execuputter

◆ Career (Level): Business (5)
◆ Skill: Charisma
◆ Need Effects: Fun 4
◆ Need Max: Fun up to 70

Interactions:

◆ Putt: Satisfies Fun, builds Charisma.

Exerto Punching Bag

◆ Career (Level): Athletic (5)
◆ Skill: Body
◆ Need Effects: Fun 6
◆ Need Max: Fun up to 80 (Punch) or 70 (Teaching Sim)

Interactions:

◆ Punch: Satisfies Fun and increases Body skill. Proficiency with the bag tied to Body Skill; at level 5, begins kicking bag too. Increases Fitness.

Exerto Selfflog Obstacle Course

◆ Career (Level): Military (4)
◆ Skill: Body
◆ Need Effects: Fun 4

Interactions:

◆ Run Course: Increase Body skill. Two Sims can run at once. Successful run satisfies Fun. Proficiency at running course tied to Body skill. Increases fitness.

Prints Charming Fingerprinting Scanner

◆ Career (Level): Law Enforcement (6)
◆ Skill: Cleaning
◆ Need Effects: Fun 4 (Scan for Prints)
◆ Need Max: Fun up to 70

note

If no Sim has used the scanned object, a random neighbor will be identified.

Interactions:

◆ Scan for Prints: Satisfies Fun and increases Cleaning skill. Sim chooses random object to scan and, if successful, detects the last Sim that used the object. Success depends on Cleaning skill.

Schokolade 890 Chocolate Manufacturing Facility

◆ Career (Level): Culinary (6)
◆ Skill: Cooking
◆ Need Effects: Fun I (Make Candies)
◆ Need Max: Fun up to 70

Interactions:

◆ Make Candies: Satisfies Fun and increases Cooking skill. As Sim builds Cooking skill, he will be able to successfully produce candy that can be sold. If the Sim using it is low skill, the machine leaves brown chocolate puddles on the floor.

◆ Steal Candy: Satisfies Hunger and Energy. Unmopped candy puddles can be tasted by toddlers, making them very hyper for a time. Autonomous only.

Simsanto Inc. Biotech Station

◆ Career (Level): Science (6)
◆ Skill: Logic
◆ Need Effects: Fun 4 (Make Medicine)
◆ Need Max: Fun up to 70

Interactions:

◆ Make Medicine: Satisfies Fun and increases Logic skill. Teen/adult/elder only; children cannot make medicine but can be taught or ask to be taught. When medicine's finished, vials are removed and placed on the machine (to be sold, used, or disposed of (see below). Factors in the quality of medicine are: Logic, Hygiene, Nice/Grouchy, and Mood. The higher they are, the stronger and more effective the medicine and the higher the price it'll fetch. The darker the color of the medicine (or virus), the stronger it is.

◆ Get Medicine: Removes medicine once it's been made.

◆ Dispose: Throw away failed medicine or virus.

◆ Sell Medicine: Sell finished medicine. Price based on quality. Virus cannot be sold.

◆ Take Medicine: If teen/adult/elder Sim is sick, she can consume finished medicine.

◆ Give Medicine To: If toddler/child Sim is sick, an teen/adult/elder can get medicine from the machine and give it to the toddler/child.

note

If Sim is bad at making medicine (low Logic, low Hygiene, a Grouchy personality, and a barely positive Mood), it's possible medicine will fail and be either simply unusable or instead yield a dangerous virus. Virus vials are green instead of blue.

Occasionally, if a Sim is very bad at making medicine, he'll mishandle the vials of virus and get very ill. See Chapter 29 for details on disease.

TraumaTime "Incision Precision" Surgical Training Station

◆ Career (Level): Medicine (4)
◆ Skill: Mechanical
◆ Need Effects: Fun 4

Interactions:

◆ Practice: Teen/adult/elder only. Satisfies Fun and increases Mechanical skill. Occasionally, a Sim pull out something she shouldn't; alarm will sound and Sim must "resuscitate" dummy. It's random whether the dummy will live, but Sim may continue regardless. Children can't use object alone.

Chapter 29
Disasters, Disease, and Death

Life isn't all juice bars and hot tubs for Sims. It's a dangerous world out there, and a Sim can get seriously hurt if he's not careful. Disaster awaits in many places, but knowledge of the dangers allows you to avoid the worst hazards.

Sims can also get seriously ill. Most of these sicknesses are unavoidable, but all can be cured with some patience and diligence. Or, perhaps, a bit of chemistry.

Finally, death is now quite inevitable for all Sims, not just those careless enough to try to repair the TV or unlucky enough to have a pool ladder mysteriously removed. Old age takes everyone someday. How a Sims dies is a direct result of how she lived, and making that moment as fruitful as possible is one of the game's major goals. Still, several vehicles for premature death must be guarded against, else the best laid plans can be cut short by cruel fate.

This chapter guides you through the most treacherous waters in a Sim's life, and all matters relating to the hereafter.

DISASTERS

Disasters are any events that cause disorder in a Sim's life and need to be remedied to stop the damage. They aren't all harrowing, but they all deserve attention.

Fire
Causes

Fire can break out any moment, but it's usually caused by unskilled cooks.

Fire can occur from several sources:

- ◆ Cooking: Ruined food has a 10 percent chance of starting a fire. Low skill cooks ruin food most frequently.
- ◆ Unattended Cooking: If a Sim gets distracted while food is in the oven, the food will burn and start a fire if left in the oven beyond its cooking time. Smoke appears before fire is triggered.
- ◆ Fireplaces: Flammable objects (i.e. made of wood or cloth) too close to a fireplace can start a fire.
- ◆ Electrocution: Any time a Sim is electrocuted during a repair, there is a chance the repaired object will ignite a fire.

Fire Behavior

Once started, a fire consumes the object that ignited it unless it's extinguished. When an object is consumed, it turns to ash and is lost. Ash piles reduce Environment score and should be cleaned up soon.

> ## note
> During a fire, Buy and Build modes are disabled so you can't move or sell items to get them away from the fire.

Fire spreads randomly to adjacent objects or floor and burns out on its own only if it has nowhere to spread.

All Sims in the house run to the fire and panic. If a toddler approaches the fire, someone usually moves the toddler to a safe location before returning to resume panicking.

note

Even if the toddler isn't moved, no harm will come to her. Toddlers and babies are completely fireproof, as are the crib and high chair.

If a Sim gets too close to a fire, there's a random chance he'll catch fire and be killed. Other Sims can click on a burning Sim and attempt to Extinguish him.

Preventing Fires

Avoid fires by controlling the risk factors:

- Inexperienced cooks shouldn't cook in a stove or toaster oven until they get some Cooking skill.
- Smoke alarms in the same room as stoves and fireplaces should be mandatory.
- Sims with low Mechanical skill should not try to repair electronic objects.
- Keep all furniture away from fireplaces.
- Keep Free Will turned on and never direct a Sim to do anything when there's something in the oven.

In the Event of Fire

If a fire breaks out, summon the fire department. A smoke alarm in the same room as the fire does this automatically. Without a smoke alarm, however, a Sim must be directed to the phone to call the fire department.

note

Often, you must cancel the Sim's autonomous panic reaction to get him to make the call. This is often the case with burglaries too.

Sims can extinguish fires themselves by canceling their panic reaction, clicking on the burning object, and choosing Extinguish. Any other fires are automatically put out as well. Sims extinguish slower than Firefighters, however, so there's a greater chance that the fire will spread if a Sim does it herself.

Burglaries

Burglaries occur between 10 p.m. and 4 a.m. approximately once every 20 nights.

The Burglar creeps into the house, cases the joint, and finds and steals up to five of the most valuable objects on the lot.

The Burglar's visit is unavoidable, but an alarm keeps him from stealing anything and automatically summons the law.

The best defense against the Burglar is a burglar alarm. When the Burglar enters a room with a burglar alarm on any of its walls, the alarm sounds. The alarm sends the Burglar into a panic, preventing him from even attempting to steal anything. It also summons the Police, who arrive in a few moments.

note

As with fires, once the Burglar appears on the lot, Buy and Build mode are disabled, preventing movement or deletion of objects he might steal.

tip

While waiting for the Police, try to route Sims to block any exits. This prevents the Burglar from escaping before the law arrives.

If there's no burglar alarm, the Burglar will steal five objects and get away scot-free unless your Sims act. If they're asleep, awaken one and direct her to call the Police. Only the Police can actually apprehend the Burglar.

No matter how the Police are summoned, the officer dashes into the house and confronts the Burglar. They tangle in an Attack interaction.

If the Burglar wins, she escapes. If the cop wins (which they do 90 percent of the time), the Burglar is apprehended.

Once the cop stows the Burglar in the squad car, Sims get a §500 reward if no objects were taken. If any objects were stolen, they instead get insurance money for the objects' depreciated value but not the objects themselves.

After a burglary, Sims who were present get a negative Memory of the event. If any Sims have a Fear of having something stolen and an object was taken, their Aspiration score is reduced. Sims may periodically cry over the Memory or talk about it. They may also lament the loss of any objects, even if the Burglar was apprehended.

There's no way to avoid burglary, but the burglar alarm at least prevents any objects being taken and any Fear realizations from the theft.

Floods

Though they pale in comparison to fire and theft, floods can cause serious problems. If leaky plumbing fixtures are left unrepaired, they create a flood that could spread over the entire level. If on the ground floor, the flood spills out to the street.

Floods punish Environment score so fix broken plumbing fixtures, especially sinks (which leak continuously when broken) ASAP.

Alien Abduction

If an adult Sim uses the Farstar e3 Telescope between 7 p.m. and 2 a.m. to Stargaze, there's a five percent chance that he'll be abducted by aliens.

Spend too much time obsessing about the heavens and they'll come take you for a ride.

While the Sim is gone, his Need meters fluctuate wildly. When he's returned three hours later, however, the Sim will be the same as when he left.

Unless, of course, the Sim in question is an adult male. Any time an adult male Sim is abducted by aliens, he always returns pregnant.

DISEASE

Several diseases can infect Sims. Adult, teen or elder Sims can get sick, but toddlers and babies can never suffer disease.

Vomiting is a sure sign of either food poisoning or pregnancy.

Disease	Symptoms	Source	Contagious?	Potentially Fatal
Cold	Coughing, Sneezing	1% chance of catching a cold anytime Sim goes to work or school	Highly	No, if untreated, becomes pneumonia
Flu	Coughing, Diarrhea	Up to 5% chance if near roaches	Highly	Yes
Pneumonia	Coughing, Fatigue	Untreated cold becomes pneumonia	Slightly	Yes
Food Poisoning	Vomiting, Nausea	5% chance anytime Sim eats spoiled food	No	Yes
Morning Sickness	Vomiting, Nausea	Pregnancy (day 1)	No	No
Virus	2 random symptoms	Mishandling of virus created with Biotech Station (Science career object), with severity determined by the Logic skill of the creating Sim and manifested by the darkness of the color of the virus's vial	Highly	Yes

Contagiousness

Many illnesses can be spread from Sim to Sim. Anywhere a contagious Sim goes, she leaves behind germs. The more contagious a disease is, the longer the germs persist. If another Sim encounters a sick Sim's germs, he has a five percent chance of catching the disease.

If a Sim has any of the contagious illnesses, the best course is to prevent other Sims from interacting with her until she's recovered.

Symptoms

Every disease features two symptoms that help in identifying precisely what sickness has befallen the Sim.

note

The only diseases with identical symptoms are food poisoning and morning sickness. If the Sim showing both these symptoms is male and hasn't recently been abducted by aliens or is female and hasn't recently engaged in a Try for Baby interaction, you can rest assured they just got some spoiled grub.

The only wild card is the Biotech Station virus that manifests two random symptoms. The earmark of this condition, however, is the symptoms. If the symptoms of a minor disease are extremely potent, the Sim probably has a virus.

The Biotech Station can be a cause of illness or a cure. Only households with an Sim successfully navigating the Science track will have one.

Symptoms are:

◆ Vomiting: Sim will attempt to vomit in a toilet but will, if necessary, vomit on the floor. Severity is determined from length of vomiting. Comfort decreases.

◆ Nausea: Sudden drop in Comfort, the degree of which indicates severity.

◆ Coughing: Sim coughs. Comfort drops; the bigger the drop, the more severe the symptom.

◆ Sneezing: Sim sneezes. Comfort drops; the bigger the drop, the more severe the symptom.

◆ Fatigue: Sudden drop in Energy. The bigger the drop, the more severe the symptom.

◆ Diarrhea: Sudden drop in Bladder. The bigger the drop, the more severe the symptom.

With this information, it's easy to play doctor and diagnose any ailing Sim.

Recovery

There are two cures to every disease: rest and medicine.

Every disease can be cured with about 12 collective (not necessarily consecutive) hours of sleep, lounging, sitting, or relaxing. In other words, satisfying Comfort and/or Energy and keeping them high when the Sim must move about are the cure-all. However, most of the time, Sims get better on their own.

Rest and relaxation are the only cure for Sims lacking a Biotech Station object. When a Sim's high on Energy, have him relax on a bed.

For a quicker cure, medicine made on the Biotech Station reward object can, depending on the disease's severity and the medicine's strength, instantly cure any disease. Teens/adults/elders can take finished medicine from the machine. Toddlers and children need a teen/adult/elder to administer the medicine.

> **note**
>
> If a disease is severe or medicine was not strong enough (made by a low Logic Sim), it may take several doses to cure the disease.

As a Sim recovers, symptoms become less severe though not less frequent.

A text message announces when a Sim is cured.

Death by Disease

If any potentially fatal disease persists for 10 days (Sim not getting sufficient rest), the Sim will die of disease. Toddlers and babies, however, can't die from disease, so they simply continue being severely sick.

DEATH

In *The Sims 2*, death is inevitable. Your Sim is going to pass on sometime, so make the most of the time she has. She can go after a long happy (or long miserable) life or her flame can be snuffed out prematurely by an act of fate or a sad consequence of the life she leads.

> **note**
>
> No matter how a Sim dies, his Aspiration Score at the time of death affects the amount of inheritance his survivors receive. Keep Aspiration score high; you never know when your Sim's last moment will be.

Ways to Die

There are nine ways a Sim can die:

> **note**
>
> Babies and toddlers cannot die.

Old Age (Elder)

When a Sim reaches the end of his life (up to 20 days after becoming an Elder), he will die of old age. This is the one cause of death that completely precludes pleading with the Reaper. When it's a Sim's time, there's nothing the living can do.

Death by old age can be sad or beautiful (if you like hula dancers, that is).

How gracefully the Sim goes depends on his Aspiration Score at the time of death.

Drowning (Child/Teen/Adult/Elder)

If a swimming Sim's Energy or Hunger Needs reach rock bottom while she's in the pool, she'll drown.

Drowning is one case in which surviving Sims may not be able to plead with the Reaper to spare the deceased's life. No pleas can occur when the Reaper is over water, so a drowned Sim can be resurrected only if she drowned very near the edge of the pool.

Electrocution (Teen/Adult/Elder)

Electrocution can occur any time a Sim repairs an electrical object. The probability of electrocution drops as the Sim rises in Mechanical skill, but the possibility is always there.

Sims aren't killed by the electrocution itself, but rather by the dramatic Need drop it causes. All Needs plummet by 50 points each upon electrocution; if three or more of them drop below -90 as a result, the Sim dies.

Burning (Teen/Adult/Elder)

Standing too close to the flames can get a Sim charred or killed.

If a Sim is close to a fire when it spreads to the tile on which he stands, he'll catch on fire. If he's not extinguished before his three Needs bottom out, he'll die and dissolve into a pile of ash.

Starvation (Teen/Adult/Elder)

Some time after a Sim's Hunger Need reaches -100 (rock bottom), she collapses and dies of hunger.

Babies, toddlers, and children can't die of Hunger. Instead they get taken away by the Social Worker.

Satellite (Teen/Adult/Elder)

While doing the Watch Cloud (daytime) or Stargaze (nighttime, not with telescope) interaction outdoors, there is a very small random chance that a satellite will fall on and crush a Sim. Nothing is left of the dearly departed but a pile of ash.

The satellite can be sold in Buy mode.

Death by Flies (Teen/Adult/Elder)

If a lot is so messy with so many fly-infested dirty objects, there is a chance all the lot's flies could converge into one giant killer super swarm.

It's not enough, however, that a lot be messy, but the Sim must be so unconcerned about the mess that he steps over a fly-infested object. If there are enough such objects on a lot, there's a random chance of a killer fly swarm any time a Sim steps over one. In this unlikely event, the flies amass around the Sim and consume him.

Disease (Child/Teen/Adult/Elder)

As described earlier, any potentially fatal disease that's uncured after 10 days will kill the Sim.

Scared to Death (Teen/Adult/Elder)

If a ghost does the autonomous Scare interaction on a Sim, it simultaneously reduces all the Sim's Needs. If, as a result, three Needs fall

below -90, the Sim may die of fright (low proba-bility). The probability of death is higher for elders than other ages. If they don't die, Sims may either Bladder fail and flee or simply flee.

Children cannot be scared to death but will likely suffer a Bladder failure (regardless of actual Bladder Need level).

Pleading with Death

When a Sim dies of anything other than old age, surviving Sims may plead with the Reaper to return the deceased to life.

Pleading with the Reaper can bring a prematurely dead Sim back to life, but only Sims with a high relationship to the deceased are likely to succeed.

While the Reaper is making the arrangements to ship the dead Sim into the hereafter, any teen, adult, or elder Sim can interact with him to plead for the deceased. Death agrees to a game of chance.

The game isn't pure chance. The Daily and Lifetime Relationship scores of the pleader to the deceased drastically affect the results:

◆ For the plea to have any chance, the surviving Sim's Daily and Lifetime Relationship scores added together must equal *at least* 25.

◆ If that total is greater than 90, the number is reduced to 90. This gives even the closest rela-tionship a 10 percent chance of failing in the plea.

◆ Reaper picks a random number. If the adjusted total Relationship score is higher than the random number, the Sim is returned to life. If not, fare thee well.

For Sims with Wants to save someone from death or to be saved from death, this weighted game of chance is crucial to the fulfillment of those Wants. Stack the odds by having the pleader have very high relationship with the soon-to-be-briefly deceased.

Mourning, Tombstones, and Urns

When a Sim dies, he leaves behind either a tomb-stone (if he dies outside) or an urn (if inside). Moving a death marker from outside to inside or vice versa changes it into the appropriate kind. Ghosts will, however, express their displeasure at having their marker moved.

Urns and tombstones allow Sims to mourn for the departed, but they also allow ghosts to visit and wreak havoc.

The kind of tombstone/urn a Sim gets depends on how and with what Aspiration score she died. Elders with at least Gold Aspiration score at passing get a special fancy marker that displays their Aspirational moniker.

Sims can use the tombstone/urn to mourn the dead Sim. Sims with high Lifetime Relationship scores toward the deceased mourn autonomously. The higher the Lifetime score, the more severely the Sim cries when mourning. Mourning is frequent the day after a death, but tails off after that.

Child or teenage Sims with low Aspiration score may autonomously smash an urn or kick a tombstone. This may also be directed for Sims who have low Lifetime score toward the deceased. The Sim gets some Fun for kicking but a lot for smashing.

Chapter 29: Disasters, Disease, and Death

Smashed urns are destroyed but still house their ghost until the shards are cleaned up.

Kicking or smashing death markers, however, has a price: ghosts who've had their markers so desecrated will be extremely disruptive (see "Ghosts," below).

Removing a tombstone or urn in Build mode or cleaning the remains of a smashed urn rids the house of the ghost tied to it.

GHOSTS

The dearly departed are still with us as long as the markers of their death reside on a lot. Ghosts can be completely benign, but will intervene in the lives of the living for several reasons, not all of them good.

Ghost Behavior

Ghosts like to scare living Sims. Don't let Sims have low Needs when ghosts are around or the fright could kill them.

Ghosts appear only at night and disappear before sunrise, always near the location of their marker (urn or tombstone) or a marker's former location if it's been moved to another spot on the lot.

tip

Ghosts, even passive ones, wake sleeping Sims. Don't, therefore, keep urns in Sims' bedrooms or they'll never get a good night's sleep.

Ghosts' appearance and general behavior reflect their manner of death:

- Burned: Red, smoking
- Drowned: Blue, leave puddles behind
- Electrocution: Yellow, spark and electrify occasionally
- Hunger: Normal but transparent; open fridge and remove five food units
- Old age: White
- Disease: Green
- Scared to death: Pink
- Death by flies: Purple
- Death by satellite: Orange

Haunting

Ghosts haunt the lot on which they died until their death marker is removed via Buy mode.

Ghosts cause various disruptions for living Sims. The higher the level of the haunting, the more often these disruptions occur. Such disruptions are:

- Making flowers wilt
- Turning on TVs and stereos

Ghosts like to haunt household objects.

They also haunt certain objects, manipulating them to the terror of the living. Ghosts can possess:

- Dining chairs: Float even if a Sim is sitting in them
- Toy xylophone: Plays by itself
- Microwave: Floats, opens, and closes
- Surgical dummy: Floats
- Tubs and shower tubs: Fill with water and bubbles; if the ghost is in a bad Mood, he'll dirty the tub
- Teddy bear: Floats and head rotates
- Table lamps: Float; if ghost is angry, may be broken

Finally, ghosts may scare living Sims (as long as they aren't Babies or Toddlers). This can cause all ages to wet their pants and/or flee. If a teen/adult/elder Sim's Needs are low enough, scaring could be fatal (see "Scared to Death," earlier in this chapter).

The level of the haunting is a factor of:

- Whether the ghost is angry (see below)
- Whether the ghost's urn or tombstone has been smashed or kicked

Ghost Anger

A relatively happy ghost is annoying, but an angry ghost can be a very big problem. Ghosts get angry for three reasons:

No Food

If a ghost died of Hunger and there are either no refrigerators on the lot or a fridge is empty, the ghost will be angry. This is displayed with a recurring refrigerator icon over the ghost's head.

To remedy this situation, buy or restock the fridge.

Spouse Remarries

If a dead Sim's spouse remarries, the dead Sim will not be very understanding. Such a ghost thinks often

about her spouse and the new interloper (with a red "X" through his face).

The only way to calm such a ghost is for the living spouse to get divorced.

Family Moves Out

If the ghost's family has moved out, the ghost will be angry at any new residents.

> **note**
>
> Tombstones/urns stay behind when Sims vacate a lot.

The only way to appease such a ghost is to move the new family out and move at least one member of the ghost's family back in.

Desecrating a Grave

If a Sim's tombstone is kicked or urn is smashed, a ghost that's already angry will haunt at the highest level.

> **tip**
>
> If you wish to keep ghosts on a lot but don't want Sims autonomously desecrating the graves, put a small fence around the markers to make them inaccessible.

Exorcism

There's no big ceremony to get rid of a ghost. Simply sell the urn/tombstone during the daytime. If the ghost is moving around the lot, the marker can't be deleted.

Part 5

All in the Family: Sims in Action

So, there it is: everything you need to know to harness the staggering power of *The Sims 2*. With the information in the previous chapters, the Sims' world is your oyster.

There is a difference, however, between having all the info crammed into your cranium and really getting how it works in practice. To demonstrate how everything works "on the ground" would transform this little guide into a multivolume reference guide, so perhaps it's better to see how things play out over a few days.

Here, therefore, for your edification: we proudly present the Ex-Machina Family and their exploits both inspiring and sordid.

Chapter 30

The Ex-Machina Family Blog

Join us and follow in the adventures of a household perilously perched on the edge of disaster. Can these three souls find happiness in their fragile domestic arrangement, and what will be the cost?

Meet Davis Ex-Machina, his wife Sangita, and their lodger (also by some bizarre coincidence surnamed Ex-Machina), Todd. They live together in a rather nice one-level, two bedroom house in Pleasantview.

Sounds nice, right? Where's the problem? The problem, friends, is in this particular household's combinations of Aspirations:

◆ Todd is a Knowledge Sim, a bookish fellow whose main concerns are with the acquisition of knowledge and experience of the unknown. He has no overriding Power Wants right now, but they'll appear as he builds skills. Anything that distracts him from skill building (e.g., love) takes him away from achieving his Aspiration.

◆ Davis is a Family Sim and desires nothing more than to interact with Sangita and have lots and lots of kids, teaching them everything he knows. He'll work in a career now to pay the bills but will become master of the house once he gets his (for now) biggest Want: a baby.

◆ Sangita is a Romance Sim and, if you've been paying attention thus far, that is going to be trouble. Single Romance Sims must do a lot of juggling to make their lives work out and avoid jealousy among the legions of lovers they require to meet their Wants. But they can do it fairly easily. Put them in a marriage, however, and the time bomb begins to tick.

Let's tune in and see what fate (in this case also known as "your humble author") has in store for these three.

Sangita gets right to work and breaks in the new bedroom with hubby, Davis.

tip

Lock in Davis's Have a Baby Want as soon as it appears.

Todd, meanwhile, does what comes naturally to him: he hops on the computer and looks for a job. He wants to enter the Medicine career track. I give it to him and he heads off to work almost immediately.

Meanwhile, the welcome wagon arrives with three friendly neighbors. One of them is an attractive redhead named Nina. After meeting all these new people, our Romantic has a Power Want to WooHoo with three different Sims. She already has one; she just needs to get the other two without Davis finding out.

Just to be sure, lock Sangita's triple WooHoo Want.

Todd, still at work, gets a lucky break on a chance card.

Todd returns from work and Sangita makes a point of getting to know him better. In the interests of good roommate-hood, surely.

While the welcome wagon warms the Ex-Machina's new home, Todd gets right to work on his skills.

Sangita, meanwhile, heads off to her first (very early) morning on the job in the Slacker career (the only one Romance Sims actively want).

While at work, Sangita too gets lucky on a chance card.

She returns later to a make out session with Davis and some very stinky dirty dishes. This lengthy series of Wants panel-driven interactions put Davis and her in Platinum Aspiration level.

Todd's doing very well with his skill building and heads off to work with a Platinum Aspiration score and a perfect Mood that's sure to get him promoted from his first tier job.

With her Platinum Mood, Sangita too has been promoted.

Unsatisfied, she and Davis (with the help of his Aspiration Reward point-purchased Thinking Cap) get to work on their skills. Davis, for his part, is working on his domestic skills: Cooking, Mechanical, and Cleaning.

Hoping to gain a bit of Logic skill, Todd spends his time with the new telescope he wanted. His lens, however, strayed a bit low of the horizon and he was caught peeping by storied neighbor, Mortimer Goth.

Davis, trying a bit too hard to be a perfect cleaning machine the first week in his new house, passes out from exhaustion, still wearing his Thinking Cap.

Sangita, still hubby-smooching her way to a Platinum Aspiration score, nabs another promotion.

---

note

When there aren't many other potential paramours around, childless Romance/Family Sim combinations align rather nicely with all the affectionate and Romantic interactions.

Sangita begins to make her move on the vivacious Nina Caliente, but is briefly interupted by some groping by Todd's work friend, Don.

After the guests leave, Todd and Sangita converse innocently enough, clad in their unmentionables.

Doing her best to stifle a giggle and cough convincingly, Sangita decides to take a day off and fraudulently calls in sick. Because her job performance is stellar, they believe her.

Without so much as a change out of her underthings, she invites Nina over for a visit. The fiery-haired neighbor accepts and arrives forth-with. Their fast friendship of Thursday blossoms quickly into a best friend-ship (Sangita's a very good socializer).

And then it happens. In the wee hours Saturday with Davis fast asleep, the first flirt goes Nina's way and she accepts.

They call it a night abuzz with their new crush.

note

Our choice for Davis's career has been an unexpectedly fortuitous one for Sangita. The Military career is excellent because it pays well in the low rungs and doesn't require any significant skills or many friends until the middle of the career. This makes it perfect for Family Sims just working until they become full-time homemakers. Because it's so physically draining, however, it also means the poor oblivious Davis sleeps a lot, giving his wandering bride plenty of room without having to leave the house.

Later that day, with Davis again asleep, Sangita establishes a foothold with Todd too (who's looking not so much the innocent bookworm now). A crush is born.

note

From now on, with two romances in the same house, Sangita must be very careful. She must keep all romantic interactions with Nina out of both men's sight and interact romantically with her own husband only when Todd isn't looking.

Playing her hot streak, Sangita invites Nina again and, on the sidewalk out front, does some serious smooching out of sight of both the men.

Davis? Still asleep.

Now Sangita's in the exciting but awkward position of being in love with (and loved by) two Sims. Either Sim may engage in autonomous romantic interactions at any time, so she can't let Nina and Davis see one another at all. She bids Nina goodnight.

Unbeknownst to Sangita, Davis is just getting up as she plants a little one on Todd to maintain their budding romance. This won't be their first close call.

On Sunday, knowing she can't have Nina visiting anymore, she arranges to meet her at a Community Lot.

There's a fortuitously located clothing store on this lot, so Sangita nonchalantly browses for duds while Nina converses with a Townie near the stairs.

Sangita ducks inside a clothing booth, ostensibly to try on a new outfit. When the coast is clear, Nina slips in too.

The other customers and the salesgirls seem to approve.

And Nina seems curiously happy about Sangita's new outfit. Weird. By the way, that makes TWO.

Back at home, Nina's Wants follow the course of the Romance Sim: success in romance breeds the hunger for more. Her most immediate Want is to meet someone new (which I oblige) and she immediately wants to flirt with him (which I ignore... for now).

Davis, on his day off but with a lot of tiring cleaning around the house, is asleep but due to wake up soon. As for the illicit in-house lovers, they haven't achieved love and just aren't quite there yet for more intimate encounters. Unless, of course, Sangita's been so successful in her pursuit of Wants that she's amassed enough Reward points to buy the Love Tub.

This object temporarily reduces the relationship requirements for all romantic interactions done inside it. Todd and Sangita climb in. Perfect!

Davis awakes mere moments after this third and final WooHoo. Had he been awake, he'd have reacted no matter where he was on the lot. Fortunately, he's blissfully oblivious and seems to be enjoying cleaning the counter as the sloppy Todd dirties it.

Davis can hold back the pull of his paternal Wants no more and engages Sangita in a bit of hopeful procreation.

Davis, sensing he'll be needed more (the cleaning has gotten away from him a bit and there could be a new family member coming) quits his very successful career.

Sangita, in a rare lone moment, ponders love. But which one? The observant may notice, Sangita has a new Want: WooHoo with FIVE different Sims.

Todd, meanwhile, is in the backyard, maxing out his Logic skill and, thus, satisfying his biggest Want.

Unless she ate a bad omelet, the mess Sangita just made in the toilet is a dead give-away: Davis is about to be very happy. Fortunately, Sangita doesn't seem to fear this new event as many Romance Sims would.

The next day, with a wardrobe and body change, there's no doubt. The Ex-Machinas are having a baby. And, with that, everyone's gotten one of the things they desire most. Now what?

And so, everyone gets one huge thing they desired. Happy ending? OK.

Well, no, actually, but not because everyone's unhappy (they are happy). It's because there's not an ending. There are no endings in The Sims 2 (unless a family dies out). Odds are, Sangita will shortly embark on a new series of even riskier romantic Wants (or else be rendered unable to keep her Aspiration score positive), Todd's feelings toward Sangita will become harder to hide and increasingly distract him from his own Aspiration. Davis seems to get what he wants (a child) and will thrive Aspirationally the more offspring he has, but his happiness teeters on remaining ignorant of Sangita's dalliances. Hers, in turn, depends on continuing them. They may both be happy only if the deception continues. But happy they can be.

Part 6

Beyond the Game

Now you know the ropes, and you've mastered the game itself. Are you ready to ascend to the next level of insight?

The chapters in this part go beyond the simulation itself. No player needs to understand these parts of the game, but (as we've learned) there's more to life than Needs:

◆ Build Mode
◆ Story Mode
◆ Understanding Sim Autonomy

Chapter 31
Build Mode

Build mode is the extraordinarily powerful mode in which houses are constructed and renovated. These tools are daunting at first, but with familiarity comes comfort, with comfort comes confidence. The heaven-sent talent for spatial design and architecture? Only nature (however you define it) and a very expensive education can give you that.

note

All general tools (Hand, Eyedropper, etc.) are explored in full in Chapter 28.

BUILD MODE AND MONEY

When building on an unoccupied lot, construction seems to cost nothing. Everything you're doing, however, is being added to the lot's purchase price. The more you add and the most expensive the components, the less affordable the resulting lot will be.

WALL TOOL (§70 PER SEGMENT)

Walls serve two very important functions. First, they separate inside space from outside space and delineate rooms. Second, they support the next floor of a building.

Structures may be up to five floors high if there's no foundation and four floors high with a foundation.

tip

Houses may actually have six floors. With or without a foundation, you can make an extra top floor by applying a tall roof. If the house's base is wide enough, there's enough head room for the area under the roof to be livable space.

Add a sixth floor to a house with a foundation by creating a basement (see "Foundations," later in this chapter for step-by-step instructions on creating basements).

The Wall tool panel contains two ways to build walls:

The Wall Tool

The Wall tool builds straight segments of wall from a fixed point to wherever you drag.

tip

Holding [Shift] switches to the Wall tool to Room tool for as long as you hold [Shift]. Holding [Control] removes walls.

Walls can be dragged straight or diagonally and intersect in both orientations. In fact, up to four walls may intersect at the same point. Diagonal walls can accommodate doors and windows but can't take wall hangings or wall lamps of any kind.

The Room Tool

The Room tool makes simple room construction very efficient.

Drag four walls at once in a rectangular shape to quickly form a room.

403

tip

Floors of a house can technically be any size, but you can't apply a roof if the area's too big. Try instead stacking smaller floors atop larger ones or building physically separate wall boxes on the same floor to break up the roof line.

DOORS AND WINDOWS

Doors and arches provide access from the outside and between rooms. Windows let in light and can provide Sims a bit of autonomous Comfort.

Doors, arches, and windows are Build mode objects, and they depreciate when added to a home and daily thereafter just as Buy mode objects do. Delete them by dragging them to the Build mode pane to "sell" them.

Doors

You can place doors on both straight and diagonal walls. Set the swing and orientation of the door *before* releasing the door by moving the mouse from one side of the wall to the other in small motions; the knob changes positions on the door and a green triangle on the door's drop shadow indicates the direction it will swing.

For Environment score purposes (see Chapter 20), a door or arch is what separates two rooms. A wall with a segment missing (even with lovely decorative pillars on either side) doesn't do the job; it's all one "room".

Doors and arches also serve as a barrier to noise. When a Sim sleeps in a room with door, no noise beyond the door (stereo or TV blaring, baby crying, the cheap dishwasher, alarm clock ringing, etc.) will awaken him.

Glass doors and ones with glass insets serve as a daytime light source exactly like a window. The amount of glass in the door dictates how much light passes through it and, thus, how much localized Environment score is increased.

Two doors have a special limitation. The EZ Evac, Inc.'s "Brick House" Men's and Women's Restroom Doors allow only the specified gender to pass through.

Single Story Windows

Windows are decorative objects that admit light during daytime hours. As such, they improve Environment score within their area of illumination.

Windows, like doors, can be attached to diagonal walls.

Windows can be placed on either straight or most diagonal walls.

Sims with low Comfort Need may autonomously Look Out windows to receive a bit of that Need.

Neat Sims (8 or higher), may autonomously clean windows as a way to kill time. It doesn't serve any Need satisfaction.

Multistory Windows

These special purpose windows span two floors of a house.

Multistory windows are best used in rooms with high ceilings that are two-stories high (actually two rooms with no floor installed on the second).

If the floor covering is installed on the second floor, tiles in front of the multistory window will be left permanently uncovered. You can leave these tiles as they are or put a railing around them for "safety."

Multistory windows are desirable because they let in oodles of light.

Arches

Arches are functionally identical to doors but all permit light, for obvious reasons. They also don't have a swing, so it doesn't matter which way they face. Despite their lack of an actual door filling their frame, they effectively exclude noise and delineate a room for Environment score.

note

See the table, "Build Mode Objects," later in this chapter, for prices.

FLOORING (§4–§19 PER TILE)

There are seven different categories of floor covering:

◆ Stone   ◆ Carpet   ◆ Wood
◆ Linoleum   ◆ Tile   ◆ Poured
◆ Brick

Though some coverings are intended to be used indoors or outdoors, there's actually no limitation on where you may use them.

tip

Floor an entire room at once by holding [Shift] before clicking on the first tile.

To be usable, a building level must have some kind of flooring applied to it. Without flooring, the upper levels are just open space (though you can suspend a ceiling light from or place a staircase to an unfloored level).

note

You can preview floor coverings and wall coverings in a room. Click on the covering to choose it, point to the wall or floor of the room you want to decorate, and hold [Shift] without clicking on the ground. If you decide you want that covering, click on the surface.

The purchase price of a floor covering determines how much it contributes to Environment score. Leaving any area unfloored squanders a large chuck of the space's Environment score, but leaving exposed the plywood floor of a foundation is a serious additional Environment score killer.

Flooring also plays a major role in creating balconies. Every floor above ground level is surrounded by a ring of translucent floor tiles. If floor covering is laid on this row, a new row appears beyond it. Two rows of floor can be extended beyond a wall without any supporting columns.

note

Laying floor tiles on the ground automatically levels uneven terrain.

Covering floors along diagonal walls (or fences) is no problem save in one situation. Clicking on a tile next to the wall covers only the half of the tile on the indicated side of the wall. Likewise, [Shift] clicking to fill the room automatically covers on the half of the tiles within the room. If, however, you click and drag to cover an area, tiles under the diagonal wall get covered on both sides of the wall. To fix the situation, [Ctrl] click on the half of the tile outside the wall to delete only that half. If the walls (or fences) are built first, then the whole room is floored at once, the floor will not poke beyond the floor (or fence).

WALL COVERINGS (§5–§15 PER WALL PIECE)

Use wall coverings to decorate walls both inside and out. You can even apply wall coverings to the outer and inner walls of foundations. You don't have to stick with the default red brick appearance.

- Brick
- Paint
- Masonry
- Wallpaper
- Siding
- Poured
- Tile
- Paneling

As with floor coverings, wall coverings contribute to Environment score, and exposed drywall actually drags down Environment score all by itself.

note

If a room has mixed variety and value of wall and floor coverings, the average value of each is used for Environment score calculation.

Putting even the cheapest wall covering on these unfinished walls will dramatically improve Environment score.

STAIRCASES

Staircases provide access between two floors. With the increased building power of *The Sims 2*, you have two choices: straight stairs and connecting stairs.

Straight Stairs

Straight stairs must have space to be built on the lower floor and room for the upper floor opening.

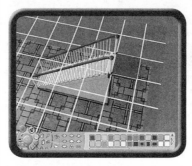

Stairs need to have open space on the floor above, even if flooring hasn't been laid yet.

Railings are placed on straight stairs by default but can be removed with the Railing tools (see page 408).

note

Straight stairs can't be used in basements because straight stairs are fixed height and basements aren't.

note

See the table, "Build Mode Objects," later in this chapter, for prices.

Connecting Stairs (§40–§85 per segment)

Connecting stairs allow extremely flexible connections between two points. Connecting stairs join when placed next to each other in the same orientation.

The most basic use for connecting stairs is from decks or foundations to flat ground. Point to the foundation/deck where you want the steps to begin at the top (there must be a top landing) and the bottom will be drawn automatically unless something's in the way.

Point to where you want the stairs to begin and the end point will be indicated in green. Click and the stairs are drawn.

If the distance is longer or the target terrain is extremely rough, drawing a connecting stair is a bit more complicated. If it can't draw the bottom landing for some reason, the stairs can't be built. Still, they do try hard; stairs will alter terrain and extend as long as they can to find a suitable ending point. If the terrain is unsuitable for building a stair landing, then you can do some terrain work to make the area more suitable.

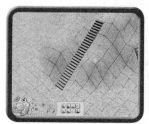 

Try clicking-and-dragging for longer stretches over rough terrain or down into ground.

If getting to point B isn't possible on a straight stretch of stairs, try building it in parts.

Use the connecting stairs on flat ground to excavate a submerged staircase.

Click and you have the first segment dug into the terrain.

Point to the first stair's bottom landing and another segment is drawn. Turn it to face the desired direction and click again.

Repeat.

How else are you going to get to that submerged pool?

You can link separated buildings and decks from upper floors with connecting stairs.

Connect these two towers via a short flight of stairs from balcony to balcony.

Using a combination of columns, raised decks, and connecting stairs, elaborately interconnected multifloor structures are possible.

Still, connecting stairs have some limitations.

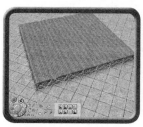 

Modular stairs can't be drawn directly from diagonal foundations or decks.

Draw a section of normal foundation or deck onto it first.

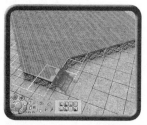

Then draw stairs from that.

Railing Tool

Use the Railing tool to add or remove rails from connecting stairs and to remove the automatically placed railings from straight stairs.

Railings finish the look of modular stairs.

The kind of railing you get is dictated by the kind of stairs, so they can't be mixed and matched.

Railings automatically draw to the length of the stairs and can be placed on each side of a stair or in the middle of a joined wide stair.

In conjunction with Ctrl, the Railing tool can remove rails from all staircases, even straight ones.

FOUNDATIONS (§2–§4 PER TILE)

Foundations aren't required for buildings (they can still be built right on the ground) but they provide greater realism and can be carved out (as described below) to make a usable basement.

Decks function almost identically to foundations but (not surprisingly) can't make basements. They have several special features, however, that foundations don't.

Draw foundations and decks by clicking and dragging. They can be either standard or diagonal. Keep in mind that diagonal foundations and decks have several quirks (mentioned throughout this chapter) that make building on them difficult.

Two foundations/ decks will join even if differently oriented.

If a foundation or deck is drawn into uneven terrain, what it does depends on where you began dragging.

Start from high ground and it builds at that elevation and creates the necessary support. This is the case if it's drawn starting at an existing foundation or deck.

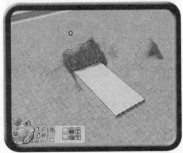

If you start from low ground, the necessary terrain is leveled to the starting tile.

note

Cover the foundation's exterior and interior walls with any wall covering. They can't, however, have doors or windows or any object attached to them.

Foundations and decks can be built over or across bodies of water...

...or drops in elevation.

note

Decks can be refloored just like foundations and can even have rooms built on them.

If you're using a column to hold up a second floor balcony of a foundation building, the column must be on a 2 x 2 section of foundation or deck too or it won't reach.

note

Decks and foundations can't be built adjacent to the sidewalk and must be two or more tiles from a lot's side and rear edges.

Decks have a special ability to build at second floor level (no higher).

Hold [Shift] and drag, and the deck will be elevated with either posts or lattice (depending on deck style) extending to the ground or down to a foundation or lower deck.

Building a Basement

One of the most interesting things you can do with foundations is make a basement. Though it's not difficult, it's far from obvious how to do it. The good news is you can learn it right here.

Build a standard foundation.

Still in the Foundations and Deck tool and holding [Ctrl], drag to erase the center of the foundation.

Going down to the lowest level ([Page Down]), it looks something like this.

Lower the terrain inside the inner wall of the foundation using the Lower Terrain tool.

Switch to the Level Terrain tool. Then, click and hold on a tile that seems to be the right depth. This levels out any included tiles to the same level as the first square. Keep leveling until the basement floor is flat.

Return to the ground floor (Page Up) and select a connectingstair. Point to the floor adjacent to the hole. A staircase draws automatically down to the basement floor. Release the mouse button.

Apply flooring to the ground level and put a railing around the opening with the Fence tool.

Cover the floor in the basement too and, if you feel like it, cover the walls.

---

note

You can decorate and wallpaper your basement walls. You can even install ceiling lights!

TERRAIN

Terrain tools enable you create differences in elevation, change ground cover, and construct bodies of (unswimmable) water.

Elevation

Use the Elevation tool for leveling, raising, and lowering the terrain.

Level Terrain Tool (§1)

With the Level Terrain tool, choose a spot of the desired elevation, click on it, and drag from it over every tile you want to be at that identical elevation.

Pick a tile and make every tile you drag over the same elevation.

tip

The resulting area is perfectly rectangular so realism might require it to be roughed up a bit with the Raise and Lower Terrain tools.

The Level Terrain tool is also useful for removing water created with the Water tool (following page).

Raise Terrain Tool (§1)

Raise Terrain tool is a circular "brush" that raises drags upward every point within its radius. The point in the middle is brought up the most. The tool comes in three different sizes for different levels of precision.

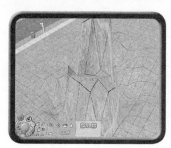

Using the Raise Terrain tool brings the ground upward.

note

With the Raise and Lower Terrain tools, holding [Shift] switches the direction of the terrain movement until [Shift] is released.

Lower Terrain Tool (§1)

Using the Lower Terrain tool pushes the ground downward.

The Lower Terrain tool works identically to the Raise Terrain tool but in the opposite direction.

Ground Cover

Change the texture of the ground beneath buildings with this tool. It works kind of like a can of spray paint, lightly coating the existing ground with the chosen covering. The longer you spray on a spot, the darker and denser the change becomes.

Ground coverings include:

- Garden Soil
- Mixed Rocks
- Grassy Growth
- Bright Burst Terrain by Dandy Lawns
- Dirt Clod
- Standard Issue Sand
- Sparse and Spotty
- Park Bark

Cover can be applied in three possible radii for different levels of precision. Remove it by holding [Ctrl] and respraying the area.

Use ground cover around objects. It looks great adorning the bases of trees and plants.

Water Tool (§1)

The Water tool lowers the level of the terrain and fills the indentation with water. The tool works in three brush sizes for varying levels of precision.

Water your lawn like you really mean it! Create a lake if that's what your muse commands.

Terrain water is for decorative/realism purposes and has no effect on Environment score.

Remove water by using the Level Terrain tool starting from the closest tile of dry land.

Sims cannot swim in water created with the Water tool.

tip

In the Garden Center, two plants (the Nine Lives Cat O' Nines and the Genetically Engineered Water Lily) can be placed only on bodies of water.

GARDEN CENTER

The Garden Center is your source for outdoor plants, including:

◆ Trees   ◆ Flowers   ◆ Shrubs

Trees beautify any lot but are most strategically useful near the curb where Sims go to work and school.

tip

Make sure that fences (taller than edging) allow entry into a flower or shrub area with an opening or a gate.

Trees (§155–§400)

Trees have a profound effect on outdoor Environment score in their immediate vicinity.

Flowers (§5–§39)

Outdoor flowers increase localized outdoor Environment score but only if they're alive. They lose their boost and further subtract from Environment score when dead.

Flowers increase Environment score but need care (from Sims or hired help) or they'll have the opposite effect.

To survive, flowers need to be watered regularly.

If not watered, flowers become increasingly wilted. Watering wilted flowers restores them to full bloom. Watering dying flowers (the last step before irretrievable death) brings them back to wilting. Dead flowers, unwatered for two days after drying out, decrease Environment score and can only be thrown away.

Overwatering flowers causes them to flood and, if watered further, die. The puddles from overwatering spawn weeds. Sims or the gardener will not autonomously overwater; you must direct them to do it.

note

Even properly watered plants spawn weeds every 12–48 hours if alive and every 4–30 hours if dead.

Flowers have the following interactions:

◆ Water: Sims autonomously water nearby flowers in need of water.

◆ Pull Weeds: Sims weed where indicated and anywhere else nearby. Decreases Energy and Hygiene.

◆ Dispose: Sim removes dead flowers and throws them in the trash.

◆ Stomp: Autonomous only from teens and children with moderate Immaturity.

Shrubs (§40–§180)

Shrubs also affect Environment score but don't need to be watered like flowers. They need to be regularly trimmed. After the first 24 hours, they become unkempt and in need of a trim. Once trimmed, they don't require further trimming for 72 hours.

Untrimmed shrubs spawn weeds.

Trimming shrubs
is hard work.

Interactions include:

◆ Trim: Available only if shrub is untrimmed. Other Sims can join. Depletes Energy and Hygiene.

◆ Use: Autonomous only. Very Outgoing or very Lazy adult male Sims with less than -40 Bladder may autonomously use shrubs as a urinal.

Someone please inform this guy that shrubs don't need to be watered.

WEEDS

Weeds reduce outdoor Environment score in their immediate vicinity. They spawn in Sims' yards from several causes:

◆ Outdoor water puddles (including Bladder accidents). Puddles evaporate in three hours and may randomly spawn weeds.

◆ Watered Flowers: Randomly after 12–48 hours.

◆ Dead Flowers: Randomly after 4–30 hours.

◆ Untrimmed Shrubs.

◆ Other Weeds: This is how they spread. The existence of one weed randomly spawns more nearby.

The only interaction for weeds is Pull. Pulling weeds reduces both Energy and Hygiene.

Weeds look unsightly and reduce Environment score.

ROOFING

Because it never rains in *The Sims 2*, there's no explicit need for roofs, but no house looks entirely realistic without one.

note

Tool automatically opens to Auto Roofs tool.

You can apply roofs manually to a dragged area or automatically with the Auto Roofs tool. Roof patterns let you decide what texture the roof will be and the Dormers tool contains a variety of roofed rooms to insert into your roofs.

Roof Types

These roofs are applied manually, but each can cover only a limited space. Otherwise, the house can't support its weight. This tool is better used for smaller structures.

There are six types of roof:

Shed Gabled Roof: Walls on three sides. Objects (including windows and doors) can be hung on the tallest of the three walls. If it's large enough, the space created by the roof is considered a room.

Shed Hipped Roof: Wall on only one side. Objects (including windows and doors) can be hung on the wall. If it's large enough, the space created by the roof is considered a room.

Short Gabled Roof: Unusable walls on either end. Not a room.

Long Gabled Roof: Unusable walls on either end. Not a room.

Hipped Roof: No walls, slopes on all four sides. Not a room.

Mansard Roof: No walls, slopes on all four sides with flat top if roof is large enough. At greater sizes, flat areas are big enough for a roof deck reachable by interior stairs. The flat area can be adorned with any floor covering. If it's large enough, the space created by the roof is considered a room.

Dormers

A dormer is a small roof that protrudes perpendicularly from a roof's gable. They're intended to accent roofs and add realism. Windows can be placed on their walls.

Dormers can be placed only through roofs, not through walls, and must be supported directly by the top of a wall or columns. Or place dormers on the ground to serve as small sheds.

Roof Patterns

Roof patterns are dictated by the surface appearance of all roofs on the lot.

Auto Roofs

The Auto Roofs tool does all the hard roofing work, deciding which roofs will fit on the given arrangement of walls. Just select the style of roof to be used.

For most builders, the Auto Roofs tool is the most useful and takes much of the uncertainty out of constructing a roof. Find several combinations of roofs in the Roof Types menu, plus one automatic-only roof and tools to delete and vary the kinds of roofs on the lot.

Use the flat tiled roof for roof decks like Pleasantview's Mr. Lothario's.

The auto roofs settings are:

◆ Hipped
◆ Short and Hipped Mix
◆ Short Gabled
◆ Tall and Short Mix
◆ Floor Tiled: This flat roof is placed on the highest enclosed rooms with no ceiling. The tiles can accommodate any floor covering. Build stairs up to it for roof decks.

Press one of these buttons to switch all roofs on the lot with one click.

Remove all roofs with one click using the Remove Roofs button or by control clicking on the roof with the Roof tool active.

Exclude existing roofs from all subsequent changes in auto roofing or remove roof commands by locking them with the Preserve Existing Roofs button.

MISCELLANEOUS

The many objects and elements in this menu don't fit neatly into any category but that doesn't mean they're not important. In fact, they're all quite important.

Columns (§70–§230)

Use columns decoratively or to support overhangs.

One column can support a five by five square (minus the corner tiles) of floor.

In THE SIMS, columns could support only three tiles by three tiles.

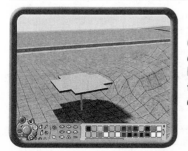

Columns in THE SIMS 2 can support a five by five square of tiles (without the corner pieces).

To support a second floor balcony of a building with a foundation, build a single tile of deck or foundation where you intended to place the column. This brings its top level with the upper floor. You can stack columns for multilevel balconies.

tip

Balconies can "float" if you later delete their supporting columns. The support is required only on initial building.

note

See the table, "Build Mode Objects," later in this chapter for prices.

Fireplaces (§600–§3,000)

Fireplaces are special Environment-enhancing objects that are installed in Build mode. If Sims interact with fireplaces, they provide Comfort and Fun but also pose a fire hazard. The choices are:

◆ Red Ember Freestanding Fireplace: §600
◆ Shiny Things, INC. "Estomago" Pot Belly Stove: §1,000
◆ Casbah Casuals Fireplace by 40 Thieves Ltd.: §2,000
◆ Gentrific "Way of the Wood" Mantel Fireplace: §2,525
◆ Gentrific "Flame-O-Rama" Fireplace: §3,000

All fireplaces except the Red Ember and the Estomago must be placed against a wall.

Stack fireplaces on upper floors to share the same chimney.

Fireplaces automatically run a chimney up through floors above and out the house's current roof level. Interior fireplaces can't be drawn if their chimney is blocked by an object or wall above. If another wall-mounted fireplace is added along the run of a chimney, it will share that chimney.

Fireplaces improve Environment score but only when they're lit. Interactions include:

◆ Light Fire: Teen/adult/elder lights a fire that stays lit 100 to 150 minutes of game time (by default).

◆ Poke: Poking a fire gives a Sim Fun and extends burn time by five minutes per poke. Poking more than three times in a row decreases fire time by 10 minutes per poke after the third. Pot belly stove can't be poked.

◆ Warm Self: Increases Comfort.

◆ View: Increases Comfort.

Swimming Pools

Swimming pools can be any size and any shape (as long as "any" means "rectangular" or "square").

A few accessories add utility to the pool and, if totally absent, leave the pool a useless (but pretty) body of water.

Swimming Pool Tool (§75 per tile)

Pools are dragged rectangular and must be larger than 2 x 2. You can remove placed pool tiles by control dragging over them with the Pool tool active. Sims can access the pool either via a ladder or diving board and can leave only via a ladder.

Pool interactions:

◆ Get In: Enter the pool either by board or ladder.

◆ Float on Back: Self-interaction. Increases Fun and increases Body skill.

◆ Swim Here: Sim swims to specific location. Increases Fun and increases Body skill.

◆ Swim: Sim swims autonomously all over the pool until ready or directed to get out. Increases Fun and increases Body skill.

Swimming pools drag in rectangular shapes. Level any uneven terrain first.

Liquidacious Lighting (§40)

Underwater lights increase Environment score at night when they auto-illuminate. They can be placed only on pool walls below water level.

Pool lights add ambiance to night swimming.

In-And-Out Ladder (§200)

Place the ladder on the edge of the pool where there's two tiles of space to exit. Without a ladder, Sims can't get out of the pool. Without either a ladder or a diving board, they can't even get in.

The ladder is the only way Sims can get out of the pool. It'd be a shame if something were to happen to it.

The ladder has only two self-explanatory interactions: Get In and Get Out.

Diving Board (§300)

The diving board is an optional pool accessory that provides an alternate way to enter the pool. Without either a diving board or a ladder, Sims can't use the pool. They will, however, dive into a pool that doesn't have a ladder, even though they'll have no way out once in the water.

Low Body skill Sims are a little hesitant about diving. When they do, it isn't any prettier.

The board has only one self-explanatory interaction (Dive). Low Body skill Sims chicken out of diving 50 percent of the time.

Fence Tool (§5—§50 per piece)

Fences behave similarly to walls. Like walls, however, they can be straight or diagonal. Though they have no specific tool for rectangular dragging, holding [Shift] while dragging makes it possible.

Fences can be placed on terrain, floors, foundations and decks. Edging, a type of fencing, can even be walked over. They can be straight or diagonal, but diagonal runs can't host a gate.

If the fence is different on either side (i.e., picket fences), the direction of the drag sets which way the fence is facing. Left-to-right faces exterior front, right-to-left faces exterior back.

Special lights (see Chapter 28) can be placed on fence posts, but lights cannot be placed on fence walls.

Gates

Gates are doors for fences, opening automatically whenever a Sim approaches.

Gates don't have to match the fence, and sometimes an odd combination works really well.

There's no requirement that a gate match the fence into which it's placed.

As with doors, set single-tile gates' swing by moving the mouse back and forth through the fence while holding the gate. The swing is indicated by a green arrow on the gate's drop shadow.

Gates cannot be placed on diagonal fences or on uneven terrain.

Build Mode Objects

Object	Purchase Price	Initial Depreciation	Daily Depreciation	Depreciation Limit
Aggressive Accents Column	§124	§18	§12	§49
Altitude Attitude, Inc. "Step-By-Step" Staircase	§1,400	§210	§140	§560
A-maze-ing Hedge	§180	§27	§18	§72
Amishim "Metropole" Column	§145	§21	§14	§58
Arch of Antiquity	§160	§24	§16	§64
Archway to a Distant Land	§144	§21	§14	§57
At Stake Picket Gate	§160	§24	§16	§64
Babbling Bougainvillea	§100	§15	§10	§40
Birch Tree Sapling	§280	§42	§28	§112
Blue Tinged Hydrangea Shrub	§90	§13	§9	§36
Boxy Lady	§150	§22	§15	§60
Breeze-easy Windows' "Double Hung" Deluxe	§90	§13	§9	§36
Brevifolito's Joshua Tree	§260	§39	§26	§104
Canonical Column	§110	§16	§11	§44
Chiclettina "Mauritania" Arch	§292	§43	§29	§116
Chiclettina "Mauritania" Beveled Glass Door	§277	§41	§27	§110
Colonial Column by Brace Yourself! Designs	§200	§30	§20	§80
Colonial Tract Arch	§650	§97	§65	§260
Colonial Tract Door	§700	§105	§70	§280
Conspicuous Views "Stained Glass with Arch"	§300	§45	§30	§120
Country Kitsch Column	§95	§14	§9	§38
Cupressus Sempervirens	§300	§45	§30	§120
Daisies of Our Lives	§10	§1	§1	§4
Daisies of Our Lives*	§5	§1	§1	§2
Diving Board	§300	§45	§30	§120
Doorway to a Distant Land	§129	§19	§12	§51
EasyShade Bay Tree	§275	§41	§27	§110
Empeerical Art Window	§280	§42	§28	§112

Build Mode Objects continued

Object	Purchase Price	Initial Depreciation	Daily Depreciation	Depreciation Limit
EZ Evac, Inc.'s "Brick House" Men's Restroom Door	§200	§30	§20	§80
EZ Evac, Inc.'s "Power Powder" Women's Restroom Door	§200	§30	§20	§80
Garden Music "Oleander"	§100	§15	§10	§40
Gate of Glorified Entry	§190	§28	§19	§76
Genetically Engineered Water Lily	§33	§4	§3	§13
Glassterpieces Privacy Window	§60	§9	§6	§24
Gothwise Staircase by I. Ron Smith	§1,550	§232	§155	§620
High Society Pillar	§230	§34	§23	§92
High-Tech Loft Window	§275	§41	§27	§110
In-And-Out Ladder	§200	§30	§20	§80
Independent Expressions, Inc., "Non-Reflective" Window	§200	§30	§20	§80
Independent Expressions, Inc., "Translucent" Window	§150	§22	§15	§60
Independent Expressions, Inc., "Big Entrance" Shop Door	§650	§97	§65	§260
Independent Expressions, Inc., "Big Entrance" Shop Window	§110	§16	§11	§44
Independent Expressions, Inc., "Showcase" Shop Window	§200	§30	§20	§80
Japanese Autumn Maple	§330	§49	§33	§132
Lafenêtre "Stately" Full-Length Shuttered Window	§250	§37	§25	§100
LafenÃªtre Shuttered Window	§175	§26	§17	§70
LafenÃªtre Window Full-Length	§220	§33	§22	§88
Longbranch Front Gate	§180	§27	§18	§72
Longbranch Side Gate	§150	§22	§15	§60
Matte & Glass Front Door	§399	§59	§39	§159
Matte & Glass Glassless Arch	§414	§62	§41	§165
Mescalito's Agave Simulado	§210	§31	§21	§84
Midnight Ride Window by Cross-Reference	§150	§22	§15	§60
Mundo Verde, Inc. Perpetual Pansies	§10	§1	§1	§4
Mundo Verde, Inc. Perpetual Pansies	§5	§1	§1	§2
Mystery of the Coral Dragon	§125	§18	§12	§50

Build Mode Objects continued

Object	Purchase Price	Initial Depreciation	Daily Depreciation	Depreciation Limit
Nice 'n Private Gate	§130	§19	§13	§52
Nine Lives Cat O' Nines	§39	§5	§3	§15
Non-Proliferating Wild Bamboo	§200	§30	§20	§80
Nopalito's Prickly Pears	§10	§1	§1	§4
Nopalito's Prickly Pears*	§5	§1	§1	§2
OakTowne "Simple Interior" Arch	§315	§47	§31	§126
OakTowne Classic Arch	§230	§34	§23	§92
OakTowne Classic Door	§173	§25	§17	§69
OakTowne Simple Interior Door	§330	§49	§33	§132
Octothorp Atrium Window	§500	§75	§50	§200
Old Yankee "4 Score" Door	§160	§24	§16	§64
Old Yankee "No Score" Arch	§175	§26	§17	§70
Open and Shut Gate	§100	§15	§10	§40
Open Sesame Door by 40 Thieves Ltd.	§375	§56	§37	§150
Papaver's Poppies	§10	§1	§1	§4
Papaver's Poppies*	§5	§1	§1	§2
Perfectly Square Gate by EnTrance	§225	§33	§22	§90
Phantastic Phlox!	§40	§6	§4	§16
Pigue Pen Metal Gate	§115	§17	§11	§46
Plainlee Palm	§290	§43	§29	§116
Pointy Things Pencil Pine Tree	§240	§36	§24	§96
Port of Ennui	§250	§37	§25	§100
Sheer Glass Window	§120	§18	§12	§48
SimCity Midbiscus	§155	§23	§15	§62
Simple Structure Staircase	§900	§135	§90	§360
Stairway to Eleven	§1,200	§180	§120	§480
Stare Stepper Staircase	§1,150	§172	§115	§460
Symmetric Poly-Molecular Matrix Window	§220	§33	§22	§88

Build Mode Objects continued

Object	Purchase Price	Initial Depreciation	Daily Depreciation	Depreciation Limit
The "Function of Plate Glass" Window	§110	§16	§11	§44
The "Light Pane"	§250	§37	§25	§100
The Literal Rose	§100	§15	§10	§40
The Simple Weeping Willow	§400	§60	§40	§160
TipTop Tulips	§10	§1	§1	§4
TipTop Tulips*	§5	§1	§1	§2
Touch of Teak "Pigalle" French Arch	§365	§54	§36	§146
Touch of Teak "Pigalle" French Door	§500	§75	§50	§200
Truly Stained-Glass Window	§130	§19	§13	§52
Up, Up, and Away Column	§90	§13	§9	§36
UpRite Column	§70	§10	§7	§28
Upwardly Mobile Staircase	§1,000	§150	§100	§400
ValueWood Lumber's "Justa Arch"	§95	§14	§9	§38
ValueWood Lumber's "Justa Door"	§80	§12	§8	§32
Vasculito's General Cactus	§225	§33	§22	§90
VIP Deluxe Arch	§515	§77	§51	§206
VIP Deluxe Double Doors	§590	§88	§59	§236
Wachowt Glass Door	§350	§52	§35	§140
Walnut Arch	§115	§17	§11	§46
Walnut Door	§100	§15	§10	§40
Well Wisher's Window	§90	§13	§9	§36
Wrought Weiler Iron Gate	§200	§30	§20	§80

Chapter 32
Story Mode and Moviemaking

Why hide your Sims under a bushel? Better to tell their stories for the world to hear.

With *The Sims 2*, there are more (and more powerful) ways than ever to tell the stories of your Sims and their constantly evolving lives.

There's also more reason than ever to tell their stories. Now that Sim families evolve through generations, living and dying and passing the torch to their offspring, Sim stories become positively epic.

Stories can be told in either pictures or in video. This chapter introduces you to both methods and describes a few extra tricks to make them even more compelling.

> **note**
>
> Find options for the snapshot and video cameras in Options: Camera Options and, as described below for the serious filmmaker, in a more esoteric place.

STORY MODE—TELLING STORIES WITH PICTURES

Story mode is where you may assemble snapshots and combine them with text to create a story of either a neighborhood or an individual family (household).

Stories become part of a family or neighborhood, always available for viewing or editing, but the real fun comes when you publish the story to *TheSims2.com*. Maybe the world will be so captivated by your Sims' story that folks keep coming back for updates, waiting with bated breath for the next installment.

Neighborhood stories can draw from every lot and family. It's the venue for the really large-scale tales.

Story mode is available from two places:

1. Neighborhood view
2. Lot view (occupied lots only)

> **note**
>
> There's one more place that Story mode makes itself felt: in the Neighborhood Preview in the Neighborhood Chooser. The first image in the neighborhood's story pops up when you select the neighborhood. This picture is unchangeable in the game but there is a way to change it. See below.

Taking Snapshots

The Camera Snapshot button is located just above Funds.

Take snapshots by pressing the Camera Snapshot button ([C] by default) when in Neighborhood or Lot view. Shots taken this way omit the user interface and show the moment exactly as framed.

Every time a snapshot is taken, it's added to the location's Snapshot bin and the neighborhood-wide Snapshot bin.

Snapshots can also be taken in Create-A-Sim. The Camera Snapshot button won't work, however, if there's an active cursor in a text entry box.

Shapshots taken in Create-A-Sim aren't added to any Snapshot bin but can, like all snapshots, be found in MY DOCUMENTS\EA GAMES\THE SIMS 2\ STORYTELLING.

Story Mode Organizer/Editor

Entering Story mode, you're first taken to the organizer.

note

In Neighborhood view, switching to Story mode starts you in a presentation of the neighborhood story. Click the Edit Neighborhood Story button to enter the organizer/editor. In Lot view, on the other hand, entering Story mode transports you directly to the organizer/editor.

The organizer is for selecting pictures to include in the album and establish in what order they appear in the story.

tip

Don't forget to name your story.

The editor is where you tell your story in words (adding text to appear with each picture), select whether the lot's story will be formatted as an album or a blog, and (if you like) upload the story to *TheSims2.com*.

Organize Story

In the organizer, snapshots incorporated into the story are shown vertically on the right and the Snapshot bins are to the left.

There are actually two Snapshot bins. One contains only snapshots taken on the current location, be it a lot or the neighborhood. The other bin holds shots from the neighborhood and every lot in it, including Community Lots.

The Organize Story tool has two Snapshot bins. One contains all unused snapshots for this location (residential lot or neighborhood). The other (marked with a "+") contains every shot from the neighborhood and all lots.

note

Snapshots may be taken on Community Lots but are available to incorporate into your family's story only via the neighborhood-wide Snapshot bin. Community Lots have no Story mode.

Family stories can include pictures from any location as long as it's within the neighborhood. Snapshots from other neighborhoods won't appear without a little hacking (see following page).

To include a snapshot in the story, highlight the picture and click the Add to Story button (it's added above whichever snapshot is highlighted in the existing story).

Once a shot is in the story, move it by clicking on it and pushing the Move Entry Up and Down buttons.

Edit Story

In Edit Story, choose in which format you'd like the story to be presented on *TheSims2.com*.

Edit Story can organize snapshots as an album...

An album is a one shot per page view while a blog is a reverse chronological multishot view.

note

Once a story is uploaded, changing the format takes effect the next time you upload story changes.

...or a blog.

Before sending your story out to the world, add words to the images in each shot's text box. Be brief and descriptive or passionate and fanciful, but let your words speak as loudly as your pictures.

Adding and Editing Snapshots Externally

Snapshots can be added to a neighborhood or family's Snapshot bin from other neighborhoods or from anywhere really (your personal photo album, a bit of artwork, etc.) but it takes a little hacking.

All snapshots are stored in *My Documents\EA Games\The Sims 2\Storytelling* in two forms: the snapshot itself and a thumbnail. You can't, however, just drop in a shot and have it appear in the Snapshot bin. To prevent duplication, every snapshot taken via the Snapshot button has a distinct alphanumeric name that attaches it to a particular neighborhood and, if any, lot. Without a properly formatted name, a snapshot won't be available.

Any digital image can take the place of a snapshot and appear in Story mode. These characters don't look like Sims.

The easy way is to take an existing picture and replace it with the one you want to include:

1. Edit the image you want to use down to 400 x 300 dpi (for the image) and make a duplicate version that's 128 x 96 (for the thumbnail).

2. In the game, take a shot of anything in the location you want the image to appear (either a lot or the neighborhood) and quit the game.

3. Go to *My Documents\EA Games\The Sims 2\Storytelling* and locate the picture and its thumbnail version.

4. Open the image and its thumbnail. In each, cut out the existing image and paste the desired image. Save.

5. Launch the game. The images have replaced the existing ones and can be used in stories for any lot in the neighborhood or the neighborhood story itself.

The composite images that adorn the three shipping neighborhoods were constructed externally and copied back into Story mode with this procedure.

Shots can also be altered by opening them in a graphics program, changing the image, and saving them under the same file name. You must change both the thumbnail and the shot for the changes to be reflected in both versions.

Change a neighborhood's image in the Neighborhood Chooser by dropping a replacement image into the neighborhood's folder. User-made neighborhoods otherwise use a generic image.

Changing the image you see when you select a neighborhood is a bit more difficult. Find that image in *My Documents\EA Games\The Sims 2\ Neighborhoods*. Each neighborhood has a folder (e.g., *N001*, *N002*, etc.) and in each folder is an image with the name of the folder plus "*_Neighborhood.png*" Thus, the image for *N001* would be "*N001_Neighborhood.png*." Convert the image you want to into a *.png* file and name it "*N###_Neighborhood.png*" in which "*###* is the neighborhood file's number. The next time the game starts, this image shows as the neighborhood's thumbnail and as the image in the pop-up window.

note

You can change the pop-up window's image for the three shipping neighborhoods, but the animated tour thumbnails in the Neighborhood Chooser are unchangeable. User-made neighborhoods use a generic image or whatever you put in the neighborhood's folder as described above.

Family Stories and Death

If the last member of a household dies, that can make a great dramatic conclusion to your story. When this happens, the story is preserved until you quit and save the now empty lot. Thus, you can end the tale with a tragic and untimely death...there won't be a dry eye on the net.

TELLING STORIES WITH VIDEOS

When still pictures are inadequate, make a movie of your Sims lives.

Start video capture by pressing the Video Capture button right above Funds.

tip

To capture video, with some videocards, you may have to turn off Smooth Edges in the Graphics Options and click Apply Changes.

When video capture is on, the screen is ringed by a yellow box. This won't, however, appear in the movie.

To begin capturing video, press Video Capture button ([V] by default). To stop capturing, press it again. Pressing B will pause video capture in progress, useful if you want to change camera framing or location within a single shot.

You may "film" your Sims either in the normal mode (the user interface, the cursor, or the social interactions menus won't appear in the film though the red pause box will if the game is stopped) or in *The Sims 2*'s special Cameraman view.

Cameraman View

To enter Cameraman view, press the Cameraman button ([Tab] by default). Cameraman view is an extra flexible camera that can zoom in much farther than the regular game camera and allow you to fly through a lot using keyboard and mouse controls. It, however, requires several keyboard controls:

Cameraman view is a much more mobile and intimate camera but it takes some practice to guide it.

♦ [Z]: Zoom In
♦ [X]: Zoom Out
♦ [A]: Start Move Left
♦ [D]: Start Move Right
♦ [W]: Start Move Forward
♦ [S]: Start Move Back
♦ [Q]: Start Lower Camera Height
♦ [E]: Start Raise Camera Height

Camera Positions

The ability to save camera positions is pretty handy when playing the game but it's really useful in moviemaking.

(tip)

Remember, you can always center the view on a Sim by right-clicking on his portrait in the toolbar or on a location or object by right-clicking on or near it. This can act as an easy jump cut in moviemaking and lets you rotate around a constant point, keeping the subject in the center of the view.

Assign camera positions by aiming the view (in either camera mode) exactly where you want it and pressing [Ctrl] and any number on the keyboard (not the keypad) from 4 through 9.

Jump right to a moment with a predefined camera position.

To move to a camera position, press the number assigned to it. Alternately, to jump from one location to a defined camera position, press [Shift] and the number.

By pre-positioning the camera in precise locations and orientations, your movies can zoom from one location to another in seconds.

The regular camera and Cameraman view each have distinct assignments for camera position, so be mindful of which mode you're in or the camera might not go where you expect it.

Movie Settings

Most settings impacting moviemaking can be found in Options: Camera. Set them as high as your computer's performance can bear.

Sound can be captured too but will decrease performance even further.

Uncompressed video produces higher quality video with less of a drag on performance, but the files it creates are gigantic. Be very cautious about capturing uncompressed video unless you have a cavernous hard drive.

You may also set the maximum capture time. If you intend to edit the video, shoot in short segments rather than one extremely long "take."

Cinematic Cheats

Several cheats can be useful for making movies with your Sims:

For that "Special Edition" feel, try putting a letterbox around your film.

Or how about "bloom?"

Or vignette?

Or filmgrain?

- Letterbox.
- Slowmotion.
- Bloom: Creates a filmic look in which everything's so bright it blurs together (à la sitcom flashbacks).
- Vignette: Creates a filmic look in which a focal point is clear but everything around it is blurry.
- Stretchskeleton: Increases or decreases Sim height compared to normal height.
- Filmgrain: Creates a film graininess.

Though not really having anything to do with moviemaking, this cheat MUST have some possibilities, don't you think?

These codes are entered in the Cheat window, accessed by pressing Ctrl + Shift + C. See Chapter 36 for details and parameters.

Saving Video

After you press the Video Capture button, everything you see is preserved in a video file on your hard drive. The size of the file varies based on the camera settings.

When the maximum video recording time ends or you press the Video Capture button again, capturing stops.

The file (saved as *.avi*) goes in *My Documents\ EA Games\The Sims 2\Movies*.

Processing Footage

Ok, great director, you've got your film "in the can" and your actors are resting in their trailers. What now?

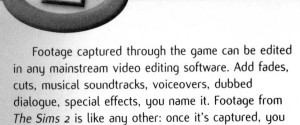
Footage captured through the game can be edited in any mainstream video editing software. Add fades, cuts, musical soundtracks, voiceovers, dubbed dialogue, special effects, you name it. Footage from *The Sims 2* is like any other: once it's captured, you may manipulate it any way you like.

Hacking the Camera

For the very adventurous, it's possible to have even more control of the video capture system's settings. Locate (and back up) the file *VideoCapture.ini* in *My Documents\EA Games\The Sims 2\Config* and open it with a text editor.

There are more picture quality and size settings here than in the in-game options menu including the power to change the system's preferred codec.

Tweak these settings at your own risk:

- PreferredCodec: Lets you choose a codec. This field is updated dynamically if your chosen codec fails to work.
- OutputFramerate: The framerate of the output AVI.
- GameFramerateForHighQuality: Sets the framerate of the game. This is used only when the quality setting is set too high. If you set it to a high number you get slow motion.
- KeyFrameEvery: Specifies that each nth frame should be a key frame.
- Folder: Specifies the folder to which the output is written. It's relative to *My Documents\EA Games\ The Sims 2*.
- FilenameBase: Specifies the beginning of the file-name. Changing this from the default "movie" might permit better organization of video files (e.g., "llamas-take").
- NoFillFrames=1: Turns off auto-filling of empty frames. Results depend on the codec.
- AudioStereoOutput: 0 for mono, 1 for stereo.

- AudioRateDivisor: 1 for 44100 Hz, 2 for 22050, etc. The maximum divisor is 8.
- SmallWidth=128: Width of video when size is set to small in the camera options.
- SmallHeight=128: Height of video when size is set to small in the camera options.
- MediumWidth=320: Width of video when size is set to medium in the camera options.
- MediumHeight=240: Height of video when size is set to medium in the camera options.
- LargeWidth=640: Width of video when size is set to large in the camera options.
- LargeHeight=480: Height of video when size is set to large in the camera options.

Additionally, settings such as zoom, pitch, orientation, etc. can also be changed for the various in-game cameras. If you're shooting in regular (not Cameraman) mode, these settings can change the camera movements you may do. Find these files at *My Documents\EA Games\The Sims 2\Cameras*. LiveCamera.txt is for the regular mode, and FirstPersonCameras.txt is for the Cameraman mode. Be very careful to back up the original files so that in case your experimentation makes some weird changes you can revert to the original default settings. An easy way to do this is to open the original with a text editor and then save them as ____.BKP, then make your modification to the file and save your new settings as ____.txt .

Sharing Your Movies

There's currently nowhere on *TheSims2.com* to host user-made movies but you can rest assured that sites will began to appear the day the game released. By the time you read these words, there should be no shortage of venues for your masterpieces.

Chapter 33
Sim Autonomy

Sims are independent creatures. Sure, they obey your every command (unless they're in a bad Mood), but they can fend for themselves if you let them. In truth, Sims are far more able now to make their own decisions and care for their own Needs thanks to developments in their autonomy system.

Autonomy comes into play any time you, the player, have not queued up an interaction for the Sim to do. "If", they think to themselves, "the bloke upstairs doesn't have any suggestions, I'll do what feels good to me." Understanding how this system operates is esoteric but can give you insight into why Sims do what they do.

Choosing what interactions to do is the major function of autonomy, but there are other systems that, though they're less important, any Sims enthusiast should yearn to know.

This chapter examines the general operation of the autonomy system and how it can benefit you as the master of your virtual people.

FREE WILL

Sims behave autonomously only if their Free Will is activated.

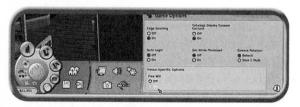

The Free Will setting is located in Options: Game Options, and applies only to the house you're in when you set it.

Free Will is enabled in the Game Options menu and is on by default. Don't turn it off unless you have a very good reason.

If Free Will is turned off, Sims just stand around when not explicitly told what to do. It actually looks kinda creepy.

The most important thing to remember about Free Will is that if it's turned off, your Sim won't lift a finger even in the event of danger or to satisfy his own Needs.

When Free Will is on, however, your Sims smartly go about their business. They give your commands priority, of course, but they fill any spare moment with activities that benefit them most.

How they make those decisions is a function of "Autonomy."

ADVERTISING

You're not aware of it, but your Sim is under constant assault. Every interaction with every object on the lot and every potential social interaction calls to your Sim, bragging about how much Need satisfaction it offers.

This call for attention is called "Advertising." It's how Sims autonomously decide what they'll do. They sift through all the possible interactions, adjust them based on the Sim's own Personality and Need levels and select the most beneficial option.

> **note**
>
> Sims' ability to choose the best advertised action is a major change from the original THE SIMS, and it's why the Need satisfaction part of the game requires less of your time than it did in the original.

> **tip**
>
> Once an interaction with an advertised item succeeds, the interaction is stored in the Sim's ineraction memory. The next time it is re-evaluated, its score is halved, which makes it less likely to happen again. This keeps Sims from choosing the same interactions over and over again.

Ad Strength and Attenuation

Each interaction's advertisement has two important features: strength and attenuation. An ad's strength is how much Need satisfaction it promises, and attenuation is how far and intensely the ad travels over distance. If an interaction's signal has low attenuation, it dissipates slowly over a great distance (can usually be heard on the entire lot). If an interaction's signal has high attenuation, its ad's strength drops quickly over a shorter distance; the Sim must be physically near such an object to hear its call.

Ads with low attenuation attract Sims from anywhere on the lot.

Interactions from objects such as beds have low attenuation, so a Sim can hear their promise of Energy satisfaction from anywhere. This makes the Sim more likely to choose a bed over a physically closer sofa or recliner. Impulse objects (e.g., reading the newspaper) have high attenuation because they're the kind of things Sims pick up and use only if they're handy.

Ads broadcast their message to specific Needs. Think of an interaction as a radio with several stations. Sitting on a sofa, for example, would broadcast on the Comfort channel while the same object's Nap interaction would be simultaneously broadcasting on the Energy channel. The Sim judges ads by how much they offer to his Needs.

That's how the ad looks from the transmitter's point of view. What the Sim hears, though, depends on many of his own personal attributes.

Personality Modifiers

Advertising affects what interactions Sims of certain Personality bents find most attractive.

Ad strength can be modified by a Sim's Personality. Not all ads have a Personality to which they advertise most strongly but most do.

Such ads have a range of strength (e.g., 10–40). How much of this promise the Sim hears depends on, for example, his Outgoing/Shy level. If he has eight points in Outgoing/Shy, he gets 80 percent of the ad's strength: in other words he hears an ad of strength 34 whereas an Outgoing/Shy 10 Sim would hear the full strength of 40.

> **note**
>
> The Outgoing/Shy 10 Sim would, as a result of the stronger signal, rank this interaction higher among his choices.

This is how certain Fun activities are deemed more attractive to specific Personality types. Reading a book from a bookshelf has its signal adjusted by the listening Sim's Playful/Serious score; the lower the score, the more of the ad the Sim will hear. Hence, only Serious Sims tend to autonomously read books. A Playful Sim would get just as much Fun out of reading but probably has many other Fun options ranking ahead of such a weak signal.

Personality, however, isn't the only factor that modifies an ad's strength.

Need Curves

A Sim's current level in a particular Need can change the strength of an ad. By this mechanism, the lower a Sim's level in a Need, the more an ad addressed to that Need will appeal.

A Sim with low Bladder Need is going to rank anything advertising Bladder satisfaction very highly on his list of possible actions.

Thus, two ads of identical strength would be scored differently for the Sim depending on his levels in each ad's addressed Need. If, for example, a Sim has -50 Hunger and 10 Hygiene and there's a Hunger ad for 20 and a Hygiene of 30, the Hunger ad would rank higher because the Need to which it's advertising is closer to failure. Thus, the more pressing a Sim's Need, the higher ads addressed to that Need rank.

Each Need boosts ads in different amounts. At a given motive level, the amount of the modification will likely be more for a Need such as Energy than a non-physical Need such as Fun.

False Advertising

Many interactions lie to get a Sim's attention, advertising to a Need they can't or won't satisfy to trick the Sim into using it. Ringing phones, for example, get Sims to answer them by advertising large amounts of satisfaction for all Needs which, of course, they have no intention of delivering.

It sounds more dastardly than it is. It's really just a way to get certain interactions the attention they need.

The Final Analysis: Find Best Action

Once an ad's signal is modified by both Personality and the Sim's current Need level, it's ranked along with all other advertising interactions that the Sim can "hear." The Sim *always* selects the highest rated interaction. This may sound obvious, but it's a major change.

If a Sim is in Need distress it's probably because you've been overruling her attempts to tend to her most imperative requirements.

In the original *The Sims*, a similar system of advertising was at play but your Sim chose differently. She would rank all advertisements and pick the top four. From these, she'd choose randomly. Thus, the player had to be mindful if the Sim had led herself astray by picking the lower of her four choices. This is how Bladder accidents happened when a perfectly good toilet was nearby.

This is no longer the case: Sims in *The Sims 2* always choose the best action available to them. That's not to say there won't still be mistakes—due primarily to player intervention or Sims' inability to choose a series of actions—but they're far less frequent.

You also may not like the order in which the Sim takes care of business ("For the thousandth time! Use the toilet and *then* shower!") but she'll rarely neglect her single most pressing Need. The trouble comes

when she's prevented (by circumstances or your intervention) from following that choice and when the second action on the list is almost as pressing as the first. With such close calls, failures are always a possibility.

THE INTERACTION QUEUE

Whenever a Sim does anything, that activity appears in the interaction queue. Sims may have as many as eight interactions queued up at one time.

Canceling an action draws a red "X" over its icon in the queue. The Sim leaves that interaction at the first chance.

Sims prioritize which interactions they'll do by who issued the interaction. User-directed interactions (that's yours) get the highest priority over interactions the Sim chose autonomously. Sims exit any autonomous interactions at the first opportunity to undertake an explicit direction.

tip

Remove interactions from the queue by left-clicking on them. A red X appears and the icon fades out. If the cancelled interaction is in progress when cancelled, the Sim may need a moment for an opportunity to exit gracefully.

Autonomous interactions queued up in front of a user directed interaction are immediately dumped, bringing the user-directed interaction to the fore.

Be careful with this power; taking priority away from Sim-initiated interactions can have consequences. If the Sim's chosen activity is to tend to a Need in dire straits, your issuing another command may be what causes the Sim's Need to fail. The oft-cited example of leaving food cooking in the oven usually arises from the issuance of a user-directed command that overrides the autonomous activity of removing the food from the oven.

Sims do user-directed interactions in order, and switch from one to another when:

◆ If it's a Need satisfying interaction, as soon as the Need is fully satisfied or the interaction's Need maximum is reached.

◆ If it's a fixed time or task interaction (e.g., cooking), as soon as he's finished with the activity.

◆ If it's a skill building interaction, as soon as a Need or overall Mood drops too low to keep using the object.

Helper interactions (represented by red Need icons) are how Sims deal with a long string of player-directed interactions.

When a Sim is busy with several user-directed interactions, he may insert a generic interaction for Bladder, Energy, Hunger, or Hygiene if they're getting too low. For instance, if he noticed that his Bladder Need was getting low, he inserts a generic icon of a toilet. This permits him to take the next open opportunity to autonomously take care of that Need with an as yet undetermined object.

Unlike other autonomous interactions, these "helper" interactions are not bumped by having user-directed interactions put behind them in the queue. They can be eliminated only by being specifically cancelled.

When the helper interaction's turn comes up, the Sim chooses the best object for satisfying the Need in question based on where he is when the interaction takes over.

DESPERATION AND IMMATURITY BEHAVIORS

Low Aspiration score gives rise to increasingly frequent and increasingly self-destructive autonomous behaviors. The differences between the kinds of behavior and a description of how they work can be found in Chapter 21.

OTHER AUTONOMOUS SYSTEMS

Several other forces are at play in how Sims behave autonomously, but none of them impact any gameplay.

Reaction

Sims have elaborate systems to react to things going on around them. Sims react to certain triggers with facial reactions, turning of the head, or other responses.

For example:

♦ Sims turn to look when another Sim enters the room. If they have a relationship, there may be a special reaction (smile or frown).

♦ They react according to Personality when another Sim has a Bladder failure.

♦ They cover their ears in the presence of a loud noise.

♦ They applaud good piano music or boo badly played music.

♦ They react to smells such as food and stinky trash.

♦ When an attack is underway, they gather around (or flee) and either cheer or boo depending on their relationships with the combatants.

♦ When they see another Sim naked, they gasp.

♦ When a Sim does something gross (e.g., stinks from low Hygiene or burps), other Sims react. Sloppy Sims may find such things amusing rather than offensive.

♦ If a Sim is talking to the Social Bunny or the Sim Shrink (either of whom only they can see), other Sims gesture that the Sim is crazy.

♦ Some events make older Sims lecture their offspring even though doing so lowers their Relationship scores.

Appraising New Objects

Whenever a new object is added to a lot, Sims may come to have a look at it and express their opinion. That opinion is based on the object's value.

Sims panicking at a fire is a function of the reaction system. Such interactions jump right to the front of the Sim's queue, but autonomous reactions aren't that pushy.

Sims rush right over to any new object and tell you what they think.

Shy Sims kvetch whenever you tell them to kiss someone, but they enjoy it in the end.

note

Object appraisal is another example of false advertising. Taking a look at the new object advertises satisfaction, which is why Sims usually drop everything to check out a new bauble.

Sims quickly become accustomed to their current standard of living and evaluate everything based on the things they already have. If the object's value is significantly less than of the median value of all other objects on the lot, the Sim will boo. If the object's value is significantly more than median value, she'll cheer. If it's close to the median value, she won't even notice.

Sims can be so shallow sometimes.

Receptivity

Based on their Personalities, Sims express resistance or pleasure when directed to do certain things. Sloppy Sims, for example, moan and groan if you direct them to clean up a mess; they'll do it, but they don't like it. The more often you tell them to do the task, the more intense the reaction becomes until they eventually give up and do the task without a reaction.

Sims with extreme Personality traits always resist, and Sims further away from the extremes resist less the more neutral they are.

Negative receptivity, especially with Sims of extreme traits, can become a major efficiency problem. They waste so much time complaining that every interaction they don't like takes longer. A severely Sloppy Sim living alone really must, therefore, have a Maid or get a Neat roommate.

Idling

Whenever a Sim has nothing to do or is deciding what to do autonomously, he does idle animations that reflect his most extreme Personality traits.

Summary

These are but a few things that Sims can do on their own, but there are many more that add richness to the world and challenge to the game.

Chapter 34
The Sims™ 2 Body Shop

The Sims™ 2 Body Shop is an astoundingly powerful tool for sculpting the physical forms of Sims for The Sims 2.

Well, that's not quite accurate. The Sims™ 2 Body Shop is, in fact, two tools that do very different things. The Sims™ 2 Body Shop consists of:

◆ Build Sims   ◆ Create Parts

BODY SHOP is divided into two parts: Build Sims and Create Parts.

note

For basic functionality and the specifics on creating custom items, consult the THE SIMS™ 2 BODY SHOP manual and online tutorials. All these items, along with a Help page and downloadable content packs, can be found at THESIMS2.COM in the Community section under Showcase.

BUILD SIMS VS. CREATE PARTS

It's important to comprehend specifically what each tool in The Sims™ 2 Body Shop does.

In brief:

◆ Build Sims: Assemble created or downloaded parts into a finished Sim. You may also duplicate any Sim in the bin and use it as the basis for another new Sim.

◆ Create Parts: Use built-in, already created, or downloaded Sim pieces to create brand new parts.

BUILD SIMS

Build Sims is where the pieces are assembled to construct a new being.

Build Sims consists of two sections:

◆ Clone Sims: Using the bin full of Sims you've downloaded or assembled, you can pick one to form the basis of a new Sim or choose to start a brand new Sim from scratch. Saved Sims may be deleted from here too.

◆ Build Sims: Once a Sim has been cloned or freshly created, you can mix and match any Genetics (eye color, skin tone, or hair), Faces (entire face or by region), Modifiers (several for each facial region), Facial Hair, Makeup, Glasses, Eyebrows, Stubble, Costume Makeup, or Clothing. These elements may have been created by you, by Maxis, or by other users.

Build Sims allows you to put together various Sim parts you've created or downloaded into one glorious, statuesque creation. You can't, of course, name these Sims or tinker with their personalities or Aspirations, but you can choose how they look.

Build Sims vs. Create-A-Sim

Much, but not all, of what can be done in Build Sims can be done in the in-game Create-A-Sim.

For example, in Build Sims, you can effectively edit finished Sims; this isn't possible in Create-A-Sim.

In Create-A-Sim, when you work your magic on a Sim from scratch or from the Sim Bin, you save that Sim into a family. Once the family is saved, that Sim exists only in that family and cannot be changed. Likewise, there's no saved original copy of your creation that you can go back to; if you want to make the same Sim with a different personality or Aspiration, you must start from scratch.

Packaging gets the file ready to share with others. To simply use your creation in your own game, packaging is unnecessary.

A packaged file can be traded among users. If you receive one, just double click on the package file and the new Sim will be saved into the right place (presuming you have *The Sims™ 2 Body Shop* or the game installed.)

> **note**
>
> Another difference between Create-A-Sim and THE SIMS™ 2 BODY SHOP is Create-A-Sim's tool to swap entire heads. These heads are a preset combination of facial features and hair shape. In THE SIMS™ 2 BODY SHOP, this must be done piecemeal.

In *The Sims™ 2 Body Shop*, however, any Sim you've completed can be cloned and modified. Though you aren't really editing the original Sim, the effect is the same: you can fix problems or create small variations and save that Sim too. The original is still available and unchanged; you may delete it and save only the altered clone if you like.

> **note**
>
> Create-A-Sim and THE SIMS™ 2 BODY SHOP handle facial alteration in different ways. When editing a face in THE SIMS™ 2 BODY SHOP, you must drag the sliders to increment the Sim's face toward the face in the thumbnail. In Create-A-Sim, on the other hand, you do the same thing by left-clicking on the thumbnail.

The Final Step: Package Sim

When a Sim is finished, you can package it either into a file or directly up to *TheSims2.com*.

CREATE PARTS

Create Parts is what really differentiates *The Sims™ 2 Body Shop* and Create-A-Sim. In Create Parts you don't change the Sim as a whole, but rather many of the components that make up a Sim. Want to create hot pink eyes? This is where you go.

Create Parts has two areas: one for beginning a new project and one to bring up an old one. Note the Change Mannequin button; it's only available at this screen and the subsequent Start New Project menu.

Create Parts consists of two tools:

- ◆ Start New Project: Take any Sim part in the catalog and alter it to your precise vision.
- ◆ Load Saved Project: Reload your own projects for further editing.

note

The Change Mannequin button lets you alter the skin color of the model on which your Sim parts will be displayed in this tool. It's available, however, in only two places.

When you click Create Parts in the main menu, you're given the option to Start New Project or Load Saved Project. Before doing either, however, note that the Change Mannequin button is darkened and can be used. It can also be pressed in the Start New Project menu.

Choose the Mannequin skin tone you want to use and click the checkmark. From now on, this will be your model.

Start New Project

Parts fall into three categories:

◆ Create Genetics: Create the color of eyes and the shape of pupils and irises, the tone of skin, and the color of hair.

◆ Create Facial Hair, Makeup, and Glasses: Generate the texture of eyebrows, the amount of men's facial hair stubble, the look of beards and mustaches, the color and pattern of makeup (blush, eye shadow, eyeliner, and lipstick), costume makeup (a.k.a. face painting/facial tattoos), and the color and texture of eyeglasses.

◆ Create Clothing: Design clothing for each sartorial category (Everyday, Formal, Undies, PJs, Swim-wear, and Athletic). You may even change an outfit's classification, for example, turn Undies into Formal (see page 439).

Create Genetics

Genetics are the basic Sim features that are passed from generation to generation: eyes, hair, and skin tone. Each is edited differently in *The Sims™ 2 Body Shop*.

Genetics include eyes, hair, and skin. Other elements of your Sims will be handed down to their children, but these are the most basic.

Skin Tone

Within each skin tone are textures for each age group, gender, and fitness level. To completely manipulate a skin tone, you must alter every file in the project folder.

To completely alter a skin tone, you must edit all of these texture files. If your goals are a bit more limited, do only the ones for the age and genders you have in mind.

note

If you want to get really snazzy, you can actually edit the arrangement or color of Sims' teeth via the skin tone files. On each facial texture you'll find a row of teeth that show when your Sim is animated in the game.

One could, for instance, paint the teeth to appear pointy for that vampiric look or give your Sim a gold tooth.

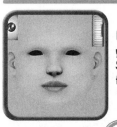

It's a subtle change, but you can fiddle with a Sim's teeth through the facial skin tone file.

note

The face texture only changes the COLOR of the face, not the shape.

Every skin tone is actually a collection of 39 files:

◆ Five textures each for male and female elders (soft, neutral, fit, face, and the head).

◆ Five textures each for male and female adults (soft, neutral, fit, face, and the head).

◆ Five textures each for male and female teens (soft, neutral, fit, face, and the head).

◆ Three textures for children (body, face, and the head).

◆ Three textures for toddlers (body, face, and the head).

◆ Three textures for babies (body, face, and the head).

If you alter only some of these files, when a Sim changes to the unmodified age or fitness level in the game, he or she will suddenly revert to the original skin tone. The same would happen for offspring; if the Sim has a child and that age is not modified, the child won't look like the parent.

> **note**
>
> You might want your Sim to have a different skin tone for different ages. If, and we're about to get really geeky here for a second, the morphology of the alien Sims you've created dictates that they don't appear alien until puberty, it'd make sense to leave the baby, toddler, and child skin tone files unchanged and alter only the ones from teen and up.

> **note**
>
> You can alter a Sim's "fit" state but it's the one fitness state that you can't select as a default in Build Sim. The only way to display the fit state in the game is to earn it by working out.

Eyes

Eyes are exported as a two files: the texture file and the alpha channel file. In the texture file, you may change the coloring and shape of the iris and the color and shape of the pupil.

Hair

A hair project contains files for each age group (except babies; they're bald) for the specified gender.

The texture files can be changed to alter the color or texture of the hair, though not the hairstyle's overall shape or configuration. Hairstyles are actually 3D models that can't be altered with *The Sims™ 2 Body Shop*.

> **note**
>
> Sims take off their hats when they shower, sleep, exercise, swim, are pregnant, or are naked for whatever reason. For Sims that use hair/hat combinations, extra textures show the hairstyle without the hat for teen, adult, and elder Sims.

Shortening hair with the alpha channel file (by coloring some of the white parts black) before and after

You can use the alpha channel file to superficially change the shape of the hair. By making parts of the image black, you can cover up parts of a hairstyle to make it look shorter or show bare patches. However, because the hairstyle is a 3D model, an alpha-channel-altered hairstyle in-game still moves as if it's longer hair.

Create Facial Hair, Makeup, and Glasses

Anything that goes *on* the face is constructed here.

Eyebrows, Stubble, and Beard

Eyebrow, stubble, and beard projects consist of colored and gray (for elders) versions of the facial hair. The texture file can be altered for color, shape, and texture of the hair.

Makeup

All makeup projects, regardless of type, export a texture and an alpha channel file. The texture file dictates the color and shading of the makeup. The alpha channel file can be changed to extend the makeup into other parts of the face (by painting parts of the file white instead of black). For example, if you want ancient Egyptian-style eye shadow, you'd extend the outer eye corners.

With makeup, you have the power to choose what ages and genders can apply it.

Right after you export the files, you can specify (in *The Sims™ 2 Body Shop*) which ages and genders you want the makeup to apply to (from toddler to elder).

Glasses

While you cannot change the *shape* of glasses or the lens colors in *The Sims™ 2 Body Shop*, you can alter the color of the frames.

The project folder contains several texture files, each of which represents a piece of the frames (the temples, the rims, etc.). Edit them all to completely change the frame color.

Clothing

Clothing of every type (Everyday, Formal, Undies, Swimwear, PJs, and Athletic) can be altered. You can even change an item's classification to have it appear as a different type.

Clothing projects consist of three files: the texture, the alpha channel, and the bump map.

Alterations to the texture file change the garment's color.

This granny dress becomes a bit more risqué with some alpha channel fiddling.

The alpha channel file lets you superficially change the shape of the garment, though drastic changes aren't possible. You can, for instance, create cut-outs to show off a little skin by painting part of the white portions black.

> **note**
>
> The ability to edit the bump map file is available only in the version of THE SIMS™ 2 BODY SHOP that ships with THE SIMS 2.

The bump map file creates the illusion of three dimensionality in the garment. If you want to make a smooth T-shirt look ribbed, for example, you could change the bump map.

Changing Clothing Classification

Want to make some manly undies into any Sims' everyday wear? In Create Parts, choose Create Clothing. Select the clothing category and specific item you wish to change, then click the Export Selected Texture button. Name the project and click the checkmark. When the clothing finishes exporting, you may select in which category your clothing will appear. Choose something other than its original category (and enter a tool tip if you like), and click the Import To Game button.

Changing clothing classification is easy: Select any additional classifications you want the garment to assume.

Now, when you go into *The Sims™ 2 Body Shop*'s Build Sim mode or Create-A-Sim in the *The Sims 2*, there'll be some real scandalous formal wear for Sims brave enough to don it.

The Final Step: Import to Game

When a project is complete, click on the Import to Game button and the part will henceforth be available in the Build Sims portion of *The Sims™ 2 Body Shop* or in Create-A-Sim in *The Sims 2*.

> ### note
> You can delete any custom content from THE SIMS™ 2 BODY SHOP or Create-A-Sim by clicking on it, and then the trash can icon nearby.

If you don't yet have *The Sims 2* installed, the appropriate files will be automatically moved over into the game when it's installed.

> ### note
> To share your project with a friend or upload it to a fansite, go to MY DOCUMENTS\EA GAMES\THE SIMS 2\SAVED SIMS and look for the filename that includes your project name. The recipient drops that file into his DOWNLOADS folder and, presto, he's got the fruits of your labor.

ADVANCED HOT KEYS

Several features dear to the hearts of Sim designers and fansite webmasters are available with a single keystroke.

> ### note
> F3, F5, F6 are available only in the version of THE SIMS™ 2 BODY SHOP that ships with THE SIMS 2.

The free camera gives you perspectives such as this.

◆ F3 : Free camera. Hold the left-mouse button and drag to move the camera. Hold the right mouse button and drag to zoom. Hold both mouse buttons and drag to pan. To return to the standard camera, press F3 again.

◆ F5 : Turns off the room background. Normally, this replaces the room background with a black void. You can customize this void by creating a pattern and saving it with the name *userBkg.bmp*. Place this file in \My Documents\EA Games\The Sims 2\. Henceforth, when you turn off the room with F5 , it will be replaced with this texture. This is very handy if you'll be posting Sims on your fansite and want to know how they'll look against your site's background.

◆ F6 : Puts the Sim in the awkward looking, but easier to view, "Bind" pose. To get out of this pose, click on any thumbnail of in the panel to the right.

◆ F7 : Jump to far zoom.

◆ F8 : Jump to close zoom.

◆ F9 : Drops the *The Sims™ 2 Body Shop* interface. Pressing again restores it.

◆ Alt + Enter : Togg+les *The Sims™ 2 Body Shop* into/out of Full Screen mode.

With a custom background and the F5 key, you can easily see how your Sim looks in any environment or against any color.

Chapter 35
Custom Content

One of the things that made *The Sims* such a roaring success was the game's openness to customization and user creativity. As much as the game gave, it got back a thousand fold from its loyal fans in the form of user-created houses, objects, walls and floors, and Sim skins.

Happily, *The Sims 2* not only continues this tradition but represents an evolutionary leap forward with the most powerful and accessible tools ever put in the hands of its players, and a game architecture that permits almost anything to be potentially customizable. Users can't currently alter *as many* parts of the game as before but can do far more with what's available to them.

You've already read about *The Sims™ 2 Body Shop*, but that's only the first example of what's possible. Many more parts of *The Sims 2* can be sculpted and shared with the world. For now, much of this altered content will come from Maxis, but time will bring more of these elements into the player community's hands.

This chapter surveys the customizable parts of the game, how to get them, how to install them, and how to share your own creations.

CUSTOM CONTENT TYPES

Myriad elements of *The Sims 2* can be customized with either user-created content or downloads from Maxis.

The items listed below are the custom content types when the game first ships. As time wears on, this list will expand considerably. Keep up with the latest news to find out when new tools become available.

Custom content includes:

◆ Build Mode Patterns (Maxis only)
◆ Collections
◆ Object Design Variations (Maxis only)
◆ Full Neighborhoods

◆ Lots (occupied and unoccupied)
◆ Music
◆ Neighborhood Decorations (Maxis only)
◆ Neighborhood Terrain (Maxis only)
◆ Objects (Maxis only)
◆ Sim Parts (eye and hair color, skin tone, clothing, etc.)
◆ Sims
◆ Stories
◆ TV Video
◆ Video/Computer Game Video

IMPORTING CUSTOM CONTENT

There are three ways to get custom content into the game:

◆ Custom Content Browser
◆ Package Installer
◆ Manually

Custom Content Browser

The Custom Content Browser built into the game is controlled in Neighborhood view.

Open the Custom Content Browser in the Neighborhood view. The button is marked by an "*".

---

tip

When importing custom content via the Custom Content Browser, it's available immediately without the need for a restart.

Via this tool, you may download Build and Buy mode objects (Maxis-made only) and user-created Sims and lots posted to *TheSims2.com*. Eventually, user-created walls, floors, objects, etc. will be available from *TheSims.com* via the browser as well.

Package Installer

The same kinds of content can come from sources other than *TheSims2.com*. If properly packaged, this content can be imported via a small program called PackageInstaller (*Program Files\EA Games\The Sims 2\CSBin\packageinstaller.exe*).

Properly packaged content can be dropped on the PackageInstaller's icon
or just double-clicked. The package installer automatically places all content in the correct folders.

tip

PackageInstaller can do its job only when neither THE SIMS 2 or THE SIMS™ 2 BODY SHOP are running. The next time you launch either program, the custom content will be installed and marked with a "*".

note

Two types of content files appear the same but aren't. "PACKAGE" files aren't installed through PackageInstaller. These game files can be dragged directly into the appropriate folder.

"SIMS2PACK" files, on the other hand, are handled by the PackageInstaller.

If you double-click on a PACKAGE file, PackageInstaller will simply refuse to do anything with it. Likewise, just dropping a SIMS2PACK file into a folder won't have any effect.

In dealing with Custom Content, especially once more elements become user-customizable, users should never have to deal with PACKAGE files.

Manually

All other content must be dragged to a location (or locations) on your hard drive. Such content becomes available only after a quit and restart.

Most such items go into a folder in your *The Sims 2* folder (found in *My Documents*) but some require slightly more elaborate procedures (detailed below).

BUILD MODE ELEMENTS

Build mode elements (wall and floor coverings, roofs, fences, and terrain cover) can be downloaded from Maxis via the Custom Content Browser.

Once installed, these items are available in the Build mode catalog.

At this time, these may be created only by Maxis.

COLLECTIONS

Collections are customized sortings of hand-picked items. For example, a collection of objects for the struggling artist or an array of skater wear.

The Collections panel in Buy and Build mode features any object/element collections from the original installation, created by you, or imported from other users.

note

If a collection includes an object that the recipient does not have (e.g., a post-release object from Maxis they haven't downloaded), it won't appear in the collection. If the object is later imported, it appears in the collection thereafter.

All installed collections, whatever the source, appear in this Collections panel, each adorned with an identifying icon. Once a custom collection is installed, it's appended to the end of this list.

Create new collections via the Create New Collection button in the panel or in the Select a Collection window.

You have an ample but limited selection of collection icons for use when creating a new collection. If you desire a custom icon, follow this procedure:

1. Quit the game.
2. Create an image for the icon. It can be 28 x 22 pixels or larger and any of .tga, .bmp, .gif, or .jpg format.
3. Save this file in *My Documents\EA Games\ The Sims 2\Collections\Icons*.
4. Restart the game, and it's available for all future collections.

To share a custom collection, locate the PACKAGE file in *My Documents\EA Games\The Sims 2\ Collections*. This is the hard part because the files names are randomly generated by the game.

tip

Sort collection files by modification date to make it easy to find the file you just made.

This PACKAGE file can be shared with other users. The recipient need only drop the file in his or her own *Collections* folder and restart the game. If the collection features a custom icon, it's carried over with the file and doesn't need to be put separately in the new user's *Icons* folder.

Collections can consist of:

◆ Buy and Build Mode Objects/Elements
◆ Clothing
◆ Sim Heads

Buy and Build Mode Collections

Buy and Build mode collections are shared by and appear in the Collections panels for both modes (just below the sort tabs) in Lot view.

All Buy and Build mode objects and many Build mode elements (floor and wall coverings, doors and windows, staircases, etc.) can be added to these mixed collections.

Clothing Collections

Assemble clothing collections in Create-A-Sim, panel 5 (Clothing). Just as with Buy and Build mode collections, clothing items can be selected for addition to the collection.

Favor a particular selection of clothing when creating your Sims? Make finding these items easier by dropping them into a clothing collection.

Head Collections

Sims' heads in the Sims Bin can be handpicked for easy location by putting them into a collection.

Generated and managed under panel 2 of Create-A-Sim (Heads), head collections give users quick access to handpicked Sims' looks. This is especially useful for players with lots of custom content Sims.

These collections are automatically filtered for gender, age, and skin tone. When working on a Sim of a given gender, age, and skin tone, you see only the heads in the collection that match all three.

DESIGN VARIATIONS

Most Buy mode objects contain design variations that alter the object's color, material, or finish.

Further variations can be added via the Custom Content Browser.

At this time, these may be created only by Maxis.

Design variations show up on an object's description panel or in the Design tool. Custom content variations are marked with a "*".

FULL NEIGHBORHOODS

Entire neighborhoods including their terrain, residential and Community Lots, families in lots, decorations, families in the Family Bin, and NPCs can be manually shared with other users.

Every neighborhood has a folder in *My Documents\EA Games\The Sims 2\Neighborhods*, each identified by the letter "N" followed by a three-digit number. All files contained in this folder feature this same prefix.

Neighborhoods can be completely changed or imported by copying files into the NEIGHBORHOOD folder in MY DOCUMENTS.

This folder can be copied to any other user's folder but will overwrite any folder with the same name in the recipient's *Neighborhood* folder. Make sure the folder has a unique number and every file in the folder is changed to reflect this new number (a lengthy process).

MUSIC

Any .mp3 or .wav file can be used in the game if copied to *My Documents\EA Games\The Sims 2\Music* and placed in the appropriate folder.

Expand music options by dropping songs into the music folders for different parts of the game.

Music folders exist for specific purposes, and the copied song will appear only in the context of the file into which it was placed. Choose from folders for: Build mode (*build*), Buy mode (*buy*), Create-A-Sim (*cas*), neighborhood (*nhood*), and the stereo channels (*hiphop, metal, pop, rnb, salsa,* and *techno*).

NEIGHBORHOOD DECORATIONS

New decorations appear in the Decorations menu.

The objects (e.g., flora, landmarks, effects, etc.) available from the Neighborhood view's Decorations menu can be added either through the Custom Content Brower or the package installer.

At this time, these may be created only by Maxis.

NEIGHBORHOOD TERRAIN

You can create a neighborhood's underlying terrain with the terrain tools in Maxis's *SimCity 4*.

The Sims 2 will import the terrain file's elevation and water, standard roads (not highways or zoning-placed roads) as long as they're straight, and intersections as long as they're at right angles.

Find a small blank city tile in any region and click Start City.

In *SimCity 4*, open a region and then a small city tile (larger won't work) and arrange the terrain features (in God mode). Next, click on Mayor mode and establish the city so you can lay out some roads (don't be stingy but make them straight. Save the city and quit the game.

Sculpt terrain and pave roads for your new neighborhood.

Locate the region folder and city file (.sc4) in *My Documents\SimCity 4\Regions* and copy it into *My Documents\EA Games\The Sims 2\SC4Terrains*.

Find your customized terrain file in the list.

Once installed, you can use the terrain file to create a new neighborhood. From the neighborhood browser, click on Create Custom Neighborhood and select the terrain file (or any other) from the list. Name it, choose the type of terrain (lush or desert), and add a description if you want.

Make the neighbor-hood's thumbnail anything you like.

Change the thumbnail that appears in the Neighborhood Chooser from the default generic image by copying a new image file (400 x 300, .png format) into the new neighborhood's folder. Name the new image "N###_Neighborhood.png" in which the ### is the number assigned to the neighborhood folder.

> **note**
>
> The terrain type (desert or lush) can be toggled later by using the TerrainType cheat (See Chapter 36).

OBJECTS (BUY AND BUILD MODE)

New objects can be either entirely new objects or modified versions of existing objects.

Import these items via the Custom Content Browser or the package installer, and they appear in Buy or Build mode.

At this time, these may only be created by Maxis.

LOTS

Lots, both occupied and vacant, can be uploaded to or from *TheSims2.com* via the Custom Content Browser.

Lots not downloaded from the browser must be installed via a package installer or manually placed in *My Documents\EA Games\The Sims 2\Lot Catalog*. If

the filename of the manually placed lot PACKAGE file is already in use in the *Lot Catalog* folder, alter the numerical portion of the filename taking care to keep the same number of characters in the file name. Proper format for the file name is: "cx_########.package".

You may package a lot to THESIM2.COM or to a file for sharing or backup purposes.

No matter the source of the file, added lots appear in the Lots and Houses Bin. The bin, in turn, is sorted by Occupied and Unoccupied Lots. Occupied lots contain the lot's family but without any of the lot's story or relationships outside the lot. Memories and family trees pertaining to non-household Sims are, however, preserved.

Lots, both occupied and unoccupied, appear in the Lots and Houses Bin.

> **note**
>
> If the Sims in the family contain any custom content parts, these are added to Create-A-Sim and THE SIMS™ 2 BODY SHOP.

SIM PARTS

Skin tone, hair color, makeup, glasses, eye color, clothing, and facial hair can all be redesigned using *The Sims™ 2 Body Shop* (see Chapter 34).

Unless they're contained in a SIMS2PACK file, copy parts files into *My Documents\EA Games\The Sims 2\Downloads*.

After installation, parts become available in both Create-A-Sim and *The Sims™ 2 Body Shop*. They're also available in mirrors on your Sims' lots for the Change Appearance interaction or, if clothing, in dressers and clothing racks.

SIMS

You can download entire Sims (minus name, personality, and Aspiration) in packaged form from the browser or any website or other user.

Once installed, the entire Sim and any custom component parts can be accessed from the Sim Bin in Create-A-Sim and in *The Sims™ 2 Body Shop*.

Custom created Sims always appear at the top of the list and are marked by the usual "*".

STORIES

Generally, stories can be uploaded only to *TheSims2.com*, but the files that make up a lot or neighborhood's story can be shared between users.

If both users have the same family in a neighborhood, one user's story for that family can be shared by copying the story's .xml document (titled

"*webentry_########*" in which the "#"s are a string of letters and numbers) and all images and thumbnails with the same id number in their file name. The recipient must copy these files into *My Documents\EA Games\The Sims 2\Storytelling*.

TV VIDEO

Sims don't really care what's on TV, so make it whatever you like.

You can place video files in *My Documents\EAGames\The Sims 2\Movies\Broadcast* and the folder for the channel on which you want the video to appear:

◆ TvChildren	◆ TvMusic
◆ TvSBN	◆ TvWorkout
◆ TvFood	◆ Commercials
◆ Games	◆ CommercialsNet

Files should be .avi of any size and codec. The larger the file, the more it will affect game performance, so keep clips down to about 15 frames per second and 128 x 128 pixels.

VIDEO/COMPUTER GAME VIDEO

Video/computer games are special purpose video but can't be altered so easily.

In the ultimate reality inversion, use your home movies as video for Sims' computer/ video games and let them appear to control YOUR family. My brain hurts.

These files must be given precise file names. Moreover, only games that have been purchased by your Sim can be viewed, so you can see your custom content only if your Sim has the games that have been altered.

note

The default game in THE SIMS 2 is SSX3. Replace its movies to see your custom content without your Sim having to buy new games.

There are three video games folders: *SSX*, *BUS*, and *SC4*. Each folder contains six files; the replacement files must bear precisely the same names (the three letters of the game's folder plus: *_ATTRACT*, *_INTRO*, *_P1LOSE*, *_P1WIN*, *_P2LOSE*, *_P2WIN*.

Place these files in *My Documents\EA Games\The Sims 2\Movies\Games* and the appropriate game folder.

note

The actual video files for video/computer games reside in the game's program file, but placing items with the same name in your MY DOCUMENTS folder overrides the program files versions. If you remove the replacement, the original will return.

UPLOADS

All of the above describes how to acquire and use content made by others. What, however, if you want to share your work with the world?

You can upload three kinds of content in-game to *TheSims2.com*:

◆ Lots: Occupied and unoccupied
◆ Stories: From neighborhood or lot
◆ Sims or Sim parts: From *The Sims™ 2 Body Shop*

note

There is no freestanding utility for packaging files; only the game and THE SIMS™ 2 BODY SHOP can do that. Anything other than the three uploadables (above), therefore, must be shared as files and manually placed in the correct folders.

All other kinds of user-created custom content can be uploaded only to Internet fan sites and shared among friends and relations.

With the staggering size of the community you've joined, however, that's a pretty big audience with a pretty big thirst for contributions.

Such elements include:

◆ Collections
◆ Full Neighborhoods
◆ Neighborhood Terrain
◆ Stories (if other user has same family)
◆ Music and Video

Read the sections above to locate the necessary files and instruct your recipients on where to put them.

Chapter 36

Appendix A: Cheats

Summon the cheat window by pressing Ctrl + Shift + C.

GENERAL CHEATS

- ◆ Exit: Closes Cheat window.
- ◆ Expand: Expands or contracts the Cheat window.
- ◆ Kaching: Adds §1,000 to household funds.
- ◆ Motherlode: Adds §50,000 to household funds.
- ◆ Help: Lists some, but not all, cheats. The list you see before you is complete.
- ◆ Autopatch (on/off): Toggles notification of available game patches.
- ◆ Moveobjects (on/off) Move unmovable objects and put them in illegal places. Causes problems, so use carefully.
- ◆ Aging (on/off): Sims won't age.
- ◆ Stretchskeleton (0.9–1.1): Increases or decreases Sim height compared to normal height. However, it might disrupt character animation.
- ◆ Vsync (on/off): turning off increases game performance but with some graphical errors as the price.
- ◆ faceBlendLimits (on/off): Turns off some automatic corrections in Make a Child that fixes freakish combinations of widely divergent facial features. Results in frequent "freak children."

NEIGHBORHOOD ONLY CHEATS

- ◆ deleteAllCharacters: At Neighborhood view only, removes every Sim from the neighborhood. Don't use it unless you have a very good reason.
- ◆ TerrainType (desert/temperate): Only in Neighborhood view. Toggles between two terrain types.

FILMMAKING CHEATS

- ◆ Slowmotion (0–8): 0 is normal speed and 8 is slower.
- ◆ boolProp enablePostProcessing (true/false): Must be true for all filmic cheats to function.
- ◆ Bloom (r g b x): Computer's video card must be able to handle pixel shaders. Creates a filmic look in which everything's so bright it blurs together (à la sitcom flashbacks). "r," "g," and "b" are color values (0–255), and "x" is the amount of blooming from 0 to 255.
- ◆ vignette (centerx centery X): Computer's video card must be able to handle pixel shaders. Creates a filmic look in which a focal point is clear but everything around it is blurry. Must first enter "boolProp enablePostProcessing true."
- ◆ filmgrain (0–1): Computer's video card must be able to handle pixel shaders. Creates a film graininess. Must first enter "boolProp enablePostProcessing true."
- ◆ letterbox (0.0–0.4): Computer's video card must be able to handle pixel shaders. Creates a letterbox view of size specified. Must first enter "boolProp enablePostProcessing true."

> ### note
> Film cheats may cause refresh problems from the NH view.

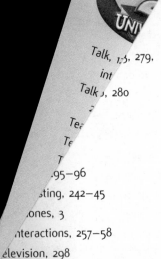